EDITOR: Dominic Bates
MANAGING EDITOR: Dan French
CONTRIBUTORS: Chris Wingrove, Kathryn Wortley,
Martin Fitzpatrick, William Lee-Wright

DESIGN AND PRODUCTION BY THINK PUBLISHING
Project Editor: Emma Jones
Sub Editors: Rica Dearman, Marion Thompson
Designer: Garry Lyons
www.thinkpublishing.co.uk

Cover photograph: Glencoe, Scotland –
©Grant Dixon/Lonely Planet Images

PRINTED AND BOUND BY BGP, COLCHESTER, ESSEX
walk BRITAIN 2008 is printed on GraphoMatt
which is manufactured using wood products certified by
the Forestry Stewardship Council.

TRADE DISTRIBUTION BY CORDEE LTD
3a de Montfort Street, Leicester LE1 7HD
☎ 0116 254 3579 Email: sales@cordee.co.uk

ACCOMMODATION ADVERTISING
Visit: www.ramblers.org.uk/accommodation

COMMERCIAL ADVERTISING
Think Publishing
The Pall Mall Deposit, 124-128 Barlby Road,
London W10 6BL
☎ 020 8962 3020
Email: advertising@thinkpublishing.co.uk

PUBLISHED BY
The Ramblers' Association
2nd Floor, Camelford House
87-90 Albert Embankment, London SE1 7TW
☎ 020 7339 8500 Fax: 020 7339 8501
Email: ramblers@ramblers.org.uk
www.ramblers.org.uk
Registered charity no. 1093577 and a company limited
by guarantee in England and Wales (no. 4458492)

Ramblers' Association Scotland
Kingfisher House, Auld Mart Business Park
Milnathort, Kinross KY13 9DA
☎ 01577 861222 Fax: 01577 861333
Email: enquiries@scotland.ramblers.org.uk
www.ramblers.org.uk/scotland

Ramblers' Association Wales
3 Coopers Yard, Curran Road, Cardiff CF10 5NB
☎ 029 2064 4308 Fax: 029 2064 5187
Email: cerdddwyr@ramblers.org.uk
www.ramblers.org.uk/wales
www.ramblers.org.uk/cymru

Ramblers Holidays
Box 43, Welwyn Garden City AL8 6PQ
☎ 01707 331133 Fax: 01707 333276
Email: info@ramblersholidays.co.uk
www.ramblersholidays.co.uk

Discounts shown in walk BRITAIN are wholly
at the discretion of the retailer and not an entitlement
to Ramblers members.

WELCOME

**Welcome to the 2008 edition of walk BRITAIN, the
official handbook and accommodation guide of the
Ramblers' Association.**

This book is divided into three parts:

THE RAMBLERS' WORK where you'll find news of all our
campaigns, recent successes and forthcoming initiatives, plus details
about how you can volunteer, join and other ways to support us.

WALKER'S TOOLKIT which contains information that's essential
for every walker – from 'how to' guides for reading maps and
reporting a footpath problem, to FAQs about rights of way and
countryside access. You'll also find clothing and equipment advice,
details of long distance paths and listings of all local Ramblers Groups.
Plus, discover our all-new, detailed city walks in London,
Birmingham, Manchester, Cardiff and Edinburgh.

ACCOMMODATION listing over 1,500 walker-friendly B&Bs,
self-catering cottages, hostels, bunkhouses, campsites and group
accommodation. There are full-colour maps to help you plan your
trips showing the location of B&Bs, long distance paths and national
parks. And regional introductions offering lots of ideas for walks and
places to visit that will inspire you to explore the British countryside.

For all the latest information about walking in Britain, visit our website
www.ramblers.org.uk which also features all the accommodation
in this book searchable by postcode, county, long distance path or
national park and is linked to our nationwide Group Walks Finder.

We hope you enjoy reading **walk BRITAIN** and find it useful.
Please let us know what you think with the feedback form on p113,
and if you're not a member of the Ramblers' Association yet, please
join us using the special offer on p21.

CONTENTS

The Ramblers' Work

THE RAMBLERS' ASSOCIATION

The Ramblers' Association is the largest and most effective organisation in Britain representing walkers' interests. We are a registered charity that promotes walking and improves conditions for everyone who walks in England, Scotland and Wales. We are dedicated to:

- **Promoting walking** The Ramblers promotes walking to everyone, especially the health and environmental benefits, so that all walkers can enjoy our wonderful heritage.
- **Safeguarding paths** Britain's unique network of public paths is all too often illegally blocked and overgrown. The Ramblers campaigns for local authorities to keep paths open and make them a pleasure to walk on.
- **Increasing access for walkers** We are at the forefront of establishing statutory rights of access for walkers to the outdoors in England, Wales and Scotland.
- **Protecting the countryside** The Ramblers is helping to protect the countryside and green spaces from harmful and polluting developments so that walkers can enjoy their tranquility and beauty.
- **Educating the public** Our work informs the public about their rights and responsibilities.

We receive no government funding and are dependent on the generosity of our members and supporters. If you would like to help, the simplest way is to join. See below for the many benefits of Ramblers membership, and read about the campaigns your money will help support over the following pages. Then either fill in the form on p21 or apply online at www.ramblers.org.uk/join.

ABOUT US

BECOME A MEMBER

Join us today, and make the most of the benefits of membership!

- **walk BRITAIN**, our annual handbook

- **walk**, our quarterly magazine

- Discretionary discounts in many outdoor stores, including 10% off at Millets, Blacks and Rohan

- Membership of a local Group with a programme of organised walks and social events. Members may also join walks and events run by any of the other 470 Ramblers Groups around the country

- Access to the Ramblers Map Library, stocking all OS Landranger and Explorer maps. Members can borrow up to ten maps at a time for a small fee plus p&p. (For more info, see p67)

Don't just take our word for it!
Whether you're an old hand or a complete beginner, we can help you get the most out of walking. Thousands of people enjoy walking more with the Ramblers every year. Here are a couple:

"I joined the MAD Walkers 20s and 30s Group in Manchester. I recently arrived here from Auckland NZ and I've found this Group to be fantastic. I've gone from knowing no one in the country to having a large network of friends and acquaintances and all thanks to the social activities, walks and weekends that have been organised."
Nardia Lloyd, Manchester

"This year I moved house from Norfolk to Somerset, and the Ramblers has been a wonderful way to meet people and see the countryside, in a way that would never have been possible otherwise. It has helped me settle in here and get to know my way around the countryside and find companionship in doing so. Despite having no car, the Ramblers is still possible because of the car-sharing offered for getting to the start of the Sunday walks. If you wonder if you'll like it, be brave and give it a go!"
Rosalind Hough, Somerset

If you love walking and you're not currently a member, then join the Ramblers today and make the most of our **walk BRITAIN** offer on p21 or apply online at www.ramblers.org.uk/join. If you're already a member, why not sign up a friend and receive £10 of Rohan vouchers to spend in-store or online. For details of this offer, look for the reply card in **walk** magazine or ☎ 020 7339 8500.

Explore the range

Collins rambler's guides

In association with **The Ramblers**

COLLINS *rambler's guide*
ben nevis & glen coe

Collins *rambler's guide*
isle of skye

Collins *rambler's guide*
yorkshire dales

COLLINS *rambler's guide*
north wales

COLLINS *rambler's guide*
peak district

Collins *rambler's guide*
lake district

richar

david leather

roly smith

john gillham & ronald turnbull

Waterproof Cover

Available at all good bookstores

PRESIDENT'S FOREWORD

There's no better way of getting some exercise, savouring the fresh air, and enjoying some of the finest landscapes in the world, than taking a walk through Britain's countryside. It's something I've loved doing all my life, and this book will help me and thousands of others to continue to do so.

But the Ramblers' Association doesn't just help to point us in the direction of a good walk or two and suggest some of the best B&Bs around. It's thanks to the Ramblers that many of Britain's footpaths are there for us to walk on at all, and the countryside has been opened up for all to enjoy.

The last ten years in particular have seen some real progress, and I was proud to be part of the government that helped bring it about. It wouldn't have happened, however, without the Ramblers and their dedicated campaigning, lobbying and researching over the years. The implementation of the Countryside and Rights of Way Act – with a right to roam over open country,

'At a time when we're increasingly concerned about our impact on the environment and our need to exercise more, what could possibly be better than going out for a walk?'

mountain and moorland – has been a milestone. Areas of wild land that were previously prohibited have been opened up for responsible access on foot, bringing opportunities for walks in new areas of countryside.

Now the need is to extend the concept of open access to Britain's coastline. We're a proud island nation, and yet we have no legal right at present in England to walk along the clifftops, across the foreshore, and around the coastline. The access we have currently is by permission, not by right. Even more absurdly, we have a right to take a boat across the foreshore when the tide is in, but not to walk across it when the tide is out. As a result, there are substantial parts of the coast where access is needlessly prohibited. Thanks largely to the Ramblers' work, the government has launched a consultation on a proposed 'coastal corridor', and I hope that we'll see this implemented within the next few years.

While nationally the Ramblers has been moving legislative mountains, at local level its members have been checking footpaths, getting obstacles removed and stiles re-built, securing rights of way, and organising local walking groups. It's this combination of practical work on the ground and effective professional work in Parliament, across Whitehall, and at Holyrood and Cardiff, that makes the Ramblers such an invaluable organisation. It really is thanks to them that we continue to be able to put on our boots and stride out into the countryside. And at a time when we're increasingly concerned about our impact on the environment around us, and our need to exercise more, what could possibly be better than going out for a walk? Happy walking!

Chris Smith

Rt Hon Lord Smith of Finsbury
President of the Ramblers' Association

PROMOTING WALKING

'Walking is the closest thing to perfect exercise. National Get Walking Day on 30 May will truly celebrate this'

The Ramblers' work to get more people walking for health and well-being has received a huge boost with the announcement of a £3.5million grant from the Big Lottery Fund's (BIG) Well-being programme. This will fund our Get Walking Keep Walking project for four years in deprived areas of Birmingham, London, Manchester and Sheffield. An additional £1million in funds is coming from Ramblers Holidays Charitable Trust and local authorities supporting the scheme.

Big funding for everyday walking

Get Walking provides free 12-week walking programmes combining information and motivation with led walks and other activities. There's also a free DIY pack available with a plan to follow by yourself. The project aims to encourage regular independent walking close to home as part of everyday life – not only health and leisure walks, but everyday trips on foot, such as to the shops, school or work. We want to see more people reaching the Chief Medical Officer's recommended minimum of 30 minutes a day of brisk walking, five days a week.

Activities and materials are targeted particularly at those who aren't already active, including people from black and minority ethnic communities, older people, those with mental health issues and families with young children (Little Legs Big Strides is a special programme for pre-school children). All walks are local, using quiet streets, urban footpaths and green spaces – so people can walk from their doorstep, school or workplace.

The scheme was piloted during 2006 and 2007 with great success. Most people stuck with the programme to the end, we had very positive feedback and nearly all users reported they have continued walking in informal groups or on their own. We've worked with around 250 participants and with a wide range of partners including councils, Sure Start centres, NHS trusts, schools, childhood obesity project MEND, Age Concern, mental health charities and black and minority ethnic groups. Two locally-based staff are already running the project in Birmingham and – thanks to BIG funding – offices in south London (covering Lambeth, Lewisham and Southwark), east London (Hackney and Tower Hamlets), Manchester and Sheffield will open this year.

Trained volunteers, as well as Ramblers Areas and Groups, play a major role in the project, such as Walking Ambassadors – keen walkers who already know the local area and want to share the joys and benefits of walking with others. Other volunteers are working on researching and writing up short, safe and attractive local walking routes – initially for organised walks, but eventually to publicise more widely in leaflets and on the web.

'We want more people exercising the recommended minimum. Within four years we'll have helped 90,000 people walk more, and trained 600 volunteers'

Within four years we'll have helped around 90,000 walk more, and trained over 600 volunteers. Around three million people will be within reach of our routes, and we will have a practical programme that can be extended to other cities when funds are available.

More projects with more walks for all

There are many other ways in which we're helping people do more walking, including the thousands of led walks run by Ramblers Areas and Groups every year. More Groups are responding to the demand for shorter and family-friendly walks, and last year new family walking Groups launched in London and the Forth Valley.

The Cerrig Camu (Stepping Stones) project in Wales – aimed at those who've attended health walks and now want to move to slightly longer walks – continues despite external funding ending. And Rail Rambles – a long-running project promoting walking via public transport by providing led walks from the Cambrian Coast Line in mid-Wales – is due for a boost this year. We're working with operator Trenau Arriva Cymru and Welsh Ramblers Groups to expand the service throughout the country.

In Scotland, we're helping Groups provide shorter, easier walks as part of our Get Fit for Tomorrow project funded by the Paths for All Partnership, attracting many new walkers, including people with busy lifestyles and those recovering from illness or injury.

Meanwhile, we've developed a pioneering partnership with Forth Valley NHS to help marginalised young men get out walking in the hills with the help of Ramblers' volunteers. Called Forth Valley Street Sport, this year we'll also be working with its sister project, Women In Sport

and Health (WISH), to provide a range of walks that suit young women (see p17 for more details).

A new national walking event

From Westminster to the local GP surgery, walking is increasingly recognised as the best prescription for curing Britain's inactivity epidemic, as well as a practical way of reducing harmful emissions and congestion. We've been keeping up the pressure on decision makers, from government departments to local authorities to the bodies responsible for the London 2012 Olympics, for more resources to help turn things round.

In previous years we've supported a National Day of Walking in the autumn, but this year we've declared National Get Walking Day on 30 May and are working with other organisations and local authorities to build it over the next few years into a truly national event celebrating walking. Walking is the closest thing to perfect exercise, the best way to access the outdoors and the most sustainable means of transport. In today's world of obesity, lack of exercise, high stress and climate change, that really is something to celebrate.

For more about promoting walking, visit www.ramblers.org.uk/walking

  Get Walking Keep Walking is part of a portfolio of projects funded by BIG through a Consortium of leading walking, cycling and health organisations. LOTTERY FUNDED *The Consortium is led by Sustrans and besides the Ramblers it includes British Cycling, CTC, Cycling England, Living Streets, London Cycling Campaign, the National Heart Forum, the National Obesity Forum, Transport 2000 and Walk 21. Visit www.getwalking.org.uk for further info.*

OUR CAMPAIGNS

IN FOCUS: WHEN THE SUN IS OUT, IT'S TIME TO WALK!

Anthony Sousa joined one of the pilot Get Walking Keep Walking programmes in Southwark, south London, hosted by a local NHS trust. "I enjoyed myself, the staff were friendly and I met lots of different people," he says. "I've been walking to work and got friends at work to start walking, too. It's been great."

Walks on the programme included Southwark Park and sections of the Thames Path National Trail, as well as lesser-known waterside walks, green spaces and footpaths around the old Surrey Docks and Bermondsey.

"Walking makes me feel fit and happy," Anthony says. "I feel great in the mornings and, using the logbook we were given, I can see I now do more and longer walks. I've cut out chocolate, drink more water and have lost about 5kg of weight. Now, when the sun is out, it's time to walk!"

FOOTPATHS IN ENGLAND AND WALES

The public rights-of-way network remains the single most important way of gaining access to the countryside, and also provides convenient routes in towns and cities – whether walking for pleasure, or simply getting from A to B. Unfortunately, the standard of the network, and how easy it is to use, varies dramatically across England and Wales. While some areas enjoy open, well-maintained paths, others struggle with paths that are difficult or impossible to use.

The Ramblers' role on footpaths is as relevant today as it ever was. Our volunteers continue to work tirelessly to improve the standard of rights of way through practical work, campaigning, path surveys and reporting problems. A key part of our work is addressing problems raised by members of the public, and pursuing them to a satisfactory resolution.

Victories in the courts

As ever, Ramblers volunteers and staff are involved in extensive casework to protect, extend and improve the path network. We have appeared at public inquiries defending routes against diversion and closure, served legal notice on highway authorities to ensure paths are kept open and maintained, and challenged through the courts adverse decisions involving rights of way.

The most important legal challenge in our history reached a successful conclusion in the House of Lords last summer (see box-out opposite). We also had a victory in the High Court when the Defence Secretary's closure of a footpath in Suffolk was declared unlawful. The path which runs through RAF Lakenheath near Mildenhall had been closed on grounds of security.

But no replacement was provided as required under the Defence Act 1842. The only 'alternative route' was a lane and the A1101 – both busy with fast-moving vehicles – and the judge ruled that in such cases, any replacement route must involve some length of newly-created footpath.

The gate debate

One recent focus for our work has been the closure of urban paths for crime prevention and anti-social behaviour reasons. For a number of authorities, closing paths seems the first and only option rather than working to keep them clean, lit and safe.

Where such paths have a public value, and in line with our desire to encourage walking for both health and environmental reasons, the Ramblers opposes these closures. We are challenging Coventry City Council in the High Court following their decision to

'For many authorities, closing paths seems the first and only option rather than working to keep them clean, lit and safe'

gate a path that is seemingly contrary both to its own policies and any legislative tests. We are campaigning for a change in the law on these gating orders so that local authorities are obliged to hold a public inquiry if a member of the public objects.

Welcoming help from more walkers

Last year, the Use Your Paths Challenge attracted more than 3,500 people to help walk all the rights of way in England and Wales, and the Footpath Guardian scheme signed up its 600th participant. These initiatives aim to encourage a wider range of walkers, whether Ramblers members or not, to take an active part in our work. This additional support is greatly appreciated, and we'll continue to develop these projects and build on their success.

Whether it's an obstacle on an individual path, or a funding cut which leads to the loss of a member of staff in a council's rights of way department, the Ramblers is there to press for the right outcome for walkers. In increasingly tight financial circumstances for local authorities, our presence is needed more than ever. Again, this work falls to our dedicated volunteers who

operate in all 171 local authority areas. Targeted campaigns are often run which look at the policies, procedures and budgets of authorities failing in their duties on rights of way. Campaigns continue this year in Cornwall, Somerset, Staffordshire, Suffolk, and Wiltshire.

Our future footpath work

Much of 2007 was spent laying the groundwork of a new footpath strategy for the 21st century. The process kicked off in March with a conference at Losehill Hall in Derbyshire attended by Ramblers volunteers from all across the organisation. We took a fundamental look at what we want to achieve and how we want to achieve it, and the findings were drawn into a consultation document looking at our aims, methods, organisation and volunteer training. The feedback to this document will help shape both the detail of our footpath work and the Ramblers' overall strategy for the coming years.

For all the latest footpath campaign news, visit www.ramblers.org.uk/footpaths

OUR CAMPAIGNS

IN FOCUS: RAMBLERS VICTORY IN THE HOUSE OF LORDS

In May last year, the Ramblers took its first ever case to the House of Lords. We were disputing the interpretation of a law since 1999 that made it unfairly easy for landowners to stop paths being recognised as public rights of way.

Prior to 1999, the law was always understood to be that if the public used a path freely for 20 years or more then it became a right of way. The only exception to this was if a landowner put up a sign stating 'no right of way',

locked gates or ordered the public off the footpath. Through these actions, which made their intention clear to the public, the route remained private.

But then a High Court ruled that a landowner could, even after 20 years of uncontested public use, defeat a claim that a right of way had come into existence by producing evidence of virtually any sort of which the public were totally unaware – such as letters to a solicitor, or directions to staff to keep people off the path.

However, in June last year, we celebrated the dramatic overturning by the Law Lords of this adverse precedent. The judgment on what has become known as the 'Dorset' case (more properly known as the Godmanchester and Drain cases) was handed down in the magnificent setting of the Chamber of the House of Lords. And to everyone's delight, all five

Lords of Appeal found in the Ramblers' favour.

This landmark ruling means that in future, actions to stop paths being recognised as public rights of way will have to be transparent. It will prevent countless paths from being lost for ever.

'This landmark ruling means all future legal actions will have to be transparent and will prevent countless paths from being lost for ever'

FREEDOM TO ROAM IN ENGLAND AND WALES

The Countryside and Rights of Way (CRoW) Act 2000, which came into force in 2005, represents one of the great achievements of the Ramblers' Association. Now, with more and more walkers getting off the beaten track and using the 936,000 hectares of mapped open country that the Act brought about, our campaigning focus has shifted.

Time for the English coast

As a proud island people, you might well assume that we all have a right to walk and be beside the sea. We do not. There is no general right for the public to walk along the coast and what we do have – our network of coastal rights of way – varies massively in both extent and quality. Indeed, even access to beaches and the foreshore is usually permissive and can be withdrawn by the landowner at any time.

We believe that the time has come to change this situation and give everyone a right of access to our beautiful coastline. Fortunately, the government shares our vision, and has spent much of the last two years investigating how the current situation can be improved.

One of the options put forward by Natural England during this consultation is the creation of a 'coastal corridor' right around England. It is our favoured option, with great potential to benefit walkers, wildlife and landowners alike. A broad corridor will give walkers the opportunity to enjoy the coast in confidence, spreading out across uncultivated headlands and away from the often-crumbling cliff edge. It will be flexible and continuous, moving inland in line with coastal erosion and linked to the rights of way network to create a wide range of new circular routes. Rolling back intensive

> 'A coastal corridor around England will bring great benefits to walkers, wildlife and landowners alike'

agriculture will create diverse new habitats for wildlife and aid conservation, improving the beauty and biodiversity of the coast and making it an even better place to walk.

With the consultation already moving in the right direction, we now need to keep up the pressure on MPs to make sure that proposals for a coastal access corridor are taken up without any watering down, and that sufficient parliamentary time is found for the new legislation to be implemented.

Promoting and securing access land

With the battle to secure access land now won, our focus has moved to promoting its use and enjoyment to

'The Welsh coast is magnificent and its value indisputable: a quarter of Wales' tourism comes from walkers of the coast'

quarter of tourist income comes from walkers of the coast. The potential is evident to all, with 40% of the Welsh coast still not having secure access even though a poll commissioned by the Ramblers showed 94% of people would like the access that we are seeking.

Our aspiration in Wales is for a coastal corridor with a presumption in favour of access and an accompanying code. We put forward this idea back in

as wide an audience as possible. Our Access Promoters project – a new initiative that sees volunteers give presentations about the benefits brought by access land in their local area – has been very successful and will be supported by new walks and promotional literature.

As we always predicted, there have been very few problems on access land and 99% of it is open for walkers at any one time. In the few places where access is threatened, we are engaged with ongoing campaigns, such as at Vixen Tor on Dartmoor (pictured, below left) where the landowner has removed a right of access after more then 50 years of public enjoyment. We are also continuing our work to open up the few areas that the CRoW Act missed. The amount of downland included on access land maps, for example, was much less than we had hoped for and work continues to try and rectify this when the next mapping exercise begins in 2010.

Coastal access in Wales

The Welsh coast is magnificent. Its landscape, history and culture are inspiring and its value to Wales indisputable, not least economically since nearly a

2005 as we feel it is the best way to give permanent, wide and erosion-proofed access. The corridor should provide secure access to beaches, cliffs, foreshore and adjacent land, plus offer safeguards for wildlife and privacy. We would also like agri-environment measures to develop the quality of coastal access.

To date we have achieved a Welsh Assembly coastal access improvement programme to create a coastal path (using existing path legislation) and improve paths around coastal communities, as well as providing new opportunities for cyclists, horse-riders and those with disabilities. Grants totalling £1.5million have already been awarded to 16 local authorities and staff appointed. At the same time, Minister Jane Davidson AM has regularly spoken of the advantages of a coastal corridor, so we look forward to this happening swiftly together with the appropriate legislation.

For further information about access and the latest news on our campaigns, visit www.ramblers.org.uk/freedom

OUR CAMPAIGNS

IN FOCUS: CAMPAIGN SUCCESS! ACCESS GRANTS REINSTATED

In March 2004, Natural England established the Access Management Grant Scheme, a project that made money available to authorities to carry out work on access land in their area. Unfortunately, when the initial three-year span of the project was reached, the funding was withdrawn, leaving much important work undone.

We lobbied Natural England for its return and, in August last year, the scheme was extended for a further year. This is vitally important to provide support for the everyday nuts-and-bolts work that keeps the countryside open and available for walkers. It lets access authorities put in gaps, gates and stiles; provides links to access land from the existing rights-of-way network; and, by funding research into improved land management, helps reduce the need for restrictions.

Securing this funding provides a great incentive to both staff and volunteers to take action. Now we can be even bolder in pushing for improvements to our access land network, safe in the knowledge that there's a dedicated pot of cash just sitting there, waiting to be used! And of course, we will be looking to support a number of volunteer-led local projects utilising this funding in the forthcoming year.

COUNTRYSIDE PROTECTION

The Ramblers' Association aims not just to keep the countryside beautiful – but to make it even more so wherever possible. Protection and enhancement go hand in hand when it comes to making sure that walkers and the wider public can benefit from our natural environment.

Our network of dedicated countryside volunteers get involved in countless campaigns to preserve and improve their favourite walking areas every year. Nationally, we seek to influence key government policies that will shape our places and landscapes for years to come.

We also recognise our responsibilities as users of the countryside to make sure future generations can enjoy the same opportunities we have. During 2008, we'll be starting work on a strategy that sees the Ramblers play our part in the drive to tackle the causes and effects of climate change.

The big picture

Major proposals from government in the last year have put countryside campaigners on red alert. Reforms to energy and planning laws could see fresh efforts to steamroller major construction projects into pristine countryside without a meaningful say from local communities.

New roads, airports and power stations – including nuclear plants and 120million wind turbines – could be taken out of the hands of local authorities and ministers, instead being given the nod by a powerful new unelected Planning Commission.

Tens of thousands of campaigners had already told the government to think again by the end of 2007, but we expect the fight to continue throughout the coming year.

An eye for detail

Meanwhile, local Ramblers Groups take action on their own patch to keep the countryside in top-class condition. Groups as far apart as Dorset and the Peak District are fighting road proposals that will damage scenic and protected landscapes, but are not guaranteed to cut congestion. And volunteers in Wales are making it easier for walkers to cut their carbon footprint by expanding a programme of Rail Rambles.

In the Scottish Highlands, we continue to call for a sustainable alternative to the unprecedented Beauly-Denny power line proposal. While in Hertfordshire and Essex, Ramblers have presented evidence showing

'Legal changes could see fresh efforts to steamroller major construction projects into pristine countryside without proper consultation'

how the noise and pollution from Stansted airport expansion will affect their local environment.

Make a difference

It's easy to help us protect and enhance the countryside we all enjoy. Next time you're out on a walk, look out for good and bad examples of how people interact with the landscape. Are new buildings in keeping with traditional styles, in proportion with natural features? Are roads located so that beauty spots are protected and noise kept to a minimum? Are signposts sensible and discreet or do they clutter and spoil the view?

Simply discussing these issues with others helps raise awareness and understanding of what we mean by countryside protection. From there it's a simple step to discovering what local decision makers might have

planned for your area, or how government policy will affect development in the future.

If you're still interested, think about signing up for our Take Action email newsletter, or our regular Countryside Update bulletin. Get in touch with your local Ramblers Group or Area and talk to the countryside secretary – perhaps even think about volunteering for the post yourself. Or contact the countryside protection team at central office (countryside@ramblers.org.uk, ☎ 020 7339 8571) or write to the usual address. Ramblers members in Scotland and Wales can receive specific information about Welsh Assembly and Scottish Parliament developments.

For all the latest news and information, visit www.ramblers.org.uk/countryside

OUR CAMPAIGNS

IN FOCUS: AFTER 60 YEARS – THE SOUTH DOWNS NATIONAL PARK AT LAST?

One of the most important ways to protect and enhance our most outstanding countryside is to designate the area as a national park. The South Downs is the last of ten scenic landscapes originally identified by Sir Arthur Hobhouse in 1947 as worthy of that status.

In 1999, the government launched a process to achieve this goal, but delays and legal challenges have meant that the dream is only finally looking like a reality. Last year, an independent inspector agreed that a new national park should indeed be established in the Downs, to the delight of campaigners, including the Ramblers' Association.

'The proposed South Downs National Park has a sting in the tail: the Western Weald, an area of outstanding natural beauty, is excluded'

There was a sting in the tail, however, when against all expectations the report concluded that the Western Weald, although part of an established area of outstanding natural beauty, should be excluded from the national park.

This year will be critical for the South Downs. The government has promised further consultation – and possibly a public inquiry – but says a final decision will be made by the autumn. National parks benefit the whole nation, with visitors coming from all over the world to see them, and their designation means the landscape's quality can be improved more easily for future generations to enjoy. The Ramblers remains a leading part of the campaign, and your help could make a difference. Keep an eye on our website for updates.

THE RAMBLERS' ASSOCIATION IN SCOTLAND

More and more people are discovering Scotland as a destination for enjoying wonderful scenery and fantastic opportunities for outdoor recreation, but it's still very easy to get away from it all.

Laying down the law for walkers
One reason people enjoy walking here is the traditional freedom of access to the outdoors – a freedom which has been secured by access legislation and is now in its fourth year. In general, the consensus is that the Land Reform Act and the accompanying Scottish Outdoor Access Code are working well in both rural and urban areas.

February sees the deadline for all local authorities and national park authorities to publish draft core path plans, which should make it easier for everyone to walk, ride or cycle on path networks leading around and between their communities and into the wider countryside. These plans will form a framework for local paths and will all be shown on OS maps.

Challenging maverick landowners
Our access work last year was dominated by the first legal test cases under the new access legislation involving a few maverick landowners who are unhappy with the situation. The Ramblers went to court with Perth & Kinross Council in a case regarding four acres of woodland at Kinfauns Castle, near Perth, and were disappointed that the sheriff found in favour of the landowner – Stagecoach founder Ann Gloag. We were also involved with Stirling Council in a court case in Stirlingshire where the landowner, Euan Snowie, sought a declaration that 40 acres of his estate should be exempt from access rights.

Wild work with government
Elsewhere, we carried on with our work to protect the wild qualities of Scotland's countryside which continues to be threatened by certain developments – whether these are giant wind turbines and powerlines in

'Last year was dominated by our first legal test cases against maverick landowners. We also developed a pioneering partnership to help marginalised young people get out hillwalking'

insensitive locations, or telecommunication masts and electrified deer-fencing. We are working with the Scottish government to develop policies that protect the wildness of our uplands for the enjoyment of future generations of walkers.

A new government, though, means a new set of MSPs and ministers to lobby. Fortunately, we also have a new president at Ramblers Scotland; Dennis Canavan was formerly an MSP and MP and was closely involved in the development of the access legislation. He is a keen walker and his parliamentary experience will be very useful in informing our future work.

Wide-reaching walks programmes
Meanwhile, we continued our work to promote the health benefits of walking, with funding from the Paths for All Partnership. With our support, local Ramblers Groups have included shorter, easier walks in their programmes and attracted many new people as a result, including those with busy lifestyles or recovering from illness or injury. We also made links with health walk groups to promote these walks as a next step for their clients, and hope to step up this work in 2008 in partnership with Paths to Health.

Last year a number of new Groups were launched in Scotland, including one especially for families in the Forth Valley area, and we encouraged all Groups to offer walks with wider public appeal and using public transport. This important work will continue with funding from Ramblers Holidays Charitable Trust.

We continue to lobby the Glasgow 2014 Commonwealth Games Bid Team about using the occasion to inspire people to walk for 30 minutes, five times a week, providing a legacy of not only a fitter, healthier city, but also Scotland as a whole. We produced an inspiring leaflet to encourage people to walk more, which was distributed at the Bid Team's events across the country.

We have also developed a pioneering partnership with Forth Valley NHS to help marginalised young people get out walking in the hills with the help of Ramblers volunteers. The project, called Forth Valley Street Sport, gives young people in Clackmannanshire who are not in education, employment or training the opportunity to participate in rewarding activities, and provides a route out of social exclusion and back into mainstream society. This year we'll also be working with Street Sport's sister project, Women In Sport and Health (WISH) to develop a range of walks to meet their specific needs.

For the latest Ramblers Scotland news, visit www.ramblers.org.uk/scotland

DATES FOR THE DIARY

JANUARY	26 Dec–2	Festival of Winter Walks, www.ramblers.org.uk/winterwalks
	2	Get Walking Keep Walking London launch, www.ramblers.org.uk/getwalking
MARCH	15–16	Ramblers Scotland Annual Conference, Stirling Highland Hotel, Stirling
	14–16	The Ordnance Survey Outdoors Show, Birmingham NEC, www.theoutdoorsshow.co.uk
APRIL	1	Get Walking Keep Walking Sheffield and Manchester launch, www.ramblers.org.uk/getwalking
	4–6	Ramblers' Association General Council, Winchester University
	12–13	Ramblers Welsh Council, Marine Hotel, Aberystwyth
MAY	1	England & Wales Local Authority Elections; London Mayoral & Assembly Elections
	2–5	Scottish Ramblers Gathering 2008, Fort William
	12–16	Walk to School Week in Scotland
	19–23	Walk to School Week in England and Wales, www.walktoschool.org.uk
	30	National Get Walking Day www.ramblers.org.uk/walking
JUNE	7–13	Green Transport Week, www.eta.co.uk
SEPTEMBER	22	In Town Without My Car Day, www.mobilityweek.eu
	20–28	Use Your Paths Week, www.useyourpaths.info
DECEMBER	26–2 Jan	Festival of Winter Walks, www.ramblers.org.uk/winterwalks

OUR CAMPAIGNS

simple *pleasures*

The world is ever-changing, but the simplest pleasures remain the same.

At the Ramblers' Association, we want to make sure that these pleasures can be enjoyed for ever.

Once you have provided for your loved ones, remembering the Ramblers in your will is a wonderful way to preserve for tomorrow the countryside that gives you such pleasure today.

www.ramblers.org.uk

GET INVOLVED

If you want to turn your love of walking into action, the Ramblers can offer some great opportunities to get stuck in. Whether you have ten minutes spare here or there or want to commit more regular chunks of time, there's always a way to make a difference.

If you're always very busy...

...Sign up to our e-newsletter

Every month you can receive our lively e-newsletter which will keep you informed about our campaigns and suggest some short, sharp actions that you can take. Visit www.ramblers.org.uk/volunteer, click on 'Sign up for our newsletter' and enter your email address to subscribe!

...Keep your eyes open for footpath problems*

Something you can do when you're out and about walking! If you come across a blocked or overgrown path, a stile or bridge that is dilapidated, or any other footpath problem, let us and the local authority know about it! Either fill in the footpath report form on p45 following the instructions on the neighbouring page. Or become a Footpath Guardian and get a colourful pack telling you what to look out for and what to do. Contact our footpath campaign team for your free pack on ☎ 020 7339 8582 or register online at www.ramblers.org.uk/footpaths/guardian.

If you've got a bit more time...

...Forgotten Paths Project*

If you have an interest in archives and research, the Forgotten Paths Project could be for you. At least 20,000 paths are at risk of being lost for ever. Volunteers with time and enthusiasm to research can help us keep these paths by identifying them. Find out more and get the Forgotten Paths pack from our footpath policy team on ☎ 020 7339 8530 or at rightsofway@ramblers.org.uk.

...Get involved with your local Group and Area

Every local Group is different, but they are all run entirely by volunteers and organise a range of activities. Leading walks is the most visible of Group activities and new leaders are always welcome. As important as leading walks is publicising them. Groups put together walks programmes, list walks on the Group Walks Finder, and publicise their activities in local information centres and through local media. Groups are active in footpath, access and countryside work: whether it's monitoring the condition of local footpaths, lobbying over developments that affect walkers, or running local campaigns to raise awareness. Many Groups also carry out practical work to improve footpaths, clearing paths or repairing stiles.

Areas work to support and coordinate the efforts of their various Groups and to ensure that the voice of the Ramblers is heard loud and clear across their patch.

Getting involved with your Area or Group is a great way to keep informed about the issues facing walkers locally and to do something about them. There are all sorts of opportunities, from traditional committee roles to shorter-term or more infrequent commitments. Whatever you would like to offer, your Area or Group will be delighted to hear from you. Contact details for all Area and Groups are listed on p85.

(* England and Wales only)

For more details of opportunities to volunteer or get involved at the Ramblers, visit www.ramblers.org.uk/volunteer

SUPPORTING US

OTHER WAYS YOU CAN HELP

Following in your footsteps –

Many people understandably find it difficult to think about what will happen when they die. Too often, this results in a failure to make the necessary arrangements. There is a perception that making a will can be a complicated and expensive chore, but the real cost could be in not having a will. In the worst case, your entire estate would revert to the government's coffers.

Once you have made provision for your loved ones, a gift to the Ramblers' Association is the ideal way to play a lasting part in ensuring that the countryside continues to be protected for future generations. And what's more, because we are a registered charity, all gifts to the Ramblers' Association are free of inheritance tax.

With the simple pleasures of a day outdoors uppermost in our mind, we are the only charity dedicated to working in the interests of walkers – a job we have done for over 70 years. If you think that is a job worth investing in, please consider leaving us a gift in your will.

For a copy of our free guide to making and updating your will, ☎ 020 7339 8511, or see the advert on p18.

RAMBLERS SHOP

Have you visited the Ramblers Shop, featuring many items popular with walkers, and often at a significant discount? Best of all, we receive a donation for every purchase you make, helping raise money for our vital charitable work. So why not visit our online shop – www.ramblers.org.uk/shop – and follow the links to make your purchases, or call the numbers opposite.

Ramblers Insurance –

UIA is an ethical insurer offering low-cost, high-quality insurance and will pledge between £5 and £15 to the Ramblers for every home, travel or motor policy taken out. You can get a no-obligation quote from ☎ 0800 013 0064, quoting reference RAMG, or buy online and save even more money.

Ramblers Credit Card –

Run by the ethically guided Co-operative Bank, we receive £15 for every new cardholder, £2.50 on first use, and donations for every transaction thereafter. ☎ 0800 002 006 to apply.

Ordnance Survey maps –

Aqua3 offers a 10% discount on both standard paper and waterproof maps, with a 10% donation to the Ramblers for each map sold. Buy online through our shop and get free p&p, or ☎ 0870 777 0791, quoting the Ramblers.

Digital mapping –

Get the latest software from Anquet at a 15% discount and a donation will also go to the Ramblers for every product sold. ☎ 0845 330 9570 and quote RA150.

Gift Aid –

giftaid it

If you say yes to Gift Aid, we can claim an extra 28p per pound donated, even on membership fees. This doesn't cost you a penny but raises hundreds of thousands of pounds for us! There is no easier or cheaper way to raise money for the Ramblers' Association. So even if you are already a member, either sign the form opposite, go to our website or ☎ 020 7339 8595.

Direct Debit –

Over 50% of members pay their subscriptions by direct debit, which saves them trouble and greatly reduces our administration costs and bank charges. To sign up, please complete the bottom half of the form opposite. Members can, if they wish, easily cancel this arrangement at any time.

Ramblers Worldwide Holidays –

Set up in 1946 to support the work of the Ramblers' Association, Ramblers Worldwide Holidays still makes a kind and considerable donation to the Ramblers' Association every year and provides generous funding for our core charitable work. For a brochure ☎ 01707 331133, or see the inside back cover advert.

Our thanks go to **Millets** for their continuing support and sponsorship of the Gear section and we would like to draw your attention to their pages (pp22–23 and pp80–83).

SPECIAL DISCOUNT MEMBERSHIP OFFER

If you are not yet a Ramblers member, use this form and receive 13 months' membership for the price of 12 for joining by Direct Debit. If you are already a member, why not introduce a friend and enjoy £10 of Rohan gift vouchers to use towards your next Rohan purchase? ☎ 020 7339 8500 for more details.

The Ramblers

IT IS A CONDITION OF THIS OFFER THAT YOU PAY BY DIRECT DEBIT

Title ....First name(s) ....Surname(s)..

Address ....

....Postcode ....

Phone number...Email ....
(I am happy for the Ramblers to contact me by email)

Date(s) of Birth ....RA Group (if you have a preference) ....

If you have no preference you will be placed in a group according to your postcode

Tick the box that suits you best: ☐ Individual £27 ☐ Joint* £36

☐ Reduced Individual+ £15 ☐ Reduced Joint*+ £20

*Joint membership is available for two adults living at the same address. +Reduced rates are available and are intended for people who, through whatever circumstances, cannot afford the standard rates. The offer is valid until December 2008. The offer is not open to existing members.

I/we agree to become a member of the Ramblers' Association, subject to its Memorandum and Articles of Association and Standing Orders.

Signature ....

gift aid it If you are a UK tax payer, please complete this section to increase the value of any donation by 28% (or 25% from 6 April 2008) at no extra cost to you.

I want the Ramblers' Association to treat this payment, and all donations I made from the date of this declaration, as Gift Aid donations.

Title .... Full name .... Date ....

Ramblers Membership Number (if currently a member) ....
You must pay an amount of Income Tax (or Capital Gains Tax) at least equal to the tax that the Ramblers' Association will reclaim on your donation (currently 28p for each £1 you pay). You can cancel this declaration at any time.

Instruction to your Bank or Building Society to pay by Direct Debit
DIRECT Debit

Please fill in the whole form and send it to: The Ramblers' Association, FREEPOST SW15, London SE1 7BR

Ramblers Membership Number (if currently a member)

Details of the Bank/Building Society

To: The Manager   Bank/Building Society

Address

Postcode

Name(s) of Account Holder(s)

Bank/Building Society account number

Originator's Identification Number 9 2 2 6 7 0

Branch Sort Code

Reference Number (for office use)

Instruction to your Bank/Building Society
– Please pay The Ramblers' Association Direct Debits from the account detailed in this Instruction subject to the safeguards assured by the Direct Debit Guarantee.

Signature(s)

Date

Banks/Building Societies may not accept Direct Debit Instructions for some types of account.

SUPPORTING US

10% DISCOUNT
at Blacks stores for all Ramblers' Association Members*

Walker's Toolkit

LONG DISTANCE PATHS

These pages give information on a selection of long distance paths and routes in Britain, offering thousands of miles of excellent walking through a huge variety of dramatic landscapes. Nearly all of them can be used as the basis for shorter walks or walked in sections, as well as a longer, single trek.

Walking advice

If you are planning your first extended walking trip, we recommend you practise on day walks before setting out, to ensure you can comfortably walk the distance you intend to cover each day. Don't forget that, unless you have arranged luggage transfer, you will probably be carrying a heavier pack than you would on a day walk.

EASY routes offer generally level walking through areas where transport and assistance are usually close at hand and, while attractive to all, are especially recommended for the less experienced or energetic.

CHALLENGING routes have sections across difficult or remote terrain, which should only be attempted by those who have a little experience and navigational skill and are properly equipped, especially in bad weather. The majority fall somewhere in

between. All routes are signed, unless otherwise stated, though standards vary. We recommend you always take a path guide and map, even when following a well-signed trail. There are now many hundreds of walking routes in Britain and only space for a selection in this guide. The Ramblers website lists many more routes, in much more detail – see www.ramblers.org.uk/info/paths.

Accommodation

All routes listed are cross-referenced in the B&B section and appear on the maps for each region. Accommodation within 3.2km/2 miles of paths listed here is indicated by a note under its location. You can also use the path listings on the Ramblers website to search for nearby accommodation.

Comprehensive accommodation lists are available for some paths via their own website or printed publication and these are indicated with the abbreviation (AC) in the listings.

Luggage carriers are listed on p73. Many accommodation providers are also willing to transfer your luggage. Look for the ! symbol in the accommodation section.

Maps

Sheet numbers refer to Ordnance Survey Explorer 1:25 000 maps. The latest editions show the exact line of route for almost all the following trails. You can buy the full range of OS Explorer maps in both weatherproof and paper versions from Aqua3 through the Ramblers website at a special discount, and we'll also receive a donation for every map sold (see p20).

Strip maps and digital maps are available for some routes. These cover the route itself and some terrain either side. For more on maps and contact details for the map publishers listed here, see p67.

Publications

Where indicated, these can be obtained from the Ramblers Bookshop (see p109) or directly from local Ramblers Areas and Groups. Publications with ISBN numbers can be ordered from bookshops and internet retailers, or direct from the publisher. Some are less widely available, in which cases we give ordering details. Where a publication is stated as available from a local council, please visit www.directgov.gov.uk for contact details of all local councils. Guides include at least sketch maps and those marked (OS) have extracts from Ordnance Survey mapping.

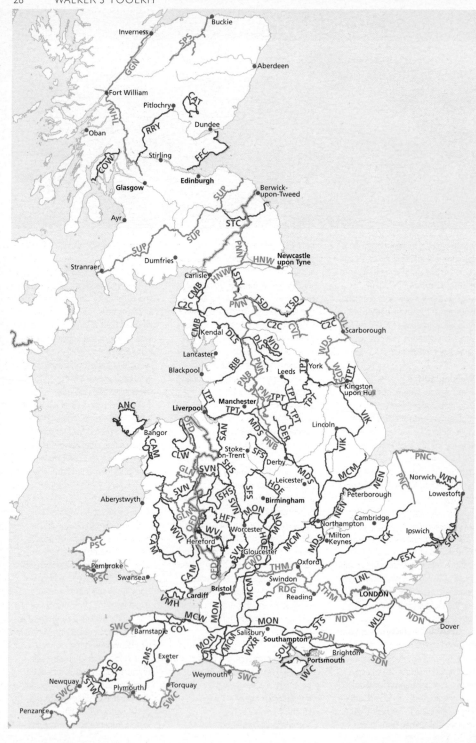

SYMBOLS AND ABBREVIATIONS

🏃 = National trail (England and Wales)
🔷 = Long distance route (Scotland)
(CLW) = Path abbreviation on maps in this book

(AC) = includes accommodation listings
(OS) = includes Ordnance Survey map extracts
TIC = Tourist/Visitor Information Centre

Cambrian Way (CAM)
Cardiff to Conwy 440km/274 miles
CHALLENGING
A spectacular but very mountainous unsigned coast-to-coast route across Wales from north to south via the Brecon Beacons, Cader Idris and Snowdonia, devised by Ramblers volunteers. Through the Beacons, partly-signed route the Beacons Way covers some of the same route but offers some easier alternatives.
MAPS OL12, OL13, OL17, OL18, OL23, 151, 152, 187, 213, 215
PUBLICATIONS CAMBRIAN WAY GUIDEBOOK (AC), 6TH EDITION DUE EARLY 2008, £5.50 FROM AJ DRAKE. BEACONS WAY GUIDEBOOK (OS), ISBN 1 902302 35 4, £12 FROM BRECON BEACONS NATIONAL PARK, VISIT WWW.BRECONBEACONSPARKSOCIETY.ORG
CONTACT CAMBRIAN WAY, 2 BEECH LODGE, 67 THE PARK, CHELTENHAM GL50 2RX, WWW.CAMBRIANWAY.ORG.UK

Cateran Trail (CAT)
Blairgowrie, Bridge of Cally and Spittal of Glenshee
101km/63 miles
A lengthy heart-shaped trail with a spur from Blairgowrie, over varied terrain from rolling pastures to the foothills of the Cairngorms with excellent views and stunning scenery throughout. Mostly moderate walking with a more challenging section from Enochdu to Spittal of Glenshee.
MAPS 381, 387, 388
PUBLICATIONS THE CATERAN TRAIL ISBN 1 898481 21 0, RUCKSACK READERS £10.99
CONTACT PERTH AND KINROSS COUNTRYSIDE TRUST ☎ 01738 475340
WWW.PKCT.ORG/CATERANTRAIL

🏃 Cleveland Way (CVL)
Helmsley to Filey Brigg
177km/110 miles
Horseshoe-shaped route that first follows the western and northern edges of the North York Moors National Park to Saltburn, then the beautiful coastline via Whitby and Scarborough: this last section is now part of the international North Sea Trail project. The whole route is accessible by public transport, and some sections are accessible for people with disabilities: contact the

CLEVELAND WAY

national trail officer for more information. The Link through the Tabular Hills connects Helmsley with the coast near Scalby via a more direct route (77km/48 miles), creating a complete circuit of the national park.
MAPS OL26, OL27, 301
PUBLICATIONS OFFICIAL GUIDEBOOK (OS), ISBN 1 854108 54 9, AURUM PRESS, £12.99 FROM OUR CENTRAL OFFICE. ALTERNATIVE GUIDEBOOK: THE CLEVELAND WAY: WITH YORKSHIRE WOLDS WAY AND LINK (OS), ISBN 1 852844 47 7, CICERONE, £12
LUGGAGE CARRIERS BRIGANTES, COAST TO COAST HOLIDAYS, SHERPA VAN
CONTACT NATIONAL TRAIL OFFICER
☎ 01439 770657
WWW.NATIONALTRAIL.CO.UK/CLEVELANDWAY (AC)

Clwydian Way (CLW)
Prestatyn, Llangollen, Corwen and Denbigh
243km/152 miles total
A roughly bottle-shaped route through splendid but little-known walking country and historic towns in the Clwydian Range and the Vale of Clwyd. The main 195km/122-mile circuit is complemented by an alternative 48km/30-mile moorland section linking Mynydd Hiraethog and Denbigh.
MAPS 255, 256, 264, 265
PUBLICATIONS GUIDEBOOK (OS), ISBN 1 901184 36 6, NORTH WALES AREA, £5.95 FROM OUR CENTRAL OFFICE
CONTACT WWW.CLWYDIANWAY.CO.UK (AC)

Coast to Coast Walk (C2C)
St Bees to Robin Hood's Bay
304km/190 miles **CHALLENGING**
Unsigned route devised by Alfred Wainwright to link the Irish Sea and the North Sea via three national parks: the Lake District, Yorkshire Dales and the North York Moors. Popular and scenic, but notably demanding, it is often cited as one of the best walks in the world by walking experts.

MAPS OL4, OL5, OL19, OL26, OL27, OL30, 302, 303, 304
WEATHERPROOF STRIP MAP (WEST), ISBN 1 85137 410 8, AND WEATHERPROOF STRIP MAP (EAST), ISBN 1 851374 40 X, HARVEY MAPS, BOTH £9.95 FROM OUR CENTRAL OFFICE. DIGITAL EXPLORER STRIP MAP £99.95 FROM MEMORY-MAP
PUBLICATIONS A COAST TO COAST WALK BY A WAINWRIGHT, ISBN 0 711222 36 3, FRANCES LINCOLN £12.99 FROM OUR CENTRAL OFFICE. ACCOMM GUIDE, £4 FROM DOREEN WHITEHEAD, BUTT HOUSE, KELD, RICHMOND DL11 6LJ, BUTTHOUSE@SUPANET.COM. CAMPING GUIDE £2.99 FROM ROCKUMENTARY PRESS, 11 CLIFF TOP, FILEY YO14 9HG, ROCKUMENTARYPRESS@YAHOO.CO.UK
LUGGAGE CARRIERS BRIGANTES, COAST TO COAST HOLIDAYS, COAST TO COAST PACKHORSE, SHERPA VAN

Coleridge Way (COL)
Nether Stowey to Porlock
58km/36 miles
A walk linking the Quantock and Brendon hills, Exmoor National Park and the Somerset coast through a landscape that inspired the Romantic poet Samuel Taylor Coleridge, including numerous delightful villages. Launched in 2005, the route is now fully signed.
MAPS OL9, 140
PUBLICATIONS FREE OVERVIEW LEAFLET FROM PORLOCK TIC ☎ 01643 863150. DETAILED DESCRIPTION AND MAPS ON WEBSITE BELOW
CONTACT WWW.COLERIDGEWAY.CO.UK

Copper Trail (COP)
Minions, Bodmin, Camelford, Five Lanes 100km/60 miles
A circuit around bleak and beautiful Bodmin Moor, including prehistoric remains, mining heritage and open access land. Launched by a local businesses partnership in 2005.
MAP 109
PUBLICATIONS GUIDEBOOK £4.95 + £1 P&P

COPPER TRAIL

FROM BEST OF BODMIN MOOR (SEE BELOW)
CONTACTS BEST OF BODMIN MOOR,
LOWER TRENGALE FARM, LISKEARD PL14 6HF
WWW.BOBM.INFO (AC) &
WWW.COPPERTRAIL.CO.UK

Cotswold Way (CWD)

Bath to Chipping Campden
163km/101 miles
Scenic, popular and undulating route
through classic English countryside
first proposed by Gloucestershire
Ramblers in the 1950s and relaunched
as a national trail last year. Part of the
Cotswold Round, a lengthy circular walk
(see Macmillan Way).
MAPS OL45, 155, 167, 179
WEATHERPROOF STRIP MAP, ISBN 1 85137 342 X,
HARVEY MAPS, £9.95 FROM OUR CENTRAL OFFICE
PUBLICATIONS GUIDE, ISBN 1 873877 10 2,
REARDON PUBLISHING, £5.95; HANDBOOK
(AC, FACILITIES, TRANSPORT), ISBN 1 873877 79 X,
GLOUCESTERSHIRE AREA, £2.95; ALTERNATIVE
GUIDE: THE COTSWOLD WAY (OS), ISBN 1 85284
449 3, CICERONE £12; OFFICIAL NATIONAL
TRAIL GUIDE (OS) ISBN 1 85410 914 6, AURUM
PRESS, £12.99: ALL AVAILABLE FROM OUR
CENTRAL OFFICE
LUGGAGE CARRIERS COMPASS, SHERPA VAN
CONTACT NATIONAL TRAIL OFFICE ☎ 01453
827004 WWW.NATIONALTRAIL.CO.UK/COTSWOLD

Cowal Way (COW)

Portavadie to Ardgartan near
Arrochar 75km/47 miles
Across the Cowal peninsula
from Loch Fyne to Loch Long, with
grassy hills, heather moorland, forest
plantations, prehistoric heritage and rich
wildlife all within easy reach of Glasgow.
Includes some more remote and
strenuous sections.
MAPS 362, 363, 364
PUBLICATIONS GUIDE £4.99 + P&P
FROM DUNOON VISITOR INFORMATION CENTRE
☎ 08707 200629 OR
WWW.SKWEBPAGES.COM/COWALWAY (AC)

Cumbria Way (CMB)

Ulverston to Carlisle 112km/70 miles
Through the heart of the Lake District
National Park via Langdale and
Borrowdale, Coniston, Derwent Water
and Caldbeck. A good introduction to
the area keeping mainly to the valleys,

with some higher exposed ground.
MAPS OL4, OL5, OL6, OL7, 315
WEATHERPROOF STRIP MAP, ISBN 1 85137 334 9,
HARVEY MAPS, £9.95 FROM OUR CENTRAL OFFICE
PUBLICATIONS GUIDE, ISBN 1 855681 97 8,
DALESMAN PUBLISHING, £2.99 FROM OUR
CENTRAL OFFICE
LUGGAGE CARRIERS BRIGANTES,
SHERPA VAN

Dales Way (DLS)

Leeds, Shipley or
Harrogate to Bowness-
on-Windermere
205km/128 miles total **EASY**
Originally inspired by local Ramblers,
this fairly easy-going, mainly waterside
trail links the Yorkshire Dales and the
Lake District. The original route runs
from Ilkley to Bowness, and three links
connect with big towns in the lower
Dales.
MAPS OL2, OL7, OL10, OL30, 297 (MAIN ROUTE),
288 (SHIPLEY), 289 (LEEDS)
WEATHERPROOF STRIP MAP, ISBN 1 85137 428 0,
HARVEY MAPS, £11.95 FROM OUR CENTRAL OFFICE
PUBLICATIONS GUIDEBOOK, ISBN 0 906886 72
4, AVAILABLE FROM ADDRESS BELOW, £5.99.
HANDBOOK (AC, FACILITIES, TRANSPORT), WEST
RIDING AREA, £1.50 FROM OUR CENTRAL OFFICE
LUGGAGE CARRIERS BRIGANTES,
SHERPA VAN
USER GROUP DALES WAY ASSOCIATION,
3 MOORFIELD ROAD, ILKLEY LS29 8BL
WWW.DALESWAY.ORG.UK (AC)

Derwent Valley Heritage Way (DER)

Ladybower Reservoir,
Bamford to Derwent Mouth, Shardlow
88km/55 miles **EASY**
Along the river Derwent from
Ladybower Reservoir in the Peak
District via the Derwent Valley Mills
World Heritage Site and the city of
Derby to its confluence with the river
Trent near Shardlow. A fascinating
combination of rich natural landscapes,
industrial heritage and famous estates.
MAPS OL1, OL24, 259, 260
PUBLICATIONS THE DERWENT VALLEY
HERITAGE WAY, ISBN 0 711729 58 1, JARROLD £11.99
(OS). BASIC ROUTE DESCRIPTION AND OVERVIEW
MAP ON WEBSITE
WWW.NATIONALHERITAGECORRIDOR.ORG.UK

Essex Way (ESX)

Epping to Harwich
130km/81 miles **EASY**
Pioneered by Ramblers and CPRE
members, this walk heads across quiet
countryside via Dedham Vale and
Constable country to finish at the Stour
estuary. The unsigned 24km/15-mile
Epping Forest Centenary Walk, created
to celebrate the centenary of the saving
of the Forest for public enjoyment,
connects Manor Park in east London
with Epping.
MAPS 174, 175, 183, 184
PUBLICATIONS GUIDE BOOKLET, ISBN 1 852812
48 6, ESSEX COUNTY COUNCIL, £3.50 FROM OUR
CENTRAL OFFICE. CENTENARY WALK GUIDE £1 +
30P P&P FROM EPPING FOREST VISITOR CENTRE
☎ 020 8508 0028
WWW.CITYOFLONDON.GOV.UK/OPENSPACES

Fife Coastal Path (FFC)

North Queensferry to Newport
on Tay 107km/67 miles
Around the firths of Forth and Tay,
through historic towns and villages,
excellent countryside and attractive
beaches, combining surfaced seaside
promenades and rougher coastal tracks.
The route is now part of the
international North Sea Trail.
MAPS 367, 370, 371
PUBLICATIONS GUIDE, ISBN 1 841830 57 7,
MERCAT PRESS, £12.99 FROM OUR CENTRAL OFFICE.
PATH MAPS AND OTHER USEFUL INFORMATION ON
WEBSITE BELOW.
CONTACT FIFE COAST AND COUNTRYSIDE TRUST
☎01333 592591 WWW.FIFECOASTALPATH.COM (AC)

Glyndŵr's Way (GLN)

Knighton to Welshpool
206km/128 miles
A beautiful route through mid-Wales
visiting many sites associated with
the fifteenth-century hero Owain
Glyndŵr. Forms a rough triangle with
Offa's Dyke Path as the third side and
Machynlleth as its westernmost point.
MAPS 201, 214, 215, 216, 239
DIGITAL EXPLORER STRIP MAP £49.95 FROM
MEMORY-MAP
PUBLICATIONS GUIDE, ISBN 1 854109 68 5,
AURUM PRESS, £12.99 FROM OUR CENTRAL OFFICE.
FOR ACCOM GUIDE SEE OFFA'S DYKE PATH
CONTACT NATIONAL TRAIL OFFICER
☎ 01597 827562
WWW.NATIONALTRAIL.CO.UK/GLYNDWRSWAY (AC)

Great Glen Way (GGN)

Fort William to Inverness
117km/73 miles
From the West Highland Way along
the fault-line of Glen Mor and the

GREAT GLEN WAY

northwest shores of Loch Lochy and Loch Ness, following the course of the Caledonian Canal. Lower level and less demanding than some other Scottish routes.
MAPS 392, 400, 416
WEATHERPROOF STRIP MAP, ISBN 1 851373 84 5, HARVEY MAPS, £9.95 FROM OUR CENTRAL OFFICE
PUBLICATIONS GUIDEBOOK, ISBN 1 898481 24 5, RUCKSACK READERS, £10.99; ACCOM & SERVICES GUIDE (AC) FREE + P&P: BOTH AVAILABLE FROM OUR CENTRAL OFFICE
LUGGAGE CARRIERS ABERCHALDER, GREAT GLEN BAGGAGE, GREAT GLEN TRAVEL, LOCH NESS INDEPENDENT HOSTELS IBHS
CONTACT GREAT GLEN WAY RANGER SERVICE
☎ 01320 366633
WWW.GREATGLENWAY.COM (AC)

Hadrian's Wall Path (HNW)

Newcastle to Bowness on Solway
130km/81 miles
From the bustling Newcastle quaysides to the remote North Pennines alongside the line of the wall built in AD122 to mark the northern limit of the Roman empire. Please help to look after the monument by following the conservation advice issued by the National Trail Office.
MAPS OL43, 314, 315, 316
WEATHERPROOF STRIP MAP, ISBN 1 851374 05 1, HARVEY MAPS, £9.95 FROM OUR CENTRAL OFFICE. DIGITAL EXPLORER STRIP MAP £49.95 FROM MEMORY-MAP
PUBLICATIONS GUIDEBOOK (OS), ISBN 1 854108 93 X, AURUM PRESS, £12.99; ESSENTIAL GUIDE (FACILITIES, TRANSPORT, SUGGESTED ITINERARIES ETC), ISBN 978 0 954734 21 3, HADRIAN'S WALL HERITAGE, £3.95; ACCOM GUIDE (AC) FREE + P&P: ALL AVAILABLE FROM OUR CENTRAL OFFICE. NUMEROUS SHORTER AND CIRCULAR WALKS GUIDES FROM NATIONAL TRAIL OFFICE (SEE BELOW)
LUGGAGE CARRIERS BRIGANTES, SHERPA VAN, WALKERS BAGGAGE TRANSFER, WALKING SUPPORT
CONTACTS NATIONAL TRAIL OFFICER
☎ 0191 269 1600
WWW.NATIONALTRAIL.CO.UK/HADRIANSWALL (AC)
HADRIAN'S WALL INFORMATION LINE
☎ 01434 322002

WWW.HADRIANS-WALL.ORG (AC)
USER GROUP HADRIAN'S WALL HERITAGE
C/O NATIONAL TRAIL OFFICER

Heart Of England Way (HOE)

Milford near Stafford to Bourton on the Water 161km/100 miles
A green route across the West Midlands linking Cannock Chase with the Cotswolds, through mainly gentle low-lying country with woodlands, canals and agricultural land.
MAPS OL45, 204, 205, 219, 220, 232, 244
PUBLICATIONS GUIDEBOOK, ISBN 0 947708 40 5, WALKWAYS, £7.50; ACCOM LIST (AC) FREE + P&P: BOTH AVAILABLE FROM OUR CENTRAL OFFICE
USER GROUP HEART OF ENGLAND WAY ASSOCIATION, 1 ALREWAS ROAD, KINGS BROMLEY, BURTON-ON-TRENT DE13 7HW
WWW.HEARTOFENGLANDWAY.ORG

HEREFORDSHIRE TRAIL

Herefordshire Trail (HFT)

Ledbury, Ross-on-Wye, Kington, Leominster and Bromyard 246.5km/154 miles
A circuit around the county visiting all the market towns, with numerous pretty villages and attractive countryside, including commons, woodlands, hills, farmlands, waterside and characteristic black and white architecture. Created by local Ramblers in partnership with Herefordshire council.
MAPS OL13, OL14, 189, 190, 201, 202, 203
PUBLICATIONS THE HEREFORDSHIRE TRAIL, BY THE HEREFORD GROUP (SEE P103), £5.95 + £2 P&P
WEBSITE WWW.HEREFORDSHIRETRAIL.COM (AC)

Icknield Way Path (ICK)

Bledlow to Knettishall Heath near Thetford 206km/128 miles
Follows prehistoric trackways from the Chilterns into East Anglia, passing many sites of archaeological interest and connecting the Ridgeway and Peddars Way as part of a lengthy off-road route along ancient ways between the Dorset coast and the Wash (see Ridgeway). The original walking route runs from Ivinghoe Beacon; there are now alternative

multi-user sections from Bledlow to Ivinghoe, running parallel to the Ridgeway, and from Aldbury to Pegsdon (Icknield Way Trail).
MAPS 181, 193, 208, 209, 210, 226, 229
PUBLICATIONS GUIDEBOOK (FROM IVINGHOE), £8 FROM OUR CENTRAL OFFICE. ACCOM LIST (AC) £1 + P&P AVAILABLE FROM DAVID NORTHRUP, 5 PERNE AVENUE, CAMBRIDGE, CB1 3RY. GREATER RIDGEWAY GUIDE: SEE RIDGEWAY.
BLEDLOW–IVINGHOE LEAFLET FROM BUCKINGHAMSHIRE COUNCIL, DOWNLOADABLE FROM WWW.BUCKSCC.GOV.UK UNDER WALKS AND RIDES
USER GROUP ICKNIELD WAY ASSOCIATION, 1 EDGEBOROUGH CLOSE, KENTFORD, NEWMARKET CB8 8QY
WWW.ICKNIELDWAYPATH.CO.UK

ISLE OF ANGLESEY COASTAL PATH

Isle Of Anglesey Coastal Path (ANC)

Llanfaethlu, Amlwch, Beaumaris, Holyhead 200km/125 miles
Fairly easy walking around the edge of Anglesey, through diverse coastal scenery mainly within an area of outstanding natural beauty, with many attractive villages. Easily accessed by bus (details in publications below).
MAPS 262, 263
PUBLICATIONS GUIDEBOOK, ISBN 1 902512 13 8, £1.50 FROM OUR CENTRAL OFFICE, OR DOWNLOAD ROUTE INFORMATION FROM WEBSITE, WWW.ANGLESEYCOASTALPATH.COM (AC)

Isle Of Wight Coastal Path (IWC)

Circular from Ryde 105km/65 miles
Popular coastal circuit round an island well-loved by walkers, via chines, saltmarshes, cliffs and holiday resorts, with plenty of accommodation and good public transport links. Connects with a number of other routes heading inland, including the 22km/14-mile Tennyson Trail from Carisbrooke to Alum Bay and the 18km/11-mile Bembridge Trail from Shide to Bembridge.
PUBLICATIONS COASTAL PATH AND INLAND TRAILS GUIDE, £3 FROM ISLE OF WIGHT TOURISM, OR DOWNLOAD ROUTE GUIDES FROM

PATHS & ACCESS

ISLAND BREAKS WEBSITE (SEE BELOW)
LUGGAGE CARRIERS BAG TAG
CONTACT ISLE OF WIGHT TOURISM
☎ 01983 813800
WWW.ISLANDBREAKS.CO.UK (AC)

London Loop (LNL)
Erith to Rainham via Kingston,
near circular around Greater
London 241km/150 miles **EASY**
A fascinating mix of waterside,
parkland, nature reserves and
countryside on the urban fringe, within
easy reach of central London by public
transport. The Loop and sister inner
orbital path the Capital Ring
(115km/72 miles via Woolwich,Crystal
Palace, Richmond and Finsbury Park,
fully opened in 2005) were pioneered
by Ramblers volunteers and the
London Walking Forum, and both are
now Transport for London strategic
walking routes.
MAPS 160, 161, 162, 172, 173, 174
PUBLICATIONS LOOP AND RING GUIDEBOOKS
(OS) £12.99 + P&P EACH FROM RAMBLERS
CENTRAL OFFICE. FREE LEAFLETS FOR MOST OF THE
LOOP AND ALL OF THE RING ALSO AVAILABLE,
☎ 0870 240 6094, HTTP://WALKLONDON.ORG.UK

Macmillan Ways (MCM)
Macmillan Way: Boston to
Abbotsbury 464km/290 miles
Macmillan Way West: Castle Cary to
Barnstaple 163km/102 miles
Abbotsbury–Langport Link:
38.5km/24 miles
Cross-Cotswold Pathway: Banbury to
Bath 138km/86 miles
Cotswold Link: Chipping Campden to
Banbury 33.5km/21 miles
A network of attractive routes linking
the south coast, Bristol channel and
North Sea coast of England, taking in
the Cotswolds, the Quantocks and
the Fens. The main route runs
diagonally across England from south
to east, while the western route links
the north Devon coast to the east
coast, or to the south coast via the
Langport link. The Cross-Cotswold
option uses one of the most popular
sections of the main route with
additional town links providing public
transport connections, while the
Cotswold Link connects with the
Cotswold Way to create the
Cotswold Round, a 331km/207-mile
circuit via Chipping Campden,
Banbury, Cirencester and Bath.
MAPS MAIN ROUTE/ABBOTSBURY LINK: OL15,
OL45, 117, 129, 142, 156, 168, 191, 206, 207, 223,
233, 234, 248, 249, 261

WEST: OL9, 129, 140, 141, 142
CROSS-COTSWOLD PATHWAY/LINK: OL45, 155, 156,
168, 179, 191, 206
PUBLICATIONS MACMILLAN WAY GUIDEBOOK
£9 FROM OUR CENTRAL OFFICE, MACMILLAN WAY
WEST GUIDEBOOK £6.25 FROM MACMILLAN WAY
ASSOCIATION (SEE BELOW). NORTH-SOUTH
SUPPLEMENT FOR THE MAIN ROUTE, GUIDES TO
OTHER LINKS AND SPURS, PLANNERS, UPDATE
SHEETS, ACCOMMODATION LISTS AND NUMEROUS
OTHER PUBLICATIONS AND MERCHANDISE FROM
USER GROUP BELOW
USER GROUP MACMILLAN WAY ASSOCIATION
☎ 01789 740852
WWW.MACMILLANWAY.ORG

Midshires Way (MDS)
Princes Risborough to
Stockport 363km/230 miles
A walking link between southern and
northern England, from the Ridgeway
in the Chilterns to the Pennine
Bridleway and Trans Pennine Trail via
historic estates, farmland and the Peak
District National Park. Generally gentle
walking incorporating sections of
numerous other trails including the
North Bucks Way, Brampton Valley
Way and High Peak Trail. In the north,
the 25km/15.5-mile Etherow–Goyt
Valley Way connects Stockport with
Longendale in the Peak District via two
country parks.
MAPS OL1, OL24, 181, 192, 207, 223, 233, 244,
246, 259, 260, 269
PUBLICATIONS MIDSHIRES WAY GUIDE
ISBN 1 850058 778 7, SIGMA LEISURE £7.95.
ETHEROW–GOYT VALLEY WAY GUIDE £2.25 FROM
TAMESIDE COUNCIL

Monarch's Way (MON)
Worcester to Shoreham
982km/610 miles
Britain's second longest signed route
follows in the footsteps of Charles II on
his flight from the Battle of Worcester,
a meandering course from the West
Midlands to the south coast taking in
many historic sights.
MAPS OL45, 116, 117, 119, 120, 121, 122, 129, 130,
131, 132, 141, 142, 143, 155, 167, 168. 204, 205, 218,
219, 220, 221, 242
PUBLICATIONS GUIDEBOOK IN THREE VOLS:
1. THE MIDLANDS, ISBN 1 869922 52 2; 2. THE
COTSWOLDS, THE MENDIPS AND THE SEA, ISBN 1
869922 28 X; 3. THE SOUTH COAST, THE DOWNS AND
ESCAPE, ISBN 1 869922 29 8, ALL MERIDIAN, ALL
£6.95. ALL AVAILABLE FROM OUR CENTRAL OFFICE.
ACCOM LIST (AC), £1 FROM MONARCH'S WAY
ASSOCIATION (SEE BELOW)
USER GROUP MONARCH'S WAY ASSOCIATION
☎ 0121 429 4397
WWW.MONARCHSWAY.50MEGS.COM

Nene Way (NEN)
Badby to Sutton Bridge
177km/110 miles **EASY**
Along the valley of the river Nene
as it first meanders through quiet
Northamptonshire countryside then
straightens out onto a canalised section
towards Lincolnshire and the Wash.
MAPS 207, 223, 224, 227, 234, 235, 249
PUBLICATIONS LEAFLET PACK BADBY TO
WANSFORD, £3 FROM OUR CENTRAL OFFICE. LEAFLET
WANSFORD TO WHITTLESEA FREE FROM
PETERBOROUGH COUNCIL PUBLIC RIGHTS OF WAY
OFFICE. LEAFLET WHITTLESEA TO SUTTON BRIDGE
FREE FROM CAMBRIDGESHIRE COUNCIL PUBLIC
RIGHTS OF WAY OFFICE

NIDDERDALE WAY

Nidderdale Way (NID)
Circular from Pateley Bridge
85 km/53 miles
Around the valley of the river Nidd, an
area of outstanding natural beauty
on the edge of the Yorkshire Dales,
including gritstone outcrops and rough,
open moorland. Much of the route has
good public transport connections:
information from Nidderdale AONB.
MAP 298
WEATHERPROOF STRIP MAP, ISBN 1 851373 92 6,
HARVEY MAPS, £6.95 FROM OUR CENTRAL OFFICE
PUBLICATIONS WALK CARD PACK, £2.95 FROM
OUR CENTRAL OFFICE
CONTACT NIDDERDALE AONB ☎ 01423 712950
WWW.VISITNIDDERDALEAONB.COM

North Downs Way (NDN)
Farnham to Dover 245km/153 miles
Along the chalk ridges and wooded
downland of Surrey into Kent, with
an optional loop via Canterbury,
often running parallel to the ancient
trackway of the Pilgrim's Way.
The 55km/24-mile St Swithun's
Way continues along the line of
the trackway from Farnham
to Winchester.
MAPS 137, 138, 145, 146, 147, 148, 150 (AND 132,
144 FOR ST SWITHUN'S WAY)
WEATHERPROOF STRIP MAPS, WEST (FARNHAM
TO THE MEDWAY) ISBN 1 851373 67 5 & EAST
(MEDWAY TO DOVER) ISBN 1 851373 79 9, HARVEY
MAPS, BOTH £9.95 FROM OUR CENTRAL OFFICE
PUBLICATIONS GUIDEBOOK (OS), ISBN 1

845130 65 0, AURUM PRESS, £12.99; ST SWITHUN'S WAY ROUTE CARD PACK: BOTH AVAILABLE FROM OUR CENTRAL OFFICE. ACCOMMODATION AND TRANSPORT DETAILS ON WEBSITE BELOW
CONTACT NATIONAL TRAIL OFFICE
☎ 01622 221525
WWW.NATIONALTRAIL.CO.UK/NORTHDOWNS (AC)
ST SWITHUN'S WAY WEBSITE
WWW.HANTS.GOV.UK/WALKING

Offa's Dyke Path (OFD)
Chepstow to Prestatyn
283km/177 miles **CHALLENGING**
A varied walk from the Severn estuary to the Irish Sea through the border country of England and Wales via Knighton, Welshpool and Llangollen, with around 100km/60 miles alongside the eighth-century earthwork of Offa's Dyke itself. Although not as challenging as more mountainous routes, there are some remote sections with rough paths and numerous ups and downs.
MAPS OL13, OL14, 201, 216, 240, 256, 265 WEATHERPROOF STRIP MAPS, SOUTH (CHEPSTOW TO KNIGHTON) ISBN 1 851374 56 6, NORTH (KNIGHTON TO PRESTATYN) ISBN 1 851374 51 5, HARVEY MAPS, BOTH £9.95 FROM OUR CENTRAL OFFICE
PUBLICATIONS OFFA'S DYKE PATH SOUTH (CHEPSTOW TO KNIGHTON) (OS), ISBN 1 854109 87 1 & OFFA'S DYKE NORTH (KNIGHTON TO PRESTATYN) (OS), ISBN 1 854109 76 6, AURUM PRESS, BOTH £12.99; OFFA'S DYKE & GLYNDŴR'S WAY ACCOM GUIDE (AC), £4.25, ROUTE DESCRIPTIONS SOUTH TO NORTH AND NORTH TO SOUTH: ALL AVAILABLE FROM OUR CENTRAL OFFICE. A CAMPING AND BACKPACKING GUIDE, CIRCULAR WALKS BOOKS AND NUMEROUS OTHER ITEMS ALL FROM OFFA'S DYKE ASSOCIATION (SEE BELOW)
LUGGAGE CARRIERS SHERPA VAN
USER GROUP/CONTACT OFFA'S DYKE ASSOCIATION ☎ 01547 528 753
WWW.OFFASDYKE.DEMON.CO.UK
NATIONAL TRAIL OFFICE ☎ 01242 533288
WWW.NATIONALTRAIL.CO.UK/OFFASDYKE (AC)

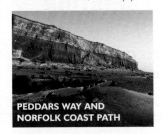

PEDDARS WAY AND NORFOLK COAST PATH

Peddars Way and Norfolk Coast Path (PNC)
Knettishall Heath near Thetford to Cromer 146km/91 miles **EASY**
Effectively two routes: the Peddars Way runs northwards through the Norfolk countryside to near Hunstanton, connecting with the Icknield Way Path to form the last link in a continuous chain of ancient trackways from the south coast. The coast path then runs eastwards via Sheringham. Many sections are suitable for people with special access needs: more information from the National Trail Office (below). Two other easy routes connect to provide a lengthy circuit of Norfolk, the 90km/56-mile Weavers Way from Cromer to Great Yarmouth via the Broads, and the 123km/77-mile Angles Way eastwards along the Waveney and Little Ouse rivers back to Knettishall Heath.
MAPS 229, 236, 250, 252, 252 (AND OL40, 238 FOR WEAVERS WAY; OL40, 230, 231 FOR ANGLES WAY)
PUBLICATIONS PEDDARS WAY/COAST PATH/WEAVERS WAY GUIDE BOOKLET (AC) AND ANGLES WAY GUIDE BOOKLET (AC) £2.70 EACH; PEDDARS WAY AND NORFOLK COAST PATH OFFICIAL GUIDEBOOK (OS) ISBN 1 8541085 2 2, AURUM £12.99: ALL AVAILABLE FROM OUR CENTRAL OFFICE. GREATER RIDGEWAY GUIDE: SEE RIDGEWAY
CONTACT NATIONAL TRAIL OFFICE
☎ 01328 850530
WWW.NATIONALTRAIL.CO.UK/PEDDARSWAY (AC)

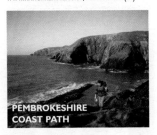

PEMBROKESHIRE COAST PATH

Pembrokeshire Coast Path (PSC)
Amroth to Cardigan 299km/186 miles
Some of the most spectacular coastal walking in Britain, mainly along clifftops and almost all within the Pembrokeshire Coast National Park, including Wales' only marine nature reserve and 17 Sites of Special Scientific Interest. Some steep climbs but also sections suitable for people with special access needs. At Cardigan the Path links with the 101km/63-mile Ceredigion Coastal Path; both paths will eventually form part of a continuous walking route around the Welsh coast.
MAPS OL35, OL36 (CEREDIGION COAST OL23, 198, 213)
PUBLICATIONS GUIDEBOOK (OS), ISBN 1 854109 75 8, AURUM PRESS, £12.99 FROM OUR CENTRAL OFFICE. EASY ACCESS GUIDE £2.95 + P&P, WALK LEAFLETS FOR INDIVIDUAL SECTIONS AND CIRCULAR WALKS, VARIOUS OTHER PUBLICATIONS FROM PEMBROKESHIRE COAST NATIONAL PARK. WALKING THE CEREDIGION COAST, FREE + P&P FROM OUR CENTRAL OFFICE OR DOWNLOADABLE FROM WWW.WALKCARDIGANBAY.COM (AC). WALKING THE CARDIGAN BAY COAST FROM CARDIGAN TO BORTH, ISBN 1 902302 09 5, KITTIWAKE £3.95
LUGGAGE CARRIERS PEMBROKESHIRE DISCOVERY, TONY'S TAXIS
CONTACT PEMBROKESHIRE COAST NATIONAL PARK ☎ 0845 345 7275 WWW.PCNPA.ORG.UK (AC)

Pennine Bridleway (PNB)
Hartington or Middleton Top to Byrness
560km/350 miles
A route for walkers as well as horse riders and cyclists, running roughly parallel to the Pennine Way but along easier paths to the west of the hilltops. The southern section, 188km/117 miles from the Peak District to the South Pennines includes the Mary Towneley Loop, a 68km/42-mile circuit around Todmorden and Bacup. A further 142km/89 miles runs from the Loop to the Fat Lamb Inn, Cumbria. The rest is mainly walkable already, though unsigned: see website for the latest situation.
MAPS SOUTHERN SECTION OL1, OL21, OL24; NORTHERN SECTION OL2, OL19, OL41 WEATHERPROOF STRIP MAP, ISBN 1 851374 06 X, HARVEY MAPS, £9.95 FROM OUR CENTRAL OFFICE
PUBLICATIONS GUIDEBOOK TO DERBYSHIRE/SOUTH PENNINES SECTION (OS), ISBN 1 854109 57 X, AURUM PRESS, £12.99; ACCOM AND SERVICES GUIDE (AC), SETTLE LOOP & MARY TOWNELEY LOOP LEAFLETS, ALL FREE + P&P: ALL AVAILABLE FROM OUR CENTRAL OFFICE
CONTACT PENNINE BRIDLEWAY TEAM
☎ 0161 237 1061
WWW.NATIONALTRAIL.CO.UK/PENNINEBRIDLEWAY (AC)

Pennine Way (PNN)
Edale to Kirk Yetholm
429km/268 miles **CHALLENGING**
A high and wild trail along the backbone of England from the Peak District to the Scottish Borders. Pioneered by Ramblers activist Tom Stephenson, it is the oldest as well as one of the toughest of Britain's signed walking trails.
MAPS OL1, OL2, OL16, OL19, OL21, OL30, OL31, OL42, OL43
HARVEY WEATHERPROOF STRIP MAPS: SOUTH (EDALE TO HORTON), ISBN 1 851374 31 0; CENTRAL (HORTON TO GREENHEAD), ISBN 1 851374 26 4; NORTH (GREENHEAD TO KIRK YETHOLM) ISBN 1 851374 21 3, £9.95 ALL HARVEY MAPS, ALL

PATHS & ACCESS

AVAILABLE FROM OUR CENTRAL OFFICE. DIGITAL EXPLORER STRIP MAP £99.95 FROM MEMORY-MAP. **PUBLICATIONS** GUIDEBOOKS SOUTH (EDALE TO BOWES) (OS), ISBN 1 854108 51 4; NORTH (BOWES TO KIRK YETHOLM) (OS), ISBN 1 854109 62 6, AURUM PRESS, BOTH £12.99; TRANSPORT AND ACCOM LIST (AC) FREE + P&P: ALL AVAILABLE FROM OUR CENTRAL OFFICE **LUGGAGE CARRIERS** BRIGANTES, SHERPA VAN **CONTACT** NATIONAL TRAIL OFFICE ☎ 0113 246 9222 WWW.NATIONALTRAIL.CO.UK/PENNINEWAY (AC) **USER GROUP** PENNINE WAY ASSOCIATION ☎ 0191 488 7789 WWW.PENNINEWAYASSOCIATION.CO.UK

Ribble Way (RIB)

Longton to the source of the Ribble near Ribblehead 114km/71 miles A riverside walk originally championed by local Ramblers from the wide-open Ribble estuary through rolling pastoral countryside via Preston and Clitheroe, then cutting through rough Pennine moorlands to reach remote Cam Fell. **MAPS** OL2, OL41 **PUBLICATIONS** 2006 GUIDEBOOK ISBN 1 85284 456 6, CICERONE £10. ROUTE MAPS ARE AVAILABLE ON LANCASHIRE COUNCIL'S WEBSITE

RIDGEWAY

Ridgeway (RDG)

Overton Hill near Avebury to Ivinghoe Beacon 137km/85 miles A route along 'Britain's oldest road' past the ancient hillforts of the North Wessex Downs, across the Thames and through the wooded countryside of the Chilterns. With the Wessex Ridgeway, Icknield Way Path and Peddars Way it forms a continuous 583km/363-mile walking route following ancient ways from the south coast to the Wash, the complete route of which is described in the *Greater Ridgeway Guide* below. **MAPS** 157, 170, 171, 181 WEATHERPROOF STRIP MAP, ISBN 1 8541373 14 4,

HARVEY MAPS, £9.95 FROM OUR CENTRAL OFFICE. DIGITAL EXPLORER STRIP MAP £49.95 FROM MEMORY-MAP **PUBLICATIONS** GUIDEBOOK (OS), ISBN 1 845130 63 4, AURUM PRESS, £12.99; RIDGEWAY COMPANION (AC), ISBN 0 953520 77 3, NATIONAL TRAIL OFFICE, £3.95 FROM OUR CENTRAL OFFICE; GREATER RIDGEWAY GUIDE (OS), ISBN 1 852843 46 2, CICERONE, £12.95 **CONTACT** NATIONAL TRAIL OFFICE ☎ 01865 810224 WWW.NATIONALTRAIL.CO.UK/RIDGEWAY (AC) **USER GROUP** FRIENDS OF THE RIDGEWAY, 18 HAMPTON PARK, BRISTOL BS6 6LH WWW.RIDGEWAYFRIENDS.ORG.UK

Rob Roy Way (RRY)

Drymen to Pitlochry 126km/79 miles Connecting the West Highland Way with the Tay valley, this unsigned route includes rich woodlands, remote moors and heaths, dramatic mountain views, impressive built heritage and sites connected with Scotland's most famous outlaw, Rob Roy MacGregor (1671-1734). **MAPS** 347, 365, 378, 386 **PUBLICATIONS** GUIDEBOOK, ISBN 1 89848126 1, RUCKSACK READERS, £10.99 FROM OUR CENTRAL OFFICE **LUGGAGE CARRIERS** BIKE AND HIKE, TROSSACHS TRANSFERS **WEBSITE** WWW.ROBROYWAY.COM (AC)

Saints' Way (STW)

Padstow to Fowey 48km/30 miles Attractive coast to coast trail across Cornwall, following a route possibly taken by the Celtic saints. **MAPS** 106, 107 **PUBLICATIONS** GUIDE, £3.99 FROM OUR CENTRAL OFFICE

Sandstone Trail (SAN)

Frodsham to Whitchurch 51km/32 miles An airy walk following the sandstone ridge that rises dramatically from the central Cheshire plain, including rock outcrops, woodlands, castles and historic churches. Can be walked easily in three sections of around 17km/10.5 miles each, with a seasonal weekend bus service. **MAPS** 257, 267 **PUBLICATIONS** FREE LEAFLET + P&P FROM OUR CENTRAL OFFICE, INFORMATION PACK (AC) FROM CHESHIRE COUNCIL COUNTRYSIDE SERVICES OR SEE WWW.CHESHIRE.GOV.UK/WALKING **LUGGAGE CARRIERS** BYWAYS BREAKS

Severn Way (SVN)

Plylimon to Bristol 360km/225 miles Britain's longest riverside walk follows the Severn from its source in the wild mid-Wales moorlands to its wide estuary on the Bristol channel via Welshpool, Shrewsbury, the World Heritage Site at Ironbridge, Worcester and Gloucester. The Way ends officially at Severn Beach (337km/210.5 miles) where a link path continues into central Bristol. **MAPS** OL14, 167, 179, 190, 204, 214, 215, 216, 218, 241, 242 **PUBLICATIONS** GUIDEBOOK £6.95 FROM RECREATION DEPARTMENT, ENVIRONMENT AGENCY, HAFREN HOUSE, WELSHPOOL ROAD, SHELTON, SHREWSBURY SY3 8BB **WEBSITE** WWW.SEVERNWAY.COM (AC)

SHROPSHIRE WAY

Shropshire Way (SHS)

Shrewsbury, Wem, Grindley Brook, Long Mynd, Ludlow 264km/165 miles total A tour devised by local Ramblers, combining bracing hill sections and celebrated sights like Wenlock Edge, the Long Mynd and the Wrekin, with gentler, more pastoral walking in the valleys. A narrow, wiggling circuit from Shrewsbury with two alternative routes is combined with a spur to Grindley Brook and the Llangollen Canal. A good network of leisure buses operates in the area: see www.shropshirehillsshuttles.co.uk. **MAPS** 203, 216, 217, 241, 242 **PUBLICATIONS** GUIDEBOOK, £6.99 FROM OUR CENTRAL OFFICE

Solent Way (SOL)

Christchurch to Emsworth 96km/60 miles Across the south of Hampshire via beaches, clifftops, marshes, heaths, ancient woodlands, riverside villages and the historic waterfronts of Southampton and Portsmouth. The Way is signed from Milford but *Pub Walks* (below) describes a route from Christchurch. The Bournemouth Coast Path, signed as European

path E9, links Sandbanks (Poole) and the South West Coast Path to Milford: the guide below includes sections with alternative clifftop and prom routes.
MAPS OL22, 119, 120 (AND OL15 FOR POOLE)
PUBLICATIONS PUB WALKS ALONG THE SOLENT WAY, ISBN 1 853067 38 5, COUNTRYSIDE BOOKS, £7.95. LEAFLET WITH ROUTE OVERVIEW, FREE + P&P FROM RAMBLERS CENTRAL OFFICE. DETAILS ALSO AVAILABLE AT WWW.HANTS.GOV.UK/WALKING. EXPLORING THE BOURNEMOUTH COAST PATH, ISBN 1 85306908 6, COUNTRYSIDE BOOKS £7.99

SOUTH DOWNS WAY

⬧ South Downs Way (SDN)
Eastbourne to Winchester
161km/101 miles
Exhilarating route along the rolling chalk downs of Sussex and Hampshire, through the heart of the future national park.
MAPS 119 (PART), 120, 121, 122, 123, 132 HARVEY WEATHERPROOF STRIP MAP £9.95 + P&P FROM OUR CENTRAL OFFICE
PUBLICATIONS GUIDE (OS), ISBN 1 85410 966 9, AURUM £12.99. ALONG THE SOUTH DOWNS WAY GUIDE IN BOTH DIRECTIONS (AC), £6 FROM OUR CENTRAL OFFICE
CONTACT NATIONAL TRAIL OFFICER
☎ 01243 558716
WWW.NATIONALTRAIL.CO.UK/SOUTHDOWNS; SOUTH DOWNS SOCIETY ☎ 01798 875073
WWW.SOUTHDOWNSSOCIETY.ORG.UK

South Tyne Trail (STY)
Source of the South Tyne near Garrigill to Haltwhistle
36.5km/23 miles **EASY**
A route created with the help of local Ramblers following the South Tyne and Tyne rivers through the remote and lesser-visited countryside of East Cumbria and the North Pennines to an end near Hadrian's Wall. From Alston to Haltwhistle it follows an old railway line with easy access. More ambitious walkers can follow the full length of both the Tyne (Garrigill to Tynemouth 133km/83 miles) and North Tyne (Hexham to Alston and Deadwater 76km/47.5 miles) as both linear and linked circular walks, using the additional publications below: note

these longer routes include more challenging sections.
MAPS OL31, OL42, OL43, 316
PUBLICATIONS SOUTH TYNE TRAIL LEAFLET £2 FROM EAST CUMBRIA COUNTRYSIDE PROJECT (BELOW). WALKING THE TYNE AND WALKING THE NORTH TYNE GUIDEBOOKS FROM NORTHUMBRIA AREA (SEE PP104–105)
CONTACT EAST CUMBRIA COUNTRYSIDE PROJECT ☎ 01228 561601, WWW.ECCP.ORG.UK

⬧ South West Coast Path (SWC)
Minehead to Poole 1014km/630 miles
Britain's longest national walking route, a spectacular and massively popular continuous path around almost the entire southwest peninsula. Although never too remote, there are some arduous clifftop sections with steep climbs and descents. The National Trail website below includes plentiful suggestions for short and easy walks as well as information about the whole trail.
MAPS OL9, OL15, OL20, 102, 103, 104, 105, 106, 107, 108, 110, 111, 115, 116, 126, 139
WEATHERPROOF STRIP MAPS: MAP 1 – MINEHEAD TO BUDE, ISBN 1 85137 422 9; MAP 2 – BUDE TO PORTREATH, ISBN 1 85137 427 2; MAP 3 – PORTREATH TO LIZARD; MAP 4 – LIZARD TO PLYMOUTH, ISBN 1 85137 437 3; MAP 5 & 6 AVAILABLE EARLY 2008, ALL HARVEY MAPS, ALL £9.95 FROM OUR CENTRAL OFFICE. DIGITAL EXPLORER STRIP MAPS, MINEHEAD TO FALMOUTH AND FALMOUTH TO POOLE, £99.95 EACH FROM MEMORY-MAP

SPEYSIDE WAY

PUBLICATIONS SOUTH WEST COAST PATH OFFICIAL GUIDES IN FOUR VOLUMES, AURUM £12.99 EACH (OS) – MINEHEAD TO PADSTOW ISBN 1 8541097 7 4, PADSTOW TO FALMOUTH ISBN 1 8541085 0 6, FALMOUTH TO EXMOUTH ISBN 1 8541076 8 2, EXMOUTH TO POOLE ISBN 1 854109 88 X; SOUTH WEST COAST PATH GUIDE (ROUTE DESCRIPTION ONLY, NO MAPS, UPDATED ANNUALLY, AC), £3.50: ALL AVAILABLE FROM OUR CENTRAL OFFICE. SOUTH WEST COAST PATH THE OTHER WAY ROUND, ROUTE DESCRIPTION FROM POOLE TO MINEHEAD TO BE USED IN CONJUNCTION WITH OTHER GUIDES, £3.50 FROM SOUTH WEST COAST PATH ASSOCIATION (SEE

BELOW) WHO CAN ALSO SUPPLY OTHER LITERATURE AND MERCHANDISE
CONTACT NATIONAL TRAIL OFFICER
☎ 01392 383560
WWW.SOUTHWESTCOASTPATH.COM (AC)
USER GROUP SOUTH WEST COAST PATH ASSOCIATION ☎ 01752 896237
WWW.SWCP.ORG.UK

⬧ Southern Upland Way (SUP)
Portpatrick to Cockburnspath
341km/212 miles **CHALLENGING**
Scenic coast to coast trail through southern Scotland via Sanquar, Moffat and Melrose, combining some remote and demanding stretches with sections suitable for families.
MAPS OL32, OL44, 309, 310, 320, 321, 322, 328, 329, 330, 345, 346
PUBLICATIONS GUIDE(OS), ISBN 1 841830 77 1, MERCAT PRESS, £16.99; ACCOM LEAFLET (AC) FREE + P&P FROM OUR CENTRAL OFFICE. SHORTER WALKS LEAFLETS FROM RANGER SERVICES OR DOWNLOADABLE FROM WEBSITE (SEE BELOW)
LUGGAGE CARRIERS
SOUTHERNUPLANDWAY.COM, WAY FORWARD
CONTACT RANGER SERVICE ☎ 01387 260184 (WEST) OR ☎ 01835 830281 (EAST)
WWW.DUMGAL.GOV.UK/SOUTHERNUPLANDWAY (AC)

⬧ Speyside Way (SPS)
Buckie to Craigellachie, Tomintoul or Aviemore 135km/84 miles total
Following the fast-flowing river Spey south from the Grampian coast through classic malt whisky country, along forest trails and an old railway track to the famous Highland resort of Aviemore.
MAPS 403, 419, 424
WEATHERPROOF STRIP MAP, ISBN 1 851373 37 3, HARVEY MAPS, £9.95
PUBLICATIONS GUIDE (INCLUDES FULL ROUTE MAP), ISBN 1 841830 46 1, MERCAT PRESS, £14.99. ACCOM GUIDE (AC) FREE; RUCKSACK READER GUIDE, ISBN 1 89848 127 0, £10.99, MOST RECENT GUIDE: BOTH AVAILABLE FROM OUR CENTRAL OFFICE
CONTACT SPEYSIDE WAY RANGER'S OFFICE
☎ 01340 881266
WWW.SPEYSIDEWAY.ORG.UK (AC)

St Cuthbert's Way (STC)
Melrose to Lindisfarne
100km/62 miles
Pilgrimage path on the border between England and Scotland, following in the footsteps of a seventh-century saint and linking the Pennine and Southern Upland Ways. Easy except for a remote upland stretch between Kirk Yetholm and Wooler.
MAPS OL16, OL44, 339, 340 HARVEY ROUTE MAP £7.95 (INCLUDED WITH GUIDE BELOW)

PUBLICATIONS GUIDE, ISBN 0 114957 62 2, THE STATIONERY OFFICE, £9.99 FROM OUR CENTRAL OFFICE
LUGGAGE CARRIERS CARRYLITE, SHERPA VAN
CONTACT JEDBURGH TIC ☎ 01835 863435
WWW.STCUTHBERTSWAY.FSNET.CO.UK (AC)

Staffordshire Way (SFS)

Mow Cop Castle to Kinver Edge 147km/92 miles
A north-south route across the county, from gritstone hills on the edge of the Peak District via the steep wooded slopes of the Churnet Valley ('Staffordshire's Rhineland'), Cannock Chase and more gentle pastoral scenery and parkland to the sandstone ridge of Kinver Edge. Sister path The Way for the Millennium, designed for easier walking, crosses at Shugborough on its way from Newport to Burton upon Trent (65km/41 miles).
MAPS OL24, 219, 242, 244, 259, 268
PUBLICATIONS GUIDEBOOK, £5 AND WAY FOR THE MILLENNIUM, £3.50; ACCOM LEAFLET (AC) FOR BOTH PATHS FREE: BOTH AVAILABLE FROM OUR CENTRAL OFFICE

Suffolk Coast And Heaths Path (SCH)

Manningtree to Lowestoft
106km/92 miles **EASY**
Through the tranquil landscapes of an area of outstanding natural beauty in a less-visited part of England: beaches, estuaries and wild heaths. The original route starts at Felixstowe, while an extension, the Stour and Orwell Walk, negotiates the river estuaries via Ipswich to Manningtree. The 96km/60-mile Sandlings Walk provides an inland alternative through the heathland between Ipswich and Southwold.
MAPS OL40, 197, 212, 231
PUBLICATIONS SUFFOLK COAST AND STOUR AND ORWELL PACKS INCLUDING PUBLIC TRANSPORT (AC), £4 EACH AND SANDLINGS WALK PACK, £4.75: BOTH AVAILABLE FROM OUR CENTRAL OFFICE
CONTACT SUFFOLK COAST AND HEATHS PROJECT
☎ 01394 384948
WWW.SUFFOLKCOASTANDHEATHS.ORG

TEESDALE WAY

Teesdale Way (TSD)

Dufton to Warrenby, Redcar
161km/100 miles
Along the Tees from its source in the Cumbrian Pennines through wild and remote moorland and gentler countryside to the industrial cityscapes of Teesside and on to the North Sea, including ten circular walks. A shorter path, the Tees Link, connects Middlesbrough Dock to High Cliff Nab, Guisborough (17km/10.5 miles) via Guisborough Forest.
MAPS OL26, OL31, 304, 306
PUBLICATIONS THE TEESDALE WAY ISBN 1 852844 61 2, CICERONE £10 (OS). TEES LINK LEAFLET FROM TEES FOREST ☎ 01642 300716
WWW.TEESFOREST.ORG.UK

THAMES PATH

Thames Path (THM)

Source of the Thames near Kemble to London and Crayford Ness
311 km/194 miles **EASY**
A splendid and very popular riverside walk pioneered by Ramblers members from the remote Cotswolds to Britain's biggest city, passing world-famous sites such as Oxford, Windsor, the central London riverfront and Greenwich. The national trail ends officially at the Thames Barrier where a well-signed 16km/10-mile extension continues eastwards towards Erith and the marshes. The whole route through London is now one of Transport for London's six strategic walking routes.
MAPS 160, 161, 168, 169, 170, 171, 172, 173, 180
DIGITAL EXPLORER STRIP MAP £99.95 FROM MEMORY-MAP
PUBLICATIONS GUIDEBOOK (OS) £12.99 + P&P, COMPANION (AC ETC) £4.75 + P&P FROM OUR CENTRAL OFFICE; THE THAMES PATH GUIDE FROM BARRIER TO SOURCE, ISBN 1 852844 36 1, CICERONE £12. FREE LEAFLETS COVERING LONDON SECTION INCLUDING EXTENSION
☎ 0870 240 6094 WWW.TFL.GOV.UK/WALKING.
CONTACT NATIONAL TRAIL OFFICE
☎ 01865 810224
WWW.NATIONALTRAIL.GOV.UK/THAMESPATH (AC)

Trans Pennine Trail (TPT)

Southport to Chesterfield, Leeds, York or Hornsea
560km/350 miles total
Multi-user route from Merseyside to Humberside via Stockport (Manchester) and Doncaster, with connecting spurs to Chesterfield via Sheffield, Leeds via Wakefield, York and Beverley linking all the major cities of northern England, interestingly mixing rural and urban walking. Much of the route, which was created with the help of local Ramblers, is wheelchair and pushchair accessible and easily reached by public transport, and the section from Liverpool to Hull is part of European path E8. Walkers following the linear coast-to-coast route from Southport to Hornsea need only route maps 1 and 3 below, while map 2 covers the central north-south spurs.
MAPS OL1, 268, 275, 276, 277, 278, 279, 285, 288, 289, 290, 291, 292, 293, 295
ROUTE MAPS:1 IRISH SEA–YORKSHIRE; 2 DERBYSHIRE & YORKSHIRE; 3 YORKSHIRE–NORTH SEA; £4.95 FROM OUR CENTRAL OFFICE
PUBLICATIONS VISITOR GUIDE (AC) £4.95 FROM OUR CENTRAL OFFICE
CONTACT TRANS PENNINE TRAIL OFFICE
☎ 01226 772574
WWW.TRANSPENNINETRAIL.ORG.UK
USER GROUP FRIENDS OF THE TRANS PENNINE TRAIL, 164 HIGH STREET, HOOK, GOOLE DN14 5PL. SEE ALSO WEBSITE ABOVE

TWO MOORS WAY

Two Moors Way (2MS)

Ivybridge to Lynmouth
166km/103 miles
An outstanding route pioneered by local Ramblers linking wild and remote Dartmoor to the spectacular North Devon coast via the Dart Valley and Exmoor. Mainly easy going with some challenging stretches and unsigned sections across the moors. The southern end links with the well-signed Erme–Plym Trail from Ivybridge to Plymouth (21km/13 miles) to provide a coast-to-coast route across Devon.
MAPS OL9, OL20, OL28, 113, 114, 127

PATHS & ACCESS

ILLUSTRATED ROUTE MAP £1.50 + 50P P&P FROM TWO MOORS WAY ASSOCIATION (SEE BELOW) **PUBLICATIONS** TWO MOORS WAY GUIDEBOOK, £4.95 AND ACCOM LIST (AC), 50P, BOTH FROM OUR CENTRAL OFFICE. ERME–PLYM TRAIL SHOWN ON OS MAPS: SEE ALSO WWW.DISCOVERDEVON.COM/WALKING **LUGGAGE CARRIERS** CAN BE ARRANGED BY ACCOMMODATION PROVIDERS LISTED IN GUIDE **USER GROUP** TWO MOORS WAY ASSOCIATION, 63 HIGHER COMBE DRIVE, TEIGNMOUTH, TQ14 9ML

Valeways Millennium Heritage Trail (VMH)

Circular from St Fagans
111km/69 miles
Meandering route through the Vale of Glamorgan, an often beautiful area rich in history in the southernmost part of Wales. Circular via Peterston-super-Ely, Barry, Cowbridge, Llantwit Major, St Bride's Major and Llanharry, with spurs to Ewenny Priory near Bridgend and St Fagans.
MAP 151
PUBLICATIONS ROUTE CARD AND BOOKLET PACK £6.99 + £1.50 P&P FROM VALEWAYS (SEE BELOW).
CONTACT VALEWAYS ☎ 01446 749000 WWW.VALEWAYS.ORG.UK

Viking Way (VIK)

Barton upon Humber to Oakham 225km/140 miles **EASY**
A trail pioneered by Ramblers volunteers from the Humber Bridge south along the Lincolnshire Wolds through territory once occupied by Vikings to Horncastle and Lincoln, finishing near Rutland Water.
MAPS 234, 247, 272, 273, 281, 282, 284
PUBLICATIONS GUIDEBOOK £2.50, FACTSHEET (AC) FREE BOTH FROM OUR CENTRAL OFFICE

Wealdway (WLD)

Gravesend to Eastbourne
129km/80 miles
Attractive and quiet walk devised by local Ramblers from the Thames estuary to the south coast via the Kent and Sussex Weald and Ashdown Forest. The southern section runs parallel and sometimes together with the Vanguard Way, a 107km/66-mile route from Croydon to Newhaven. At Croydon you can continue along the Wandle Trail for 19km/12 miles to join the Thames Path at Wandsworth.
MAPS 123, 135, 147, 148, 163 (AND 146, 161 FOR VANGUARD WAY/WANDLE TRAIL)
PUBLICATIONS GUIDEBOOK IS OUT OF PRINT. VANGUARD WAY GUIDEBOOK, £2.95 FROM OUR

CENTRAL OFFICE. WANDLE TRAIL MAP FREE FROM SUTTON LIBRARY ☎ 020 8770 4700

WESSEX RIDGEWAY

Wessex Ridgeway (WXR)

Marlborough to Lyme Regis
219km/136 miles
From deepest Wiltshire along ancient paths via the edge of Salisbury Plain and Cranbourne Chase to the Dorset Coast. Connects with the Ridgeway as part of a series of trails linking Wessex and East Anglia.
MAPS 116, 117, 118, 130, 143, 157
PUBLICATIONS GUIDE (OS), ISBN 1 8541061 3 9, AURUM, £12.99. GREATER RIDGEWAY GUIDE: SEE RIDGEWAY

West Highland Way (WHL)

Milngavie, Glasgow to Fort William
153km/95 miles **CHALLENGING**
A popular trail following old drove, military and coach roads from the edge of Scotland's biggest city via its largest freshwater loch, Loch Lomond, and first national park, to the foot of its tallest mountain, Ben Nevis, connecting with the Great Glen Way. Two riverside walkways effectively extend the walk in the south through Glasgow city centre and beyond: the Kelvin-Allander Walkway from Milngavie to the Clyde near the Tall Ship (14.5km/9 miles), and the Clyde Walkway from Partick station to the Falls of Clyde at New Lanark (64km/40 miles).
MAPS 347, 348, 364, 377, 384, 392 (AND 335, 342 AND 343 FOR THE WALKWAYS)
HARVEY ROUTE MAP £9.95 (INCLUDED WITH GUIDE BELOW) FROM OUR CENTRAL OFFICE.
DIGITAL EXPLORER STRIP MAP £49.95 FROM MEMORY-MAP
PUBLICATIONS GUIDEBOOK, ISBN 1 841831 02 6, MERCAT PRESS, £14.99; ACCOM LEAFLET (AC) FREE: BOTH FROM OUR CENTRAL OFFICE. FIT FOR LIFE! MAP INCLUDING ALL GLASGOW WALKWAYS AND THE CLYDE WALKWAY LEAFLET PACK, BOTH FREE FROM GLASGOW TIC ☎ 0141 204 4400
LUGGAGE CARRIERS AMS, SHERPA VAN, TRAVEL-LITE, TROSSACH TRANSFERS INDEPENDENT HOSTELS IBHS

CONTACT WEST HIGHLAND WAY RANGER ☎ 01389 722199 WWW.WEST-HIGHLAND-WAY.CO.UK (AC)

Wherryman's Way (WRY)

Norwich to Great Yarmouth
56km/35 miles **EASY**
Links Norwich to the coast and Angles Way through the heart of the unique landscapes of the Broads along the river Yare, once plied by boats known as wherries. This route launched in 2005 and also boasts public art and good public transport connections, including a riverbus.
MAPS OL40
CONTACT WWW.WHERRYMANSWAY.NET

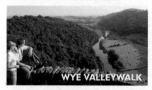

WYE VALLEY WALK

Wye Valley Walk (WVL)

Chepstow to Plynlimon, Hafren Forest 218km/136 miles
Along the the river Wye via Monmouth, Hereford, Builth Wells and Rhayader to the source deep in rugged and remote Hafren Forest, crisscrossing the border of England and Wales along dramatic limestone gorges and through rolling countryside and uplands.
MAPS OL13, OL14, 188, 189, 200, 214
PUBLICATIONS GUIDEBOOK £9 + FREE ACCOM LIST (AC) FROM OUR CENTRAL OFFICE
CONTACT WYE VALLEY AONB ☎ 01600 713977 WWW.WYEVALLEYAONB.ORG.UK OR WWW.WYEVALLEYWALK.ORG

Yorkshire Wolds Way (WDS)

Hessle, Kingston upon Hull to Filey
127 km/79 miles
One of the least-known national trails, but well worth getting to know, this route runs through rolling chalk hills between the North Sea coast and the Humber estuary. Some easy access sections are described on the website below.
MAPS 293, 294, 300, 301
PUBLICATIONS GUIDEBOOK (OS), ISBN 1 854109 86 3, AURUM PRESS, £12.99 FROM OUR CENTRAL OFFICE. CIRCULAR WALKS GUIDES AVAILABLE FROM NATIONAL TRAIL OFFICE (SEE BELOW)
CONTACT NATIONAL TRAIL OFFICER ☎ 01439 770657 WW.NATIONALTRAIL.CO.UK/YORKSHIREWOLDSWAY (AC)

EUROPEAN LONG DISTANCE PATHS

E-paths are designated by the European Ramblers' Association (ERA). They largely follow sections of existing trails and are not usually signed in their own right except at major junctions. Route names shown in red below indicate that the route has a full entry in the LDPs section; otherwise brief details of further information sources are given. For an overview of the E-paths, visit www.era-ewv-ferp.org or see our website. E-paths are also now shown on OS Explorer maps.

E2 Atlantic–Mediterranean

Stranraer–Harwich or Dover 1400km/875 miles
The main route takes in the Southern Uplands, Pennines, Yorkshire coast, Wolds and Fens to connect with the ferry for Hoek van Holland. A western branch visits the Peak District, Cotswolds, Thames Valley and North Downs on its way to Dover (this branch continues from Oostende but there is currently no direct ferry: an alternative is the ferry to Calais and the E9 coastal path). The two routes rejoin in the Belgian Kempen and continue along the celebrated GR5 via the Ardennes, Lake Geneva and the French Alps to the Mediterranean coast at Nice. An Irish section to the Galway coast is planned, making a total length of 4,850km/3,030 miles.

FROM STRANRAER
SOUTHERN UPLAND WAY TO MELROSE 258KM/161 MILES
ST CUTHBERT'S WAY TO KIRK YETHOLM 51KM/32 MILES
PENNINE WAY TO MIDDLETON IN TEESDALE 180KM/113 MILES

EASTERN ROUTE VIA HARWICH
TEESDALE WAY AND TEES LINK TO GUISBOROUGH 125KM/77.5 MILES
CLEVELAND WAY TO FILEY 99KM/62 MILES
YORKSHIRE WOLDS WAY TO HESSLE THEN VIA HUMBER BRIDGE TO BARTON UPON HUMBER 131KM/82 MILES
VIKING WAY TO RUTLAND WATER 233KM/146KM
HEREWARD WAY TO ELY 117KM/73 MILES: INFORMATION FROM RUTLAND, PETERBOROUGH AND CAMBRIDGESHIRE COUNCILS. AN IMPROVED AND NEWLY-SIGNED ROUTE FOR THE HEREWARD WAY THROUGH PETERBOROUGH OPENED IN 2006.
FEN RIVERS WAY TO CAMBRIDGE 27KM/17 MILES: GUIDE FROM CAMBRIDGE GROUP (P100)
ROMAN ROAD LINK TO LINTON 18KM/11 MILES: NOT YET SIGNED AND NO GUIDE, BUT THE ROMAN ROAD IS OBVIOUS ON OS MAPS.
ICKNIELD WAY PATH TO STETCHWORTH 15KM/9.5 MILES
STOUR VALLEY PATH TO STRATFORD ST MARY 83KM/52 MILES: GUIDE £3.50

ERA|EWU|FERP

FROM DEDHAM VALE AND STOUR VALLEY AONB ☎ 01473 264263 WWW.DEDHAMVALESTOURVALLEY.ORG
ESSEX WAY TO RAMSEY THEN LINK PATH TO HARWICH INTERNATIONAL 28KM/17.5 MILES

WESTERN ROUTE VIA DOVER
PENNINE WAY TO STANDEDGE 200KM/125 MILES OLDHAM WAY TO MOSSLEY 15KM/9.5 MILES: CONTACT OLDHAM COUNCIL
TAMESIDE TRAIL TO BROADBOTTOM 13KM/8 MILES: CONTACT TAMESIDE COUNCIL
ETHEROW GOYT VALLEY WAY TO COMPSTALL 8KM/5 MILES: SEE MIDSHIRES WAY (GOYT WAY) TO MARPLE 4KM/2.5 MILES
PEAK FOREST CANAL TO DISLEY 4KM/2.5 MILES: CONTACT BRITISH WATERWAYS ☎ 01923 201120 WWW.BRITISHWATERWAYS.CO.UK
GRITSTONE TRAIL TO RUSHTON SPENCER 33KM/20.5 MILES: CONTACT CHESHIRE COUNCIL
STAFFORDSHIRE WAY TO CANNOCK CHASE 76KM/47.5 MILES
HEART OF ENGLAND WAY TO BOURTON-ON-THE-WATER 159KM/99.5 MILES
OXFORDSHIRE WAY TO KIRTLINGTON 41KM/25.5 MILES: GUIDEBOOK £5.99 FROM OXFORDSHIRE COUNCIL
OXFORD CANAL WALK TO OXFORD 16KM/10 MILES: CONTACT BRITISH WATERWAYS OR SEE WWW.WATERSCAPE.COM/OXFORD_CANAL
THAMES PATH TO WEYBRIDGE 146KM/91 MILES
WEY NAVIGATION TO GUILDFORD 25KM/15.5 MILES: CONTACT NATIONAL TRUST ☎ 01483 561389 WWW.NATIONALTRUST.ORG.UK
NORTH DOWNS WAY TO DOVER 193KM/120.5 MILES

PATHS & ACCESS

E8 Atlantic–Istanbul

Liverpool–Hull 300km/188 miles

In Britain this path entirely follows the Trans Pennine Trail (see p35), connecting via the Dublin ferry with the Irish Waymarked Ways network. From Rotterdam it heads for the Rhine Valley, the Romantische Straße, the Northern Carpathians and the Bulgarian Rodopi mountains to Svilengrad on the Turkish border, a total of 4,390km/ 2,750 miles, though some of the eastern section of the route is incomplete.

E9 European Coastal Path

Plymouth–Dover 711km/444 miles, plus Isle of Wight loop 68km/43 miles

Along or parallel to the south coast of England, including some of its most famous coastal sites. The path provides an alternative to the mainland route of the E9, with which it connects by ferry at Roscoff, Calais and several points between. Additionally, it links the Saxon Shore Way and South West Coast Path to provide a continuous signed route of almost 1,000 miles around southern England from Gravesend to Minehead. The complete route will eventually stretch 5,000km/3,125 miles from Capo de São Vincente in the southwest corner of Portugal to Narva-Jõesuu on the Baltic coast at the Estonian–Russian border.

FROM PLYMOUTH
SOUTH WEST COAST PATH AND FERRY TO POOLE 343KM/214 MILES
BOURNEMOUTH COAST PATH (SEE SOLENT WAY) TO MILFORD ON SEA 30KM/19 MILES
SOLENT WAY TO LYMINGTON 11KM/7 MILES

ISLE OF WIGHT LOOP VIA FERRY TO YARMOUTH
ISLE OF WIGHT COASTAL PATH TO THE NEEDLES 11KM/7 MILES
TENNYSON TRAIL (SEE IOW COASTAL PATH) TO CARISBROOK 21KM/13 MILES
LINK TO NEWPORT 5KM/3.5 MILES
BEMBRIDGE TRAIL (SEE IOW COASTAL PATH) TO BEMBRIDGE 18KM/11 MILES
ISLE OF WIGHT COASTAL PATH TO RYDE 13KM/8 MILES THEN FERRY TO PORTSMOUTH

MAIN ROUTE
SOLENT WAY TO PORTSMOUTH, REJOINING ISLE OF WIGHT ALTERNATIVE 60KM/37.5 MILES.

SOLENT WAY TO LANGSTONE HARBOUR, HAVANT 16KM/10 MILES
STAUNTON WAY TO QUEEN ELIZABETH COUNTRY PARK 19KM/12 MILES: CONTACT HAMPSHIRE COUNCIL
SOUTH DOWNS WAY TO JEVINGTON 111KM/69.5 MILES
1066 COUNTRY WALK TO RYE 56KM/35 MILES: CONTACT BATTLE TIC
☎ 01424 773721
SAXON SHORE WAY TO DOVER 65KM/39 MILES: 2006 GUIDEBOOK FROM KENT COUNCIL

RIGHT TO ROAM FAQs

Where does the legislation apply?

The Countryside and Rights of Way (CRoW) Act provides a legal right of access to approximately one million hectares of open, uncultivated countryside in England and Wales, which is defined in the legislation as mountain, moor, heath and down, as well as registered common land.

How can I find out where I can walk?

Ordnance Survey has re-issued all of its Explorer maps to show access land, which is indicated by a light yellow area surrounded by a narrow pale-orange border. Orange 'i' symbols pinpoint access information points. To avoid confusion, a border of light magenta dashes now represents the boundaries of national parks.

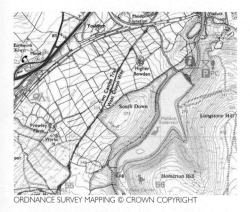

ORDNANCE SURVEY MAPPING © CROWN COPYRIGHT

In addition, Natural England provides an open access website where walkers can find details of access land throughout the country. While in Wales the Countryside Council for Wales hosts a similar resource. See p43 for details.

What am I allowed to do on access land?

The law provides a right of access for walkers only and does not confer any additional rights for cyclists or horse-riders, (though where additional rights are currently allowed or tolerated, they are likely to continue). Dogs are permitted on some areas of open country, but must be kept on a lead on access land between 1 March and 31 July and at any time in the vicinity of livestock. Furthermore, dogs may be banned temporarily or permanently from some areas of land. Access at night is permitted but may be subject to local restrictions. Walkers are responsible for their own safety at all times.

How is access managed locally?

Access is managed by local authorities or, in national parks, by the national park authority. They have the power to enact and enforce bylaws that will apply to open access land in their jurisdiction, subject to consultation with the relevant local access forum and countryside body. They also have powers to set up the necessary infrastructure to make the new access land easily available to walkers, including the power to appoint wardens, erect and maintain notices and improve means of access.

What is a local access forum?

Local access forums, made up of landowners, users and others with an interest in the land, have been established to advise access authorities on the local application of the law. This may mean commenting on access management, or the need for signage, or the necessity or otherwise of a proposed long-term local access restriction.

Are landowners able to close their land for any reason?

The Act allows landowners to close their land for up to 28 days a year (including some Saturdays and Sundays) for any reason. Natural England and the Countryside Council for Wales should be informed of these closures and can make the information publicly available. Landowners may apply for further closures or restrictions, on a temporary or permanent basis, for public safety, land management or fire risk. There may also be restrictions to protect wildlife or areas of historic interest or on the grounds of national security.

What should I do if I see a misleading notice?

Please contact your local authority using the problem report form on p45, and then inform the Ramblers' Association in England or Wales.

What if there is no way onto the access land?

Access authorities must provide ways of getting to access land, ideally in consultation with the landowner but by order if necessary. If you find there is no way of getting to the access land then please contact your local authority using the problem report form on p45, and then inform the Ramblers' Association.

For more access advice, visit www.ramblers.org.uk/freedom

PATHS & ACCESS

RIGHTS OF WAY FAQs

What is a right of way?

A right of way is a path that anyone has the legal right to use on foot, and sometimes using other modes of transport.

 Public footpaths are open only to walkers, and may be waymarked with yellow arrows

 Public bridleways are open to walkers, horse-riders and pedal cyclists, and may be waymarked with blue arrows

 Restricted byways are open to walkers, horse-riders, pedal cyclists and horse-drawn carriages and may be waymarked with purple arrows

Byways Open to All Traffic (BOATs) are open to all classes of traffic including motor vehicles, though they may not be maintained to the same standard as ordinary roads, and may be waymarked with red arrows

Legally, a public right of way is part of the Queen's highway and subject to the same protection in law as all other highways, including trunk roads.

What are my rights on a public right of way?

Your legal right is to 'pass and repass along the way'. You may stop to rest or admire the view, or to consume refreshments, providing you stay on the path and do not cause an obstruction. You can also take with you a 'natural accompaniment' which includes a pram, or pushchair, or a manual or powered wheelchair (mobility scooter) provided you follow the regulations for taking these vehicles on ordinary roads. However, there is no guarantee that the path's surface will be suitable for pushchairs and wheelchairs. You can take a dog with you, but you must ensure it is under close control. Note that there is no requirement for stiles to be suitable for use by dogs.

How do I know whether a path is a public right of way or not?

The safest evidence is the official 'definitive map' of public rights of way. These maps are available for public inspection at the offices of local surveying authorities (county or unitary councils). In addition, public rights of way information derived from them is shown by the Ordnance Survey on its Explorer and Landranger maps. Some rights of way are not yet shown on definitive maps. These can quite properly be used, and application may be made to surveying authorities for them to be added to the map. The inner London boroughs are not required to produce definitive maps, but this doesn't mean there are no rights of way there.

How does a path become public?

In legal theory most paths become rights of way because the owner 'dedicates' them to public use. In fact, very few paths have been formally dedicated, but the law assumes that if the public uses a path without interference for some period of time – set by statute at 20 years – then the owner had intended to dedicate it as a right of way. A public path unused for 20 years does not cease to be public (except possibly in Scotland). The legal maxim is 'once a highway, always a highway'.

Paths can also be created by agreement between local authorities and owners or by compulsory order, subject (in the case of objection) to confirmation by the Secretary of State for the Environment, Food and Rural Affairs, or the National Assembly for Wales.

Can a landowner put up new gates and stiles where none exist presently?

No. Not without seeking and getting permission from the local authority and then complying with any conditions to that permission. Maintaining stiles and gates is primarily the owner's responsibility, but the local authority must contribute 25% of the cost if asked and

RIGHTS OF WAY FAQs

may contribute more if it wishes. If stiles and gates are not kept in proper repair the authority can, after 14 days' notice, do the job itself and bill the owner.

How wide should a path be?
The path should be whatever width was dedicated for public use. This width may have arisen through usage, or by formal agreement, or by order, for example if the path has been diverted. The width may be recorded in a statement accompanying the definitive map but in many cases the proper width will be a matter of past practice on that particular path.

Is it illegal to plough up or disturb the surface of a path so as to make it inconvenient to use?
Yes, unless the path is a footpath or bridleway that runs across a field (as opposed to alongside a field edge). In this case the landowner can plough or otherwise disturb the path surface provided it is not reasonably convenient to avoid doing so. The path must be restored within 24 hours of the disturbance, or within two weeks if this is the first such disturbance for a particular crop. The restored path must be reasonably convenient to use, have a minimum width of 1m for a footpath or 2m for a bridleway, or the legal width (see above) if known, and its line must be clearly apparent on the ground.

What about crops growing on or over a path?
The landowner has a duty to prevent a crop (other than grass) from making the path difficult to find or follow. The minimum widths given above apply here also, but if the path is a field-edge path they are increased to 1.5m for a footpath, 3m for a bridleway. You have every right to walk through crops growing on or over a path, but stick as close as you can to its correct line. Report the problem to the local authority: it has the power to prosecute the landowner or cut the crop and send the owner the bill for the work.

Can a farmer keep a bull in a field crossed by a public path?
Only a bull of up to ten months in age. Bulls over ten months of a recognised dairy breed (Ayrshire, British Friesian, British Holstein, Dairy Shorthorn, Guernsey, Jersey and Kerry) are banned from fields crossed by public paths under all circumstances. All other bulls over ten months are banned unless accompanied by cows or heifers. If any bulls act in a way that endangers the public, an offence may be committed under health and safety legislation.

What is an obstruction on a path?
Anything which interferes with your right to use it, for example a barbed wire fence across the path or a heap of manure dumped on it. Dense undergrowth is not normally treated as an obstruction but is dealt with under path maintenance. Highway authorities have a duty 'to prevent as far as possible the stopping up or obstruction' of paths.

Can I remove an obstruction to get by?
Yes, provided that you are a bona fide traveller on the path and have not gone out for the specific purpose of moving the obstruction, and that you remove only as much as is necessary to get through. If you can easily go round the obstruction without causing any damage, then you should do so. But report the obstruction to the local authority, and/or the Ramblers (see p44).

Are horses allowed on public paths?
Horse-riders have a right to use bridleways, restricted byways and byways open to all traffic. They have no right to use footpaths, and if they do they are committing a trespass against the owner of the land, unless the use is by permission. If use of a footpath by riders becomes a nuisance the local authority can ban them with a traffic regulation order or byelaw. This makes such use a criminal offence rather than an act of trespass.

Are pedal cyclists allowed on public paths?
Pedal cyclists have a right to use bridleways, restricted byways and byways open to all traffic, but on bridleways they must give way to walkers and riders. Like horse-riders, they have no right to use footpaths and if they do so they are committing a trespass against the owner of the land, unless use is by permission. As with horse-riding (see above), use of any right of way by cyclists can be controlled by traffic regulation orders and bylaws imposed by local authorities. Infringement

PATHS & ACCESS

of bylaws or orders is a criminal offence. Under the Highways Act 1835, it is an offence to ride a bicycle on the pavement at the side of a road, and under the Fixed Penalty Offences Order 1999 a person who rides on a pavement can be fined on the spot by a police officer.

Is it illegal to drive cars or motorcycles on public paths?

Anyone who drives a motor vehicle on a footpath, bridleway or restricted byway without permission is committing an offence. This does not apply if the driver stays within 15 yards of the road, only goes on the path to park and does not obstruct the right of passage. The owner of the land, however, can still order vehicles off even within 15 yards from the road. Races or speed trials on paths are forbidden. Permission for other types of trials on paths may be sought from the local authority, if the landowner consents.

What is trespass?

A person who strays from a right of way (or access land – see Right to roam FAQs, p39), or uses it other than for 'passing and repassing' commits trespass against the landowner.

In most cases, trespass is a civil rather than a criminal matter. A landowner may use 'reasonable force' to compel a trespasser to leave, but not more than is reasonably necessary. Unless injury to the property can be proven, a landowner could probably only recover nominal damages by suing for trespass. But of course you might have to meet the landowner's legal costs. Thus, a notice saying 'Trespassers will be Prosecuted', aimed for instance at keeping you off a private drive, is usually meaningless. Criminal prosecution could only arise if you trespass and damage property. However, under public order law, trespassing with an intention to reside may be a criminal offence under some circumstances. It is also a criminal offence to trespass on railway land, sometimes on military training land, and land specifically designated under the Serious Organised Crime and Police Act 2005.

A fuller version of this text is available as a factsheet (FS7) from the Ramblers Bookshop (see p109) and on our website. *Rights of Way: a guide to law and practice* is the definitive guide to rights of way law published by the Ramblers and Opens Spaces Society (see p38)

OUTDOOR ACCESS IN SCOTLAND FAQs

What is the Land Reform (Scotland) Act?

The Land Reform (Scotland) Act 2003 establishes a statutory right of responsible access and is accompanied by the Scottish Outdoor Access Code (see p43). For a full explanation visit www.ramblers.org.uk/scotland.

How does the Act affect my access to the Scottish countryside?

There has long been a general presumption of access to all land unless there is a very good reason for the public to be excluded. The access legislation confirms this presumption, and walkers in Scotland now have a statutory right of access to all land, except for areas such as railway lands, quarries, harbours, airfields and defence land where other laws apply. Walkers should act responsibly when exercising their right of access, and follow the Scottish Outdoor Access Code (see p43).

Are there rights of way in Scotland?

Yes, but they are less extensive than in England and Wales because there is a tradition of access to most land. Rights of way do exist, but there is no legal obligation on local authorities to record them, so they don't appear on Ordnance Survey maps, though paths and tracks are shown on these maps as geographical

features and you have a right to walk on most of these. ScotWays keeps a catalogue of rights of way, signs many of them, and maps and describes the major rural routes in its publication *Scottish Hill Tracks*. It is expected that Core Paths will largely supersede the existing arrangements for rights of way.

What is a Core Path?

Local authorities have new duties and powers to develop Core Path Networks by adopting and improving existing paths and creating new ones. Councils have until February 2008 to produce plans for these networks. Core paths will eventually appear on OS Explorer maps. Scottish Natural Heritage and local authorities have developed The Scottish Paths Record database as a tool to help develop path networks.

THE COUNTRYSIDE CODE

RESPECT – PROTECT – ENJOY
If you follow the Countryside Code wherever you go, you'll get the best enjoyment possible and you'll help to protect the countryside now and for future generations.

Be safe – plan ahead and follow any signs
Even when going out locally, it's best to get the latest information about where and when you can go; for example, your rights to go onto some areas of open land may be restricted while work is carried out, for safety reasons, or during breeding season. Follow advice and local signs, and be prepared for the unexpected.

Leave gates and property as you find them
Please respect the working life of the countryside, as our actions can affect people's livelihoods, our heritage, and the safety and welfare of animals and ourselves.

Protect plants and animals, and take your litter home
We have a responsibility to protect our countryside now and for future generations, so make sure you don't harm animals, birds, plants or trees.

Keep dogs under close control
The countryside is a great place to exercise dogs, but it's every owner's duty to make sure their dog is not a danger or nuisance to farm animals, wildlife or other people.

Consider other people
Showing consideration and respect for other people makes the countryside a pleasant environment for everyone – at home, at work and at leisure.

For the full code, including advice for land managers, visit www.countrysideaccess.gov.uk or contact Natural England (☎ 0845 600 3078 www.naturalengland.org.uk) or Countryside Council for Wales (☎ 0845 130 6229 www.ccw.gov.uk)

SCOTTISH OUTDOOR ACCESS CODE

Everyone has the right to be on most land and water for recreation, education and for going from place to place, providing they act responsibly. These access rights and responsibilities are explained in the Scottish Outdoor Access Code.

The key points are:

When you're in the outdoors
• take personal responsibility for your own actions and act safely
• respect people's privacy and peace of mind

• help land managers and others to work safely and effectively
• care for your environment and take your litter home
• keep your dog under proper control
• take extra care if you're organising an event or running a business

If you're managing the outdoors
• respect access rights
• act reasonably when asking people to avoid land management operations
• work with your local authority and other bodies to help integrate access and land management
• respect rights of way and customary access

For more detailed advice, visit www.outdooraccess-scotland.com or contact Scottish Natural Heritage (☎ 01463 725000 www.snh.org.uk)

HOW TO REPORT A PATH PROBLEM

What is a path problem?

There are many types of footpath problem – too many to list here – but the selection below gives a good idea of the type of problem that should be reported. If you have any doubts, please contact our central office.

- **Natural vegetation** – undergrowth, overgrowth, hedgerow encroachment, overhanging branches, fallen trees, etc.
- **Path 'furniture'** – missing or broken stiles, bridges, gates, signposts, waymarks, etc.
- **Agriculture-related** – ploughing, cropping, manure, slurry, etc.
- **Man-made problems** – barbed wire, buildings, fences, walls, rubbish, rubble, etc.
- **Miscellaneous** – misleading notices, dangerous animals, surface problems, etc.

Reporting the problem

When you come across a path problem on a walk in England and Wales, simply follow these steps:

1. Note down the location and details of the problem. Grid references are very useful (help with these can be found on p69). Photos are useful too, so if you've got your camera take a few shots of the problem.

2. Write to the Public Rights of Way Officer at the relevant highway authority. (Highway authorities are the county, unitary, metropolitan, or London borough council for the area in question – i.e. not district, town, parish, or community councils. Visit www.directgov.gov.uk for full listings.) Use the form opposite, or a letter or email is just as good. Outline the details of the problem you encountered, giving as much information as possible. Remember to include your contact details.

3. Make a copy of your form or letter to the highway authority and send this to our central office. This will be forwarded to our local footpath secretary for information. You can also do this online at www.ramblers.org.uk/footpaths/report.html.

4. If possible, we would encourage you to go out and check on any promised action and satisfy yourself that the problem has been resolved.

5. If the problem has not been resolved within a reasonable timescale (say, three months), write again to the highway authority requesting action.

And in Scotland?

In Scotland, access authorities now have a duty to uphold access rights to land generally as well as paths. Contact the access officer in the relevant local authority area or national park (see the access section of www.ramblers.org.uk/scotland). Copy any correspondence to the Ramblers Scotland office and to your Group's access and footpath officer. For further advice ☎ 01577 861222 or email enquiries@scotland.ramblers.org.uk

Enjoy protecting your local footpaths? Then see p19 for details of how to become a Footpath Guardian

PATH OR ACCESS PROBLEM REPORT FORM

Please complete this form to report a footpath or access problem following the instructions opposite.

WHERE WAS THE PROBLEM? Please give as much information as you can

Path report ☐	**Access report** ☐
District..	Nearest Town/Village....................................
Parish/Community	....
From (place)	....
Grid ref.	Grid ref. ....
To (place)	....
Grid ref.	(and if applicable) Grid ref. ....
Path Nº if known......................................	....

Date problem encountered ....

County/unitary authority ....

WHAT WAS THE PROBLEM? Be precise: quote grid references for any specific point or draw a sketch map if you think it will help. If anyone spoke to you, please give details, including their name and address if known

PLEASE GIVE YOUR DETAILS

Name..

Address..

Email..

Telephone .... **Tick box for more Report Forms** ☐

Send this form to
Your relevant local highway authority **and** the Ramblers' Association,
2nd Floor, 87-90 Albert Embankment, London SE1 7TW
☎ 020 7339 8500 • Fax 020 7339 8501

Sidebar: PATHS & ACCESS

Explore
Lee Valley Regional Park

The Park is a regional and national destination for sport and leisure stretching for 10,000 acres between Ware in Hertfordshire down to the river Thames at the East India Dock Basin, and provides activities which suit all ages, tastes and abilities.

For more information all about the Park and what you can do call 0845 677 0601* or visit
www.leevalleypark.org.uk
*local rate number

Area Map

▲ = Places to Stay

1. Rye Meads Nature Reserve & Rye House Gatehouse
2. Dobbs Weir
3. Lee Valley Boat Centre & Lee Valley Leisure Pool
4. The Old Mill & Meadows
5. Lee Valley Park Farms
6. YHA Lee Valley Cheshunt
7. Cornmill Meadows Dragonfly Sanctuary
8. Abbey Gardens
9. Rammey Marsh
10. Gunpowder Park
11. Lee Valley Camping & Caravan Park, Sewardstone
12. Myddelton House Gardens
13. Lee Valley Camping & Caravan Park, Picketts Lock
14. Lee Valley Athletics Centre
15. Picketts Lock Golf Course
16. Tottenham Marshes
17. Walthamstow Marsh Nature Reserve
18. Lee Valley Ice Centre
19. Lee Valley Riding Centre
20. Middlesex Filter Beds & Nature Reserve
21. Lee Valley WaterWorks Nature Reserve & Golf Centre
22. Three Mills
23. Bow Creek Ecology Park
24. East India Bock Basin

Lee Valley Park

Open spaces and sporting places

CITY WALKS

The city walks described here are designed to be city escapes – easy, linear routes that avoid busy streets and lead the walker out of their urban surroundings and into the countryside. All can be embarked upon at any point along their length and contain several drop-out points, and all visit green spaces that make ideal venues for shorter health walks.

In addition to the route description, it is recommended you carry with you the relevant street map or OS Explorer map for which grid references and numbers are given. All durations are approximate and do not include breaks or exploration time. Any information not essential to the route description (such as historical background or local attractions) is shown in italics.

For more city walks and links to footpaths across the country, visit **www.ramblers.org.uk/info**.

LONDON

THREE WINDMILLS WALK FROM BATTERSEA TO THE NORTH DOWNS

A gently hilly walk through three of London's finest parks, and a hidden gem of ancient woodland with several fine panoramic views to savour, plus visits to a working windmill, two sphinx and a notorious prison en route.

Distance: 25.5km/16 miles
OS map: 161
Duration: 7-10 hours
Accessibility: Good paths throughout with gentle inclines. The Dulwich Woods footpath may be muddy after rainy weather
Drop-out points: Herne Hill station (5 miles), Sydenham Hill station (8.5 miles), Crystal Palace station (10.5 miles)

1 Start at Clapham Junction railway station (TQ273754) and turn left out of the St John's Hill main exit and up Lavender Hill. At Battersea Library, turn right up Lavender Walk, past the old bakery buildings, turn left at the top and cross Battersea Rise at the traffic lights into the corner of Clapham Common and follow the path ahead. Take the zebra crossing over The Avenue and continue along the path *to the Grade II-listed Victorian bandstand (TQ285748), which was newly restored last year.*

2 Take the path at 11 o'clock with the café to your left and follow it for several minutes. To your right is the Windmill pub – *the first of three windmills on this route, the pub is actually named after one demolished here in the 18th century. Walk to the left of Long Pond – probably London's oldest model yachting site built in the 1870s – cross the road, follow the path over the grass and turn right at the road. To your left is the Holy Trinity*

church where the Clapham Sect congregated, led by the abolitionist William Wilberforce. Cross the road at the traffic lights, walk right then first left into Crescent Grove (TQ294752). *This private estate is well worth a detour to admire the superb 19th-century Regency-style townhouses and gardens.*

3 Exit the estate and take the next left down Crescent Lane, across Abbeville Road and Park Hill and turn right by the TA centre onto King's Avenue. Continue ahead, then left before the bus shelter into an alley through a small estate. Turn right onto Lyham Road and, just after John Ashley Close, turn left through a brick doorway (TQ303743) – *the public gate to Brixton Prison, Britain's oldest operational prison built in 1820 and the first women-only facility.* Continue past the main gate and on your left you'll see Brixton Windmill. To get to it, turn left on Brixton Hill and take the next left to the end of Blenheim Gardens. *The windmill pre-dates the prison by four years and was still operational in the 20th century.*

4 Retrace your steps to Brixton Hill, turn left and then right at the traffic lights down Brixton Water Lane. Cross over the junction and turn right through the gates of Brockwell Park (TQ314746). *Formerly the country estate of a wealthy glass merchant, the old manor has great views and a café serving refreshments.*

5 Leave the park by the east exit on Norwood Road and head down Rosendale Road, *passing under a fine Victorian brick railway arch and another steel bridge.* Turn left after the school onto Turney Road, over the junction, under another bridge and then first right down Burbage Road into Dulwich Village.

6 Turn right at the roundabout through the gates (TQ332737) and head down the impressive paved route to the Old College *built in 1618 for poor boys by Edward Alleyn, a bankside theatre owner and master of bear baiting.* Turn left at the war memorial and cross the road into Dulwich Park through the stately Old College Gate. Follow the path round to the right, over the bridge – *noticing an unmistakable Barbara Hepworth sculpture among the trees to your left* – and exit the park by Queen Mary's Gate on your right. Walk right to the crossroads, turn left by the Mill Pond down College Road, *admiring the lavish Charles Barry-designed chapel and spire of the college to your right,* until you reach the tollgate, *the only operational tollgate in London.*

7 Turn left up bucolic Grange Lane, past the allotments and golf club and turn right through a kissing gate into ancient Dulwich Woods (TQ339726). Continue ahead 100m and turn right at the litterbin in the clearing. Head down the hill, through the gate and walk right into the leafy grandeur of Sydenham Hill. Turn left up the hill past tantalising, nay inaccessible, woodland to your left. Keep left to the end of the road, turn left and follow Crystal Palace Park Road to the park entrance (TQ345713) on your right opposite Chulsa Road.

8 Turn right and follow the path around the concert bowl and up onto the Terraces with fantastic views off to the south-east. Head down the main, central steps – *all that remains of the former Great Exhibition building of 1854* – turn right at the car park, follow the Capital Ring signs for Crystal Palace station, and turn left onto Anerley Road – *look out for the amusing anecdote above the door to the Paxton Arms Hotel opposite.* Take the second right for Hamlet Road, then left onto Maberley Road, and continue down to the entrance of South Norwood Lake Park at a sharp right (TQ340697). Head down the path and right around the serene angling lake to the clubhouse exit. Turn left onto Avenue Road and right at the end, walking towards then along the high street. Turn left at the traffic lights, under the bridge, then second left up Albert Road a fair way and left into South Norwood Country Park via the signposted footpath 644 (TQ348681).

9 Follow the gravel path, cross the tramlines and continue along the Waterlink Way cycle route alongside and then back over the tramlines. Cross the grass to rejoin the Waterlink Way at the Arena tram station, go past the golf range, over the A222 and onto Baywood Avenue with the beautiful Long Lane Wood and bird sanctuary to your left. After the short row of houses on your right, turn right into the playing fields (TQ355673) and walk due south, *noticing the bright white sails of Shirley Windmill (TQ355651, via Postmill Close) in the near distance. Fully restored, it opens to the public on the first Sunday of every month, June to October, 1-4pm.*

CITY WALKS

10 At the tarmacked path, turn left and exit the park on Woodmere Avenue, following it down onto Orchard Avenue, over the A232 by the eye-catching art deco library, down Hartland Way to meet up with the London Loop on Shirley Church Road. Turn right and follow the signposts through the delightful Pinewoods, over the crossroads and back on a woodland trail to the summit of

Addington Hill (TQ353644) where superb views of the capital reach as far as Parliament Hill and the Docklands.

11 To continue walking, head east down the hill to meet with the Vanguard Way, or return to the crossroads for frequent buses to Croydon/Norwood, or take a tram from Coombe Lane station on the south side of the hill.

FOUR MORE LONDON ESCAPE ROUTES

LEE VALLEY WALK, EAST INDIA DOCK TO WARE (42KM/26 MILES)
As well as visiting some fascinating industrial heritage and the famous Hackney Marshes, part of this north-east London green corridor includes a canalside walk through the 2012 Olympic site, although access may be restricted. For an overview, visit www.leevalleypark.org.uk.

GRAND UNION CANAL WALK, PADDINGTON TO BUCKINGHAMSHIRE SECTION (37KM/23 MILES)
A picturesque start in well-heeled Little Venice, the towpaths of the famous London-Birmingham canal pass industrial landmarks and impressive country parks before arriving at rural Denham. Visit www.waterscape.com/ Grand_Union_Canal for more details.

THAMES PATH – PUTNEY TO HAMPTON COURT SECTION (35KM/22 MILES)
This beautiful stretch of the national trail following the river's south bank from Putney includes a stretch known as 'Arcadian Thames' around Richmond with pastoral views to the west protected by a 1902 Act of Parliament. Visit thames-landscape-strategy.org.uk or see p35 for more information.

NEW RIVER PATH, ISLINGTON INTO HERTFORDSHIRE (45KM/28 MILES)
Following an early 17th-century artificial watercourse, much of this waymarked route is along grassy riverbank and includes a three-mile heritage section south of Stoke Newington through parks and streets. To download a full route description, Google "New River Path" and click on the Thames Water weblink.

BIRMINGHAM

WATERWAYS ESCAPE TO THE HILLS: DIGBETH TO THE LICKEYS

Beginning at the birthplace and former industrial heart of the city, this gentle river and canalside walk follows a green corridor south into the Worcestershire countryside and finishes with a steep climb up to the Lickey Hills.

Distance: 21km/13 miles
OS map: 220
Duration: 5-7 hours
Accessibility: Good, easy-going footpaths up to Goodrest Lane; the rural footpaths and stiles from then on may be increasingly inaccessible for wheelchair users or those with pushchairs
Drop-out points: Bourneville station (4.5 miles), Primrose Hill – 35 bus (8 miles)

1 Leave New Street station via the city centre exit (SP071864), cross the road and enter the recently-built Bull Ring shopping centre. Walk straight through, keeping left, to the far exit and turn right, down the steps, past the Lord Nelson statue – *where you can admire the panoramic view* – towards the open-air markets and St Martin's Church – *the city's oldest, dating to the 13th century.* (For a step-free alternative, take the lift in the shopping centre to the lower level.)

2 Head left along the rear of the church, then right down Moat Lane and second left onto Upper Mill Lane, before turning right onto Digbeth High Street. Continue straight on, past the coach station, and into the historic area of Deritend

where the road crosses the culverted River Rea (SP077864). *Notice the handsome Victorian facade of the Bird's custard factory on your left (now a media and arts complex), and The Old Crown pub dating from 1368 a few paces on.*

3 At the next set of traffic lights (by the Peugeot garage) turn right and head down Allcester Street. *This is the city's Irish Quarter which is being extensively redeveloped as part of the Eastside project. Old warehouses and Ireland-themed pubs survive among the new high-rise flats. St Anne's Catholic Church, on your right, was JRR Tolkien's childhood church, and further down, the Paragon Hotel is a fine example of a Victorian 'Rowton House' or working men's hostel, once frequented by Orwell and mentioned in 'Down and Out in Paris and London'.* Follow the road around to the right and take the second road on the left – Charles Henry Street. Proceed to the end and turn left along Gooch Street to the bridge over the Rea (SP073852) – *where it is claimed the first Saxon settlers made their homes on the river's banks.*

4 Turn right at the bridge onto Cumberland Avenue following the course of the culverted river, over the busy main road, and along the grassy bank next to the cycle path into Calthorpe Park. Keep to the black railings along the river, through the playground by

Camp for less
on sites with more

The Camping and Caravanning Club

The friendly Club

Damage Barton Club Site

£5 off your stay on one of our award-winning UK Club Sites

If you love camping as much as we do, you'll love staying on one of The Camping and Caravanning Club's 101 UK Club Sites. And with this £5 voucher, you can stay for less. If you're already a member, feel free to use this voucher on your next holiday. If you're not a member, use the voucher to try a Club Site and experience life as a Club member.

There's just one thing: once you've discovered the friendly welcome, the excellent facilities and clean, safe surroundings, you'll probably want to join anyway!

To book your adventure or to join The Club
call **0845 130 7633**
quoting code **0924** or visit
www.campingandcaravanningclub.co.uk

- More choice of highly maintained, regularly inspected sites
- Friendly sites that are clean and safe, so great for families
- Preferential rates – recoup your membership fee in just 6 nights' stay
- Reduced site fees for 55's and over and special deals for families
- Exclusive Member Services including specialist insurance and advice.

£5 off voucher · £5 off voucher · £5 off voucher · £5 off voucher · £5 off voucher

£5 off your site fee with this voucher. Simply present this voucher when you arrive on any Camping and Caravanning Club UK Club Site. Ref **0924**

The Camping and Caravanning Club

The friendly Club

the pavilion and cross the road into Eastwood Road *(with Edgbaston Cricket Ground towering behind)*. Follow the road around into Willow Crescent and turn right onto Cannon Hill Road into Cannon Hill Park (SP069841). *This expansive park boasts an excellent nature centre and café. Look out for the Grade II-listed bandstand, bridge and 16th-century Golden Lion Inn – relocated brick by brick from Digbeth in 1911 and in need of urgent repairs.*

5 Follow the cycle route/River Rea Walkway south through the park and its latter stretches of wildflower meadow and woodland, and on for another mile along a narrow riverside track to Moor Green Lane (or use the hard-surfaced track running parallel on the opposite side of the river). Cross over and continue on the path, over Cartland Road into Hazelwell Recreation Ground – *former site of two*

18th-century mills whose remains can still be seen in the head race channels in the Rea. Cross over the footbridge (SP057812) by the allotments on your left and turn left onto Hunt's Road. Follow it round to the right, turn left at the junction and then first right onto Mary Vale Road. Walk up the hill and turn right before the bridge into the purple entrance for Bourneville station and the Worcester and Birmingham Canal towpath. *The Cadbury's chocolate factory still dominates this area having relocated from the city centre in 1879 and Bourneville was subsequently planned as a model village for its workers. The last commercial traffic to use the adjacent canal in the 1960s probably brought chocolate crumb to the factory.*

6 Walk right along the towpath with the canal on your left, crossing the bridge at Pershore Road to the opposite side (or use the slip road) and again at Lifford Lane. *Notice the picturesque Grade II-listed Junction House where the canal*

meets the Stratford Canal (SP053793). The roving bridge next to it allowed a horse and cart to continue along the towpath uninterrupted. This is now a popular leisure route for narrowboaters on the Stourport Ring, so say hello as they pass! Continue along this leafy, green section of the towpath and go up the steps at the next bridge (SP049783) or continue 200m to the tunnel entrance and take the steep ramp up the bank and return to the road using the cycle track.

8 Go over the stile directly opposite (or take the less overgrown track to the right of the cottage which runs parallel) and follow the route as it descends to the right until you reach a white gate. Turn right here and follow the signs for the North Worcestershire Path (NWP) over the stile, through the fields and out to the road. Turn right and then left after 10m to rejoin the NWP around the back of the farmhouse and up – and then down – High Hill to the A441 main road. Turn left, following the grass verge for 50m and cross over when you can, then over Longbridge Road at the roundabout. (Caution! Take care, this is a very busy road.) Follow the Birmingham Road for 100m, and turn immediately right after the entrance to Groveley Hall back onto the NWP (SP028765). (Beware! The stile and signpost are missing.)

7 Turn left and head up Primrose Hill, following it over Longdales Road to the right of the cemetery. After 50m, turn right through a kissing gate (SP052776) and over the stile onto the footpath (or take the bridleway which runs parallel). Keep right along the field until the path reaches the road and turn right along Goodrest Lane, then right again after the stables into a field and rejoin the footpath heading diagonally left across the field. Turn left at the far corner and follow the fence on your right, over the stile into Redhill Farm (SP045766) and out to the road. (Warning! From this point on, wheelchair users or those with pushchairs may find the rural footpaths and stiles increasingly inaccessible.)

9 Head through the little coppice, over the stile into the field, keeping right, and continue following the path across several fields and into a grange. At the T-junction with another path, turn right, following the NWP with the sounds of ducks and geese on the Upper Bittell Reservoir behind the trees. *This reservoir feeds the Worcester and Birmingham Canal and once acted as an insurance policy, keeping the canal usable during times of drought. Now it is popular for sailing and birdwatching – a young Bill Oddie was a regular visitor.*

10 Go over the stile, keeping left along the field for 150m, then left over another stile through a small coppice and straight across the field ahead. Turn left at the NWP signpost along the perimeter, over the stile and turn left down the tarmac lane. Head straight on, keeping right, through the railway underpass and past the church on your left (SP012753). *The beautiful St Michael & All Angels was founded in 1066 and parts of the building date back to the 15th century. The grounds and graveyard are well worth a few minutes' exploration.*

12 To return to the city centre, take the 62 bus which runs regularly from Rednal, or a train from Barnt Green. Both are another 10–15 minutes' walk downhill via well-signposted footpaths and bridleways.

11 After 50m, turn right through the kissing gate and follow the NWP up the field, veering left and across the bridleway. Continue along the right-hand side of the field *(looking back downhill to see the impressive Georgian-fronted Cofton Hall behind you)*, over the bluff, then out of the field through the kissing gate and up the steep drive to Barnt Green Road. Cross opposite to begin the steep, densely wooded climb to the summit of Cofton Hill and the Lickey Hills Country Park visitor centre (SO996754). *This 524-acre forest and heathland site has spectacular views from its three hilltops and has been a traditional Bank Holiday escape for Brummies since its creation 100 years ago.*

CITY WALKS

THREE MORE BIRMINGHAM ESCAPE ROUTES

RIVER REA HERITAGE TRAIL (22.5KM/ 14 MILES)

Discover far more about the archaeology and ecology of the city's vital river from its source in the peaceful Waseley Hills to the confluence with the River Tame near bustling Spaghetti Junction.

Visit www.riverreatrail.org.uk for a superb array of in-depth resources on the river and a downloadable trail leaflet.

THE ILLEY WAY (7.2KM/4.5 MILES)

A lovely half-day walk from Woodgate Valley Country Park to Waseley Hills Country Park that takes you deep into the countryside. Rare meadow plants, babbling brooks, historic remains and

ancient bluebell woodlands can all be found along its length.

Download a leaflet from Worcestershire County Council's website www.worcestershire.gov.uk (search under 'Illey Way').

THE BIRMINGHAM GREENWAY (37KM/23 MILES)

The southern stretch of this easy, unsigned route offers a variation on the route described above, but extends north via numerous green spaces up to Watford Gap.

An excellent guide by Ramblers stalwart Fred Willits containing transport details, sketch maps and historical background is available from our central office, priced £4.95.

MANCHESTER

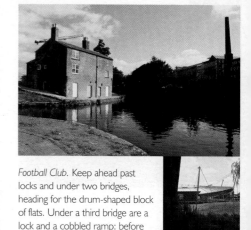

CITY TOWPATH TO PENNINE PIKE:
PICCADILLY STATION TO MOSSLEY

The Ashton Canal passes through industrial relics of the city's past and the new architecture of its future; riverside strolls in a park discover a lovely vale; and country paths by canal and river combine to escape the city and find a dramatic viewpoint on the edge of the hills.

Distance: 17km/10.5 miles

OS map: 277

Duration: 5-7 hours

Accessibility: Good paths throughout. Piccadilly Station to Edge Lane accessible to buggies and wheelchairs; some hills. Daisy Nook Country Park has several accessible routes

Drop-out points: Alan Turing Way (1.5 miles), Edge Lane (3.5 miles), Daisy Nook Country Park (6 miles), Ashton/Oldham Road (7 miles), Lees Road (9 miles) – all have bus links to city and rail network

I Starting from Piccadilly Station concourse (SJ848979) descend the vehicle ramp until you reach a junction. Turn right up Ducie Street until passing over a bridge you meet a wall end on. Keep right, turning towards a crane and a footbridge, and once there head left along the Ashton Canal towpath. *Important early warehouses remain either side of Ducie Street, and the elegant canal aqueduct dates from 1794.*

2 Lock No.1 is reached just under a road. Beyond it, pass either side of the lock-keeper's cottage and continue up the canal. *Early 19th-century tourists to this area were both awestruck and horrified by its concentration of cotton mills, some of which remain.* After approximately 10-15 minutes' walking two gasometers appear, then the massive structure of the City of Manchester Stadium to your right. *Home to the 2002 Commonwealth Games and now Manchester City*

Football Club. Keep ahead past locks and under two bridges, heading for the drum-shaped block of flats. Under a third bridge are a lock and a cobbled ramp: before these turn left up a tarmac path to Stuart Street.

3 Bear left, following the wall to the entrance to Philips Park (SJ870989). Pass a lodge and veer left before a dry water-fountain to descend to a crossroads of tarmac paths. Go straight across then head right under trees. The River Medlock in its channel becomes visible to your left. The path follows its fence-line and skirts an open space with central beds. Where the path continues to meet a footbridge, instead turn right, ascending steeply through a gate to reach a plateau. Turn left towards the red brick viaduct: the path passes

through its one open arch. *Philips Park opened in 1846, a pioneering municipal park. Two modern play areas will satisfy any junior ramblers.*

4 Cross the road beyond the kissing gate. Beyond another kissing gate are two routes. **If on foot**, ascend the steps on the left before turning right on a single track that gradually curves left through trees. After crossing the narrow brick viaduct, descend sharply via steps to your right. Then turn left on a broad, straight track heading gently downhill. **If with buggies or wheelchairs**, ignore the steps and head gently uphill on a broad cobbled road, gradually narrowing before reaching a galvanised kissing gate at the crest of the hill. With a pylon at your left, descend the steep path before heading left downhill on a track through woodland. Continue until you arrive at a junction of tracks amidst boulders. Turning right, descend a broad, straight track heading gently downhill.

5 At a junction of paths keep right to cross the footbridge (SJ881995) over the river before heading left on a broad, tarmac path. Keep straight ahead on this path (running parallel to the river) for approximately 10-15 minutes until a low brick building appears on the right, and Edge Lane road beyond. *Clayton Vale contains ponds, woods and many paths; The Bay Horse Inn (SJ891995) on Edge Lane offers refreshments.*

6 Cross Edge Lane and ascend a steep, cobbled path between trees. Pass the Clockhouse Mews and Old Farm before a path veers left across the grass area. Keep right, just behind houses and gardens, towards a pylon. Behind runs a railway line; the path runs alongside, through woodland and behind houses. Care should be taken on some slippery boardwalks.

7 As the path emerges ascend right up a badly worn road (Sunnyside Avenue). At Parvet Avenue turn left, then left again onto a footpath at the end of the row of houses (SJ899995). Beyond a kissing gate a track enters woodland; keep going and before another kissing gate turn left to cross a footbridge over the railway. Descend steep steps and then note a second set descending right to cross a footbridge over a stream. Ascend steeply until the path forks and keep left; the path soon reaches the valley edge close by a pylon, with increasingly impressive views.

8 Continue on this clear path until, under power lines, it arrives between a hedge and a barbed wire fence. Cross the stile ahead and bear left on a farm track. Cross the stile immediately before and to the left of a bridge and turn left alongside an overgrown canal (SJ912998). *The Hollinwood Branch Canal once linked with the Ashton canal to transport coal to Manchester's mills.*

9 Follow the towpath until it reaches the footbridge over the M60; cross then continue to a kissing gate and Stannybrook Road beyond. Enter Daisy Nook Country Park (SD920005) and, past the visitor centre *(which serves excellent teas, and has maps of the many routes in the park)* follow the path in its cutting. At a stone slope on the left descend right by a gate. Keep ahead on an undulating path through woodland, ignoring paths to the river on the left, until reaching a broad track beyond a stile. Turn left over the river bridge.

10 The track – now a road – ascends: with the high sandstone viaduct ahead take the path on the left that climbs to its level; find the overgrown canal and head right along its towpath. Pass under the A627 road and continue *(passing a Willy Wonkaesque factory (SD932013)* – keeping the fence-line close by your left and the river a distance to your right.

11 Emerging at a road, turn right across Greenfield Bridge before entering the woods opposite. When the path rejoins the road follow it gently uphill, past the industrial relics, until the two brick chimneys of Park Bridge are ahead. *A heritage centre tells the story of the world-class ironworks that once thrived in this quiet vale.* Keep right at the fork, ascending and cresting Alt Hill Road *(the house on your right was once a station, hence the name!)* before descending left past the Old Post Office. At the bridge (SD942023) take the narrow path to the right of the river.

12 At a grassy junction of tracks keep ahead, pass the ruin, and keep right of the channel to ascend into birch woods with outcrops opposite. At a stile Hartshead Pike – a tall tower – is dead ahead; a path at one o'clock passes some reeds on the left, then crosses them on decking and heads straight for the pike. Join a farm track arriving from the left and continue to a T-junction by a house (SD948023); bear left then left again as a stile and narrow path lead up to a road.

13 Cross to a stile to the left. Advance at 11 o'clock towards a sports field, veering right before the house to cross a stile at a fence junction. Continue with the fence at your right until the field corner, turn left towards the tower, and continue by the fence as before. Keep ahead past holly bushes, ignoring a path on the right, until a stile leads to decking over reeds.

14 Cross the decking and take the path that goes directly uphill, gradually veering right towards telegraph wires and a stile. With the tower in view, cross the farm road and ascend directly up the slope on the path between fence and wall. At the summit turn right to reach the tower (SD961024) and see the vast panorama of hills and city. *The Pike is steeped in legend, and was a beacon station from Roman times. Four counties are visible from its summit.*

15 From the tower retrace your steps but descend right down a walled path to a farm. Turn left, then right downhill between further farm buildings, to cross a stile hard by a gate. Head left of the pylon, then keep the wall at your right to reach a road. Descend; just after the house a footpath strikes out at one o'clock across a field: take it, crest the hill and descend through heather to a bus stop on Mossley Road (SD968023). *Buses return to Manchester from this stop, helpfully opposite a pub. Paths into the Peak District National Park are readily accessible from Mossley; regular bus and rail services link the town with Manchester and Yorkshire.*

THREE MORE MANCHESTER ESCAPE ROUTES

CITY WALKS

THE IRK VALLEY (9KM/5.5 MILES)

A fascinating walk from Victoria Station to Blackley Forest along Manchester's 'forgotten river', gradually being reclaimed from industry. Roadside elements lessen before trails reach the lovely Blackley Forest. Footpaths link the route to Heaton Park and the Rochdale Way beyond Middleton.

Visit www.irkvalley.info/walking.htm for further details and downloadable maps.

IRWELL VALLEY SCULPTURE TRAIL (48KM/30 MILES)

This varied route stretches from the River Irwell's ship canal docks to its source high in the West Pennine hills. The northern trail is excellent, but the entire route includes some startling and surprising works of art.

Visit www.irwellsculpturetrail.co.uk or contact Salford City Council (☎ 0161 794 4711) for further details.

CHESHIRE RING CANAL WALK (155KM/96 MILES)

The Ashton, Rochdale and Bridgewater Canals all provide easy walking from the city. This route links them with three other historic canals to provide a loop through rural Cheshire and the fringes of the Dark Peak.

Visit www.waterscape.com and search for 'Cheshire Ring' for further information, or contact British Waterways' Pennine and Potteries Office ☎ 01782 785703.

CARDIFF

GRAVES AND PARKS ARC

An easy, shaded level walk that arcs from west to east across the city taking in two of the capital's most famous parks and a Victorian cemetery.

Distance: 8km/5 miles
OS map: 151
Duration: 2-3 hours
Accessibility: Good, level footpaths throughout
Drop-out points: Blackweir (2 miles), Roath Park north (3.5 miles)

the park is a regular 'love-in' for tree-huggers and contains over 700 varieties of tree, including many nominated as Champion Trees (exceptional for their size or historical significance).

1 Start at Cardiff Central station (ST182758), turn left down Wood Street and then right at the Millennium Stadium and walk along the Millennium Walkway (gates open 7am to 7pm, except on event days. Alternatively, cross the river bridge, turn right and walk alongside the river). Cross over Castle Street to the Animal Wall and enter Bute Park at West Gate Lodge (ST178765). *The park was originally part of the grounds of Cardiff Castle. In 1776, the first Marquis decided to restore the castle back to habitable condition and engaged Capability Brown to landscape the area. But its current appearance and gardens owe most to the design carried out by the Bute Estate in the late Victorian era. (The head gardeners then were Andrew Pettigrew and son Andrew Alexander Pettigrew who are buried in Cathays Cemetery which we visit later.) Today*

2 Take the central path past the Gorsedd stone circle. *The central stone slab is apparently from a megalithic monument found in the park.* Follow the path round to the right until you come to a small bridge over a stream. *This is a Dock Feeder Canal, constructed between 1836 and 1841, and it follows the line of the medieval millstream that fed water to the corn mills of Cardiff.* Take the small path just before the bridge on the left-hand side; alternatively a concrete path runs parallel. *Watch out for the giant Gunnera manicata along*

EXIT
by Salomon

SALOMON

the bank and listen for the sound of strings and oboes as you pass the Welsh College of Music and Drama.

3 It'll take you around 20 minutes to reach the sports ground changing rooms, at which point you should strike off the path across the cricket fields (or around the edge if there's a game on) towards the woods beyond. Either of the paths through the woods will lead you to the weir (ST172781). *The bridge that spans the 40ft weir looks like a mini version of Norman Foster's Millau Bridge in France. The annual salmon migration begins in September, and Blackweir is an ideal position to watch them attempting to leap up the weir (although it's rare that any are successful). If you cross the bridge you can double-back along the Taff Trail to central Cardiff.*

4 Just before the bridge, a path to the right takes you deeper into the woods. Follow this path to a T-junction then turn left. *The path you have joined may look like a converted railway line, but is in fact the filled-in section of the once proud Glamorgan Canal that transported iron and coal from the south Wales valleys to Cardiff docks.* After about five minutes' walk you will come across another little bridge and the park's exit to the right leading to Llys Tal-y-Bont Road, then Parkfield Road and the first drop-out point. *The Maindy pub on the main road here opens at 2pm, or you can catch a bus back to central Cardiff.*

5 To continue, cross the main road and walk to the end of Canada Road. Cross over Whitchurch Road and head down Llanishen Street. The pedestrian entrance to Cathays Cemetery is opposite and to the left (ST179787). *This is one of the largest Victorian cemeteries in Britain. Opened in 1859, it was billed by the local press as a place 'that would form the principal walk of the inhabitants of Cardiff'.* It's easy to get lost among the gravestones, so if you'd like to find out about the 'residents' you can pick up the Cathays Cemetery Heritage Trail booklet in the information shed: look for the copper roof of the Mortuary Chapel and head towards it. Here you'll also find the main entrance and toilets.

6 Leave the cemetery and turn left down Fairoak Road. A brisk five-minute walk, skirting the roundabout, past YHA Cardiff, and under the Eastern Avenue bridge, will take you to the west entrance of Roath Park – *where there are buses back to central Cardiff. There are a number of options here depending on your mood: 12 more Champion Trees to discover (numbered), a Victorian conservatory, rose gardens and a large children's play area.* For this route though, take the left-hand path towards Roath Park Lake. Five minutes' walk will take you to the south shore of the lake, with a boathouse, café, toilets and the Scott Memorial (ST185793).

Captain Scott's famous Antarctic expedition departed from Cardiff on 15 June 1910. The Terra Nova was originally to sail from London, but was moved to Cardiff partly because of easy access to coal, but mainly due to some 'dubious' dealings by Scott's second in command, Lt 'Teddy' Evans, who exploited his connection with the city as part of a fundraising exercise. The lighthouse and scale-model of the Terra Nova were constructed three years after Scott's death in 1912, as a memorial to the ill-fated expedition.

7 You can walk the extra mile or so around the lake, but you 'may be gone some time'. *(Regular evening walks are organised by the Park Ranger Service to view bats circling the lake.)* Instead, cross the promenade and head back along the east side of the park. Take the left-hand track up into the rockery to avoid the crowds. Follow the path all the way to the south-east exit and cross the

Ty Draw Road at the traffic lights – an entrance to the Pleasure Gardens can be seen to the left. Head in and follow the path along the left bank of the stream past the little bridge, tennis courts and bowling green until you come to the south-east exit.

8 Cross over Alder Road and the little iron bridge to get to the recreation ground. From here you can follow the path to the left along the banks of the stream, or head across the field making a beeline for the distant steeple of St Andrews church. Approximately 10 minutes should see you safely to the south end of the park where there is a community centre (ST192781), toilets and another children's play area, marking the final destination for this walk. Buses leave here to Queen's Street for a little post-walk shopping or tipple.

THREE MORE CARDIFF ESCAPE ROUTES

THE TAFF TRAIL – BRECON TO CARDIFF (88KM/55 MILES)

A multi-purpose route along the Taff valley using old railway lines, canals and forestry paths linking the Brecon Beacons with Cardiff Bay via Merthyr Tydfil and Pontypridd.

For further information, visit www.tafftrail.org.uk or contact the parks service at Cardiff Council ☎ 029 2068 4000, parks@cardiff.gov.uk

FOREST FARM COUNTRY PARK (VARIOUS WALKS)

Situated close to the M4 junction, this 60-acre park is a slice of peaceful countryside within the north-west of the city and boasts ancient woodland, important wetlands and a nature reserve.

Download a park guide and walking map from www.forestfarm.org.uk or visit www.glamorganwalks.com/coryton.htm for an alternative route and details of many other walks in the region.

CARDIFF CENTENARY WALK (3.6KM/ 2.2 MILES)

This popular tourist walk may not take you far from the city's centre, but it does visit some of Cardiff's most celebrated and historic landmarks, as well as some well-kept secrets. ☎ 08701 211258 or get a free leaflet by emailing tourism@cardiff.gov.uk.

EDINBURGH

SHOPS TO SHORE WALK FROM CITY TO PORTOBELLO

From Edinburgh's heart to Edinburgh's seaside, this walk lets you discover some of the city's fascinating history and explore some less trodden paths while taking in fine landscapes and fresh sea air.

Distance: 8km/5 miles
OS map: 350
Duration: 2-3 hours
Accessibility: On excellent paths throughout, this walk is easy with only a few gentle hills
Drop-out points: Scottish Parliament (1 mile), Duddingston (4 miles)

1 Set off from the Waverley Bridge Exit of Waverley Station (NT257738) and turn left. Go right at the mini-roundabout, heading up the steep Market Street alongside Princes Street Gardens. Turn left, skirting the impressive

Museum on the Mound, and then follow the road to the right onto Bank Street. At the top, turn left on to the Royal Mile (Lawnmarket), passing the High Court of Justiciary and the statue of Hume on the left. This

simple route follows the Royal Mile – *on the east side of a once-active volcano and carved out by the Ice Age* – towards the sea in the distance. *The name is believed to originate from the current High Street, which was once called Via Regis or 'Way of the King'.*

2 *To the right is the Lothian Regional Chambers, which at the request of a local sheriff, was modelled on a temple he saw in the Acropolis in Athens in the early 19th century. A church has also stood here for over 1,000 years – today it is the impressive St Giles' Cathedral.* Continue down the cobbled street flanked by six- and seven-storey buildings, *which is always packed with street performers during the annual Festival.* Behind, you will catch a glimpse of the famous castle

walls. *The many gaps between the buildings on this route are called closes, which once divided the enclosures used to house livestock, and are great to explore.* Continue past the City Chambers and a stone Wellhead on your right. *It provided water from Comiston springs to the citizens of the city from 1675 and was restored in 1997 with the addition of basins and drinking water.*

3 Continue straight on at the North/South Bridge junction, passing a number of souvenir shops and eating establishments to reach the Story Telling Centre and John Knox House on your left (NT261737). *Of particular interest is the mix of old and new,*

including the almost Shakespearean-style features, sundial and intricate finishing on the stone and wood. When you meet the road at The World's End pub, continue straight on to Canongate. *The pub and the neighbouring close take their name from the wall erected here after the Battle of Flodden in 1513 to protect the citizens of the Burgh. If you look closely, you will see brass cobbles which mark where the ancient gates used to be.*

4 Continue downhill passing the Canongate Kirk, *where local man and famous Scots poet, Robert Fergusson is buried. History tells that Robert Burns never met Fergusson but so respected his work he paid for a gravestone, which the Fergussons could not afford.* At the roundabout, follow the

road round to the right onto Horse Wynd, from where you can see the hulk of Arthur's Seat and the white dome of Dynamic Earth. The Palace of Holyrood and the Queen's Gallery here are also worth a visit. Continue alongside the Scottish Parliament building – *a controversial, though impressively modern blend of angular shapes in steel, wood and granite* – and the pools, towards the car park on the left. Go right at the roundabout, following the cycle path uphill around the side of Arthur's Seat. *On the right is a play park and at the top, stunning views of the Salisbury Crags and the grassy hills.*

5 When you meet the roundabout, turn right and then left at the next roundabout, walk over the grass and cross the road to join a wooded path (NT270726). (For wheelchair or buggy users, a path along the opposite side of the road meets the same path.) Ahead, turn right onto the cycle path and after a short distance turn right at the crossroads. *Once part of 'The Innocent Railway' – a horse-drawn line between Edinburgh and Dalkeith – this wide, tarmac path is well away from the road and surprisingly peaceful.* Ahead in the distance, you will see the quaint tower of Duddingston Church. Continue on this path for some time until you meet the road.

7 A sign *(and some quaint cobbled streets)* mark your arrival in Portobello. Passing the beautiful St John's Church on the right, you meet Portobello High Street. Continue straight on, passing the public toilets on your left until you reach Portobello beach and promenade (NT307741). *With golden sand and impressive views of Fife and the Lothian coastline, it is hard to believe this beach is so near to the city. Useful public signposts will help you find your way around and there are ample places for refreshments and meals.*

6 Cross the road and turn left, following the sign for Duddingston village. Continue on this road, passing by residential areas, to meet a junction and continue straight down Duddingston Road. You will soon come upon a gate for Figgate Park on your left (NT293732), *a lovely park with a variety of flowers and saplings as well as grasslands and benches.* Enter here and follow the path, with the stream *(known locally at the 'Figgie Burn')* on your left. Continue under the bridge and keep straight until you meet the loch – *look out for nesting birds on the island* – before continuing straight on a gradual uphill path to exit the park at Baileyfield Road. Turn right, walk to the junction and then turn left onto Southfield Place, heading towards the rail bridge.

8 To return to the city centre, head back up the street on to Portobello High Street. Lothian Bus 49 leaves regularly from the front of City Hall and stops at North Bridge (just off Princes Street).

FOUR MORE EDINBURGH ESCAPE ROUTES

WATER OF LEITH WALKWAY FROM BALERNO TO LEITH (19KM/12 MILES)

A popular route for both locals and tourists. Probably the most walked section is from Roseburn to Canonmills, passing the picturesque Dean Village.

Visit the Water of Leith Visitor Centre at www.waterofleith.org.uk/find/find.shtm or ☎ 0131 455 7367 daily from 10am to 4pm.

PENICUIK TO MUSSELBURGH (17.5KM/ 11 MILES)

This cycle path is mainly flat and off road with a number of interesting historical and natural attractions en route. For a shorter route, you can start from the cycle path at Arthur's Seat, near the city centre, following the old railway line to Musselburgh.

Visit walking.visitscotland.com/ walks for more about this and numerous other routes.

HAYMARKET TO FORTH ROAD BRIDGE (14.5KM/9 MILES)

A series of well-signposted cycle paths connect the city to this beautiful viewpoint, passing by the historic Dalmeny House. Set off from the office buildings to the west of Haymarket Station to join the Roseburn Path. From the Forth Road Bridge, you can retrace your steps to Dalmeny to return to the city by train.

Visit www.cycling-edinburgh.org.uk/ escape.htm for further details.

CITY CENTRE TO THE BOTANIC GARDEN (8KM/5 MILES)

A gentle walk from the junction of Princes Street and the Mound, featuring the fine Georgian architecture of the New Town and passing the Gallery of Modern Art to lead to the Botanic Gardens.

Visit walking.visitscotland.com/walks for complete details and many other routes.

MAPS FOR WALKERS

Ordnance Survey maps

The best and most comprehensive walkers' maps of Britain are the 1:25 000 scale Ordnance Survey (OS) Explorer series in orange covers. They include a range of geographical features and landmarks at a high level of detail, including field boundaries, heights shown as contours and 'spot heights', railway stations and tram stops. They also show rights of way (and core paths in Scotland in the most recent editions), permissive paths, many long distance paths, off-road cycle paths, open access land, locations of shorter circular walks and nature trails, information centres and visitor attractions.

Another OS series, 1:50 000 Landranger maps in pink and silver covers, also include footpaths and selected tourist attractions, but show less detail; OS is now marketing them as maps for planning days out rather than navigating on the ground. Bookshops, information centres, larger newsagents and even some garages stock their local OS sheets. Maps can also be bought from specialist retailers, over the internet or direct from the OS, who can also supply a free Mapping Index showing all the sheet numbers.

Ordnance Survey ☎ 0845 605 0505
www.ordnancesurvey.co.uk

Or buy OS maps online from **Aqua3** through the Ramblers website and earn a 10% discount with free postage. The Ramblers receives a 10% donation for every map sold this way.

Other paper maps

While no other publisher covers all of Britain at detailed scales, a number of other specialist publishers do offer maps of use to walkers. The most important is Harvey who produces very clear specialist walkers' maps of certain popular upland areas and long distance paths at 1:25 000 and 1:40 000 scales. The maps also usually include useful information and addresses, and most are printed on weatherproof paper.

Harvey Maps ☎ 01786 841202 (credit card hotline)
www.harveymaps.co.uk

In urban areas street atlases can be more useful than OS maps. The Philips series is probably the best for walkers since most rights of way and other off-road paths, parks and open spaces – and even some promoted routes – are clearly shown.

Philips ☎ 01903 828503 (mail order)
www.philips-maps.co.uk

Electronic maps

Electronic mapping systems for home PCs enable you to print OS maps at a variety of scales, to plan and annotate routes, and link up to a GPS or pocket PC to take out on your walk – but make sure your hardware is compatible with the system you want to buy. The main suppliers are:

Anquet Maps ☎ 0845 330 9570
www.anquet.co.uk

Hillwalker (ISYS) ☎ 0845 166 5701
www.hillwalker.org.uk

memory-map ☎ 0870 740 9040
www.memory-map.co.uk

TrackLogs www.tracklogs.co.uk

Mapping websites allowing you to view extracts from Landranger and street maps by grid reference, postcode or place name include www.streetmap.co.uk, www.multimap.com, www.map24.co.uk and the OS site.

Learning more about maps

In addition to the map and compass tutorial on the next page of this book, the free *Map Reading Made Easy* from OS is an excellent brief introduction and is downloadable from their website.

Two particularly useful books are available from the Ramblers Bookshop (see p109 to order). *Navigation and Leadership: a manual for walkers* is the Ramblers' official bible on the use of map and compass and leading group walks. Julian Tippett's *Navigation for Walkers* is a great beginners' guide which includes OS map extracts, (the author also helped produce the tutorial overleaf).

See the Maps section on our website which lists navigation course providers and suggestions for further reading. This information is also available as a printed fact sheet – FS2 (see p109).

MAPS & TRANSPORT

Ramblers map library...

Our central office has the complete range of Ordnance Survey Explorer 1:25,000 and Landranger 1:50,000 maps available to loan to **members only** for a small fee.

A maximum of 10 can be borrowed at any one time, for a period of four weeks from the date of issue.

☎ 020 7339 8500 or visit www.ramblers.org.uk/membership/maplibrary.html to order.

HOW TO USE A MAP AND COMPASS

For effective navigation, in addition to the appropriate maps, you should also carry:

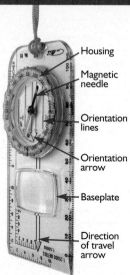

Housing

Magnetic needle

Orientation lines

Orientation arrow

Baseplate

Direction of travel arrow

- a **compass** – in lowland areas you could rely purely on map-reading skills, but using map and compass together, provided you have the basic skills, will help you follow your route with much more accuracy, particularly in woods. In the hills a compass is essential, especially when visibility is poor. Choose an **orienteering** or **protractor** compass with a rectangular baseplate of reasonable size so it can be turned while wearing gloves, and clearly marked km/m scales that can be read in poor light
- a reliable **watch**, to help judge speed, monitor progress and plan for future journeys
- a **torch**, especially on short winter days
- something to **protect** non-waterproof maps, such as a polythene bag or map case.

A **GPS** will provide an accurate check of position at any time, and can be programmed to provide directions for a complete route. It is, though, essential to be well practised in its use.

Map interpretation

Maps are simply an accurate picture of the ground as seen from above, scaled down from life size and with symbols to show particular features and landmarks. On a 1:25 000 map such as an OS Explorer, one unit of length on the map represents 25,000 units on the ground, so 1cm on the map represents 25,000cm, that is 250m or 0.25km on the ground. On a 1:50 000 map, 1cm on the map represents 500m on the ground.

To find out what features the different **symbols** represent (buildings, different kinds of church, electricity pylons, roads and railways, woods, orchards, scrub or marsh and so on) consult the key shown on the map. The best way to learn these symbols is to relate them to the way they appear on the ground.

Some map markings do not show on the ground, such as council boundaries (unless these follow a physical feature such as a river or ditch), contours and grid lines. Rights of way marked on maps will often be visible as a distinct path or track on the ground, but in less well-walked areas the path may not be visible. **Footpaths and bridleways** are marked as green dashes on Explorer maps (magenta on Landranger). Remember: although a good map will remain useful for at least a few years, the landscape is ever-changing and you should not be surprised if some features on the ground do not agree with your map.

To measure the approximate distance of your route, take a piece of thin string and lay it carefully along the exact route on the map, then lay it straight along the scale line on the map's margin. With practice, you'll soon learn to estimate the distances involved by eye, but don't forget the extra effort of climbing hills when calculating how long the route will take to walk.

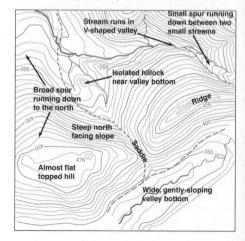

Contours are lines connecting points of equal height above sea level. Together with spot heights, they are the means used by the map-maker to portray the shape of the land, its height, the form taken by hills and valleys, steepness of slopes and so on. On Explorer maps, the interval between contours is 5m in lowland areas and 10m where mountainous. At random points along many of the contour lines a number is shown to indicate its height, always printed so that the top of the number points uphill. Every fifth contour line is printed more thickly than the others. The closer together contours are the steeper the ascent or descent for the walker. **Spot heights** – shown as a number beside a dot – appear at strategic points, often along roads where they level out

How to take or locate a six-figure grid reference

What is the grid reference of the church?

1. Identify the 1km square containing the church. Do this by selecting its left and bottom sides (imagine a letter 'L' bounds the square).
2. Take the numbers on the edge of the map for these two sides (downstroke of the 'L' first, as you would write it). This gives: 31_25_ (Note: 3125 is the four-figure grid reference of the square).
3. Now an extra figure must be added to each pair of numbers to specify to the nearest 100m where the church lies within the square. Estimate the number of tenths (100m) the church lies from the two sides, once again starting with the downstroke. It is seven-tenths from the downstroke and four-tenths from the horizontal stroke, so the six-figure grid reference is: 317254.

To find a point on a map using a six-figure grid reference, simply do the reverse. Start with the eastings (the first three figures) and then move up the northings (the last three). A helpful reminder is the saying: "go along the corridor and then up the stairs".

Many compasses also contain a **romer** – a rectangular scale on the clear plastic baseplate – that makes estimating the tenths easier, though make sure you have the correct romer for the scale of your map.

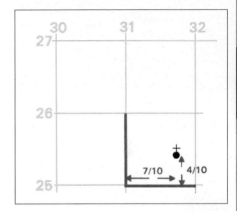

at the top or foot of a hill. These can be a useful guide where contour height numbers are infrequent.

Grid references

All OS maps are criss-crossed by vertical and horizontal **grid lines** (coloured blue on Explorer maps) which are 4cm apart on 1:25 000 scale maps and 2cm apart on the 1:50 000 scale. A **grid reference** uses six figures to identify a particular spot on a map that is 100 metres square. The first three specify the vertical lines (the eastings) and the second three the horizontal (the northings). Sometimes four-figure grid references are used to give a rough location (the map grid square).

Using the compass

There are three basic techniques detailed here that should be mastered with a compass:

- **Setting the map** – aligning the map in the direction you are facing so features on the map match those on the ground.
- **Travelling on a bearing** – walking over open ground on a bearing taken from the map.
- **Checking the direction of the path** – e.g. at a junction in a wood where you can see no other landmarks to help you.

Setting the map

Setting the map (or orientating the map) helps relate the map to the countryside by turning the map so that your direction of travel is at the top. When done, all features

on the map and on the ground are seen to lie in the same direction from your current position, and the north edge of the map points to north on the ground.

The map can be set by aligning it to prominent features in the landscape, or by compass. Simply place the compass on your map in any orientation (or even just drop it into your map case). Then rotate the map and compass together so the compass needle aligns with any north-pointing grid line, with the red end of the needle pointing to the top of the map (ignore all other parts of the compass).

MAPS & TRANSPORT

Travelling on a bearing

If you want to travel from your present position to a landmark you cannot see due to poor visibility, use the following procedure:

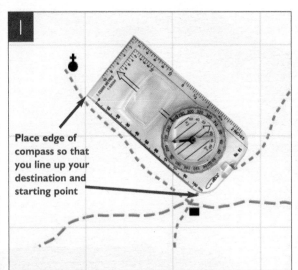

1

Place edge of compass so that you line up your destination and starting point

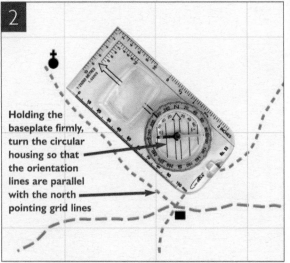

2

Holding the baseplate firmly, turn the circular housing so that the orientation lines are parallel with the north pointing grid lines

3

Take the compass off the map, and hold it as shown.
Turn your body to align the red end of the compass needle to the red end of the orientating arrow ('red on red').
The direction of travel arrow now points along the path to take.

NB *You can also use this procedure to check the direction of a path.*

MAPS & TRANSPORT

FALKE

ERGONOMIC SPORT SYSTEM

ACHILLES PROTECTION

OPTIMUM PRESSURE DISTRIBUTION

ASYMETRIC TOE BOX

MOISTURE MANAGEMENT

PUBLIC TRANSPORT

Help avoid pollution and congestion by combining walking and public transport. You can plan more flexible walks such as linear walks, and forget worries like parking, car crime and whether or not you should have a pint along the way.

For information about **train** services and fares, including an online journey planner, use:
National Rail ☎ 0845 748 4950, textphone 0845 605 0600 www.nationalrail.co.uk

For long distance **coaches**, use:
National Express ☎ 08705 808080
www.nationalexpress.com
Scottish Citylink ☎ 08705 505050 www.citylink.co.uk

For **local transport** information, including online journey planners for local bus, metro/underground, tram/light rail and ferries, use:
Transport Direct www.transportdirect.info
Transport for London ☎ 020 7222 1234
www.tfl.gov.uk
Traveline ☎ 08712 002233 www.traveline.org.uk

There is an increasing number of services for **countryside visitors**, especially in popular areas during the summer. They often run on Sundays and bank holidays and offer economical ticket deals for those planning linear walks. See the information section of our website, and:
Countrygoer www.countrygoer.org

Travel information for people with **disabilities** is available from:
Door to Door www.dptac.gov.uk/door-to-door

We encourage **Ramblers Areas and Groups** to organise walks by public transport wherever possible. Ramblers walk leaders in need of advice on organising walks by public transport should contact the countryside protection team at our central office, who can put you in touch with our network of regional transport contacts.

If cars are necessary to get to a Group walk, then check that there are adequate parking facilities at the starting point. If possible, this should be an official car park avoiding places where several parked vehicles may cause inconvenience to residents or businesses.

MAPS & TRANSPORT

LUGGAGE CARRIERS

Aberchalder (Scotland) ☎ 01809 501411
AMS (Scotland) ☎ 01360 312840
www.ams-scotland.com
Bag Tag (Isle of Wight) ☎ 01983 861559
www.bagtagiow.co.uk
Bike and Hike (Scotland) ☎ 01877 339788
www.bikeandhike.co.uk
Brigantes (North of England) ☎ 01729 830463
www.brigantesenglishwalks.com
Byways Breaks
(North West & Welsh Borders)
☎ 0151 722 8050 www.byways-breaks.co.uk
CarryLite (St Cuthbert's Way) ☎ 01434 634448
www.carrylite.com
Coast to Coast Holidays
(C2C, Herriot's and Cleveland Ways)
☎ 01642 489173
www.coasttocoast-holidays.co.uk
Coast to Coast Packhorse
☎ 017683 71777 www.cumbria.com/packhorse
Compass Holidays (England)
☎ 01242 250642 www.compass-holidays.com

Great Glen Baggage Transfer (Scottish Highlands)
☎ 01320 351322
http://uk.geocities.com/greatglenbaggagetransfer/bags
Great Glen Travel (Scottish Highlands)
☎ 01809 501222 www.greatglentravel.com
Loch Ness Travel (Scottish Highlands)
☎ 01456 450550 www.lochnesstravel.com
Sherpa Van Project (UK-wide) ☎ 0871 520 0124
www.sherpavan.com
southernuplandway.com (Southern Scotland)
☎ 0870 835 8448 www.southernuplandway.com
Tony's Taxis (Pembrokeshire) ☎ 01437 720931
www.tonystaxis.co.uk
Travel-Lite (West Highland Way) ☎ 0141 956 7890
www.travel-lite-uk.com
Walkers' Baggage Transfer Company
(Hadrian's Wall Path) ☎ 0870 990 5549
www.walkersbags.co.uk
Walking Support (UK-wide) ☎ 01896 822079
www.walkingsupport.co.uk
**For details of more UK luggage carriers, visit
www.ramblers.org.uk/info/contacts/hols.html**

Remember why you bought great gear in the first place?

Because it kept water out, warmth in and all the layers underneath dry.

But that was then. Now, it's probably lost a lot of its original water repellent finish. So it doesn't keep you anything like as comfortable.

Here's how to turn back time: The Granger's range of waterproofing, cleaners and conditioners.

They put back the comfort that time and the weather take away.

Restoring performance. And allowing your gear to work better, for longer. Just like you remember.

To learn more about our complete, environmentally responsible range,
visit **www.grangers.co.uk** or call us on **01773 521 521**.

WHAT TO WEAR WALKING

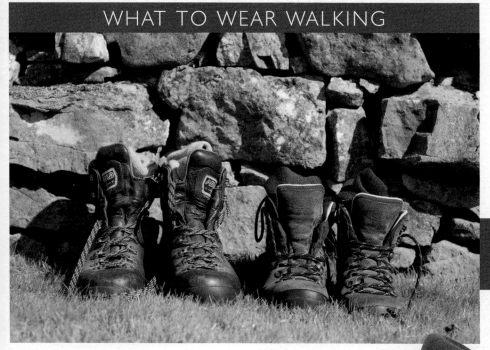

A huge range of clothing is available to make your walking easier, safer and more comfortable, and most walkers find the gear that suits them through experience. **The golden rules** are: be comfortable, dress for the sort of weather and terrain you are likely to meet, and never underestimate the changeability of British weather.

It's advisable to buy your outdoor gear from a specialist supplier who can give you expert advice (such as Millets, whose stores we list on pp81 and 83). A directory of suppliers is available on the Ramblers website **www.ramblers.org.uk/info/equipmentshops**

Footwear – boots or shoes?

Feet are probably the most important part of a walker's body, so treat them with care. If you want to walk regularly in all kinds of weather, especially on longer walks out in the countryside, you should invest in specialist walking footwear.

- **Walking boots** with tough moulded soles are the best all-round solution, protecting and keeping feet warm and dry, providing grip and supporting the ankles – essential on steep slopes.

Meindl boots

- **Walking shoes** are a lighter alternative to boots, offering tough protective soles with good grip, but no ankle support.
- **Good quality trainers** are cheap and lightweight, but usually not waterproof and give limited support and protection.
- **Walking sandals** for lowland use in summer have solid soles suitable for a variety of surfaces, but give no ankle support and less protection from undergrowth and sharp rocks, so should be used with great discretion.

Bridgedale socks

Socks

Boots are more comfortably worn with good walking socks. Modern socks are often made from synthetic looped material, and have extra padding around toes and heels to cushion impact without potentially irritating raised seams. Some even 'wick' sweat outwards or are waterproof.

THE PROFESSIONAL'S CHOICE

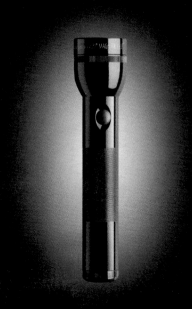

MAGLITE® LED

SETTING THE STANDARD

MAG-LED™ Technology

BRILLIANT WHITE LIGHT

FOCUS FROM FLOOD TO SPOT

POWERFUL PROJECTING BEAM

STANDARD ALKALINE BATTERIES

LIFETIME GUARANTEE

CALL 0116 234 4644 FOR DETAILS OF YOUR NEAREST STOCKIST.

WWW.MAGLITE.COM

Some walkers wear two pairs of socks – a thin cotton or synthetic pair next to the skin, and a thicker pair on top. This helps cushion the feet and prevent blisters. Good walking socks are tough enough to last a while. Discard heavily worn or holed socks; don't attempt to repair them. On long walks, bumps, holes and darning stitches can cause irritation and blistering.

Clothing – waterproof and windproof wear

In the British climate, a good quality **waterproof** (not just showerproof) and windproof jacket or anorak is essential. Look for something with at least a hood (or provision for a hood to be attached) and spacious pockets for maps and snacks. A cheap lightweight cagoule is adequate, but if you plan to do a lot of walking, consider a jacket made from 'breathable' material which allows sweat out but stops rain getting in.

To stop trousers and socks getting wet or muddy, consider waterproof **overtrousers**, or **gaiters** – knee-high waterproof leggings that attach to the boot. Both have their champions, but can be difficult to put on or remove.

Inner layers

The basic principle of outdoor clothing is the **layering** system. Several thin layers are more useful than one thick sweatshirt or large jumper, since warm air is trapped between layers and provides better insulation, and you can add or remove layers according to the weather and level of activity.

The **base layer** nearest the skin is best made of thin synthetic material with the capability of 'wicking' moisture away from the skin and drying quickly. Natural fibres like cotton are not recommended, since they absorb sweat and make you clammy. Wicking base layers work especially well with breathable jackets.

Between the base layer and jacket you can add one or more **insulating layers**, usually made of an open-weave or knit fabric. An ordinary sweatshirt, jersey or high-street fleece will suffice, but a good fleece specially designed for outdoor use

Berghaus base layers, fleeces and waterproof jackets

could offer more warmth and comfort. Some are also windproof, keeping you warmer in cold winds even without a top layer, and a zipped front allows you to alter ventilation.

Trousers

Tracksuit bottoms or everyday casual trousers are fine for the average lowland walk, though can irritate and chafe on long walks. Modern synthetic **walking trousers** are popular among regular walkers, being lightweight, loose-fitting and quick-drying, with handy pockets. Some walkers wear walking shorts in fine weather, though long trousers offer better protection against brambles, nettles and ticks and should always be carried in case the weather changes.

Rohan walking trousers

GEAR

We **don't recommend denim jeans** for long walks in the countryside as they restrict movement, lack pocket space, chafe when wet and take a long time to dry. They have a high wind-chill factor, meaning you can get very cold in them, especially when they get wet.

Head and hands

Up to 40% of body heat is lost through the head, so it is essential to protect your head and ears. A **warm hat** is a must in winter, especially in the hills, and can be worn under a jacket hood.

When sunny, wear a **sunhat** and use **sun cream** on your face and any bare patches of skin. You may be out in the sun for long periods without shelter, and even with a cooling wind or in cold weather you can still burn.

Gloves are important in cold weather, especially for those with circulatory problems. To walk comfortably and with good posture you should be able to swing your arms freely, so putting your hands in your pockets is not an option.

See the Ramblers Bookshop on p109 to order factsheet FS3 for more details about walkers' clothing and equipment, and a buyer's guide

WHAT EQUIPMENT TO TAKE

Karrimor and Aztec backpacks

Equipment checklist

On lowland walks you should also consider carrying:

- ☑ **Map**, **compass** and **navigation equipment** (See How to use a map and compass, pp68-70)
- ☑ Full **water bottle** and/or thermos flask adequate for your walk
- ☑ **Extra clothing**, including hat and gloves, especially in winter
- ☑ **Food**, unless you're absolutely sure you can eat on the way
- ☑ **Emergency rations**
- ☑ A **first aid kit** and any medicines you might need
- ☑ Optionally, a **mobile phone**

And don't forget to make room for non-essential items that might make your walk more enjoyable, such as a notebook, pencil, camera, guidebooks etc.

Rucksacks

Wherever you walk, rucksacks or backpacks are the best means of carrying what you need – they leave your hands free and are far more comfortable than a shoulder bag over a long distance. Modern rucksacks are made of tough, waterproof nylon or polyester fabric and lightweight alloy frames.

The simplest rucksack is a small daysack, which is usually frameless and has only shoulder straps, so that all weight is carried on the shoulders. Larger, more sophisticated travel packs and backpacks have frames, hip-belts and chest-straps to help distribute weight more evenly across the back. Many models now have ventilation features to avoid a sweaty back, and some are designed especially to fit women or children.

Always choose the best size rucksack for the purpose. A daysack of around 20 litres capacity is fine for walks of a day or less, but quickly become uncomfortable across the shoulders if too heavily loaded. For weekends and short breaks, or when you need to carry more equipment, there are various medium-sized packs of 30-55 litres. For longer holidays or serious backpacking with camping equipment, large packs with a capacity of 55-75 litres are available. You should also look for additional features, such as ice-axe loops, key clips and concealed security pockets.

Leki Walking Pole

Garmin GPS

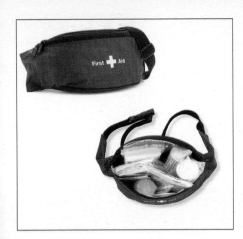

First Aid Kit

A basic first aid kit should include:

- ☑ 10 **plasters** in various sizes
- ☑ 2 **large sterile dressings** for severe bleeding
- ☑ 1 **medium sterile dressing** for larger wounds
- ☑ 4 **triangular bandages** to support suspected broken bones, dislocations and sprains
- ☑ 1 **eye pad** in case of a cut to the eye
- ☑ 4 **safety pins** to secure dressings
- ☑ **Disposable gloves** for good hygiene

Ready-made first aid kits for walkers are available from outdoor shops and **St John Supplies** ☎ 020 7278 7888 www.stjohnsupplies.co.uk.

For more demanding walks in hills or mountains you may need additional equipment, such as:

- ☑ A **survival bag** – a heavy-duty bag for body insulation in an emergency
- ☑ **Torch** and spare batteries
- ☑ **Whistle**
- ☑ **Water purification tablets**
- ☑ **High-energy rations**, such as mint cake, chocolate and dried fruit

If you are likely to encounter heavy snow or ice, wear a pair of heavy-duty winter walking boots that can be fitted with **crampons** – metal spike attachments that give a better grip in icy conditions that are not suitable for all boots – and carry an **ice axe**. Learn how to use them both properly – in the hands of a novice they can cause, rather than prevent, accidents (see appropriate courses on our website www.ramblers.org.uk).

Many hillwalkers carry a **kisu** shelter or **bothy bag**. Like a tent without poles, it is made of lightweight waterproof nylon with a draw cord around the base, is big enough to sit inside and allows two or more people to share bodyheat. Available in a range of sizes, you should carry one that is adequate for the size of your party.

GEAR

LOCAL MILLETS STORES

ABERDEEN	167/168 Union Street AB11 6BB	01224 596230
ABERGAVENNY	Unit 3 Cibi Walk NP7 5AJ	01873 858944
ABERYSTWYTH	3 Great Darkgate Street SY23 1DE	01970 612119
ALDERSHOT	1/2 Wellington Centre GU11 1DB	01252 345979
ALTRINCHAM	101 George Street WA14 1RN	0161 9269794
AMBLESIDE	Unit 12 Market Cross Shopping Centre LA22 9BT	01539 433956
ANDOVER	29 High Street SP10 1LJ	01264 324877
ASHFORD	Unit 24 Park Mall TN24 8RY	01233 634192
AYR	58 High Street KA7 1PA	01292 610516
BAKEWELL	Unit 3 Rutland Square DE45 1BZ	01629 815143
BALLYMENA	Unit 33 Fairhill BT43 6UG	02825 646098
BANBURY	9 High Street OX16 5DZ	01295 263189
BANGOR	261 High Street LL5 71PB	01248 361263
BARNSTAPLE	91 High Street EX31 1HR	01271 342937
BASILDON	21A Town Square SS1 41BA	01268 272771
BASINGSTOKE	11/12 Potters Walk RG21 7GQ	01256 364649
BATH	25/28 High Street BA1 5AJ	01225 471500
BEDFORD	3 West Arcade, Church Street MK40 1LQ	01234 357375
BELFAST	1 Cornmarket BT1 4DA	02890 242264
BEVERLEY	16 Butcher Row HU17 0AE	01482 868132
BEXLEYHEATH	119 The Broadway DA6 7HF	0208 3035089
BICESTER	26/27 Crown Walk OX26 6HY	01869 324854
BIGGLESWADE	2 Market Square SG18 8AP	01767 312089
BIRKENHEAD	32/34 Borough Pavement CH41 2XX	0151 6661350
BIRMINGHAM	35 Union Street B2 4SR	0121 6431496
BISHOP AUCKLAND	63/65 Newgate Street DL14 7EW	01388 602555
BISHOP STORTFORD	26 South Street CM23 3AT	01279 651452
BLACKPOOL	22 Church Street FY1 1EW	01253 628430
BODMIN	27/31 Fore Street PL31 2HT	01208 79003
BOGNOR REGIS	38 London Road PO21 1PZ	01243 837340
BOLTON	53/55 Victoria Square BL1 1RY	01204 366563
BOSCOMBE	13 Sovereign Centre BH1 4SX	01202 300720
BOSTON	16 Market Street PE21 6EH	01205 361753
BOURNEMOUTH	39 Old Christchurch Road BH1 1DS	01202 295911
BRACKNELL	46 High Street RG12 1LL	01344 485 524
BRADFORD	43A Darley Street BD1 3HN	01274 725343
BRAINTREE	86/88 High Street CM7 1JP	01376 554742
BRECON	16 High Street LD3 7AL	01874 624634
BRENTWOOD	7 Chapel High CM14 4RY	01277 223669
BRIDGEND	Brackla State Centre CF31 1EB	01656 657945
BRIDGWATER	5 Fore Street TA6 3NQ	01278 422243
BRIGHTON	Unit 3 Air Street BN1 3FB	01273 777125
BRIGHTON	153 Western Rd BN1 2DA	01273 329435
BRISTOL	10 Broadmead BS1 3HH	0117 9221167
BRISTOL	9/10 Transom House BS1 6A	0117 925 4892
BROMLEY	65 High Street BR1 1JY	0208 460 0418
BURGESS HILL	Unit 77, Church Walk, The Martlets RH15 9BQ	01444 258448
BURNLEY	64/66 St James Square BB11 1NH	01282 831803
BURTON ON TRENT	12 St Modwens Walk DE14 1HL	01283 562488
BURY ST EDMUNDS	2 Buttermarket IP33 1DB	01284 755521
BUXTON	53/55 Spring Gardens SK17 6BJ	01298 25660
CAMBRIDGE	18/19 Sidney Street CB2 3HG	01223 307406
CANTERBURY	47 Burgate CT1 4BH	01227 479698
CARDIFF	10 Duke Street CF10 1AY	02920 390887
CARLISLE	59 English Street CA3 8JU	01228 529206
CARMARTHEN	1 Red Street SA31 1QL	01267 235906
CHELMSFORD	34 High Chelmer CM1 1XR	01245 269989
CHELTENHAM	117 High Street GL50 1DW	01242 520692
CHESHAM	35 High Street HP5 1BW	01494 791920
CHESTER	15/17 Northgate CH1 1HA	01244 329331
CHICHESTER	4 South Street PO19 1EH	01243 786627
CHIPPENHAM	17/18 High Street SN15 3ER	01249 652533
CHISWICK	167 Chiswick High Road W4 2DR	0208 9945807
CIRENCESTER	34 Cricklade street GL7 1JH	01285 651250
COLCHESTER	17/18 High Street CO1 1DB	01206 574615
COLCHESTER	16 Short Wyre Street CO1 1LN	01206 577040
COVENTRY	19 Smithford Way CV1 1FY	02476 837048
COVENTRY	41 Smithford Way CV1 1FY	02476 224841
CRAWLEY	16 Haslett Avenue RH10 1HS	01293 541003
CREWE	7 Queensway CW1 2HH	01270 255446
CROYDON	52 High Street CRO 1YB	0208 688 6066
CROYDON	3 High Street CRO 1QA	0208 688 7830
CWMBRAN	14 Monmouth Walk NP44 1PE	01633 871279
DARLINGTON	5/7 East Row DL1 5PZ	01325 485806
DERBY	1 East Street DE1 2AU	01332 342368
DEVIZES	29 The Brittox SN1 01AJ	01380 730281
DONCASTER	54 High Street DN1 1BE	01302 739659
DORCHESTER	16 Cornhill DT1 1BQ	01305 251637
DORKING	5 South Street RH4 2DY	01306 887227
DUMFRIES	28 Munches street DG1 1ET	01387 739954
DUNDEE	23 Cowgate DD1 2HS	01382 223744
EAST GRINSTEAD	23 London Road RH19 1AL	01342 300977
EASTBOURNE	146/148 Terminus Road BN21 3AN	01323 728340
EDINBURGH	12 Frederick Street EH2 2HB	0131 220 1551
ELGIN	Unit 13 St Giles Centre IV30 1EA	01343 556550
ELTHAM	122 Eltham High Road SE9 1BJ	0208 8502822
ELY	26 Market Place CB7 4NT	01353 664023
ENFIELD	21 Palace Gardens EN2 6SN	0208 363 1682
EPSOM	17 High Street KT19 8DD	01372 721557
EVESHAM	33 Bridge Street WR11 4SQ	01386 446759
EXETER	207 High Street EX4 3EB	01392 255811
EXMOUTH	42 Chapel Street EX8 1HW	01395 267144
FALMOUTH	11 Market Strand TR11 3DB	01326 313348
FAREHAM	80/82 Osborne Mall, Hampshire PO16 0PW	01329 283088
FARNBOROUGH	Unit 5/7 The Mead GU14 7RT	01252 371663
FARNHAM	2/3 West Street, Surrey GU9 7DN	01252 711338
FELIXSTOWE	52 Hamilton Road IP11 7AJ	01394 672203
FLEET	158 Fleet Road GU51 8BE	01252 620636
GATESHEAD	31 The Galleria NE11 9YP	0191 460 3153
GLASGOW	Unit 2B Sauchiehall Street G2 3ER	0141 332 5617
GLENROTHES	56 Unicorn Way, Kingdom Centre KY7 5NU	01592 753217
GLOUCESTER	4 Southgate Street GL1 2DH	01452 412803
GRAVESEND	Unit 4 Anglesea Centre DA11 0AU	01474 362889
GREAT YARMOUTH	20/21 Market Place NR30 1LY	01493 857040
GREENOCK	45 Hamilton Way PA15 1RQ	01475 726425
GRIMSBY	22 Baxtergate, Freshney Place DN31 1QL	01472 362449
GUERNSEY	9 The Pollett GY1 1WZ	01481 725888
GUILDFORD	21 Friary Street GU1 4GH	01483 573476
HALIFAX	11 Crown Street HX1 1TT	01422 342644
HAMILTON	17 Duke Street ML3 7DT	01698 284691
HANLEY	10/12 Upper Market Square ST1 1NS	01782 214560
HARLOW	5 Eastgate CM20 1HP	01279 438165
HARROGATE	15/15A Beulah Street HG1 1QH	01423 526677
HARROW	324A Station road HA1 2DX	0208 4273809
HASTINGS	12/13 York Building, Wellington Place TN34 1NN	01424 203589
HAVERFORDWEST	Perrots Road Haverfordwest SA61 2HD	01437 767300
HAVERHILL	17 High Street CB9 8AD	01440 713682
HAYWARDS HEATH	98 South Street RH16 4LJ	01444 457214
HEMEL HEMPSTEAD	221 The Marlowes HP1 1BH	01442 265218
HEREFORD	12/14 Eign Gate HR4 0AB	01432 264196
HERTFORD	18 Fore Street SG14 1BZ	01992 584427
HEXHAM	24 Fore Street,Hexham NE46 1LZ	01434 608324
HIGH WYCOMBE	4/5 Church Street HP11 2DE	01494 522100
HITCHIN	26 Market Place SG5 1DT	01462 432567
HORSHAM	18 West Street RH12 1TV	01403 262851
HULL	24/26 King Edward Street HU1 3SS	01482 210389
HUNTINGDON	Unit 5 St Germain Walk PE29 3FG	01480 413554
ILFORD	154 High Road IG1 1LL	0208 478 7341
INVERNESS	24 High Street IV1 1JQ	01463 714387
IPSWICH	16 Hacket Street IP4 1AY	01473 254704
IPSWICH	14/16 Carr Street IP4 1EJ	01473 211797
KENDAL	26/28 Highgate LA9 4SX	01539 736866
KENSINGTON (London)	176 Kensington High Street W8 7RG	0207 9377101
KESWICK	85/87 Main Street, Cumbria CA12 5DT	01768 775524
KETTERING	3/5 Newland Street NN16 8JH	01536 481261
KIDDERMINSTER	21 The Bull Ring DY10 2AZ	01562 740127

GEAR

One Earth
Eco-friendly gear for the outdoors

Eco-friendly gear for the outdoors

Introducing One Earth, the first eco-friendly range of clothing, camping gear and accessories for the outdoors. We've used eco-friendly fibres, fabrics and production techniques to bring them to you, so you can enjoy the outdoors and have a minimal impact on your environment.

The One Earth range is available online and at selected Millets stores. Please visit www.millets.co.uk for details

Exclusively at **Millets** the outdoor store   millets.co.uk

KINGS LYNN	Unit SU 17a The Vancouver Centre Kings Lynn PE30 IDE	01553 776 169
KINGSTON	3/5 Thames Street KTI IPH	0208 546 5042
LANCASTER	7 Cheapside LAI ILY	01524 841043
LEEDS	117/118 Kirkgate LSI 6BY	0113 242 9892
LEEDS	Unit 24 St Johns Centre, 110 Albion Street LS2 8LQ	0113 2342395
LEEDS - WHITEROSE	Unit 28 Whiterose Centre LSII 8LU	0113 276 1149
LEEK	34 Derby Street ST13 5AB	01538 383731
LEICESTER	121/123 Granby Street LEI 6FD	0116 254 2402
LEIGH	Unit 33 Spinning Gate Centre, Ellesmere St WN7 4PG	01942 671944
LEIGHTON BUZZARD	47 High Street LU7 IDN	01525 371623
LETCHWORTH	5 Commerce Way, Garden Sq Shopping Centre SG6 3DN	01462 679583
LEWISHAM	205 Lewisham High Street SE13 6LY	0208 852 1909
LICHFIELD	19 Tamworth Street WS13 6JP	01543 262003
LINCOLN	321/322 High Street LN5 7DW	01522 567317
LIVERPOOL	15 Ranelagh Street LI IJW	0151 709 7017
LIVINGSTONE	Unit 68, Almomdvale Centre EH54 6HR	01506 437 728
LLANDUDNO	80 Moystn St LL30 2RP	01492 875 810
LLANELLI	42 Stepney Street SAI5 3YA	01554 751657
LOUGHBOROUGH	4 Market Street LEII 3EP	01509 236413
LOUTH	78 East Gate LNII 9PG	01507 602711
LOWESTOFT	71 London Road North NR32 ILS	01502 572239
LUTON	Unit 125 Arndale Centre LUI 2TN	01582 724514
LYMINGTON	52 High Street SO41 9AG	01590 675144
MACCLESFIELD	45 Mill St SK11 6NE	01625 427477
MAIDSTONE	Unit 34A Fremlin Walk ME14 IQT	01622 754465
MANCHESTER	133 Deansgate M3 3WR	01618 351016
MANCHESTER	Unit 49 Arndale Centre M4 2HU	0161 832 7547
MANCHESTER	200 Deansgate M3 3NN	0161 833 0349
MANSFIELD	48 Westgate NG18 IRR	01623 629446
MERRY HILL	11 Merry Hill, Brierley Hill DY5 IQX	01384 261671
MIDDLESBROUGH	40 Linthorpe Road TSI IRD	01642 240863
MILTON KEYNES	21/23 Crown Walk MK9 3AH	01908 672322
MONMOUTH	21 Monnow Street NP25 3EF	01600 719187
NEATH	12 Queen Street SAII IDL	01639 637216
NEWARK	25 Middlegate NG24 IAL	01636 640842
NEWBURY	68/69 Northbrook Street RG13 IAE	01635 40070
NEWCASTLE U LYME	53 High Street ST5 IPN	01622 754465
NEWCASTLE U TYNE	121/125 Grainger Street NEI 5AE	0191 232 1100
NEWPORT (Gwent)	3 Llanarth Street, Gwent NP20 IHS	01633 246 309
NEWPORT (Isle of Wight)	21 St James Square PO30 IUX	01983 525995
NEWRY	Unit 30, Buttercrane Quay BT35 8HJ	02830 263565
NEWTON ABBOT	17 Queen Street TQ12 2AQ	01626 353405
NEWTOWNABBEY	Unit 70/71, Abbey Centre BT37 9AQ	02890 865520
NORTHAMPTON	24 Market Square NNI 2DX	01604 621898
NORWICH	9/11 St Stephens Street NRI 3QN	01603 622708
NORWICH	Boston House, 5 Orford Hill NRI 3QB	01603 625645
NOTTINGHAM	12 Exchange Walk NGI 2NX	01159 417456
NUNEATON	14/15 Abbey Gate Centre CVII 4HL	02476 385625
OBAN	71 George Street PA34 5NN	01631 571122
ORPINGTON	178 High Street BR6 0JW	01689 826794
OXFORD	42/43 Queen Street OXI IET	01865 790676
PAIGNTON	37/39 Victoria Street TQ4 5AD	01803 529578
PAISLEY	29 The High Street PAI 2AF	0141 8471013
PENZANCE	105 Market Jew Street TRI8 2LE	01736 363204
PERTH	182/186 High Street PHI 5PA	01738 622248
PETERBOROUGH	47 Bridge Street PEI IHA	01733 341371
PETERBOROUGH	97 Bridge Street PEI IHG	01733 561000
PETERSFIELD	8 Rams Walk GU32 3JA	01730 260317
PLYMOUTH	39/40 New George Street PLI IRW	01752 665521
PONTYPRIDD	80 Taff Street CF37 4SD	01443 400086
POOLE	9 Kingland Crescent BHI5 ITA	01202 661307
PORTSMOUTH	213/215 Commercial Road POI 4BJ	02392 851653
PRESTON	28 Market Place PRI 2AR	01772 884433
PRESTON	23 Miller Arcade PRI 2QA	0177 2250242
PUTNEY	98 High Street SWI5 IRB	0208 788 2300
RAMSGATE	8 Queen Street CTII 9DR	01843 594220

READING	4/5 St Mary's Butts RGI 2LN	0118 959 5228
REDCAR	15/17 High Street TS10 3BZ	01642 483924
REDDITCH	12 Kingfisher Walk B97 4EY	01527 595229
REDHILL	29 High Street RHI IRD	01737 765177
RHYL	60/62 High Street LLI8 IET	01745 353178
ROMFORD	Unit 6A The Brewery RMI IAU	01708 748345
ROTHERHAM	18 Howard Street S60 IQU	01709 382502
RUGBY	Unit 28 Clock Towers Shopping Centre CV21 3JT	01788 578 106
SAFFRON WALDEN	37/39 King Street CB10 IEU	01799 529343
SALISBURY	38/39 Old George Mall SPI 2AF	01722 341 583
SCARBOROUGH	6/7 Westborough YOII IUH	01723 367869
SCUNTHORPE	116 High Street DNI5 6HB	01724 849890
SHEFFIELD	71 The Moor SI 4PF	0114 2722194
SHREWSBURY	6/7 Mardol Head SYI IHD	01743 353686
SITTINGBOURNE	119 High Street ME10 4AQ	01795 472544
SKIPTON	30 Sheep Street BD23 IHX	01756 793754
SLOUGH	186/188 High Street SLI IJS	01753 520981
SOUTHAMPTON	104 East Street SO14 3HH	02380 228797
SOUTHEND	4/19 York Road SSI 2BH	01702 463316
SOUTHPORT	4/8 Tulketh Street, Merseyside PR8 IAQ	01704 534017
SOUTHSEA	5 Palmerston Road PO5 3QQ	02392 732461
ST ALBANS	19/21 French Row AL3 5DZ	01727 856328
ST HELENS	2/4 Cotham Street WAI0 ISQ	01744 739941
STAFFORD	13 Gaolgate Street STI6 2BQ	01785 251912
STAINES	IIIA High Street TWI8 4PQ	01784 469820
STAMFORD	63 High Street PE9 2LA	01780 481346
STIRLING	20/22 Murray Place FK8 IDQ	01786 451141
STOCKPORT	29/31 Princes Street SKI ISU	0161 477 4160
STRATFORD UPON AVON	Unit 21A Town Square Shopping Centre CV37 6JN	01789 414857
STROUD	34 Kendrick Street GL5 IAQ	01453 764646
SUDBURY	14 North Street CO10 IRB	01787 375883
SUTTON	86 High Street SMI IJG	0208 643 4251
SUTTON COLDFIELD	56 The Parade B72 IDS	01213 554931
SWANSEA	234 High Street SAI INZ	01792 655637
SWINDON	Sub Unit 4 The Parade SNI IBA	01793 514941
TAUNTON	20 East Street TAI 3LP	01823 332782
TELFORD	207 Dean Street TF34BT	01952 201002
THANET	Unit 6a Westwood Cross, Thanet, Kent CTI0 2BF	01843 861760
TONBRIDGE	70 High Street TN9 ISD	01732 355247
TORQUAY	49 Union Street TQI IET	01803 297588
TROWBRIDGE	40 The Shires BAI4 8AT	01225 762871
TRURO	11 Pydar Street TRI 2AX	01872 240973
TUNBRIDGE WELLS	3/7 Camden Road TNI 2PS	01892 519891
UCKFIELD	136 High Street TN22 IQN	01825 766176
WALSALL	9 The Bridge, West Midlands WSI ILR	01922 624462
WARRINGTON	28 Golden Square Shopping Centre WAI IQE	01925 417050
WATFORD	Unit A8 The Harlequin Centre WD7 2TB	01923 212427
WEST THURROCK	Unit 338 Lakeside Shopping Centre RM20 2ZH	01708 864366
WESTON-S-MARE	98 High Street BS23 IHS	01934 621930
WEYMOUTH	74 St Mary Street DT4 8PJ	01305 786002
WHITEHAVEN	19/20 King Street CA28 7LA	01946 694655
WIGAN	24/26 Market Street WNI IHX	01942 245330
WIMBLEDON	34 The Broadway SWI9 0BB	0208 946 6644
WINCHESTER	149 High Street SO23 9AY	01962 841970
WINDSOR	42 Peascod Street SL4 IDE	01753 620405
WITNEY	Unit 18A, Woolgate OX28 6AP	01993 778775
WOKING	31 Commercial Road GU21 6XR	01483 721551
WOKINGHAM	37 Peach Street RG4 0IXJ	01189 798097
WOLVERHAMPTON	2 Wulfrun Centre WVI 3HF	01902 423797
WORCESTER	7/8 The Shambles WRI 2RF	01905 25672
WORTHING	95 Montague Street BNII 3BN	01903 236066
WREXHAM	24 Queen Street LLII IAL	01978 261261
YATE	5 West Walk BS37 4AX	01454 312823
YEOVIL	22 Middle Street BA20 ILY	01935 423156
YORK	4/6 Market Street YOI 8ST	01904 620618
YORK	Unit 3, Queens House, Micklegate YOI 6JH	01904 653567

GEAR

RAMBLERS AREAS AND GROUPS

AREA
Areas bring together and coordinate the charitable work of the Groups. They often represent us in discussions with local authorities.

GROUPS
Groups carry out our work in their 'patch' and organise programmes of led walks.

BOARD OF TRUSTEES

The Board of Trustees takes overall responsibility for the policies of the charity and appoints the Chief Executive.

GENERAL COUNCIL
General Council is the Annual General Meeting of the organisation. Each Area sends delegates who can present and vote on motions. The Board of Trustees is elected at General Council.

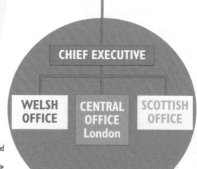

CHIEF EXECUTIVE

WELSH OFFICE   **CENTRAL OFFICE London**   **SCOTTISH OFFICE**

you

Where you live determines which Area you fall into and your automatic Group allocation (although you may request for this to be changed). Being part of a Group and Area gives you the opportunity to get further involved in the activities of each.

Staff provide support to Areas and Groups, coordinate national campaigns and lobbying, promote us and our work to the public and undertake day-to-day administration.

The Ramblers' structure

The Ramblers' Association operates across the whole of Britain, although Scotland and Wales have their own devolved structure within the organisation. It is a democratic organisation where members have a say and become involved in our work. Our network of Areas and Groups gives us a fantastic combination of a strong national voice and effective local action.

There are just over 50 Areas. These largely correspond to county boundaries in England and to other regional boundaries in Scotland and Wales. Each Area, and each subsidiary Group within it, is managed and run entirely by volunteers.

Area and Group activities

Our Groups carry out conservation work in their localities, walk and socialise together. Each Group listed organises its own programme of led walks. Most walks are now on the Group Walks Finder www.ramblers.org.uk/walksfinder, otherwise you can request a programme by sending a SAE to the Group secretary.

Many work from home so if you telephone, please do so at reasonable times.

Many Groups also publish details of upcoming walks and activities on their own websites, which are all linked from www.ramblers.org.uk/info/localgroups.

A variety of walks offered

Most Groups and Areas offer a mixed programme of long and short walks, but some offer regular programmes of shorter, easier walks and/or walks aimed at families with young children, generally no more than 8km/5 miles and taken at an easy pace. We've marked these with ● in the listings. For more information about these walks contact the Area or Group directly or see www.ramblers.org.uk/walking.

There are also a number of Groups for people in their 20s and 30s known as hike 20–30s Groups. These are highlighted in blue.

All Group details listed were correct in October 2007 but changes may take place during the year.

ENGLAND

AVON
Bath & North East Somerset; Bristol and South Gloucester

AREA SECRETARY
Jill Fysh, 43a Springfields, Ableton Lane, Severn Beach, Bristol BS35 4PP
☎ 01454 633001 jillfysh@aol.com
www.avon-ramblers.org.uk

GROUP SECRETARIES
Bath Mrs Marilyn Wright, 47 Dovers Park, Bathford, Bath BA1 7UD
☎ 01225 858047
wright_marilyn@hotmail.com
www.bathra.org.uk
Bristol ● Mr Roy Mathias, 2 Oakwood Avenue, Henleaze, Bristol BS9 4NS
www.bristolramblers.org.uk
Brunel Walking & Activity
Miss Kathryn Easlick, 17 Sherston Close, Bristol BS16 2LP
kathryn.eastlick@airbus.com
brunelwalking.org.uk
Kingswood Mrs Nicola Phelps, 10 Cloverlea Road, Warmley, Bristol BS30 8LF ☎ 0117 985 8825
ronphelps@supanet.com
www.kingswoodramblers.pwp.
blueyonder.co.uk
Norton Radstock Mrs Sally Haddon, 4 Dymboro Close, Midsomer Norton, Bath BA3 2QS
Severnside Mrs Gill King, 42 Riverside Park, Severn Beach, Bristol BS35 4PN
www.severnside-ramblers.org.uk
Southwold (Yate) Miss Sharifa Naqui, 3 Brake Close, Bradley Stoke, Bristol BS32 8BA ☎ 01179 697246
sharifa.naqui@ukgateway.net
www.southwold-ramblers.co.uk

BEDFORDSHIRE
AREA SECRETARY
Mr John Hartley, 57 The Paddocks, Leighton Buzzard LU7 2SX
☎ 01525 372525
linda_andjohnh@hotmail.com

GROUP SECRETARIES
Ivel Valley Brian Gubbins (chairman), 21 Leyside, Bromham, Bedford MK43 8NE ☎ 01234 823603
info@ivelvalleywalkers.org.uk
www.ivelvalleywalkers.org.uk
Ivel Valley Under 40s
ivelvalleyu40@tiscali.co.uk
www.ivelvalleywalkers.org.uk/
u40s/index1.html
Lea & Icknield Miss Sarah Lewis, 21 Simpson Close, Leagrave, Luton LU4 9TP ☎ 01582 847273

Leighton Buzzard Mr John Hartley, 57 The Paddocks, Leighton Buzzard LU7 2SX ☎ 01525 372525
leightonramblers2.mysite.wanadoo-members.co.uk
North Bedfordshire Mrs Linda Tongue, 25 Field Cottage Road, Eaton Socon, St Neots PE19 8HA ☎ 01480 350345
lindatongue@yahoo.co.uk
Ouse Valley Mrs Brenda Leaf, 117 High Street, Blunham MK44 3NW
☎ 01767 640623
www.ousevalleyramblers.co.uk

BERKSHIRE
AREA SECRETARY
Mr Cliff Lambert, Marandella, 1 Lawrence Mead, Kintbury, Hungerford RG17 9XT ☎ 01488 608108

GROUP SECRETARIES
Berkshire Walkers Ian Montague
☎ 07762 054207
berkshirewalkers@yahoo.co.uk
www.berkshirewalkers.org.uk
East Berkshire ● Dr Gerald Barnett, 9 Fremantle Road, High Wycombe HP13 7PQ ☎ 01494 522404
gerbarn@talktalk.net [membership enquiries, Mrs Margaret Welch ☎ 01753 662139] www.eastberksramblers.org
Loddon Valley Mr David Turner, 9 Meadow Walk, Wokingham RG41 2TG ☎ 01189 784364 turnerd@freeuk.com
www.lvra.org.uk
Mid Berkshire Ms Elizabeth Cuff, Donkey Pound Cottage, Beech Hill, Reading RG7 2AX ☎ 0118 988 2674
www.mbra.org.uk
Pang Valley Dr C Howlett, 3 Western Elms Avenue, Reading RG30 2AL
☎ 0118 9590436
chris.r.howlett@btinternet.com
South East Berks Mr John Moules, 50 Qualitas, Roman Hill, Bracknell RG12 7QG ☎ 01344 420015
john.moules@ntlworld.com
West Berkshire ● Mr Fred Carter, Elvira, Main Street, West Ilsley, Newbury RG20 7AW ☎ 01635 281621
fred_kathcarter@btinternet.com
www.wberksramblers.org.uk
Windsor & District Miss JM Clark, 7 Dyson Close, Windsor, SL4 3LZ
☎ 01753 866545

BUCKINGHAMSHIRE & W MIDDLESEX
Buckinghamshire, plus the London boroughs of Brent, Ealing, Harrow, Hillingdon and Hounslow

AREA SECRETARY
Mr Tom Berry, 128 Park Lane, South Harrow HA2 8NL ☎ 020 8422 3284

westlondongroup@yahoo.co.uk
www.bucks-wmiddx-ramblers.org.uk

GROUP SECRETARIES
Amersham & District Mrs Madeleine Moody, White Cottage, 93 St Leonard's Road, Chesham Bois, Amersham HP6 6DR ☎ 01494 727504
Aylesbury & District Jim Cornwell, 41 Archer Drive, Aylesbury HP20 1ER
☎ 01296 336588
Chiltern 20s–30s Walking
www.chilterns2030s.co.uk or visit www.ramblers.org.uk/info/localgroups or contact our central office for current details
Chilterns Weekend Walkers
Mr Chris Candy, 7 Thanestead Court, London Road, Loudwater, High Wycombe HP10 9QS [membership enquiries ☎ 01442 212519]
www.chilternsww.co.uk
Hillingdon ● Ms Vivien Kermath, 92 Hill Road, Pinner HA5 1LE
☎ 020 8866 1062 Vivkermath@aol.com
www.hillingdonramblers.org.uk
Milton Keynes & District Mr John West, 45 Blackdown, Fullers Slade, Milton Keynes MK11 2AA
☎ 01908 564055
john.f.west@btinternet.com
www.mkramblers.org.uk
North West London Ms Carole Swithern ☎ 020 8429 4946
caroleswithern@yahoo.co.uk
The Hike MK Mr Bryan Mitcham, 20 Curlew, Watermead, Aylesbury HP19 0WG
www.mk-northbucks2030s.org.uk
West London Mr Tom Berry, 128 Park Lane, South Harrow HA2 8NL
☎ 020 8422 3284
westlondongroup@yahoo.co.uk
www.btinternet.com/
~westlondongroupra
Wycombe District ● Mr John Shipley, 192 Wycombe Road, Great Missenden HP16 0HJ ☎ 01494 862699
bee_bee17@talktalk.net

CAMBRIDGESHIRE & PETERBOROUGH
AREA SECRETARY
Ms Jill Tuffnell, 62 Beche Road, Cambridge CB5 8HU ☎ 01223 362881
www.cambsandpeterboroughramblers.
org.uk

GROUP SECRETARIES
Cambridge Ms Jill Tuffnell, 62 Beche Road, Cambridge CB5 8HU
☎ 01223 362881
East Cambridgeshire Mrs Sue Summerside, Mow Fen Hall, 4a Silt Road,

Littleport Ely CB6 1QD ☎ 01353 861435
Fenland Mrs S L Ledger, 18 Alexandra
Road, Wisbech PE13 1HS
☎ 01945 587135
Huntingdonshire Mr William
Thompson, 2 Bankers Walk, Ramsey,
Huntingdon PE26 1EG ☎ 01487 812022
Peterborough Ms Christine Kirby,
49 Elter Walk, Peterborough PE4 7TZ
☎ 01733 321944
Peterborough Younger Walkers
Mr Stephen Abbott, 11 Culme Close,
Oundle, Peterborough PE8 4QQ
☎ 01832 270086 www.pyw.org.uk
WalkCambridge Mr Dan Worgan, The
Cottage, Little St Marys, Long Melford,
Suffolk CO10 9HX
walkcambridge@yahoo.co.uk
www.walkcambridge.org

CHESHIRE
See Merseyside & West Cheshire,
South & East Cheshire, and North &
Mid-Cheshire Areas

CORNWALL
AREA SECRETARY
Mrs Christine James, Chy-Vean, Tresillian,
Truro TR2 4BN ☎ 01872 520368
www.racornwall.org.uk

GROUP SECRETARIES
Bude/Stratton Mr Peter Judson,
Meadowcroft, Bagbury Road, Bude,
Cornwall EX23 8QJ ☎ 01288 356597
Camel District (Wadebridge)
Mrs Daphne Windle, 4 Sarahs Close,
Padstow PL28 8BJ ☎ 01841 533283
www.racamelgroup.org.uk
Caradon Ms C Craze, 3 Culverland Park,
Liskeard, Cornwall PL14 3HY
☎ 01579 348973
Carrick ● Mr JB Jennings, 7 Moresk
Close, Truro, Cornwall, TR1 1DL
☎ 01872 278317
Newquay Mr Chris Owen, 2 Pengannel
Close, Newquay, Cornwall TR7 2AT
Restormel ● Mrs Jane Sloan, Brouard
Cottage, Fore Street, Grampound, Truro
TR2 4QT ☎ 01726 883214
West Cornwall (Penwith & Kerrier)
Mrs Sylvia Ronan, Trebant, Ludgvan
Churchtown, Penzance, Cornwall
TR20 8HH ☎ 01736 740542
sylvronan@btinternet.com

CUMBRIA
See Lake District Area

DERBYSHIRE
West Derbyshire, Amber Valley,
Derby, South Derbyshire and Erewash
districts of Derbyshire. See also
Nottinghamshire, South Yorkshire &
North East Derbyshire, and
Manchester Areas

AREA SECRETARY
Mr Martin Pape, Stable Grange, Rock
House Grounds, Cromford, Matlock
DE4 3RP ☎ 01629 820265
emartinpape@aol.com
www.derbyshireramblers.org.uk

GROUP SECRETARIES
Amber Valley Mrs Margaret Siddons,
Overdene, Ridgeway Lane, Nether
Heage, Nr Belper, Derbyshire DE56 2JT
www.ambervalleyramblers.org.uk
Derby & S Derbyshire Mr Chris
Vaughan, 13 Evans Avenue, Allestree
DE22 2EL ☎ 01332 558552
sec@derbyramblers.org.uk
www.derbyramblers.org.uk
Derbyshire Dales Miss Amanda Higton,
4 Paddocks Close, Pinxton, Nottingham
NG16 6JR ☎ 01773 783658
Amanda-higton@ntlworld.com
www.derbyshiredalesramblers.org.uk
Derbyshire Family Rambling ●
Mr Greg Lunn ☎ 01332 700184
www.derbyshirefamilyrambling.org.uk
Erewash District Tony Beardsley,
14 York Avenue, Sandiacre, Nottingham
NG10 5HB ☎ 0115 917 0082
aebbooks@ntlworld.com
www.erewashramblers.org.uk

DEVON
AREA SECRETARY
Mrs E M Linfoot, 14 Blaydon Cottages,
Blackborough, Cullompton EX15 2HJ
☎ 01884 266435
website.lineone.net/~devon.ramblers

GROUP SECRETARIES
Devon Bootlegs
devonbootlegs@yahoo.co.uk
www.geocities.com/devonbootlegs
East Devon Mr Andy Mack, 3 Cadbury
Gardens, East Budleigh, Budleigh Salterton
EX9 7EU ☎ 01395 442748
Exeter & District Frans & Christine
Ahlheid, 26 Countess Wear Road, Exeter
EX2 6LP ☎ 01392 496645
frans.ahlheid@virgin.net

Moorland Mr Michael Willis, Reaper's
Cottage, Cockington Village, Torquay
TQ2 6XA ☎ 01803 690511
m.willis995@btinternet.com
North Devon Mrs Pauline Newbound,
Mauretania, Town Bridge, Burrington,
Umberleigh EX37 9LT ☎ 01769 520421
website.lineone.net/
~northdevon.ramblers
Plymouth Mrs Gill Seymour
☎ 01752 562818
info@plymouthramblers.org.uk
www.plymouthramblers.org.uk
South Devon Mrs Carole Woolcott,
The Lodge, 43 Seymour Drive,
Watcombe, Torquay TQ2 8PY
☎ 01803 313430
www.southdevonramblers.com
South Hams Mr Mick Warne,
17 Hedingham Gardens, Roborough,
Plymouth PL6 7DX ☎ 01752 774289
Tavistock Ms Nina Jones, Hogstor
Cottage, Chillaton, Lifton, Devon PL16 0JE
[membership enquiries, Mrs Randall
☎ 01822 018660]
Teignmouth & Dawlish Mrs Anne
Mccallister, 21 Southdowns Road, Dawlish
EX7 0LB ☎ 01626 864046
anne@mccallister.fsnet.co.uk
Tiverton Maureen Cox, 18 Anstey
Crescent, Tiverton EX16 4JR
☎ 01884 256395
Totnes Mrs Elizabeth Evans, 7 North
Street, Totnes TQ9 5NZ
☎ 01803 840403

DORSET
AREA SECRETARY
Mr Jim Scott, 'Bankside', Holt Lane, Holt,
Wimborne BH21 7DQ ☎ 01202 885870
www.dorset-ramblers.co.uk

GROUP SECRETARIES
Dorset Young Walkers Miss Cheryl
Hadnutt, Flat 4, 51 St Albans Avenue,
Bournemouth BH8 9EG
☎ 07765 497887 dywra@hotmail.com
www.dorsetyoungwalkers.org.uk

East Dorset Mrs Margaret Kettlewell, 12 Limited Road, Bournemouth BH9 1SS ☎ 01202 522467 [membership enquiries 01202 691709] marg788@ntlworld.com

North Dorset Mr A T Combridge, Green Bushes, North Road, Sherborne, Dorset DT9 3JN ☎ 01935 812809

South Dorset Mr Stan Faris, 4 Long Acre, New Street, Portland, Dorset DT5 1HH ☎ 01305 820957 stan@stanfaris.wanadoo.co.uk

West Dorset Mrs Jacqueline Stow, 21 Glebe Court, Beaminster, DT8 3EZ ☎ 01308 863081

DURHAM

See Northumbria and North Yorkshire & South Durham Areas

EAST YORKSHIRE & DERWENT

East Riding of Yorkshire, York and the old rural districts of Derwent, Easingwold, Flaxton, Malton, Norton, and Filey; part of Scarborough, Ryedale and Hambleton

AREA SECRETARY
Mr Malcolm Dixon, 8 Horseman Avenue, Copmanthorpe, York YO23 3UF ☎ 01904 706850 m.s.dixon@talktalk.net www.eastyorkshireramblers.org.uk

GROUP SECRETARIES
Beverley Ms J Cavill, 1 Friary Walk, Eastgate, Beverley, East Yorkshire, HU17 0HE ☎ 01432 888096

Driffield Mr John Jefferson, Delamere, 2 Spellowgate, Driffield, YO25 5BB ☎ 01377 252412 john@spellowgate.fsnet.co.uk

East Yorks Get Your Boots On Miss Nancy Sydenham, 23 Ash Street, York YO26 4UR ☎ 07749 840885 www.gybo.org.uk

Howden & Goole Dr Marian Thomas, 46 Boothgate Drive, Howden, East Yorks DN14 7EW ☎ 01430 431766 thomas.marian@btinternet.com

Hull & Holderness Visit www.ramblers.org.uk/info/localgroups or contact our central office for current details

Pocklington Mr A F Ashbridge, 4 Burnaby Close, Molescroft, Beverley, East Yorkshire, HU17 7ET ☎ 01482 861215

Ryedale Mrs Wendy Borman, 18 Town End Close, Pickering YO18 8JB ☎ 01751 477325

Scarborough & District Visit www.ramblers.org.uk/info/localgroups or contact our central office for current details

York Miss Vera Silberberg, 41 North Parade, Bootham, York YO30 7AB

☎ 01904 628134 vsilberberg@fish.co.uk www.communigate.co.uk/york/ yorkramblers2

ESSEX

Essex, plus London boroughs of Waltham Forest, Redbridge, Havering, Barking & Dagenham, and Newham

AREA SECRETARY
Visit www.ramblers.org.uk/info/ localgroups or contact our central office for current details

GROUP SECRETARIES
Basildon Greenway Mrs Joyce Cleary (membership secretary), 48 Hollyford, Billericay CM11 1EG ☎ 01277 625493

Brentwood Mr Mick Dodge, 27 Bruce Grove, Wickford SS11 8RB ☎ 01268 765475 [membership enquiries, ☎ 01277 220781 mickdodge@aol.com www.brentwoodramblers.org.uk

Chelmer & Blackwater www.chelmerandblackwater-ramblers.org.uk or visit www.ramblers.org.uk/info/localgroups or contact our central office for current details

Colchester Mr K J Clark, Vine Cottage, 366 London Road, Stanway, Colchester CO3 8LU www.colchester-ramblers.ccom.co.uk

East Essex Friends ● Mrs Jan Palmer, 6 Victoria Road, South Woodham Ferrers, Chelmsford CM3 5LR ☎ 01245 321050 www.eastessexfriends.plus.com

Essex Friends ● Ms Carole Bartlett, 12 Lawford Lane, Writtle, Chelmsford CM1 3EA ☎ 01245 420887

Essex Young Ramblers Miss Nicola Smith, 6 Seabrook Road, Great Baddow, Chelmsford CM2 7JF, visit www.ramblers.org.uk/info/localgroups or contact our central office for further details

Havering & East London Mr Ken Richards, 26 Arundel Road, Harold Wood, Romford RM3 0RT ☎ 01708 375559 www.havering-and-eastlondon-ramblers.org.uk

Lea Valley Friends ● Mrs Margaret Brown ☎ 020 8529 1602 lvfwalkers2001@hotmail.com www.communigate.co.uk/london/ leavalleyfriendswalkinggroup

Maldon & Dengie Hundred Ms Jill McGregor, 29 Doubleday Drive, Heybridge, Maldon CM9 4TL ☎ 01621 842595 jill.mcgregor@itsyourhome.co.uk www.maldondengieramblers.org.uk

North West Essex Mr David Harvey, 18 Clydesdale Road, Braintree, Essex CM7 2NX ☎ 01376 342090

Redbridge ● Mrs Maureen Gourley, 49 Severn Drive, Upminster RM14 1QF ☎ 01708 640747 www.redbridgeramblers.org.uk

Rochford & Castle Point Mrs Janet Paton, 11 Arundel Gardens, Rayleigh SS6 9GS ☎ 01268 786620 www.btinternet.com/~bta.wga/ rochford-ramblers

South East Essex Mr Jim Folwell, 27 South Crescent, Prittlewell, Southend-on-Sea SS2 6TB www.e-cox.fsnet.co.uk

Stort Valley Ms Heather McNaughton, 123 Red Willow, Harlow CM19 5PD ☎ 07711 570248 secretary_svwalking@yahoo.co.uk www.geocities.com/stortvalleywalkers

Tendring District Mrs Ann Jones, Wayside, Hall Road, Great Bromley, Colchester CO7 7TS www.tendringramblers.co.uk

Thurrock Mr Stan Dyball, 29 Bishops Road, Corringham, Stanford Le Hope, Essex SS17 7HB ☎ 01375 676442

Uttlesford Mrs Ann Corke, Roston House, Dunmow Road, Thaxted, Dunmow CM6 2LU ☎ 01371 830654

West Essex Mr Mike Whitley, 62 Beresford Road, Chingford, London E4 6EF ☎ 020 8524 2737 www.westessexramblers.org.uk

GLOUCESTERSHIRE

AREA SECRETARY
Mrs Mavis Rear, 106 Malleson Road, Gotherington, Cheltenham, Gloucestershire GL52 9EY ☎ 01242 674470 mavis.rear@tesco.net

GROUP SECRETARIES
Cirencester Mrs Karen Appleby, 46 Rendcomb Drive, Cirencester GL7 1YN karen.appleby@openwork.uk.com

Cleeve Mrs Diana Terry, 18 Pecked Lane, Bishops Cleeve, Cheltenham GL52 8JQ ☎ 01242 674288

Forest of Dean Mrs Olive Jeanes, Beechenhurst, Church Road, Undy, Caldicot NP26 3HF ☎ 01633 889460 olivepjeanes@btinternet.com myweb.tiscali.co.uk/deanforest

Gloucester Mrs Rosemary Parker, 62 Ermin Park, Brockworth, Gloucester GL3 4DP ☎ 01452 618404

Gloucestershire Walking Group www.gwg.org.uk or visit www.ramblers.org.uk/info/localgroups or contact central office for current details

Mid-Gloucestershire Mrs Sheila Houston, 22 Leckhampton Road, Cheltenham GL53 0AY sheilahouston22@yahoo.co.uk

North Cotswold Mr Simon Mallatratt, 1 Willow Road, Willersey, Broadway

WR12 7QE ☎ 01386 853722
simonmallatratt@yahoo.co.uk
South Cotswold Bernard Smith,
139 Thrupp Lane, Thrupp, Stroud
GL5 2DQ ☎ 01453 884 013
smith.bernard@tesco.net
www.southcotswoldramblers.org.uk

HAMPSHIRE
AREA SECRETARY
Mr David Nixon, 27 Brading Avenue,
Southsea PO4 9QJ ☎ 023 9273 2649
dnixon27@waitrose.com
www.hants.gov.uk/hampshireramblers

GROUP SECRETARIES
Alton Mrs Sarah Hinde, Millhurst,
11 Anstey Mill Lane, Alton, GU34 2QP
☎ 01420 87774
sarahandpatric@yahoo.co.uk
Andover Mrs Nesta Baird, 3 Hazel
Close, Andover SP10 3PT
☎ 01264 336788 nestascb3@yahoo.co.uk
www.andoverramblers.hampshire.org.uk
Eastleigh Mrs P D Beazley, 16 Windover
Close, Bitterne, Southampton SO19 5JS
☎ 02380 437443 secretary@eastleigh
ramblers.wanadoo.co.uk
www.hants.org.uk/eastleighramblers
Hampshire 20s–30s Walking Group
Miss Gillian Nield gmnield@hotmail.com
www.hants.gov.uk/hantswalk2030
Meon Visit www.ramblers.org.uk/
info/localgroups or contact our central
office for current details
New Forest Mrs Audrey Wilson,
16 West Road, Dibden Purlieu,
Southampton SO45 4RJ
☎ 023 8084 6353
www.newforestramblers.org.uk
North East Hants Mrs Mary Hill,
25 Church Road West, Farnborough,
Hants GU14 6QF ☎ 01252 547429
North Hampshire Downs Mr Mike
Taylor, 19 Inkpen Gardens, Lychpit,
Basingstoke RG24 8YQ ☎ 01256 842468
taylor@mgksb.wanadoo.co.uk
www.hants.org.uk/ramblersnhd
Portsmouth Mrs M G Haly,
95 Winstanley Road, Stamshaw,
Portsmouth PO2 8JS ☎ 023 92693874
www.portsmouth-
ramblers.hampshire.org.uk
Romsey Mr Tom W Radford,
67 Rownhams Lane, North Baddesley,
Southampton SO52 9HR ☎ 02380
731279 tom.radford@virgin.net
www.romseynet.org.uk/ramblers/
ramblers.htm
South East Hants ● Mrs Adina Burton,
5 Lancaster Way, Waterlooville PO7 7NG
☎ 023 9225 3301
kenandadina@talktalk.net
www.hants.org.uk/sehantsramblers

Southampton Mr John Catchlove,
4 Sandringham Court, 18 Winn Road,
Southampton SO17 1EN
☎ 023 8055 3883
www.southamptonramblers.org.uk
Waltham ● Mrs W E Bassom,
3 Mayfair Court, Botley, Southampton,
SO30 2GT ☎ 01489 784946
Wessex Weekend Walkers
www.wessexweekendwalkers.org.uk
or visit www.ramblers.org.uk/info/
localgroups or contact our central office for
current details
Winchester Mrs Penny Farncombe,
7 Fairfax Close, Winchester SO22 4LP
☎ 01962 620126
pennymf.ra@ntlworld.com
www.wramblers.hampshire.org.uk

HEREFORDSHIRE
AREA SECRETARY
www.herefordshireramblers.org.uk
or visit www.ramblers.org.uk/info/
localgroups or contact our central office

GROUP SECRETARIES
Hereford Mr Arthur Lee, 61 Bredon
Grove, Malvern, Worcs WR14 3JS
☎ 01684 575044 arthurlee@sky.com
Leadon Vale Isobel Gibson, 41 Jubilee
Close, Ledbury, Herefordshire HR8 2XA
☎ 01531 635139
isobel.gibson@talk21.com
Mortimer Mrs Pat Bickerton,
35 Mortimer Drive, Orleton, Ludlow,
Shropshire SY8 4JW ☎ 01568 780827
patbickerton@btinternet.com
Ross-on-Wye ● Visit www.ramblers.
org.uk/info/localgroups or contact our
central office for current details

HERTFORDSHIRE & NORTH MIDDLESEX
Hertfordshire, plus London boroughs of
Barnet, Enfield and Haringey

AREA SECRETARY
Mr D S Allard, 8 Chilcourt, Royston
SG8 9DD ☎ 01763 242677
www.ramblers-herts-
northmiddlesex.org.uk
GROUP SECRETARIES
Dacorum Mr Norman Jones, 47 Cedar
Walk, Hemel Hempstead HP3 9ED
☎ 01442 211794
www.dacorumramblers.com
East Hertfordshire Miss P A
Hemmings, 16 Smiths Green, Debden,
Saffron Walden CB11 3LP
www.easthertsramblers.co.uk
Finchley & Hornsey Mrs Julia Haynes,
33 Links Road, Cricklewood, London
NW2 7LE [membership enquiries,
Mrs V Mallindine ☎ 020 8883 8190]
www.ramblers-herts-
northmiddlesex.org.uk

North Hertfordshire Mrs Frances Fakes
ff331@tiscali.co.uk www.ramblers-herts-
northmiddlesex.org.uk
North London & South Herts
Mr M Noon, 100 Wynchgate, London
N14 6RN ☎ 020 8886 0348
[membership enquiries, ☎ 020 8441
0920] www.ramblers-herts-
northmiddlesex.org.uk
Royston Mrs Katherine Heale,
4 The Brambles, Royston SG8 9NQ
www.ramblers-herts-
northmiddlesex.org.uk
Watford & Three Rivers Mrs VM
Buckley, 4 Firbank Drive, Watford
WD19 4EL ☎ 01923 222591
www.ramblers-herts-
northmiddlesex.org.uk

INNER LONDON ●
AREA SECRETARY
Clare Wadd, 43 Wolsey Drive,
Kingston-upon-Thames KT2 5DP
☎ 020 8546 2812
secretary@innerlondonramblers.org.uk
www.innerlondonramblers.org.uk

GROUP SECRETARIES
Blackheath
blackrammemsec@googlemail.com
www.blackheathramblers.org.uk
Hammersmith & Wandsworth
Mrs M Jones, 27 Rannoch Road, London
W6 9SS ☎ 07796 684522 [membership
enquiries, Mr Esbester ☎ 020 8646 5545]
Hampstead Mr KD Jones, Flat 4,
144 Agar Grove, Camden, London
NW1 9TY ☎ 020 7485 2348 [evenings
only] kevin_jones@onetel.com
www.hampsteadramblers.org.uk
Kensington, Chelsea & Westminster
Ms Rita Kandela ☎ 020 7486 7447
ritakandela@aol.com [membership
enquiries, Susan Gunning, 54a Fulham
Road, London SW3 6HH
☎ 020 7589 6600
gunningsusan@hotmail.com]
users.whsmithnet.co.uk/kcw.ramblers
Metropolitan Walkers
secretary@metropolitan-walkers.org.uk
www.metropolitan-walkers.org.uk or visit
www.ramblers.org.uk/info/localgroups

or contact our central office for current details

North East London Ms S Milsome, 2 Thames Village, Hartington Road, London W4 3UE ☎ 020 8994 0171 nelr.co.uk

South Bank Mr J K Pestle, 50 Doverfield Road, London SW2 5NB ☎ 020 8674 1657 [evenings] johnpestle@btinternet.com www.southbankramblers.org.uk

ISLE OF WIGHT
AREA SECRETARY

Mrs Jenny Mitchell, 6 Northcliff Heights, Northcliff Gardens, Shanklin PO37 6ES ☎ 01983 861238 jenreflex@yahoo.co.uk

GROUP SECRETARIES

Isle of Wight Mr David Skelsey, Madeira, Hunts Road, St Lawrence, Ventnor PO38 1XT ☎ 01983 854540 wdskelsey@aol.com

Wight Sole Mr Gary Clarke, 70 Newport Road, Cowes PO31 7PN ☎ 01983 299511 wightsole@yahoo.co.uk www.wightsole.org.uk

KENT
AREA SECRETARY

Mr Arthur Russ, 7 Barnfield Road, Riverhead, Sevenoaks TN13 2AY ☎ 01732 453863 arthurruss@waitrose.com www.kentramblers.org.uk

GROUP SECRETARIES

Ashford (Kent) [membership enquiries, David Gatward ☎ 01580 762355 rambleon@orange.net] ashford-ramblers.org.uk ashford-ramblers.org.uk

Bromley Miss Barbara Phelps, 60 St Georges Road West, Bromley BR1 2NP barbara.phelps@btopenworld.com

Canterbury Mr R Cordell, 162 Broadway, Herne Bay CT6 8HY ☎ 01227 361 902 raycordell162@hotmail.com

Dartford & Gravesham Ms Joyce Gathercole, 10 Amberley Road, London SE2 0SF ☎ 020 8310 2453

East Kent Walking Mr Mike Harries, 99 Newbury Avenue, Maidstone ME16 0RE ☎ 01622 763685 or 07742 444779 mike@harries1962.freeserve.co.uk www.ekwg.co.uk

Maidstone Mr PD Royall, 18 Firs Close, Aylesford, Maidstone ME20 7LH ☎ 01622 710782 [membership enquiries, W Williams ☎ 01634 371906] www.maidstoneramblers.org.uk

Medway Mrs D M Ashdown, 94a Hollywood Lane, Wainscott, Rochester ME3 8AR

North West Kent Mr Tim Wilson, Flat 11 Maybury, 58 Wickham Road, Beckenham BR3 6RQ ☎ 020 8658 9616 timothy.wilson93@ntlworld.com

Sevenoaks Ms Sylvia Penzer, 62 Oakhill Road, Sevenoaks TN13 1NT ☎ 01732 461536 gands.penzer@virgin.net

Tonbridge & Malling ● Miss B Stead, 43 Copse Hill, Leybourne, West Malling ME19 5QR

Tunbridge Wells Ms Judith Sanbach, 36 Sandown Park, Tunbridge Wells TN2 4RN ☎ 01892 822494

West Kent Walking Mr N Houghton, 69 Penfold Road, Folkestone CT19 6DQ home.freeuk.net/wkwo

White Cliffs Mrs R Hodges, 25 William Avenue, Folkestone CT19 5TL ☎ 01303 258022 rhonahodges@hotmail.com

LAKE DISTRICT
Cumbria, plus Lancaster district of Lancashire

AREA SECRETARY

Peter Jones, 44 High Fellside, Kendal LA9 4JG ☎ 01539 723705 pcj111@googlemail.com www.ralakedistrict.ukf.net

GROUP SECRETARIES

Carlisle Mrs Mabel Little, 29 Kelvin Grove, Morton Park, Carlisle CA2 6HE ☎ 01228 529650 See area website for further details

Furness Mrs Pam Leverton, 6 Churchill Drive, Millom LA18 5DD ☎ 01229 772217 See area website for further details

Grange over Sands Mrs Wendy Bowen, Hollyhow, Hazelrigg Lane, Newby Bridge, Ulverston LA12 8NY ☎ 015395 31785 See area website for further details

Kendal ● See area website for further details or visit www.ramblers.org.uk/info/localgroups or contact our central office for current details

Lancaster Ms Joy Greenwood, 25 Connaught Road, Lancaster LA1 4BQ ☎ 01524 32816 joygreenwood25@yahoo.co.uk See area website for further details

Penrith Mr Dave Dixon, Oaklea, Beacon Edge, Penrith CA11 8BN ☎ 01768 863155 davedixon@talktalk.net www.penrithramblers.org.uk

Summit Good Mr Rob Milligan, 12 Brackenfield, Bowness-on-Windermere LA23 3HL ☎ 07773 986512 robmilligan@ukonline.co.uk www.summittgood.blogspot.com

West Cumbria Mr Mike Murgatroyd, Briar Lodge, Brundholme Road, Keswick

CA12 4NL ☎ 017687 75755 mjmurgatroyd@onetel.com See area website for further details

LANCASHIRE
See Lake District, Mid Lancashire and North East Lancashire Areas

LEICESTERSHIRE & RUTLAND
AREA SECRETARY

Mr John Jackson, 87 Coleridge Drive, Enderby, Leics LE19 4QH ☎ 0116 2865735 john@johncjackson.wanadoo.co.uk uk.geocities.com/ramblingjohn/Leics.html

GROUP SECRETARIES

Coalville ● Mr K M Pare, 103 Tressall Road, Whitwick, Coalville LE67 5QE ☎ 01530 833967 webmail@coalvilleramblers.org.uk www.coalvilleramblers.org.uk

Hinckley Mrs Barbara Elliston, 20 Surrey Close, Burbage, Hinckley LE10 2NY ☎ 01455 238881 www.hinckleyramblers.cjb.net

Leicester Mr David Siddons, 88 Grange Road, Wigston, Leicester LE18 1JJ ☎ 0116 2887457 ramblers@rutlanduk.fsnet.co.uk leicesterramblers.co.uk

Leicestershire & Rutland Walking Ms Jo Pagett, 21 Riverside Walk, Asfordby, Melton Mowbray LE14 3SD ☎ 01664 812934 secretary@lrwg.org.uk www.lrwg.org.uk

Loughborough & District Mrs Joyce Noon, 8 Ribble Drive, Barrow-upon-Soar, Loughborough LE12 8LJ ☎ 01509 414519 uk.geocities.com/ramblingjohn/Loughborough.html

Lutterworth Mrs Y Coulson, 12 Elmhirst Road, Lutterworth, Leics LE17 4QB ☎ 01455 552265

Melton Mowbray ● Gill Lant, 94 Scalford Road, Melton Mowbray LE13 1JZ ☎ 01664 500516 jbgramblers@btinternet.com www.meltonramblers.org.uk

Rutland Mrs Margaret Wright, 7 Forsells End, Houghton-on-the-Hill, Leics LE7 9HQ ☎ 0116 243 2550

LINCOLNSHIRE
AREA SECRETARY

Stuart Parker, 129 Broughton Gardens, Brant Road, Lincoln LN5 8SR ☎ 01522 534655 s.w.parker@btinternet.com www.lincscountyramblers.co.uk

GROUP SECRETARIES

Boston Mr RM Warren, 6 Gilder Way, Fishtoft, Boston PE21 0QS

RAMBLERS GROUPS & PUBLICATIONS

☎ 01205 351854
www.lincscountyramblers.co.uk
Gainsborough Mr MA Clapham, 69
Beckett Avenue, Gainsborough DN21 1EJ
☎ 01427 615871
www.lincscountyramblers.co.uk
Grantham Mr Derek Booles,
4 Dovedale Close, Grantham NG31 8EA
☎ 01476 403533
Grimsby & Louth Mrs Joan Johnson,
50 Gayton Road, Cleethorpes
DN35 0HN ☎ 01472 509396
grimsbylouth.ramblers@ntlworld.com
uk.geocities.com/tjrambler
Horncastle Mr Gordon Vessey, 51 Elm
Crescent, Burgh-le-Marsh PE24 5EG
☎ 01754 810049
www.lincscountyramblers.co.uk
Lincoln ● Mrs Mary Glen, 130 Fulmar
Road, Lincoln LN6 0LA ☎ 01522 689387
www.lincscountyramblers.co.uk
Lincolnshire Walking Mr Stephen Lait,
37 Hope Street, Lincoln LN5 7UJ
☎ 01522 874221
www.lincswalkinggroup.org.uk
Scunthorpe Mrs Janet Atkinson,
30 Conference Court, Scunthorpe
DN16 3SZ ☎ 01724 350118
www.lincscountyramblers.co.uk
Skegness Mrs Glenys Malcolm,
9 Winston Drive, Skegness PE25 2RE
☎ 01754 899878
www.users.madasafish.com/~skegnessra
Sleaford ● Mr Dave Houghton,
19 Eastgate, Heckington, Sleaford
NG34 9RB ☎ 01529 461220
dave-houghton@tiscali.co.uk
www.lincscountyramblers.co.uk
Spalding Ms Jean Weller, 10 Miles Bank,
Spalding PE11 3EZ ☎ 01775 762192
Stamford Visit www.ramblers.org.uk/
info/localgroups or contact our central
office for current details

LONDON
For inner London boroughs see Inner
London Area; for outer London
boroughs, see Buckinghamshire & West
Middlesex, Essex, Hertfordshire &
North Middlesex, Kent, and
Surrey Areas

MANCHESTER & HIGH PEAK
Former Greater Manchester, plus High
Peak district of Derbyshire

AREA SECRETARY
www.manchester-ramblers.org.uk or visit
www.ramblers.org.uk/info/localgroups or
contact our central office for current details

GROUP SECRETARIES
Bolton Ms Pat Hall, 92 Bradshaw Road,
Bolton BL2 3EW ☎ 01204 300602

pat.hall1@ntlworld.com
homepage.ntlworld.com/boltonramblers
Bury Mrs Megan Smith, 87 Bankhouse
Road, Bury BL8 1DY ☎ 0161 764 8598
Mad Walkers (Manchester & District) Mr John Ireland, 13 Rawson
Road, Bolton BL1 4JG ☎ 01204 496310
johnaj.ireland@virgin.net
www.madwalkers.org.uk
New Mills Mr John Biggins, 39 Grasmere
Crescent, High Lane, Stockport SK6 8AL
☎ 0161 427 7303
www.nmramblers.freeserve.co.uk
Oldham Janet Hewitt, 2 Hillside Avenue,
Carrbrook, Stalybridge SK15 3NE
☎ 01457 834769
www.oldhamramblers.org.uk
Rochdale ● Mrs S Blatcher, 5 Enfield
Close, Rochdale OL11 5RT
☎ 01706 641041
Stockport Mrs L Sangster, 98 Mile End
Lane, Great Moor, Stockport SK2 6BP
☎ 0161 4838774
www.stockportramblers.org.uk
Wigan & District Mrs M A Newall,
4 Rydal Close, Blackrod, Bolton BL6 5EH
☎ 01204 691790 jmnewall@yahoo.co.uk
uk.geocities.com/wiganramblers@
btinternet.com

MERSEYSIDE & WEST CHESHIRE ●
Merseyside, plus Chester and Ellesmere
Port districts of Cheshire

AREA SECRETARY
Miss G F Thayer, 53 Bramwell Avenue,
Prenton, Wirral CH43 0RQ
☎ 0151 608 9472

GROUP SECRETARIES
Cestrian (Chester) Ms F Parsons,
32 Wetherby Way, Little Sutton,
South Wirral CH66 4NY
☎ 0151 3391178
Liverpool Mrs M Hems, 19 Moorcroft
Road, Liverpool L18 9UG
☎ 07980 856101
www.liverpoolramblers.co.uk
Merseyside 20s–30s Walkers
Jo Bremner, 28 Sutton Road,
Wallasey, Wirral CH45 5BD
☎ 07968 505303
joannebremner@yahoo.co.uk
www.fillyaboots.org.uk
Southport Mr D Wall, 8 Sulby Close,
Southport PR8 4TJ ☎ 01704 564831
St Helens Mrs Carol Walsh,
48 South Street, Thatto Heath,
St Helens WA9 5QF
☎ 01744 601608
carol.walshram@blueyonder.co.uk
Wirral Mr Gordon Clarke, 19 Stevenson
Drive, Wirral CH63 9AH
☎ 0151 334 3435
www.wirralramblers.org.uk

MID LANCASHIRE
Lancashire: Blackpool, Fylde, Preston,
South Ribble, Chorley, West Lancashire
and Wyre boroughs

AREA SECRETARY
Mr D Kelly, 4 Buttermere Close,
Bamber Bridge, Preston PR5 4RT
☎ 01772 312027
www.lancashire-ramblers.org.uk

GROUP SECRETARIES
Chorley Mrs J Tudor Williams, Oaklands,
5 The Bowers, Chorley PR7 3LA
www.chorleyramblers.com
Fylde David Stokes, 7 Cedar Close,
Newton With Scales, Kirkham PR4 3TZ
☎ 01772 671134
www.fylderamblers.org.uk
Garstang & District Mrs C Stenning,
20 Meadowcroft Avenue, Catterall,
Garstang PR3 1ZH ☎ 01995 601478
Lancashire Walking Mrs R Kirk,
68 Broadriding Road, Shevington, Wigan
WN6 8EX ruth.kirk@blueyonder.co.uk
www.lypwc.org.uk
Preston Mr A Manzie, 3 Ruthin Court,
Dunbar Road, Ingol, Preston PR2 3YE
☎ 01772 736467
prestonra@prestonra.co.uk
www.prestonra.co.uk
South Ribble Mr BA Kershaw, 2 Moss
Way, New Longton, Preston PR4 4ZQ
West Lancashire Mr WG Wright, 49
Riverview, Tarleton, Preston PR4 6ED
☎ 01772 812034
www.westlancsramblers.org.uk

NORFOLK
AREA SECRETARY
Mr Brian Ansell, 44 The Street, Rockland
St Mary, Norwich NR17 7AH
☎ 01508 538654 ansell44@tiscali.co.uk
homepage.ntlworld.com/bcmoore/
NorfolkRA

GROUP SECRETARIES
Fakenham Mrs Brenda Gibson,
Tithe Cottage, The Street, Little Snoring,
Fakenham NR21 0AJ ☎ 01328 878672
Great Yarmouth Mrs Annie Sharrock,
Aldebaran, The Street, West Somerton
NR29 4EA ☎ 01493 393671
annie.pas@btopenworld.com

King's Lynn Mrs Sue Berman, 12 Kendle Way, King's Lynn PE30 3XX
Mid-Norfolk Mrs Carole Jackson, Mandola, Mill Street, Elsing, Dereham NR20 3EJ ☎ 01362 637752
alwynandcarole@my-emails.com
Norwich Mr Derek Goddard, 49 Lindford Drive, Eaton, Norwich NR4 6LR ☎ 01603 506906
dgoddard@my-emails.com
homepage.ntlworld.com/bcmoore/NorwichRA
Sheringham & District ● Mrs Edwina Moore, 20 Creake Road, Sculthorpe, Fakenham NR21 9NG ☎ 01328 862771
Southern Norfolk Mrs Jean Aldridge, Miller's Cottage, Wacton Common, Long Stratton, Norwich NR15 2UP ☎ 01508 530289
Wensum Mr Tony Smith, 3 Priors Drive, Old Catton, Norwich NR6 7LJ ☎ 01603 423085

NORTH & MID CHESHIRE

The district of Vale Royal and the western part of Macclesfield district

AREA SECRETARY
Ms Christina Goddard, 15 Lowfield Gardens, Glazebury, Warrington WA3 5LY ☎ 01925 765 639
christinag@dsl.pipex.com
nmc-ramblers.org.uk

GROUP SECRETARIES
Halton Mr Norman Lidbury, 50 Deepdale Drive, Rainhill, Prescot L35 4NW ☎ 0151 4260925
n.lidbury@blueyonder.co.uk
nmc-ramblers.org.uk
North & Mid Cheshire Under 40 Mrs Sarah Talbot, 217 Edgeley Road, Stockport SK3 0TL
www.cheshirewalkers.org.uk
Vale Royal and Knutsford Mrs Daphne Armitage, Birchtree Bungalow, Red Lane, Appleton, Warrington WA4 5AB
nmc-ramblers.org.uk
Warrington Mrs Bernadette Elebert, Yellow Lodge, Park Lane, Higher Walton, Warrington WA4 5LW
bernielebert@hotmail.com
nmc-ramblers.org.uk

NORTH EAST LANCASHIRE

Lancashire: Ribble Valley, Pendle, Burnley, Rossendale, Blackburn and Hyndburn districts

AREA SECRETARY
Mrs Sue Baxendale, 101 Blackburn Road, Clayton-Le-Moors, Accrington BB5 5JT ☎ 01254 235049

GROUP SECRETARIES
Blackburn & Darwen Miss Glenda Brindle, 103 School Lane, Guide, Blackburn ☎ 01254 671269
mgbrindle@btinternet.com
www.ramblersassociationblackburnanddarwen.co.uk
Burnley & Pendle Mrs Janet Lofthouse, Briercliffe Road, Burnley ☎ 01282 435352
jlofthouse1@ntlworld.com
Clitheroe ● Mr Ben Brown, 2 Chorlton Terrace, Barrow, Whalley, Clitheroe, Lancs BB7 9AR ☎ 01254 822851
Hyndburn Mrs Sue Baxendale, 101 Blackburn Road, Clayton-Le-Moors, Accrington BB5 5JT ☎ 01254 235049
www.hyndburnramblers.co.uk
Rossendale Mr Peter Aizlewood, Lynwood, 265 Haslingden Old Road, Rossendale BB4 8RR ☎ 01706 215085
peter.aizlewood@ntlworld.com
www.rossendaleramblers.com

NORTH YORKS & SOUTH DURHAM

Cleveland: Co Durham except Derwentside, Durham and Chester-le-Street districts; North Yorkshire: present Richmondshire district and the former urban and rural districts of Bedale, Helmsley, Kirkbymoorside, Northallerton, Pickering, Stokesley, Thirsk and Whitby now forming part of the Hamberton and Rydedale districts. See also West Riding, and East Yorks & Derwent Areas

AREA SECRETARY
Dr David Leyshon, 11 Ripley Road, Norton, Stockton-on-Tees TS20 1NX ☎ 01642 553796
david.leyshon@btinternet.com

GROUP SECRETARIES
Barnard Castle Mrs E Vlaming-Helmer, Hollincroft, Romaldkirk, Barnard Castle DL12 9EL ☎ 01833 650192
helmerrupert@aol.com
www.barnardcastleramblers.org.uk
Cleveland ● Mr Alan Patterson, 141 Castle Road, Redcar TS10 2NF ☎ 01642 474864
Crook & Weardale Mrs K Berry, 11 Wood Square, Bishop Auckland DL14 6QQ ☎ 01388 608979
members.aol.com/crookramblers
Darlington Mr Bryan Spark, 3 Thirlmere Grove, West Auckland, Bishop Auckland DL14 9LW ☎ 01388 834213
bspark@addisonandco.co.uk
Darlington Dales & Hills Simon Cummings, 20 Burnhope, Newton Aycliffe, Co Durham DL5 7ER ☎ 01325 320911 [evenings only]
darlingtonhiking@hotmail.co.uk
www.darlingtonhiking.co.uk

Northallerton Mr Martin Davies, West House, Great Smeaton, Northallerton DL6 2EH ☎ 01609 881659
Martdavies_6@btinternet.com
www.members.aol.com/nragroup
Richmondshire Mrs V Darwin, 4 Sycamore Avenue, Richmond DL10 4BN ☎ 01748 822 845
www.richmondshireramblers.com

NORTHAMPTONSHIRE

AREA SECRETARY
Mr Roy Talbot, 17 Spring Lane, Flore, Northampton NN7 4LS ☎ 01327 340836 Roytalbot@onetel.com
www.northants-area-ra.info

GROUP SECRETARIES
Daventry Steve Ellis, 25a Sutton Street, Flore NN7 4LD ☎ 01327 341428
Kettering Mrs Rita East, 38 Hawthorn Avenue, Mawsley, Kettering NN14 1TH ☎ 07830 188725
info@kra-g.org kra-g.org
Northampton Miss Joanne Hammond, 37 Knights Court, Little Billing, Northampton NN3 9AT ☎ 01604 518517
Northants 20s–30s Walking Mr John Hadley, 19 St Peters Avenue, Rushden NN10 6XW
secretary@letsgetreadytoramble.org.uk
www.letsgetreadytoramble.org.uk
Wellingborough & District Mr Jim Timpson, Midways, The Promenade, Wellingborough NN8 5AL ☎ 01933 224750
Jimjaq@rumpus.freeserve.co.uk
www.wellingboroughramblers.org.uk

NORTHUMBERLAND

See Northumbria Area below

NORTHUMBRIA ●

AREA SECRETARY
Ms Rachel Orange, Roseberry Cottage, Littleburn Lane, Langley Moor, Durham DH7 8HA ☎ 0191 3782962
rachelorange2701@hotmail.com
northern.ra-area.org.uk

GROUP SECRETARIES
Alnwick Mr Colin McClure, The Acorns, Acklington Road, North Broomhill, Morpeth NE65 9XD ☎ 01670 763006
colsyl95@hotmail.co.uk
northern.ra-area.org.uk
Berwick Mrs G Hanham
g.hanham@virgin.net
Chester le Street Mr Brian Stout, 37 Kirkstone Drive, Lambton, Durham DH1 1AH ☎ 0191 3864089
Derwentside Mrs Sheila Jeffreys, 7 Ferndene Court, Moor Road South, Newcastle-upon-Tyne, Tyne & Wear

NE3 INN ☎ 0191 285 8442
Sheila@jeffreyss.fsnet.co.uk
Durham City Dr Cliff Ludman, 5 Church
Street, Durham DH1 3DG
☎ 0191 386 6886
cliff.ludman@ramblers.durhamcity.org.uk
Gateshead Mrs Hilary Clark, 15 Shibdon
Park View, Blaydon NE21 5HA
☎ 0191 4143643
Hexham Mrs Rosalind Blaylock,
10 Quatre Bras, Hexham,
Northumberland NE46 3JY
☎ 01434 604639
Morpeth Miss Margaret Siggins,
17 Kingswell, Carlisle Lea, Morpeth,
Northumberland NE61 2TY
☎ 01670 518031
Northumbria Family Walking ●
Mrs Simin Cooper, 3 Roydon Avenue,
Sunderland SR2 7TB ☎ 0191 5108851
simincooper@talk21.com
Northumbria Short Circuits ●
Mrs Mary Moore, 2 Kingsway Avenue,
Gosforth, Newcastle-upon-Tyne NE3 2HS
☎ 0191 285 6890
mtmoore@waitrose.com
Northumbria Walking Ms Gill Atkinson
northumbria_walking_group@hotmail.com
Ponteland Mr Colin Braithwaite,
105 Western Way, Ponteland, Newcastle-
upon-Tyne NE20 9LY ☎ 01661 822929
Sunderland Mrs Pat Jackson,
73 Houghton Road, Hetton-Le-Hole,
Houghton Le Spring DH5 9PQ
☎ 0191 5260434
Tyneside Mrs Pennie Porter,
16 Northfield Road, Gosforth, Newcastle-
upon-Tyne NE3 3UL ☎ 0191 2135707
penny@angerton.fsnet.co.uk

NOTTINGHAMSHIRE
AREA SECRETARY
Mr Rod Fillingham, 1 Albany Close,
Arnold, Nottingham NG5 6JP ☎ 0115
9204066 rod@fillingham.f9.co.uk
www.nottsarearamblers.co.uk

GROUP SECRETARIES
Broxtowe Liz Pritchett (acting),
17 Buxton Avenue, Carlton, Nottingham
☎ 0115 987 6268 liz.pritchett@tiscali.co.uk
www.broxtoweramblers.co.uk
Collingham Ms Anne Burns, 2 Brewers
Wharf, Newark NG24 1ET
anneburns39@ntlworld.com
Dukeries Mr A Gamble, 35 Greenwood
Crescent, Boughton, Newark NG22 9HX
☎ 01623 861376
www.nottsarearamblers.co.uk/Groups/
Dukeries/Dukeries.htm
Gedling ● Mrs Jenny Fillingham, 1 Albany
Close, Arnold, Nottingham NG5 6JP
☎ 0115 9204066
jenny@fillingham.f9.co.uk

Hucknall Ms Sarah Smith, 306 Belper
Road, Stanley Common, Ilkeston DE7 6FY
☎ 07968 267846 sarahs306@aol.com
www.nottsarearamblers.co.uk/Groups/
Hucknall/hucknall.htm
**Mansfield & Sherwood Walking
Group** Mr Malc Lawson, 2 Northfield
Drive, Mansfield, Nottingham NG18 3DD
☎ 01623 460941
secretary@mansfield-ramblers.co.uk
www.mansfield-ramblers.co.uk
Newark Mr Richard Legg, 43 Ropewalk,
Southwell, Nottingham NG25 0AL
☎ 01636 812318
www.newarkramblers.co.uk
Nottingham Mrs Margo Cameron,
46 Sandford Road, Nottingham NG3 6AJ
☎ 0115 8718927
www.nottsarearamblers.co.uk/Groups/
Nottingham/nottingham.htm
Notts Derby Walking Mr Ian Bell,
86 Ladygrove, Ambergate, Derbyshire
DE56 2JS ☎ 01773 852603
ian@ladygrove86.demon.co.uk
www.ndwg.co.uk
Notts Weekend Walkers
Kevin Matthews, 44 The Downs,
Silverdale, Nottingham NG11 7DY
☎ 0115 914 5653
notts.walkers@ntlworld.com
Ravenshead Mrs Polly Hill, 8 Lea Road,
Ravenshead ☎ 01623 409686
Retford Mrs Judith Anson, Townrows
Farm, High Street, Elkesley DN22 8AJ
☎ 01777 838 763 andyrperry@mac.com
www.nottsarearamblers.co.uk/Groups/
Retford/Retford.htm
Rushcliffe Mr Richard Parrey, 61 West
Leake Road, Kingston On Soar
NG11 0DN ☎ 0115 9830730
richard.parrey@btinternet.com
www.theburks.org/ramblers
Southwell Mrs Margaret Gash,
4 Waterside, North Muskham, Newark
NG23 6FD ☎ 01636 677017
Vale of Belvoir Dr Angela Turner,
9 Maple Close, Radcliffe-On-Trent,
Nottingham NG12 2DG
☎ 0115 9334436
www.nottsarearamblers.co.uk/Groups/Vale
%20of%20Belvoir/vob.htm
Worksop Mrs Cherry Keates, 46 Snipe
Park Road, Bircotes, Doncaster
DN11 8DG
www.nottsarearamblers.co.uk/Groups/
Worksop/worksop%20group.htm

OXFORDSHIRE
AREA SECRETARY
Mrs Susan Maguire, Jennyanydots,
112 Reading Road, Henley-on-Thames
RG9 1DN ☎ 01491 575682
susan.maguire@tiscali.co.uk
www.ramblers-oxon.org.uk

GROUP SECRETARIES
Bicester & Kidlington Mr Colin
Morgan, 11 Spruce Drive, Bicester
OX26 3YE ☎ 01869 369603
colin.morgan278@talktalk.net
Cherwell Hazel Lister, 3 Bowling Green,
Farthinghoe, Brackley NN13 5PQ
☎ 01295 710227
hazel@lister8280.fsbusiness.co.uk
Didcot & Wallingford Mrs J Tilling,
The Cedars, Brookfield Close, Wallingford
OX10 9EQ ☎ 01491 839221
janicetilling@aol.com
Henley & Goring Eileen Burroughs,
43 Elizabeth Road, Henley-on-Thames
RG9 1RA ☎ 01491 572490 [membership
enquiries, Tony Brown ☎ 01491 575500]
Oxford Ms Melissa Perot, 35 Boulter
Street, Oxford OX4 1AX ☎ 01865
727775 missaperot@yahoo.com
Oxon 20s–30s Walking Miss Sam Band,
4 Chestnut Road, Oxford OX2 9EA
www.oxon2030walkers.org
Thame & Wheatley Mrs J E Noyce,
27 Worminghall Road, Ickford, Aylesbury,
Bucks HP18 9JB ☎ 01844 339969
Vale of White Horse Mr Patrick
Lonergan, 35 Cherwell Close, Abingdon
OX14 3TD ☎ 01235 202784
patlon@ntlworld.com
West Oxfordshire Mrs Eileen Lukes,
46 Spencer Avenue, Yarnton, Kidlington
OX5 1NQ eileenlukes@yahoo.co.uk

SHROPSHIRE
AREA SECRETARY
Mrs Marion Law, 3 Mead Way, Shifnal
TF11 9QB ☎ 01952 462855
marionlaw@rapidial.co.uk
www.shropshireramblers.org.uk

GROUP SECRETARIES
Market Drayton Mrs Heather Morris,
10 Golf Links Lane, Wellington, Telford
TF1 2DS ☎ 01952 242910
Oswestry Mr Peter Carr, Tre Tylluan,
Dolybont, Llanrhaeadr Ym Mochnant,
Oswestry SY10 0LJ ☎ 01691 780722
epc@uwclub.net
Shrewsbury & Mid-Shropshire
Mrs Chris Cluley, Birches Farm, Clun,
Craven Arms, Shropshire SY7 8NL
☎ 01588 640243
Shropshire Young Ramblers Miss
Rachael Chadwick, 23 Beaumaris Road,
Newport TF10 7BN ☎ 07929 591222
www.syr.org.uk
South Shropshire ● Ms Susan Sharp,
Brookside, Eagle Lane, Cleobury
Mortimer, Kidderminster DY14 8RA
☎ 01299 271099 susan@eaglelane.co.uk
Telford & East Shropshire Mrs Anne
Sumner, 18 Shrewsbury Road, Edgmond,
Newport, Shropshire TF10 8HU
☎ 01952 810444

Sheffield 20s–30s The Circle,
Rockingham Way, Sheffield S1 4FW
sheffieldwalkinggroup@hotmail.com
www.sheffieldwalkinggroup.org.uk

STAFFORDSHIRE
Staffordshire, plus Dudley, Sandwell,
Walsall and Wolverhampton districts of
former West Midlands

AREA SECRETARY
Mr Graham Evans, 65 Pacific Road,
Trentham, Stoke-on-Trent ST4 8RS
☎ 01782 642872
gsevans@gsevans.f9.co.uk
homepages.tesco.net/~staffsra

GROUP SECRETARIES
Biddulph Mr N Oakden, Dukes Well,
Cloudside, Congleton CW12 3QG
☎ 01260 226617
www.biddulphra.freeuk.com
Bilston Mrs Jackie Tyler, 50 Wellington
Place, Wednesfield, Willenhall WV13 3AB
☎ 01902 633849
www.bilstonramblers.org.uk
**Black Country 20s–30s Walking
Group** Ms Sarah Andrews, 33 Lapwing
Close, Walsall WS6 7LL
bcwg@hotmail.co.uk
www.blackcountrywalkinggroup.
netfirms.com
Chase & District ● Mr Roy
Roobottom, 10 Beaconside Close,
Stafford ST16 3QS ☎ 01785 211148
East Staffordshire ● Mrs Jane King,
39 Faraday Avenue, Stretton,
Burton-on-Trent DE13 0FX ☎ 01283
543483
Leek Mrs Shirley Lunt, 17 Rennie
Crescent, Cheddleton, Leek ST13 7HD
☎ 01538 360907 www.raleek.co.uk
Lichfield Mr Malcolm Day, 2 Fontenaye
Road, Coton Green, Tamworth B79 8JZ
☎ 01827 700590
lichfield.ramblers.users.btopenworld.com
Mid Staffordshire Mrs Shirley Benn,
11 Porlock Avenue, Stafford ST17 0HS
☎ 01785 603646
midstaffs.ra@ntlworld.com
homepage.ntlworld.com/brian.benn/ra
Sandwell Vivien Du Bois, 47 Gladys
Road, Smethwick B67 5AW
☎ 0121 4296148 vdubois@excite.com
www.sandwellramblers.org.uk
Staffordshire Walkers
www.staffs-walkers.org.uk or visit
www.ramblers.org.uk/info/localgroups or
contact our central office for current details
Stoke/Newcastle Mr Richard Clamp,
61 Downing Avenue, Basford, Newcastle
ST5 0LB ☎ 01782 621541 [membership
enquiries ☎ 01782 787948]
Stone Mr G Greensides, Ambleside,
111 Lichfield Road, Stone ST15 8QD
☎ 01785 813067

SOMERSET
AREA SECRETARY
Mr Rod Porter, 132 Wellington Road,
Taunton TA1 5LA ☎ 01823 321783
rodporter2002@aol.com
www.somersetramblers.org.uk

GROUP SECRETARIES
Clevedon Mrs Sue Shewan,
25 Honeylands, Portishead, Bristol
BS20 6RB ☎ 01275 848075
www.somersetramblers.org.uk
Family Countryside Walkers ●
Mary Henry, 22 Linden Grove, Taunton
TA1 1EF ☎ 01823 333369
Mendip Ms Lisa Sutton, 26 West Street,
Wells BA5 2HG ☎ 01749 678806
lisa@mendipramblers.co.uk
www.mendipramblers.co.uk
Sedgemoor Mrs Nicky Hewitt
☎ 01278 684676
nickyhewett@aol.com
Somerset Walking & Activity Group
swag02@googlemail.com
www.funwithswag.org.uk
South Somerset ● Mr Ian Rendall,
3a Tintern, Abbey Manor Park, Yeovil
BA21 3SJ ☎ 01935 421235
www.somersetramblers.co.uk/
southsom.htm
Taunton Deane Mr Robert Camp,
7 Wilton Close, Taunton TA1 4EZ
☎ 01823 331058
robert.camp1@ukonline.co.uk
www.tauntonramblers.org.uk
West Somerset Mr Geoffrey Taylor,
1 Culvercliffe Court, Minehead TA24 5UP
☎ 01643 705288 geoff@woodclose.co.uk
Woodspring Ms Diane Smith, 45 The
Badgers, St Georges, Weston Super Mare
BS22 7RF ☎ 01934 518082

SOUTH & EAST CHESHIRE
Cheshire: Crewe & Nantwich and
Congleton districts, plus eastern section
of Macclesfield district

AREA SECRETARY
Visit www.ramblers.org.uk/info/localgroups
or contact our central office for
current details
GROUP SECRETARIES
Congleton Mrs Anne Wheater, 35 Back

Lane, Congleton, Cheshire CW12 4PY
☎ 01260 273536 wheaterk@aol.com
East Cheshire Jenny Irwin, 9 Green Villa
Park, Wilmslow SK9 6EJ
walk@ramblerseastcheshire.org.uk
www.ramblerseastcheshire.org.uk
South Cheshire Mr P Callery,
45 Broughton Lane, Wistaston, Crewe
CW2 8JR ☎ 01270 568714
www.ramblerssouthcheshire.org.uk

SOUTH YORKS & NE DERBYSHIRE
Former South Yorkshire, plus North
East Derbyshire: Chesterfield and
Bolsover districts of Derbyshire

AREA SECRETARY
Mr Terry Howard, 334 Manchester Road,
Crosspool, Sheffield S10 5DQ
☎ 0114 2665438
www.syned-ramblers.org.uk

GROUP SECRETARIES
Barnsley & Penistone Mrs C Wood,
25 Cloverlands Drive, Mapplewell,
Barnsley S75 6EB ☎ 01226 384041
Bolsover District Ms Daeana Walker,
53 Somerset Drive, Brimington,
Chesterfield S43 1DL ☎ 078170 45266
daeanawalker@yahoo.co.uk
**Chesterfield & North East
Derbyshire** Mr Graham Wright,
26 Ashford Road, Dronfield-Woodhouse
S18 8RQ ☎ 01246 233179 [Basil Merry]
bjmerry@tinyworld.co.uk
www.chesterfieldramblers.org.uk
Chesterfield 20s–30s Miss Rachael
Burnett, 29 Cross London Street, New
Whittington, Chesterfield S43 2AG
www.chesterfieldyoungramblers.co.uk
Dearne Valley Sue Haywood [acting],
84 Clayfield View, Mexborough, South
Yorks ☎ 01709 586870
www.dearnevalleyramblers.org.uk
Doncaster ● Mr David Gadd, 5 Wong
Lane, Tickhill, Doncaster DN11 9NH
www.doncasterramblers.org
Rotherham Metro District Mrs V
Wills, 19 Martin Rise, Thorpe Hesley,
Rotherham S61 2UE
☎ 0114 225 7498
www.doncasterramblers.org
Sheffield ● Mrs Sheila Thompson,
61 Seagrave Road, Sheffield S12 2JS
☎ 0114 2655111
www.sheffield.ramblers.care4free.net

george.greensides@tesco.net
www.stoneramblers.com
Stourbridge ● Mrs Daphne Pearce,
17 Ibstock Drive, Stourbridge DY8 1NW
☎ 01384 359463
Walsall Mrs Anne Ball, 33 Berryfields,
Aldridge, Walsall WS9 0EL
☎ 01922 863672
Wolverhampton Mr Geoff Lewis,
73 Albert Road, Wolverhampton
WV6 0AG ☎ 01902 422531
geoff@lewis02.co.uk wton-ra.atspace.com

SUFFOLK
AREA SECRETARY
Mr Phil Snelling, 12 Market Place,
Lavenham CO10 9QZ ☎ 01787 248 079
phil.snelling@amec.com
www.suffolkramblers.org.uk

GROUP SECRETARIES
Alde Valley Anne Hubert-Chibnall,
133 High Street, Wickham Market,
Woodbridge IP13 0RD ☎ 01728 747966
tulasim@visa.com
Bury St Edmunds Mrs JM Bolwell, 42
Cloverfields, Sandpit Lane, Thurston, Bury
St Edmunds IP31 3TJ ☎ 01359 231301
www.burystedmundsramblers.org.uk
Ipswich & District ● Mr Ian Dolby,
469 Norwich Road, Ipswich IP1 5DS
☎ 01473 412742
www.ipswichramblers.co.uk
Newmarket & District Mrs CC Lee,
Corner Cottage, Sharps Lane, Horringer,
Bury St Edmunds IP29 5PW
☎ 01284 735971 cclwalk@aol.com
www.newmarketramblers.co.uk
Stour Walking Mr David Collings, 34 St
Agnes Way, Kesgrave, Ipswich IP5 1JZ
david.2.collings@bt.com
www.stourwalkinggroup.co.uk
Stowmarket Mrs JJ Thompson,
2 Harvest Close, Haughley,
Stowmarket IP14 3PZ
www.stowmarketramblers.org.uk
Sudbury Mrs Ingrid Kay, 6 Chaplin Walk,
Great Cornard, Sudbury CO10 0YT
☎ 01787 370019
ingrid@ingridkay.wanadoo.co.uk
www.sudburyra.freeserve.co.uk
Waveney Mrs Anne Crosland,
16 Holmere Drive, Church Meadows,
Halesworth IP19 8TR ☎ 01986 873662

croslandanne@btinternet.com
www.waveneyramblers.co.uk

SURREY
Surrey, plus London boroughs of
Richmond, Kingston, Merton, Sutton
and Croydon

AREA SECRETARY
Mr David Ross, 10 Shortheath Road,
Farnham GU9 8SR ☎ 01252 725888
david_ross_gu9@btinternet.com

GROUP SECRETARIES
Croydon Mrs Ann Toomey, 77 Abercairn
Road, London SW16 5AF ☎ 020 8679
5604 www.croydonramblers.org.uk
East Surrey Mrs Lisa Dunning,
143 Hillbury Road, Warlingham CR6 9TG
☎ 01883 622827
lisa-dunning@raworth.co.uk
www.eastsurreyramblers.org.uk
Epsom & Ewell ● Mr David Newman,
56a Acacia Grove, New Malden KT3 3BU
☎ 0208 949 3471
david.mayumi@virgin.net
www.epsomandewellramblers.co.uk
Farnham & District Ms Gaynor Ross,
10 Ridgway Hill Road, Farnham GU9 8LS
☎ 01252 722930
gaynorross@ferdys.freeserve.co.uk
www.farnhamramblers.org.uk
Godalming & Haslemere
Mrs Cynthia Chard, 1 Hill House, Ockford
Road, Godalming GU7 1QX
☎ 01483 416907
www.godalmingandhaslemereramblers.
org.uk
Guildford Mr Phillip Mansley,
40 Guildown Road, Guildford GU2 4EY
☎ 01483 854451
phillipmansley@ntlworld.com
www.guildfordramblers.org.uk
Kingston ● Mr Martin Lake, 87
Porchester Road, Kingston-upon-Thames
KT1 3PW ☎ 0208 541 3437
walker@martinlake.plus.com
www.geocities.com/kingstonramblers
Mole Valley Mrs J Kucera, 33 Durfold
Drive, Reigate RH2 0QA
☎ 01737 221244 [membership enquiries,
Mrs Marles ☎ 01372 454012]
myweb.tiscali.co.uk/molevalleyramblers
Reigate Mr Glyn Jones, 12 Briars Wood,
Horley RH6 9UE ☎ 01293 773198
glyn.thelma@virgin.net
www.reigateramblers.org.uk
Richmond Mr Vic Lewis, 6 St James'
Avenue, Hampton Hill, Hampton
TW12 1HH ☎ 020 8979 8458
ramblers@hampton-hill.fsnet.co.uk
www.richmondramblers.org.uk
Staines Pat Pratley, 76 Hetherington Rd,
Charlton Village, Shepperton TW17 0SW
☎ 01932 711355

www.stainesramblersgroup.org.uk
Surrey Area Weekend Walkers
Mr Dave Lambert, 29 Castle House,
1 Overton Road, Sutton SM2 6QE
secretary@saww.org.uk www.saww.org.uk
Surrey Heath Mr Laurence Welch,
\2a Rorkes Drift, Mytchett, Camberley
GU16 6EQ ☎ 01252 678012
laurence.welch@ntlworld.com
www.surreyheathramblers.org.uk
Surrey Under 40s Mrs Paula Maddison,
52 Down Road, Guildford GU1 2PY
☎ 07959 585587
www.surreyyoungwalkers.org.uk
Sutton & Wandle Valley ●
Peter Rogers, 8 Claygate Court, All Saints
Road, Sutton SM1 3DB ☎ 020 8641 4339
[membership enquiries ☎ 020 8643 2605]
peterogs@aol.com
mysite.orange.co.uk/wandleramblers
Woking & District ● Mrs Janet
Mannan, Stantor, Oak End Way,
Woodham, Addlestone KT15 3DT ☎
01932 343038 janetmannan@yahoo.com
web.ukonline.co.uk/wokingramblers

SUSSEX
AREA SECRETARY
Mr Nigel Sloan, Kervesridge, Kerves Lane,
Horsham RH13 6ES ☎ 01403 258055
[enquiries, ☎ Anne Parker 01243 536080]
nigelsloan2001@yahoo.co.uk
www.sussex-ramblers.org.uk

GROUP SECRETARIES
Arun-Adur Ms Julie O'Neil, 11 Thornhill
Way, Mile Oak, Portslade, Brighton
BN41 2YY ☎ 01273 416381
www.arun-adur-ramblers.org.uk
Beachy Head Miss M O'Brien,
Southease, Folkington Lane, Folkington,
Polegate BN26 5SA ☎ 01323 482068
Brighton & Hove ● Mrs FM Leenders,
14 Middle Road, Brighton BN1 6SR
☎ 01273 501233
www.brightonandhoveramblers.org.uk
Crawley & North Sussex Mrs V
Sherrington, 37 Cook Road, Crawley
RH10 5DJ ☎ 01293 535852
Heathfield & District Mrs R Brown,
Chant House, Eridge Lane, Rotherfield,
Nr Crowborough TN6 3JU
☎ 0189 285 2153
High Weald Walkers Mr Clive
Grumett, Greenways, Ashdown Road,
Forest Row RH18 5BN ☎ 01342 825518
clivegrumett@btinternet.com
www.highwealdwalkers.com
Horsham & Billingshurst Angie
Alderson, 34 Glovers Road, Reigate
RH2 7LA www.sussex-
ramblers.org.uk/horsham/horsham.php
Mid Sussex ● Mrs Margaret Carroll,
8 Daynes Way, Burgess Hill RH15 9RH
☎ 01444 244259

margaretcarroll@talktalk.net
Rother Ms Lesley Hayes, 36 Paynton
Road, St Leonards-on-Sea TN37 7DY
☎ 01424 437775
www.rotherramblers.org.uk
South West Sussex Mrs Anne Parker,
11 Palmers Field Avenue, Chichester
PO19 6YE ☎ 01243 536080
anne_parker@tiscali.co.uk
southwestsxramblers.mysite.wanadoo-
members.co.uk
Sussex Young Walkers Ms B Bruzon &
Mr D Hammond, 30 Northiam Road,
Eastbourne BN20 8LP
☎ 01323 639172

WARWICKSHIRE
AREA SECRETARY
Mr Michael Bird, 16 Melford Hall Road,
Solihull B91 2ES ☎ 0121 705 1118

GROUP SECRETARIES
Bear Steven Bick, 1 Donalbain Close,
Heathcote, Warwick CV34 6GD
☎ 01926 400842
stephen@sbick.wanadoo.co.uk
www.bearwalkinggroup.co.uk
Castle Bromwich Mr Andrew Moore
☎ 07779 205183
cbr.website@googlemail.com
www.castlebromwichramblers.btik.com
City of Birmingham ● Mr Roger
Gibbs, 40 Roman Way, Rowley Regis
B65 9RB ☎ 0121 559 8479
www.birminghamramblers.org.uk
Coventry ● Mr Tom O'Sullivan,
94 Dunhill Avenue, Coventry CV4 9PX
☎ 02476 471404
tom.osullivan1@btinternet.com
www.coventryra.org.uk
Mid Warwickshire Mrs Beryl Shone,
23 Stephenson Close, Old Milverton Rd,
Leamington Spa CV32 6BS
☎ 01926 335999
www.midwarksramblers.org
Rugby Mr Tony Harris, 16 Fishers Close,
Kilsby, Rugby CV23 8XH
☎ 01788 822996
anthony.harris2@btinternet.com
Solihull Mrs Sheila Woolley
☎ 0121 7055753
www.solihullramblers.co.uk
South Birmingham Ms Jackie
Spearpoint, 63 Oak Farm Road,
Birmingham B30 1ET ☎ 0121 4591479
jackie.spearpoint@virgin.net
www.sbramblers.pwp.blueyonder.co.uk
Southam Mr Colin Haywood,
44 Pendicke Street, Southam CV47 1PF
☎ 01926 812820
Stratford upon Avon Mrs Judy
Leavesley, 16 Icknield Row, Alcester
B49 5EW ☎ 01789 764798
www.stratfordramblers.com

Sutton Coldfield Mr Geoff Jones,
3 Shenstone Close, Four Oaks, Sutton
Coldfield B74 4XB ☎ 0121 353 0405
obrigado1087@tiscali.co.uk
www.suttoncoldfieldramblers.co.uk
West Midlands Walking Mr Andy Page,
28 Seymour Close, Coventry CV3 4ER
☎ 02476 304825 andy_page@fsmail.net
www.wmwg.co.uk

WEST MIDLANDS
See Warwickshire and
Staffordshire Areas

WEST RIDING
AREA SECRETARY
Gwendoline Goddard, 9 Butlers Wharf,
Hebden Bridge HX7 8AF
☎ 01422 842558
gwendoline.goddard@3-c.coop

GROUP SECRETARIES
Bradford Mr Malcolm Pitt, 1 Highfield
Close, East Morton, Keighley BD20 5SG
☎ 01274 567030
Calderdale Mrs Diane Hall, 11 School
Close, Ripponden, Halifax HX6 4HP
☎ 01422 823440
Castleford & Pontefract Mr Chris
Halton, The Grange, 38 Regent Street,
Castleford WF10 5RN ☎ 01977 515469
Craven Ms Diane Lindsay, 8 Deganwy
Drive, Huddersfield HD5 0NG
Harrogate ● Mrs Clare Sandercock,
3 Burrell Close, Wetherby LS22 6YA
☎ 01937 520174
cmsandercock@djinter.net
www.willouby.demon.co.uk/ramblersassoc
iation/harrogategroup.htm
Huddersfield Mr John Lieberg,
11 Woodroyd Avenue, Honley,
Huddersfield HD9 6LG ☎ 01484 662866
lieberg1@tiscali.co.uk
Keighley Mrs Pat Verity, 5 Appleton
Close, Bingley BD16 3LY
☎ 01274 563439 verity@waitrose.com
Leeds Ms JB Morton, 6 Lawns Green,
New Farnley, Leeds LS12 5RR
☎ 0113 279 0229
jeanne.morton@ntlworld.com
www.leedsramblers.co.uk
Leeds & Bradford 20s–30s
secretary@takeahike.org.uk [membership
enquiries, membership@takeahike.org.uk]
www.takeahike.org.uk
Lower Wharfedale The Revd David
Morling, Lorindell, 61 Layton Lane,
Rawdon, Leeds LS19 6RA
☎ 0113 250 3488 david@morling.co.u
North Kirklees Michael Church,
58 Alexandra Crescent, Birkdale Road,
Dewsbury, West Yorkshire WF13 4HL
☎ 01924 462811 church_mj@yahoo.com
Ripon Ms Barbara Jordan, 10 Red Bank
Drive, Ripon, North Yorks HG4 2LF

☎ 01765 604431
b_a_jordao@yahoo.com
Wakefield Ms Jeanette Douglas, 19
Clifton Avenue, Stanley, Wakefield WF3
4HB ☎ 01924 820732 wfgra@aol.com
Wetherby & District Ms Anthea Lunn,
18 Milnthorpe Close, Braham, Wetherby
LS23 6TG anthea.lunn@bl.uk
[membership enquiries, Ms Ursula Turner,
23 Beeches End, Boston Spa, Wetherby
LS23 6HL ursula@andut.co.uk]

WILTSHIRE & SWINDON
AREA SECRETARY
Mrs Joan Crosbee, 2 Kennet View,
Fyfield, Marlborough SN8 1PU
☎ 01672 861359 joancrosbee@tesco.net
www.ramblers-wilts.org.uk

GROUP SECRETARIES
Chippenham Mrs Kathleen Parkinson,
6 Silbury Road, Curzon Park, Calne
SN11 0ES ☎ 01249 811445
rogerbarnes@lineone.net www.ramblers-
wilts.org.uk/chip.htm
Mid Wiltshire Mrs Valerie Thomas,
6 Orchard Close, Devizes SN10 5JU
☎ 01380 725214
val@dhtdev.freeseve.co.uk
www.ramblers-wilts.org.uk/mid.htm
North East Wilts ● Mr Peter Gallagher,
10 Folkestone Road, Swindon SN1 3NH
☎ 01793 537472 peg.456@virgin.net
www.ramblers-wilts.org.uk/northeast.htm
South Wiltshire Mr Brian Abel,
27 Richards Way, West Harnham,
Salisbury SP2 8NT ☎ 01722 506561
brian.abel@ntlworld.com
www.ramblers-wilts.org.uk/swilts.htm
West Wiltshire Mrs Elizabeth Weaver,
174a Winsley Road, Bradford-on-Avon
BA15 1NY ☎ 01225 868091
www.ramblers-wilts.org.uk/wwilts.htm
Wiltshire Wanderers Martin Lucas,
10 Foreman Street, Calne SN11 8PE
☎ 01249 816467 mart75@yahoo.com
www.ramblers-wilts.org.uk/ypg.htm

WORCESTERSHIRE
AREA SECRETARY
Mr RA Hemmings, 25 Whinfield Road,
Worcester WR3 7HF
☎ 01905 451142
richard_a_hemmings@lineone.net

GROUP SECRETARIES
Bromsgrove Jean Deakin, 106 Salwarpe
Road, Charford, Bromsgrove, Worcs
B60 3HS ☎ 01527 875385
Evesham Ms DK Harwood [acting],
12 Queen's Rd, Evesham WR11 4JN
www.communigate.co.uk/worcs/
ramblersevesham

Redditch Mrs Ann Hawkins,
58 Cherington Close, Redditch B98 0BB
Worcester ● Tanya Willson, 5 Russell
Close, Powick, Worcester WR2 4QE
☎ 01905 831163
tanya1207@btinternet.com
Worcestershire 20s–30s Ms Alison Hill,
1 Trafalgar House, Nelson Road,
Worcester WR2 5BN ☎ 01905 426792
ramblers20-30@fsmail.net
www.worcesterwalkers.org.uk
Wyre Forest ● Hugh Buttress, 132 Elan
Avenue, Stourport-on-Severn, Worcester
DY13 8LR ☎ 01299 878181

WALES

CARMARTHENSHIRE
AREA SECRETARY
Mr David Foot, Ty Isaf, Taliaris, Llandeilo
SA19 7DE ☎ 01550 777623
margaret@margaretbeauchamp.freeserve.
co.uk mysite.wanadoo-
members.co.uk/beauchamp/index.html

GROUP SECRETARIES
Carmarthen & District Mr David Bush,
31 Eldergrove, Llangunnor,
Carmarthenshire, Dyfed SA31 2LQ
☎ 01267 230994
david.bush@btinternet.com
Dinefwr ● Mr David Foot, Ty Isaf, Taliaris,
Llandeilo SA19 7DE ☎ 01550 777623
mysite.freeserve.com/beauchamp/
index.html
Llanelli ● Mrs Nina Clements
☎ 01554 810979 llanelliramblers.org.uk
www.llanelliramblers.org.uk

CEREDIGION
AREA SECRETARY
Anne Macmillan, Maes Y Wawr, Rhyd Y
Gwin, Llanfarian, Aberystwyth SY23 4DD
amacmi2606@aol.com

GROUP SECRETARIES
Aberystwyth ● Shirley Kinghorn, 16
Bryn Glas, Llanbadarn, Aberystwyth, Dyfed
SY23 3QR ☎ 01970 624965
www.ceredigionramblers.org.uk/
AberystwythGroup
Cardigan & District ● Mrs Kathy Gill,
Abersylltyn, Cwm Cou, Newcastle Emlyn,
Dyfed SA38 9PN ☎ 01239 710858
mysite.wanadoo-members.co.uk/cardigan/
index.html
Lampeter ● Mr Phillip Lodwick,
Penrhyn, Cwmann, Lampeter SA48 8ET
☎ 01570 422181 philcer@btinternet.com

DYFED
See Carmarthenshire, Ceredigion and
Pembrokeshire Areas

GLAMORGAN
Bridgend, Cardiff, Rhondda, Cynon Taff,
Swansea, Vale of Glamorgan and
West Glamorgan

AREA SECRETARY
Mr John Thomas, 7 Parc Afon, Porth
CF40 1JF ☎ 01443 681082
tigerbayramblers@hotmail.com
www.glamorganramblers.org.uk

GROUP SECRETARIES
Bridgend & District ● Mr John
Sanders, 3 Bryn Rhedyn, Pencoed,
Bridgend
CF35 6TL ☎ 01656 861835
john@pencoed9.wanadoo.co.uk
www.bridgendramblers.org.uk
Cardiff ● Ms Diane Davies, 9 Cyncoed
Rise, Cyncoed, Cardiff CF23 6SF
secretary@cardifframblers.org.uk
www.cardifframblers.org.uk
Cynon Valley ● Mr Allan Harrison,
8 Stuart Street, Aberdare CF44 7LY
☎ 01685 881824
allan.harrison1@btopenworld.com
alex-penyfai.homecall.co.uk
Maesteg Mr Stephen Luke, 33 Maiden
Street, Cwmfelin, Maesteg CF34 9HP
☎ 07818 445606 lukee@btinternet.com
Merthyr Valley ● Mr Andrew Richards,
8 St Davids Close, Penpedairheol,
Hengoed CF82 8BL ☎ 01443 833719
ajeffreyrichards@yahoo.co.uk
Neath Port Talbot Mr David Davies,
21 Cwrt Coed Parc, Maesteg CF34 9DG
☎ 01656 733021
www.neathporttalbotramblers.org.uk
Penarth & District Lorraine Davies,
3 Barrians Way, Barry CF62 8JG
☎ 01446 407595
lorraine.davies@ntlworld.com
uk.geocities.com/jungjames@btinternet.
com/penarth/penarth.html
Taff Ely ● Mr Jeff Brown, 2 Shadow
Wood Drive, Miskin, Pontyclun CF72 8SX
☎ 01443 239743
jeff_tjbrown@btinternet.com
www.apyule.demon.co.uk/taffely.htm
Tawe Trekkers Mr Doug Morgan,
32 Eaton Crescent, Swansea SA1 4QL
☎ 07766 652837 tawe@hotmail.co.uk
www.tawetrekkers.org.uk
Tiger Bay Ramblers ● Ms Nina Ley
☎ 02920 628892
secretary@tigerbayramblers.org.uk
www.tigerbayramblers.org.uk
Vale of Glamorgan ● Mr Ian Fraser,
44 Millfield Drive, Cowbridge CF71 7BR

☎ 01446 774706
ian.fraser@elwa.org.uk
www.valeofglamorganramblers.co.uk
West Glamorgan Mrs Zetta Flew,
8 Meadow Croft, Southgate, Swansea
SA3 2DF ☎ 01792 232060
zettaflew@hotmail.com
www.westglamorganramblers.org.uk

GREATER GWENT
Blaenau Gwent, Caerphilly,
Monmouthshire, Newport and Torfaen

AREA SECRETARY
Mr Adrian Sheehan, 6 Wood Crescent,
Rogerstone, Newport NP10 0AL
☎ 01633 896275
adrian.sheehan@btinternet.com

GROUP SECRETARIES
Gelligaer ● Mrs Dolores Price,
26 Tyn Y Coed, Ystrad Mynach,
Caerphilly CF82 7DD ☎ 01443 813220
dolores.p@virgin.net
www.ramblersgelligaergroup.co.uk
Islwyn Ms Maggie Thomas, 15 Carlton
Terrace, Cross Keys, Newport NP11 7BU
☎ 01495 273057 maggie.thomas@virgin.net
www.islwyn-ramblers.co.uk
Lower Wye Mrs Dawn Davies,
5 Crown Meadow, Coal Way,
Coleford, Glos GL16 7HF
☎ 01594 837157
rdawndavies@hotmail.co.uk
North Gwent ● Miss Liz Kennedy
☎ 07976 913083
northgwentramblers@yahoo.co.uk
www.northgwentramblers.co.uk
Pontypool Mrs Barbara Whitticase,
Glantawell, Llanfihangel Talyllyn, Brecon,
Powys LD3 7TH ☎ 01874 658386
www.pontypool-ramblers.co.uk
South Gwent Mr Ken Phillips,
39 Penylan Close, Bassaleg, Newport
NP10 8NW ☎ 01633 894172
information@south-gwent-ramblers.co.uk
south-gwent-ramblers.co.uk

NORTH WALES
Isle of Anglesey, Conwy, Denbighshire,
Flintshire, Gwynedd and Wrexham

AREA SECRETARY
Mr Ron Williams, 11 Fron Las, Holywell
CH8 7HX ☎ 01352 715723
ronanol@macunlimited.net

GROUP SECRETARIES
Bangor-Bethesda Mr Neville Fernley,
Fedw Crymlyn Aber, Llanfairfechan,
Gwynedd LL33 0LU ☎ 01248 354724
Nevfern@talk21.com
Berwyn ● John & Sue Kay, Erw Fain,
Llantysilio, Llangollen LL20 8BU
gmoss@ukonline.co.uk
www.berwynra.org.uk

Caernarfon/Dwyfor ● Canon Edmund Plaxton, 1 & 2 Tyn Y Maes, Y Fron, Upper Llandwrog, Caernarfon LL54 7BW ☎ 01286 880188 Edmundrachel@aol.com

Clwydian ● Mr Eldryd Ankers, 14 Bron Yr Eglwys, Mynydd Isa, Mold CH7 6YQ ☎ 01352 754659 clwydianramblers@ woodlawn.wanadoo.co.uk

Conwy Valley ● www.conwyvalleyra.org.uk or visit www.ramblers.org.uk/info/localgroups or contact our central office for current details

Deeside ● Mr Jim Irvine, 30 St Davids Drive, Connahs Quay, Flintshire CH5 4SR ☎ 01244 818577 deesideramblers@btinternet.com www.deesideramblers.org.uk

Eryri 20.30 Mrs Delyth Roberts, Tre Wen, Groeslon, Waunfawr, Caernarfon LL55 4EZ ☎ 01286 650295 walk20.30@btopenworld.com www.eryri2030.org.uk

Meirionnydd ● Mr Peter Butterworth, Sarn Waun, Dyffryn Ardudwy LL44 2BH ☎ 01341 247693 pjbutterworth@btinternet.com

Vale of Clwyd ● Mr Malcolm Wilkinson, 49 Victoria Road West, Prestatyn LL19 7AA ☎ 01745 888137 malcolmray@supanet.com www.voc-ramblers.org.uk

Walkers on Wales Ms Neus Ferrer, 21 Hilltop View Road, Wrexham LL12 7SF ☎ 01978 366435 www.walkersonwales.fsnet.co.uk

Wrexham ● Mrs Anne Cooper, 33 Fford Llywelyn, Smithy Lane, Wrexham LL12 8JW ☎ 01978 312515 llwelyn.cooper@btinternet.com

Ynys Mon ● Mrs Rhiannon Pritchard, 14 Llanfaes, Llanfaes, Beaumaris LL58 8RH ☎ 01248 490534

PEMBROKESHIRE

AREA SECRETARY
Mrs Rose Taylor, 17 Gaddarn Reach, Neyland, Milford Haven, Pembs SA73 1PW ☎ 01646 600 225 taylor@stratocu.fsnet.co.u

GROUP SECRETARIES
Pembrokeshire ● Mrs Rose Taylor, 17 Gaddarn Reach, Neyland SA73 1PW ☎ 01646 600225 taylor@stratocu.waitrose.com www.pembrokeshireramblers.org.uk

POWYS

AREA SECRETARY
Mr KM Jones, 1 Heyope Road, Knucklas LD7 1PT ☎ 01547 520266 secretary@powysramblers.org.uk www.powysramblers.org.uk
GROUP SECRETARIES
4 Wells Mr Derek Cosslett, 2 Gilfach

Cottage, Newbridge On Wye, Llandrindod Wells LD1 6HS ☎ 01597 860519 fourwells@gmail.com fourwells.powysramblers.org.uk

East Radnor Mr KM Jones, 1 Heyope Road, Knucklas LD7 1PT ☎ 01547 520266 secretary@powysramblers.org.uk

Welshpool ● Mr Matthew & Gwyneth Prosser, 29 Court Close, Abermule, Powys SY15 6NU ☎ 01686 630428 mprosser@countrywidefarmers.co.uk

SCOTLAND

ARGYLL & BUTE
See Strathclyde, Dumfries & Galloway Area

CENTRAL FIFE & TAYSIDE
See Forth Valley, Fife & Tayside Area

DUMFRIES & GALLOWAY
See Strathclyde, Dumfries & Galloway Area

FORTH VALLEY, FIFE & TAYSIDE
Angus, City of Dundee, Clackmannanshire, Falkirk, Fife, Perth & Kinross, and Stirling

AREA SECRETARY
Mr David Galloway, 5 Doocot Road, St Andrews, Fife KY16 8QP ☎ 01334 475102

GROUP SECRETARIES
Blairgowrie & District Miss Agnes Mcruvie, 5 Grampian Crescent, Kirriemuir, Angus DD8 4TW ☎ 01575 572415

Brechin Jenny Ross, 17 Dalhousie Street, Brechin DD9 7BB ☎ 01356 623419 jenny.x.ross@gsk.com

Broughty Ferry Miss M Cameron, 19 Gillies Place, Broughty Ferry, Dundee DD5 3LE ☎ 01382 776250

Dalgety Bay & District ● Mr David Thomson, Sand Dollar House, High Street, Aberdour, Burntisland KY3 0SW ☎ 01383 860324 davidthomson@tesco.net www.dalgetybayramblers.org.uk

Dundee & District Mrs AC Cowie, 32 Ballindean Terrace, Dundee, Tayside DD4 8PA ☎ 01382 507682

Forfar & District Mrs Jenny Mcdade, Lamees, 2a Dalhousie Street, Carnoustie DD7 6EJ ☎ 01241 855481

Forth Valley Family Walking ●
Mrs Nicola Glennie, 19 Bevan Drive, Alva

FK12 5PD ☎ 01259 769316 nicola.glennie@hotmail.co.uk

Glenrothes Mr Doug Jolly, 16 Orchard Drive, Glenrothes, Fife KY7 5RG ☎ 01592 757039 douglas_jolly@virgin.net

Kinross & Ochil Karen Bernard, 4 St Serfs Place, Crook Of Devon, Kinross KY13 0PL ☎ 01577 842246

Kirkcaldy Mr WH Gibson, Flat 5, 2 Darney Terrace, Kinghorn, Fife KY3 9RF ☎ 01592 891 319

Perth & District Miss E J Bryce, 2 Hawarden Terrace, Jeanfield, Perth PH1 1PA ☎ 01738 632645 perthramblers.blogspot.com

St Andrews & North East Fife ● Ms PJ Ritchie, 63 St Michaels Drive, Cupar, Fife KY15 5BP ☎ 01334 653667

Stirling, Falkirk & District Ms JA Cameron, 17 Buchany, Doune FK16 6HD ☎ 01786 841178

Strathtay Clair Robertson, West Wing, Pitnacree, Ballinluig, Perthshire PH9 0LW ☎ 01887 840324

Tayside Trekkers Ms Donna Wilkinson, Top Flat Left (3/f), 49 Lyon Street, Dundee DD4 6RA ☎ 07796 692847 www.taysidetrekkers.co.uk

West Fife Mrs ME Wrightson, 24 Orwell Place, Dunfermline KY12 7XP ☎ 01383 729994

GRAMPIAN
Aberdeenshire, City of Aberdeen, Moray

AREA SECRETARY
Anne Macdonald, 15 Garthdee Drive, Aberdeen AB10 7JB ☎ 01330 823 255

GROUP SECRETARIES
Aberdeen ● Miss Alison Mitchell, 32 Gordon Road, Mannofield, Aberdeen AB15 7RL ☎ 01224 322580 alisonmmitchell@talktalk.net www.aberdeenramblers.org.uk

Inverurie Ms MT Corley, 60 Gray Street, Aberdeen AB10 6JE ☎ 01224 318672

Moray ● Mrs EM Robertson, Abbey Bank, Station Road, Urquhart, By Elgin, Moray IV30 8LQ ☎ 01343 842489

Stonehaven Mr I Forbes, 11 Burnside Gardens, Stonehaven AB39 2FA ☎ 01569 766553

HIGHLAND & ISLANDS
Highland, the Western Isles, Orkney and Shetland

AREA SECRETARY
www.highlandramblers.org.uk or visit www.ramblers.org.uk/info/localgroups or contact our central office for current details
GROUP SECRETARIES
Badenoch & Strathspey Mr Stewart

RAMBLERS GROUPS & PUBLICATIONS

Brown, Acarsaid, Mossie Road, Grantown-on-Spey, Moray PH26 3HW ☎ 01479 873747 acarsaidmor@supanet.com www.highlandramblers.org.uk/ badenochandstrathspey

Inverness Mrs Moira Livingstone, 'Nooralain', 21 Green Drive, Inverness IV2 4EX ☎ 01463 231985 analbo@dsl.pipex.com www.highlandramblers.org.uk/inverness

Lochaber & Lorn Mrs Jean O'Brien, Flat 1, 75-83 High Street, Fort William PH33 6DG ☎ 01397 701957 jean_t_o'brien@hotmail.co.uk www.highlandramblers.org.uk/ lochaberandlorn

LOTHIAN & BORDERS
City of Edinburgh, East Lothian, Midlothian, Scottish Borders, West Lothian

AREA SECRETARY
Senga Macrae, 13 Finlay Avenue, East Calder, Livingston EH53 0RP ☎ 01506 880980 www.lothian-borders-ramblers.org.uk

GROUP SECRETARIES
Balerno Mr RJ Bayley, 65 Silverknowles Drive, Edinburgh EH4 5HX www.lothian-borders-ramblers.org.uk/Balerno.htm
Coldstream Ms Georgina Jahre, The Anchorage, Main Street, Leitholm TD12 4JN ☎ 01890 840723 www.lothian-borders-ramblers.org.uk/Coldstream.htm
East Berwickshire Mrs E Windram, 20 Hinkar Way, Eyemouth, Berwickshire TD14 5EQ ☎ 018907 51048 www.lothian-borders-ramblers.org.uk/EastBerwickshire.htm
Edinburgh ● Miss Bridget Read ☎ 0131 447 8339 www.lothian-borders-ramblers.org.uk/Edinburgh.htm
Edinburgh Young Walkers Sarah Emmerson ☎ 0131 553 5303 edinburghyoungwalkers@hotmail.com
Linlithgow ● Mr John Davidson, 16 Friars Way, Linlithgow EH49 6AX ☎ 01506 842504 www.lothian-borders-ramblers.org.uk/Linlithgow.htm
Livingston ● Mrs V McGowan, 4 Larbert Avenue, Deans, Livingston EH54 8QJ ☎ 01506 438706 www.lothian-borders-ramblers.org.uk/Livingston.htm
Midlothian Walkers Mrs Cheryl Prior, 37 Bevan Road, Mayfield, Dalkeith EH22 5PZ www.lothian-borders-ramblers.org.uk/Midlothian.htm
Musselburgh Mr GC Edmond, 54 Northfield Gardens, Prestonpans

EH32 9LG ☎ 01875 810729 www.lothian-borders-ramblers.org.uk/Musselburgh.htm
North Berwick ● Mrs IR Mcadam, 23 Gilbert Avenue, North Berwick EH39 4ED ☎ 01620 893657 www.lothian-borders-ramblers.org.uk/NorthBerwick.htm
South Queensferry Mr Nigel Southworth, 47 Middleton Road, Uphall, Broxburn EH52 5DF ☎ echonige@yahoo.co.uk www.lothian-borders-ramblers.org.uk/SouthQueensferry.htm
Tweeddale Miss Anne Hogarth, 8 Leyden Grove, Clovenfords, Galashiels TD1 3NF www.lothian-borders-ramblers.org.uk/Tweeddale.htm

PERTH & KINROSS
See Forth Valley, Fife & Tayside Area

SCOTTISH BORDERS
See Lothian & Borders Area

STIRLING
See Forth Valley, Fife & Tayside Area

STRATHCLYDE, DUMFRIES & GALLOWAY
Argyll & Bute, City of Glasgow, Dumfries & Galloway, East, North & South Ayrshire, East & West Dunbartonshire, East Renfrew, Inverclyde, North & South Lanarkshire, Renfrewshire

AREA SECRETARY
Elizabeth Lawie, Burnside Cottage, 64 Main Street, Glenboig, Lanarkshire ML5 2RD ☎ 01236 872959

GROUP SECRETARIES
Bearsden & Milngavie Mr Andrew Summers, 47 Burnbrae Avenue, Bearsden, Glasgow G61 3ET ☎ 0141 9426505 lilias@asummers.wanadoo.co.uk www.bearsdenandmilngavieramblers.co.uk
Biggar Mrs Sue Wigram, The Granary, Annieston Farm, Symington, Biggar ML12 6LQ ☎ 01899 308920
Clyde Valley Mr Gordon Kelly, 4 Windermere Gardens, Hamilton, Lanarkshire ML3 7HL ☎ 01698 427566 secretary.cvr@scotsol.plus.com www.clydevalleyramblers.org
Cumbernauld & Kilsyth ● www.ckramblers.org.uk or visit www.ramblers.org.uk/info/localgroups or contact our central office for current details
Cunninghame ● Mrs Jacqueline Taylor, Ingleside, 83 Kings Rd, Beith, Ayrshire KA15 2BN ☎ 01505 502977 www.cunninghameramblers.org.uk

Dumfries & Galloway Jean Snary, 7 Birchwood Place, Lockerbie Road, Dumfries DG1 3EB ☎ 01387 267450
Eastwood www.eastwood-ramblers.org.uk or visit www.ramblers.org.uk/info/localgroups or contact our central office for current details
Glasgow Ms Colette Yvonne, 5 Airlie Street, Glasgow G12 9RH ☎ 0141 5760420
Glasgow Region Under 40 First Footers (GRUFF) www.geocities.com/GRUFF_RAMBLERS or visit www.ramblers.org.uk/info/localgroups or contact our central office for current details
Helensburgh & W Dunbartonshire Una Campbell, 5 Dalmore House, Dalmore Crescent, Helensburgh G84 8JP ☎ 01436 673726 www.hwdramblers.me.uk
Inverclyde ● Mr Alex Wooler, 37 Margaret Street, Greenock PA16 8BU ☎ 01475 727849 awooler@hotmail.com www.inverclyderamblers.org.uk
Isle of Bute Mrs Monica Brooks, Stevenson House, Ascog, Isle Of Bute PA20 9ET ☎ 01700 500554 monica.brooks@btopenworld.com
Kilmarnock & Loudoun Ms M Bush, 14 Goatfoot Road, Galston, Ayrshire KA4 8BJ ☎ 01563 821331 www.freewebs.com/kilmarnockand loudounramblers
Mid Argyll & Kintyre Mrs Brenda Nicholson, 14 Wilson Road, Lochgilphead, Argyll PA31 8TR ☎ 01546 603026
Moffat Mrs Sheila Bowman, Victoria Cottage, Victoria Place, Moffat DG10 9AG ☎ 01683 221440
Monklands Ms C McMahon, 4 Blackmoor Place, New Stevenston, Motherwell ML1 4JX ☎ 01698 833983 christine.mcmahon@scott-moncrieff.com www.monklandsramblers.org.uk
Paisley Ms Nicole Stevens, 23 Grants Way, Paisley, Renfrewshire PA2 6AT ☎ 0141 8841268 nicolestevens1@lycos.com
SLOW – S Lanark Older Walkers Ms MA Rankin, 18 Cherrytree Crescent, Larkhall, Lanarkshire ML9 2AP ☎ 01698 885995
South Ayrshire Mrs K Graham, 113 Logan Drive, Troon KA10 6QE ☎ 01292 311704
Stranraer & The Rhins Mr John McCulloch, Aberdale, Bridge Of Aldouran, Leswalt, Stranraer DG9 0LW ☎ 01776 870247 j.mcculloch@virgin.net
Strathkelvin Mr Alan Connor, 15 Westermains Avenue, Kirkintilloch, Glasgow G66 1EJ

LOCAL RAMBLERS PUBLICATIONS

The books and guides listed – by country, then county – cover a huge range of walks, from short circular strolls to long distance paths. All are written and published by local Ramblers Groups with local walking knowledge, and are available by mail order directly from the addresses shown. Where no p&p charge is shown, this is included in the price.

Publications specifically about long distance paths can be found listed in the section on p25.

Titles published or revised in 2007 are marked *NEW.*

ENGLAND

Walk East Midlands
edited by Chris Thompson of Nottinghamshire Area. ISBN 1-85058-824-4. This book brings together the expertise of six Ramblers Areas to create the definitive volume of circular walks in this English region. Offering 50 walks, most with short and long options, all with public transport links, avoiding the obvious honeypots of the Peak District and exploring instead the surprisingly varied landscapes of Derbyshire, Leicestershire, Lincolnshire, Northamptonshire, Nottinghamshire and Rutland, from flat fens to limestone uplands, river valleys and lush woodlands. Published jointly with Sigma Leisure ☎ 01625 531035, www.sigmapress.co.uk. *£8.95, order from bookshops or Sigma Leisure.*

BEDFORDSHIRE
Leighton Buzzard Millennium Walks (Leighton Buzzard Group). 10 tried and tested walks from gentle strolls to day treks, illustrated in full colour with OS map extracts.
Free + first class stamp from 8 Carlton Grove, Leighton Buzzard LU7 3BR.

BERKSHIRE
The Chairman's Walk around the perimeter of West Berkshire
edited by Geoff Vince. ISBN 1-901184-59-5. A series of 25 linear walks, each of about 7km/4 miles, grouped in 10 sections and completing a 158km/98-mile circuit. Guide contains maps, route guides, public transport and local interest information and photographs.
£7 + £1 p&p from West Berks Ramblers, 38 Kipling Close, Thatcham RG18 3AY. Cheques to West Berks Ramblers.

Rambling for Pleasure Footpath Maps for East Berkshire:

Cookham & District
ISBN 1-874258-11-2. A superb area of walking country in the Thames Valley easily accessible by rail.
£1 + 50p p&p.
Hurley & District
ISBN 1-874258-14-7. Highlights the dense network of footpaths linking the Thames Path with the quiet meadows and wooded slopes surrounding Warren Row and Knowl Hill.
£1 + 50p p&p.
Windsor & The Great Park revised full-colour 6th edition
ISBN 1-874258-18-X. The only guide to show all the paths and areas open to the public on foot in the Park, plus footpaths in surrounding areas and other features of interest.
£1 + 50p p&p (see below for address).

Rambling for Pleasure Guides:

Along the Thames, revised 6th edition
ISBN 1-874258-19-8. 24 walks of 3km/2 miles to 9.5km/6 miles between Runnymede and Sonning.
£2.95 + 60p p&p.
Around Reading – 1st and 2nd series
ISBN 1-874258-12-0 and ISBN 1-874258-16-3. Two books each of 24 easy country walks of 5km/3 miles to 16km/10 miles through Berkshire, Oxfordshire and north Hampshire, within an 11km/7-mile radius of Reading.
£4.95 + 75p p&p.
In East Berkshire, revised 2nd edition
ISBN 978-1-874258-19-3. 24 mainly flat walks of 5km/3 miles to 12km/7.5 miles around Maidenhead, Wokingham, Bracknell and Ascot, including six from stations.
£4.95 + 75p p&p.
Kennet Valley & Watership Down
ISBN 1-874258-13-9. 24 walks of 4km/2.5 miles and 11km/7 miles exploring the hidden countryside between Reading, Newbury and Basingstoke. Some modest hills.
£4.95 + 75p p&p. All Rambling for Pleasure Guides and Maps from East Berks

RA Publications, PO Box 1357, Maidenhead SL6 7FP. Cheques to East Berks RA Publications.
The Secrets of Countryside Access
by Dave Ramm. ISBN-10: 1-874258-20-1, ISBN-13: 978-1-874258-20-9. An illustrated guide to finding, using and enjoying country paths. A mine of information, full of practical advice, explained in simple terms and attractively presented with over 200 illustrations.
£4.95 + £1 p&p.
Three Castles Path
ISBN 1-874258-08-2. A 96km/60-mile route from Windsor to Winchester with six circular walks.
£4.95 + 60p p&p.
Both from East Berks RA Publications, PO Box 1357, Maidenhead SL6 7FP. Cheques to East Berks RA Publications.

21 Walks for the 21st Century
Walks on the Berkshire/Wiltshire border of between 8km/5 miles and 14.5km/9 miles, on a set of colour laminated cards with maps, directions, points of interest and transport details.
£6 + £1 p&p from West Berks Group, 38 Kipling Close, Thatcham RG18 3AY. Cheques to West Berks Ramblers.

BIRMINGHAM & THE BLACK COUNTRY
Birmingham Greenway
by Fred Willits. ISBN 1-869922-40-9. From the southern to the northern boundary of Birmingham, using footpaths, riversides and towpaths.
£4.95 + £1 p&p.
Waterside Walks in the Midlands
by Birmingham Ramblers. ISBN 1-869922-09-3. 22 walks by brooks, streams, pools, rivers and canals in Derbyshire, Shropshire, Staffordshire, Warwickshire and Worcestershire.
£4.95 + £1 p&p.
More Waterside Walks in the Midlands
by Birmingham Ramblers. ISBN 1-869922-31-X. A second collection of Midlands walks.
£5.95 + £1 p&p.

NEW Ramblers' Choice
edited by Peter Groves. ISBN
978-1-869922-54-2. Favourite
walks in the Midlands by
members of the City of
Birmingham Group.
*£5.95 + £1.50 p&p. All from Meridian
Books Sales Office, 8 Hartside Close, Luckley,
Halesowen B63 1HP.
meridian.books@tiscali.co.uk.*
☎ *0121 4294397.*

BUCKINGHAMSHIRE
**Best Walks in Bucks by Bus
and Train**
Although the printed edition is no longer
available, up-to-date detailed route
descriptions are now available online at
www.bucks-wmiddx-ramblers.org.uk.
Walks in South Bucks
by West London Ramblers. Seventeen
short walks.
*£1.50 from 128 Park Lane, Harrow HA2
8NL. Cheques to West London Group
Ramblers' Association.*

CAMBRIDGESHIRE
Guide to the Fen Rivers Way
Describes this 80km/50-mile route, part of
E2 (see p37), from Cambridge to Ongar
Hill, on the Wash north of King's Lynn, with
some circular walks of 6.5km/4 miles to
13km/8 miles linked to the main route.
*£4.50 from 52 Maids Causeway, Cambridge
CB5 8DD. Cheques to Cambridge Group of
the Ramblers' Association.*

**Twenty Rambles in Huntingdonshire
Revisited**
by Huntingdonshire Ramblers. ISBN 1-
901184-77-3. Walks in lowland countryside
in the former county, 8km/5 miles to
21km/13 miles, spiral bound in handy
pocket size, sketch maps, no public
transport details. Revised and updated
second edition of a book first published
in 1998.
*£4 + 50p p&p from 8 Park View,
Needingworth, St Ives PE27 4TJ. Cheques to
Huntingdonshire Group Ramblers.*

Walks in East Cambridgeshire
ISBN 0-9522518-0-9. Circular
lowland walks from 9.5km/6 miles to
19km/12 miles.
Walks in South Cambridgeshire
ISBN 0-9522518-3-3. Circular
lowland walks from 8km/5 miles to
19km/12 miles.
**Walks on the South Cambridgeshire
Borders**
ISBN 0-9522518-2-5. 20 easy to moderate
walks from 8km/5 miles to 19km/12 miles

along the boundaries with Essex,
Hertfordshire and Bedfordshire.
*All £4.50 each from 52 Maids Causeway,
Cambridge CB5 8DD. Cheques to Cambridge
Group of the Ramblers' Association.*

CORNWALL
**The Maritime Line: Trails from the
Track Walk**
Card pack detailing nine walks, 3km/
2 miles to 11km/7 miles, with most 8km/
5 miles or under, generally easy-going, and
all connecting with the Maritime Line, one
of Cornwall's attractive branch lines running
from Truro on the Great Western main line
to Falmouth Docks. Includes linear walks
linking all the stations between Truro and
Penmere, and some circular options.
Attractive and clear mapping, route
descriptions and background information.
A joint project of Carrick Group and the
Devon & Cornwall Rail Partnership.
*Free from local stations and information
centres, or send an SAE to Carrick Ramblers,
7 Moresk Close, Truro TR1 1DL.*

Rambles in the Roseland
(6 walks 4km/2.5 miles to 9km/5.5 miles)
**Six Circular Coast and Country
Walks on the Lizard**
(6.5km/4 miles to 11km/7 miles)
**Six Coastal Walks with Inland
Returns in or on The Lizard**
(5.5km/3.5 miles to 13km/8 miles)
**Six Coastal Walks with Inland
Returns in Penwith Book 1**
(3km/2 miles to 11km/7 miles)
**Six Coastal Walks with Inland
Returns in Penwith Book 2**
(3km/2 miles to 11km/7 miles)
Six Walks around Falmouth 1
(3km/2 miles to 11km/7 miles)
Six Walks around Falmouth 2
(3km/2 miles to 11km/7 miles)
Six North Cornwall Walks 1
(5km/3 miles to 9.5km/6 miles)
Six North Cornwall Walks 2
(5.5km/3.5 miles to 13km/8 miles)
Six Walks from Truro
(6.5km/4 miles to 11km/7 miles)
**Wendron's Church and
Chapels Walks**
(6 walks 6.5km/4 miles to 8km/5 miles).
*All £1.25 each from Publicity Officer, 2
Lanaton Road, Penryn TR10 8RB. Cheques to
Cornwall Area, Ramblers' Association. Penwith
and Lizard books also available from Trebant,
Ludgvan, Churchtown, Penzance TR20 8HH.
Cheques to Penwith/Kerrier Ramblers.*

**Six North Cornwall Walks Book 1
Six North Cornwall Walks Book 2**
Six short walks in each. Mainly around
6.5km/4 miles to 9.5km/6 miles.

*Each £1.50 from Pridham House,
Molesworth Street, Wadebridge PL27 7DS.
Cheques to Ramblers' Association
Camel District.*

CUMBRIA
The Cumbria Way
by John Trevelyan. ISBN 1-855681-97-8
(Lake District Ramblers/Dalesman).
Concise guide to this popular 112kmk/
70-mile route from Ulverston to Carlisle,
with sketch maps, route description and
background information.
*£2.99 from Lakeing, Grasmere, Ambleside
LA22 9RW. Cheques to Lake District RA.*

**More Walks Around Carlisle and
North Cumbria**
ISBN 1-904350-43-6 (Carlisle Ramblers).
Well-stuffed book of 37 circular and linear
walks including countryside, coast and
Hadrian's Wall. From 4km/2.5 miles to
23km/14 miles, with quite a few options
under 8km/5 miles. Some public transport
walks, several starting from Carlisle itself and
several of the walks interconnect for more
options. Sketch maps, background details.
*£4 from Little Gables, Brampton CA8 2HZ.
Cheques to Ramblers' Association.*

**Walks Around Carlisle &
North Cumbria**
ISBN 0-9521458-0-4 (Carlisle Ramblers).
17 fairly easy walks of between 8km/5 miles
and 14.5km/9 miles in the lowland
countryside around Carlisle, including the
Eden Valley and Hadrian's Wall.
*£3.50 post free to members, + 50p p&p
to non-members from 24 Currock Mount,
Carlisle CA2 4RF. Cheques to
Carlisle Ramblers.*

Walks from the Limestone Link
ISBN 0-904350-41-X. 17 easy walks of
between 2km/1.5 miles and 16km/10 miles
in the beautiful limestone area north of
Lancaster, and the 19km/12-mile Limestone
Link path. Includes maps and sketches.
*£2.95 + 45p p&p each from 116 North
Road, Carnforth LA5 9LX. Cheques to
Ramblers' Association Lancaster Group.*

**Walks in the Kendal Area Book 1,
3rd edition**
ISBN 0-904350-40-1. Eighteen low-level
walks within 16km/10 miles of Kendal.
**Walks in the Kendal Area Book 3,
2nd edition**
ISBN 0-904350-37-1. Mostly lower-level
walks of between 6.5km/4 miles and
24km/15 miles within 16km/10 miles
of Kendal.
Each £2.95 + 50p p&p.

NEW Walks in South Lakeland
revised edition of *Walks in the Kendal Area
Book 2*. 17 mainly low-level walks within
16km/10 miles of Kendal. Walks vary from
6.5km/4 miles to 19km/12 miles.
*£2.85 + 50p p&p. All three from
6 Orchard Close, Sedgwick, Kendal LA8 0LJ.
Cheques to RA Kendal Group.*

DERBYSHIRE
Chesterfield Round Walk
devised by Chesterfield and Northeast
Derbyshire Group and written by Rob
Haslam. A colour leaflet, including maps,
of this new 55km/34-mile walk around
Chesterfield, launched in June 2005.
*£1.50 + 50p p&p (badge on completion
£3.50 + 50p p&p) from Membership
Secretary, 11 Halesworth Close, Walton,
Chesterfield S40 3LW. Cheques to
Chesterfield and North East Derbyshire
Ramblers' Group.*

**Walks Through Derbyshire's
Gateway**
Favourite walks of the Bolsover Group
in their own backyard. Five leaflets
with clear maps and route descriptions,
each describing a single circular walk
of between 6.5km/4 miles and
13km/8 miles.
*Free from local outlets or send an SAE
to 34 Lime Tree Avenue, Glapwell,
Chesterfield S44 5LE.*

Our Favourite Walks
See under Staffordshire.

DEVON
John Musgrave Heritage Trail
56km/35-mile route created from a
generous legacy left by former South
Devon Group chairman John Musgrave.
The Trail is split into four managable
sections of between 9km/5.5 miles to
8km/11 miles each. The guide provides
detailed commentary of local heritage,
maps and transport links along the way.
*£3 from the secretary of the South Devon
Ramblers, The Lodge, 43 Seymour Drive,
Watcombe, Torquay, Devon TQ2 8PY.
Cheques to Ramblers' Association
South Devon Group.*

Walks Around Dawlish
by Teignmouth and Dawlish Ramblers,
published with Dawlish Town Council.
Leaflet pack of seven illustrated walks
around the town.
*£2 from Dawlish Town Council, The Manor
House, Old Town Street, Dawlish EX7 9AP.
☎ 01626 863388. Cheques to Dawlish
Town Council.*

DORSET
**A Rambler's Guide to the Dorset
Jubilee Trail**
ISBN 1-901184-04-8. A comprehensive
guide with maps to this 145km/90-mile
walk across Dorset from Forde Abbey to
Bokerley Dyke.
*£4.50 + 50p p&p from Jubilee Trail
Contact, 19 Shaston Crescent, Dorchester
DT1 2EB. Cheques to Ramblers' Association
Dorset Area.*

Channel to Channel
See under Somerset.

ESSEX
Camulodunum
by Colchester Ramblers. 40km/25 miles
around Colchester via Great Horkesley and
Mersea Road. No printed guide, but a full
route description, updated in 2004, is
available at www.colchester-
ramblers.ccom.co.uk/diy.htm

The Ramblers Millennium Walk
37km/23-mile walk around Southend-on-
Sea and district.
*£1 + A5 SAE from Southend Borough
Council Leisure Services Department,
Civic Centre, Victoria Avenue, Southend-
on-Sea SS2 6ER. Cheques to Southend
Borough Council.*

**15 Walks in South East Essex for all
the Family**
ISBN 1-901184-17-X
**17 More Walks in and around South
East Essex**
ISBN 1-901184-50-1

**Short Walks in the area of
Southend-on-Sea**
Walks of 6.5km/4 miles to
14.5km/9 miles.
*£2.25 each including postage from
146 Kenneth Road, Thundersley SS7 3AN.
Cheques to SE Essex Group RA.*

GLOUCESTERSHIRE
AND BRISTOL
**Bristol Backs: Discovering Bristol
on Foot**
compiled by Peter Gould, jointly published
with Bristol City Council. ISBN 1-901184-
52-8. 27 walks of between 3km/2 miles
and 17.5km/11 miles in the city, including
street-based heritage walks, green trails,
waterside strolls and a sculpture trail, with
plentiful background descriptions.
£6.99 + £1.50 p&p.
Bristol Triangular City Walk
A 28km/18-mile circuit of the city starting at
Temple Meads station, easily walked as

three sections of between 6 km/4 miles
and 13km/8 miles connected by public
transport. Includes the waterfront,
Durdham Downs, Avon Gorge and Blaise
Castle Estate, as well as the heart and
history of the city, developed by Bristol
Group in association with the City Council.
Connects with South Bristol Circular Walk
(see below).
*Colour leaflet £1.50.
Both from 57 Somerset Road, Bristol BS4
2HT. Cheques to Bristol Group Ramblers'
Association. (Leaflet is free from local outlets.)*

Cirencester Circuit
A moderate 16km/10-mile walk around
Cirencester.
£1 + 40p p&p
Walks Around Cirencester
A moderate 9.5km/6-mile walk from
Cirencester to Duntisbourne.
*80p + 40p p&p from 80 Melmore Gardens,
Cirencester GL7 1NS. Cheques to Cirencester
Ramblers.*

**Cotswold Way Handbook &
Accommodation List**
ISBN 1-901184-62-5.
*£2.95 + 50p p&p from Mail Order
Secretary, Tudor Cottage, Berrow, Malvern
WR13 6JJ. Cheques to Ramblers' Association
Gloucestershire Area.*

**Favourite South Cotswold Walks
Book One**
by South Cotswold Ramblers. 18 attractive
half-day walks, several of which can be
combined into day walks, in the Cotswolds
Area of Outstanding Natural Beauty. A fully
revised and extended issue of a best selling
book first published in 1995.
£3 + 95p p&p.
**More Favourite Walks in the
South Cotswolds**
Fifteen fully graded and illustrated walks
of between 3km/2 miles and 22.5km/
14 miles in the Cotswolds Area of
Outstanding Natural Beauty.
*Special offer price £3 + 50p.
Both from Southcot, The Headlands, Stroud
GL5 5PS. Cheques to South Cotswold
Ramblers. See also
www.southcotswoldramblers.org.uk/books for
further information and updates.*
Forest of Dean East
*40p + 30p p&p from Mail Order Secretary,
Tudor Cottage, Berrow, Malvern WR13 6JJ.
Cheques to Ramblers' Association
Gloucestershire Area.*
The Glevum Way
by Gloucester Ramblers. A 38.5km/
24-mile circular route around Gloucester
originally launched in 1995. New colour

leaflet now available, dividing the Way into five sections with transport connections *available free from Gloucester TIC* ☎ *01452 396572.*

North Cotswold Diamond Way

Thirty sparkling short walks by Elizabeth Bell (North Cotswold Group). Revised edition presenting this 96km/60-mile circular route via Moreton-on-Marsh, devised to celebrate the Ramblers' diamond jubilee in 1975, as 30 linked shorter (around 8km/5 mile) circular walks. Varied terrain, gently undulating with no steep hills, stone villages, open fields, streams and pleasant rural views. *£6.95 + £2 p&p from Holly Tree House, Evenlode GL56 0NT. Cheques to Ramblers' Association North Cotswold Group.*

Samaritans Way South West

A Walk from Bristol to Lynton by Graham Hoyle. Linking Bristol with the Cotswold Way National Trail at Bath, the Mendips, Cheddar, the Quantocks, Exmoor National Park and the South West Coast Path at Lynton, 160km/100 miles. Pocket guide with overprinted old OS map extracts. *£5.45 from Samaritans Way SW Association, 6 Mervyn Road, Bristol BS7 9EL or email samaritansway@aol.com Cheques to Samaritans Way SW.*

Six Walks in Chipping Sodbury

by South Gloucestershire Council and Southwold Ramblers. Leaflets are Work and Play, Golf Course and Common, The Sodbury Round, Old Sodbury and Kingrove Common, Kingrove Common and Codrington, Paddocks and Ponds. *Free from Chipping Sodbury Tourist Information Centre, The Clock Tower, Chipping Sodbury BS37 6AH.* ☎ *01454 888686.*

South Bristol Circular Walk

devised by Neil Buriton. A 37km/23-mile route following quiet streets and paths around the south of the city, from Temple Meads station via Troopers Hill, Whitchurch, Dundry and Clifton Bridge. The route offers beautiful views of the city centre, the Avon Valley, Stockwood Nature Reserve, Dundry Hill and Ashton Court. Lots of opportunities to split the walk into smaller sections via public transport, and a connection with the Bristol Triangular City Walk (see above). Developed by Bristol Group and Bristol council. Excellent free colour booklet with maps, route description, photos. *Free from Bristol TIC.*

Waymarked Trails in the Forest of Dean and Highmeadow Woods

Attractive leaflet describing two circular walks, the Beechenhurst Trail and the Highmeadow Trail. *60p + 30p p&p, as North Cotswold Diamond Way above.*

Walk West

by Geoff Mullett (Avon Area). Thirty country walks of between 6.5km/4 miles and 22.5km/14 miles within easy reach of Bristol and Bath, including some in south Wales.

Walk West Again

by Geoff Mullett. ISBN 1-901184-61-7. A second volume of walks from 6.5km/4 miles to 19km/12 miles, within easy reach of Bristol and Bath. *£7.99 each from 12 Gadshill Drive, Stoke Gifford, Bristol BS34 8UX. Cheques to Geoff Mullett. For information and updates visit walk-west.members.beeb.net.*

Yate Walks Leaflets

by Yate Town Council and Southwold Ramblers. Three leaflets: Brimshaw Manor Walk, Stanshawes Walk and Upstream & Downstream Walk. *Free from Yate Town Council, Poole Court, Poole Court Drive, Yate BS37 5PP.* ☎ *01454 866506.*

HAMPSHIRE

Avon Valley Path

55km/34-mile route from Salisbury to Christchurch. *£2.99 from 9 Pine Close, Dibden Purlieu, Southampton SO45 4AT. Cheques payable to Ramblers' Association New Forest Group.*

NEW **Eastleigh Walks** by Eastleigh Ramblers. ISBN 978-1-901184-97-6. Six walks on the edge of Southampton Water, of 6km/3.75 miles to 14.5km/9 miles in length. Illustrated with sketch maps. *£3 + 50 p&p from 16 Market Buildings, High Road, Southampton SO16 2HX. Cheques to Eastleigh Ramblers Group.*

King's Way

by Pat Miles. ISBN 0-861460-93-X (Meon Group). A 72km/45-mile walk from Portchester to Winchester, divided into easy stages. *£3.25 + £1 p&p from 19 New Road, Fareham PO16 7SR. Cheques to Ramblers' Association Meon Group.*

More Than the New Forest

by New Forest Ramblers. ISBN

1-901184-75-7. Not a guide book, but a collection of forest lore and walking anecdotes, from prehistory to the National Park, illustrated with cartoons. *£1.*

Walking the Wessex Heights

Detailed maps and route descriptions for a 123km/77-mile route and 14 circular walks. *£1.99.*

Walks Around the New Forest National Park

Seventeen newly surveyed and updated short- and medium-length routes into the heart of the new National Park and along its borders, plus carefully researched route maps, times and walk directions. *£3.50 + 50p&p. All from 9 Pine Close, Dibden Purlieu, Southampton SO45 4AT. Cheques payable to Ramblers' Association New Forest Group.*

Rural Rambles from the villages around Alton

by Alton and District Ramblers. Ten circular walks from 9.5km/6 miles to 16km/10 miles starting from villages, including details of places of interest, pubs and public transport. Ideal for visitors to east Hampshire and Jane Austen's house at Chawton.

Walks From Alton

Ten walks from 6km/3.75 miles to 14km/8.75 miles through typical Hampshire landscapes, all starting in the town. *£3.50 for both from Green Bank, Wilsons Road, Headley Down, Bordon GU35 8JG. Cheques to Alton and District Ramblers.*

12 Walks in and Around Winchester, updated edition

Moderate-level walks in town and countryside varying from 3km/2 miles to 14.5km/9 miles. *£2 + 50p p&p from Underhill House, Beech Copse, Winchester SO22 5NR. Cheques to Winchester Ramblers.*

HEREFORDSHIRE

The Herefordshire Trail

by Hereford Ramblers. ISBN 1-901184-73-0. A 246km/154-mile circuit of Herefordshire visiting all eight market towns in the county, some delightful villages and attractive countryside. Ringbound colour guide dividing the route into 15 manageable sections of around 16km/10 miles each, most with public transport connections, with detailed route descriptions, tempting photos and very clear maps. *£5.95 + £2 p&p from The Book Secretary, 98 Gorsty Lane, Hereford HR1 1UN. Cheques to the Hereford Group of the Ramblers' Association.*

HERTFORDSHIRE

Ten Walks in North Herts
by North Hertfordshire Ramblers.
ISBN 0-900613-90-4. Ten mainly easy
walks of 9.5km/6 miles for enjoyment in
all seasons, most accessible by public
transport and each a personal favourite
of one of the Group.
*£2.50 + 21p p&p from 55 Derby Way,
Stevenage SG1 5TR. Cheques to North Herts
Ramblers Group.*

ISLE OF WIGHT

**12 Favourite Walks on the Isle
of Wight**
**12 More Favourite Walks on the
Isle of Wight**
**12 Walks from Country Towns on
the Isle of Wight**
Walks of between 5km/3 miles and
14.5km/9 miles, with simple maps and
route descriptions, all suitable for the
infrequent walker.
*All £2 + 40p p&p each from Dibs,
Main Road, Rookley, Ventnor PO38 3NQ.
Cheques payable to Mrs Joan Deacon.*

Vectis Trail
by Isle of Wight Ramblers, originally
devised by Barbara Aze and Iris Evans.
A 120km/75-mile mainly inland
exploration of the Isle of Wight devised
by local Ramblers, this route predates
many of the excellent signed walking
routes that now crisscross this well-loved
island. This fully revised and updated guide
splits the route into six sections between
transport points with sketch maps, full
route descriptions and plenty of helpful
practical information.
*£2.50 including postage and packaging
from Mike Marchant, Merry Meeting,
Ryde House Drive, Binstead Road, Ryde,
Isle of Wight PO33 3NF. Cheques to
Isle of Wight Ramblers' Association.*

KENT

**Ashford Ring Walk and
7 Loop Walks**
by Fred Wright (Ashford Group).
A 35km/22-mile loop circling Ashford,
linking outer villages, and connected by
seven loops of around 13km/8 miles
to the town centre.
*£2.50 from 93 Rylands Road, Kennington,
Ashford TN24 9LR. Cheques to
Ashford Ramblers.*

**Walks to Interesting Places in
Sussex & Kent** and **Walks in
the Weald (Heathfield &
District Group)**
See under Sussex.

LANCASHIRE &
MANCHESTER

Cown Edge Way (Manchester Area)
32km/20-mile walk in six sections from
Hazel Grove, Stockport to Gee Cross,
Woodley, with notes on history, fauna and
flora, maps and drawings.
*£1 from 31 Wyverne Road,
Manchester M21 0ZW. Cheques to RA
Manchester Area.*

**The Hodder Way With Circular
Walks Along The Hodder**
by Clitheroe Ramblers. ISBN 1-901184-
86-2. A new medium-distance walk
(43km/27 miles) from the source of the
Hodder to its confluence with the Ribble,
described as eight circular walks (mainly
around 11km/7 miles) and two walks to
the centre of Great Britain.
£4.50.
**25 Walks in the Ribble and Hodder
Valleys**
by Clitheroe Ramblers. ISBN 1-901184-
72-2. 25 walks from 6.5km/4 miles to
9.5km/6 miles all selected by members of
the Group.
*£5.99. Both from 1 Albany Drive, Salesbury,
Blackburn BB1 9EH. Cheques to The
Ramblers' Association Clitheroe Group
Social Account.*

Rambles Around Oldham
by Oldham Ramblers. 20 easy walks of
between 6.5km/4 miles and 16km/10
miles, all connecting with bus services,
including Sites of Biological Importance.
*£3.50 + 50p p&p from 682 Ripponden
Road, Oldham OL4 2LP. Cheques to Oldham
Ramblers Book Account.*
Walks Around Heywood
by S Jackson and D M Williams (Rochdale
Group). 20 easy to moderate walks of
5km/3 miles to 10km/6 miles in Heywood
and surrounding area, with public transport
details and local information.
*£3 + 50p p&p from 152 Higher Lomax
Lane, Heywood OL10 4SJ. Cheques to
Ramblers' Association Rochdale Group.*

Walks from the Limestone Link
ISBN 0-904350-41-X. 17 easy walks of
between 2km/1.5 miles and 16km/10
miles in the beautiful limestone area north
of Lancaster, and the 19km/12-mile
Limestone Link path. Includes maps
and sketches.
£2.95 + 45p p&p.
Walks in the Lune Valley
ISBN 0-904350-39-8. 14 walks of
between 4km/2.5 miles and 24km/15
miles, and the Lune Valley Ramble, 37km
up the north bank of the river and

38.5km/24 miles down the south bank.
Includes maps and sketches.
£2.95 + 45p p&p.
Walks in North West Lancashire
15 easy walks of between 6.5km/4 miles
and 14.5km/9 miles in the areas
surrounding the rivers Lune, Keer and
Wyre and parts of Silverdale and Arnside
and Forest of Bowland AONBs, including
sketch maps and notes on public transport.
£2.95 + 45p p&p.
**More Walks in North West
Lancashire**
ISBN 0-904350-46-0. 21 walks of
between 5km/3 miles and 14.5km/9 miles
in the areas surrounding the rivers Lune,
Keer and Wyre and parts of Silverdale and
Arnside and Forest of Bowland AONBs,
including sketch maps and notes on public
transport. Most are easy but nine are in
access areas and include rough walking.
£2.95 + 45p p&p.
Walks Round Lancaster City
ISBN 0-904350-45-2. Five easy walks
between 7km/4miles and 8km/5 miles
from the city centre which can be
combined into one 24km/15-mile walk
through the surrounding countryside.
*£1.50 + 40p p&p. All from 116 North
Road, Carnforth LA5 9LX. Cheques to
Ramblers' Association Lancaster Group.*

LINCOLNSHIRE

Country Walks in Kesteven
by NSP Mitchell (new for 2002). 30
circular walks, many with shorter options,
from 2.5km/1.5 miles to 14.5km/9 miles,
within a 24km/15-mile radius of Grantham.
Walk descriptions and sketch maps. This
book has been revised and expanded
many times since its original appearance
in 1975.
*£3.50 post free from Tweedsdale, Aviary
Close, Grantham NG31 9LF. Cheques to
Grantham Ramblers.*
Danelaw Way
by Brett Collier. A 100km/60-mile walk in
five stages between Lincoln and Stamford,
the 'burghs' of the ancient Danelaw, plus a
circular route from Ryhall. The spiral bound
guide has a detailed route description,
sketch maps, background and extracts from
poetry related to the route.
*£5.95 + 80p p&p from 39 Fiskerton Rd,
Reepham, Lincoln LN3 4EF. Cheques to
Lincoln Group Ramblers' Association.*

Gingerbread Way
A Grantham Perimeter Country Walk
(Grantham Group). 40km/25-mile
challenging circuit developed to celebrate
the Ramblers' Golden Jubilee in 1985. The
name of the path refers to the gingerbread

RAMBLERS GROUPS & PUBLICATIONS

biscuit, a Grantham speciality. Booklet with route description and OS 1:50 000 map. *£1.20 post free from Tweedsdale, Aviary Close, Grantham NG31 9LF. Cheques to Grantham Ramblers.*

Lindsey Loop
by Brett Collier. ISBN 1-901184-13-7 (2nd edition). 154km/96 miles through the Lincolnshire Wolds AONB between Market Rasen and Louth, in eight stages. £5.95 + 70p p&p.
Sew-on badge for this route
£1.25 + p&p.
Plogsland Round
by Brett Collier. ISBN 1-901184-41-2. A 75km/47-mile circular walk around Lincoln. £5.50 + 60p p&p
Viking Way and Danelaw Way and Plogsland Round sew-on badges
£1.25 each + SAE.
All from 2 Belgravia Close, Lincoln LN6 0QJ. Cheques to Lincoln Group Ramblers' Association.

Our Favourite Walks
See under Staffordshire.

The Silver Lincs Way Linking Grimsby & Louth
A 40km/25-mile walk through the Lincolnshire Wolds via Ludborough using footpaths, bridleways and quiet lanes. A parallel bus service offers good public transport connections. Established by Grimsby/Louth Ramblers to mark their 25th anniversary, in conjunction with the Lincolnshire Wolds countryside service and with funding from Awards for All.
Circular Walks from the Silver Lincs Way
Linking paths and circular options from the Silver Lincs Way, giving a choice of walks from 3km/2 miles up to 21.5km/13.5 miles. *Both colour leaflets with maps, points of interest and route descriptions, free from local information outlets or by sending an SAE to 50 Gayton Road, Cleethorpes DN35 0HN.*

Towers Way
by Alan Nash, Janet Nash, Tony Broad. A meandering 160km/100-mile route linking 40 churches between Barton-upon-Humber and Lincoln Cathedral, as an alternative to the Viking Way. *Route description available from 39 Fiskerton Road, Reepham, Lincoln LN3 4EF; publication to follow.*

LONDON
Highlights of Surrey
Includes some walks in south London: see under Surrey.

Rural Walks around Richmond
by Ramblers' Association Richmond Group. 21 walks of between 3km/2 miles and 24km/15 miles, many with various short options, in a London borough rich in green space, including Richmond Park, Bushy Park, Barnes and the Thames. Eight walks have details of wheelchair-accessible sections, including one route that is accessible throughout. *£1.80 + 45p p&p from 59 Gerard Road, London SW13 9QH. Cheques to Margaret Sharp.*

NORFOLK
Angles Way
edited by Sheila Smith. ISBN 1-901184-84-6. 125km/78-mile route following the Waveney Valley along the Norfolk/Suffolk border from Great Yarmouth in the Norfolk Broads to Knettishall Heath in the Suffolk Brecks, and completing the circuit of the Peddars Way National Trail and Weavers Way. Includes maps, accommodation and public transport information.
Iceni Way
edited by Sheila Smith. ISBN 1-901184-64-1. 134.5km/84-mile route from Knettishall Heath in Breckland to the coast at Hunstanton along the Little and Great Ouse Valleys. First 24km/15miles from Knettishall to Thetford is a useful footpath link for Peddars Way or Angles Way with transport and other facilities in Thetford. Guide includes maps, accommodation details and transport information.

 NEW Nelson's Heritage Walks
by Allan Jones, reprinted 2007. ISBN 1-901184-80-3. 16 circular walks between 5km/3 miles and 16km/10 miles, throughout Norfolk, all with a Nelson theme.
North Norfolk Rambles
edited by Allan Jones. ISBN 1-901184-88-9. 16 walks covering coast, country and city in the area around Hunstanton, Cromer and Norwich, 9km/5.5 miles to 17km/10.5 miles and all from car parks, with sketch maps.
Southern Norfolk Rambles
edited by Allan Jones. ISBN 1-901184-87-0. 16 walks in the Broads and Brecks, 9.5km/6 miles to 17.5km/11 miles and all from car parks, with sketch maps.
Walking the Peddars Way & Norfolk Coast Path with Weavers Way
edited by Ian Mitchell. ISBN 978-1-901184-95-2. Concise guide covering a total distance of 239km/149 miles, the National Trail from Knettishall Heath to Holme-next-the Sea then along the coast to Cromer, and an inland route from Cromer

to Great Yarmouth. Combined with the Angles Way they provide a circular route of 364km/227 miles. Guide includes maps, accommodation and public transport information.

NEW West Norfolk Walkaway 2
edited by Allan Jones, reprinted 2007. ISBN 1-901184-55-2. 16 circular walks between 7km/4.5 miles to 19km/12 miles in the area bounded by King's Lynn, Hunstanton, Wells, Fakenham, Swaffham and Downham Market.
West Norfolk Walkaway 3
edited by Allan Jones. ISBN 1-901184-89-7. 16 easy circular walks between 8km/5 miles to 15km/9.5 miles in the area of the Peddars Way, between King's Lynn and Fakenham. Sketch maps, route descriptions and details of local features, with sketch maps and details of local features.
All £2.70 each + 30p p&p each from Caldcleugh, Cake Street, Old Buckenham, Attleborough NR17 1RU. Postage is free if three or more guides are ordered together. Cheques to Ramblers' Association Norfolk Area.

NORTHUMBERLAND
A Walk Round Berwick Borough
by Arthur Wood. ISBN 978-0-9545331-1-3. A 120-mile circuit of Berwick Borough, through beautiful scenery in a land bearing witness to a turbulent history. It passes five castles, a palace and a mountain. A hand-drawn and lettered pocket book. £4.95.
Berwick Walks
by Arthur Wood. ISBN 978-0954533-0-6 (ISBN-10: 0-9545331-0-0). A beautifully hand-drawn and calligraphed pocket book with 24 town, coastal, countryside and riverside walks within a 19km/12-mile radius of Berwick upon Tweed, many of them shorter walks . £4.95. *Both from Berwick Group, 5 Quay Walls, Berwick-upon-Tweed TD15 1HB. Cheques to Ramblers' Association.*

Walking the Tyne: Twenty-five Walks from Mouth to Source
by JB Jonas (Northumbria Area). ISBN 1-901184-70-6. A route along all 133km/83 miles of this great river, divided into 25 linked, mainly circular walks of 8km/5 miles to 14.5km/9 miles, with suggestions for lunch stops, time estimates, public transport details, and notes on stiles, terrain and places of interest. Follows the North Tyne from Hexham to the source. £5.50.

Walking the North Tyne: Seventeen walks from Hexham to the Source
by JB Jonas (Northumbria Area). ISBN 1-901184-82-X. Complementing *Walking the Tyne* by the same author, this volume follows the North Tyne branch of the river through remote northern countryside from Hexham to the source near Deadwater in the Kielder Forest area, including a walk alongside Kielder Water. Divided into sections, most of which are circular (3km/2 miles to 12km/7.5 miles). Total length of the walk is 76km/47.5 miles. Sketch maps, photos, route description and practical information.
£5. Both from 8 Beaufront Avenue, Hexham NE46 1JD. Cheques to JB Jonas, profits to Ramblers' Association.

SHROPSHIRE
Ramblers Guide to the Shropshire Way
by Shropshire Ramblers. ISBN 1-946679-44-4. Guidebook with useful background information and clear sketch maps.
£6.99 + £1.50 p&p from Pengwern Books, 23 Princess St, Shrewsbury SY1 1LW. Cheques to Pengwern Books.

SOMERSET
Channel to Channel Seaton–Watchet
by Ken Young. 80km/50-mile rural walk across the southwest peninsula at its narrowest point, via the Blackdown Hills.
£2 + 50p p&p from K Young, 14 Wilton Orchard, Taunton TA1 3SA. Cheques to Somerset Area Ramblers' Association.

Somerset Walks
by Taunton Deane Ramblers, illustrated by Ann Sharp. ISBN 1-901184-69-2. 16 circular walks 6.5km/4 miles to 22.5km/14 miles, including the Quantocks, Blackdown Hills, Brendon Hills, Somerset Levels and Exmoor, with notes on things to look out for, tea shops and pubs, but all from car parks.
£2.95 + 50p p&p from Greenway Thatch, North Curry, Taunton TA3 6NH. Cheques to Taunton Deane Ramblers.

Walking for Pleasure
Edited by Mike Emmett (Taunton Deane Group). 14 circular walks exploring the hidden countryside in and around Taunton Deane, 6.5km/4 miles to 10.5km/6.5 miles.
£2 + 50p p&p from Fairacre, West Hatch, Taunton TA3 5RJ. Cheques to Mike Emmett.

Walks Around Shepton Mallet
compiled by Mendip Group and published by Shepton Mallet Town Council. 13 circular walks of between 5km/3 miles to 18km/11 miles, all starting at Mendip District Council car park. Includes colour photographs, OS map extracts, clear route descriptions and historical reference.
£3.95 from Shepton Mallet Town Council, 1 Park Road, Shepton Mallet BA4 5BS.
☎ *01749 343984. Cheques to Shepton Mallet Town Council.*

Yeovil's Green Bypass
Leaflet guide to a 2km/1.5-mile fully accessible traffic-free walking and cycling route across town linking Pen Mill Station with Yeovil Country Park and the Westlands Area. Produced by the Heart of Wessex Rail Partnership in collaboration with South Somerset Group.
Free from Yeovil Visitor Information Centre
☎ *01935 845946 or download at www.heartofwessex.org.uk.*

STAFFORDSHIRE
Our Favourite Walks
12 walks of between 11km/7 miles and 22.5km/14 miles, mainly in Staffordshire but venturing into Derbyshire and Shropshire.
£2.95 + 35p p&p or A5 SAE from Liz Charlton at 48 Bluebell Hollow, Walton on the Hill, Stafford ST17 0JN. Cheques to Ramblers' Association Mid Staffs Group.

Walks Around Stone
(Stone Ramblers). 12 walks each from Westridge Port and from Downs Banks, between 1.5km/1 mile and 11km/7 miles with route descriptions, maps and guidance on healthy walking in plastic cover.
£3 + 50p p&p from 1 Vanity Close, Oulton, Stone ST15 8TZ. Cheques to Ramblers' Association Stone Group.

SUFFOLK
Cornard and Beyond
by Laurie Burroughs. ISBN 1 901194 65 X (Sudbury Group). Four short easy walks of 6.5km/4 miles or less through the countryside around Cornard.
Glemsford and Beyond
by Lesley Pilbrow (Sudbury Group). A4 route cards with three walks of 6.5km/4 miles to 9.5km/6 miles, all starting at Glemsford's 15th-century church.
Both £1.20 + 50p p&p each from 6 Chaplin Walk, Great Cornard, Sudbury CO10 0YT. Cheques to Sudbury and District Ramblers.

East Suffolk Line Walks: Station to Station Ipswich to Lowestoft
by Roger Wolfe. ISBN 0-9547865-0-5. 11 varied and attractive walks linking the stations along the East Suffolk Line through both remote rural areas and parkland on the urban fringe, ranging from a short stroll beside a tidal estuary (2.5km/1.5 miles) to a lengthy field path and woodland walk (16km/10 miles). All the walks link together so you can join together sections to taste or even treat the route as a single long distance path of over 112km/70 miles. Jointly published by the East Suffolk Travellers Association, Suffolk Area and Railfuture.
£2 from East Suffolk Travellers Association, 15 Clapham Road South, Lowestoft NR32 1RQ or downloadable at www.eastsuffolklinewalks.co.uk

NEW **Melford and Beyond**
by Lesley Pilbrow. Four walks, 8-12km/5-7.5 miles in length, all starting at Long Melford, Suffolk.
£1.20 + 50p p&p from Mrs I Kay, 6 Chaplin Walk, Great Conard, Sudbury CO10 0YT. Cheques to Sudbury and District Ramblers.

Rural Rambles Round Beccles
(Waveney Ramblers) 12 walks, 5.5km/3.5 miles to 13km/8 miles.
Rural Rambles Round Lowestoft
(Waveney Ramblers) 11 walks, 6.5km/4 miles to 16km/10 miles.
Rural Rambles Round Southwold
(Waveney Ramblers) 12 walks, 8km/5 miles to 13km/8 miles.
All £1.80 + 35p p&p each, address as Waveney Way below.
Waveney Way
(Waveney Ramblers) 115km/72-mile circular walk from Lowestoft.
£2.10 + 35p p&p from 1 Church Close, Redenhall, Harleston IP20 9QS. Cheques to Ramblers' Association.

SURREY
Four Stations Way
18.5km/11-mile route via stations from Godalming to Haslemere. Illustrated in both directions on two laminated A4 cards.
£1.50 + 50p p&p from Kate Colley, 6 Hill Court, Haslemere GU27 2BD. Cheques to Godalming and Haslemere RA Group.

The Highlights of Surrey
A series of 48 online walks originally devised by members of Surrey Area to mark the Millennium. Lengths from 3km/2 miles to 13.5km/8.5 miles with some linking walks, and 30 of the walks starting from train stations. The walk descriptions are in simple route-card style and you will need to be able to use an OS map.
surreyhilitewalks.mysite.wanadoo-members.co.uk

Twenty-five Favourite Walks in West Surrey & Sussex
by Godalming & Haslemere Ramblers, revised edition. ISBN 1-901184-63-3.

Variety of circular walks offering both short and long options between 5.5km/3.5 miles and 25.5km/16 miles.
£4.95 + 60p p&p from Elstead Maps UK Ltd, 11 The Bramley Business Centre, Station Road, Bramley, Guildford GU5 0AZ. ☎ *01483 898099. Cheques to Elstead Maps.*

Another Twenty-five Favourite Walks in Surrey, Sussex & Hampshire
by Godalming & Haslemere Ramblers. ISBN 978-1-901184-81-5. 25 circular walks offering longer and shorter options.
£4.95 + 60p p&p. Visit www.godalmingandhaslemereramblers.org.uk/ Guides.htm for up-to-date details or contact Godalming & Haslemere Group secretary (p94).

SUSSEX
Sussex Diamond Way
Midhurst-Heathfield. 96km/60-mile walk across the county.
Free + £1 p&p.
Walks to Interesting Places in Sussex & Kent
(Heathfield Ramblers). ISBN 0-900613-99-8. 21 walks from 4km/2.5 miles across easy terrain, including some linear walks returning on preserved railways.
£3.50.
Walks in the Weald, revised 2nd edition
36 walks from 5km/3 miles to 16km/ 10 miles (average 10km) across varied terrain.
£3.50. All from Cobbetts, Burnt Oak Road, High Hurstwood, Uckfield TN22 4AE. Cheques to Heathfield and District RA Group.

Twenty-five Favourite Walks in West Surrey & Sussex
Another Twenty-five Favourite Walks in Surrey, Sussex & Hampshire
See under Surrey.

WILTSHIRE
Avon Valley Path
See under Hampshire.

The Kennet & Avon Wiggly Walks Guide
Three walks 3km/2 miles to 19km/ 12 miles, along the beautiful Vale of Pewsey and the Kennet and Avon Canal, connecting with Wigglybus services from Devizes. Produced by the Kennet and Avon Canal Rural Transport Partnership with assistance from the Ramblers.
Free from ☎ *01249 460600.*

Northeast Wiltshire Group Publications:
Nine Downland Walks between Swindon and Marlborough
Between 5km/3 miles and 12km/7.5 miles.
£2.20.
Ten walks from village pubs near Swindon
by Pat Crabb. Short circular walks of 2km/1.5 miles to 8km/5 miles with bus routes given where appropriate.
£2.20.
11 Short Walks in North East Wiltshire
by Phil Claridge. Circular walks of 7km/ 4.5 miles to 9km/5.5 miles.
£2.20.
12 Walks around Marlborough
Between 5.5km/3.5 miles and 14.5km/ 9 miles.
£2.20.
20 Walks around Swindon
by Northeast Wiltshire Ramblers
Between 3km/2 miles and 12km/7.5 miles, within a 30km/20-mile radius of Swindon.
£2.50.
All from 21 Brynards Hill, Wootton Bassett, Swindon SN4 7ER. Cheques to Ramblers' Association NE Wilts Group.

Sarum Way
A circular walk around Salisbury and Wilton.
Booklet £3.50 from 27 Richard Way, Salisbury SP2 8NT. Cheques to South Wilts Ramblers Group.

South Wiltshire Group Publications:
Eight easy walks in the Salisbury Area route card pack
Ten shorter walks in the Salisbury Area booklet
Ten longer walks in the Salisbury Area route card pack
£3.50 each from 27 Richard Way, Salisbury SP2 8NT. Cheques to Ramblers' Association W3.

NEW **Ten Walks Around Devizes**
Varied walks of between 6.5km/4 miles and 11km/ 7 miles, with maps, illustrations and historical notes.
£2 + 50p p&p from 1 Copings Close, Devizes SN10 5BW. Cheques to Ramblers' Association Mid Wilts Group.

12 More Walks Around Chippenham
by Chippenham Ramblers. A selection of 5km/3-mile to 14.5km/9-mile walks.
£2.50 from 11A High Street, Sutton Benger SN15 4RE. Cheques to RA Chippenham Group.

West Wiltshire Group Publications:
Ten Walks in West Wiltshire
10 circular walks between 6.5km/4 miles and 17.5km/11 miles, including some near railway stations, with OS maps.
£2.50.
Walking in West Wiltshire Book 2
10 circular walks between 6.5km/4 miles and 11km/7 miles, including some near railway stations, with sketch maps.
£1.25.
Walking in West Wiltshire Book 3
10 circular walks between 8km/5 miles and 16km/10 miles, including some near railway stations, with sketch maps.
£1.25.
All from 68 Savernake Avenue, Melksham SN12 7HE. Cheques to West Wilts Ramblers' Association.

21 Walks for the 21st Century
See under Berkshire.

WORCESTERSHIRE
Bromsgrove Ramblers
48km/30-mile circuit around Bromsgrove from Wychbold via Chaddesley Corbett and Alvechurch, devised to celebrate the 30th anniversary of the Group. Leaflet has route description and overview map and would need to be used in conjunction with the local OS map.
£1.50 from 13 Victoria Road, Bromsgrove B61 0DW. Cheques to Ramblers' Association Bromsgrove Group.

Walks in the Vale of Evesham, 2nd edition
12 walks, all reasonably easy, of between 2.5km/1.5 miles and 11.5km/7.25 miles, in and around Evesham.
£3 + A5 1st class SAE, from 12 Queens Road, Evesham WR11 4JN. Cheques to RA Vale of Evesham Group.

YORKSHIRE
Airedale Way
by Douglas Cossar. ISBN 0-900613-95-5. An 80km/50-mile riverside walk from Leeds to Malham Tarn in the Dales, in 11 sections, 10 of them walkable as circular walks, with addtional walks in Airedale.
£4.50 + £1 p&p from 11 Woodroyd Avenue, Honley, Holmfirth HD9 6LG. Cheques to West Riding Area Ramblers' Association.

Car-Free Countryside Walks Accessible From York
by Patsy Pendegrass. ISBN 1-904446-04-3 (East Yorkshire and Derwent Area). 15 walks from stations or bus stops over a wide area within easy reach of York, all

8km/5 miles to 19.5km/12 miles, some with shorter options.
£4.99 from local bookshops or from the author (+ 50p p&p) at 92 The Village, Haxby, York YO32 2JL. Cheques to PM Pendegrass. All profits to Ramblers' Association.

Chalkland Way
by Ray Wallis (Hull RA). 66km/40-mile circular walk through the chalk hills of the Yorkshire Wolds from Pocklington, including chalk wolds, arable land and woodland. A few steep hills but not too strenuous.
Colour leaflet free + A5 SAE to R Wallis, 75 Ancaster Avenue, Kingston upon Hull HU5 4QR. Badge available from the same source.

Country Walks in Mirfield, Emley, Thornhill and Denby Dale
by Douglas Cossar and John Lieberg. ISBN 1-901184-30-7. 17 circular walks of between 6km/3.75 miles and 12km/7.5 miles, with sketch maps, route descriptions, photos and public transport details.
£4.75 + £1 p&p, as Airedale Way (above).

Dales Way Handbook
edited by West Riding RA. An annually updated guide to accommodation and transport along the path between Ilkley and Windermere.
£1.50 + £1 p&p, as Airedale Way (above).

Danum Trail
A series of walks linking villages and towns in Doncaster borough, readily accessible by public transport and creating an 80km/50-mile walk from Dome Leisure Park Doncaster to the Glass Park, Kirk Sandall, taking in the Earth Centre, short sections of the Trans Pennine Trail, historic villages and open countryside. Colour foldout leaflet with map of the route and notes on places of interest.
£1.30 from 31 Broom Hill Drive, Doncaster DN4 6QZ. Cheques to Ramblers' Association Doncaster Group.

Dearne Valley Group Walks
(Dearne Valley Ramblers). Seven free walks leaflets: Conisborough to Sprotborough (9.5km/6 miles easy); River Don Walk from Sprotborough via Cusworth (13km/8 miles easy); Elsecar and Wentworth (12km/7.5 miles easy); Swinton and Rawmarsh (8km/5 miles easy to moderate); Dearne Valley Ramble (11km/7 miles easy to moderate); Broomhill, Bolton & Wath (6.5km/4 miles easy); Swinton & Wath (8km/5 miles easy to moderate). Each has sketch map and route description. *Free + SAE from 6*

Ruskin Avenue, Mexborough S64 0AU, or downloadable from www.dearnevalleyramblers.org.uk

East Riding Walks
(East Yorkshire and Derwent Ramblers). Four circular routes of around 14.5km/9 miles each with full description and photo, in a plastic case.
£2 from 2 Spellowgate, Driffield YO25 7BB. Cheques to J Jefferson.

Harrogate Dales Way Link
32km/20 miles from Valley Gardens, Harrogate to Bolton Abbey, linking to the Dales Way.
A5 leaflet, 30p + SAE. Sew-on badge available on completion, £1.50 + SAE.

Harrogate Ringway
(Harrogate Ramblers). 33.5km/21-mile circular trail around this spa town, starting from Pannal via Knaresborough, in easy stages with public transport connections.
A5 leaflet, 30p + SAE. Sew-on badge available on completion, £1.50 + SAE. Both from 20 Pannal Ash Grove, Harrogate HG2 0HZ. Cheques to Harrogate RA Group.

Kirklees Way
Circular walk around Huddersfield and Dewsbury.
£2.70 + £1 p&p, as Airedale Way above.

Knaresborough Round
32km/20-mile circular walk round this ancient town, in two stages with bus connections.
A5 leaflet, 30p + SAE. Sew-on badge available on completion. £1.50, as Harrogate Dales Way above.

Minster Way
by Ray Wallis (Hull RA). An 83km/50-mile signed walk established in 1980 between the Minsters of Beverley and York, crossing the Yorkshire Wolds and Vale of York. A good variety of countryside, not too strenuous but with hills up to 180m. Guidebook with maps and colour photos, dividing the route into three sections.
£4 + 55p p&p from 75 Ancaster Avenue, Hull HU5 4QR. Cheques payable to R Wallis. Badge and accommodation list available from same source.

Penistone Line Trail Sheffield to Huddersfield
by the Penistone Line Partnership, supported by South Yorkshire and North Derbyshire Area. 95km/60 miles divided into several sections ranging from

2.5km/1.5 miles to 7.5km/4.75 miles, all between stations on this attractive railway branch through the south Pennines, linking Lincoln and Huddersfield. Route descriptions, background on the line, overprinted OS maps.
£4.95 + 55p (or £2.95 + 55p p&p for Ramblers or Partnership members) from PLP, St Johns Community Centre, Church Street, Penistone S36 9AR. Cheques to Penistone Line Partnership.

The Ramblers' Association Book of Kiddiwalks: Thirty short family rambles in and near West Yorkshire
70th Jubilee Edition, by West Riding Ramblers. ISBN 0-900613-88-2. Easy walks 1.5km/1 mile to 6.5km/4 miles, devised principally with young families in mind, with lots of interest along the route, including some suitable for pushchairs. The book includes sketch maps, route descriptions, background notes and photos. All walks are accessible by public transport, with details included. A welcome new edition for this popular guide covering every part of West Yorkshire as well as the southern Yorkshire Dales.
£5.99 + £1 p&p, as Airedale Way (above).

Ramblers' Bradford Volume 1
by Douglas Cossar. ISBN 1-901184-22-6. 20 circular walks 3km/2 miles to 16km/10 miles, covering the whole of the district with an introduction to a variety of landscapes and a wealth of history, accessible by public transport.
£4.95 + £1 p&p.

Ramblers' Leeds Volume 1 East of Leeds
by Douglas Cossar. ISBN 1-901184-23-4. 25 mostly circular walks, 5.5km/3.5 miles to 18.5km/11.5 miles, accessible by public transport.
£4.95 + £1 p&p.

Ramblers' Leeds Volume 2 West of Leeds
by Douglas Cossar. ISBN 1-901184-24-2. 24 mainly circular walks, 4km/2.5 miles to 14.5km/9 miles, offering a variety of landscapes and using the extensive footpath network in the area, accessible by public transport.
£5.95 + £1 p&p. All as Airedale Way (above).

Rambles Around Ripon
by Ripon Ramblers. 15 varied countryside walks 2km/1.5 miles to 20km/13 miles.
£3.60 + 70p p&p. Cheques to Rambles Around Ripon.

Ripon Rowel Walk
by Les Taylor. 80km/50-mile circular route

from Ripon Cathedral via Masham, with
12 circular walks of between 5km/3 miles
and 24km/15 miles along the way.
£4.95 + 70p p&p. Cheques to The
Ripon Rowel.
Both from 10 Pine Walk, Ripon, HG4 2LW.
Order both at the same time and get them
for £8 + 70p p&p.

Rotherham Ring Route
by Rotherham Metro Ramblers. An
80km/50-mile circular walk through the
gently rolling landscape around the
boundary of Rotherham borough including
many fine country parks. Pack of 10 leaflets
in a plastic wallet plus bus details and
additional useful information for beginners.
£2 + £1 p&p from Rotherham Visitor Centre,
40 Bridge Gate, Rotherham S60 1PQ.
☎ 01709 835904. Cheques to Rotherham
TIC. Badges and completion cards from
same source.

Sheffield Country Walk,
3rd edition
by Sheffield Group and Sheffield City
Council. 87km/54.5 miles through the
countryside round Sheffield via Eckington,
Dronfield, Burbage, Grensoside and
Meadowhall, in 10 sections of around
8km/5 miles each, linked by public
transport, all with separate colour route
cards in an attractive folder.
£3.95 + 55p p&p from Ramblers'
Association Sheffield Group, 33 Durvale
Court, Sheffield S17 3PT. Cheques to
Ramblers' Association Sheffield Group.

Yorkshire Wolds Way
Accommodation Guide
(E Yorks & Derwent Area).
95p + SAE from Mrs SM Smith,
65 Ormonde Avenue, Kingston upon Hull
HU6 7LT.

Wakefield Way
by Douglas Cossar (West Riding Ramblers).
ISBN 1-901184-74-9. Describes a
120km/75-mile loop around the boundary
of Wakefield district in West Yorkshire, from
Anglers Country Park via Gawsthorpe,
Castleford, Pontefract and South Kirkby.
Easily walked as 24 shorter walks
(5.5km/3.5 miles to 13.5km/8.5 miles),
both circular and linear, with public
transport connections.
£5.99 + p&p, as Airedale Way above.

Walking with the Ramblers
in Sheffield
Free colour leaflets with local walks around
Sheffield, all accessible by public transport.
1. Deepcar Circular 11km/7 miles.

2. Mayfield and Porter Valleys 6.5km/
4 miles, easy.
3. Iron Age to Steel Age (Meadowhall to
Crabtree Pond) 5km/3 miles, mainly
surfaced paths with no obstructions.
4. Herdings Circular 6.5km/4 miles, easy
but numerous stiles, recommended for
families.
5. Lodge Moor Circular 13km/8 miles.
Includes open country and access land.
6. Moscar Moor 8km/5 miles. Includes
open moorland and access land.
From local outlets or contact Sheffield Group
☎ 01709 586870 or download from
www.sheffield.ramblers.care4free.net

Walks in and around Kirklees
ISBN 978-1-901184-93-8. 12 varied,
hand-illustrated walks in
Huddersfield/Holmfirth area by
Huddersfield Group.
£2.90 + £1 p&p, as Airedale Way (above).
More Walks in and around Kirklees
ISBN 978-1-901184-94-5. 15 varied,
hand-illustrated walks in
Huddersfield/Holmfirth area by
Huddersfield Group.
£2.90 + £1 p&p, as Airedale Way (above).
All from JM Lieberg, 11 Woodroyd Avenue,
Honley, Holmfirth HD9 6LG. Cheques to
West Riding Area Ramblers' Association.

WALES
The Pioneer Ramblers 1850-1940
by David Hollett (North Wales Ramblers).
ISBN 1-901184-54-4. The history of
walking is full of vivid incidents and striking
characters, many of them captured in this
new book. Thus George Allen, who
walked a thousand miles to advance
vegetarianism, shares a cover with
Lawrence Chubb, the severely conservative
first secretary of the Open Spaces Society,
and the young communists who trespassed
on Kinder Scout in 1932 jostle with
Victorian mountaineers and natural history
enthusiasts. The pictures are a delight.
£8.95 + £1 p&p from 69 Wethersfield
Road, Prenton CH43 9YF. Cheques to North
Wales Area RA.

CEREDIGION
Cardigan Centre for Walkers –
Aberteifi Canolfan Cerddwyr
by Cardigan and District Ramblers.
Collection of 11 graded walks of between
5km/3 miles and 16km/10 miles in and
around Cardigan, with connecting bus
service information, on attractive cards in a
pack. Bilingual Welsh/English.
£5.50 + 50p p&p from G Torr, Parc-y-Pratt,
Cardigan SA43 3DR. Cheques to Cardigan
and District Ramblers.

Lampeter Walks – Llwybrau Llanbed
by Lampeter Ramblers. ISBN 1-901184-
58-7. Revised edition of this book of 16
walks 2.5km/1.5 miles to 13km/8 miles,
with route maps, background notes on
geographical and historical context and
accommodation listings, with colour
illustrations and line drawings by Robert
Blayney. Bilingual Welsh/English.
£2.50 + £1 p&p from David Lloyd, Awelfan,
Bryn Road, Lampeter SA48 7EE. Cheques to
Lampeter Ramblers. Or you can order from
www.lampeter.org/english/walks/index.html

DENBIGHSHIRE
Clwydian Way
by David Hollett. ISBN 1-901184-36-6.
Circular route around Denbighshire,
looping through some of the best, but
relatively unknown, walking country in
the region, including details of 12 short
circular walks.
£5.95 + £1.55 p&p from PO Box 139,
Llanfairpwllgwyngyll LL61 6WR. Cheques to
The Ramblers' Association North Wales Area.

GLAMORGAN
Bunny Walk Leaflets
Free. Produced by the Taff Ely (Llantrisant)
Group. Six A4-sized leaflets with details of
short 4km/2.5-mile to 6.5km/4-mile walks
around the Llantrisant area in Rhondda
Cynon Taf.
PDF electronic copies of the walks are
available for download at
www.apyule.demon.co.uk/walkindex.htm

Capital Walks, More Capital Walks
and The Capital Walk
Cardiff Group has produced two books of
countryside walks around Cardiff, with a
total of 30 short circular walks between
about 5km/3 miles and 18km/11.5 miles.
These link up into a circular Capital Walk
around the city of 61km/38 miles starting
from Swanbridge.
Both books are out of print, but walk
descriptions are available to download from
the website at www.cardifframblers.org.uk

Valeways Millennium Heritage Trail
by B Palmer and G Woodnam (Vale of
Glamorgan Group). 99km/62-mile circular
walk with spurs linking up places of
historical, geographic and geological interest,
developed by a partnership of the
Ramblers' Association, Vale of Glamorgan
Council and other organisations. Pack with
booklet and 16 route cards with map and
details in easy sections.
£6.99 + £1.50 p&p from Valeways, Unit 7
BCEC, Skomer Road, Barry CF62 9DA.
Cheques to Valeways.

Walk West
See under Gloucestershire and Bristol

Walking Around Gower, 4th edition
by Albert White (West Glamorgan Ramblers). ISBN 0-951878-01-8. 10 circular walks of between 8km/5 miles and 21km/13 miles around the Gower peninsula, going out along the coast and returning inland, including extensive notes on scenery, wildlife and history.

Walking Around Northern Gower and the Swansea Valley
by Peter Beck and Peter J Thomas, based on an original work by Albert White. ISBN 0-951878-11-5. 10 circular walks that can be split into 25 shorter circuits, giving options of between 8km/5 miles and 21km/13 miles, in the former mining area north of Swansea and the Gower peninsula. Includes overprinted OS maps and extensive background notes.
Both £7.50 each post free from Peter Beck, 24 Hazelmere Road, Sketty, Swansea SA2 0SN. Cheques to The Ramblers' Association.

MONMOUTHSHIRE
NEW **Lower Wye Rambles**
3rd edition
by Lower Wye Group. 16 walks in the Lower Wye Valley between Chepstow and Monmouth. 4-14km/2.5-9 miles, some linking together to make longer walks and including parts of the Wye Valley Walk, with clear colour maps. Proceeds fund local footpath improvements.
£3.75 from 3 Mount Way, Chepstow NP16 5EG. Cheques to Lower Wye Group RA.

Walk West
See Gloucestershire and Bristol

POWYS
Walks You Will Enjoy
Pack of 18 walks in east Radnorshire and northwest Herefordshire on laminated pocket-sized cards.
£4.50 (£3.75 to Ramblers members) from East Radnor Publications, 1 Heyope Road, Knucklas LD7 1PT. Cheques to East Radnor Publications.

SCOTLAND
Dunbartonshire and Lanarkshire
Explore and Enjoy East Dunbartonshire
Milngavie Area Walks by Bearsden and Milngavie Ramblers. A joint project with East Dunbartonshire Council. Eight local walks, each with OS map extracts.
Available free from the council's access officer ☎ 0141 578 8520 or www.eastdunbarton.gov.uk

Walk Strathkelvin
by John Logan (Strathkelvin Ramblers) with introduction by Cameron McNeish, historical essays by Don Martin and nature notes by Ian McCallum. ISBN 1-901184-44-7. Handsome book of over 70 walks, mainly short and easy walks taking half an hour to two hours, plus longer walks in the Campsies, canalside and disused railway line trails, illustrated with over 40 maps.
£7.99 from Strathkelvin Ramblers, 25 Anne Crescent, Lenzie, Kirkintilloch G66 5HB. Cheques to Strathkelvin Ramblers.

FIFE
Cupar Walks
Explore Fife's Farming Heritage by St Andrews Ramblers. Free colour leaflet offering a large variety of walks around this historic market town and out into the surrounding countryside. 14 different routes, ranging from 3km/2 miles to 14km/9 miles, and from surfaced paths in parks to rough country and woodland tracks. Maps, detailed route descriptions, photos. Produced in association with ScotWays and funded by Scottish Natural Heritage and Sport Scotland.
Send 22cm x11cm SAE to 63 St Michaels Drive, Cupar KY15 5BP, or contact St Andrews TIC ☎ 01334 472021.

Accommodation

HOW TO USE THE ACCOMMODATION GUIDE

The accommodation guide is divided into eight English regions, Wales and Scotland. Each section contains:

- an introduction with lots of **ideas for walks** and places to visit, including details of long distance paths and national parks in the region, plus news of local Ramblers Group activities
- a **map** of the area showing the locations of all B&Bs listed, long distance paths and national parks
- and the accommodation **listings**.

NB – *All locations of the accommodation are indexed at the back of the book (see pp281-287).*

The listings

The listings are organised by country/region then alphabetically by county or unitary authority. Some smaller authorities are banded together – see the map on p115 for a complete breakdown.

Entries are listed by 'place' situated – a village, town or hamlet. If the place is in a national park or within two miles of a long distance path listed on p25, the national park or path is cross-referenced after the place name.

The six-figure grid references given refer to OS Landranger maps, scale 1:50 000. Most are generated from postcode so can be inaccurate in sparsely populated areas.

Bed & Breakfast

The prices shown are based on single occupancy of a room, per person, per night (including any single supplement). Where no single room is available, the per person cost will be significantly less for two people sharing. A range of prices may be shown for variations between low/high season.

Some B&Bs may be closed in the winter or early spring – please always phone ahead before arrival.

Self-catering

Prices for self-catering accommodation vary greatly by season – we give the lowest and highest per week. Where a proprietor lets more than one property, the price of the cheapest in low season and the most expensive in high season is given. Tourist board awards may be different for each property let, in which case we show the range of awards given.

Group, hostels, bunkhouses, campsites and other

There is a variety of accommodation types, standards, prices and sizes listed. Some are self-catering (SC), others provide meals (BB, DBB, FB),

and include hotels, hostels, university halls of residence, cabins and farmhouses. Some centres listed are primarily for groups but should all be open to individuals, too. For each we state the cheapest and most expensive rates available within seasonal variations. Here is a an explanation of a few common categories of establishment:

Bunkhouse Barn A converted farm building. Stoves/cooking facilities provided. Toilets may be chemical. Separate male/female sleeping areas, but little privacy. Bunk beds provided.

Bunkhouse Other kinds of converted buildings, simply but comfortably furnished. Cooking facilities and utensils provided. Separate male/female sleeping areas with beds or bunks. Showers and drying facilities provided.

Campsite May be for tents only, plus tourers, or have hook-up facilities for caravans. Some sites have static caravans available. Some provide meals on-site.

Camping Barn A converted farm building providing basic shelter. Little or no privacy. Limited facilities. Toilets may be chemical. Sleeping areas usually not divided between sexes and there are wooden sleeping platforms. Often described as 'stone tents'.

Independent Hostel A privately-run hostel. Standards vary. Some provide meals but majority are self-catering. Sheet sleeping-bag liners usually required.

Outdoor Centre Often for groups only.

YHA A member of the Youth Hostels Association.

Tourist Board classifications

The AA, RAC, VisitBritain, VisitScotland and the Wales Tourist Board rate all accommodation using a common set of standards and give a star rating: '★–★★★★★'. Each organisation has its own special award scheme: we only display VisitBritain's Silver ⑤ and Gold ⑥ awards in this guide.

In 2004, VisitBritain produced a national rating for meeting the needs of walkers and cyclists in consultation with the Ramblers and others. ⓦ indicates a Walkers' Welcome or Cyclists' Welcome award. However all accommodation listed here should welcome walkers.

Further Information

Any deposit paid to establishments is non-refundable in all circumstances, and any amount paid by credit card may be non-returnable.

Finally, a disclaimer. The information in the guide is based on details received from proprietors during 2007. The Ramblers' Association cannot be held responsible for errors or omissions.

An EASY formula to STAY DRY ✓

Nikwax® + washing machine = clean, waterproofed, breathable clothing

EASIER

Wash and proof in a washing machine.
It's **EASY**.

SAFER

No propellant gases or fluorocarbons, non-toxic and environmentally safe.
It's **WATERBASED**.

DRIER

Maintains and enhances the waterproofing of your gear so you stay warm and **DRY** in wet weather

NIKWAX
WATERPROOFING

For more information call **01892 786400** and quote WB01
To **WIN** a Nikwax® product visit **www.nikwax.net**

RECOMMENDATION/FEEDBACK FORM

Much of the accommodation listed in this book comes from members' recommendations. Since we are unable to independently assess establishments, this is a vital resource for us. Please keep them coming by filling in the form below and posting it to us.

FOUND SOME GOOD DIGS THAT AREN'T IN THE GUIDE? ☐

or

HAVE A COMPLAINT ABOUT ACCOMMODATION IN THIS EDITION? ☐

Your name and address ....

....

....

Name and full postal address of the establishment ....

....

....

....

....

Email (if known) ....

Comments...

....

....

....

WHAT DO YOU THINK OF walk BRITAIN 2008?

....

....

....

....

THANK YOU. PLEASE RETURN THIS FORM TO THE PUBLICATIONS TEAM:
RAMBLERS' ASSOCIATION, 2ND FLOOR CAMELFORD HOUSE
87-90 ALBERT EMBANKMENT, LONDON SE1 7TW

ACCOMMODATION GUIDE

PÁRAMO
DIRECTIONAL
CLOTHING SYSTEMS

You
trust them...

Outdoor Instructors and Search & Rescue Teams were the first to fully appreciate Páramo. Today they remain the focus of our developmen By satisfying their needs we can be sure that all active people gain the most from o garment design. Our success lies in providing a faster reaction to climate and activi changes than any other bran we know. If you need convincing, ask a Páramo wearer if they'd ever go back to conventional outdoor gea

" *All our handlers are issued Páramo Jackets and Salopettes as standard because of their high performance.*

James Coles

Call-out co-ordinator SARDA (Southern Scotland)

GOLD 2007
walk
READER AWARDS
www.ramblers.org.uk

...They trust
Páramo

PÁRAMO *– Leaders in comfort and performance*

▷ Find out more about Páramo's unique advantages – ring **01892 786444**
for our latest activity catalogue or go online at **www.paramo.co.uk**

ANALOGY
WATERPROOF
NIKWAX

KEY MAP OF COUNTRIES AND REGIONS

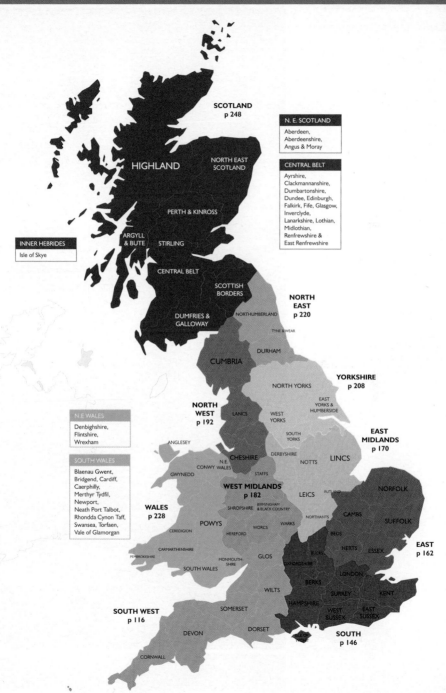

SCOTLAND
p 248

N. E. SCOTLAND

Aberdeen,
Aberdeenshire,
Angus & Moray

CENTRAL BELT

Ayrshire,
Clackmannanshire,
Dumbartonshire,
Dundee, Edinburgh,
Falkirk, Fife, Glasgow,
Inverclyde,
Lanarkshire, Lothian,
Midlothian,
Renfrewshire &
East Renfrewshire

HIGHLAND

NORTH EAST
SCOTLAND

PERTH & KINROSS

INNER HEBRIDES

Isle of Skye

ARGYLL
& BUTE   STIRLING

CENTRAL BELT

SCOTTISH
BORDERS

DUMFRIES &
GALLOWAY

NORTHUMBERLAND

**NORTH
EAST**
p 220

TYNE & WEAR

DURHAM

CUMBRIA

NORTH YORKS

YORKSHIRE
p 208

EAST
YORKS &
HUMBERSIDE

N.E WALES

Denbighshire,
Flintshire,
Wrexham

SOUTH WALES

Blaenau Gwent,
Bridgend, Cardiff,
Caerphilly,
Merthyr Tydfil,
Newport,
Neath Port Talbot,
Rhondda Cynon Taff,
Swansea, Torfaen,
Vale of Glamorgan

**NORTH
WEST**
p 192

LANCS

WEST
YORKS

SOUTH
YORKS

ANGLESEY

DERBYSHIRE

**EAST
MIDLANDS**
p 170

CHESHIRE

N.E.
CONWY WALES

NOTTS

LINCS

GWYNEDD

STAFFS

WEST MIDLANDS
p 182

LEICS

RUTLAND

NORFOLK

WALES
p 228

SHROPSHIRE

BIRMINGHAM
& BLACK COUNTRY

NORTHANTS

CAMBS

SUFFOLK

POWYS

WORCS

WARKS

BEDS

CEREDIGION

HEREFORD

HERTS

ESSEX

EAST
p 162

CARMARTHENSHIRE

BUCKS

PEMBROKESHIRE

MONMOUTH-
SHIRE

GLOS

OXFORDSHIRE

LONDON

SOUTH WALES

BERKS

KENT

WILTS

SURREY

SOUTH WEST
p 116

SOMERSET

HAMPSHIRE

WEST
SUSSEX

EAST
SUSSEX

DEVON

DORSET

ISLE OF
WIGHT

SOUTH
p 146

CORNWALL

SOUTH WEST

Long Distance Paths

**See Paths & Access p25 for full
details of LDPs and waymarks**

National Parks

Dartmoor

Exmoor

THE REMOTE AND ISOLATED SANDS OF
FISHERMAN'S BAY IN CORNWALL

WALK...   ...THE COTSWOLD WAY

Nearly 50 years since it was first mooted by Ramblers member Tony Drake, and nine years after successfully lobbying government to designate it, the Cotswold Way has officially launched as a national trail. And it's not difficult to see why: the 164km/102-mile route follows the beautiful Cotswold escarpment south from Chipping Campden in Gloucestershire to the World Heritage City of Bath. En route are the historic wonders of Belas Knap Neolithic burial chamber, Sudeley Castle and Hailes Abbey.

For more information, visit www.nationaltrail.co.uk/cotswold where you can purchase the official guide or see p101 for Gloucestershire Area's guidebook.

VISIT...
...THE GHOST VILLAGE OF TYNEHAM

The Ministry of Defence evacuated the Dorset hamlet of Tyneham in 1943 promising to return it to its residents after the war. But the army stayed and the small collection of buildings in this pretty valley at the foot of the Purbeck Range was left to the ravages of time. Only the medieval church and schoolhouse have been preserved, the pupils' schoolwork still abandoned on their desks. Equally eerie is the 1920s-style telephone box bought by the post office just weeks before the evacuation and still sealed like a time-capsule with its exterior brightly repainted. Surrounded by nearly 3,000ha of SSSI grassland, cliffs and beaches which make up the Lulworth Range, access is only permitted on weekends and holidays.

Visit www.access.mod.uk for walk descriptions on this and 13 other MoD sites.

SEE...   ...DOLPHINS OFF THE COAST PATH

If you want to spot a dolphin while walking, then head for the South West Coast Path. The waters off the Cornish peninsula are the richest for cetaceans (i.e. dolphins, whales and porpoises) in England, and nearshore sightings of the UK's estimated 500 bottlenose dolphins are possible all year round, especially off Land's End. The best places to watch are from prominent headlands and bays that offer uninterrupted views of the sea.

The Sea Watch Foundation recommends 20 known hotspots. For details, visit www.seawatchfoundation.org.uk where you can also download a guide to identifying species, check recent sightings or submit your own to help scientists monitoring cetacean distribution.

LOCAL RAMBLERS GROUPS... Bath Group is actively supporting a new shared-use path from Bath to neighbouring villages in the south using a disused Victorian railway under Combe Down. The four-mile Two Tunnels Greenway is the subject of a Sustrans lottery bid. Visit www.twotunnels.org.uk for further info... **For full details of the recently-created John Musgrave Heritage Trail, visit South Devon Group's website (see p86). The Group purchased a small wood at Great Hill to form part of this beautiful route.**

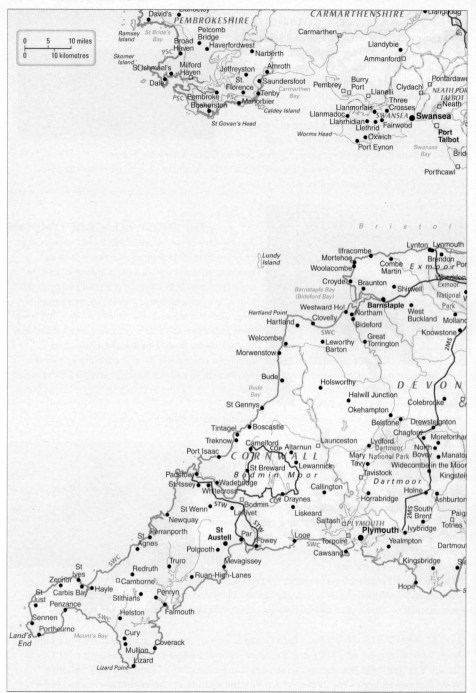

MAP 119

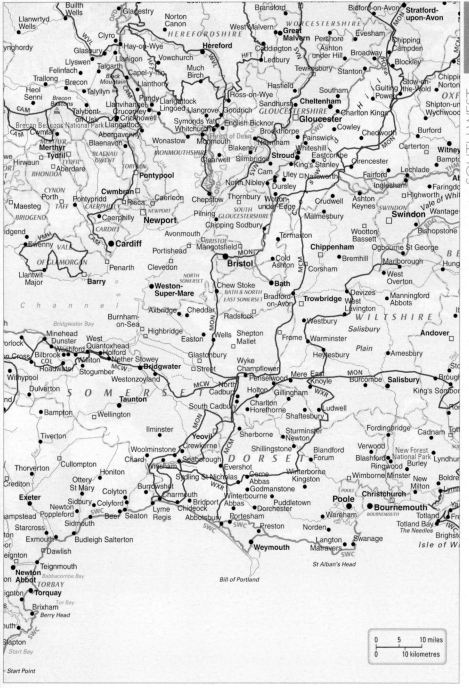

BED & BREAKFAST

CORNWALL

● Boscastle
SOUTH WEST COAST PATH

The Old Coach House, Tintagel Road, PL35 0AS ☎ 01840 250398
(Mrs Jackie Horwell) www.old-coach.co.uk Map 190/098906
£27-£30 D3 T3 F2 ✕ nearby ▯D▯ ▯B▯ ⊗ 🐾 ♨ 🚗 ! 🛏 ♿ F ★★★★

Lower Meadows, Penally Hill, PL35 0HF ☎ 01840 250570
(Anne & Adrian Prescott) www.lowermeadows.co.uk Map 190/101913
£34-£46 D4 T1 ✕ nearby ▯D▯ ▯B▯ ⊗ 🐾 ♨ 🚗 ! ★★★★

Orchard Lodge, Gunpool Lane, PL35 0AT ☎ 01840 250418 (Shelley Barratt)
www.orchardlodgeboscastle.co.uk Map 190/099906
£27.50-£50 D3 T2 ✕ nearby ▯D▯ ▯B▯ ⊗ 🐾 ♨ 🚗 ! ★★★★

● Bude
SOUTH WEST COAST PATH

Pencarrol Guest House, 21 Downs View, EX23 8RF ☎ 01288 352478
(M & E Payne) pencarrolbude@aol.com Map 190/207071
£29-£34 S2 D3 T1 F1 ✕ nearby ▯D▯ ▯B▯ ⊗ 🐾 ♨ 🚗 ! ★★★★

Harefield Cottage
Upton, EX23 0LY ☎ 01288 352350 (Sally-Ann Trewin)
www.coast-countryside.co.uk Map 190/202048
£25-£33 S2 D2 T1 ✕ £20, 6:30pm
▯V▯ ▯D▯ ▯B▯ ⊗ 🐾 ♨ 🚗 ! 🛏 ★★★★Ⓢ

Harefield Cottage is only 250 yards from the South West Coast Path. Luxurious bedrooms. A hot tub in the garden to relax your weary muscles. Excellent homecooked meals on request. We offer a pick-up-and-drop service with luggage transfer.

Tee-side Guest House, 2 Burn View, EX23 8BY ☎ 01288 352351
(Mrs June Downes) www.tee-side.co.uk Map 190/208066
£30-£40 S1 D2 T3 ✕ nearby ▯D▯ ▯B▯ ⊗ 🐾 ♨ 🚗 ! F ★★★★

Surf Haven, 31 Downs View, EX23 8RE ☎ 01288 353923 (Jan Penn)
www.surfhaven.co.uk Map 190/210070
£30-£35 D5 T2 F2 ✕ ▯V▯ ▯D▯ ▯B▯ ⊗ 🐾 ♨ 🚗 ! 🛏 ★★★★

● Cawsand
SOUTH WEST COAST PATH

Wringford Down, Hat Lane, PL10 1LE ☎ 01752 822287 (Andrew Molloy)
www.wringforddown.co.uk Map 201/427501
£32.50-£40 D4 F8 ✕ £14.75, 6pm ▯V▯ ▯D▯ ▯B▯ ⊗ 🐾 ♨ 🛏 ★★★

● Falmouth
SOUTH WEST COAST PATH

Hawthorne Dene Hotel, Pennance Road, TR11 4EA ☎ 01326 311427
(Jonna Hartland) www.hawthornedenehotel.com Map 204/804320
£40 S2 D6 T1 F1 ✕ £18, 6:30pm ⋙(Falmouth Town)
▯V▯ ▯D▯ ▯B▯ ⊗ 🐾 ♨ 🚗 ! ♿ F ★★★★Ⓢ

● Fowey
SOUTH WEST COAST PATH & SAINTS' WAY

4 Daglands Road, PL23 1JL ☎ 01726 833164 (John & Carol Eardley)
www.jabedesign.co.uk/keverne Map 200/123518
£30-£35 D2 ✕ ▯D▯ ▯B▯ ⊗ 🐾 ♨ ! 🛏 Ⓜ

● Golberdon
Keadeen, Golberdon, PL17 7LT ☎ 01579 384197 (Mrs Geraldine Parkyn)
www.keadeen.co.uk Map 201/329714
£25 S1 D2 T2 F1 ✕ £12, 7pm ▯V▯ ▯D▯ ▯B▯ ⊗ 🐾 ♨ 🚗 🛏

● Hayle
SOUTH WEST COAST PATH

54 Penpol Terrace, TR27 4BQ ☎ 01736 752855 (Mrs Anne Cooper)
jacoop@talktalk.co.net Map 203/558374
£25-£35 S1 D1 T1 ✕ nearby ⋙(Hayle) ▯D▯ ⊗ 🐾 ♨ 🚗 ! Ⓜ

● Lanivet
SAINTS' WAY

Willowbrook, Old Coach Road, Lamorick, PL30 5HB ☎ 01208 831670
(Tony & Elaine Barnaby) www.willowbrookbandb.co.uk Map 200/037646
£30-£65 S1 D2 T1 ✕ £13, 7pm
▯V▯ ▯D▯ ▯B▯ ⊗ 🐾 ♨ 🚗 ! ★★★★

● Liskeard
COPPER TRAIL

Elnor Guest House, 1 Russell Street, PL14 4BP ☎ 01579 342472
(Mr & Mrs B J Slocombe) www.elnorguesthouse.co.uk Map 201/250642
£26-£40 S4 D1 T1 F3 ✕ nearby ⋙(Liskeard)
▯D▯ ▯B▯ ⊗ 🐾 ♨ 🛏 ★★★

● Looe
SOUTH WEST COAST PATH

Marwinthy Guest House, East Cliff, PL13 1DE ☎ 01503 264382
(Eddie Mawby) www.marwinthy.co.uk Map 201/256533
✕ ⋙(Looe) ▯D▯ ▯B▯ 🛏

Schooner Point B&B
Schooner Point, 1 Trelawney Terrace, PL13 2AG ☎ 01503 262670
(Paul & Helen Barlow) www.schoonerpoint.co.uk Map 201/252536
£25-£30 S1 D2 T1 ⋙(Looe)
▯D▯ ▯B▯ ⊗ 🐾 ♨ ★★★★

We are pleasantly situated close to Looe town with splendid river views. Our immaculate rooms are recently decorated and carpeted.
Hearty breakfasts, including vegetarian and vegan options. Early starts welcome.
All rooms en-suite or with private facilities.
No card facilities.

Kantana Guest House, 7 Trelawney Terrace, PL13 2AG ☎ 01503 262093
(Rick & Sandra Blanks) www.kantana.co.uk Map 201/252536
£20-£35 S2 D2 T1 F1 ✕ nearby ⋙(Looe) ▯D▯ ▯B▯ ⊗ 🐾 ♨

Haven House,
Barbican Hill, PL13 1BQ ☎ 01503 264160 (Edwina Arkell)
www.visitlooe.co.uk Map 201/255533
£25-£30 D2 F1 ✕ £15, 7pm ⋙(Looe)
▯V▯ ▯D▯ 🐾 ♨ 🚗 ! ★★★

Fantastic views over historic fishing harbour of Looe, two minutes from restaurants, South West Coast Path and sandy beach.

Two spacious double rooms in contemporary style.
Run to a 'green' environmentally friendly ethos.

Emphasis on local produce and genuine Cornish welcome.

SOUTH WEST

● Mevagissey
SOUTH WEST COAST PATH

Honeycombe House, 61 Polkirt Hill, PL26 6UR ☎ 01726 843750
(Ian & Val Soper) www.honeycombehouse.com Map 204/015446
£27 S1 D3 T1 ✗ nearby ▣ Ⓑ ⊗ 🐕 🛁 🚗 ! ★★★★

● Morwenstow
SOUTH WEST COAST PATH

Cornakey Farm
EX23 9SS ☎ 01288 331260 (Monica Heywood)
Map 190/208157
£24-£25 D1 T1 F1 ✗ £12, 6:30pm
Ⓥ Ⓓ Ⓑ ⊗ 🐕 🛁 🚗 ! ★★★

Cornakey Farm is in the far north-east of Cornwall, directly overlooking the Atlantic Ocean. The farm consists of 220 acres, some of which forms part of the coastal footpath. Good home cooking. Guests welcome to wander around farm.

The Bush Inn
Crosstown, EX23 9SR ☎ 01288 331242 (The Pub)
www.bushinn-morwenstow.co.uk Map 190/208150
£45 D1 T1 ✗ £12, 7:30pm
Ⓥ Ⓓ Ⓑ ⊗ 🐕 🛁 🚗 🏍 Ⓕ

A 13th-century freehouse in a stunning location just off the South West Coast Path.

Once a haunt for smugglers and wreckers, this historic pub has provided sustenance for weary travellers for hundreds of years and is situated halfway between Bude and Hartland on one of the most dramatic stretches of the north Cornish coast.

Open all day serving homecooked food and Cornish real ales. Children and dogs welcome. Self-catering available.

● Mullion
SOUTH WEST COAST PATH

Trenance Farmhouse, TR12 7HB ☎ 01326 240639 (Jennifer Tyler Street)
www.trenancefarmholidays.co.uk Map 203/673185
£33-£37 D4 T1 ✗ Ⓓ Ⓑ ⊗ 🐕 🛁 ! 🏍

● Newlyn
SOUTH WEST COAST PATH

Mordros, 10 Tolcarne Terrace, Newlyn, TR18 5PS ☎ 01736 351357
(John Watson) johnwatson_artist@yahoo.co.uk Map 203/463290
£20-£30 D1 ✗ nearby ▟▟▟(Penzance) Ⓓ Ⓑ ⊗ 🐕 🛁 🚗 !

● Newquay
SOUTH WEST COAST PATH

Chichester, 14 Bay View Terrace, TR7 2LR ☎ 01637 874216 (Sheila Harper)
freespace.virgin.net/sheila.harper Map 200/813614
£22 S1 D3 T2 F1 ✗ nearby ▟▟▟(Newquay) Ⓓ 🐕 🛁 ★★Ⓜ

Roma Guest House, 1 Atlantic Road, TR7 1QJ ☎ 01637 875085
(Mrs P Williams) www.romaguesthouse.co.uk Map 200/803616
£25-£27 S1 D2 T1 F2 ✗ £12, 6pm ▟▟▟(Newquay)
Ⓥ Ⓓ Ⓑ ⊗ 🐕 🛁 ! ★★★★

The Three Tees , 21 Carminow Way, TR7 3AY ☎ 01637 872055
(Greg & Fiona Dolan) www.3tees.co.uk Map 200/823622
£30-£35 D3 T2 F4 ✗ nearby ▟▟▟(Newquay)
Ⓓ Ⓑ ⊗ 🐕 🛁 ! 🏍 ★★★

Dewolf Guest House, 100 Henver Road, TR7 3BL ☎ 01637 874746
(Meryl & Mark Dewolfreys) www.dewolfguesthouse.com Map 200/828620
£25-£40 S2 D2 F2 ✗ nearby ▟▟▟(Newquay)
Ⓑ ⊗ 🐕 🛁 🚗 🛁 Ⓕ ★★★★Ⓜ

Fairways Guest House, 16 St Georges Road, TR7 1RE ☎ 01637 873 015
(Joanne Benton) www.fairwaysnewquay.co.uk Map 200/807615
£27.50-£40 S6 D4 T2 F2 ✗ nearby ▟▟▟(Newquay) Ⓑ 🐕 🛁 !

● Padstow
SOUTH WEST COAST PATH & SAINTS' WAY

Trevorrick Farm
St Issey, PL27 7QH ☎ 01841 540574 (Mr & Mrs M Benwell)
www.trevorrick.co.uk Map 200/922732
£39.50-£44.50 D2 T1 ✗
Ⓓ Ⓑ ⊗ 🛁 ! ★★★Ⓦ

Trevorrick Farm is a small holding located in an AONB close to Padstow with an excellent pub/restaurant only half-a-mile away. Good access to footpaths. Facilities include a heated indoor pool (seasonal).

● Pendoggett
SOUTH WEST COAST PATH

Lane End Farm, Pendoggett, PL30 3HH ☎ 01208 880013
(Linda and Nab Monk) nabmonk@tiscali.co.uk Map 200/026793
✗ nearby Ⓓ Ⓑ ⊗ 🐕 🚗 ! ★★★★

● Penryn
SOUTH WEST COAST PATH

62 St Thomas Street, TR10 8JP ☎ 01326 374473
(Brian & Penny Ward) Map 204/786341
£18 S1 D2 T1 F1 ✗ nearby ▟▟▟(Penryn) Ⓓ 🐕 🚗 🏍 Ⓜ

● Penzance
SOUTH WEST COAST PATH

Glencree House, 2 Mennaye Road, TR18 4NG ☎ 01736 362026
(Helen Cahalane) www.glencreehouse.co.uk Map 203/469297
✗ ▟▟▟(Penzance) Ⓓ Ⓑ ⊗ 🐕 ! 🏍 Ⓜ

● Porthcurno
SOUTH WEST COAST PATH

Sea View House, The Valley, TR19 6JX ☎ 01736 810638 (Chris Bishop)
www.seaviewhouseporthcurno.com Map 203/383227
£33-£36 S1 D4 T2 ✗ £15, 5pm
Ⓥ Ⓓ Ⓑ ⊗ 🐕 🛁 ! ★★★★Ⓜ

Rose Cottage, The Valley, TR19 6JY ☎ 01736 810082 (Chris Hatton)
chrisswcpa.co.uk Map 203/382229
£25-£30 S1 D2 F1 ✗ nearby Ⓓ ⊗ 🐕 🛁 🚗 ! Ⓜ

● Ruan-High-Lanes
SOUTH WEST COAST PATH

New Gonitor Farm
TR2 5LE ☎ 01872 501345 (Mrs R Dingle)
rosemary@newgonitorfarm.wanadoo.co.uk Map 204/905416
£25-£30 D1 T1 ✗ nearby
Ⓓ Ⓑ ⊛ 🐾 ♿ 🏛 ★★★★

Stay at our comfortable farmhouse in the beautiful Roseland. Wonderful coastal walks and NT gardens within the local area. Also, Lost Gardens of Heligan and Eden Project. En-suite rooms, traditional farmhouse fare.

● St Agnes
SOUTH WEST COAST PATH

Driftwood Spars
Trevaunance Cove, Quay Road, TR5 0RT ☎ 01872 552428 (Louise Treseder)
www.driftwoodspars.com Map 204/721513
£43-£60 S1 D9 T1 F4 ✗ £10, 7pm
Ⓥ Ⓑ ⊛ 🐾 ♿ ! 🏛 ★★★★

This 17th-century building is located 100 yards from the beach and is adjacent to the coastal path with some rooms that offer a seaview. It is a delightful pub serving excellent food, real ale and has a fish restaurant.

● St Austell
SOUTH WEST COAST PATH

Spindrift, London Apprentice, PL26 7AR ☎ 01726 69316 (Linda Mcguffie)
www.spindrift-guesthouse.co.uk Map 200/007501
£25-£70 D1 F2 ✗ nearby Ⓓ Ⓑ ⊛ ♿ 🏛 ★★★

● St Blazey
SAINTS' WAY & SOUTH WEST COAST PATH

Palm Garden House, 3 Tywardreath Highway, PL24 2RW ☎ 01726 816112
(Pat Taylor) website.lineone.net/%7eroy10/new%5findex.htm Map 200/077556
£25 S1 D2 T1 F1 ✗ £7.50, 7pm 🚌 (Par)
Ⓥ Ⓓ ⊛ 🐾 ♿ ! 🏛

● St Cleer
COPPER TRAIL

Redgate Smithy
Redgate, PL14 6RU ☎ 01579 321578 (Clive & Julie Ffitch)
www.redgatesmithy.co.uk Map 201/227685
£40 D2 T1
Ⓓ Ⓑ ⊛ 🐾 ♿ ! 🏛 ★★★★

Welcoming B&B situated above beautiful Golitha Falls on Southern edge of Bodmin Moor. Excellent walking, on moor or coast. On Copper Trail. Area abounds with Cornish mining heritage and birds and wildlife on the moor. Lovely woodland garden. Brochure available.

● St Gennys
SOUTH WEST COAST PATH

Bears & Boxes Country Guest House, Penrose, Dizzard, EX23 0NX
☎ 01840 230318 (Robert & Francoise Holmes)
www.bearsandboxes.com Map 190/170986
£29.50 S4 D4 T1 F1 ✗ £13, 5pm Ⓥ Ⓓ Ⓑ ⊛ 🐾 ♿ ! 🏛

● St Just
SOUTH WEST COAST PATH

Bosavern House
TR19 7RD ☎ 01736 788301 (Allan & Corinne Collinson)
www.bosavern.com Map 203/371305
£30-£38 S1 D3 T2 F2 ✗ nearby
Ⓓ Ⓑ ⊛ 🐾 ♿ 🏛 ! ★★★★

C.17th country house offering centrally heated, comfortable accommodation. Most bedrooms have sea or moorland views; en-suite or private facilities. Lounge with log fire, TV and bar. Drying facilities. Home cooking using local produce. Half-mile from the coast path.

● St Neot
COPPER TRAIL

Little Keasts Farmhouse Bed and Breakfast, Little Keasts, Draynes, PL14 6RY
☎ 01579 320645 (Karen & John Popplewell)
www.littlekeasts.co.uk Map 201/214691
£50-£60 D2 Ⓓ Ⓑ ⊛ ♿ 🚌

● St Wenn
SAINTS' WAY

Tregolls Farm
PL30 5PG ☎ 01208 812154 (Mrs Marilyn Hawkey)
www.tregollsfarm.co.uk Map 200/983661
£28-£30 D1 T1 F1 ✗ £13, 7pm
Ⓥ Ⓓ Ⓑ ⊛ 🐾 ♿ 🚌 ! ♿ ★★★★

Grade II-listed farmhouse with beautiful countryside views from all windows. Two guest bedrooms. Farm trail links up to Saints' Way footpath. Pets' corner. Eden, Helligan, Fowey and Padstow all within 25 minutes' drive.

● Tintagel
SOUTH WEST COAST PATH

Bosayne Guest House, Atlantic Road, PL34 0DE ☎ 01840 770514
(Julie & Keith Walker) www.bosayne.co.uk Map 200/050890
£25-£30 S3 D2 T1 F2 ✗ nearby Ⓓ Ⓑ ⊛ 🐾 ♿ ! ★★★Ⓦ

● Treknow
SOUTH WEST COAST PATH & COPPER TRAIL

Michael House Vegetarian Guest House, Trelake Lane, PL34 0EW
☎ 01840 770592 (Vanessa Lackford)
www.michael-house.co.uk Map 200/057866
✕ £17.50, 7:30pm Ⓥ Ⓓ Ⓑ ⊗ 🐾 ♿ ! ▤

Tregosse House
PL34 0EP ☎ 01840 779230 (Richard Hart)
www.tregossehouse.co.uk Map 200/052866
£42-£52 D2 T1 ✕ nearby
Ⓓ Ⓑ 🐾 ♿ ▤ ! ★★★

A beautiful Victorian detached property only 150 yards from the South West Coast Path – ideal location to explore the north Cornwall coast. Every room has panoramic sea views, en-suites, colour TV/DVDs and tea/coffe making facilities.

● Truro
The Bay Tree, 28 Ferris Town, TR1 3JH ☎ 01872 240274 (Ann Talbot)
Map 204/821448
£30 S1 D1 T2 F1 ✕ nearby ₩(Truro) ⊗ ♿ ▤

● Zennor
SOUTH WEST COAST PATH

Trewey Farm, TR26 3DA ☎ 01736 796936 (Mrs N I Mann)
Map 203/454384
£30-£35 S1 D2 T1 F2 ✕ nearby Ⓓ Ⓑ 🐾 ♿

The Tinners Arms, TR26 3BY ☎ 01736 796927 (Richard Motley)
www.tinnersarms.com Map 203/454385
£40-£45 S2 D2 ✕ £12, 6:30pm Ⓥ Ⓓ Ⓑ ⊗ 🐾 ♿ !

DEVON

● Bideford
SOUTH WEST COAST PATH

The Mount, Northdown Road, EX39 3LP ☎ 01237 473748 (Andrew Laugharne)
www.themountbideford.co.uk Map 180/449269
£32.50-£36 S2 D2 T2 F2 ✕ nearby
Ⓓ Ⓑ ⊗ 🐾 ♿ ! ♿ Ⓕ ★★★★Ⓢ

● Braunton
SOUTH WEST COAST PATH

North Cottage, 14 North Street, EX33 1AJ ☎ 01271 812703 (Mrs Jean Watkins)
north_cottage@hotmail.com Map 180/485367
£25 S2 D2 T1 F1 ✕ nearby Ⓓ Ⓑ 🐾 ♿ ▤ Ⓜ

The Firs, Higher Park Road, EX33 2LG ☎ 01271 814358 (Alison Benning)
www.bennings.co.uk Map 180/498364
£30-£35 D1 T1 ✕ nearby Ⓓ Ⓑ ⊗ 🐾 ♿ ! ▤

The Brookfield, South Street, EX33 2AN ☎ 01271 812382 (Chris Brookes)
www.thebrookfield.co.uk Map 180/487362
£40 S2 D3 T3 Ⓑ ♿

The Laurels, 26 Church Street, EX33 2EL ☎ 01271 812872 (Thelma Crook)
Map 180/489369
£25 D1 T2 ✕ nearby Ⓓ ⊗ 🐾 ♿ ▤

● Brixham
SOUTH WEST COAST PATH

Nods Fold B&B, Mudstone Lane, TQ5 9EQ ☎ 01803 856138
(Linda & Doug McRae) www.nodsfold.co.uk Map 202/930555
£40-£45 D1 ✕ nearby Ⓓ Ⓑ ⊗ 🐾 ♿ ♿ !

● Clovelly
SOUTH WEST COAST PATH

The New House, EX39 5TQ ☎ 01237 431303 (Beryl Grant)
www.clovelly.co.uk Map 190/317248
£27.50 D2 T3 F2 ✕ £12, 7pm Ⓥ Ⓑ ⊗ 🐾 ★★Ⓜ

● Combe Martin
EXMOOR
SOUTH WEST COAST PATH

Mellstock House, Woodlands, EX34 0AR ☎ 01271 882592 (Paul Wade)
www.mellstockhouse.co.uk Map 180/575473
£36-£38 S1 D4 T1 F1 ✕ £14, 7pm
Ⓥ Ⓓ Ⓑ ⊗ 🐾 ♿ ▤ ! ★★★★

Blair Lodge Guest House
Moory Meadow, EX34 0DG ☎ 01271 882294 (Rachel Brown)
www.blairlodge.co.uk Map 180/578472
£27.50-£30 S1 D6 T2 F1 ✕ £10.50, 6:30pm
Ⓥ Ⓓ Ⓑ ⊗ 🐾 ♿ ▤ ! ★★★★Ⓦ

A very homely, licensed guesthouse on the South West Coast Path and on the edge of Exmoor. Superbly placed for endless walks with fantastic scenery, we offer excellent homemade meals, sea views and are just yards from the beach!

● Dartmouth
DARTMOOR
SOUTH WEST COAST PATH

Hill View House, 76 Victoria Road, TQ6 9DZ ☎ 01803 839372 (Suzanne White)
www.hillviewdartmouth.co.uk Map 202/872512
£38.50-£56 D3 T2 ✕ nearby ₩(Kingswear) Ⓓ Ⓑ ⊗ ♿ ★★★★Ⓖ

● Drewsteignton
DARTMOOR

The Old Inn
Drewsteignton, EX6 6QR ☎ 01647 281276 (Charlotte Hammick)
www.old-inn.co.uk Map 191/735908
£50-£70 D4 T1 ✕ £20, 7pm
Ⓥ Ⓓ Ⓑ ⊗ 🐾 ♿ !

The Old Inn is in the centre of Drewsteignton village, with the Two Moors Way passing its front door. Walkers welcome, luggage transportation and evening meals can be arranged if booked in advance. Look forward to seeing you, Charlotte.

● Exeter
Park View Hotel, 8 Howell Road, EX4 1LG ☎ 01392 271772 (Mr & Mrs Batho)
www.parkviewexeter.co.uk Map 192/917933
£28-£45 S1 D7 T3 F2 ✕ nearby ₩(Exeter Central)
Ⓓ Ⓑ ⊗ 🐾 ♿ ★★★

The Old Mill, Mill Lane, Alphington, EX2 8SG
☎ 01392 259977 (Lesley Marchant)
www.smoothhound.co.uk/hotels/oldmillg.html Map 192/915903
£18-£19 S1 D1 T1 F2 ✕ nearby ⁂(Exeter St Davids) 🅳 ⊗ ♿ 🚻

● Exmouth
SOUTH WEST COAST PATH

Sholton Guest House, 29 Morton Road, EX8 1BA ☎ 01395 277318
(Ann Jones) bobbyann@xln.co.uk Map 192/999807
✕ 5pm ⁂(Exmouth) 🅳 🅱 ⊗

● Hartland
SOUTH WEST COAST PATH

West Titchberry Farm, Hartland Point, EX39 6AU
☎ 01237 441287 (Yvonne Heard)
£25-£30 D1 T1 F1 ✕ £12, 6:30pm
🆅 🅳 🅱 ⊗ 🐾 ♿ 🚗 ‼

Elmscott Farm
EX39 6ES ☎ 01237 441276 (Mrs Thirza Goaman)
john.goa@virgin.net Map 190/231215
£28-£30 D1 T1 F1 ✕ £12, 6pm
🆅 🅳 🅱 ⊗ 🐾 ♿ 🚗 ‼ ★★★★

Elmscott is a working farm on the beautiful South West Coast Path. The farmhouse offers spacious accommodation with every comfort for guests. Ideal for walking holidays, with local pubs and tourist attractions nearby. Sign-posted from A39 approximately four miles.

Gawlish Farm
EX39 6AT ☎ 01237 441320 (Jill George)
Map 190/256263
£30-£48 D2 T2 ✕ £14, 6:30pm
🆅 🅳 🅱 ⊗ 🐾 ♿ 🚗 ‼ ★★★★

A charming farmhouse set in idyllic countryside only a stroll away from the coastal path. Traditional homecooked evening meals are available. Bedrooms in the style of Laura Ashley and Jane Churchill await you.

● Hillhead
SOUTH WEST COAST PATH

Raddicombe Lodge
Kingswear Road, TQ5 0EX ☎ 01803 882125 (Kay Sowerby)
www.raddicombelodge.co.uk Map 202/905539
£24-£32 S1 D4 T2 F2 ✕ £15, 5pm
🆅 🅳 🅱 ⊗ 🐾 ♿ ‼ 🏕

Luxury 4 star with all en-suite rooms. Midway between Kingswear & Brixham. Close to South West Coast Path and River Dart Trail. Sea and country views. Relaxing garden and sitting room, comfortable dining room. Drying room for kit and boots.

● Holsworthy

Leworthy Farmhouse
Pyworthy, EX22 6SJ ☎ 01409 259469 (Mrs Pat Jennings)
www.leworthyfarmhouse.co.uk Map 190/322012
£40 D4 T2 F1 ✕ nearby
🅳 🅱 ⊗ 🐾 ♿ 🚗 ‼ ★★★★⑤

Charming Georgian farmhouse in idyllic backwater. Delightful en-suite rooms, fresh milk, fresh flowers, pretty china. Peaceful lounge with books, ticking clocks, comfy old sofas, Chinese carpets. Scrumptious breakfasts: porridge, kippers, haddock, free-range eggs, local bacon. Warm welcome assured.

● Hope Cove
SOUTH WEST COAST PATH

The Cottage Hotel
TQ7 3HJ ☎ 01548 561555
www.hopecove.com Map 202/676401
£39-£76 S5 D7 T18 F5 ✕ £17.95, 7:30pm
🆅 🅳 🅱 🐾 ♿ 🚗 ★★⑤

Hotel enjoys a magnificent position in this pretty, secluded fishing village. By heritage coastline and National Trust Land. Ideally situated for walks. Log fire in winter. Drying facilities. Group rates available. Friendly and efficent service. Dinner included in above tariff.

● Ilfracombe
SOUTH WEST COAST PATH

The Woodlands, Torrs Park, EX34 8AZ ☎ 01271 863098 (Mike Lurcock)
www.woodlandsdevon.com Map 180/511472
£30-£40 S4 D6 T2 F1 ✕ nearby 🅳 🅱 ⊗ 🐾 ♿ ‼ 🏕 ★★★⑤

Lyncott House, 56 St Brannock's Road, EX34 8EQ ☎ 01271 862425
(John & Carol Pearson) www.lyncotthouse.co.uk Map 180/515468
£35-£45 D3 T2 ✕ £15, 5pm 🆅 🅳 🅱 ⊗ 🐾 ♿ ★★★★

Wellbeing Coastal Retreat, Torrs Park, Ilfracombe, EX34 8AZ ☎ 01271 863663
or 07834 043965 (Susan David) wellbeingbandb.com Map 180/511472
£35-£45 D2 T1 F1 ✕ nearby 🅳 🅱 🐾 ♿ 🚗 ‼ ★★★★⑤ Ⓦ

Coastal Fringes Guest House, 76 St Brannocks Road, EX34 8EQ
☎ 01271 865096 (David & Marianna Holdsworth)
www.coastalfringes.com Map 180/515468
£25-£28 D2 🅱 ⊗ ♿

Marine Court
Hillsborough Road, EX34 9QQ ☎ 01271 862920 (Helen Golinski)
www.marinecourthoteldevon.co.uk Map 180/528473
£27.50-£32.50 S1 D4 T1 F2
🅱 ⊗ 🐾 ♿ 🚗 ‼ 🏕

Marine Court is a four-star, AA-accredited, family-run guest house situated in a pleasant position just off the South West Coast Path and in easy walking distance of the picturesque harbour. All rooms en-suite. Parking. Sea Views. Fully licensed.

● Ivybridge

DARTMOOR
TWO MOORS WAY

Hillhead Farm, Ugborough, PL21 0HQ ☎ 01752 892674 (Mrs Jane Johns)
www.hillhead-farm.co.uk Map 202/674564
£35 D2 T1 ✕ nearby Ⓓ Ⓑ ⊛ 🍴🛏🚗!🛁 ★★★★Ⓢ

● Kingsbridge

SOUTH WEST COAST PATH

Ashleigh House, Ashleigh Road, TQ7 1HB ☎ 01548 852893
(Sue & Richard Agar) www.ashleigh-house.co.uk Map 202/730439
£36.50-£40 D5 T1 F2 ✕ nearby Ⓓ Ⓑ ⊛ 🍴🛏🚗!🛁 ★★★Ⓦ

Keynedon Barton Bed and Breakfast, Keynedon Barton, Sherford, TQ7 2AS
☎ 01548 531124 (Rosemary Heath)
www.kingsbridge-holiday-cottage.co.uk Map 202/775433
£26-£29.50 D2 T1 ✕ nearby Ⓓ ⊛ 🍴🛏🚗🛁

● Knowstone

TWO MOORS WAY

West Bowden Farm, EX36 4RP ☎ 01398 341224 (Mrs J Bray)
www.westbowden.ukf.net Map 181/833224
£27-£32 S2 D5 T2 F2 ✕ £12, 6:30pm
Ⓥ Ⓓ Ⓑ ⊛ 🍴🛏🚗!🛁🐾 ★★★★

Gossip Cottage, EX36 4RY ☎ 01398 341114 (Elizabeth Todd)
tim.todd@virgin.net Map 181/826230
£25 T1 ✕ nearby Ⓑ 🍴🛏🚗!🛁

● Lynmouth

EXMOOR
SOUTH WEST COAST PATH & TWO MOORS WAY

Tregonwell & The Olde Sea-Captain's House
1 Tors Road, EX35 6ET ☎ 01598 753369 (Mr & Mrs C & J Parker)
www.smoothhound.co.uk/hotels/tregonwl.html Map 180/727494
£28-£40 S1 D7 T1 ✕ nearby
Ⓓ Ⓑ ⊛ 🍴🛏🚗!🛁

"England's B&B of the Year" ('04). Warm welcome guaranteed at the best place for Exmoor ramblers. Elegant Victorian riverside guesthouse snuggled in wooded valleys, waterfalls, England's highest clifftops and most enchanting harbour. Garaged parking. Group discounts. Four flags (DTT).

Glenville House
2 Tors Road, EX35 6ET ☎ 01598 752202 (Tricia & Alan Francis)
www.glenvillelynmouth.co.uk Map 180/727494
£28-£30 S1 D4 T1 ✕ nearby
Ⓓ Ⓑ ⊛ 🍴🛏!★★★★Ⓦ

Elegant Victorian house in idyllic riverside setting. Lovely licensed B&B. Tastefully decorated bedrooms. Picturesque harbour and village. Dramatic Exmoor scenery and spectacular valley & coastal walks. Peaceful, tranquil, romantic – a very special place.

Rockvale Hotel, Hollerday Drive, Lee Road, EX356HQ ☎ 01598 752279
(Alwyn Tasker) www.rockvalehotel.co.uk Map 180/718495
£27-£29 S2 D7 T2 F2 ✕ £19, 7pm
Ⓥ Ⓓ Ⓑ ⊛ 🍴🛏 ★★★

The Bath Hotel
EX35 6EL ☎ 01598 752238 (Mrs S L Hobbs)
www.bathhotellynmouth.co.uk Map 180/723496
£39 S1 D10 T7 F4 ✕ £19, 7pm
Ⓥ Ⓓ Ⓑ ⊛ 🍴🛏!🛁 ★★

The Bath Hotel is perfectly situated in the heart of Lynmouth close to the harbour. After completing one of the many enjoyable walks in the area you can return to the hotel and stroll around our beautiful village.

River Lyn View
26 Watersmeet Road, EX35 6EP
☎ 01598 753501 (Carol Sheppard)
www.riverlynview.com Map 180/725493
£35 D3 T1 ✕ nearby Ⓓ Ⓑ ⊛ 🍴🛏🚗!🛁 ★★★

River Lyn View offers comfortable B&B. Rooms are en-suite and overlook the East Lyn River on the edge of Exmoor near Lynmouth's picturesque harbour with its spectacular coastal views. Ideal for walking holidays. Major credit cards accepted. Email: riverlynview@aol.com

● Lynton

EXMOOR
SOUTH WEST COAST PATH & TWO MOORS WAY

The Denes
15 Longmead, EX35 6DQ ☎ 01598 753573 (John McGowan)
www.thedenes.com Map 180/715495
£23-£27.50 D3 T2 F2 ✕ £16, 7pm
Ⓥ Ⓓ Ⓑ ⊛ 🍴🛏🚗!★★★★Ⓢ

Glorious place. Good food. Great value. An ideal base for exploring Exmoor or stopover for SW Coast Path trekkers. Drying facilities. Car parking. Licensed. Evening meals. En-suite rooms available. From £23-£27.50pppn. Open all year. Major credit cards accepted.

Chough's Nest Hotel
North Walk, EX35 6HJ ☎ 01598 753 315 (John Hodges)
www.choughsnesthotel.co.uk Map 180/718497
£42 S2 D4 T4 F1
Ⓓ Ⓑ ⊛ 🍴🛏🚗!★★

An idyllic cliff-top retreat, right in the heart of Exmoor. Our well-appointed bedrooms have their own individual charm and character, along with captivating sea and coastal views. All rooms are en-suite with TV, clock-radio, hospitality tray and big fluffy towels.

For an explanation of the symbols and abbreviations used in this guide, see the Key on the fold-out flap at the back

Lorna Doone House
4 Tors Road, EX35 6ET ☎ 01598 753354 (Mrs Sharon Hobbs)
www.lornadoonehouse.co.uk Map 180/726493
£45 D2 T2 F2
D B ⊗ 🛪 🛆 🏃 🔥

Lorna Doone House is situated by the River Lyn at the start of the walk to Watersmeet. At Lorna Doone you will find friendly service and extra touches to make your stay as enjoyable as possible. Ideal for small groups.

North Walk House
North Walk, EX35 6HJ ☎ 01598 753372 (Anne & Kelvin Jacobs)
www.northwalkhouse.co.uk Map 180/718497
£40 S1 D4 T1
D B ⊗ 🛪 🛆 🔥 🚗 ! ★★★★ Ⓜ

Luxury guest accommodation situated on Exmoor. En-suite facilities with fantastic sea views, very comfortable beds and Egyptian cotton linen and digital television, parking, organic food, packed lunches, self-guided walking holidays, drying facilities, central heating, log fires, comfortable lounge, internet connection.

Highcliffe House
Sinai Hill, EX35 6AR ☎ 01598 752235 (Mike & Karen Orchard)
www.highcliffehouse.co.uk Map 180/719492
£65-£75 D6 T1 ✕ nearby
D B ⊗ 🛆 ! ★★★★★Ⓢ

Fantastic house situated 600ft above the rugged Exmoor coastline close to the SW Coastal Path with stunning views across the Bristol Channel to Wales. Fantastic walking on the moor from coastal paths to wooded valleys and waterfalls.

● Manaton
DARTMOOR
TWO MOORS WAY

Hazelcott B&B, TQ13 9UY ☎ 01647 221521 (Nigel Fisher)
www.dartmoordays.com Map 191/751822
✕ £17.50 V D B ⊗ 🛪 🛆 ! 🔥

Wingstone Farm, TQ13 9UL ☎ 01647 221215 (Juliette Rich)
www.wingstonefarm.co.uk Map 191/747811
£25-£30 S1 D2 ✕ nearby D ⊗ 🛪 🛆 ! 🔥

LOST? NEED A MAP?
Why not use the Ramblers Map Library?
A complete range of Ordnance Survey Explorer and Landranger maps for members of the Ramblers, now available in paper and waterproof editions.

If you are not a member, visit:
www.ramblers.org.uk/join

● Molland
EXMOOR
TWO MOORS WAY

West Lee Farm
Molland, EX36 3NJ ☎ 01398 341751 (Maggi Woodward)
www.westleefarm.co.uk Map 181/816268
£30-£35 D1 T1 ✕ £12, 7pm
D B ⊗ 🛪 🛆 🚗 ! 🔥 ★★★★

A working farm on the southern edge of Exmoor on the Molland Estate.

An ideal base for walking and relaxing.

Warm, friendly atmosphere with large, comfortable bedrooms, each with en-suite and colour TV, own lounge and dining room. Kennels/stabling facilities.

● Moretonhampstead
DARTMOOR
TWO MOORS WAY

Great Slon Combe Farm, TQ13 8QF ☎ 01647 440595 (Mrs Trudie Merchant)
www.greatsloncombefarm.co.uk Map 191/736862
£32-£35 D2 T1 ✕ nearby D B ⊗ 🛪 🛆 🚗 ! 🔥 ★★★★Ⓢ

Cookshayes Country Guest House
33 Court Street, TQ13 8LG ☎ 01647 440374 (Tracy Williams)
www.cookshayes.co.uk Map 191/751860
£25-£27.50 S1 D5 T3 F1 ✕ £16, 5pm
V D B ⊗ 🛪 🛆 🔥

Cookshayes stands in a half-acre of well-tended gardens, with views of the surrounding moors and countryside. There is parking within the grounds and we hope our guests will enjoy the gardens when they feel the need to relax.

● Newton Abbot
Branscombe House B&B, 48 Highweek Village, TQ12 1QQ ☎ 01626 356752
(Miles Opie) www.branscombe-house.co.uk Map 191/845721
✕ 🚶(Newton Abbot) D B ⊗ 🚗 !

● Newton Poppleford
SOUTH WEST COAST PATH

Newland House, 35 Temple Street, EX10 9BA ☎ 07855953739 (David Leach)
sheshe@fsmail.net Map 192/126881
£20-£28 S1 D2 T2 F1 ✕ nearby D B ⊗ 🛪 🛆 🚗 !

● North Bovey
DARTMOOR
TWO MOORS WAY

Lower Hookner Barn, TQ13 8RS ☎ 01647 221282 (Jenny Pryce-Davies)
lowerhookner@hotmail.com Map 191/714825
£27-£29 S1 D1 T1 ✕ £11, 7:30pm
V D B ⊗ 🛪 🛆 🚗 ! 🔥 ᴴ

● Okehampton
DARTMOOR

Northlake, Stockley, EX20 1QH ☎ 01837 53100 (Pam Jeffrey)
www.northlakedevon.co.uk Map 191/610953
£22.50-£25 S1 D1 T1 D B ⊗ 🛪 🛆 🔥 ! 🔥

SOUTH WEST

The Barton
Belstone, EX20 1RA ☎ 01837 840891 (Lucinda Walsh)
thebarton-dartmoor.co.uk　Map 191/619935
£30-£40　D2 T1 ✕ nearby
🄳 🄱 ⊗ 🐾 👤 🛁 🏠

Located in delightful Belstone, within the Dartmoor National Park. Ideally situated for walking as Dartmoor really is on your doorstep, look out for ponies and sheep as you go! After a day on the moor, ease away those aches and pains with powerful showers, a deep bath and comfortable beds in quality surroundings. Good traditional foods and ales can be found at the popular village pub opposite.

● Ottery St Mary
Fluxton Farm, EX11 1RJ ☎ 01404 812818 (Mrs E A Forth)
www.fluxtonfarm.co.uk　Map 192/086934
£25-£27.50　S2 T3 ✕ nearby 🄳 🄱 ⊗ 🛁 🏠 ★★

● Paignton
SOUTH WEST COAST PATH
Culverden Guest House, 4 Colin Road, TQ3 2NR ☎ 01803 559786
(Mr & Mrs Mortlock) www.culverdenhotel.co.uk　Map 202/893614
£21-£28　S2 D3 T1 F2 ✕ nearby ⋘(Paignton)
🄱 ⊗ 🐾 👤 🛁 🏠 ★★★Ⓦ

Harbour Lodge Guest House, 4 Cleveland Road, TQ4 6EN ☎ 01803 556932
(Peter Lloyd)　www.harbourlodge.co.uk　Map 202/893601
£24-£32　D3 T1 F1 ⋘(Paignton) 🄱 ⊗ 🐾 👤 ★★★

● Plymouth
SOUTH WEST COAST PATH
The Caledonia, 27 Athenaeum Street, The Hoe, PL1 2RQ ☎ 01752 229052
(David & Karen Marshall) www.thecaledonia.co.uk　Map 201/474541
£25-£30　S1 D5 T4 F1 ⋘(Plymouth) 🄱 ⊗ 🐾 👤 🛁 🄵 ★★★★

● Seaton
SOUTH WEST COAST PATH
Beach End, 8 Trevelyan Road, EX12 2NL ☎ 01297 23388 (Hilary Bevis)
Map 192/251899
£45-£47.50　D2 T1 ✕ nearby 🄳 🄱 ⊗ 👤 ! ★★★★Ⓢ Ⓜ

● Shirwell
The Spinney Guest House, EX31 4JR ☎ 01271 850282 (Mrs Janet Pelling)
www.thespinneyshirwell.co.uk　Map 180/590370
✕ £16　🅅 🄳 🄱 ⊗ 🏠 Ⓢ

● Sidmouth
SOUTH WEST COAST PATH
Ryton Guest House, 52-54 Winslade Road, EX10 9EX ☎ 01395 513981
(Mrs G Bradnam)　www.ryton-guest-house.co.uk　Map 192/126885
£25-£35　S3 D1 T2 F4 ✕ nearby 🄳 🄱 ⊗ 🐾 👤 ! 🏠 ★★★

● Slapton
SOUTH WEST COAST PATH
Old Walls, TQ7 2QN ☎ 01548 580516 (V J Mercer)
Map 202/823449
£26-£30　S1 D1 T1 F1 ✕ nearby
🄳 🄱 ⊗ 🐾 👤 🚗 ! 🏠 Ⓜ

● Teignmouth
SOUTH WEST COAST PATH
Brunswick House, 5 Brunswick Street, TQ14 8AE
☎ 01626 774102 (Margrethe & Pete Hockings)
margrethehockings@hotmail.com　Map 192/941727
£25-£30　S1 D4 T3 F1 ✕ nearby ⋘(Teignmouth)
🄳 🄱 ⊗ 🐾 👤 🏠

● Thorverton

Thorverton Arms
Thorverton, EX5 5NS ☎ 01392 860205 (Melissa Pearse)
www.thethorvertonarms.co.uk　Map 192/925020
£30-£32.50　S1 D3 T1 F1
⊗ 🐾 🚗 ! 👤 🛁 👤 ★★★

16th-century coaching inn located in the picturesque village of Thorverton (seven miles from Exeter) in Devon. We are in the heart of the English countryside on the Exe Valley Way and on the Land's End to John O'Groats route.

● Torquay
SOUTH WEST COAST PATH

Mount Edgcombe
23 Avenue Road, TQ2 5LB ☎ 01803 292310 (Pam Cole)
www.mountedgcombe.co.uk　Map 202/905642
£40-£60　D5 T1 F4 ✕ £15, 6:30pm ⋘(Torquay)
🅅 🄳 🄱 ⊗ 🐾 👤 🚗 ! 🏠 👤 ★★★★Ⓦ

Pam and David, owners of the Mount Edgcombe, are keen walkers themselves and can provide perfect accommodation for a walking break in South Devon. We offer facilities for walking groups or individuals. Fully guided walking holidays or self guided breaks.

● West Buckland
MACMILLAN WAY WEST
Huxtable Farm, EX32 0SR ☎ 01598 760254 (Jackie & Antony Payne)
www.huxtablefarm.co.uk　Map 180/665308
£36-£45　D3 T1 F2 ✕ £25, 7pm
🅅 🄳 🄱 ⊗ 🐾 👤 🚗 ! ★★★★Ⓢ Ⓦ

● Woolacombe
SOUTH WEST COAST PATH
Clyst House, Rockfield Road, EX34 7DH ☎ 01271 870220 (Ann Braund)
Map 180/455441
£30　S1 D1 T1 ✕ nearby 🄳 ⊗ 👤

Lundy House Hotel
Chapel Hill, EX34 7DZ ☎ 01271 870372 (Tim Cole)
www.lundyhousehotel.co.uk Map 180/454447
£28-£45 D3 T1 F5 ✗ £15, 7pm
Ⓥ Ⓓ Ⓑ ☻ 🐾 ♿ 🚗 ! ♿ Ⓕ

Lundy House Hotel is set directly on the North Devon coastline, with views across to Lundy island. Terraced gardens onto the South West Coast Path. Home cooked food and big breakfasts. Dogs and dirty boots welcome.

DORSET

● Bere Regis
Vest Acres, West Street, DT11 9AT ☎ 01929 471293 (Mr & Mrs Jenkins)
www.westacres-bedandbreakfast.co.uk Map 194/854978
.30 D1 T1 ✗ nearby ☻ 🐾 ♿ 🚗 ! ♿ Ⓕ

● Bournemouth
SOUTH WEST COAST PATH

t Michaels Guest House, 42 St Michaels Road, Westcliff, BH2 5DY
☎ 01202 557386 (Mrs E Davies)
www.stmichaelsfriendlyguesthouse.co.uk Map 195/082910
.22-£25 S1 D2 T2 F1 ✗ £6, 6pm 🚍 (Bournemouth) Ⓥ Ⓓ ☻ 🐾 ♿ ♿

levonshire Guest House, 40 St Michaels Road, BH2 5DY
☎ 01202 291610 (Mrs K Ferns) Map 195/082910
.23-£27 S1 D3 T2 F1 ✗ nearby 🚍 (Bournemouth) Ⓓ ☻ 🐾 ♿ ♿

The Norfolk Royale Hotel
Richmond Hill, BH2 6EN ☎ 01723 374374 (Central Reservations)
www.norfolk-royale.co.uk Map 195/086913
£80-£129 S9 D38 T38 F3 ✗ £29.50, 7pm 🚍 (Bournemouth)
Ⓥ Ⓓ Ⓑ ☻ 🐾 ♿ 🚗 ! ★★★★

Perfectly positioned in the heart of Bournemouth and only a short walk through beautiful gardens to golden beaches, The Norfolk Royale Hotel makes an excellent choice for ramblers seeking to enjoy the many walks around Bournemouth's coastline and countryside.

● Bridport
SOUTH WEST COAST PATH & MONARCH'S WAY

Britmead House
154 West Bay Road, DT6 4EG ☎ 01308 422941 (A Hardy)
www.britmeadhouse.co.uk Map 193/465912
£40-£50 D4 T2 F2 ✗ nearby
Ⓓ Ⓑ ☻ ♿ 🚗 ! ♿ ★★★★

An elegant Edwardian house, situated within walking distance of West Bay harbour and the South West Coast Path, part of the World Heritage Site. We offer comfortable ensuite accommodation with many thoughtful extras. Parking, non-smoking. Dogs welcome by arrangement.

Eypes Mouth Country Hotel
Eype, DT6 6AL ☎ 01308 423300 (Kevin & Glenis French)
www.eypesmouthhotel.co.uk Map 193/448914
£55-£60 S2 D12 T3 F1 ✗ £24.50, 7pm
Ⓥ Ⓓ Ⓑ ☻ 🐾 ♿ 🚗 ! ♿ ★★

The hotel nestles between the clifftops and downland that form the Heritage Coastline. Close to SW Coast Path, the hotel enjoys stunning seaviews, peace and tranquility, superb food using the best local produce and offers a high standard of hospitality.

Fleet Cottage, 152 West Bay Road, DT6 4AZ ☎ 01308 458698
(Janice Warburton) www.fleetcottage.co.uk Map 193/465915
£35-£40 S2 D2 T2 F2 Ⓓ Ⓑ 🐾 ♿ 🚗 ♿

Green Lane House, Dorchester Road, DT6 4LH ☎ 01308 422619
(Christine Prideaux) greenlanehouse@aol.com Map 193/483932
£30 S1 D1 T1 F1 ✗ £12, 6pm Ⓥ Ⓓ Ⓑ ☻ 🐾 ♿ 🚗 ♿

Eypeleaze Bed & Breakfast, 117 West Bay Road, DT6 4EQ ☎ 01308 423363
(Ann Walker) www.eypeleaze.co.uk Map 193/467912
✗ nearby Ⓓ Ⓑ ☻ 🐾 ! ★★★★

Stonehaven, First Cliff Walk, West Bay, DT6 4HH ☎ 01308427035
(Christine Bourne) Map 193/458905
£28-£35 D1 T1 Ⓓ ☻ ♿

● Chideock
SOUTH WEST COAST PATH & MONARCH'S WAY

Rose Cottage, Main Street, DT6 6JQ ☎ 01297 489994 (Sue & Mick Kelson)
www.rosecottage-chideock.co.uk Map 193/423927
£40 D1 T1 ✗ nearby Ⓓ Ⓑ ☻ 🐾 ♿ ★★★★

Bay Tree House
Duck Street, DT6 6JW ☎ 01297 489336 (Jane James)
www.baytreechideock.co.uk Map 193/419929
£45 D1 T1 ✗ nearby
Ⓓ Ⓑ ☻ 🐾 ♿ ★★★★ Ⓢ

Bay Tree House is just a ten-minute walk from the Coast Path at Seatown. Both rooms have en-suite facilities and are extremely comfortable. There are three pubs and a hotel within walking distance for evening meals. Stunning views and walking.

● Dorchester
MACMILLAN WAY

Churchview Guest House
Winterbourne Abbas, DT2 9LS ☎ 01305 889296
www.churchview.co.uk Map 194/618905
£31-£37 SI D4 T3 FI
🄳 🄱 ⊗ 🐾👌🛇🚗❗🎒 ★★★★Ⓢ

Michael and Jane
Deller offer a
memorable stay
at beautiful 17c.
Churchview.

Character bedrooms with TV and hospitality trays, delicious breakfasts and
home cooked evening meals with relaxation provided by two comfortable
lounges and licensed bar.

The Guest House is also ideal for Groups wishing to explore dramatic West
Dorset. We can cater for up to 17 (and more by arrangement with local
B&Bs); Group discounts available.

● Gillingham
North Lodge, Wavering Lane West, SP8 5NH ☎ 01747 821215 (Janet Adams)
www.dorsetbreak.co.uk Map 183/792268
£30-£36 D2 TI ✖ nearby 🚍(Gillingham) 🄳 🄱 ⊗ 🐾👌🚗❗

● Ludwell
WESSEX RIDGEWAY

Cedar Lodge, 5 Dewey's Place, SP7 9LW ☎ 01747 829240 (Lorraine Dewey)
www.cedarlodge.org.uk Map 184/902227
£40 S3 D3 T3 FI 🄳 🄱 ⊗ 🐾👌🚗❗★★★Ⓦ

Birdbush Farm, SP7 9HH ☎ 01747 828252 (Mrs Ann Rossiter)
annrossiter@fsmail.net Map 184/913229
✖ 🄳 🄱 ⊗ 🐾🚗❗

● Lyme Regis
SOUTH WEST COAST PATH, WESSEX RIDGEWAY & MONARCH'S WAY

Lucerne, View Road, DT7 3AA ☎ 01297 443752 (Owen Keith Lovell)
lymeregis.com/lucerne Map 193/338923
£32-£36 SI D3 T2 🄳 🄱 ⊗ 👌🚗❗★★★★

Charnwood Guest House, 21 Woodmead Road, DT7 3AD ☎ 01297 445281
(Wayne & Ann Bradbury) www.lymeregisaccommodation.com Map 193/339924
£30-£45 SI D4 T2 🄱 ⊗ 👌 ★★★★Ⓜ

● Poole
SOUTH WEST COAST PATH

The Laurels, 60 Britannia Road, BH14 8BB ☎ 07837 737368 (Mrs North)
www.thelaurelsbandb.freeservers.com Map 195/033913
£35 SI D2 TI FI ✖ nearby 🚍(Parkstone) 🄳 🄱 ⊗ 👌

● Portesham
SOUTH WEST COAST PATH

Bridge House, 13 Frys Close, DT3 4LQ ☎ 01305 871685 (Thea Alexander)
www.bridgehousebandb.co.uk Map 194/602858
£29-£30 D2 ✖ nearby 🄳 🄱 ⊗ 👌🚗❗★★★★

● Puddletown
Zoar House, DT2 8SR ☎ 01305 848498 (Mrs J Stephens)
Map 194/762942
£22-£25 SI DI TI FI ✖ nearby 🄳 🄱 ⊗ 🐾👌🎒

● Shaftesbury

Cat 'n Mouse Cottage
39 The Street, SP7 9PE ☎ 01747 855389 (Connie Mercer)
Map 183/850253
£35 D2 ✖ nearby 🚍(Gillingham, Dorset)
🄳 🄱 ⊗ 🐾👌🚗❗🎒

Welcoming, 300-year-old country home.
Breakfast includes homemade and local
produce. Comfortable antique beds.
Luxurious fluffy towels, lashings of hot water
for relaxing baths after countryside walks.
Maps and local walk information available.
Friendly dogs free! Welcome cream tea.

● Sherborne
MACMILLAN WAY

Honeycombe View, Lower Clatcombe, DT9 4RH ☎ 01935 814644 (Mrs D Bower)
honeycombower@talktalk.net Map 183/637179
£30 T2 ✖ nearby 🚍(Sherborne) 🄳 🄱 ⊗ 👌🚗 ★★★

● Shillingstone
WESSEX RIDGEWAY

Pennhills Farm, Sandy Lane, Off Lanchards Lane, DT11 0TF ☎ 01258 860491
(Mrs Rosemary Watts) Map 194/819102
£26 SI DI TI FI 🄳 🄱 ⊗ 🐾👌🚗❗🎒👌 ★★★

● Stoborough
Ashcroft, 64 Furzebrook Road, BH20 5AX ☎ 01929 552392 (Eileen Cake)
www.ashcroft-bb.co.uk Map 195/928850
£27-£35 DI TI FI ✖ nearby 🚍(Wareham)
🄳 🄱 ⊗ 🐾👌🚗 ★★★★

● Swanage
SOUTH WEST COAST PATH

Hermitage Guesthouse, 1 Manor Road, BH19 2BH ☎ 01929 423014
(Susan Pickering) www.hermitage-online.co.uk Map 195/031785
£25-£26 D2 TI F4 ✖ nearby 🄳 ⊗ 👌🎒 Ⓜ

The Limes
48 Park Road, BH19 2AE ☎ 01929 422664
www.limeshotel.com Map 195/033783
£32.50-£37.50 S3 D2 T4 F3 ✖ nearby
🄳 🄱 ⊗ 👌🚗❗🎒 ★★★

Swanage – just off coast path.
Close to town and beach.
Wonderful walks.
Car park, laundry facilities.
Open all year for B&B.
Families, groups and pets welcome.
Email: info@limeshotel.net

Sandhaven, 5 Ulwell Rd, BH19 1LE ☎ 01929 422322 (Janet Foran)
www.sandhaven-guest-house.co.uk Map 195/030798
£30-£35 SI D3 TI F3 ✖ nearby
🄳 🄱 ⊗ 🐾👌🎒 ★★★

Sandringham Hotel, 20 Durlston Rd, BH19 2HX ☎ 01929 423076
(Mr & Mrs T Silk) www.smoothhound.co.uk/hotels/sandringham.html
Map 195/033782 🅱 ⛟🐾🌿

Beachway Private Hotel, 19 Ulwell Road, BH19 1LF ☎ 01929 423077
(Mrs Helen Holt) beachway.19ulwellroad@fsmail.net Map 195/030799
£20-£28 S1 D3 T1 F2 ✗ nearby 🅳 🅱 🐾👶🌿

The Oxford, 3-5 Park Road, BH19 2AA ☎ 01929 422247 (Robin Creed)
www.theoxfordswanage.co.uk Map 195/032784
£35-£60 S2 D4 T2 F4 ✗ nearby 🅱 ⊗ 🐾👶 ★★★

● Sydling St Nicholas
WESSEX RIDGEWAY
City Cottage, DT2 9NX ☎ 01300 341300 (Mrs J Wareham)
Map 194/632994
£21 S1 D1 ✗ nearby 🅳 🐾

Magiston Farm, DT2 9NR ☎ 01300 320295 (Mrs Barraclough)
Map 194/637967
£20 S2 D1 T2 ✗ £12, 7pm 🆅 🅳 🅱 🐾👶🌿 ★★★

● Upwey
Friar Barn, DT3 4EN ☎ 01304 816071 (Jackie Faulkner)
www.friarbarn.co.uk Map 194/659855
£30 S1 D1 T1 F2 ✗ nearby 🚶(Upwey) 🅳 ⊗ 🐾👶🚗!

● Verwood
NEW FOREST
Squirrels Oak, 2 Penrith Close, BH31 6XE ☎ 01202 821397 (Susan Lawes)
www.squirrelsoak.co.uk Map 195/084082
£30 S2 D2 ✗ nearby 🅳 🅱 🐾👶!🌿

● Wareham
Hyde Cottage, Furzebrooke Rd, Stoborough, BH20 5AX ☎ 01929 553344
(D & J Bryer) www.hydecottage.com Map 195/927853
£27-£35 S1 D1 T1 F1 ✗ £12, 7pm 🚶(Wareham)
🆅 🅳 🅱 ⊗ 🐾👶🚗! ★★★★

● Weymouth
SOUTH WEST COAST PATH
Channel View Guest House, 10 Brunswick Terrace, DT4 7RW ☎ 01305 782527
(Martin & Alison Weller) www.channelviewweymouth.co.uk Map 194/682799
✗ 🚶(Weymouth) 🅳 🅱 ⊗!

Riviera Hotel
Bowleaze Cove, DT3 6PR ☎ 01305 836600 (Liz Walden)
www.rivierahotelweymouth.co.uk Map 194/705819
£30-£45 S7 D33 T34 F39 ✗ £10.95, 6pm 🚶(Weymouth)
🆅 🅱 ⊗ 🐾👶!👶 🅵

The Riviera Hotel is a well-known Dorset landmark that has welcomed
holidaymakers to its stunning location for over 70 years.

This chalet style hotel is set just above Bowleaze Cove on the Dorset Coast
Path and is just two-and-a-half miles from Weymouth.

Cunard Guest House, 45/46 Lennox Street, DT4 7HB ☎ 01305 771546
(Mr & Mrs Harris) www.cunardguesthouse.co.uk Map 194/681798
£25-£30 S1 D5 T1 F1 ✗ nearby 🚶(Weymouth)
🅳 🅱 ⊗ 🐾👶!★★★★Ⓜ

Greenwood Guest House, 1 Holland Rd, DT4 0AL ☎ 01305 775626
(Sharon Arnold) www.greenwoodguesthouse.co.uk Map 194/674793
✗ 🚶(Weymouth) 🅳 🅱 ⊗ 🐾🚗!🌿

GLOUCESTERSHIRE

SOUTH WEST

● Aust
The Old Piggery, Aust Road, BS35 4HG ☎ 07967 146743 (Lorna Fussell)
theoldpiggery@yahoo.co.uk Map 172/558870
£30-£40 D2 T1 🚶(Severn Beach) 🅳 🅱 ⊗ 🐾👶🚗!

● Blakeney
The Cock Inn, Nibley Hill, GL15 4DB ☎ 01594 510239 (Andy Jeffs)
www.thecockinnblakeney.co.uk Map 162/665065
£30 S1 D3 T2 F1 ✗ £9.50, 6pm 🚶(Lydney) 🆅 🅳 🅱 ⊗ 🐾👶

● Brookthorpe
COTSWOLD WAY

Brookthorpe Lodge
Stroud Road, GL4 0UQ ☎ 01452 812645 (Robert & Diana Bailey)
www.brookthorpelodge.demon.co.uk Map 162/835128
£30-£32.50 S3 D3 T3 F1 ✗ nearby
🅳 🅱 ⊗ 🐾👶🚗!♿★★★

Elegant Georgian country guest house,
situated at the foot of the Cotswold
escarpment. Family-run, excellent
breakfasts, rooms with nice views. Near
Cotswold Way, ideal for Gloucester,
Cheltenham, Stratford-upon-Avon and
Bath. Private off-road parking.

● Cam
COTSWOLD WAY

Foresters
31 Chapel Street, GL11 5NX ☎ 01453 549996 (Mrs Victoria Jennings)
foresters@freeuk.com Map 162/750002
£32-£40 D2 T2 F1 ✗ £12, 7:30pm 🚶(Cam & Dursley)
🆅 🅳 🅱 🐾👶🌿★★★★

18th-century cosy former village inn with
walled garden. Spacious en-suite beamed
bedrooms, four-poster, visitor lounge. Excellent
walking on our doorstep and a wealth of
attractions, villages, cities. Westonbirt,
Slimbridge, Bath, Berkeley Castle nearby.
Junction 13/14 M5. 10% off seven nights.

WALKS FROM
YOUR DOORSTEP!
Check out our new City Walks section and see a side
of your town that you never knew existed.
Pages 47–65.

● Charlton Kings
COTSWOLD WAY

22 Ledmore Road, GL53 8RA ☎ 01242 526957 (Geraldine White)
www.cotswoldstudio.co.uk Map 163/967207
£30 SI DI TI ✗ nearby ⋙(Cheltenham) ⅅ Ⓑ ⊗ 🍳🛏🐾🚗❗Ⓜ

Charlton Kings Hotel
London Road, GL52 6UU ☎ 01242 231061
www.charltonkingshotel.co.uk Map 163/977201
£65 S2 D5 T5 FI ✗ £14, 7pm
Ⓥ ⅅ Ⓑ ⊗ 🍳🛏🐾⚓ ★★★

Ideally situated on edge of town, half-a-mile from Cotswold Way. Most rooms have views of the Cotswold Hills.
Set in an acre of gardens, ample parking.
Restaurant open every night.
Completely non-smoking. Wifi available.
Conde Nast Johansens Recommended. enquiries@charltonkingshotel.co.uk

● Chedworth
MONARCH'S WAY & MACMILLAN WAY

The Vicarage, GL54 4AA ☎ 01285 720392 (George & Pattie Mitchell)
canongeorgemitchell@btinternet.com Map 163/052118
£26-£30 SI TI ✗ nearby ⅅ Ⓑ ⊗ 🍳🛏🚗 ★★★

● Cheltenham
COTSWOLD WAY

Tickford Cottage, 20 Moorend Crescent, GL53 0EL ☎ 01242 572290
(Annie Grocott) anniegrocott@waitrose.com Map 163/944205
£25 TI ✗ nearby ⋙(Cheltenham) ⅅ Ⓑ ⊗ 🍳🛏Ⓜ

● Chipping Campden
COTSWOLD WAY & HEART OF ENGLAND WAY

Weston Park Farm, Dovers Hill, GL55 6UW ☎ 01386 840835
(Mrs J Whitehouse) www.cotswoldcottages.uk.com
£45 DI FI ✗ nearby ⅅ Ⓑ ⊗ 🍳🛏🚗❗ ★★★

● Chipping Sodbury
MONARCH'S WAY & COTSWOLD WAY

The Moda Hotel, I High Street, BS37 6BA ☎ 01454 312135 (Jo Macarthur)
www.modahotel.com Map 172/726822
£58.50-£98 S4 D5 FI ✗ nearby ⋙(Yate)
ⅅ Ⓑ ⊗ 🍳🛏🐾 ★★★★

● Cirencester
MONARCH'S WAY

Royal Agricultural College
GL7 6JS ☎ 01285 652531 (Conference Department)
www.rac.ac.uk/ Map 163/004011
✗ £19, 5pm
Ⓥ ⅅ Ⓑ 🐾 ★★★

Beautiful college venue, set in the spectacular Cotswold countryside. Accommodation available for small groups all year round, and for larger groups during the college vacation period. Catering staff to service all culinary needs: breakfast, brunch, dinner, and everything in between.

● Clearwell
WYE VALLEY WALK

Tudor Farmhouse Hotel, High Street, GL16 8JS ☎ 01594 833046 (Hari Fell)
www.tudorfarmhousehotel.co.uk Map 162/573080
ⅅ Ⓑ 🍳🛏❗🐾 ★★★

● Cold Ashton
COTSWOLD WAY

Toghill House Farm, BS30 5RT ☎ 01225 891261 (D Bishop)
www.toghillhousefarm.co.uk Map 172/731724
£48-£52 D5 T3 F3 ⅅ Ⓑ ⊗ 🍳🛏🐾🚶 ★★★★

● Coleford
OFFA'S DYKE & WYE VALLEY WALK

Bells Hotel, Lords Hill, GL16 8BE ☎ 01594 832583 (Felicity Jones)
www.bells-hotel.co.uk Map 162/579105
£35-£45 S6 D2 T30 FI4 ✗ £7.50, 6pm Ⓥ ⅅ Ⓑ ⊗ 🍳🛏🐾❗🐾🚶 Ⓕ

● English Bicknor
WYE VALLEY WALK

Dryslade Farm, GL16 7PA ☎ 01594 860259 (Mrs Daphne Gwilliam)
www.drysladefarm.co.uk Map 162/579149
£27-£32 D2 TI ⅅ Ⓑ ⊗ 🍳🛏🚗❗🐾

● Fairford
THAMES PATH

Kempsford Manor, GL7 4EQ ☎ 01285 810131
www.kempsfordmanor.co.uk Map 163/158969
£35-£40 S2 D2 FI ✗ £17.50, 7:30pm Ⓥ ⅅ Ⓑ ⊗ 🍳🛏🚗🐾 ★★★

● King's Stanley
COTSWOLD WAY

Old Chapel House, Broad Street, GL10 3PN ☎ 01453 826289 (Jean Hanna)
www.geocities.com/bandbinuk Map 162/813033
£25 S2 DI TI FI ✗ £6, 6:30pm ⋙(Stonehouse) Ⓥ ⅅ Ⓑ ⊗ 🍳🛏

Valley Views, 12 Orchard Close, Middleyard, GL10 3QA ☎ 01453 827458
(Mrs Pam White) www.valley-views.com Map 162/819032
£28-£36 D2 TI ✗ £7, 7pm ⋙(Stonehouse)
Ⓥ ⅅ Ⓑ 🍳🛏🚗❗ ★★★★Ⓦ

● Lechlade
THAMES PATH

Cambrai Lodge, Oak Street, GL7 3AY ☎ 01367 253173 (Mr John Titchener)
www.cambrailodgeguesthouse.co.uk Map 163/214998
£27.50 D3 T3 ✗ nearby ⅅ Ⓑ ⊗ 🍳🛏❗🐾 ★★★★

● Nibley
SEVERN WAY & WYE VALLEY WALK

Old Nibley Farmhouse B&B
Nibley Hill, GL15 4DB ☎ 01594 516770 (Marian Buckmaster)
www.oldnibleyfarmhouse.co.uk Map 162/667066
£25-£55 SI D2 T2 ⋙(Lydney)
ⅅ Ⓑ 🍳🛏🐾❗🐾 ★★★★Ⓦ

300-year-old former farmhouse now providing beautifully decorated and extremely comfortable accommodation for the discerning traveller. Breakfasts, from croissants and coffee to the full English. Large garden to relax in; ample off-road parking for six cars. Three lovely cats!

SOUTH WEST

● North Nibley
COTSWOLD WAY

Nibley House
North Nibley, GL11 6DL ☎ 01453 543108 (Diana A Eley)
www.nibleyhouse.co.uk Map 162/737958
£30 D2 T2 F1 ✕ 5pm
Ⓥ Ⓓ Ⓑ ⊛ 🐾 🛏 ⛽ ! 🔥

Relax... splendid views.
Relax... 2.5 acres of garden.
Relax... 400 years of history.
Relax... Hospitality.
Relax... where to stay on the Cotswold Way?
Relax... You've found it.

● Painswick
COTSWOLD WAY

Skyrack, The Highlands, GL6 6SL ☎ 01452 812029 (Wendy Hodgson)
wendyskyrack@hotmail.com Map 162/868105
£30 S1 D1 T1 ✕ nearby Ⓓ Ⓑ ⊛ 🐾 🛏 ⛽ ! 🔥 ★★★

Orchard House, 4 Court Orchard, GL6 6UU ☎ 01452 813150
(Mrs Barbara Harley) www.painswick.co.uk Map 162/866095
£25-£30 D1 T1 ✕ nearby Ⓑ ⊛ 🛏 ⛽ ! Ⓜ

Cardynham House, The Cross, GL6 6XX ☎ 01452 814006 (John Paterson)
www.cardynham.co.uk Map 162/867096
£50-£59 D6 T2 F1 ✕ £18, 6:30pm Ⓥ Ⓑ ⊛ 🛏 ★★★★

Wren's Nest, 3 Painswick Heights, Yokehouse Lane, GL6 7QS ☎ 01452 812347
(Patricia Moroney) bsimplybetter@tiscali.co.uk Map 162/873086
£30-£45 S1 D1 T1 ✕ £15, 7pm Ⓥ Ⓓ Ⓑ ⊛ 🐾 🛏 ⛽

● Slimbridge
SEVERN WAY

May Cottage, Shepherd's Patch, GL2 7BP ☎ 01453 890820
(Peter & Sue Gibson) www.smoothhound.co.uk/hotels/maycottage1
Map 162/721044 ✕ Ⓓ Ⓑ ⊛ 🐾

● Southam
COTSWOLD WAY

Pigeon House Cottage, next Tithe Barn, Southam Lane, GL52 3NY
☎ 01242 584255 (B J Holden)
www.pigeonhousecottage.co.uk Map 163/973255
£35 D1 T2 ✕ nearby Ⓓ Ⓑ ⊛ 🐾 🛏 ⛽ !

● Stanton
COTSWOLD WAY

Shenberrow Hill, Sheppey Corner, WR12 7NE
☎ 01386 584468 (Mrs Angela Neilan)
www.broadway-cotswolds.co.uk/shenberrowhillbb.html Map 150/071342
£37.50-£40 S1 D3 T2 F2 ✕ nearby
Ⓓ Ⓑ ⊛ 🐾 🛏 ⛽ ! 🔥 ★★★★

● Stow-on-the-Wold
HEART OF ENGLAND WAY, MONARCH'S WAY & MACMILLAN WAY

Corsham Field Farm House, Bledington Road, GL54 1JH
☎ 01451 831750 (Robert Smith)
www.corshamfield.co.uk Map 163/217250
£35-£45 D2 T2 F3 ✕ nearby Ⓓ Ⓑ ⊛ 🛏

● Stroud
COTSWOLD WAY

Pretoria Villa, Wells Road, Eastcombe, GL6 7EE ☎ 01452 770435
(Mrs Glynis Solomon) www.bedandbreakfast-cotswold.co.uk Map 163/891044
£35 D1 T2 Ⓓ Ⓑ ⊛ 🐾 🛏 ⛽ ! ★★★★Ⓢ

1 Woodchester Lodge, Southfield Road, GL5 5PA ☎ 01453 872586
(Anne Brooke-Smith) www.woodchesterlodge.co.uk Map 162/841027
£32-£38 S2 D2 T1 F1 ✕ £10, 7pm 🚍(Stroud)
Ⓥ Ⓓ Ⓑ ⊛ 🐾 🛏 ⛽ ! ★★★★

● Uley
COTSWOLD WAY

Old Crown Inn
GL11 5SN ☎ 01453 860502 (Ben Gwyer)
www.theoldcrownuley.com Map 162/792986
£40 S2 D2 T2 F2 ✕ £8.95, 7pm
Ⓥ Ⓑ 🐾 🛏 ⛽ ! 🔥

Quiet village pub just off the cotswold way, situated on the village green of Uley, serving six real ales and traditional pub food with comfortable accommodation and a hearty breakfast. A warm welcome awaits you.

● Upper Hasfield
SEVERN WAY

Rural Cottage B&B, Rust's Meadow, Hasfield Road, GL19 4LL
☎ 01452 700814 (Liz Dawson) Map 162/809279
£25 D1 T1 Ⓓ Ⓑ ⊛ 🐾 🛏 ⛽ ! 🔥

● Winchcombe
COTSWOLD WAY

Gower House, 16 North Street, GL54 5LH ☎ 01242 602616 (Mrs S Simmonds)
cotswolds.info.com.uk Map 150/025284
£27.50 D1 T2 ✕ nearby Ⓓ Ⓑ ⊛ 🐾 🛏 ! ★★★★Ⓜ

Blair House, 41 Gretton Road, GL54 5EG ☎ 01242 603626 (Mrs S Chisholm)
www.blairhousewinchcombe.co.uk Map 150/023287
£32 S2 D1 T1 Ⓓ Ⓑ ⊛ 🛏 Ⓜ

Glebe Farm, Wood-Stanway, GL54 5PG ☎ 01386 584791 (Ann Flavell-Wood)
www.woodstanway.co.uk Map 150/065313
£32 D1 T2 ✕ £19.50, 6:30pm Ⓥ Ⓓ Ⓑ 🐾 🛏 🔥

Wood Stanway Farmhouse, Wood Stanway, GL54 5PG ☎ 01386 584318
(Maggie Green) www.woodstanwayfarmhouse.co.uk Map 150/063312
£35 D1 T1 F2 ✕ £13.50, 6:30pm Ⓥ Ⓓ Ⓑ 🐾 🛏 ⛽ !

One Silk Mill Lane, GL54 5HZ ☎ 01242 603952 (Jenny Cheshire)
jenny.cheshire@virgin.net Map 150/026284
£35 S1 D1 T1 ✕ nearby Ⓓ Ⓑ ⊛ 🐾 🛏 ⛽ !

Gaia Cottage, 50 Gloucester St, GL54 5LX ☎ 01242 603495
(Brian & Sally Simmonds) gaia.cottage@yahoo.co.uk Map 150/022282
£25-£28 D1 T1 ✕ nearby Ⓓ ⊛ 🐾 🛏 ⛽ ! ★★★★

● Wotton-under-Edge
COTSWOLD WAY

Cotswold Way B&B, Holywell Farm, Valley Road, GL12 7NP
☎ 07887 520890 / 01453 845071 (Mrs Maggie Sampson)
www.webspawner.com/users/cotswoldwaybb Map 162/761935
£50-£55 D3 F1 ✕ nearby Ⓓ Ⓑ ⊛ 🐾 🛏 ⛽ ! 🔥

SOMERSET

● Axbridge
Waterside, Cheddar Road, BS26 2DP ☎ 01934 743182 (Gillian Aldridge)
www.watersidecheddar.co.uk Map 182/438545
£30-£35 D2 T2 ✕ £10, 6pm Ⓥ Ⓓ Ⓑ ⊗ 🐾 ♨ 🧺 ♿ Ⓕ ★★

● Bath
COTSWOLD WAY
Cranleigh, 159 Newbridge Hill, BA1 3PX ☎ 01225 310197
www.cranleighguesthouse.com Map 172/724656
£40-£60 S1 D3 T3 F2 ✕ nearby ₩(Bath Spa)
Ⓓ Ⓑ ⊗ 🚗 ★★★★

Number 30 Crescent Gardens
BA1 2NB ☎ 01225 337393 (David Greenwood)
www.numberthirty.com Map 172/744650
£59-£79 S2 D3 T1 ✕ nearby ₩(Bath Spa)
Ⓓ Ⓑ ⊗ 🐾 ♨ ★★★★Ⓢ Ⓜ

Fully refurbished Victorian house located within a
five-minute walk of the centre.
All en-suite, light and airy rooms.
Great English or vegetarian breakfasts.
Non-smoking throughout.
Minimum 2 nights at weekends.

Athole Guest House, 33 Upper Oldfield Park, BA2 3JX ☎ 01225 320000
(Dr Wolfgang Herrlinger) www.atholehouse.co.uk Map 172/742641
£37.50-£52 S2 D4 T2 F1 ✕ nearby ₩(Bath Spa)
Ⓓ Ⓑ ⊗ ♨ 🚗 ! ★★★★★Ⓖ Ⓦ

Lindisfarne Guest House
41a Warminster Road, BA2 6XJ ☎ 01225 466342 (Ian & Carolyn Tiley)
www.bath.org/hotel/lindisfarne.html Map 172/776658
£39-£45 D2 T1 ₩(Bath Spa)
Ⓑ ⊗ 🐾 ♨ 🚗 ! ★★★★

Get a great welcome at our family-run
B&B 1.5 miles out of Bath near lovely
canal-side walks and access to Bath
skyline walk. Full English and
continental breakfast. All en-suite
rooms with colour TV/DVD, hospitality
tray and very comfortable beds.

Devonshire House, 143 Wellsway, BA2 4RZ ☎ 01225 312495 (Louise Fry)
www.devonshire-house.uk.com Map 172/746631
£45-£63 D3 T2 F1 ✕ nearby ₩(Bath Spa) Ⓓ Ⓑ ⊗ 🐾 ♨ ★★★

● Bridgwater
MACMILLAN WAY
Cokerhurst Farm, 87 Wembdon Hill, TA6 7QA ☎ 01278 422330
(Mrs D Chappell) cokerhurst.co.uk Map 182/279378
£38 D1 T1 F1 ✕ nearby ₩(Bridgwater) Ⓓ Ⓑ ⊗ 🐾 ♨ 🚗 ! ★★★★

● Charlton Horethorne
MACMILLAN WAY & MONARCH'S WAY
Beech Farm, Sigwells, DT9 4LN ☎ 01963 220524 (Susan Stretton)
stretton@beechfarmsigwells.freeserve.co.uk Map 183/642231
£20-£25 S1 D1 T1 F1 Ⓓ Ⓑ ⊗ 🐾 ♨ 🚗 ! 🧺

● Cheddar
Constantine, Lower New Road, BS27 3DY ☎ 01934 741339
(Sue & Barry Mitchell) Map 182/450531
£22 S1 D2 F1 ✕ nearby Ⓓ Ⓑ ⊗ 🐾 ♨ ★★★

● Chew Stoke
MONARCH'S WAY
Orchard House, Bristol Road, BS40 8UB ☎ 01275 333143 (Mrs Ann Hollomon)
www.orchardhouse-chewstoke.co.uk Map 172/561618
£27-£35 S1 D1 T2 F1 ✕ nearby Ⓓ Ⓑ 🐾 ♨ 🚗 ! ★★★

Breach Hill Farm, Breach Hill Common,, BS40 8YG ☎ 01761 462411
(Margaret Wilson) jmwilson@surfree.co.uk Map 172/539598
£20 D1 ✕ £15, 5:30pm Ⓓ ⊗ 🐾 ♨ 🚗 ! Ⓜ

● Crewkerne
MONARCH'S WAY
Honeydown Farm, Seaborough Hill, TA18 8PL ☎ 01460 72665
(Catherine Bacon) www.honeydown.co.uk Map 193/430072
£30-£40 D2 T1 ✕ £16, 7pm ₩(Crewkerne)
Ⓥ Ⓓ Ⓑ ⊗ 🐾 ♨ 🚗 ! ★★★★

● Dunster
EXMOOR
SOUTH WEST COAST PATH & MACMILLAN WAY WEST
Wanneroo Farm, Timberscombe, TA24 7TU ☎ 01643 841493 (Lucie Allison)
www.wanneroofarm.co.uk Map 181/955421
£25-£30 D1 T1 F1 ✕ nearby
Ⓓ Ⓑ ⊗ 🐾 ♨ 🚗 🧺 ★★★★

The Yarn Market Hotel
High Street, TA24 6SF ☎ 01643 821425 (Penny Bale)
www.yarnmarkethotel.co.uk Map 181/992437
£40-£60 S6 D16 T5 F2 ✕ £20, 7pm ₩(Dunster)
Ⓥ Ⓓ Ⓑ ⊗ 🐾 ♨ 🚗 ! 🧺 ★★★Ⓦ Ⓜ

Our family-friendly hotel is set in the
beautiful, medieval village of Dunster,
within Exmoor National Park. Offers
a wide opportunity of walks direct
from the door. Magnificent views &
magnificent scenery. Pet-friendly.
Group bookings welcome.

● Holford
MACMILLAN WAY
Forge Cottage, Holford, TA5 1RY ☎ 01278 741215 (Susan Ayshford)
susanayshford@yahoo.co.uk Map 181/156411
£20 D2 T1 ✕ nearby ⊗ 🐾 ♨

● Ilminster
Best Western Shrubbery Hotel, Station Road, TA19 9AR ☎ 01460 52108
(Stuart Shepherd) www.shrubberyhotel.com Map 193/355147
£65-£80 D11 T10 F2 ✕ £20, 7:30pm
Ⓥ Ⓓ Ⓑ ⊗ 🐾 ♨ 🚗 ! 🧺 ♿ Ⓕ ★★★

● Minehead
EXMOOR
SOUTH WEST COAST PATH & MACMILLAN WAY WEST
The Parks Guesthouse, 26 The Parks, TA24 8BT ☎ 01643 703547
(Bryan & Sarah Leaker) www.parksguesthouse.co.uk Map 181/964462
£45 D3 T2 F2 ✕ £19, 7pm Ⓥ Ⓓ Ⓑ ⊗ 🐾 ♨ 🚗 ! ★★★★Ⓢ Ⓦ

Kenella House, 7 Tregonwell Rd, TA24 5DT ☎ 01643 703128
(Steve and Sandy Poingdestre) www.kenellahouse.co.uk Map 181/972461
£30-£35 D4 T2 ✕ £15, 7pm Ⓥ Ⓓ Ⓑ ⊛ 🐾 👶 🚗 ! ★★★★

The Wayside B&B, The Wayside, Bilbrook, TA24 6HE ☎ 01984 641669
(Rosalind Hoare) www.thewayside.co.uk Map 181/032410
£27-£39 D2 ✕ nearby Ⓑ ⊛ 🐾 👶 ★★★★Ⓢ Ⓜ

● Nether Stowey
COLERIDGE WAY, MACMILLAN WAY & SOUTH WEST COAST PATH
The Old Cider House, 25 Castle Street, TA5 1LN ☎ 01278 732228 (Ian Pearson)
www.theoldciderhouse.co.uk Map 181/191397
£45 D2 T3 ✕ £13.50, 5:30pm Ⓥ Ⓓ Ⓑ ⊛ 🐾 👶 🚲 ★★★★

Stowey Brooke House
18 Castle Street, TA5 1LN ☎ 01278 733356 (Jackie Jones)
www.stoweybrookehouse.co.uk Map 181/191397
£40-£45 S2 D2 T1 F1 ✕ nearby
Ⓓ Ⓑ ⊛ 👶 ★★★★★

An excellent base for exploring the beautiful Quantock Hills and the dramatic west Somerset Coast. Luxury accommodation. Deeply comfortable beds. Bathrooms made for relaxing. Breakfast using the best local produce. A truly special place to stay after a day's walking.

● North Cadbury
MACMILLAN WAY & MONARCH'S WAY
Ashlea House, High Street, BA22 7DP ☎ 01963 440891 (Mr & Mrs J Wade)
www.ashleahouse.co.uk Map 183/635274
£32-£36 D1 T1 ✕ £16, 7pm
Ⓥ Ⓓ Ⓑ ⊛ 🐾 👶 🚗 ! ★★★★Ⓢ

● Porlock
EXMOOR
SOUTH WEST COAST PATH & COLERIDGE WAY
The Lorna Doone Hotel, High Street, TA24 8PS ☎ 01643 862404
(Mrs AH Thornton) www.lornadoonehotel.co.uk Map 181/887469
£35 D13 ✕ £14, 6pm Ⓥ Ⓓ Ⓑ ⊛ 🐾 👶 ! 🚲

Glen Lodge
Hawkcombe, TA24 8LN ☎ 01643 863371 (Meryl Salter)
www.glenlodge.net Map 181/884459
£40-£55 D4 T1 ✕ nearby
Ⓓ Ⓑ ⊛ 🐾 👶 🚗 !

Glen Lodge is perfectly situated a short walk from Porlock and is set within 20 acres of gorgeous gardens with stunning views. Leads directly onto local walks. Paths to Dunkery, Ley Hill and other Exmoor spots straight from the door.

● Roadwater
EXMOOR
COLERIDGE WAY

Trinity Cottage Bed & Breakfast
TA23 0QY ☎ 01984 641676 (Abigail Humphrey)
www.trinitycottage.co.uk Map 181/031382
£38 D2 T1 ✕ £17, 7pm
Ⓥ Ⓓ Ⓑ ⊛ 🐾 👶 🚗 ! 🚲 ★★★★

Quiet, attractive, comfortable en-suite accommodation on the Coleridge Way and within Exmoor National Park. Excellent local walks. Pick-up and drop-off services available making a convenient base. Delicious breakfasts and a smile to great you!

● South Cadbury
MACMILLAN WAY & MONARCH'S WAY
Lower Camelot B&B, South Cadbury, BA22 7HA ☎ 01963 440581 (Julie Verney)
www.southcadbury.co.uk Map 183/632255
£42.50 S3 D3 T2 ✕ nearby Ⓓ Ⓑ ⊛ 🐾 👶 ! Ⓕ

● Stogumber
COLERIDGE WAY

The White Horse Inn
High Street, TA4 3TA ☎ 01984 656277 (John Trebilcock)
www.whitehorsestogumber.co.uk Map 181/098373
£32 D1 T1 ✕ £10, 7pm
Ⓥ Ⓓ Ⓑ ⊛ 🐾 👶 🚗 ! 🚲 ★★★

The White Horse Inn is a traditional village freehouse on the edge of the Quantock Hills. Excellent homemade food and local real ales to refresh you after exploring the numerous local walks in this glorious part of the West Country.

● Watchet
COLERIDGE WAY

St Audries Bay Holiday Club
West Quantoxhead, TA4 4DY ☎ 01984 632515
www.staudriesbay.co.uk Map 181/112430
£18.50-£23.50 S6 D6 T20 F4 ✕ £8, 7pm
Ⓥ Ⓓ Ⓑ ⊛ 🐾 👶 ♿ Ⓕ ★★★★

Family-owned and run, award-winning holiday park, near Exmoor and the Quantocks. Situated in beautiful surroundings on the Somerset coast. Fantastic views across the sea with beach access. Indoor pool, leisure facilities, bar, resturant, on-site shop. 15 miles from M5.

● Wells
MONARCH'S WAY
Cadgwith House, Hawkers Lane, BA5 3JH ☎ 01749 677799
(Elspeth Fletcher) www.cadgwithhouse.co.uk Map 182/559462
£35-£40 D2 F1 ✕ nearby Ⓓ Ⓑ ⊛ 🐾 👶 🚗 ! 🚲 ★★★★

The Crown At Wells & Anton's Bistrot, Market Place, BA5 2RP
☎ 01749 673457 (Adrian Lawrence) www.crownatwells.co.uk Map 182/550457
£55-£60 S2 D9 T4 F2 ✕ £15, 6pm
Ⓥ Ⓓ Ⓑ ⊗ 🐾🔥♨🐕★★Ⓦ Ⓜ

● Wheddon Cross
EXMOOR
COLERIDGE WAY & MACMILLAN WAY WEST
Exmoor House, TA24 7DU ☎ 01643 841432 (Rosi Davis)
www.exmoorhouse.com Map 181/924388
£39-£59 D3 T3 Fl ✕, 7pm Ⓥ Ⓓ Ⓑ ⊗ 🐾🔥 ★★★★Ⓦ

● Wincanton
MONARCH'S WAY & MACMILLAN WAY
Foxgloves, Coombe Street, Pen Selwood, BA9 8NF ☎ 01747 840680
(Penny Varnes) www.foxglovesb-b.co.uk Map 183/765312
£25-£35 Tl Fl ✕ nearby Ⓓ Ⓑ ⊗ 🐾🔥🚗!

● Winsham
MONARCH'S WAY & WESSEX RIDGEWAY
Fulwood House, Ebben Lane, TA20 4EE ☎ 01460 30163 (Elizabeth & Carl Earl)
carleton.earl@virgin.net Map 193/377066
£35 D2 ✕ nearby Ⓓ Ⓑ ⊗ 🐾🔥🚗 ★★★★Ⓜ

WILTSHIRE

● Ashton Keynes
THAMES PATH & COTSWOLD WAY
The Firs, High Road, SN6 6NX ☎ 01285 860169 (Karen Shaw)
thefirsbb@yahoo.co.uk Map 163/045941
£32-£35 S2 D2 Tl ✕ nearby
Ⓓ Ⓑ ⊗ 🐾🔥🚗!♨ ★★★Ⓜ

● Bremhill
Lowbridge Farm, SN11 9HE ☎ 01249 815889 (Elizabeth Sinden)
Map 173/987737
£26-£30 Sl Dl Tl Fl ✕ £10.50, 7pm Ⓥ Ⓓ 🐾🔥🚗!♨

● Devizes
WESSEX RIDGEWAY & RIDGEWAY

Rosemundy Cottage
London Road, SN10 2DS ☎ 01380 727122 (Mr A Aldridge)
www.rosemundycottage.co.uk Map 173/014621
£35 S4 D4 T2 F2 ✕ nearby
Ⓓ Ⓑ ⊗ 🐾🔥🚗!♨Ⓕ ★★★★

Alongside the Kennet and Avon Canal, just off Wessex Ridgeway, and a short walk to the town centre. Facilities include guest office, sitting room and a garden with seasonal heated pool and BBQ. All rooms en-suite. Four-poster and ground floor rooms available. Good base for varied walks.

● Heytesbury
WESSEX RIDGEWAY
The Resting Post, 67 High Street, BA12 0ED ☎ 01985 840204
(Felicity McLellan) www.therestingpost.co.uk Map 184/926425
£50 D2 Tl Ⓓ Ⓑ ⊗ 🐾🔥🚗!★★★★

● Inglesham
THAMES PATH
Evergreen, 3 College Farm Cottages, SN6 7QU ☎ 01367 253407
(Mr & Mrs G Blowen) www.evergreen-cotswolds.co.uk Map 163/204959
£30-£32.50 S2 Dl ✕, 5pm Ⓓ Ⓑ ⊗ 🐾🔥!★★★Ⓢ

● Manningford Abbots
Huntleys Farm, SN9 6HZ ☎ 01672 563663 (Mrs Margot Andrews)
meg@gimspike.fsnet.co.uk Map 173/145593
£25-£30 Dl Fl ✕ £15, 7:30pm ⋙(Pewsey)
Ⓥ Ⓓ Ⓑ ⊗ 🐾🔥🚗!♨ ★★★★

● Marlborough
WESSEX RIDGEWAY

Browns Farm
SN8 4ND ☎ 01672 515129 (Hazel J Crockford)
www.marlboroughholidaycottages.co.uk Map 173/198678
£25 D2 Tl Fl ✕ nearby
Ⓓ Ⓑ ⊗ 🐾🔥

Attractive farmhouse set on the edge of the Savernake Forest. Large comfortable rooms offering views over open farmland. Ideal base for walkers and cyclists. Close to the Ridgeway, Averbury and Wansdyke.

● Mere
MONARCH'S WAY
Castleton House, Castle St, BA12 6JE ☎ 01747 860446 (Gail Garbutt)
www.castletonhouse.com Map 183/811323 ✕ £15 Ⓥ Ⓓ Ⓑ 🐾🚗!

● Ogbourne St George
RIDGEWAY
Foxlynch, Bytham Road, SN8 1TD ☎ 01672 8413070
(Mr G H Edwins) Map 173/190740
£20 Dl Fl ✕ nearby Ⓓ Ⓑ ⊗ 🐾🔥🚗!♨

Parklands Hotel & Restaurant
SN8 1SL ☎ 01672 841555 (Mark Bentley)
www.parklandshoteluk.co.uk
£55-£65 S2 D4 T4 F2 ✕ £14.10, 7pm
Ⓥ Ⓓ Ⓑ ⊗ 🐾🔥🚗!♨♿

Set in the tiny village of Ogbourne St George, Parklands Hotel offers comfortable, peaceful accomodation and an excellent restaurant in a family-run hotel.

Conveniently located for the Ridgeway path. Visit websiet for more details.

● Salisbury
Hayburn Wyke Guest House, 72 Castle Road, SP1 3RL ☎ 01722 412627
www.hayburnwykeguesthouse.co.uk Map 184/142309
D3 T2 F2 ✕ nearby ⋙(Salisbury) Ⓓ Ⓑ ⊗ 🔥♿

● Tisbury
WESSEX RIDGEWAY
Cools Farm, East Knoyle, SP3 6DB ☎ 01747 830720 (Maggie Edwards)
www.coolsfarm.co.uk Map 184/901296
£35-£40 D2 Tl Fl Ⓓ Ⓑ 🐾🔥🚗!♨

SELF-CATERING

CORNWALL

● Ashton
SOUTH WEST COAST PATH

Chycarne Farm Cottages ☎ 01736 762473 (Pauline & Graham Ross)
www.chycarne-farm-cottages.co.uk Map 201/383683
£110-£470 Sleeps 1-4. 9 cottages. ⊗ 🐾 Short breaks available

● Boscastle
SOUTH WEST COAST PATH

Forth Cottage & Pendee ☎ 01726 72091 (Mrs A Boyd)
alixboyd@tiscali.co.uk Map 190/076891
£210-£800 Sleeps 1-6. 2 courtyard cottages. ⊗ 🐾 Short breaks available ★★★

● Callington
COPPER TRAIL

Berrio Mill ☎ 01579 363252 (Ivan & Carolyn Callanan)
www.berriomill.co.uk Map 201/361710
£210-£650 Sleeps 2-4. 2 cottages. ⊗ ♿ 🖂 Short breaks available Ⓦ

● Crackington Haven

Crackington Manor ☎ 01840 230397 (Crackington Manor)
crackington.manor@virgin.net Map 190/150956 . 🐾

● Fowey
SOUTH WEST COAST PATH & SAINTS' WAY

Tor Side
☎ 01726870909 (Sheila Nelson)
stevennelson07@aol.com Map 200/144522
£290-£645 Sleeps 1-9. 1 house.
⊗ Short breaks available

Hidden in the tranquil depths of rural Cornwall lies Tor Side, situated above the picturesque Pont Creek.

Set amid the 2,800 acres of National Trust protected woodlands, Tor Side is the gateway to exploring unspoilt Cornwall and the surrounding Daphne Du Maurier Country.

Hall Walk is a mere five-minute walk away, and the South West Coast Path offers the chance to explore neighbouring Fowey and St Catherine's Castle.

Fowey lies a mere ferry ride across the river, and offers boat trips, marine adventures and kayak expeditions up the river.

Pont Creek is a hidden paradise waiting to be explored.

Fowey Harbour Cottages ☎ 01726 832211 (David Hill)
www.foweyharbourcottages.co.uk Map 200/125520
£150-£1000 Sleeps 2-6. 10 cottages and flats.
🐾 Short breaks available ★★★

● Launceston

Eastgate Barn ☎ 01566 782573 (Jill Goodman)
www.eastgatebarn.co.uk Map 201/286760
£295-£475 Sleeps 2-4. 1 cottage.
⊗ Short breaks available ★★★★Ⓦ

● Liskeard
SOUTH WEST COAST PATH & COPPER TRAIL

Cutkive Wood Holiday Lodges ☎ 01579 362216 (Andy Lowman)
www.cutkivewood.co.uk Map 201/292676
£200-£550 Sleeps 1-6. 6 lodges. ⊗ 🐾 Short breaks available

● Looe
SOUTH WEST COAST PATH

Summercourt Cottages
☎ 01503 263149 (Philippa and Mac Hocking)
www.holidaycottagescornwall.tv Map 201/279547
£150-£615 Sleeps 2-5. 6 cottages.
🐾 Short breaks available ★★★★

Six converted stone barns in an area of oustanding natural landscape, east of Looe and right on the SW Coast Path. Close to beaches and historical houses and gardens. All fully-equipped with central heating.

● Mullion
SOUTH WEST COAST PATH

Trenance Farm Cottages ☎ 01326 240639 (Jennifer Tyler Street)
www.trenancefarmholidays.co.uk Map 203/672185
£210-£750 Sleeps 2-6. 9 cottages. 🐾 Short breaks available ★★★Ⓦ

● Newquay
SOUTH WEST COAST PATH & SAINTS' WAY

Newquay Bay Holidays
☎ 01637 859595 (Newquay Bay Holidays)
www.newquaybayholidays.co.uk Map 200/812616
£220-£1200 Sleeps 2-8. 30 cottages, apartments, lodges, houses.
⊗ ♿ 🐾 Short breaks available ★★★★★

Whether you are seeking peace and quiet amid nature's beauty or long solitary walks along the wild coastline, Cornwall offers so much for the visitor throughout the year, and Newquay and her surrounds offer the perfect base to begin exploring.

● Padstow
SOUTH WEST COAST PATH & SAINTS' WAY

Yellow Sands ☎ 01841 520376 (Mr M Dakin)
www.yellowsands.net Map 200/897745
£210-£1250 Sleeps 2-8. 5 house and apartments.
⊗ 🐾 Short breaks available ★★★★

SOUTH WEST

Bosca Brea

☎ 01208 814472 (Mrs Alison Mitchell)
alisonm.trevalsa@btinternet.com Map 200/897745
£215-£395 Sleeps 1-4. 1 holiday cottage.
Short breaks available

Detached bungalow in peaceful hamlet of Tregonce. Views across Little Petherick Creek and towards Padstow from half-acre private grounds. Close access to Saints' Way, Camel Trail and SW Coast Path. Wadebridge and Padstow, surfing and sandy beaches approx' five miles.

● Polzeath
SOUTH WEST COAST PATH

Mermaids Purse, Scirocco ☎ 01763 837341 / 07808 078834
(Ros Renwick) www.polzeathbeachhouse.co.uk Map 200/938790
£125-£1400 Sleeps 1-6. Beachhouse, luxury garden apartment, caravan.
Ⓢ ⓑ 🐾 Short breaks available

● Porthleven
SOUTH WEST COAST PATH

Pennti-an-Goelann ☎ 01326 281515 (Wendy Rochefort)
www.cornwall-online.co.uk
£230-£550 Sleeps 1-4. 1 cottage. Ⓢ Short breaks available

● St Austell
SOUTH WEST COAST PATH

Spindrift ☎ 01726 69316 (Mrs McGuffie)
www.spindrift-guesthouse.co.uk Map 200/002527
£250-£600 Sleeps 1-4. Bungalow, cottage & house.
Ⓢ 🐾 Short breaks available ★★★

● St Dennis

Ginny ☎ 01726 821715 (Ginny)
ginzi@hotmail.co.uk Map 200/950577
£120-£320 Sleeps 1-2. 1 studio apartment. Ⓢ 🐾 Short breaks available

● St Just
SOUTH WEST COAST PATH

Cornish Cocoons ☎ 01733 787276 (Siobhan Hayles)
www.cornishcocoons.co.uk Map 203/364304
£250-£1495 Sleeps 1-5. 4 cottages/apartments/beach chatlets.
Ⓢ 🐾 Short breaks available

● St Wenn
SAINTS' WAY

Tregolls Farm Cottages

☎ 01208 812154 (Mrs Marilyn Hawkey)
www.tregollsfarm.co.uk Map 200/983661
£235-£850 Sleeps 2-8. 4 converted barns.
Ⓢ ⓑ Short breaks available ★★★★

Quality barn conversion in a picturesque valley overlooking fields of cows and sheep. Farm trail links up with Saints' Way footpath. Pets corner. Games room. BBQs. Central heating and log burners. Only 20 minutes' drive from Eden to Padstow.

● Wadebridge
DARTMOOR
SOUTH WEST COAST PATH

Seaweed

☎ 01377 236 039 (Nash)
www.cornwall-online.co.uk/seaweed-polzeath
Map 200/935794
Ⓢ ⓑ Ⓕ

Situated 100 yards from the coastal path and Polzeath Beach, this light, bright, well-furnished bungalow is ideal to explore spectacular North Cornwall coastpaths, Camel Estuary, Port Isaac, Padstow, Bodmin Moor. One double, one twin and sofa-bed in sitting room. Rayburn.

DEVON

● Appledore

Number 5 Hillcliff Terrace ☎ 01600 716418 (Jennifer Frecknall)
www.appledore-holiday.co.uk Map 180/461303
£225-£525 Sleeps 1-6. 1 terraced house. Ⓢ 🐾 Short breaks available

● Berrynarbor

Smythen Farm Coastal Cottages

☎ 01271 882875 (Jayne Elstone)
www.smythenfarmholidaycottages.co.uk Map 180/560468
£95-£894 Sleeps 2-7. 4 cottages.
🐾 Short breaks available ★★★

Four cottages, 2-7 berth, set in an area of outstanding natural beauty overlooking the sea.

Heated covered swimming pool in a suntrap enclosure. Spacious lawns and gardens. Children's play area with 12m x 5m all-weather games room with full-size pool & table-tennis tables, darts and football machine. Also, for younger children, inflatable bouncy castle and ball-pond.

Free pony rides. 14-acre recreation field and dog walk.

The village of Berrynarbor is two miles, with store, an inn welcoming children, and quality eating places. 3/4/5-night breaks available.

● **Branscombe**

SOUTH WEST COAST PATH

4 Nestlecombe ☎ 01484323146 (Jean Parker)
www.branscombeholidaylet.co.uk Map 192/203888
£210-£420 Sleeps 2-4. 1 apartment. Ⓧ Short breaks available

● **Dartmouth**

SOUTH WEST COAST PATH

Norton Park ☎ 07802 308030 (Julie Nesbit-Bell)
www.chalets-dartmouth.co.uk Map 202/868508
£150-£450 Sleeps 1-5. 3 chalets.
Ⓧ Short breaks available

de Beers – The Barn ☎ 01803 712170 (Suzie de Beer)
www.debeersdartmouth.com Map 202/816521
£304-£795 Sleeps 2-6. 1 barn conversion.
Ⓧ 🐾 Short breaks available

● **Down Thomas**

SOUTH WEST COAST PATH

Becalmed
☎ 01989 770725 (Mrs J Davis)
jackienicholsonx@yahoo.co.uk
Map 201/503498
£150-£425 Sleeps 1-4. 1 chalet. Ⓧ

'Becalmed' (photo shows view from chalet).

Cosy, modern chalet on cliffs of the South West Coast Path overlooking the waters of Plymouth Sound. West-facing, the windows and patio enjoy glorious sunsets. Within minutes of the beaches, the chalet's position provides ample opportunity for walking the footpaths of the South Hams and Dartmoor.

Completely refurbished with all modern facilities, two bedrooms (one double, one twin), lounge with dining area, new shower-room and fully-equipped fitted kitchen with washer/dryer. Charges inclusive of heating and electricity. Food baskets arranged for walkers on request for a small extra charge. Brochure on request. Closed Jan-Feb.

● **Galmpton**

SOUTH WEST COAST PATH

Jenny Wren ☎ 024 76460917 (Rosalind Fletcher)
www.jennywren-brixham.co.uk Map 202/886558
£200-£415 Sleeps 1-4. 1 chalet bungalow.
Ⓧ 🐾 Short breaks available

● **Hartland**

SOUTH WEST COAST PATH

Yapham Cottages
☎ 01237 441916 (Jane Young)
www.yaphamcottages.com Map 190/255234
£280-£795 Sleeps 2-4. 3 cottages.
Ⓧ Short breaks available ★★★★

Set in landscaped gardens within seven acres of lovely grounds, including ancient woodland walk.

Guided walks can be arranged.

Situated on the breathtaking, unspoilt Hartland Peninsula, Yapham enjoys complete tranquility yet is perfect for visiting nearby tourist attractions; Exmoor, Dartmoor, The Eden Project, Lundy Island.

Our cottages are beautifully furnished and include central heating. Excellent homecooked meals available. Delicious cream tea on arrival, plus chocolates and flowers. 'Taxi' service available.

● **Holsworthy**

The Barn at Southcombe Farm
☎ 01409 253761 (Eileen Clark)
www.southcombe.net Map 190/354032
£400-£575 Sleeps 4-6. 1 barn conversion.
Ⓧ Short breaks available ★★★★

Southcombe is a small thoroughbred stud farm providing high quality accommodation set against a background of important wildlife conservation areas. Southcombe's location is picturesque, secluded and peaceful yet provides a superb location from which to explore Devon and Cornwall.

● **Honiton**

Twistgates Farm
☎ 01404 861173 (Mrs Gray)
www.twistgatesfarm.co.uk Map 192/163025
£195-£650 Sleeps 1-5. 3 self-catering cottages.
Ⓧ 🐾 Short breaks available

Three cottages that combine quality and comfort with traditional character, set in the Blackdown Hills, an AONB. Quiet, peaceful lanes and paths surround us or, within easy driving distance, enjoy the South West Coastal Path, Jurassic Coast and national parks.

Please mention **walk BRITAIN**
when booking your accommodation

SOUTH WEST

Odle Farm Holiday Cottages

☎ 01404 861105 (Karen Marshallsay)
www.odlefarm.co.uk Map 192/163025
£240-£860 Sleeps 2-5. 4 cottages.
Ⓢ ⊞ Short breaks available ★★★★Ⓦ

Set in 10 acres of the unspoilt Otter Valley, an excellent area for walking and cycling. Very comfortable accomodation. Hydrotherapy spa, underfloor heating and all mod cons. Complimentary cake, tea tray and pint of milk on arrival. Other local amenities nearby.

● Lustleigh
DARTMOOR
TWO MOORS WAY

Little Cedars

☎ 01647 277 245 (Jeanette Lee)
cedarsweb.co.uk Map 191/781811
£250-£550 Sleeps 2-6. 1 bungalow.
Ⓢ ⊞ Short breaks available

Dartmoor National Park. Bungalow sleeps maximum six. Three bedrooms. Off-road parking, two cars, private garden, good views. Quiet location outskirts of popular village. Woodland and moor walking from bungalow. Golf, climbing, fishing, coast and surfing easy distance. Well equipped, modern.

● Lyme Regis
SOUTH WEST COAST PATH & WESSEX RIDGEWAY

Symondsdown Cottages ☎ 01297 32385 (Stuart & Jenny Hynds)
www.symondsdownholidaycottages.co.uk Map 193/331925
£190-£620 Sleeps 2-6. 6 cottages. ⊞ Short breaks available

● Moretonhampstead
DARTMOOR
TWO MOORS WAY

Budleigh Farm

☎ 01647 440835 (Judith Harvey)
www.budleighfarm.co.uk Map 191/754862
£155-£530 Sleeps 2-6. 7 barn conversions.
Ⓢ ⊞ Short breaks available ★★

Climb our hill and admire Dartmoor from the site of an Iron Age fort. There's not much left of the fort, but the view is stunning.
Visit historic cities, secret villages, tumbling streams and superb beaches. Admire bluebell woods and wild flowers, roam Dartmoor and sleep soundly after walking the Tors. Short breaks.

● Oare
EXMOOR

Cloud Farm

☎ 01598 741234 (Jill Harman)
www.doonevalleyholidays.co.uk
Map 181/800477
⊞

Cloud Farm's idyllic riverside setting in the tranquility of the Exmoor National Park's Doone Valley provides perfect 'away-from-it-all' holidays and short breaks all year round.

Three farmhouse cottage accommodations, all newly refurbished, set in an unspoilt paradise for walking, relaxing, exploring, watching wildlife, or riding from our stables (all ages/levels).

Excellent base for touring nearby villages and walking the South West Coast Path. Shop, off-licence, tearooms, gardens, laundry facilities on-site.

● Okehampton
DARTMOOR

East Hook Holiday Cottages

☎ 01837 52305 (Mrs M E Stevens)
www.easthook-holiday-cottages.co.uk Map 191/588966
£175-£650 Sleeps 2-6. 3 Devon country cottages.
⊞ Short breaks available ★★★★Ⓦ

On the Tarka Trail/fringe of Dartmoor with beautiful panoramic view of the National Park, near Abbeyford Woods.

Quiet/peaceful in own parkland only half-a-mile from Okehampton. Idyllic country cottages with oak beams, log fires, comfortable, wonderful charm and ambience.

● Parracombe
EXMOOR
SOUTH WEST COAST PATH

Voley Farm Cottages ☎ 01598763315 (Susan Brown)
voleyfarm.com Map 180/642459
£232-£693 Sleeps 1-6. 2 cottage.
Ⓢ Short breaks available

● Princetown
DARTMOOR

Middlemoor ☎ 01752361134 (Sandra Michaelson)
s.thomson-michelson@sky.com Map 191/588734
£120-£420 Sleeps 4-6. 1 cottage.
Ⓢ ⊞ Short breaks available

● Sidmouth
SOUTH WEST COAST PATH

Anstis Court ☎ 07855501315 (Barbara Smith)
www.selfcateringinsidmouth.co.uk Map 192/124890
£195-£470 Sleeps 1-3. 1 apartment.
🚭 Short breaks available ★★★★ Ⓜ

● Tavistock
DARTMOOR

Langstone Manor ☎ 01822 613371 (Jane Kellett)
langstone-manor.co.uk Map 191/472753
🚭 🐾 Short breaks available

● Teignmouth
SOUTH WEST COAST PATH

Bowden Close House ☎ 01803 328029 (Mrs Rae Farquharson)
www.bowdenclose.co.uk Map 192/932733
£230-£570 Sleeps 1-4. 6 apartments.
🚭 Short breaks available ★★★

● Trentishoe
EXMOOR
SOUTH WEST COAST PATH

South Dean Cottage ☎ 01598763732 (Trevor & Vicki)
www.southdeancottage.co.uk Map 180/725485
£400-£500 Sleeps 1-6. 1 cottage.
🚭 🐾 Short breaks available

● Widecombe-in-the-Moor
DARTMOOR

Wooder Manor Holiday Homes
☎ 01364 621391 (Mrs Angela Bell)
www.woodermanor.com Map 191/711766
£180-£1200 Sleeps 2-12. 5 cottages.
🚭 ♿ Ⓕ 🐾 Short breaks available ★★★

Cottages in picturesque valley, surrounded by moors and granite tors. Peaceful location with lovely walks from doorstep. Clean and well-equipped. Central heating. Gardens. Easy parking. Open all year. Good food at local inns. Brochure. Sleeps 2-4, 4-6, 8-12. Groups welcome.

● Witherage
TWO MOORS WAY

Newhouse Farm Cottages
☎ 01884 860266 (Mr Keith Jenkins)
www.newhousecottages.com
£235-£1575 Sleeps 2-40. 8 cottages.
🚭 🐾 Short breaks available

Eight beautifully converted well equipped Grade 11-listed stone barns sleeping 2-40 people, the perfect place to relax & unwind, peaceful location, with abundant wildlife, enjoy our indoor heated swimming pool and 23 acres of land to roam.

DORSET

● Abbotsbury
MACMILLAN WAY WEST & SOUTH WEST COAST PATH

Gorwell Farm ☎ 01305 871401 (Mrs J M Pengelly)
www.gorwellfarm.co.uk Map 194/575852
£250-£1075 Sleeps 1-8. 6 cottages.
🚭 ♿ Ⓕ 🐾 Short breaks available ★★★★

● Beaminster
WESSEX RIDGEWAY

Culverhayes Bungalow ☎ 01903201773 (David Sykes)
sykesrd@gmail.com Map 193/473013
£70-£280 Sleeps 2-5. 1 detached bungalow. 🚭 Ⓜ

● Bridport
SOUTH WEST COAST PATH

Lancombes House ☎ 01308 485375 (Adrian Semmence)
www.lancombes-house.co.uk/34.html Map 194/500968
£310-£1600 Sleeps 2-30. 5 cottages.
🚭 ♿ Ⓕ 🐾 Short breaks available ★★★★ Ⓦ

Rudge Farm
☎ 01308 482630 (Mike Hamer)
www.rudgefarm.co.uk Map 194/528903
£280-£835 Sleeps 2-6. 10 cottages.
🚭 Short breaks available ★★★★

Rudge Farm is an ideal walking base for the beautiful Bride Valley and is just over two miles from Dorset's World Heritage coastline.

The old farm buildings have been converted into ten well-equipped, comfortable cottages arranged around a flower decked cobbled yard enjoying views across the valley towards the coast. There are a number of leisure facilities on the farm including a tennis court and games barn.

● Corfe Castle
SOUTH WEST COAST PATH

Knaveswell Farm Cottage
☎ 01929 422918 (Joanna Dyer)
www.knaveswellfarmcottage.co.uk Map 195/004807
£250-£700 Sleeps 2-6. 1 detached cottage.
🚭 🐾 Short breaks available ★★★

Detached 2-bedroom character cottage on working dairy farm, nestling under the Purbeck Hills between Corfe Castle and Swanage. Spacious kitchen, lounge/diner with woodburner, one double bedroom, one family room and bathroom. Garden and parking, ideal location for walkers.

● Dorchester

Sandyholme Holiday Park ☎ 01305 852677 (Reception)
www.sandyholme.co.uk Map 194/682932
£160-£550 Sleeps 2-6. 25 caravans. 🐾

● Langton Matravers
SOUTH WEST COAST PATH

April Cottage ☎ 01929 405520 (Roger & Jo Jupp)
www.aprilcottage-dorset.co.uk Map 195/994787
£275-£800 Sleeps 2-8. 1 cottage. ⊗ Short breaks available Ⓜ

● Marshwood

Colmer Farmhouse
☎ 01297 678652 (Stephen Bowditch)
www.colmerfarmhouse.co.uk Map 193/383997
£250-£580 Sleeps 1-6. 1 farmhouse.
🐾 Short breaks available

Colmer Farmhouse has three footpaths on its doorstep, plus glorious walks along the coast, an Aga to dry clothes and boots if need be. Sleeps six in three large bedrooms.
Separate lounge, kitchen and dining room. 15th-century, lots of character.

● Poole
SOUTH WEST COAST PATH

Sunny Cottage ☎ 01202 253563 (John Samways / Nikki Froud)
www.sunnycottage-poole.co.uk Map 195/018903
£300-£550 Sleeps 1-4. 1 house. ⊗ Short breaks available

● Portland
SOUTH WEST COAST PATH

Church Ope Studio
☎ 01305 860428 (Douglas Stem)
www.churchopestudio.com
£210-£400 Sleeps 2-3. 1 self-contained studio.
⊗ ♿ 🐾 Short breaks available

Church Ope Studio lies metres away from the South West Coast Path overlooking the beautiful Church Ope Cove. Self-contained studio accomodation en-suite with on-site parking. Ideal location for bird watching and cliff walks in quiet setting.

● Sixpenny Handley

The Stable Barn ☎ 01725 552860 (Richard Hickinbotham)
hickinbotham@btinternet.com Map 195/974136
£150-£250 Sleeps 2. 1 barn cottage. ⊗ Short breaks available

● Sturminster Newton

Hillyground Cottage Holidays
☎ 01258 473890 (Catherine Walker and Liz Wray)
www.hillyground.co.uk Map 194/781134
£170-£392 Sleeps 1-3. 2 chalet.
⊗ ♿ 🐾 Short breaks available

Two comfortable chalets in large garden, overlooking River Stour in Blackmore Vale (AONB).

Within easy reach of Jubilee Trail, Hardy Way, ancient monuments (e.g. Hambledon Hill, Maiden Castle & Badbury Rings) and local nature and river trails. 40min drive to coast.

● Swanage
SOUTH WEST COAST PATH

Sandhaven ☎ 01929 422322 (Janet Foran)
www.sandhaven-guest-house.co.uk Map 195/017786
£350-£750 Sleeps 1-6. 1 cottage.
⊗ 🐾 Short breaks available ★★★★

Melton Lodge Holidays ☎ 01929 422440 (Geoff Chambers)
meltonlodge.co.uk Map 195/030797
£170-£650 Sleeps 2-8. 4 apartments. ⊗ Short breaks available

● Weymouth
SOUTH WEST COAST PATH

Palulu – The WindBreak ☎ 01256 761247 (Rise Rytlewski)
www.palulu.co.uk Map 194/696816
£210-£550 Sleeps 2-4. 1 beach front chalet. ⊗ Short breaks available

GLOUCESTERSHIRE

● Chipping Campden
COTSWOLD WAY

Cotswold Cottages ☎ 01386 840835 (Mrs J Whitehouse)
cotswoldcottages.uk.com Map 151/159403
£200-£600 Sleeps 2-5. 2 coachhouse and flat.
⊗ 🐾 Short breaks available ★★★

● Dursley
COTSWOLD WAY

Two Springbank ☎ 01453 543047 (Mrs F A Jones)
lhandfaj32lg@surefish.co.uk Map 162/757993
£186-£267 Sleeps 4. 1 cottage. ⊗ Short breaks available

● Elkstone
COTSWOLD WAY

The Grannery ☎ 01242 870375 (Mrs Lois Eyre)
www.cottageguide.co.uk/grannery Map 163/968116
£195-£315 Sleeps 1-2. 1 west wing of a house.
⊗ 🐾 Short breaks available

● Mitcheldean

The Old Dairy ☎ 01594 543737 (Lorraine Morgan)
www.olddairycottage.com Map 162/644175
£179-£279 Sleeps 2-3. 1 cottage.
⊗ ♿ 🐾 Short breaks available ★★★★

● Stanton
COTSWOLD WAY

Charity Farm
☎ 01386 584339 (Mrs V Ryland)
www.charitycottage.com Map 150/064343
£250-£575 Sleeps 2-6. 2 cottages.
Short breaks available ★★★

Charming Cotswold stone cottages in picturesque village on the Cotswold Way. Pretty gardens offer 'al fresco' dining. Village pub serves food and Broadway has a selection of pubs and restaurants. Walk the hills or visit National Trust houses and gardens.

● Stow-on-the-Wold
HEART OF ENGLAND WAY & MONARCH'S WAY

Uphome Cottage ☎ 01451 831284 (Sally Godman)
www.cotswoldbreaks.co.uk Map 163/222256
£300-£600 Sleeps 1-4. 1 cottage.
Short breaks available ★★★★

● Stroud
COTSWOLD WAY

The Barn ☎ 01453 824659 (Fleur Alvares)
www.middleyard.co.uk Map 162/817031
£280-£575 Sleeps 1-6. 1 cottage.
Short breaks available ★★★★

● Uley
COTSWOLD WAY

Stouts Hill Resort
☎ 07783 943633 (George Stewart)
www.stoutshill.co.uk Map 162/790977
£250-£500 Sleeps 28-64. 14 apartments and cottages.
Short breaks available ★★★Ⓢ

Welcome to this Cotswold gem; a country house set in 27-acre parkland with 14 apartments & 5 cottages. Why not take advantage of our Ramblers' Breaks, November to March at the special price of £25pppn (min' 2 nights).

● Winchcombe
COTSWOLD WAY

Folly Cottages
☎ 01386 584741 (Maggie Campbell)
www.follycottages.co.uk Map 150/025284
£300-£490 Sleeps 2-8. 2 cottages.
Short breaks available ★★★★

Appealing cottages, both situated a minute's walk from the shops, restaurants and pubs of Winchcombe with its close proximity to the Cotswold, Windrush, Wychavon, Warden and Gloucestershire Ways.

SOMERSET

● Cheddar

Home Farm
☎ 01934 842078 (Chris & Sue Sanders)
www.homefarmcottages.com
Map 182/462527
Short breaks available

Four beautifully converted stone barns with original beams. Set in two acres of an area of outstanding natural beauty, and surrounded by farm and National Trust land. Many local walks. All cottages are comfortable, warm and fully equipped.

Sungate Holiday Apartments ☎ 01934 842273 (Mrs M M Fieldhouse)
sungateholidayapartments.co.uk Map 182/462527
£160-£200 Sleeps 1-5. 4 apartments. Short breaks available

● Crewkerne
MONARCH'S WAY

Mrs Z Morgan ☎ 01460 77259
zenamorgan@hotmail.com Map 193/445094
£100-£150 Sleeps 2-4. 1 property.

● Dunster
EXMOOR
SOUTH WEST COAST PATH, COLERIDGE WAY & MACMILLAN WAY WEST

The Courtyard ☎ 01643 821113 (Angela Morecroft)
www.thecourtyarddunster.co.uk Map 181/991436
£195-£220 Sleeps 1-2. 1 cottage. Short breaks available ★★★

● Porlock
EXMOOR
SOUTH WEST COAST PATH & MACMILLAN WAY WEST

The Cleeve
☎ 07767 474247 (Kevin Bramhill)
www.the-cleeve.co.uk Map 181/885462
£4000-£5600 Sleeps 1-28. 1 mansion.
Short breaks available

Luxuriously furnished and equipped imposing Victorian hunting lodge. Uniquely set in large secluded private grounds above a valley, once the seat of Saxon kings. Open fires, dining for 28, two lounges, six bathrooms, big Aga + conventional cooker. Fantastic setting, spectacular ancient woodland with stream, hills and views with trails straight from the door. Village conveniently close with pubs, restaurants, sports (football, tennis, cricket, bowls), playground and shops two minutes' walk.

The Pack Horse
☎ 01643 862475 (Linda & Brian Garner)
www.thepackhorse.net Map 181/879465
£275-£535 Sleeps 2-6. 4 apartments, one cottage.
🛏 Short breaks available ★★★

Apartments and cottage situated in this unique location alongside the shallow river Aller overlooking the famous Pack Horse Bridge. Immediate access from our doorstep to the beautiful surrounding countryside, pretty villages, spectacular coast and Exmoor. Open all year. Private parking.

● Roadwater
EXMOOR
COLERIDGE WAY

Lyndale
☎ 01984 641426 (John Middleton)
www.cottageguide.co.uk/lyndale Map 181/031382
£240-£475 Sleeps 1-6. 1 cottage.
Ⓧ 🛏 Short breaks available Ⓜ

Character cottage on Coleridge Way. Two bedrooms: double and twin. Cosy living room with woodburner and two sofas, one converts to double bed. TV/DVD/CD player. Dining room seats six. Kitchen with dishwasher, oven and fridge-freezer. Private parking, garden. Inn nearby.

● Taunton
MACMILLAN WAY WEST & COLERIDGE WAY

Spring Cottage ☎ 01823 451542 (Nicky Withers)
quantockonline.co.uk Map 182/238323
£165-£250 Sleeps 2-3. 1 cottage. Short breaks available

WILTSHIRE

● Devizes
WESSEX RIDGEWAY & RIDGEWAY

Tichborne's Farm Cottages ☎ 01380 862971 (Jon Nash)
www.tichbornes.co.uk Map 173/046602
£280-£455 Sleeps 2-4. 3 cottages. Ⓧ 🛏 Short breaks available ★★★★

● Marlborough
RIDGEWAY & WESSEX RIDGEWAY

Dairy Cottage
☎ 01672 515129 (Hazel & Mark Crockford)
www.marlboroughholidaycottages.co.uk Map 174/207665
£300-£650 Sleeps 6-8. 1 cottage.
Ⓧ 🛏 Short breaks available ★★★

Dairy Cottage is situated on Brown's Farm, a working beef/arable farm. Set on edge of Savernake Forest overlooking open farmland, it offers peace and tranquility for a true north Wiltshire holiday.

Modern, spacious, well-equipped bungalow with open fire awaits you.

GROUPS, HOSTELS, BUNKHOUSES, CAMPSITES & OTHERS

CORNWALL

● Liskeard
COPPER TRAIL

Cutkive Wood Holiday Lodges, St Ive, PL14 3ND ☎ 01579 362216
(Andy & Jackie Lowman) www.cutkivewood.co.uk Map 201/292676
SC £200-£550 per week Sleeps 1-30. 6 lodges. Ⓓ ☺ 🛏

● Mullion
SOUTH WEST COAST PATH

Franchis Holidays
Cury Cross Lanes, TR12 7AZ ☎ 01326 240301 (Kate D'Arcy)
www.franchis.co.uk Map 203/695206
SC £10-£15 per night. Sleeps 1-6.
Campsite, caravans & chalets.

Franchis nestles between farm & woodland in an area of outstanding natural beauty, perfectly situated for visiting all of West Cornwall, the Lizard & walking the South West Coast Path. 70 pitches, seven static caravans & five chalets available.

DEVON

● Lynton
EXMOOR
SOUTH WEST COAST PATH & TWO MOORS WAY

Cloud Farm
Oare, EX35 6NU ☎ 01598 741234
www.doonevalleyholidays.co.uk Map 180/794468
£5-£7.50 per night Sleeps 1-100. Camping & caravan site.
Ⓓ ★★★

Cloud Farm's idyllic riverside setting in the tranquility of the Exmoor National Park's Doone Valley provides perfect 'away-from-it-all' camping all year.

Three spacious riverside camping/caravan fields, set in an unspoilt paradise for walking, relaxing, exploring, watching wildlife, or riding from our stables (all ages/levels).

Excellent base for touring nearby villages and walking the South West Coast Path. Shop selling food and camping supplies. Laundry facilities and new shower block on-site.

● Tavistock

DARTMOOR

TWO MOORS WAY

Langstone Manor Park, Moortown, PL19 9JZ ☎ 01822 613371
www.langstone-manor.co.uk Map 191/524738
SC £15-£50 per night Sleeps 1-6. Campsite.
Ⓥ Ⓓ ⊗ ⇆ ! ⌂ ★★★★Ⓦ

DORSET

● Swanage

SOUTH WEST COAST PATH

Sandringham Hotel, 20 Durlston Roadd, BH19 2HX
☎ 01929 423076 (Mr & Mrs Silk)
www.smoothhound.co.uk/hotels/sandringham.html Map 195/033782
BB, DBB £30-£40 per night Sleeps 1-25. Hotel, group accommodation.
Ⓥ ⊗ ⇆ ⇆ !

GLOUCESTERSHIRE

● Drybrook

Greenway Farm, Puddlebrook Road, GL17 9HW ☎ 01594 543737
(Lorraine Morgan) www.greenwayfarm.org Map 162/645184
SC £4.50-£13 per night Sleeps 1-55. Campsite.
Ⓓ ⊗ ⇆ ⌂ & Ⓕ ★★★★

SOMERSET

● Dunster

EXMOOR

SOUTH WEST COAST PATH, COLERIDGE WAY & MACMILLAN WAY WEST

Yarn Market Hotel, High Street, TA24 6SF ☎ 01643 821425 (Penny Bale)
www.yarnmarkethotel.co.uk Map 181/992437
BB, DBB £30-£50 per night Sleeps 1-60. Hotel. ⋙(Dunster)
Ⓥ Ⓓ ⊗ ⇆ ⇆ ! ⌂ ★★★Ⓦ Ⓜ

SOUTH

Long Distance Paths

Icknield Way Path ....ICK

Isle of Wight Coastal Path ....IWC

London Loop ....LNL

Macmillan Way ....MCM

Midshires Way ....MDS

Monarch's Way ....MON

North Downs Way ....NDN

Ridgeway ....RDG

Solent Way ....SOL

South Downs Way ....SDN

Thames Path ....THM

Wealdway ....WLD

**See Paths & Access p25 for full
details of LDPs and waymarks**

National Parks

New Forest

South Downs*

AN AUTUMNAL PATH IN THE
NEW FOREST, HAMPSHIRE

WALK...   ...THE GREEN CHAIN

From Richmond Park to Hampstead Heath, the capital boasts some superb green spaces. But perhaps less well-known are the more than 300 smaller parks and commons of south-east London that make up the Green Chain between the eastern stretches of the Thames and Crystal Palace. Brought together by 27km/16.5 miles of interlinked walks, it encompasses woodland, palace gardens, bird-rich wetlands, and some fine historical architecture. There are some surprises too: look out for fossils at Lesnes Abbey woods or the roost of Indian ring-necked parakeets that have made Hither Green Cemetery their home.

A detailed route pack can be ordered at www.greenchain.com which also gives an excellent overview of the ten devised walks and itineraries for family days out.

VISIT...   ...SAMPHIRE HOE

This 75-acre beauty spot at the foot of the Dover cliffs, just off the North Downs Way, is based on the mound of spoil dug from the Channel Tunnel. The site was first used as a platform for the Dover to Folkestone railway in 1843 after blowing up part of the cliff, and was later home to a short-lived colliery. Then it became the staging post for two failed chunnel attempts (the first in 1882) before being landscaped and planted with wildflowers. A 2km, wheelchair-accessible circuit takes you through the hoe and along the bracing seawall with fantastic views of the famous cliff-face. Adders and lizards can be seen in summer as well as the occasional grazing sheep.

Visit www.samphirehoe.com or ☎ 01304 225649 for details of visitor times.

SEE...   ...COBSTONE MILL

There's more than one silver-screened reason why this landmark windmill in Ibstone, Buckinghamshire, might be familiar to you, but its starring role as the workshop of *Chitty Chitty Bang Bang*'s inventor Caractacus Potts is probably the most famous. Built around 1816, it enjoys some of the best views of the surrounding Chilterns and overlooks the chocolate-box village of Turville – itself a regular backdrop for the TV series *The Vicar of Dibley*. You're sure to spot red kites at close quarters as you descend into the village, where you can stop for a pint at the splendid Bull & Butcher before joining the Chilterns Way.

Buckinghamshire & West Middlesex Group gives details of some excellent walks in the region at www.bucks-wmiddx-ramblers.org.uk.

LOCAL RAMBLERS GROUPS... Inner London Area is compiling a small library of self-guided walks around London on their website (see p88), where you'll also find details of their family walks, Saturday strolls and summer waterways walks – all open to the public... **The guide to the picturesque, 96.6km/60-mile Milton Keynes Boundary Walk has been revived by Milton Keynes & District Group and is freely downloadable from their website (see p85)**... Members of West Berkshire Group have worked with the local council to produce a map of walking short-cuts in Newbury. Download it from West Berkshire Council's website www.westberks.gov.uk or ☎ 01635 519505.

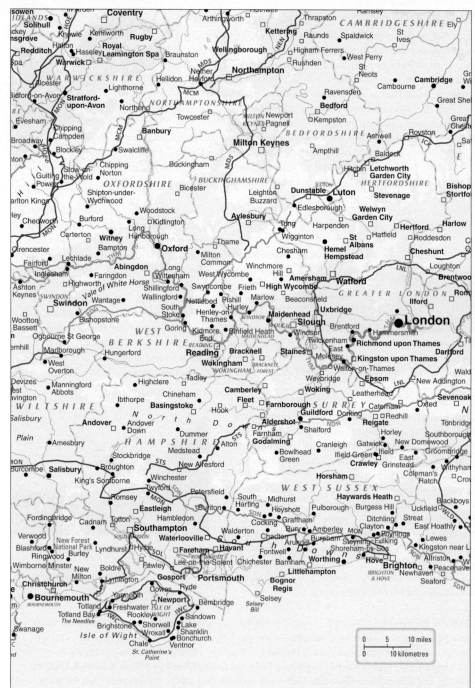

MAP   149

SOUTH

BED & BREAKFAST

BERKSHIRE

● Reading
THAMES PATH & RIDGEWAY

The New Inn, Chalkhouse Green Road, RG4 9AU ☎ 01189723115 (Rae Rose)
thenewinnrestaurant.co.uk Map 175/700791
£75-£110 D5 F1 ✖ £20, 7pm ▰▰(Reading) Ⓥ Ⓑ ⊛ 🐾👜🛁♿Ⓕ

BUCKINGHAMSHIRE

● Amersham
CHILTERN WAY & RIDGEWAY

Mrs Pat Orme, 49 Lowndes Avenue, HP5 2HH ☎ 01494 792647 (Mrs P Orme)
pageormelowndes@tiscali.co.uk Map 165/957022
£28-£30 S1 T1 ✖ nearby ▰▰(Chesham) ⊛ 🐾👜🛁 ★★★

● Edlesborough
RIDGEWAY

Ridgeway End, 5 Ivinghoe Way, LU6 2EL ☎ 01525 220405 (Mr & Mrs Lloyd)
www.ridgewayend.co.uk Map 165/974183
✖ Ⓓ Ⓑ ⊛ 🐾🚗!

● Marlow
THAMES PATH

Merrie Hollow
Seymour Court Hill, Marlow Road, SL7 3DE ☎ 01628 485663
(Mr & Mrs B Wells) bandb@thamesinternet.com Map 175/837889
£35 S2 D2 T1 ✖ £15, 7pm ▰▰(Marlow)
Ⓥ Ⓓ Ⓑ ⊛ 🐾🚗🛁

Secluded country house in large garden.
150 yards off B482 Marlow to Stokenchurch Road.
Easy access to M4,M40 and M25 also to London and Oxford.

● Princes Risborough
RIDGEWAY

Red Lion Public House and Bed & Breakfast, Upper Icknield Way, HP27 0LL
☎ 01844 344476 (Tim Hibbert)
www.theredlionwhiteleaf.co.uk Map 165/819041
£40 D2 T2 ✖ £10, 7pm ▰▰(Princes Risborough or Monks Risborough)
Ⓥ Ⓑ ⊛ 🐾👜🛁♿

● West Wycombe
The Swan Inn, HP14 3AE ☎ 01494 527031
Map 175/829945
£30 S1 D1 T1 F1 ✖ nearby ▰▰(Saunderton) ⊛

HAMPSHIRE

● Broughton
MONARCH'S WAY

Kings, Salisbury Road, SO20 8BY ☎ 01794 301458 (Ann Heather)
Map 185/300336
£25 D1 T1 ✖ £10, 8pm Ⓥ Ⓓ Ⓑ 🐾🛁🚗!

● Dummer

Oakdown Farm
RG23 7LR ☎ 01256 397218 (Mrs E Hutton)
Map 185/587472
£25-£30 D1 T2
Ⓓ ⊛ 🐾🛁🚗!👜 ★★★Ⓜ

Wayfarer's Walk 200 metres.
North of Junction 7 M3.
Secluded position.
Evening meal locally.
Lifts available.
Car parking.

● Hambledon
MONARCH'S WAY

Mornington House, Speltham Hill, PO7 4RU ☎ 023 9263 2704
(Mr & Mrs Lutyens) Map 196/644149
£25 T2 ✖ nearby Ⓓ 🐾🛁🚗👜

● Ibthorpe
TEST WAY

Staggs Cottage, Windmill Hill, Hurstbourne Tarrant, SP11 0BP
☎ 01264 736235 (Mr & Mrs Norton)
www.staggscottage.co.uk Map 185/374536
£30-£40 D1 T2 ✖ £10, 6pm Ⓥ Ⓓ ⊛ 🐾🛁🚗👜 ★★★★Ⓜ

● King's Somborne
MONARCH'S WAY

High View, 12 Nutcher Drove, SO20 6PA ☎ 01794 388626 (Frances Shone)
pjshone@btinternet.com Map 185/363313
✖ nearby Ⓓ Ⓑ ⊛ 🐾🚗!👜

● Lymington
NEW FOREST
SOLENT WAY

Honeysuckle House, 24 Clinton Road, SO41 9EA ☎ 01590 676635
(Mrs P Farrell) www.newforest.demon.co.uk/honeysuckle.htm Map 196/322962
£30-£35 D1 ✖ nearby ▰▰(Lymington Town) Ⓓ Ⓑ ⊛ 🐾🛁👜

● Lyndhurst
NEW FOREST
SOLENT WAY

Stable End, Emery Down, SO43 7FJ ☎ 023 8028 2504 (William & Mary Dibben)
dibbenfam@aol.com
£30-£35 D1 T1 ✖ nearby ▰▰(Ashurst) Ⓓ Ⓑ ⊛ 🛁🚗!★★★★

Heather House, Southampton Rd, SO43 7BQ ☎ 02380 28 4409 (Ann Evans)
www.heatherhouse.co.uk Map 196/304082
£30-£37.50 S1 D6 T2 F1
✖ nearby ▰▰(Ashurst/Brockenhurst) Ⓓ Ⓑ 🐾🛁🚗Ⓕ ★★★

Burwood Lodge
27 Romsey Road, SO43 7AA ☎ 023 8028 2445 (Betty Tennant)
www.burwoodlodge.co.uk Map 196/299083
£35 S1 D3 T1 F2 ✕ nearby
🅳 🅱 ⊗ 🐾 🖐 🚗 ♿ 🅵 ★★★★Ⓢ

Delightful Edwardian house set in half acre grounds. Family-run guest house offering comfort and hospitality. Guest lounge, excellent breakfast and close to shops, pubs and restaurants. Ideal for cyclist and walkers. Private parking.

● Medstead
Plum Cottage, Hattingley Road, GU34 5NQ ☎ 01420 563741
(Jean Westmacott) www.plumcottagehampshire.com
✕ £6, 7pm ⋙(Medstead) 🆅 🅳 🐾 🚗 ! 🍴 ♿

● Petersfield
SOUTH DOWNS
SOUTH DOWNS WAY
Heath Farmhouse, Sussex Road, GU31 4HU ☎ 01730 264709
(Mrs P Scurfield) www.heathfarmhouse.co.uk Map 197/757224
£30-£35 D1 T1 F1 ⋙(Petersfield)
🅳 🅱 ⊗ 🐾 🖐 🚗 ! 🍴 ★★★★Ⓦ

I The Spain, Sheep St, GU32 3JZ ☎ 01730 263261 (Jennifer Tarver)
www.1thespain.com Map 197/748232
£38-£40 D2 T1 ✕ nearby ⋙(Petersfield) 🅳 🅱 ⊗ 🐾 🖐 🚗 🍴 ★★★★

● Twyford
SOUTH DOWNS WAY & MONARCH'S WAY
Orchard House, Orchard House, Manor Road, Twyford, SO21 1RJ
☎ 01962 712067 (Susan Flemons) www.orchardhousetwyford.co.uk Map 185/479242
£40 S3 D3 T1 ✕ nearby ⋙(Shawford) 🅱 ⊗ 🐾 🖐 🚗 ★★★

● Winchester
SOUTH DOWNS WAY & MONARCH'S WAY
St Margaret's, 3 St Michael's Road, SO23 9JE ☎ 01962 861450
(Mrs Brigid Brett) www.winchesterbandb.com Map 185/479290
£27.50-£45 S2 D1 T1 ✕ nearby ⋙(Winchester) 🅳 ⊗ 🖐 ★★★

ISLE OF WIGHT

● Bonchurch
ISLE OF WIGHT COASTAL PATH

The Lake Hotel
Shore Road, PO38 1RF ☎ 01983 852613
www.lakehotel.co.uk Map 196/572778
£42 S1 D8 T6 F5
✕ £12, 7pm ⋙(Shanklin) 🆅 🅳 🅱 ⊗ 🐾 🖐 ! 🍴 ★★★★

Visiting beautiful Bonchurch? Comfortable en-suite accommodation in a country house in beautiful two acre garden, 400 yards from sea. Same family run for over 40 years with assured first class food/service and comfort. Special four night break including car-ferry, dinner/breakfast £175.

● Brighstone
ISLE OF WIGHT COASTAL PATH
Buddlebrook Guest House, Moortown Lane, PO30 4AN
☎ 01983 740381 www.buddlebrookguesthouse.co.uk
Map 196/426832
£25-£30 D2 T1 ✕ nearby 🅳 🅱 ⊗ 🖐 🚗 ! 🍴

● Chale
ISLE OF WIGHT COASTAL PATH
Cortina, Gotten Lane, PO38 2HQ ☎ 01983 551292 (Mrs E L Whittington)
Map 196/487791
£35 D1 T1 ✕ nearby 🅳 ⊗ 🐾 🚗 !

Butterfly Paragliding, Sunacre, The Terrace, PO38 2HL ☎ 01983 731611
(Miranda Botha) www.paraglide.uk.com Map 196/484774
£20 T2 ✕ nearby 🅳 ⊗ 🐾 🖐 🚗 ! Ⓖ

● Freshwater
ISLE OF WIGHT COASTAL PATH
Rockstone Cottage, Colwell Chine Road, PO40 9NR ☎ 01983 753723
www.rockstonecottage.co.uk Map 196/329876
£36-£60 D2 T2 F1 ✕ nearby
🅳 🅱 ⊗ 🐾 🖐 🚗 ! ★★★★Ⓢ Ⓜ

Seahorses, Victoria Road, PO40 9PP ☎ 01983 752574 (Mrs Brenda Moscoff)
www.seahorsesisleofwight.com Map 196/341866
£26-£32 D1 T1 F2 ✕ nearby
🅳 🅱 ⊗ 🐾 🖐 🚗 ! 🍴 ★★★★

● Rookley
Sundowner B&B, Niton Road, PO38 3NX ☎ 01983 721350
(Pauline & Peter Wade) www.sundowner.iowight.com Map 196/508835
£24-£27.50 D2 T1 F1 ✕ nearby 🅳 🅱 ⊗ 🐾 🖐 🚗 🍴

● Sandown
ISLE OF WIGHT COASTAL PATH
Heathfield House, 52 Melville St, PO36 8LF ☎ 01983 400002
(Mike or Jackie Sollis) www.heathfieldhousehotel.com Map 196/595841
✕ ⋙(Sandown) 🅳 🅱 ⊗ 🐾

● Shanklin
ISLE OF WIGHT COASTAL PATH
The Edgecliffe, Clarence Gardens, PO37 6HA ☎ 01983 866199
(Mick & Dru Webster) www.wightonline.co.uk/edgecliffehotel
Map 196/585820
£25-£33 S2 D4 T1 F3 ✕ £11.95, 6:30pm ⋙(Shanklin)
🆅 🅳 🅱 ⊗ 🐾 🖐 ★★★★

The Grange by the Sea, 9 Eastcliff Road, PO37 6AA ☎ 01983 867 644
(Jenni Canakis) www.thegrangebythesea.com Map 196/582811
£65-£73 S1 D8 T6 F2 ✕ nearby ⋙(Shanklin)
🅳 🅱 ⊗ 🖐 ♿ 🅵 ★★★★

St Brelades Hotel, 15 Hope Road, PO37 6EA ☎ 01983 862967 (Don Hobbs)
www.st-brelades-hotel.co.uk Map 196/585818
£25-£33 S2 D6 T3 F4 ✕ nearby
⋙(Shanklin Station) 🅳 🅱 ⊗ 🐾 🖐

● Shorwell Newport
ISLE OF WIGHT COASTAL PATH
Presford Farm, Shorwell, PO30 3LW ☎ 01983 551216 (Jill Fryer)
www.presfordfarm.co.uk Map 196/463821
£30-£35 S1 D1 T1 ✕ nearby 🅳 🅱 ⊗ 🖐 Ⓦ

SOUTH

● Totland
ISLE OF WIGHT COASTAL PATH

The Hermitage
Cliff Road, Totland Bay, PO39 0EW
☎ 01983 752518 (David & Jane Blake)
www.thehermitagebnb.com Map 196/020864
£30-£35 D2 T1 F1 ✕ £15, 7pm Ⓥ Ⓓ Ⓑ ⊛ 🐾👶♨ ⌂ ! ⛲

The Hermitage: a beautiful 1880s Victorian home in west Wight (an area of outstanding natural beauty), situated between the coastal path and the cliff edge immediately above Totland Bay. An ideal centre for enjoying all the country walks.

● Wroxall
Will-o-Wisp Bed & Breakfast, Castle Road, PO38 3DU ☎ 01983 854241
(Hazel Wood) www.will-o-wisp.co.uk Map 196/552801
£27.50 D1 ✕ nearby ₩(Shanklin)
Ⓓ Ⓑ ⊛ 🐾👶 ⌂ ! ★★★★

KENT

● Bilsington
SAXON SHORE WAY

Willow Farm, Stone Cross, TN25 7JJ ☎ 01233 721700 (Mrs Hopper)
www.willowfarmenterprises.co.uk Map 189/028366
£35 T1 F1 Ⓓ ⊛ 🐾 ⌂ ! ★★★

● Charing
NORTH DOWNS WAY

23 The Moat, TN27 0JH ☎ 01233 713141 (Margaret Micklewright)
m.micklewright@btinternet.com Map 189/954492
£27 T1 ✕ nearby ₩(Charing) Ⓓ Ⓑ ⊛ 👶 ⌂ Ⓜ

● Chilham
NORTH DOWNS WAY & STOUR VALLEY PATH

The Old Alma, Canterbury Road, CT4 8DX ☎ 01227 731913
(Mrs Jo Niven) oldalma@aol.com Map 179/079538
£35-£45 D3 ✕ nearby ₩(Chilham)
Ⓓ Ⓑ ⊛ 🐾👶 ⌂

Homelea, Canterbury Road, CT4 8AG ☎ 07951 496836 (Fiona Ely)
www.members.lycos.co.uk/canterburyhotels/ Map 179/084543
£40-£85 D2 T2 F1 ✕ nearby ₩(Chilham)
Ⓓ Ⓑ ⊛ 🐾👶 ⌂ ! ★★★★★

● Cranbrook
The Hollies, Old Angley Road, TN17 2PN ☎ 01580 713106
(Mrs D M Waddoup) digsw@talktalk.net Map 188/775367
£27.50 S1 D1 T1 F1 ✕ nearby ₩(Staplehurst)
Ⓓ Ⓑ ⊛ 🐾👶 ⌂ ⛲♿ Ⓕ

● Detling
NORTH DOWNS WAY

Detling Coach House Hotel, Scragged Oak Road, ME14 3HB ☎ 01622 737590
(Emma or Pan Tang) www.detlingcoachhouse.co.uk Map 178/799591
£50 S2 D3 T3 ✕, 5pm ₩(Bearsted)
Ⓥ Ⓓ Ⓑ ⊛ 🐾👶 ⌂ ★★★

● Dover
NORTH DOWNS WAY

Amanda Guest House, 4 Harold Street, CT16 1SF ☎ 01304 201711
www.amandaguesthouse.homestead.com Map 179/320418
£20-£25 D1 T1 F1 ₩(Dover Priory) Ⓓ ⊛ ★★★

Bleriot's, 47 Park Avenue, CT16 1HE ☎ 01304 211394 (M J Casey)
www.bleriots.net Map 179/316422
✕ ₩(Dover Priory) Ⓑ

● Etchinghill
NORTH DOWNS WAY

One Step Beyond, Westfield Lane, CT18 8BT ☎ 01303 862637
(John & Jenny Holden) johnosb@rdplus.net Map 179/166394
£25-£30 S2 D1 F1 ✕ nearby ₩(Sandling, Kent)
Ⓑ ⊛ 🐾👶 ⌂ !

● Harrietsham
NORTH DOWNS WAY

Homestay, 14 Chippendayle Drive, ME17 1AD ☎ 01622 858698
(Barbara Beveridge) www.kent-homestay.info Map 189/870527
✕ nearby ₩(Harrietsham) Ⓓ Ⓑ ⊛ 🐾 ⌂ !

● Kingsdown
Gardeners' Rest, Nemesis, Queensdown Road, CT14 8EF ☎ 01304 371449
(Mr & Mrs Upton) www.holidaysdeal.co.uk Map 179/373477
£50-£55 D1 F1 ✕ £17.50, 7pm
Ⓥ Ⓓ Ⓑ ⊛ 🐾👶 ⌂ ★★★★★Ⓖ

● Lympne
Corner House, Aldington Road, CT21 4LF ☎ 01303 268108 (Denise Jorgensen)
www.cornerhouselympne.co.uk Map 179/119349
£30-£40 D2 T1 ✕ nearby ₩(Westenhanger)
Ⓓ Ⓑ ⊛ 🐾👶 ⌂ !

● New Romney
Broadacre Hotel, North Street, TN288DR ☎ 01797 362381 (Lyndon Smith)
www.broadacrehotel.co.uk Map 189/063248
£48-£52 S3 D4 T2 ✕ £17, 5pm
Ⓥ Ⓑ ⊛ 🐾👶 ★★

● Rochester
NORTH DOWNS WAY

St Martin, 104 Borstal Road, ME1 3BD ☎ 01634 848192 (Mrs H Colvin)
icolvin@stmartin.freeserve.co.uk Map 178/736673
₩(Rochester) Ⓓ Ⓑ ⊛ 🐾 ⌂ ! 👶 Ⓜ

● Sandwich
Ilex Cottage, Temple Way, Worth, CT14 0DA ☎ 01304 617026 (Mrs Stobie)
www.ilexcottage.com Map 179/335560
£40-£45 D1 T2 ✕ nearby ₩(Sandwich)
Ⓓ Ⓑ ⊛ 🐾👶 ⌂ ! ♨♿ Ⓕ ★★★★

Le Trayas, Poulders Road, CT13 0BB ☎ 01304 611056 (Mrs R A Pettican)
www.letrayas.co.uk Map 179/322576
£25 D1 T2 ✕ nearby ₩(Sandwich) Ⓓ Ⓑ ⊛ 🐾👶 ⌂ !

PENNY FOR YOUR THOUGHTS:
Found somewhere good that's not in the guide?
Use the Recommendation/Feedback Form on p113.

LONDON

● Brentford
THAMES PATH

Primrose House, 56 Boston Gardens, TW8 9LP ☎ 020 8568 5573
(Garrie & Constance Williams) www.primrosehouse.com Map 176/164786
£43-£53 D2 T2 ⚶(Brentford) B ⊗ ♿ 🚗 ! ★★★★

● Central London
THAMES PATH

Cardiff Hotel
5-9 Norfolk Square, W2 1RU
☎ 020 7723 3513 (Debbie & Andrew Davies)
www.cardiff-hotel.com Map 176/268812
£49-£55 S26 D24 T6 F5 ✕ nearby ⚶(Paddington) B ⊗ ♿ ★★★

15 minutes from Heathrow Airport by express train, the Cardiff overlooks a quiet garden square just 2 minutes walk from Paddington station. Rooms have TV, phone, hairdryer, tea making facilities and wireless internet access. Hearty English breakfast included.

● Hammersmith
THAMES PATH

91 Langthorne St, SW6 6JU ☎ 020 7381 0198 (Brigid Richardson)
www.londonthameswalk.co.uk Map 176/236770
£25-£40 S1 D2 T1 ✕ nearby ⚶(Hammersmith)
D B ⊗ 🛁 ★★★

● Richmond-upon-Thames
LONDON LOOP

Ivy Cottage, Upper Ham Road, Ham Common, TW10 5LA ☎ 020 8940 8601
(David Taylor) www.dbta.freeserve.co.uk Map 176/178717
£26-£30 S1 D1 T2 F1
✕ nearby D B ⊗ 🍴 ♿ 🚗 ! 🛁 ★★★

OXFORDSHIRE

● Faringdon
THAMES PATH

Sudbury House Hotel, 39 Street, SN7 8AA ☎ 01367 241272 (Andrew Ibbotson)
www.sudburyhouse.co.uk Map 164/294954
£75-£95 D39 T10 F2 ✕ £23.50, 5pm
V D B ⊗ 🍴 ♿ 🚗 ! 🛁 ♿ F ★★★

● Goring-on-Thames
RIDGEWAY & THAMES PATH

Perch & Pike, The Street, RG8 0JS ☎ 01491 872415 (Neil Dorsett)
www.perchandpike.co.uk Map 174/599834
£80 D3 T1 ✕ £14, 7pm ⚶(Goring & Streatley)
V D B ⊗ 🍴 ♿ 🚗 !

Northview House, Farm Rd, RG8 0AA ☎ 01491 872184 (I. Sheppard)
hi@goring-on-thames.freeserve.co.uk Map 175/603808
£25-£30 S1 D2 T1 F1 ✕ nearby ⚶(Goring & Streatley)
D ⊗ 🍴 ♿ 🛁 Ⓜ

● Henley-on-Thames
THAMES PATH & RIDGEWAY

Lenwade, 3 Western Road, RG9 1JL ☎ 01491 573468 (Mrs J Williams)
www.w3b-ink.com/lenwade Map 175/760817
£35-£37.50 D2 T1 ✕ nearby ⚶(Henley-on-Thames)
D B ⊗ 🍴 ♿ 🚗 ! ★★★★★Ⓦ Ⓜ

● Long Wittenham
THAMES PATH

Witta's Ham Cottage, High Street, OX14 4QH ☎ 01865 407686
(Mrs Jill Mellor) bandb@wittenham.com Map 164/546937
£36-£38 S1 D1 T1 ✕ nearby ⚶(Culham)
D ⊗ 🍴 ♿ 🚗 ! ★★★★Ⓢ

● Nettlebed
RIDGEWAY

Park Corner Farm House, RG9 6DX ☎ 01491 641450 (Mrs S Rutter)
parkcorner_farmhouse@hotmail.com Map 175/688891
£27.50-£30 S1 T1 ✕ nearby D ⊗ 🍴 ♿ 🚗 ! 🛁 ★★★

● Nuffield
RIDGEWAY

14 Bradley Road, RG9 5SG ☎ 01491 641359 (Diana Chambers)
dianamc@waitrose.com Map 175/681882
£30 D2 T1 ✕ nearby D B ⊗ 🍴 ♿ 🚗 ! 🛁

● Pishill
RIDGEWAY

Bank Farm, RG9 6HS ☎ 01491 638601 (Mrs E Lakey)
e.f.lakey@btinternet.com Map 175/713898
£25 D2 T1 ✕ nearby D ⊗ 🍴 ♿ 🚗 !

● Shillingford
THAMES PATH

The Kingfisher Inn, 27 Henley Road, OX10 7EL ☎ 01865 858595
(Alexis or Mayumi) www.kingfisher-inn.co.uk Map 164/595928
£62 D5 T1 ✕ £10, 7:30pm
V D B ⊗ 🍴 ♿ 🚗 ! ★★★★

● Shipton-under-Wychwood
Court Farm, Mawles Lane, OX7 6DA ☎ 01993 831515 (Belinda Willson)
www.courtfarmbb.com Map 163/279177
£40-£45 D2 T1 ✕ nearby ⚶(Shipton-under-Wychwood)
D B ⊗ 🍴 ♿ 🚗 🛁 ♿ ★★★★Ⓢ

● Swalcliffe
MACMILLAN WAY

Grange Farm Bed & Breakfast
Swalcliffe Grange, OX15 5EX
☎ 01295 780206 (Barbara Taylor)
www.swalcliffegrange.com Map 151/372369
✕ nearby B ⊗ 🍴

Enjoy warm hospitality and peaceful surroundings in 18th century farmhouse.

● **Swyncombe**

RIDGEWAY

Pathways, Cookley Green, RG9 6EN ☎ 01491 641631 (Mrs Ismayne Peters)
ismayne.peters@tesco.net Map 175/695901
£30 D1 T2 ✗ £15, 7pm Ⓥ Ⓓ Ⓑ ⊛ 🐾 ♿ 🚗 !

● **Wallingford**

THAMES PATH & RIDGEWAY

B & B at Little Gables, 166 Crowmarsh Hill, OX10 8BG ☎ 01491 837834
(Jill & Tony Reeves) www.stayingaway.com Map 175/627887
£45-£55 S2 D3 T3 F2 ✗ nearby ⋙(Cholsey)
Ⓓ Ⓑ ⊛ 🐾 ♿ ! ♿ ★★★★Ⓦ

Huntington House, 18 Wood Street, OX10 0AX ☎ 01491 839201
(Julie & Mike Huntington) hunting311@aol.com
Map 175/607891 ✗ Ⓓ Ⓑ ⊛ 🐾 !

Alouette Bed & Breakfast, 2 Caldicott Close, Shillingford, OX10 7HF
☎ 01865 858600 (Wendy Seymour) www.alouettebandb.co.uk
Map 164/596928
£40-£45 S2 D2 T1 F1 ✗ nearby Ⓓ Ⓑ ⊛ 🐾 ♿ 🚗 ! ★★★★

● **Wantage**

RIDGEWAY

Lockinge Kiln Farm, The Ridgeway, Chain Hill, OX12 8PA ☎ 01235 763308
(Mrs Stella Cowan) www.lockingekiln.co.uk Map 174/423833
£25-£30 D1 T2 ✗ £12.50, 6:30pm Ⓥ Ⓓ ⊛ 🐾 ♿ !

Regis Guesthouse, Regis House, 12 Charlton Road, OX12 8ER ☎ 01235 762860
(Mrs Millie Rastall) regisguesthouse.com Map 174/404879
£40-£45 D2 T2 F1 ✗ £15, 7pm
Ⓥ Ⓓ Ⓑ ⊛ 🐾 ♿ ! Ⓕ ★★★Ⓢ

SURREY

● **Dorking**

NORTH DOWNS WAY

5 Rose Hill, RH4 2EG ☎ 01306 883127 (Margaret Walton)
www.altourism.com/uk/walt.html Map 187/166491
£40-£70 D1 T1 F1 ✗ £16, 6pm ⋙(Dorking North)
Ⓥ Ⓓ Ⓑ ⊛ 🐾 ♿ 🚗 ! ★★★★

Claremont Cottage
Rose Hill, RH4 2ED
☎ 01306 885487 (Mrs Julie Hedge) www.claremontcott.co.uk
Map 187/164489 £55-£60 S3 D2 T1
✗ nearby ⋙(Dorking) Ⓑ ⊛ 🐾 ♿ 🚗 ★★★★

Olde worlde cottage, former coach house and stable, with modern amenities. Very close to town centre, yet peaceful location down own lane. Off road parking available for cars. All rooms with en-suite. Easy access to London, M25 and beauty spots.

● **Guildford**

NORTH DOWNS WAY

25 Scholars Walk, Ridgemount, GU2 7TR ☎ 01483 531351 (Dr Prime)
Map 186/988498
£45-£55 S2 ✗ nearby ⋙(Guildford) Ⓓ ⊛ ♿

Highfield House, 18 Harvey Rd, GU1 3SG ☎ 01483 534946 (Mike & Jo Anning)
mj.anning@clara.co.uk Map 186/001494
£30 D1 T1 ✗ nearby ⋙(Guildford) Ⓓ Ⓑ ⊛ ♿ 🚗 Ⓜ

● **Hampton Court**

THAMES PATH

Hurst Meadow B & B, 42 Rivermead, KT8 9AZ ☎ 020 8783 1252
(Sue Stannard) www.hurstmeadow.co.uk Map 119/251746
£35-£40 S1 T2 F1 ✗ £10, 7pm ⋙(Hampton Court)
Ⓥ Ⓓ ⊛ 🐾 ♿ 🚗 ! Ⓜ

● **Horley**

The Lawn Guest House, 30 Massetts Rd, RH6 7DF ☎ 01293 775751
(Adrian Grinsted) www.lawnguesthouse.co.uk Map 187/283428
✗ ⋙(Horley/Gatwick) Ⓓ Ⓑ ⊛ 🚗 🏠 ★★★★Ⓢ

Rosemead Guest House
19 Church Road, RH6 7EY ☎ 01293 784965 (Miss Fiona Stimpson)
www.rosemeadguesthouse.co.uk Map 187/279429
£38-£45 S2 D1 T1 F2 ✗ nearby ⋙(Horley/Gatwick)
Ⓓ Ⓑ ⊛ 🐾 ♿ 🚗 ! 🏠 ★★★★Ⓢ

A warm welcome awaits you at this non-smoking Edwardian guesthouse. Five minutes from Gatwick Airport. 24-hour courtesy transfers. Full English breakfast 7:30-8:30am. CTV and full central heating. Private bathrooms in all rooms. Holiday parking available. Families welcome.

Southbourne Guest House
34 Massetts Road, Gatwick, RH6 7DS ☎ 01293 771991 (Tony Breen)
www.southbournegatwick.com Map 187/280428
£45 S2 D3 T3 F4 ✗ nearby ⋙(Horley)
Ⓑ ⊛ 🚗 ♿ ! Ⓕ ★★★★

A warm welcome awaits you in our family-run guesthouse. Ideally located for Gatwick Airport and exploring Surrey, Sussex and London. Five minutes' walk from Horley train station, restaurants, shops and pubs. 30 minutes by train from London and five minutes from Gatwick.

The Corner House Gatwick
72 Massetts Road, RH6 7ED ☎ 01293 784574 (Chris Smith)
www.thecornerhouse.co.uk Map 187/278427
£39-£49 S5 D8 T4 F4 ✗ £7.50, 8pm ⋙(Horley/Gatwick)
Ⓥ Ⓓ Ⓑ ⊛ 🐾 ♿ 🚗 ! 🏠 ♿ Ⓕ ★★★★

Family run hotel offering quality accommodation, bar/restaurant and 24hr transfers to Gatwick Airport. Holiday parking available.

● **Oxted**

NORTH DOWNS WAY

Meads, 23 Granville Road, RH8 0BX ☎ 01883 730115 (Helen Holgate)
www.bandbmeads.co.uk Map 187/399530
£48 D2 T1 ✗ nearby ⋙(Oxted) Ⓓ Ⓑ ⊛ 🐾 ♿ 🚗 !

● Shalford
NORTH DOWNS WAY

The Laurels, 23 Dagden Road, GU4 8DD ☎ 01483 565753
(Mrs M J Deeks) Map 186/000475
£26 S1 D1 T1 ✕ £9, 7pm ⋘(Shalford)
Ⓥ Ⓓ Ⓑ ⊗ 🐾 🛁 🚗 ！🏠 ★★★Ⓦ Ⓜ

EAST SUSSEX

● Alfriston
SOUTH DOWNS
SOUTH DOWNS WAY & WEALDWAY

Dacres, BN26 5TP ☎ 01323 870447
(Mrs Patsy Embry) Map 199/518028
£42 T1 ✕ nearby ⋘(Berwick) Ⓓ Ⓑ ⊗ 🛁 ！

5 The Broadway, BN26 5XL ☎ 01323 870145 (Mrs Janet Dingley)
janetandbrian@dingley5635.freeserve.co.uk Map 199/516030
£28-£33 S1 D1 T1 Ⓓ Ⓑ ⊗ 🐾🛁 🚗 ！

Wychmount House Bed and Breakfast, 19 Kings Ride, BN26 5XP
☎ 01323 871088 (Fran Wates) www.wychmounthouse.co.uk Map 199/518029
£25-£35 S1 F1 ✕ nearby ⋘(Berwick) Ⓓ ⊗ 🐾🛁 🚗 ！🏠

Winton Fields, Alfriston, BN26 5UJ ☎ 01323 870306 (Heather Hurst)
heatherhurst1@googlemail.com Map 199/518038
£25-£35 D1 T1 ✕ £8, 7pm ⋘(Berwick) Ⓥ Ⓓ Ⓑ ⊗ 🐾🛁 🚗 ！🏠

● Colemans Hatch
Gospel Oak, TN7 4ER ☎ 01342 823840 (Mrs L Hawker)
lindah@thehatch.freeserve.co.uk Map 187/447327
£28-£40 D1 T1 ✕ £14, 7pm
Ⓥ Ⓓ Ⓑ ⊗ 🐾🛁 🚗 ！🏠 ★★★Ⓜ

● Eastbourne
SOUTH DOWNS WAY & WEALDWAY

Brayscroft House, 13 South Cliff Avenue, BN20 7AH ☎ 01323 647005
www.brayscrofthotel.co.uk Map 199/609980
✕ £14 ⋘(Eastbourne) Ⓥ Ⓓ Ⓑ ⊗ 🐾🚗 🏠 Ⓖ

Southcroft, 15 South Cliff Ave, BN20 7AH ☎ 01323 729071 (Andrew Johnson)
www.southcrofthotel.co.uk Map 199/609980
£38 S1 D3 T2 ✕ £12, 6pm ⋘(Eastbourne)
Ⓥ Ⓓ Ⓑ ⊗ 🐾🛁 🚗 ！★★★★Ⓢ

Courtlands Hotel
3-5 Wilmington Garden, BN21 4JN
☎ 01323723737 (Mrs.Bawa) www.courtlandseastbourne.com
Map 199/611982 ✕ £17, 6:30pm
⋘(Eastbourne) Ⓥ Ⓓ 🐾🚗 ！🛁 ★★

Courtlands Hotel has large free car park, 45 en-suite bedrooms, located within 100 yards of the Seafront, one mile from the town centre. Opposite to the Congress Conference Centre, Winter Gardens, Devonshire Park Theatre and Tennis courts. Pets welcome.

Beach Haven, 61 Pevensey Road, BN21 3HS ☎ 01323 726195
(Christine & Ken Martin) www.beach-haven.co.uk Map 199/617992
£30-£35 S3 D2 T2 ✕ £10, 6pm ⋘(Eastbourne)
Ⓥ Ⓓ Ⓑ ⊗ 🐾🛁 ★★★

Meridale Guest House, 91 Royal Parade, BN22 7AE ☎ 01323 729686
(Jane Bradley) www.meridaleguesthouse.co.uk Map 199/622998
£28-£30 D3 T1 F2 ✕ nearby ⋘(Eastbourne)
Ⓓ Ⓑ ⊗ 🐾Ⓜ

The Berkeley, 3 Lascelles Terrace, BN21 4BJ ☎ 01323 645055 (Tony Scott)
www.theberkeley.net Map 199/612984
£39-£45 S2 D4 T3 F4 ✕ nearby ⋘(Eastbourne)
Ⓑ ⊗ 🐾🛁 🏠 ★★★★★

● Hailsham
WEALDWAY

Longleys Farm Cottage, Harebeating Lane, BN27 1ER ☎ 01323 841227
(David & Jill Hook) www.longleysfarmcottage.co.uk Map 199/598105
£26-£30 D1 T1 F1 ✕ nearby Ⓓ Ⓑ ⊗ 🐾🛁 🚗 ★★★

● Hastings

White Cottage
Battery Hill, Fairlight, TN35 4AP ☎ 01424 812528 (John & June Dyer)
www.whitecottagebb.co.uk Map 199/873123
£30-£45 D2 T1 ✕ nearby
Ⓓ Ⓑ ⊗ 🛁 🚗 ★★★★

We are a peaceful, friendly B&B with beautiful gardens for our guests to enjoy. We have three doubles and one twin room, all en-suite (two with sea views). Tea/coffee making facilities and TV in all rooms. Extensive breakfast menu.

● Horam
WEALDWAY

Oak Mead Nursery, Cowden Hall Lane, TN21 9HG
☎ 01435 812962 (Mrs Barbara Curtis) Map 199/597162
£24 S1 D1 T1 Ⓓ Ⓑ ⊗ 🐾🛁

● Lewes
SOUTH DOWNS
SOUTH DOWNS WAY

Bethel, Kingston Ridge,, BN7 3JX ✕ 01273 478658 (Tim & Nancy Lear)
www.bethelbandb.co.uk Map 198/387085
£45 D1 T2 ✕ nearby ⋘(Lewes)
Ⓓ Ⓑ ⊗ 🐾🛁 🚗 ！

Berkeley House, 2 Albion Street, BN7 2ND ☎ 01273 476057 (Roy Patten)
www.berkeleyhouselewes.co.uk Map 198/418102
£50-£65 D2 F1 ⋘(Lewes)
Ⓓ Ⓑ ⊗ 🛁 ★★★★

Bevern Bridge Farm, South Chailey, BN8 4QH
☎ 01273 401846 (Graham Botting) www.bevernbridgefarm.com
Map 198/395163 £35-£45 S1 D4 ✕
£20 , 7:30pm ⋘(Cooksbridge) Ⓥ Ⓓ Ⓑ 🐾🛁 🚗

● Rye
Little Saltcote, 22 Military Rd, TN31 7NY ☎ 01797 223210
(Barbara & Denys Martin) www.littlesaltcote.co.uk Map 189/923212
£31.50-£36.75 D2 F2 ✕ nearby ⋘(Rye)
Ⓓ Ⓑ ⊗ 🐾🚗 ！🏠 ★★★★

SOUTH

The Windmill Guest House
Ferry Road, TN31 7DW ☎ 01797 224027 (Brian Elliott)
www.ryewindmill.co.uk Map 189/916203 £50-£70
D4 T4 ✕ nearby ▥(Rye)
Ⓓ Ⓑ ⊛ 🐴 ♨ ⛁ 🛴 ★★★★

Rye's famous windmill provides the backdrop to this welcoming B&B at the end of the 1066 Walk and very close to The Saxon Way Tour. Just a two-minute walk from the town with fabulous restaurants, tea rooms and quaint pubs.

● Streat
SOUTH DOWNS
SOUTH DOWNS WAY

North Acres, BN6 8RX ☎ 01273 890278 (Mrs Valerie Eastwood)
www.northacres-streat.co.uk Map 198/353154
✕ ▥(Plumpton) Ⓓ Ⓑ ⊛ 🐴 🚗 ⚑

WEST SUSSEX

● Amberley
SOUTH DOWNS
SOUTH DOWNS WAY

Burpham Country House
The Street, BN18 9RJ ☎ 01903 882160 (Jackie Penticost)
www.burphamcountryhouse.com Map 197/041090
£40-£70 S1 D9 T3 ✕ £25, 7pm ▥(Arundel)
Ⓥ Ⓓ Ⓑ ⊛ 🐴 ♨ ⛁ ★★★★

Burpham Country House offers luxury guest house accommodation in the heart of the South Downs near Arundel. You can park and walk directly onto the Downs. We have ten en-suite rooms, and our restaurant is open Wednesday–Saturday.

Woodybanks Cottage, Crossgates, BN18 9NR ☎ 01798 831295
(Mr & Mrs G Hardy) www.woodybanks.co.uk Map 197/041136
£35-£45 D2 F1 ✕ nearby ▥(Amberley)
Ⓓ ⊛ 🐴 ♨ ⛁ 🚗 Ⓕ ★★★★

● Arundel
SOUTH DOWNS
SOUTH DOWNS WAY & MONARCH'S WAY

Arden Guest House, 4 Queen's Lane, BN18 9JN ☎ 01903 882544 (Terry
Meathrel) terryandann@talktalkbusiness.net Map 197/019068
£34 S1 D4 T3 ✕, 5pm ▥(Arundel) Ⓑ ⊛ ♨

Dellfield, 9 Dalloway Road, BN18 9HJ ☎ 01903 882253 (Mrs J M Carter)
jane@heron-electric.com Map 197/006064
£22-£24 S1 T1 ✕ nearby ▥(Arundel) Ⓓ Ⓑ ⊛ 🐴 ♨ 🚗

● Barnham
SOUTH DOWNS

High Trees B&B, High Trees, Lake Lane, Barnham, PO22 0AE ☎ 01243 553008
(Janet Reeves) hightreesbandb.mysite.orange.co.uk Map 197/966047
£30 D1 F1 ✕ nearby ▥(Barnham) Ⓑ ⊛ 🐴 ♨ 🚗

● Burgess Hill
The Homestead, Valebridge Road, RH15 0RQ ☎ 0800 064 0015
(Sue & Mike Mundy) www.burgess-hill.co.uk Map 198/324208
£40 S1 D1 T1 ✕ nearby ▥(Wivelsfield) Ⓓ Ⓑ 🐴 ♨ ⛁ 🛴 ★★★★

● Clayton
SOUTH DOWNS
SOUTH DOWNS WAY

Dower Cottage, Underhill Lane, BN6 9PL ☎ 01273 843363 (Mrs C Bailey)
www.dowercottage.co.uk Map 198/309136
£50 S1 D2 T1 F2 ✕ nearby ▥(Hassocks) Ⓓ Ⓑ ⊛ 🐴 ♨

● Cocking
SOUTH DOWNS
SOUTH DOWNS WAY

The Blue Bell, Bell Lane, GU29 0HN ☎ 01730 813449 (Ashley Finch)
www.thebluebell.org.uk Map 197/877175
£45-£90 D2 T1 ✕ £8.95, 5pm Ⓥ Ⓑ ⊛ 🐴 ♨ ⛁

Downsfold, Bell Lane, Cocking, GU29 0HU ☎ 01730 814376 (Malcolm Hunt)
www.downsfold.co.uk Map 197/876176
£33 D1 T1 ✕ nearby ⊛ 🐴 🚗 ⚑ 🛴

● Ditchling
SOUTH DOWNS
SOUTH DOWNS WAY

South Cottage, 2 The Drove, BN6 8TR ☎ 01273 846636
(Sonia Stock) Map 198/326153
£32-£35 D2 T1 ✕ nearby ▥(Hassocks) Ⓓ ⊛ 🐴 ♨ 🚗 ♨

● Graffham
SOUTH DOWNS WAY

Brook Barn, GU28 0PU ☎ 01798 867356 (Mr & Mrs S A Jollands)
brookbarn@hotmail.com Map 197/929180
£37.50-£65 D1 ✕ nearby Ⓓ Ⓑ ⊛ 🐴 ♨ ⛁ 🛴 Ⓕ ★★★★★Ⓢ

● Heyshott
SOUTH DOWNS
SOUTH DOWNS WAY

Little Hoyle, Hoyle Lane, GU29 0DX ☎ 01798 867359 (Robert & Judith Ralph)
www.smoothhound.co.uk/hotels/littlehoyle Map 197/906187
£32.50-£45 D1 ✕ nearby Ⓓ Ⓑ ⊛ 🐴 ♨ 🚗 ⚑ ★★★★

● Pulborough
SOUTH DOWNS
SOUTH DOWNS WAY

Barn House Lodge, Barn House Lane, RH20 2BS ☎ 01798 872682
(Sue Harvey-Jones) www.barnhouselodge.co.uk Map 197/052185
£35-£40 D1 T1 ✕ nearby ▥(Pulborough) Ⓓ Ⓑ ⊛ 🐴 🚗 ★★★★

● South Harting
SOUTH DOWNS
SOUTH DOWNS WAY

Torberry Cottage, Torberry Farm, GU31 5RG ☎ 01730 826883
(Mrs Maggie Barker) www.visitsussex.org/torberrycottage Map 197/767200
£35-£40 D1 T1 Ⓓ Ⓑ ⊛ 🐴 ♨ 🚗 ⚑ ★★★★

● Steyning
SOUTH DOWNS
MONARCH'S WAY & SOUTH DOWNS WAY

5 Coxham Lane, BN44 3LG ☎ 01903 812286 (Mrs J Morrow) Map 198/176116
£20 S1 T2 ✕ nearby Ⓓ Ⓑ ♨ 🚗 ⚑

Uppingham, Kings Barn Villas, BN44 3FH ☎ 01903 812099
(Mrs Diana Couling) www.uppingham-steyning.co.uk Map 198/182111
£30 S2 D1 T1 ✗ £10, 5pm Ⓥ Ⓓ Ⓑ ⊛ 🐾🏃🚶 ‼ 🏠 Ⓦ Ⓜ

● Walderton
SOUTH DOWNS
MONARCH'S WAY

Hillside Cottages
Cooks Lane, PO18 9EF ☎ 02392 631260 (Robina Richter)
www.hillside-cottages.co.uk Map 197/790107
£25-£35 D1 T1 ✗ nearby
Ⓓ Ⓑ ⊛ 🐾🏃🚶 ‼ ★★★★Ⓦ

Hillside Cottages offers a friendly welcome, delicious homecooked food and a pretty garden with downland views. The Monarch's Way, South Downs Way, South Coast Cycle Route and Kingly Vale National Nature Reserve are nearby. Plus good pub around the corner. Easy parking.

SELF-CATERING

HAMPSHIRE

● Sway
NEW FOREST

Hackney Park Mount Pleasant ☎ 01590 682049 (Mrs Helen Beale)
hackneypark@tiscali.co.uk Map 195/278980
£165-£410 Sleeps 1-6. 3 cottages/flats. ⊛ 🛏 Short breaks available

ISLE OF WIGHT

● Brighstone
ISLE OF WIGHT COASTAL PATH

Sea Breeze Cottage
☎ 01983 740993 (Ginny Peckham)
www.seabreeze-cottage.co.uk Map 196/419821
£250-£590 Sleeps 1-5. 1 modern cottage. ⊛ Short breaks available
★★★★ "A walker's paradise"

Two-bedroomed and recently refurbished to a high standard with extensive sea views in an AONB. 250m from panoramic coastal path and beach and close to downland trails. Patio. Communal garden. Complimentary ferry collection for foot passengers.

● Freshwater
ISLE OF WIGHT COASTAL PATH

Underwood ☎ 01926 336842 (Karen Grainger)
www.60scoastalhouse.co.uk Map 196/340862
£700-£1945 Sleeps 1-10. 1 house. ⊛ Short breaks available ★★★★

The Deyne ☎ 01983 753302 (Pauline Evans)
www.thedeyne.com Map 196/349860
£160-£380 Sleeps 2. 2 self-contained apartments. Short breaks available

Afton Barns
☎ 01920 822600 (Susan Lankester) www.aftonbarns.co.uk
Map 196/351865
£350-£680 Sleeps 1-5. 1 barn conversion.
⊛ 🛏 Short breaks available ★★★

Lovely 3-bedroomed barn conversion at the foot of Afton Down AONB. Excellent base for walking in west Wight, especially Tennyson Trail and Needles. Well-equipped, bright airy rooms and private west-facing garden. Freshwater Bay 10 minutes' walk.

● Godshill
Godshill Park House ☎ 01983 840271 (Nora Down)
www.godshillpark.co.uk Map 195/171147
£240-£1030 Sleeps 2-7. 1 wing of country house.
Short breaks available ★★★★

● Shanklin
ISLE OF WIGHT COASTAL PATH

Greystones
☎ 019830863921 (Mrs C Jones)
greystones-iow.co.uk Map 196/582811
£280-£280 Sleeps 1-2. 1 annexe.
⊛ 🛏 Short breaks available

Newly-renovated annexe with own entrance situated in enclosed courtyard of beautiful Georgian house in Shanklin Old Village.

Entrance lobby with storage, bedsit room with twin singles, separate shower room. Excellent transport links and amenities. Walks, beaches, theatre, restaurants, all nearby.

● Ventnor
ISLE OF WIGHT COASTAL PATH

Garden House
☎ 07887 848146 (Philip Barton)
www.holidaylets.net/properties/13874 Map 196/569779
£475-£1050 Sleeps 1-8. 1 house.
⊛ Short breaks available ★★★★

A family holiday house ideally suited for walkers and families alike.

Within five minutes you can reach superb walking (no car required) onto the Isle of Wight Coastal Path or onto the beautiful Downs.

SOUTH

● **Whitwell**

ISLE OF WIGHT COASTAL PATH

Maytime Cottage
☎ 01403211052 (Jonathan McCulloch) www.maytimecottage.co.uk
Map 196/513788
£290-£770 Sleeps 2-6. 2 cottages.
🐕 🛏 Short breaks available ★★★★

Maytime Cottage and Plum Tree Cottage are two period stone farm cottages in stunning countryside, nestling under the downs within an area of outstanding natural beauty.

Both cottages are spacious with three bedrooms, large living areas, woodburning stoves, central heating and are equipped to a high standard.

Beaches two miles. Pub one mile. Shop one mile. Superb walking with several paths right from the door. Well behaved dogs welcome.

KENT

● **Ashford**

NORTH DOWNS WAY

Kennington House ☎ 01233 636251 (Jenny Marshall)
jennifermarshall@tiscali.co.uk Map 189/025448
£225-£325 Sleeps 2-4. 2 apartments. 🐕 Short breaks available Ⓜ

● **Deal**

The Gulls
☎ 01304 371449 (Mr & Mrs Upton) www.holidaysdeal.co.uk.
£250-£450 Sleeps 2-5.
1 apartment.
🐕 🛏 Short breaks available ★★★★

Luxury, 2nd floor self-contained apartment. Spacious 2 bedroom/2 bathroom. Opposite Saxon Shore Way, Cycle Route 1 & 2, and bandstand. Sleeps five adults. Private parking. All services, linen and towels included. Fully fitted kitchen, washer dryer, dishwasher, central heating. Sea Views.

● **Ramsgate**
Coastguards Cottage ☎ 01634 722444 (Julie Collins)
www.coastguardscottages.co.uk
£300-£650 Sleeps 1-6. 1 cottage. Short breaks available

Please mention **walk BRITAIN**
when booking your accommodation

OXFORDSHIRE

● **Shipton-under-Wychwood**
King Johns Barn ☎ 01993 878075 (Vicky Greves)
www.kingjohnsbarn.co.uk Map 163/278177
£330-£610 Sleeps 2-10. 2 cottages. 🐕 🛏 Short breaks available

EAST SUSSEX

● **Alfriston**

SOUTH DOWNS, SOUTH DOWNS WAY & WEALDWAY

Martlets ☎ 01323 870451 (Rosalind Danesi)
rosalindanesi@hotmail.com Map 199/518030
£400-£550 Sleeps 1-6. 1 ground floor of private house. 🐕 🛏 Short breaks available

● **Rye**

Cadborough Farm
☎ 01424 814823 (Jane Apperly)
www.cadborough.co.uk Map 189/883216
£265-£395 Sleeps 1-2. 5 cottages.
🐕 🛏 Short breaks available

Cadborough Farm holiday cottages offer luxury accommodation just one mile from Rye, East Sussex. Located in the grounds of a farm, yet only 15 minutes walk from the town centre and surrounded by wonderful diverse walks.

● **Seaford**

SOUTH DOWNS WAY

Claremont ☎ 01323 873526 (susan stacey)
dog.crazy3@hotmail.co.uk Map 199/496988
£150-£400 Sleeps 1-4. 1 apartment. 🐕 Short breaks available

● **Staplecross**
Mill Cottage ☎ 01424427693 (Mrs Hend Finlay)
www.mill-cottages.co.uk Map 199/781224
£285-£480 Sleeps 1-4. 1 cottage. 🐕 🛏 Short breaks available ★★★★

WEST SUSSEX

● **Henfield**

SOUTH DOWNS & SOUTH DOWNS WAY

New Hall
☎ 01273 492546 (Mrs M W Carreck) www.newhallcottage.co.uk
Map 198/218155
£280-£440 Sleeps 3-5. 1 flat and 1 cottage)
🐕 🛏 Short breaks available

Self-contained flat and 17th-century cottage in two wings of manor house, set in three and half acres of mature gardens, surrounded by farmland and footpaths. Half mile from river Adur and Downslink path. Approximately, two miles from South Downs Way.

GROUPS, HOSTELS, BUNKHOUSES, CAMPSITES & OTHERS

BUCKINGHAMSHIRE

● Bletchley

The Old Dairy Farm, Orchard Mill Lane, MK17 9BF ☎ 01908 274206 (Ashley Wiggins) wiblang@aol.com Map 152/882308
SC £6-£8 per night Sleeps 1-50. Caravan/campsite. ♨(Bletchley) ⊗ ♨ க. F

ISLE OF WIGHT

● Shanklin
ISLE OF WIGHT COASTAL PATH

YMCA, Isle of Wight, Winchester House, Sandown Rd, PO37 6HU
☎ 01489 772215 www.ymca-fg.org/iow/index.htm Map 196/588826
SC, BB, FB £12.50-£28.50 per night Sleeps 10-135. Lodge and main house.
♨(Lake) Ⅴ ⊗ ♨

● Yarmouth
ISLE OF WIGHT COASTAL PATH

Warner Norton Grange Coastal Resort
Halletts Shute, PO41 0SD ☎ 01983 760323 (Melanie Cox)
www.nortongrange.co.uk Map 196/344897
DBB £35-£66 per night Sleeps 1-392. Chalets.
♨ ♨ ! க. F ★★★ Exclusively for Adults!

Warner Norton Grange Coastal Resort offers short breaks inclusive of dinner, bed & breakfast, use of our leisure facilities and live entertainment. Monday 8th October 2007 - 4 night Walking Package available, only from only £194pp.

KENT

● Ringwould
NORTH DOWNS WAY

Rippledown
Ripple Down House, Dover Road, Ringwould, CT14 8HE ☎ 01304 364854
www.rippledown.com Map 179/361484
BB £18-£22.50 per night Sleeps 8-19. Hostel. ♨(Walmer)
Ⅾ ⊗ ♨ க. F ★★★

The Old Stables offers group accommodation (bed & self-service breakfast) for 8 minimum to 19 maximum in five various sized bedrooms in part of Rippledown Environmental Education Centre. Organised events and training courses during the year. Advance booking required.

● Sittingbourne
Palace Farm Hostel & Campsite, Down Court Road, Doddington, ME9 0AU
☎ 01795 886200 (Graham or Liz) www.palacefarm.com Map 178/935577
BB £12-£22 per night Sleeps 1-30. Hostel.
Ⅾ ⊗ ♨ ♨ க. F ★★★ⓌⓂ

WEST SUSSEX

● Washington
SOUTH DOWNS
SOUTH DOWNS WAY

Washington Caravan & Camping Park, London Road, RH20 4AJ
☎ 01903 892869 (Max F Edlin) www.washcamp.com Map 198/121133
SC £5.75-£8 per night Sleeps 1-250. Camping & caravan site. ♨(Worthing)
♨ ♨ க. F ★★★★

SOUTH

EAST

Long Distance Paths

Essex Way ....ESX

Icknield Way Path ....ICK

London Loop ....LNL

Nene Way ....NEN

Peddars Way & Norfolk
Coast Path ....PNC

Suffolk Coast &
Heaths Path ....SCH

Wherryman's Way ....WRY

**See Paths & Access p25 for full
details of LDPs and waymarks**

National Park

The Broads

THURNE DYKE WIND PUMP WHICH DRAINS
MARSHLAND ON THE NORFOLK BROADS

WALK...   ...ST ALBANS WAY

The renowned long-distance walker John Merrill devised this new 40km/25-mile route after researching medieval pilgrimages in the region. He became convinced that pilgrims would have made the journey from Waltham Abbey to St Alban's Cathedral for more than 1,700 years, paying homage to the shrine of England's first martyr. Following parts of the Lee and New rivers, the route visits historic parkland, woodland, Roman ruins, and the picturesque hamlet of North Mymms – home of the most complete 14th-century church in England. Modern-day pilgrims can complete the journey in a day or break halfway at Potters Bar.

For a detailed guidebook, contact The John Merrill Foundation on ☎ 01992 762776 or visit www.johnmerrillwalkguides.com

VISIT...   ...FINESHADE WOOD

Part of the patchwork remains of the Royal Forest of Rockingham, a medieval hunting forest that stretched across eastern Northamptonshire, this ancient mixed broadleaf and conifer woodland near Stamford bears testament to centuries of coppicing and evidence of Roman-era iron smelting. But Fineshade's newest attraction is The Lodge visitor centre – a converted set of 18th-century buildings using eco-friendly technology and local materials. Three new trails between 2 and 6 miles in length lead from its doors and make an excellent detour from the nearby Jurassic Way.

For more information, including a downloadable map, visit www.forestry.gov.uk/rockinghamforest or ☎ 01780 444920 for a free leaflet with over 250 miles of walks in the area.

SEE...   ...KINGFISHERS AT CHAFFORD GORGES

It's not often an Essex housing estate is recommended as a prime location for spotting one of the British countryside's most iconic birds. But then Chafford Gorges, near the Lakeside Shopping Centre in Grays, Essex, isn't your average nature reserve. Plumb in the middle of the Chafford Hundred housing development, the 200 acres of former quarries was bought by The Wildlife Trusts and officially opened to

visitors last year, and its grassland, lakes and woodland play host to abundant wildlife including orchids, bats, newts and pintail ducks. Holes in the chalk cliffs provide ideal roosts for kingfishers which can be seen darting at their sub-aquatic prey all-year-round.

Visit www.essexwt.org.uk for further information or call the visitor centre on ☎ 01375 484016.

LOCAL RAMBLERS GROUPS... Suffolk Area has helped establish the East Suffolk Line Walks – a series of 13 rail rambles along the scenic Ipswich-to-Lowestoft line. An excellent website, www.eastsuffolklinewalks.co.uk, gives full details of all routes and a free booklet to download or order... **North Hertfordshire Group has created the Stevenage Outer Orbital Path – a new, waymarked 27-mile loop through countryside around the town...** Colchester Group (see p87) and Ouse Valley Group (see p85) both have details of local DIY walks on their website.

EAST

MAP 165

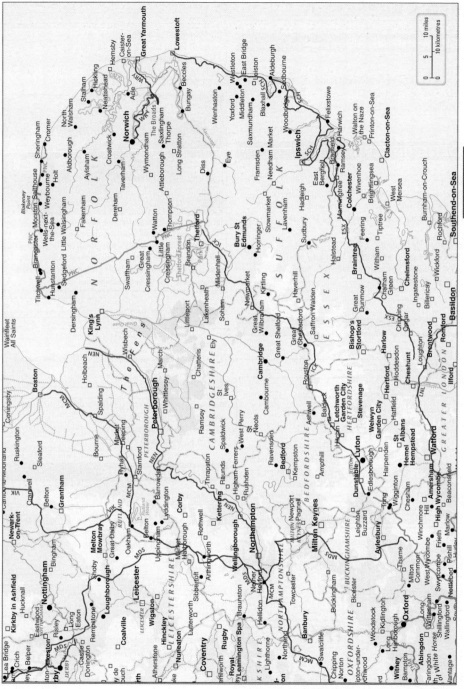

BED & BREAKFAST

BEDFORDSHIRE

● Ravensden
Tree-Garth, Church End, MK44 2RP ☎ 01234 771745 (Sue & Bruce Edwards)
www.treegarth.co.uk Map 153/079547
£30 S1 D1 T1 ✕ nearby Ⓓ ⊛ 🐾🛏🚗 ★★★

CAMBRIDGESHIRE

● Cambridge
The Gwydir House, 145 Gwydir Street, CB1 2LJ ☎ 01223 356615
(Mrs M Sanders) www.thegwydirhouse.co.uk/index.php Map 154/462579
£20-£25 T1 ✕ nearby ⋙(Cambridge) Ⓓ ⊛ 🐾🛏🚗!

● Great Wilbraham
The Sycamore House, 56 High Street, CB1 5JD ☎ 01223 880751
(B W & E A Canning) www.thesycamorehouse.co.uk Map 154/549572
✕ Ⓓ Ⓑ ⊛ 🐾🚗 🐾 Ⓜ

ESSEX

● Bradfield
ESSEX WAY

Emsworth House
Station Road, CO11 2UP ☎ 01255 870860 (Penny Linton)
www.emsworthhouse.co.uk Map 168/142310
£45-£55 S1 D1 T1 F1 ✕ nearby
Ⓓ Ⓑ ⊛ 🐾🛏🚗!🐾 ★★★★

Lovely family home with outstanding views over the countryside and River Stour. Ideal for holidays and short breaks. Very convenient for travelling to Europe via Harwich and ideally situated for exploring East Anglia and Constable Country.

HAVE YOU TRIED OUR GROUP WALKS FINDER YET?

You can search our online database and get details of thousands of Group walks the length and bredth of Britain, all led by Ramblers walk leaders and linked to the accommodation finder.

Visit www.ramblers.org.uk/walksfinder

● Chelmsford
ESSEX WAY

The Windmill Inn & Restaurant
Chatham Green, CM3 3LE ☎ 01245 361 188 (Elaine Rollings)
www.windmillmotorinn.co.uk Map 167/715151
£58 D5 T2
Ⓑ ⊛ 🐾🛏🚗!🐾 Ⓕ ★★★

The Windmill Inn & Restaurant. Bed & Breakfast accommodation on the Essex Way. Lovely double and twin rooms, all en-suite. Free Wi-Fi throughout. Traditional home cooked food with á la carte evening menu all freshly prepared to order. Friendly and relaxed cosy atmosphere. Sunday Lunch (booking advisable). 01245 361188 Chatham Green, Little Waltham, Chelmsford, Essex, CM3 3LE www.windmillmotorinn.co.uk

● Great Chesterford
ICKNIELD WAY PATH
Mill House, CB10 1NS ☎ 01799 530493 (Mrs Christine King)
Map 154/504431
£20 S1 D4 T1 ✕ nearby ⋙(Gt Chesterford) Ⓓ Ⓑ ⊛ 🐾🛏🚗 🐾

● Wrabness
ESSEX WAY
Woodview Cottage, Wrabness Road, CO12 5ND ☎ 01255 886413 (Anne Cohen)
www.woodview-cottage.co.uk Map 168/191310
£40 S1 D1 F1 ✕ £4 , 6pm ⋙(Wrabness)
Ⓥ Ⓓ Ⓑ ⊛ 🐾🛏🚗 🐾 ★★★★Ⓢ

HERTFORDSHIRE

● Baldock
ICKNIELD WAY
The Three Tuns Hotel, 6 High Street, Ashwell, SG7 5NL ☎ 01462742107
(Claire Stanley) www.tuns.co.uk Map 153/270397
£39-£62 S1 D4 T1 ✕ £11, 6:30pm ⋙(Ashwell) Ⓥ Ⓓ Ⓑ ⊛ 🐾🛏🚗

● Tring
RIDGEWAY, CHILTERN WAY & HERTFORDSHIRE WAY
The Greyhound, Chesham Road, HP23 6EH ☎ 01442 824631 (Paul Phillips)
paul@maltukltd.com Map 165/938101
£45 S3 D2 F2 ✕ £12, 6pm ⋙(Tring) Ⓥ Ⓓ Ⓑ ⊛ 🐾🛏🚗!🐾🛏

NORFOLK

● Acle
Fern House B&B, The Street, NR13 3QJ ☎ 01493 754142 (Mrs Denise Kett)
terrygkett@tiscali.co.uk Map 134/401105
✕ ⋙(Acle) Ⓥ Ⓓ Ⓑ ⊛ 🐾🚗!🐾 Ⓜ

● Aldborough
Butterfly Cottage, The Green, NR11 7AA ☎ 01263 768198
(Mrs Janet Davison) www.butterflycottage.com
Map 133/184343
Ⓓ Ⓑ ⊛ 🐾 🚗 ! 🕭

● Cromer
PEDDARS WAY & NORFOLK COAST PATH

Incleborough House Luxury Bed and Breakfast
Lower Common, East Runton, NR27 9PG ☎ 01263 515939 (Nick Davies)
www.incleboroughhouse.co.uk Map 133/197424
£105 D2 T1 ✕ £15, 7pm ᴍ(Cromer)
Ⓥ Ⓓ Ⓑ ⊛ 🐾 👶 🚗 🕭 Ⓕ ★★★★★

Looking for a little bit of heaven? Look no further.

Five-star luxury in every respect, and wheelchair friendly.

There's everything you could wish for!

Glorious countryside, a beach 300 metres away and the most beautifully restored house oozing charm and character. Sumptuous bedrooms offer every luxury from LCD TVs, to the most comfortable beds you will ever experience.

A warm welcome and delicious food in a stunning location.

● Dersingham
PEDDARS WAY & NORFOLK COAST PATH

Holkham Cottage
34 Hunstanton Road, PE31 6HQ ☎ 01485 544562 (Jane Taggart)
www.holkhamcottage.co.uk Map 132/685305
£24-£30 S1 D3 T2 F1 ✕ £12.50, 6pm
Ⓥ Ⓓ Ⓑ ⊛ 🐾 🚗 ! 👶 & Ⓕ ★★★★

Located in the picturesque village of Dersingham, close to Royal Sandringham and the unspoilt coastline of Norfolk, Holkham Cottage B&B is ideally situated for touring west Norfolk which offers glorious walks, birdwatching, historic houses and country pursuits.

● Diss
Cobwebs, 6 Riverside, Denmark Street, IP22 4BE ☎ 01379 641388
(Suzanne and Stephen Kayne) www.cobwebsbandb.co.uk
Map 144/111794
£35 S1 D1 F1 ᴍ(Diss) Ⓓ Ⓑ ⊛ 🐾 👶 🚗 !

● Hickling
Black Horse Cottage, The Green, NR12 0YA ☎ 01692 598691
(Yvonne Pugh) www.blackhorsecottage.com
Map 134/410234
✕ Ⓓ Ⓑ ⊛ 🐾 🚗 !

● Little Walsingham
PEDDARS WAY & NORFOLK COAST PATH
St David's House, Friday Market, NR22 6DB ☎ 01328 820633
(Mrs J Renshaw) www.stdavidshousewalsingham.co.uk Map 132/933366
£28-£32 D1 T2 F1 ✕ £14, 5pm
Ⓥ Ⓓ Ⓑ ⊛ 🐾 👶 🚗 🕭 ★★★

● Morston
PEDDARS WAY & NORFOLK COAST PATH
Scaldbeck Cottage, Stiffkey Road, NR25 7BJ ☎ 01263 740188 (E Hamond)
ned@hamond.co.uk Map 133/004440
£30 D1 T1 ✕ nearby Ⓓ ⊛ 👶 🚗 !

Butterfly Guest House
240 Thorpe Road, NR1 1TW ☎ 01603 437740 (Lynn Wardle)
Map 134/251084
£30-£40 S1 D3 T3 F1 ✕ nearby ᴍ(Norwich)
Ⓓ Ⓑ ⊛ 👶 & ★★★Ⓜ

Restored Edwardian house one mile from Norwich city centre. On main bus route. Close to Broads, local pubs and restaurants. In conservation area. Private car park with CCTV. Colour TV in all rooms. Business and leisure guests welcome. Cards accepted.

● Norwich
De Vere Dunston Hall, Ipswich Road, NR14 8PQ ☎ 01508 470689
www.devere.co.uk/heritage/dunston-hall/ Map 134/222022
£54.50-£59.50 D139 T10 F18 ✕ £17, 7pm
Ⓥ Ⓓ Ⓑ ⊛ 🐾 👶 🚗 ! 🕭 & Ⓕ

● Salthouse
PEDDARS WAY & NORFOLK COAST PATH
Cumfus Bottom, Purdy Street, NR25 7XA ☎ 01263 741118 (Angela Holman)
Map 133/073437
£26-£30 D2 T1 ✕ nearby Ⓓ Ⓑ 🐾 👶 ! 🕭

● Sedgeford
PEDDARS WAY & NORFOLK COAST PATH

The King William IV
Country Inn & Restaurant, Heacham Road, PE36 5LU
☎ 01485 571765 (Reception) www.thekingwilliamsedgeford.co.uk
Map 132/709365 £50-£60 S4 D4 T4 F2 ✕ £8, 7pm
Ⓥ Ⓓ Ⓑ ⊛ 🐾 👶 🚗 ! 🕭 ★★★★Ⓢ Ⓦ

Popular traditional country inn. Close to north Norfolk's beautiful coastline, Peddars Way, RSPB Bird Reserves & Golf. High standard en-suite accommodation with super kingsize beds. Extensive menu & daily specials served in two restaurants. Bar & garden. Welcoming & friendly atmosphere.

FROM YOUR DOORSTEP!
Check out our new City Walks section and see a side of town that you never knew existed: **pp47–65.**

EAST

Magazine Wood
Magazine Wood, Peddars Way, Sedgeford, PE36 5LW
☎ 07786235977 (Pippa Barber)
www.magazinewood.co.uk Map 132/722371
£80-£95 DI ✕ nearby [D] [B] 🍴 🛁 !

A luxury B&B located on Peddars Way with independent access and forming part of a beautiful home with stunning views across the wash. Fitted to five-star standards with desk, flat panel TV, mini-bar, bath, power shower and underfloor heating.

● Sheringham
PEDDARS WAY & NORFOLK COAST PATH

Elmwood, 6 The Rise, NR26 8QA ☎ 01263 825454
(Glenys Gray) Map 133/160426
£40 DI TI ✕ nearby ﹏(Sheringham) [D] [B] ⊛ 🛁 🛏 ! 🐾 Ⓜ

The Beaumaris Hotel
15 South Street, NR26 8LL ☎ 01263 822370
(Alan & Hilary Stevens) www.thebeaumarishotel.co.uk Map 133/155431
£55-£58 S5 D8 T8 ✕ £20, 7pm ﹏(Sheringham)
[V] [D] [B] ⊛ 🍴🛁🛏!🛁 ★★

21 en-suite bedrooms with television, telephone, tea and coffee and hairdryers. Spacious, tastefully-appointed restaurant.

Excellent choice featuring local fish and crabs in season. Á la carte and vegetarian menus available. Bar and lounge.

The Pheasant Hotel
Coast Road, Kelling, NR25 7EG ☎ 01263 588382
pheasanthotelnorfolk.co.uk Map 133/098427
£49.50-£52.50 D17 T11 F1 ✕ £15, 6pm
[V] [D] [B] ⊛ 🍴🛁🛏🛁[F] ★★Ⓢ

A delightful privately-owned hotel set in two acres of grounds between Sheringham and Blakeney, surrounded by Kelling Heath. The Pheasant is the perfect place to enjoy the beautiful Norfolk coastline, with walks starting from the hotel door. All rooms are en-suite with most on the ground floor. The restaurant has an enviable reputation and bar meals are available in the fully-licensed bar. Phone now for special offers.

● Thompson
PEDDARS WAY & NORFOLK COAST PATH

College Farm, IP24 1QG ☎ 01953 483318 (Lavender Garnier)
collegefarm83@amserve.net Map 144/933966
£30 D2 TI ✕ nearby [D] [B] ⊛ 🍴🛁

Thatched House, Mill Road, IP24 1PH ☎ 01953 483577 (Brenda Mills)
www.thatchedhouse.co.uk Map 144/919967
£30 DI T2 ✕ nearby [D] [B] ⊛ 🍴🛁🛏!🛁🛁[F] Ⓜ

SUFFOLK

● Beccles
Catherine House, 2 Ringsfield Road, NR34 9PQ ☎ 01502 716428
(Mr & Mrs W T Renilson) Map 156/418897
✕ ﹏(Beccles) [D] [B] 🍴 ★★★★

Pinetrees, Park Drive, NR34 7DQ ☎ 01502 470796 (Sue Bergin)
www.pinetrees.net435900
£40-£45 D3 ✕ nearby ﹏(Beccles)
[D] [B] ⊛ 🍴!🛁[F] ★★★★

● Darsham
SUFFOLK COAST & HEATHS PATH

Four Seasons Lodge
Leiston Road, IP17 3NS ☎ 01728 648105 (Joanna Tuck)
www.four-seasonslodge.co.uk Map 156/435673
£30-£35 S1 D2 T1 F1 ✕ £15, 6pm ﹏(Darsham)
[V] [D] [B] ⊛ 🍴🛁🛏!🛁[F] ★★★★

Tastefully refurbished ground floor accomodation, set in rural location overlooking Westleton Heathlands and RSPB reserve. Cosy lounge with log burner. Central heating throughout. Lovely garden. Pubs close by. En-suite rooms. Friendly hosts. Excellent Food. Local produce!

● East Bergholt
ESSEX WAY

Rosemary, Rectory Hill, CO7 6TH ☎ 01206 298241
(Mrs Natalie Finch) Map 155/073344
£29 T3 ✕ nearby ﹏(Manningtree)
[D] ⊛ 🍴🛁🛏🛁 ★★★

● Eye
Goode House B&B, Goode House, Lambseth Street, IP23 7AG ☎ 01379 870863
(Peter or Claire) peterdavies@goodworks.co.uk Map 144/144739
£25 S2 D2 ✕ nearby [D] [B] ⊛ 🍴🛁🛏!

● Framsden
Greggle Cottage, Ashfield Rd, IP14 6LP ☎ 01728 860226 (Jim & Phil Welland)
wellands@ukgateway.net Map 156/194609
£25-£30 S1 DI TI [B] ⊛ 🍴🛁🛏!🛁

● Lavenham
Brett Farm, The Common, CO10 9PG ☎ 01787 248533 (Mrs M Hussey)
www.brettfarm.com Map 155/923491
£32.50 DI TI FI ✕ nearby ﹏(Sudbury)
[D] [B] ⊛ 🍴🛁🛏!★★★★

● Reydon
SUFFOLK COAST & HEATHS PATH

Number 49, 49 Halesworth Road, IP18 6NR ☎ 01502 725075 (Miss E A Webb)
www.southwold.info Map 156/498770
£50-£70 DI TI ✕ nearby [D] [B] ⊛ 🍴🛁🛏!🛁

● Saxmundham

Georgian Guest House, 6 North Entrance, IP17 1AY ☎ 01728 603337
(Iain and Gill Bray) www.thegeorgian-house.com Map 156/385634
£45-£55 D4 T1 F2 ✕ £14.50, 7pm ₩(Saxmundham)
Ⓥ Ⓓ Ⓑ ⊗ 🐾 ♨ 🚗 ! ♿ Ⓕ ★★★★★Ⓢ

● Sudbourne

Long Meadows, Gorse Lane, IP12 2BD ☎ 01394 450269
(Mrs A Wood) Map 156/412532
£26-£28 S1 D1 T1 ✕ £10, 7:30pm
Ⓥ Ⓓ Ⓑ ⊗ 🐾 ♨ 🚗 ! 🐾 ★★★

● Sudbury

Hillview Studio, 58 Clarence Road, CO10 1NJ ☎ 01787 374221 / 07779 854199
(Sue Butcher) sooteapot@hotmail.com Map 155/873420
£37-£40 T1 ✕ nearby ₩(Sudbury) Ⓓ Ⓑ ⊗ ♨ 🚗 ! ♿ Ⓕ ★★★

● Woodbridge

Deben Lodge, Melton Road, IP12 1NH ☎ 01394 382740 (Rosemary Schlee)
Map 169/278498
£24-£27 S2 T2 ✕ nearby ₩(Woodbridge) Ⓓ ⊗ ♨ 🐾 ★★Ⓦ

SELF-CATERING

ESSEX

● New Polzeath
SOUTH WEST COAST PATH

Craig Var ☎ 01763 837341 (Ros Renwick)
www.polzeathbeachhouse.co.uk Map 154/488383
£650-£2350 Sleeps 1-12. 1 family house. ⊗ 🐾 Short breaks available

NORFOLK

● Great Yarmouth
THE BROADS

Clippesby Hall ☎ 01493 367800 (John Lindsay)
www.clippesby.com Map 134/502090
£209-£949 Sleeps 2-8. 17 cottages and lodges. 🐾 ★★★★

● Mautby

Lower Wood Farm Country Cottages ☎ 01493 722523 (Jill Nicholls)
www.lowerwoodfarm.co.uk Map 134/471114
£325-£1425 Sleeps 4-9. 7 cottages.
⊗ ♿ Short breaks available ★★★★★

● Thorpe Market
PEDDARS WAY & NORFOLK COAST PATH

Thorpewood Cottages ☎ 01263 834493 (Paula Black)
www.thorpewoodcottages.co.uk Map 133/240356
£205-£508 Sleeps 2-4. 5 cottages. ⊗ Short breaks available ★★★

● West Raynham

Pollywiggle Cottage ☎ 01603 471990 (Marilyn Farnham-Smith)
www.pollywigglecottage.co.uk Map 132/869250
£290-£890 Sleeps 1-8. 1 cottage. ⊗ Short breaks available ★★★★Ⓦ

SUFFOLK

● Badingham

Workhouse Cottage ☎ 01728 688343 (Patricia Illingworth)
www.workhousecottage.com Map 156/311689
£290-£400 Sleeps 1-3. 1 cottage. ⊗ Short breaks available

● Tattingstone
SUFFOLK COAST & HEATHS PATH

The Garden Cabin ☎ 01473 328371 (Susan Hemmings)
heronwire@tiscali.co.uk Map 169/136378
£150-£250 Sleeps 1-2. 1 cabin. ⊗ ♿ Ⓕ 🐾 Short breaks available

GROUPS, HOSTELS, BUNKHOUSES, CAMPSITES & OTHERS

ESSEX

● Feering

Prested Hall, Prested Hall Chase, CO5 9EE ☎ 01376 573300
www.prested.co.uk Map 168/882196
BB DBB £65 per night Sleeps 1-22. Hotel, group accommodation.
₩(Kelvedon) Ⓥ Ⓓ ⊗ 🐾 🚗 Ⓕ ★★★★Ⓜ

NORFOLK

● Deepdale
PEDDARS WAY & NORFOLK COAST PATH

Deepdale Backpackers and Camping, Burnham, PE31 8DD ☎ 01485 210256
www.deepdalefarm.co.uk Map 132/803443
SC £4.50-£12.50 per night Sleeps 1-500. Independent hostel & campsite.
Ⓓ ⊗ 🐾 🐾 ♿ Ⓕ ★★★★Ⓦ

EAST

EAST MIDLANDS

Long Distance Paths

See Paths & Access p25 for full details of LDPs and waymarks

National Park

Peak District

WATCHING THE SUN SET OVER
DERBYSHIRE FROM STANAGE EDGE

WALK...
...THE KINDER SCOUT TRESPASS TRAIL

Part of last year's 75th anniversary celebrations of the seminal mass trespass was the creation of this 22.5km/14-mile circular walk from New Mills, retracing the protesters' steps to Kinder where they scuffled with the Duke of Devonshire's gamekeepers. As well as providing a fascinating social insight into the walking movement and prohibitive landscape of 1930s Britain, the route also takes in some of the Peak District's most famous views and includes the award-winning Millennium Walkway – the 160m aerial path spanning Torrs Gorge.

Visit the excellent accompanying website www.kindertrespass.com for a downloadable trail guide and a wealth of resources examining the historical and cultural legacy of the event that brought about the country's first national park and the recent right to roam.

VISIT...
...SALCEY FOREST

Near the Northamptonshire village of Hartwell, this once great royal hunting forest was created for Henry VIII with some of the veteran oaks – affectionately known as 'druids' – thought to be over 500 years old. But walkers can now enjoy views that even the king himself couldn't have commanded, thanks to a 300m walkway 15 metres up that winds among the branches offering thrilling views of the forest's diverse fauna. Eight miles of footpaths on the ground are easily accessible for wheelchair users. Both the Midshires Way and Milton Keynes Boundary Walk pass through the forest.

For further information, visit www.forestry.gov.uk/salceyforest or ☎ 01780 444920.

SEE...
...DERBYSHIRE'S WELL DRESSINGS

Between May Day holiday and September, villages all over the Peak District will take part in the ancient tradition of well dressing. Rooted in the pagan worship of water gods, springs and wells thought to have healing powers were dedicated to saints in early Christian time (such as St Ann's Well in Buxton) and would be elaborately decorated at an annual ritual. It is thought that the practice was resurrected in Derbyshire during the Black Death, and today local villagers take months to plan and create their intricate designs using natural materials. Berries, leaves, moss, bark and even whole flowers are mounted on to soft clay held in a wooden frame that lasts no longer than a fortnight. Fortunately, walkers can encounter a new spectacle almost every week during the summer months.

For a searchable calendar of well dressing events, visit www.visitpeakdistrict.com or call Buxton TIC (☎ 01298 25106).

LOCAL RAMBLERS GROUPS... With financial help from the Ramblers, the Penistone Line Trail offers some attractive linear walks in South & West Yorkshire and North Nottinghamshire, leaving from train stations along the scenic route between Sheffield and Huddersfield. Visit www.penline.co.uk or ☎ 01226 761782 for further details and to buy their excellent guide... **Chesterfield & North East Derbyshire Group continue to improve and maintain the 54.5km/34-mile Chesterfield Round Walk they founded and waymarked two years ago. Visit www.chesterfieldroundwalk.org.uk or ☎ 0870 741 9255 to order a leaflet.**

EAST MIDLANDS

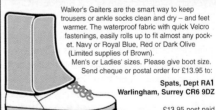

MAP 173

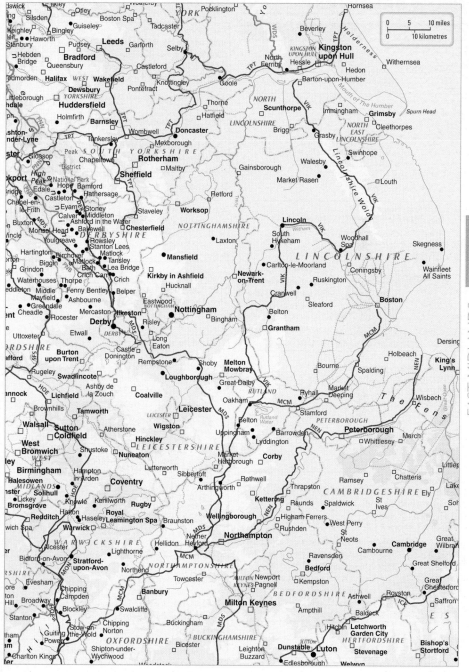

BED & BREAKFAST

DERBYSHIRE

● Ashbourne

PEAK DISTRICT

PENNINE WAY

Compton House, 27-31 Compton, DE6 1BX ☎ 01335 343100 (Jane Maher)
www.comptonhouse.co.uk Map 119/180464
£25-£35 D3 T1 F1 ✗ nearby
Ⓑ ⊛ ♨ ☺ ⇋ ! ★★★★

Mona Villas B&B, Church Lane, Middle Mayfield, DE6 2JS ☎ 01335 343773
(John Parker) www.mona-villas.fsnet.co.uk Map 119/149448
£30-£35 D2 T1 ✗ nearby
Ⓓ Ⓑ ⊛ ♨ ☺ ⇋ ৬ Ⓕ ★★★★

Beresford Arms Hotel
Station Road, DE6 1AA ☎ 01335 300035 (David Dougan)
www.beresford-arms.demon.co.uk Map 119/178464
£30-£40 S6 D6 T6 F3 ✗ £12, 5pm
Ⓥ Ⓓ Ⓑ ⊛ ♨ ☺ ⇋ ♨ ৬

The Tissington Trail starts directly opposite the hotel, so after a hearty breakfast you can enjoy the trail, where you will not fail to be entranced by the breathtaking scenery of the English Peak District.

Dove Top Farm, Coldeaton, Alsop-en-le-Dale, DE6 1QR
☎ 01335310472 (Ann Wainwright) dovetopfarm.co.uk
Map 119/147566 £28 D1 F1 ✗ £12, 7pm
Ⓥ Ⓓ Ⓑ ⊛ ♨ ☺ ⇋

● Ashford-in-the-Water

PEAK DISTRICT

PENNINE WAY

River Cottage
The Duke's Drive, DE45 1QP ☎ 01629 813327 (John and Gilly Deacon)
www.rivercottageashford.co.uk Map 119/192697
£39-£44 S1 D3 T1 ✗ nearby
Ⓓ Ⓑ ⊛ ☺ ! ★★★★★Ⓢ Ⓦ

Stylish, mainly 18th-century riverside cottage in arguably the prettiest village in the Peak District National Park.
Great walks from our doorstep, eateries within easy walking distance, a superb local produce breakfast and beautifully appointed rooms furnished with antiques.

● Bakewell

PEAK DISTRICT

Rowson House Farm, Rowson Farm, Church Street, Monyash, DE45 1JH
☎ 07971 038702 (Garry Mycock) www.rowsonhousefarm.com Map 119/151664
£25-£35 S3 D3 T3 F1 ✗ nearby
Ⓓ Ⓑ ⊛ ♨ ☺ ⇋ ! ☺

● Bamford

DERWENT VALLEY HERITAGE WAY

Pioneer House
Station Road, S33 0BN ☎ 01433 650638 (Janet Treacher)
pioneerhouse.co.uk Map 110/207826
£27.50-£35 D2 T1 ✗ nearby ☛(Bamford)
Ⓓ Ⓑ ⊛ ♨ ☺ ⇋ ! ★★★★Ⓢ Ⓦ Ⓜ

Friendly and comfortable, en-suite B&B in stunning Hope Valley.

Hearty breakfasts to start your day with lots of maps/guidebooks available.

Close to Castleton, Hathersage and Hope, with Edale and the start of the Pennine Way nearby. Shortbreaks available.

● Birchover

PEAK DISTRICT

Poppy Cottage, Main Street, Birchover, DE4 2BN ☎ 01629 650847
(Alison Wagstaff) www.poppycottagebandb.co.uk Map 119/238622
£60 D1 Ⓓ Ⓑ ⊛ ♨ ☺ ⇋ ! ★★★★Ⓦ

● Buxton

PEAK DISTRICT

MIDSHIRES WAY

The Old Manse, 6 Clifton Road, Silverlands, SK17 6QL ☎ 01298 25638
(TW & PA Cotton) www.oldmanse.co.uk Map 119/063734
£22-£26 S1 D4 T1 F1 ✗ £12, 6:30pm ☛(Buxton)
Ⓥ Ⓓ Ⓑ ⊛ ♨ ☺ ★★★★

Portland Hotel
32 St Johns Road, SK17 6XQ
☎ 01298 22462 (Robert Harwood)
www.portlandhotelbuxton.net Map 119/054734
£40 S5 D8 T9 ☛(Buxton) Ⓓ Ⓑ ♨ ☺ ৬

Rambler-friendly, Peak District National Park hotel.

- 22 en-suite rooms with singles available (no single supplement).
- Real ale bar.
- Traditional, fresh local food.
- BB or DBB rates available.
- Competitive rates for groups.
- Packed lunches available if required.
- Drying facilities.
- Open socialising area available.
- Modern but homely atmosphere with friendly and efficient service.
- Car and coach parking and bike storage available.
- Across the road from the famous Buxton Opera House.

Please contact us to ascertain availability: portland.hotel@btinternet.com

Linden Lodge, 31 Temple Rd, SK17 9BA ☎ 01298 27591 (Mrs Eileen Blane)
www.lindentreelodge.co.uk Map 119/052727
£27-£35 D1 T1 ᴧᴧ(Buxton) Ⓓ Ⓑ ⊗ 🐾 ☕ ★★★★Ⓦ

Kingscroft Guest House
10 Green Lane, SK17 9DP ☎ 01298 22757 (David Sedgwick)
Map 119/056727
£40 S2 D5 T2 ✕ nearby ᴧᴧ(Buxton)
Ⓓ Ⓑ 🐾 ☕ 🛏 🚗 ! 🐾 ★★★★Ⓢ Ⓦ

We welcome you to stay in our late Victorian luxury guesthouse, in a central yet quiet position in Buxton, at the Peak District's heart. Comfortable surroundings with period decor and furnishings.
Enjoy our hearty, delicious home-cooked and veggie breakfasts.

● Calver
PEAK DISTRICT
DERWENT VALLEY HERITAGE WAY

Pear Tree Cottage
Main Street, S32 3XR ☎ 01433 631243 (Dianne Payne)
diannepayne1@aol.com Map 119/238745
£26 S2 D1 ✕ nearby ᴧᴧ(Grindleford)
Ⓓ Ⓑ ⊗ 🐾 ☕ 🚗 !

18th-century cottage in quiet village backing onto open countryside. Footpaths from door. Comfy beds & good breakfasts with own free-range eggs await. Vegetarian option available. Three excellent pubs in village offering good food & real beer. Chatsworth two miles. On Derwent Valley Heritage Way.

● Castleton
PEAK DISTRICT
PENNINE WAY

Bargate Cottage B&B, Market Place, S33 8WQ ☎ 01433 620201 (Fiona Saxon)
www.bargatecottage.co.uk Map 110/150827
£45-£55 D2 T1 ✕ nearby ᴧᴧ(Hope) Ⓓ Ⓑ ⊗ 🐾 ☕ 🚗 ! ★★★★

Ye Olde Nags Head
Cross Street, S33 8WH
☎ 01433 620248 (Nigel Birks)
www.yeoldenagshead.com Map 110/151829
£40 D8 T1 F1 ✕ £9, 7pm ᴧᴧ(Hope) Ⓥ Ⓓ Ⓑ ⊗ 🐾 ☕ ★★★

Traditional, family-run 17th-century inn. En-suite rooms from £25pp. Four-posters & jacuzzis. Delicious home-cooked food, famous all-you-can-eat weekend carvery, cosy bar with real fire, real ales. Leave your car behind. Secure cycle storage. Parking.

Dunscar Farm Bed & Breakfast, Castleton, S33 8WA ☎ 01433 620483
(Janet Glennerster) dunscarfarm.co.uk Map 110/137833
£28-£30 D3 T1 F1 ᴧᴧ(Hope) Ⓓ Ⓑ ⊗ ☕ ! 🛏 Ⓕ ★★★★

Four Seasons Bed and Breakfast, Spital House, How Lane, S33 8WJ
☎ 01433 620 655 (Jenny Humphreys) www.4seasonsbb.co.uk Map 110/152830
£32.50-£45 D6 T2 F3 ✕ nearby ᴧᴧ(Hope)
Ⓓ Ⓑ ⊗ ☕ ! 🐾 🛏 Ⓕ

● Chapel-en-le-Frith
PEAK DISTRICT
PENNINE BRIDLEWAY & PENNINE WAY

Forest Lodge
Forest Lodge, 58 Manchester Road, SK23 9TH ☎ 01298 812854
(Noreen Preen) www.forestlodge.org.uk Map 110/051804
£28-£33 D2 T1 ✕ nearby ᴧᴧ(Chapel-en-le-Frith)
Ⓑ ⊗ 🐾 ☕ 🚗 ★★★★

Offering high quality B&B accommodation, Forest Lodge is a delightful Edwardian house, ideally located within walking distance of the town centre. Three beautifully-decorated en-suite rooms and a large sitting room for guests to relax in. Excellent breakfast. Private parking.

High Croft Guesthouse
High Croft, Manchester Road, SK23 9UH ☎ 01298 814843 (Elaine Clarke)
www.highcroft-guesthouse.co.uk Map 119/041799
£50-£65 D4 F2 ✕ nearby ᴧᴧ(Chapel-en-le-Frith)
Ⓓ Ⓑ ⊗ 🐾 ☕ 🚗 ! 🐾 ★★★★★Ⓢ Ⓦ

A luxurious country house set in 1.5 acres of peaceful, mature gardens, adjoining Chapel-en-le-Frith golf course and Combs Reservoir with magnificent views and superb walks from the door. Four beautiful en-suite rooms, sitting room, elegant dining room, extensive breakfast menu.

● Crich Carr
PEAK DISTRICT
MIDSHIRES WAY

Riverdale, Middle Lane, DE4 5EG ☎ 01773 853905 (Mrs V A Durbridge)
www.riverdaleguesthouse.co.uk Map 119/336542
✕ £12 ᴧᴧ(Whatstandwell)
Ⓥ Ⓓ Ⓑ ⊗ 🐾 🚗 🛏 Ⓦ

● Edale
PEAK DISTRICT
PENNINE WAY

Mam Tor House, Hope Valley, S33 7ZA ☎ 01433 670253 (Caroline Jackson)
www.mamtorhouse.co.uk Map 110/123858
£25 D1 T2 F1 ✕ nearby ᴧᴧ(Edale)
Ⓓ ⊗ 🐾 ☕ 🐾 ★★★

● Eyam
PEAK DISTRICT
DERWENT VALLEY HERITAGE WAY

Crown Cottage, Main Road, S32 5QW ☎ 01433 630858 (Janet Smith)
www.crown-cottage.co.uk Map 119/215766
£35-£45 D3 T1 ✕ nearby ᴧᴧ(Grindleford)
Ⓓ Ⓑ ⊗ 🐾 ☕ ! ★★★★

● Foolow
PEAK DISTRICT

Housley Cottage, Housley, S32 5QB ☎ 01433 631505 (Kevin Tighe)
www.housleycottages.co.uk Map 119/194760
£27-£40 D2 T1 F1 ✕ nearby
Ⓑ ⊗ 🐾 ☕ ★★★★

EAST MIDLANDS

● Glossop
PEAK DISTRICT
PENNINE WAY

Birds Nest Cottage, 40 Primrose Lane, SK13 8EW ☎ 01457 853478
(Lynda Ledwith) www.birdsnestcottage.co.uk Map 110/025939
£25-£30 S1 D1 T2 F1 ⚶(Glossop) Ⓓ Ⓑ ⊗ 🐾👜 ᗩ

● Grangemill
PEAK DISTRICT
PENNINE BRIDLEWAY

Avondale Farm, DE4 4HT ☎ 01629 650820 (Louise Wragg)
www.avondalefarm.co.uk Map 119/244577
£27.50 T1 ✗ nearby Ⓓ Ⓑ ⊗ 👜 ᗩ ! 🐾 ★★★★Ⓢ

● Hartington
PEAK DISTRICT

Bank House, Market Place, SK17 0AL ☎ 01298 84465
(Mrs H Harrison) Map 119/128604
£32 S1 D2 T1 F1 ✗ £14.50, 6:30pm
Ⓥ Ⓓ Ⓑ ⊗ 🐾👜 ᗩ ! ★★★★

● Hathersage
PEAK DISTRICT
DERWENT VALLEY HERITAGE WAY & PENNINE WAY

Cannon Croft
Cannonfields, S32 1AG ☎ 01433 650005 (Mrs Sandra Oates)
www.cannoncroft.fsbusiness.co.uk Map 110/226815
✗ nearby ⚶(Hathersage)
Ⓓ Ⓑ ⊗ 🐾👜 ★★★★Ⓖ Ⓦ

Award-winning B&B recommended by
Holiday Which?, Country Walking and
Food and Travel magazines. AA Highly
Commended, VB Gold Award. Famous
breakfasts (eg sundancer eggs, whisky
porridge.) Private parking, exceptional
cleanliness & friendly caring attention. See website for full details.

The Winnats B&B, The Winnats, Cannonfields, S32 1AG ☎ 01433 651 810
(Meryl Skyrme) www.peakdistrictbedandbreakfast.co.uk Map 110/225815
£30 D2 T2 ✗ nearby ⚶(Hathersage) Ⓓ Ⓑ ⊗ 🐾👜 ᗩ !

● Hayfield
PEAK DISTRICT
PENNINE WAY

The Lantern Pike Inn, 45 Glossop Road, Little Hayfield, SK22 2NG
☎ 01663 747590 (Stella) www.lanternpikeinn.co.uk Map 110/034879
£40-£55 D3 T2 ✗ £10, 5pm Ⓥ Ⓑ ⊗ 🐾👜 ᗩ ! Ⓜ

● Hope
PEAK DISTRICT
PENNINE WAY

Causeway House B&B
Back Street, S33 8WE ☎ 014433 623 291 (Janet Steynberg)
www.causewayhouse.co.uk Map 110/150829
£29.50-£45 S1 D3 T1 F2 ✗ nearby ⚶(Hope)
Ⓓ Ⓑ ⊗ 🐾👜 ᗩ ! 🐾 ★★★Ⓦ

Causeway House B&B is one of the
oldest houses in Castleton, a 15th-
century 'cruck cottage' with huge
original oak timbers. The house is
built of warm stone. The rooms are
very comfortable with splendid
views of the beautiful Peaks.

Round Meadow Barn
Parsons Lane, S33 6RB
☎ 01433 621347 (Gill & Geof Harris)
www.roundmeadowbarn.com Map 110/185831
£25-£35 D2 T1 F1 ✗ nearby ⚶(Hope) Ⓓ Ⓑ ⊗ 🐾👜 ᗩ 🐾

This recently converted barn lies
within its own four-and-a-half-acre
grounds, surrounded by the
dramatic hill scenery of Derbyshire's
Peak National Park. Easy access to
the Pennine Way, Kinder Scout and
Derwent and Ladybower Dams.

● Matlock
PEAK DISTRICT
DERWENT VALLEY HERITAGE WAY, MIDSHIRES WAY & PENNINE BRIDLEWAY

Riverbank House, Derwent Avenue, DE4 3LX ☎ 01629 582593
bookings@riverbankhouse.co.uk Map 119/299599
✗ ⚶(Matlock) Ⓓ Ⓑ ⊗ 🐾 Ⓜ

Sunnybank Guest House
37 Clifton Road, Matlock Bath, DE4 3PW ☎ 01629 584621 (Jane Bounds)
www.visitpeakdistrictbedandbreakfast.co.uk Map 119/293578
£32-£35 S1 D4 T2 F1 ⚶(Matlock Bath)
Ⓓ Ⓑ ⊗ 🐾👜 ᗩ ★★★★Ⓢ

A warm and friendly
welcome awaits you at
Sunnybank.

Characterful,
comfortable and
charming, situated at
the end of a quiet cul-
de-sac on the edge of
Matlock Bath.

Set amid peaceful woodland surroundings with stunning views of the Derwent
Valley. We offer an extensive and delicious breakfast menu (Peak District
cuisine) served in our attractive dining room. Spotlessly clean and an ideal
base for walkers and cyclists. Come, relax and enjoy!

Sheriff Lodge, Dimple Road, DE4 3JX ☎ 01629 760760 (Kate & Alan Richmond)
www.sherifflodge.co.uk Map 119/295606
£44-£55 D2 T2 ✗ nearby ⚶(Matlock) Ⓓ Ⓑ ⊗ 🐾👜 ᗩ ★★★★Ⓖ

Glendon
Knowleston Place, DE4 3BU ☎ 01629 584732 (Mrs S Elliott)
sylvia.elliott@tesco.net Map 119/301598
£29.50-£35 D2 TI FI ✕ nearby ⋘(Matlock)
Ⓓ Ⓑ ⊗ 🐾👤👣 ★★★★

Comfortable and well-equipped accommodation in a Grade 2 listed building by the river and park. Just a short, tree-lined walk into town, bus and rail stations. Hearty breakfasts with fresh eggs from our own hens. Ample private parking.

● **Monsal Head**
PEAK DISTRICT

Castle Cliffe
DE45 INL ☎ 01629 640258 (Neil & Jackie Mantell)
www.castle-cliffe.com Map 119/185715
£30-£40 D3 T2 F2 ✕ nearby
Ⓓ Ⓑ ⊗ 🐾👤👣🚗! ★★★★

Stunning position overlooking the beautiful Monsal Dale.

Noted for it's friendly atmosphere, hearty breakfasts and breathtaking views. Walk straight from the door in any direction to experience the Peak District at its finest.

Join us for tea and homemade cakes in the garden or by a roaring log fire in winter. Choice of dinner venues within an easy stroll. Guest lounge available. Groups welcome. Plenty of car parking space.

● **Risley**
MIDSHIRES WAY
Braeside Guest House, 113 Derby Road, DE72 3SS ☎ 01159 395885
(Mrs Lisa Grundy) www.braesideguesthouse.co.uk Map 129/457357
£45 D4 T2 ✕ nearby Ⓓ Ⓑ ⊗ 🐾👤👣 ★★★★

● **Rowsley**
PEAK DISTRICT
Eastfield, Chatsworth Road, DE4 2EH ☎ 01629 734427
www.east-field.co.uk Map 119/260662
£22 DI T2 ✕ Ⓓ ⊗ 🐾👤🚗! Ⓜ

● **Thorpe**
PEAK DISTRICT
Jasmine Cottage, DE6 2AW ☎ 01335 350465 (Liz Round) Map 119/155502
£30-£40 DI TI ✕ nearby Ⓓ Ⓑ ⊗ 🐾👤🚗

● **Whaley Bridge**
MIDSHIRES WAY
Springbank Guest House, 3 Reservoir Rd, SK23 7BL ☎ 01663 732819
(Margot Graham) www.whaleyspringbank.co.uk Map 110/009813
£35 D2 T2 FI ✕ nearby ⋘(Whaley Bridge) Ⓓ Ⓑ ⊗ 🐾👤🚗! ★★★★

LEICESTERSHIRE

● **Great Dalby**
MIDSHIRES WAY
Dairy Farm, 8 Burrough End, LE14 2EW ☎ 01664 562783 (Mrs L Parker)
www.dairy-farm.co.uk Map 129/744141
✕ Ⓓ Ⓑ ⊗ 🐾👤!👣

● **Market Harborough**
The Bull's Head, Arthingworth, LE16 8JZ ☎ 01858 525637 (Sandy Hopcraft)
www.thebullsheadonline.co.uk Map 141/754812
£50-£65 SI D3 T5 F2 ✕ £10, 7pm
Ⓥ Ⓓ Ⓑ ⊗ 🐾👤👣🚗!👣👣 Ⓕ ★★★Ⓦ

LINCOLNSHIRE

● **Belton**
De Vere Belton Woods, Belton, NG32 2LN ☎ 01476 593200
www.devere.co.uk/heritage/belton-woods/ Map 130/923393
£39.50-£44.50 D7I T65 ✕ £22.50, 7pm
Ⓥ Ⓓ Ⓑ ⊗ 🐾👤🚗!👣👣 Ⓕ

● **Grasby**
VIKING WAY
Little Hen Bed & Breakfast, Brigg Road, DN38 6AQ ☎ 01652 629005
(Polly Durrant) www.littlehen.co.uk Map 111/089049
£35 T2 ✕ nearby Ⓑ ⊗ 🐾👤🚗! ★★★★

● **Lincoln**
VIKING WAY
Old Rectory Guest House, 19 Newport, LN1 3DQ ☎ 01522 514774
(Tony Downes) Map 121/975722
£35 SI D3 TI FI ✕ nearby ⋘(Lincoln)
Ⓓ Ⓑ ⊗ 👤👣 ★★★

Stables Bed & Breakfast, 32 Saxon Street, LN1 3HQ ☎ 01522 851750
www.stablesbandb.com Map 121/974723
£45-£55 SI DI TI ✕ nearby ⋘(Lincoln)
Ⓓ Ⓑ ⊗ 🐾👤🚗

● **Market Rasen**
VIKING WAY

Waveney Cottage
Willingham Road, LN8 3DN ☎ 01673 843236 (Mrs J Bridger)
www.waveneycottage.co.uk Map 113/111890
£30-£35 DI T2 ✕ nearby ⋘(Market Rasen)
Ⓓ Ⓑ ⊗ 🐾👤🚗 ★★★★

Comfortable, smoke-free en-suite accommodation offering a choice of delicious breakfasts. Hospitality tray, hairdryer and TV in all rooms. Walking distance to all amenities, providing an ideal base to explore the beauty and peace of the Lincolnshire Wolds (AONB).

EAST MIDLANDS

● **Ruskington**
Sunnyside Farm, Leasingham Lane, NG34 9AH ☎ 01526 833010
(Daphne Luke) www.sunnysidefarm.co.uk Map 121/074502
£25 S1 D1 T1 ✕ nearby ⚌(Ruskington)
▢ Ⓑ ⊛ 🐾♨➡!🛏 ★★★

● **Skegness**
Sandgate Hotel, 44, Drummond Road, PE25 3EB ☎ 01754 762667 (Chris
Thornley) www.sandgate-hotel@tiscali.co.uk Map 122/568629
£22-£25 S2 D2 T3 F2 ✕ 5:30pm ⚌(Skegness)
Ⓥ ▢ Ⓑ ⊛ 🐾♨➡ ★★★

● **South Hykeham**
VIKING WAY
Wellbeck Cottage B&B, 19 Meadow Lane, LN6 9PF ☎ 01522 692669
(Mrs Margaret Driffill) maggied@hotmail.co.uk Map 121/938645
✕ £10 ⚌(North Hykeham) Ⓥ ▢ Ⓑ ⊛ 🐾➡🛏 ★★★★Ⓦ

● **Swinhope**
VIKING WAY

Hoe Hill House Bed & Breakfast
Swinhope, LN8 6HX ☎ 01472 399366 (Sally Ward)
www.hoehill.co.uk Map 113/217955
£35 D2 T1 ✕ nearby
▢ Ⓑ ⊛ 🐾♨➡!🛏 ★★★★Ⓦ

Former farmhouse with original features set in unspoilt countryside on Lincolnshire Wolds and close to the Viking Way. Enjoy our award-winning breakfasts and local produce along with excellent facilities. Happy to help with luggage and transport.

● **Walesby**
VIKING WAY
Blaven, Walesby Hill, LN8 3UW ☎ 01673 838352 (Jacqy Braithwaite)
www.blavenhouse.co.uk Map 113/135924 ▢ Ⓑ ⊛ 🐾➡

NORTHAMPTONSHIRE

● **Sibbertoft**
The Wrongs, LE16 9UJ ☎ 01858 880886 (Mrs M J Hart)
www.brookmeadow.co.uk Map 141/666829
✕ ▢ Ⓑ ⊛ 🐾➡!🛏

NOTTINGHAMSHIRE

● **Mansfield**
Bridleways Holiday Homes & Guest House, Newlands Road, Forest Town, NG19 0HU
☎ 01623 635725 (Gillian & Michael Rand)
www.stayatbridleways.co.uk Map 120/579624
£35 S5 D2 T1 F1 Ⓑ ⊛ ♨ঙ Ⓕ ★★★

● **Rempstone**
MIDSHIRES WAY
Guesthouse at Rempstone, Main Street, LE12 6RH ☎ 01509 881886
(Mark Cosgrove) www.guesthouse-rempstone.co.uk Map 129/577243
£30 S5 D4 T4 F2 ✕ £7, 7pm Ⓥ ▢ Ⓑ ⊛ 🐾♨➡!ঙ

RUTLAND

● **Belton-in-Rutland**
MACMILLAN WAY

The Old Rectory
LE15 9LE ☎ 01572 717279
www.theoldrectorybelton.co.uk Map 141/814010
£25-£30 S1 D2 T3 F1 ✕ nearby
▢ Ⓑ ⊛ ♨➡!🛏 ★★★

On MacMillan Way, Leicestershire and Rutland Rounds. Edge of village overlooking Eyebrook Valley. Rooms both in the main house and annexe, mostly ensuite and at various rates. Local pub approx' 150yds. Excellent farmhouse breakfast, packed lunch by arrangement.

● **Oakham**
MACMILLAN WAY & VIKING WAY
The Old Wisteria Hotel, 4 Catmose Street, LE15 6HW ☎ 01572 722844
(Emad Saleeb) www.wisteriahotel.co.uk Map 141/862086
£55-£65 S7 D18 ✕ £12.50, 6pm ⚌(Oakham)
Ⓥ ▢ Ⓑ ⊛ 🐾♨🛏ঙ Ⓕ ★★★

Barleythorpe Training & Conference Centre
Barleythorpe, LE15 7ED ☎ 01572 723711 (Rebecca Myatt/Cate Carter)
www.barleythorpe.com Map 141/847098
£52.75 S2 T20 ✕ £17.65, 7pm ⚌(Oakham)
Ⓥ ▢ Ⓑ ⊛ 🐾♨!ঙ Ⓕ ★★★

Set in five acres of grounds in beautiful Rutland countryside, Barleythorpe offers groups a welcoming, peaceful location with en-suite bedrooms, spacious residents' lounge, licensed bar, free car parking and evening meals by prior arrangement. Minimum 12 guests per night.

The Noel @ Whitwell, Main Road, LE15 8BW ☎ 01780 460347
(Claire Latham) www.thenoel.co.uk Map 141/925088
£55-£70 S1 D3 T1 F3 ✕ £15, 6:30pm ⚌(Oakham) Ⓥ Ⓑ 🐾♨🛏ঙ ★★★

17 Northgate
LE15 6QR ☎ 01572 759271 (Dane Gould)
17northgate.co.uk Map 141/858089
£50 D1 T1 ✕ nearby ⚌(Oakham)
▢ Ⓑ ⊛ 🐾♨➡ ঙঙ ★★★★Ⓜ

A recently renovated 300-year-old thatched farmhouse in the centre of Oakham with two newly built en-suite rooms with their own patios, off-road parking and private entrance.

Very close to all the shops, pubs, restaurants and Rutland Water.

For an explanation of the symbols and abbreviations used in this guide, see the Key on the back cover's fold-out flap.

SELF-CATERING

DERBYSHIRE

● Ashbourne

PEAK DISTRICT

PENNINE BRIDLEWAY & PENNINE WAY

Offcote Grange Cottage Holidays
☎ 01335 344795 (Pat Walker) www.offcotegrange.com
Map 119/190438
£1200-£1995 Sleeps 10-14. 2 cottages.
Short breaks available ★★★★★

Hillside Croft and Billy's Bothy.

Two large, luxurious five-star five-bedroom detached country cottages in peaceful rural locations, own landscaped gardens within beautiful scenery.

Patio and BBQs. Private parking. Each with separate lounge and dining rooms, exceptional farmhouse kitchens, quality bath/shower rooms. Billy's Bothy is all en-suite.

An excellent walking area, central Derbyshire, ideal base for all attractions. Close to Chatsworth House/Carsington Water.
Relaxation room and sauna. Cinema screen available.

Sandybrook Country Park
☎ 01335 300000 (Pinelodge Holidays Ltd)
www.pinelodgeholidays.co.uk/sandybrook.ihtml Map 119/178482
£260-£1040 Sleeps 2-8. 41 pinelodges.
F Short breaks available ★★★★

Luxurious pinelodges with glorious views.

Excellent base for Peak District.

Children's adventure playground, soft play, indoor pool with spa and sauna.

Woodland walk. The Coach House bar and restaurant serves an extensive menu and takeaways.

The luxurious, well equipped pinelodges have satellite television and CD players. Each has a verandah with garden furniture. All linen is included. Weeks and short breaks available year round.

● Bakewell

PEAK DISTRICT

Rock House ☎ 01298 872418 (Paul Steverson)
www.rockhouse-peakdistrict.co.uk Map 119/214686 .
£295-£450 Sleeps 2-7. 1 cottage.
Short breaks available ★★★ Ⓦ

● Belper

PEAK DISTRICT

DERWENT VALLEY HERITAGE WAY

Chevin View
☎ 07773 197783 (Mrs T Sowerby)
www.spacelocations.co.uk Map 119/351474
£395-£445 Sleeps 1-7. 1 cottage.
Short breaks available ★★★ Ⓦ

Luxury listed, spacious cottage with contemporary design. Excellent location for walks around Belper, world heritage sites and Peak District.
Three bedrooms and two bathrooms, modern kitchen and bathrooms. Broadband internet access. Peaceful conservation area, close to train and bus stations.

● Buxton

PEAK DISTRICT

MIDSHIRES WAY

Town house ☎ 0151 342 7673 (Stan Orton)
stan.orton@btinternet.com Map 119/059731
£350-£600 Sleeps 6-8. 1 town centre-house. Short breaks available Ⓜ

Victoria Lodge ☎ 01260 297429 (Stewart Price)
www.victorialodge.info Map 119/058730
£500-£750 Sleeps 4-16. 1 self-catering house.

● Castleton

PEAK DISTRICT

PENNINE WAY

Riding House Cottages ☎ 01433 620257 (Denise Matthews)
www.peak-district-holiday-cottages.co.uk Map 110/149829
£350-£530 Sleeps 2-4. 2 cottages. Short breaks available ★★★★★

● Curbar

PEAK DISTRICT

Curbar Cottages ☎ 01433 631885 (Dr Morrissy)
curbarcottages.com Map 119/251746
£190-£300 Sleeps 2-4. 2 cottages. Short breaks available

● Earl Sterndale

PEAK DISTRICT

PENNINE BRIDLEWAY & MIDSHIRES WAY

Wheeldon Trees Farm Holiday Cottages ☎ 01298 83219 (Deborah and Martin Hofman) www.wheeldontreesfarm.co.uk Map 119/103661
£325-£620 Sleeps 1-24. 7 cottages. Short breaks available Ⓦ

● Eyam

PEAK DISTRICT

DERWENT VALLEY HERITAGE WAY

Dalehead Court Country Cottages
☎ 01433 620214 (Mrs Dorothy Neary)
www.peakdistrictholidaycottages.com Map 119/212766
£195-£520 Sleeps 2-6. 3 cottages.
Short breaks available ★★★★★

Historic Eyam. A fine house, a delightful 17th-century barn and cosy cottage overlooking Derbyshire's most historic village square. Exceptional decor/furnishings, walled courtyard garden and private parking. Village inn, shops two minutes. Breaks from £115.
Phone for a brochure or email: laneside@lineone.net

EAST MIDLANDS

Fenny Bentley

PEAK DISTRICT

Swallows Cottage
☎ 01335 350238 (Angela Hughes)
freespace.virgin.net/hughes.priory/
Map 119/185503
£225-£480 Sleeps 4-6. 1 cottage. Short breaks available ★★★

Peak District National Park near Ashbourne. Peaceful, comfortable stone cottage, sleeps up to six (plus baby). Central heating, open fire, games room, garden. Within easy reach of Dovedale and Alton Towers. Open all year, 3/4-night short breaks available.

Hope

PEAK DISTRICT

PENNINE WAY & PENNINE BRIDLEWAY

Laneside Farm Holiday Cottages
☎ 01433 620214 (Mrs Dorothy Neary)
www.peakdistrictholidaycottages.com Map 110/172835
£195-£420 Sleeps 2-4. 4 cottages.
Short breaks available ★★★★★

Riverside setting. Award-winning conversion of 3 beamed farm barns into delightful self-catering cottages. River/hill walks abound. Train/buses nearby for walk and ride-back options. Conveniently located near village amenities. Breaks from £110. Phone/email for brochure (laneside@lineone.net)

Farfield Farm Cottages ☎ 01433 620640 (Mrs Gill Elliott)
www.farfield.gemsoft.co.uk Map 110/172835
£250-£575 Sleeps 2-5. 3 cottages.
Short breaks available ★★★★

Watergates Caravan ☎ 01433 620110 (Gill Owen)
gillrav4@tiscali.co.uk Map 110/171833
£260-£400 Sleeps 1-4. 1 caravan.

Oaker Farm Holiday Cottages ☎ 01433 621955 (Julie Hadfield)
www.oakerfarm.co.uk Map 110/167850
£250-£495 Sleeps 2-4. 3 cottage. Short breaks available ★★★★

Matlock

PEAK DISTRICT

DERWENT VALLEY HERITAGE WAY, MIDSHIRES WAY & PENNINE BRIDLEWAY

Carpenters Cottage
☎ 0115 9233455 (Iris & Bob Wilmot)
www.carpenters-cottage.com Map 119/310600
£220-£400 Sleeps 1-5. 1 cottage.
Short breaks available ★★★★

Warm, well-equipped, two bathroom, three bedroom, fully modernised cottage in sensitively converted 18th-century mill complex. Small sunny garden with lovely views down Lumsdale valley. Many doorstep walks. Parking for two cars. Short stroll to Matlock, pubs, restaurants and parks.

The Log Cabin Walker Wood ☎ 01629 825687 (Simone Jordan)
martinkinsella@supanet.com Map 119/328547
£175-£330 Sleeps 1-4. 1 log cabin. Short breaks available

Darwin Forest Country Park
☎ 01629 732428 (Pinelodge Holidays Ltd)
www.pinelodgeholidays.co.uk/darwin_forest.ihtml Map 119/288588
£260-£1040 Sleeps 2-8. 85 pinelodges.
Short breaks available

Set in 44 acres of stunning woodland, an excellent base for exploring the Peak District. Tennis courts, children's play areas, indoor pool with gym, spa, sauna, steam room.
The Forester's Inn serves an extensive menu and takeaways. Handy shop and wine store. The luxurious, well equipped pinelodges have satellite television and CD players.
Each has a verandah with garden furniture. All linen is included.
Weeks and short breaks available year round.

Parwich

PEAK DISTRICT

MIDSHIRES WAY

Parwich Lees Holiday Cottages ☎ 01335 390 625 (Jane Gerard-Pearse)
www.parwichlees.co.uk Map 119/172548
£214-£1213 Sleeps 2-10. 3 cottages. Short breaks available ★★★

Sheen

PEAK DISTRICT

Sheen Cottage
☎ 01270 874979 (Janice Mills)
www.sheencottage.co.uk Map 119/110609
£220-£420 Sleeps 1-4. 1 cottage.
Short breaks available

Lovely Grade II-listed cottage. Modernised to high standards with much character and charm. Clean, warm and welcoming. Excellent for exploring White Peak. Adjoins quiet pub serving good food. Includes heating, electricity, coal, logs and bed linen.

Sutton-on-the-Hill

Windlehill Farm ☎ 01283 732377 (Keith & Joan Lennard)
www.windlehill.btinternet.co.uk Map 128/240349
£160-£520 Sleeps 1-6. 2 cottage and apartment.
Short breaks available ★★★★ Ⓦ

Tideswell

PEAK DISTRICT

PENNINE BRIDLEWAY

1 Primrose Cottages ☎ 01332 831352 (Nick and Joanna Watson)
www.tideswellcottage.co.uk Map 119/151752
£250-£400 Sleeps 2-7. 1 cottage. Short breaks available

LEICESTERSHIRE

● Sibbertoft
Brook Meadow Chalets ☎ 01858 880886 (Mrs M J Hart)
www.brookmeadow.co.uk Map 141/675826
£180-£490 Sleeps 2-6. 3 chalets. ⊗ ⑤ 🛁 Short breaks available ★★★

LINCOLNSHIRE

● Horncastle
VIKING WAY
Cottage One ☎ 01507 578263 (Sandra Willerton)
thewillertons@hotmail.co.uk Map 122/226742
£140-£180 Sleeps 1-3. I cottage. 🛁 Short breaks available

● Market Rasen
VIKING WAY
Meadow Farm House ☎ 01673 885909 (Nick Grimshaw)
www.meadowfarmhouse.co.uk Map 121/130837
£220-£370 Sleeps 1-4. I cottage. ⊗ ⑤ Short breaks available ★★★★

RUTLAND

● Oakham
MACMILLAN WAY & VIKING WAY
The Old Wisteria Hotel, 4 Catmose Street, LE15 6HW ☎ 01572 722844
(Emad Saleeb) www.wisteriahotel.co.uk Map 141/862086
DBB £47.50 per night Sleeps 15-45. Hotel, group accommodation.
🚶(Oakham) Ⓓ ⊗ 🐾 ★★★

GROUPS, HOSTELS, BUNKHOUSES, CAMPSITES & OTHERS

DERBYSHIRE

● Buxton
PEAK DISTRICT
MIDSHIRES WAY
Bushey Heath Farm, Tideswell Moor, SK17 8JE ☎ 01298 873007 (Rod Baraona)
www.busheyheathfarm.co.uk Map 119/146785
SC £4-£15 per night Sleeps 1-110. Campsite & bunkhouse barn. Ⓓ ⊗ 🐾 🛁

● Calver
PEAK DISTRICT
DERWENT VALLEY HERITAGE WAY
Cliff College, Calver, S32 3XG ☎ 01246 584206 (Ian Phipps)
www.cliffcollege.org Map 119/250740
BB, DBB £18.49-£47.29 per night Sleeps 1-150. College buildings, dormitories.
🚶(Grindleford) Ⓥ Ⓓ ⊗ 🐾 ⑤ Ⓕ

● Wirksworth
PEAK DISTRICT
The Glenorchy Centre, West Derbyshire United Reformed Church, Coldwell
Street, DE4 4FB ☎ 01629 824323 (Mrs EM Butlin)
www.glenorchycentre.org.uk Map 119/287541
SC £10 per night Sleeps 10-20. Converted church building. 🚶(Cromford) Ⓓ

EAST MIDLANDS

WEST MIDLANDS

Long Distance Paths

Heart of England ....HOE

Herefordshire Trail ....HFT

Macmillan Way ....MCM

Monarch's Way ....MON

Offa's Dyke Path ....OFD

Sandstone Trail ....SAN

Severn Way ....SVN

Shropshire Way ....SHS

Staffordshire Way ....SFS

Wye Valley Walk ....WVL

**See Paths & Access p25 for full
details of LDPs and waymarks**

VIEW FROM THE MALVERN HILLS
TO THE COTSWOLDS

WALK...   ...THE NEWCASTLE WAY

Staffordshire's most recent long distance route stretches 40km/25 miles from the hill-top castle of Mow Cop on the Staffordshire-Cheshire border to the Shropshire Union canal at Market Drayton, providing a new link with the Staffordshire Way and numerous astonishing views. Well waymarked with oak signs, the footpath passes through some of Newcastle-under-Lyme's historic coal mines and iron works dotted among the scenic farmland and rough moors.

Staffordshire County Council's excellent guide is free to download from their website www.staffordshire.gov.uk (search for 'Newcastle Way'), or ☎ 01785 277264, and breaks the route down into pleasant half-day sections with full details of public transport links and amenities throughout.

VISIT...   ...THE CLUN GREEN MAN FESTIVAL

In *A Shropshire Lad*, AE Housman called Clun 'the quietest place under the sun'. And it still is, with the exception of the May Day weekend when the whole town turns out for the Clun Green Man Festival. On the Sunday the main square is filled with singers, dancers and performers – all with a medieval flavour. Then the next day, the Green Man begins a procession through the town, battling the Frost Queen on the bridge to bring spring to the valley, before arriving at Clun Castle and the beginning of a May Fair with over 40 craft stalls and attractions.

Visit www.clungreenman.org.uk for a full programme of events and more about walking in this beautiful region.

SEE...

...THE ROCK HOUSES AT KINVER EDGE

Home to the last occupied troglodyte dwellings in England, this 164-metre sandstone ridge west of Stourbridge would have commanded stunning views for its residents before their eviction in the 1950s. Surrounded by 300 acres of heath and woodland, visitors can now see a fully-restored rock house complete with Victorian furniture and fittings – one of 11 that were recorded occupied as early as 1777 (with Holy Austin Rock known to be a hermitage for over a century before then). The Staffordshire Way follows the ridge to its summit, which is also the site of an Iron Age hill fort.

Visit www.nationaltrust.org.uk for more details or ☎ 01384 872553.

LOCAL RAMBLERS GROUPS... City of Birmingham Group organises an annual walk with the Birmingham Sports Club for the Disabled known as the 'Meerkats walk' because everyone looks out for each other. Visit their website (see p95) or ☎ 0121 749 1227 for details of this year's event and how to join in... **Staffordshire Area gives a comprehensive list of grid-referenced access points in the Peak Park on their website (see p93) to help plan your right to roam walks**... Stone Group offers a Walking for Health programme of walks open to all every Tuesday morning at Westbridge Park. Contact them for more details (see p93).

WEST MIDLANDS

MAP   185

BED & BREAKFAST

BIRMINGHAM & THE BLACK COUNTRY

● Solihull
HEART OF ENGLAND WAY

Ivy House, Warwick Road, Heronfield Knowle, B93 0EB ☎ 01564 770247
(Mr & Mrs J Townsend) www.ivyhouseguesthouse.co.uk Map 139/194750
£40 S1 D2 T3 F1 ✗ nearby ⋙(Dorridge)
B ⊗ ⌂ ♨ ★★★

HEREFORDSHIRE

● Gladestry
OFFA'S DYKE

Gobe Farm, Gladestry, HR5 3PW ☎ 01544 370606 (June Lloyd)
www.gobefarm.co.uk Map 148/226545
£26.50-£36.50 D2
D ⊗ 🖐 ⌂ 🚗 ! ♨ Ⓜ

● Hay-on-Wye
OFFA'S DYKE

Baskerville Arms Hotel, HR3 5RZ ☎ 01497 820670 (Dave Slade)
www.baskervillearms.co.uk Map 148/214438
£30-£40 S1 D9 T2 F1 ✗ £10, 6pm
V D B ⊗ 🖐 ⌂ 🚗 ! ♨ Ⓜ

● Kington
OFFA'S DYKE & HEREFORDSHIRE TRAIL

Southbourne, Newton Lane, HR5 3NF ☎ 01544 231706 (Geoff & Patsy Cooper)
www.southbournebandb.co.uk Map 148/290570
£25 S1 D2 T2 ✗ £12, 7pm V D ⊗ 🖐 🚗 !

● Ledbury
HEREFORDSHIRE TRAIL

Wall Hills House, Hereford Road, HR8 2PR ☎ 01531 632833
(David & Jennifer Slaughter) www.wallhills.com Map 149/701386
⋙(Ledbury) D B ⊗ 🖐

Church Farm
Coddington, HR8 1JJ ☎ 01531 640271 (Jane West)
www.dexta.co.uk Map 149/718426
£40 D2 T1 F2
D B ⊗ ⌂ ♨

Come and enjoy our 16th-century listed,
timber-framed farmhouse, on a working farm.
Warm welcome and relaxed atmosphere
assured. Lovely garden, immediate access to
wonderful walks, inglenook fireplace. Aga-
cooked breakfasts. Ledbury/Malvern Hills
four miles. En-suite/shared accommodation.

● Ross-on-Wye
WYE VALLEY WALK & HEREFORDSHIRE TRAIL

Sunnymount, Ryefield Road, HR9 5LU ☎ 01989 563880
(Denise & Bob Robertson) sunnymount@tinyworld.co.uk Map 162/606242
£30-£35 D4 T2 ✗ nearby
D B ⊗ 🖐 ⌂ 🚗 ! ♨ ★★★★

● Vowchurch
HEREFORDSHIRE TRAIL

Yew Tree House, Vowchurch, HR2 9PF ☎ 01981 251195
(John or Sue Richardson) www.yewtreehouse-hereford.co.uk Map 149/396367
£30-£35 D1 T1 F1 ✗ £20, 7pm V D B
⊗ 🖐 ⌂ 🚗 ! ★★★★Ⓖ

● Weobley
HEREFORDSHIRE TRAIL & WYE VALLEY WALK

Highbury House, Norton Canon, HR4 7BH ☎ 01544 318556 (Susanne Pavey)
highburyguesthouse.com Map 148/377485
£30 D2 T2 F1 D B ⊗ 🖐 ⌂ 🚗 ! 🏠 ★★★★Ⓢ

SHROPSHIRE

● Abdon
SHROPSHIRE WAY

Earnstrey Hill House, SY7 9HU ☎ 01746 712579 (Mrs Jill Scurfield)
Map 137/587873
£30-£37 D1 T2 ✗ £18.50, 6pm V D B ⊗ 🖐 ⌂ 🚗 !

● Bishop's Castle
SHROPSHIRE WAY

The Old Brick Guesthouse, 7 Church Street, SY9 5AA ☎ 01588 638471
(Norm & Rosie Reid) www.oldbrick.co.uk Map 137/323885
£35-£40 D2 T1 F2 ✗ nearby D B ⊗ 🖐 ⌂ 🚗 ! 🏠 ★★★

Old Time, 29 High Street, SY9 5BE ☎ 01588 638467 (Jane Carroll)
www.oldtime.co.uk Map 137/323888
£30-£35 D2 T1 ✗ nearby D B ⊗ 🖐 ⌂ 🚗 ! 🏠 ★★★Ⓦ

The Porch House, 33/35 High Street, SY9 5BE ☎ 01588 638854
(Gill and John Lucas) www.theporchhouse.com Map 137/323888
£45 D1 T1 ✗ nearby D B ⊗ 🖐 ⌂ 🚗 !

Middle Woodbatch Farm, Woodbatch Road, SY9 5JT ☎ 01588 630141
(Mary & Steven Austin) www.middlewoodbatchfarm.co.uk Map 137/314883
£25 D1 T2 F1 ✗ £10, 7pm V D B 🖐 🚗 ! 🏠

Magnolia, 3 Montgomery Road, SY9 5EZ ☎ 01588 638098
(Elizabeth Ronan and Geoff Grimes) www.magnoliabishopscastle.co.uk
Map 137/324893
£40 S3 D3 T3 ✗ nearby D B ⊗ 🖐 ⌂ 🚗 ! ★★★★Ⓖ Ⓦ

Claremont, Bull Lane, SY9 5DA ☎ 01588 638170 (Audrey Price)
www.priceclaremont.co.uk Map 137/324890
£30-£40 D1 T2 ✗ nearby D B ⊗ 🖐 ⌂ 🚗 !

● Cardington
SHROPSHIRE WAY

Enchmarsh Farm, Leebotwood, SY6 7JX ☎ 01694 771371 or 07967 976164
(Sandra Allsop) www.virtual-shropshire.co.uk/enchmarsh Map 137/501964
£23 S4 D2 T4 F2 ✗ £12, 7pm ⋙(Church Stretton)
V D B ⊗ 🖐 ⌂ 🚗 ! 🏠

● Church Stretton
SHROPSHIRE WAY

Belvedere Guest House, Burway Road, SY6 6DP ☎ 01694 722232 (Ewa Lovejoy)
www.belvedereguesthouse.co.uk Map 137/451941
£27-£31 D4 T1 F2 ✗ nearby ⋙(Church Stretton)
D B ⊗ 🖐 ⌂ 🚗 ! 🏠

Brookfields Guest House
Watling Street North, SY6 7AR ☎ 01694 722314 (Angie & Paul Bradley)
www.churchstretton-guesthouse.co.uk Map 137/459937
£40 S1 D5 TI ✕ nearby ⚶(Church Stretton)
Ⅴ Ⅾ Ⓑ ⊛ 🍴 👶 🚗 ! ★★★★★Ⓢ

Large comfortable Edwardian house and grounds, ample parking. Stroll to town and train station. Luxury en-suite bedrooms. Ideal base for walkers and tourers. Special rates for weekly or party bookings. Evening meals provided for groups of six or more.

The Longmynd Hotel
Cunnery Road, SY6 6AG ☎ 01694 722244
www.longmynd.co.uk Map 137/449935
£53-£63 S6 D23 T15 F6 ✕ £24.95, 6:45pm ⚶(Church Stretton)
Ⅴ Ⅾ Ⓑ ⊛ 🍴 👶 🏊 ⚴ ★★

Breathtaking views, fine restaurant and bar facilities. Ideal location for walking the Shropshire hills and touring the area. Special interest packages and many amenities available (including outdoor heated pool, sauna, table tennis, pool table, pitch & putt course). Book online at www.longmynd.co.uk

Sayang House, Hope Bowdler, SY6 7DD ☎ 01694 723981
(Patrick & Madeline Egan) www.sayanghouse.com Map 137/476924
£30-£35 D2 TI ✕ £15, 7pm ⚶(Church Stretton)
Ⅴ Ⅾ Ⓑ ⊛ 🍴 👶 🚗 ! 🏇 ★★★★

Old Rectory House, Burway Road, SY6 6DW ☎ 01694 724462 (Mike Smith)
info@oldrectoryhouse.co.uk Map 137/452938
£26-£28 D2 TI ✕ nearby ⚶(Church Stretton)
Ⅾ Ⓑ ⊛ 🍴 👶 ★★★

Ragdon Manor, Ragdon, SY6 7EZ ☎ 01694 781389 (Wendy Clark)
www.ragdonbandb.co.uk Map 137/455915
£28-£30 D1 TI ⚶(Church Stretton)
Ⅾ Ⓑ ⊛ 🍴 👶 🚗 🏇 ★★★★

Lawley House Bed and Breakfast, Lawley House, Smethcott, SY6 6NX
☎ 01694 751236 (Mrs Jacqueline Scarratt)
www.lawleyhouse.co.uk Map 137/452995
£25-£35 S1 D2 T2 Ⅾ Ⓑ ⊛ 🍴 👶 🚗 ! ★★★★

● Clun
SHROPSHIRE WAY & OFFA'S DYKE

Crown House
Church Street, SY7 8JW ☎ 01588 640780 (Reg Maund & Judy Bailey)
www.smoothhound.co.uk Map 137/300805
£30 S1 D1 TI ✕ nearby
Ⅾ Ⓑ ⊛ 🍴 👶 🚗 ! 🏇 ★★★★Ⓜ

Walking the Shropshire Way or Offa's Dyke? If you visit Clun, visit us! We welcome muddy boots, wet anoraks and happy people. We have superb accommodation in a self-contained annexe. Lifts and luggage transfers by arrangement.

Clun Farm House, High Street, SY7 8JB ☎ 01588 640432
(Anthony & Sue Whitfield) www.clunfarmhouse.co.uk Map 137/302808
£32.50-£35 S2 D1 TI FI ✕ £25, 7:30pm
Ⅴ Ⅾ Ⓑ ⊛ 🍴 👶 🚗 ! 🏇

The White Horse Inn, The Square, SY7 8JA ☎ 01588 640305 (Jack Limond)
www.whi-clun.co.uk Map 137/300808
Ⅾ Ⓑ 🍴 🚗 ! 🏇 ★★★

● Gobowen
Clevelands, Station Road, SY11 3JS ☎ 01691 661359 (Miss O Powell)
Map 126/302334
£19-£20 S2 D1 ✕ nearby ⚶(Gobowen) ⊛ 🏇

● High Ercall
SHROPSHIRE WAY
The Mill House, Shrewsbury Road, TF6 6BE ☎ 01952 770394 (Judy Yates)
www.ercallmill.co.uk Map 126/584163
£35 D1 TI FI Ⅾ Ⓑ ⊛ 🍴 👶 🚗 ! 🏇 ★★★★

● Ironbridge
SHROPSHIRE WAY
Post Office House, 6 The Square, TF8 7AQ ☎ 01952 433201 (Janet Hunter)
hunter@pohouse-ironbridge.fsnet.co.uk Map 127/673034
£40-£42 D1 TI FI ✕ nearby
Ⅾ Ⓑ ⊛ 🍴 👶 🚗 ! 🏇 ★★★

● Oswestry
OFFA'S DYKE
BJ's, 87 Llwyn Rd, SY11 1EW ☎ 01691 650205 (Barbara Williams)
barbarajoyce.williams@talktalk.net Map 126/294303
£25 D1 TI ✕ nearby Ⅾ ⊛ 🍴 👶 🚗 ★★

● Shrewsbury
SHROPSHIRE WAY
Abbey Court House, 134 Abbey Foregate, SY2 6AU ☎ 01743 364416
(Mrs V.A Macleod) www.abbeycourt.biz Map 126/503122
✕ ⚶(Shrewsbury) Ⓑ 🍴 ★★★★

STAFFORDSHIRE

● Cheddleton
STAFFORDSHIRE WAY
Prospect House Guest House, 334 Cheadle Road, ST13 7BW ☎ 01782 550639
(Rolf & Jackie Griffiths) www.prospecthouseleek.co.uk Map 118/967506
✕ £14 Ⅴ Ⓑ ⊛ 🍴 🚗 !

● Endon
STAFFORDSHIRE WAY
Hollinhurst Farm, Park Lane, ST9 9JB ☎ 01782 502633 (Mrs J Ball)
www.smoothhound.co.uk/hotels/hollinhurst.html Map 118/942531
£22 D2 TI FI ✕ nearby Ⓑ ⊛ 🍴 👶 🚗 ! 🏇 ⚴ ★★★

● **Grindon**
PEAK DISTRICT

Summerhill Farm
ST13 7TT ☎ 01538 304264 (Mrs P Simpson)
www.summerhillfarm.co.uk Map 119/083534
£25-£30 D2 T1 F1 ✕ £12, 6:30pm
Ⓥ Ⓓ Ⓑ ⊛ 🐾 ♨ 🚗 ★★★

Tastefully furnished, en-suite facilities, tea/coffee, colour TV. Amid rolling countryside overlooking the Dove and Manifold Valleys. Wonderful for walkers. Ideally situated for Buxton, Chatsworth House and the Potteries. Excellent pubs nearby. Email: info@summerhillfarm.co.uk, or visit our website.

WARWICKSHIRE

● **Hampton-in-Arden**
HEART OF ENGLAND WAY
The White Lion, High Street, B92 0AA ☎ 01675 442833 (Liz Thorne)
www.thewhitelioninn.com Map 139/203808
£49 D5 T3 ✕ £15, 7pm 🚌 (Hampton-in-Arden)
Ⓥ Ⓓ Ⓑ ⊛ 🐾 ♨ 🚗 ! 🎒

● **Hatton**
HEART OF ENGLAND WAY
Northleigh House, Five Ways Road, CV35 7HZ ☎ 01926 484203 (Viv Morgan)
www.northleigh.co.uk Map 139/222689
£35-£50 D7 T2 F2 ✕ £8, 7pm 🚌 (Hatton)
Ⓥ Ⓓ Ⓑ ⊛ 🐾 ♨ 🚗 ! 🎒 ♿ Ⓕ ★★★★

● **Kenilworth**
Banner Hill Farmhouse, Rouncil Lane, CV8 1NN ☎ 01926 852850
(Mrs Patricia Snelson) Map 140/268708
£20 S2 D2 T4 F2 ✕ nearby Ⓓ Ⓑ 🐾 ♨ 🚗 ! 🎒 ♿

● **Warwick**
Haseley Coach House Motel, Haseley, Nr Hatton, CV35 7LS ☎ 01926 484222
(Jane Richards) www.haseleycoachhouse.com Map 151/238679
£45-£49.50 D7 T1 F2 ✕ nearby 🚌 (Warwick Parkway)
Ⓓ Ⓑ 🐾 ♨ 🚗 ! 🎒 ♿ ★★★

WORCESTERSHIRE

● **Ashton-under-Hill**
Holloway Farm House, WR11 7SN ☎ 01386 881910 (M Sanger-Davies)
www.hollowayfarmhouse.btinternet.co.uk Map 150/998382
£30 T1 F1 ✕ nearby Ⓓ Ⓑ ⊛ 🐾 ♨ 🚗 ! 🎒

● **Broadway**
COTSWOLD WAY
Old Station House, Station Drive, WR12 7DF ☎ 01386 852659 (Pam Trueman)
www.broadway-cotswolds.co.uk/oldstationhouse.html Map 150/090380
£45 S2 D4 T2 ✕ nearby
Ⓓ Ⓑ ⊛ 🐾 ♨ ! ★★★★ⓢ

Brook House, Station Road, WR12 7DE ☎ 01386 852313
(Mrs Marianne Thomas) www.brookhousebandb.co.uk Map 150/090379
£35-£60 S1 D2 T1 F1 ✕ nearby Ⓓ Ⓑ ⊛ 🐾 ♨ 🎒

● **Bromsgrove**
MONARCH'S WAY

Old Rose and Crown Hotel
Rose Hill, Lickey, B45 8RT ☎ 0121 453 3502 (Andrew Hodges)
www.oldroseandcrown.com Map 139/995757
£25-£40 S4 D8 T6 F3 ✕ nearby 🚌 (Longbridge)
Ⓓ Ⓑ 🐾 ♨ 🚗 ! 🎒 ♿

Set in 500 acres of Country Park, comfortable bedrooms, excellent local ameneties and only 10 minutes drive off Monarch's Way via complimentary shuttle bus from Hagley Worcestershire. Drying and storage room available. Call the hotel now to check availablity.

● **Clifton-upon-Teme**
Pitlands Farm, WR6 6DX ☎ 01886 812220 (Diane Mann)
www.pitlandsfarm.co.uk Map 138/728609
£26-£32 T2 F1 ✕ nearby Ⓓ Ⓑ ⊛ 🐾 ♨ 🚗 ! ★★★★

● **Great Malvern**
SEVERN WAY
Sidney House, 40 Worcester Road, WR14 4AA ☎ 01684 574994
www.sidneyhouse.co.uk Map 150/775463
£25-£30 S1 D4 T2 F1 ✕ nearby 🚌 (Great Malvern)
Ⓓ Ⓑ 🐾 ♨ 🎒 ★★★

Croft Guest House, Bransford, WR6 5JD ☎ 01886 832227 (Mrs Ann Porter)
www.croftguesthouse.com Map 150/795524
£27-£38 D3 T1 F1 ✕ £12, 7pm
Ⓓ Ⓑ ⊛ 🐾 ♨ 🎒 ★★

● **Tenbury Wells**
HEREFORDSHIRE TRAIL
Kyre Equestrian Centre & B&B, Lower House Farm, Vine Lane, WR15 8RL
☎ 01885 410233 (Anne Durston-Smith)
www.kyre-equestrian.co.uk Map 138/615649
£25-£35 S1 D1 T2 ✕ nearby Ⓓ Ⓑ ⊛ 🐾 ♨ 🚗 ! 🎒

● **West Malvern**
Harmony House, 184 West Malvern Rd, WR14 4AZ ☎ 01684 891650
(Catherine Bower) harmonyhousemalvern.com Map 150/763465
£27.50-£35 S1 D2 T2 F1 🚌 (Malvern Link) Ⓓ Ⓑ ⊛ 🐾 ♨ 🚗 🎒 ★★★

SELF-CATERING

HEREFORDSHIRE

● Kington
OFFA'S DYKE & HEREFORDSHIRE TRAIL

Crossing Cottage ☎ 01625 582550 (N Passey)
www.crossingcottage.info Map 148/290557
£240-£440 Sleeps 1-6. ⊗ ♨ Short breaks available

● Ross-on-Wye
WYE VALLEY WALK & HEREFORDSHIRE TRAIL

Woodredding Farm Cottages
☎ 01531 660257 (Brian Robbins) www.woodredding.co.uk
Map 149/640298
£250-£550 Sleeps 2-6. 2 cottages.
⊗ Short breaks available ★★★

One bedroom cottage and a three bedroom cottage in a tastefully converted cider mill. Both comfortable, well-equipped and centrally-heated, with views of open countryside and the Malvern Hills. Ideal base for the Forest of Dean and Wye Valley.

● Bishop's Castle
SHROPSHIRE WAY & OFFA'S DYKE

The Firs ☎ 01588 638560 (Maureen Thuraisingham)
www.thefirscolebatch.co.uk Map 137/329895
£195-£295 Sleeps 2-4. 1 bungalow. ⊗ ♨ Short breaks available ★★★

The Porch House
☎ 01588 638854 (Gill and John Lucas)
www.theporchhouse.com Map 137/329895
£180-£300 Sleeps 1-2. 2 apartments.
⊗ Short breaks available

Elizabethan town house in centre of Bishop's Castle. Renovated to very high standard yet retaining 16th-century character. Facilities for walkers and cyclists, off-street parking and cycle storage. Full details on website.

● Knighton
OFFA'S DYKE

The Garden Lodge ☎ 01547 529542 (Sue & Roger Morris)
sue.morris07@btinternet.com Map 127/746268
£175-£250 Sleeps 1-3. 1 bungalow.
⊗ ♨ Short breaks available

● Ludlow
SHROPSHIRE WAY & HEREFORDSHIRE TRAIL

Mrs Jean Mellings ☎ 01584 873315 (Mrs Jean Mellings)
www.shropshirecottage.co.uk Map 137/511867
£370-£800 Sleeps 2-6. 1 cottage.
♨ Short breaks available

Mocktree Barns
☎ 01547 540441 (Clive & Cynthia Prior)
www.mocktreeholidays.co.uk Map 137/424755
£195-£455 Sleeps 1-6. 5 cottages.
⊗ F ♨ Short breaks available ★★★Ⓦ

Best Value award-winning, comfortable cottages in lovely peaceful countryside. Gardens, wildlife, super views, great walks. Offa's Dyke, Mortimer Trail, Herefordshire Trail, Shropshire Hills all nearby. Maps and advice. Groups welcome. Disabled-friendly. Good food nearby. Short breaks (three nights minimum).

Hinds Cottage ☎ 01568 770242 (Hazel Newby)
www.hindscottage.co.uk Map 137/380690
£200-£375 Sleeps 1-4. 1 barn conversion.
⊗ ♨ Short breaks available

Sutton Court Farm
☎ 01584 861305 (Jane Cronin)
www.suttoncourtfarm.co.uk Map 137/527742
£210-£499 Sleeps 2-6. 6 cottages.
⊗ ♿ F ♨ Short breaks available ★★★★ⓌⓌ

Six special cottages set around a peaceful, rural, courtyard in the Corvedale. Walk from the door or explore further afield in the beautiful south Shropshire countryside. Enjoy a cream tea or evening meal on your return (by prior arrangment).

STAFFORDSHIRE

● Calton
PEAK DISTRICT

Field Head Farmhouse Holidays
☎ 01538 308352 (Janet Hudson)
www.field-head.co.uk Map 119/105500
£620-£1285 Sleeps 12-14. 1 farm house.
⊗ ♨ Short breaks available ★★★★

This Grade II-listed farmhouse with stables, set within its own grounds, with open views is situated midway between the historic towns of Leek and Ashbourne and within the Southern Peak District and the Staffordshire Moorlands.

● Oakamoor
STAFFORDSHIRE WAY

The Annexe at the Old Furnace ☎ 01538 703331 (Annette Baxter/John Higgins)
www.oldfurnace.co.uk Map 119/059449
£175-£315 Sleeps 1-3. 1 cottage. ⊗ ♨ Short breaks available ★★★

● Winkhill

Broomyshaw Country Cottages ☎ 01538 308298 (Mr & Mrs Saul)
www.broomyshaw.co.uk Map 119/060512
£120-£595 Sleeps 2-18. 3 stone-built cottages.
♿ ♨ Short breaks available ★★★

WEST MIDLANDS

WORCESTERSHIRE

● Great Malvern
SEVERN WAY

Greenbank ☎ 01684 567328 (Mr D G Matthews)
matthews.greenbank@virgin.net Map 150/781461
£150-£230 Sleeps 1-4. 1 self-contained garden flat.
⊗ 🛁 Short breaks available ★★★

Rosehill Cottage ☎ 01684 561074 (Mrs Gwyn Sloan)
sloaniain@hotmail.com Map 150/781461
£200-£230 Sleeps 1-2. 1 studio. ⊗ 🛁 Short breaks available

GROUPS, HOSTELS, BUNKHOUSES, CAMPSITES & OTHERS

HEREFORDSHIRE

● Ledbury
HEREFORDSHIRE TRAIL

Berrow House Camping/Bunkhouse, Hollybush, HR8 1ET ☎ 01531 635845
www.berrowhouse.co.uk Map 150/763368
SC £8 per night Sleeps 1-15. Camping, bunkhouse & hostel.
▰▰(Ledbury) Ⓓ ⊗ 🛁 ♿

SHROPSHIRE

● Church Stretton
SHROPSHIRE WAY

Longmynd Hotel, Cunnery Road, SY6 6AG ☎ 01694 722244 (Rowena Jones)
www.longmynd.co.uk Map 137/449935
DBB £48-£70 per night Sleeps 20-100. Hotel, group accommodation.
▰▰(Church Stretton) Ⓥ Ⓓ ⊗ 🐾 🛁 ♿

● Craven Arms
SHROPSHIRE WAY

Sallow View, 1 Park Lane, SY7 9AB ☎ 01588 673295 (Mr Steve Rudge)
www.sallowview.co.uk Map 137/422825
SC £210-£280 per week Sleeps 1-4. Static holiday caravan.
▰▰(Craven Arms) Ⓓ ⊗ 🐾

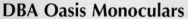

NORTH WEST

Long Distance Paths

Coast to Coast Walk C2C

Cumbria Way ....CMB

Dales Way ....DLS

Hadrian's Wall Path ....HNW

Midshires Way ....MDS

Pennine Bridleway ....PNB

Pennine Way ....PNN

Ribble Way ....RIB

Sandstone Trail ....SAN

Staffordshire Way ....SFS

Teesdale Way ....TSD

Trans Pennine Trail ....TPT

**See Paths & Access p25 for full
details of LDPs and waymarks**

National Parks

Lake District

Peak District

Yorkshire Dales

CAULDRON SNOUT ON
THE RIVER TEES, NORTH PENNINES

WALK...
...THE CLITHEROE CIRCULAR WALKS

These four new, easy interlinking walks are set among the beautiful countryside along the Ribble Valley in Lancashire. Ranging from two to five miles in length, each route pays visit to a wealth of local attractions, including Brungerley sculpture park, Crosshill Quarry nature reserve, a community woodland, Waddow Hall and Clitheroe Castle.

The attractive hand-drawn leaflets that accompany each walk illustrate the rich plant and birdlife that can be spotted along the way and are ideal for families. Download them all from the Ribble Valley Borough Council website www.ribblevalley.gov.uk (search for 'Clitheroe walks') or pick them up at the Clitheroe TIC (☎ 01200 425566).

VISIT...   ...ARNSIDE KNOTT

Just outside the Lake District National Park, this distinctive 522ft limestone hill is renowned for its striking views over Morecambe Bay and the Kent Viaduct, and its woodland and orchid-strewn grassland is a haven for rare wildlife, such as the Scotch argus butterfly. But during the warm summer nights, it's the dancing light display of thousands of female glow worms (actually beetles) trying to attract a mate that draws in the visitors.

The National Trust – which owns the site – sometimes runs guided glow worm walks and also offers an excellent 3km/2-mile circular route around the hill downloadable from its website www.nationaltrust.org.uk. Plus there are plenty more walking opportunities in the neighbouring Arnside and Silverdale AONB.

NORTH WEST

SEE...   ...GORMLEY'S IRON MEN

Staring out at the windswept waters of the Mersey estuary, the eerie, partially-submerged silhouettes of 100 rusted iron men are scattered over 2 miles of beach at Crosby in Anthony Gormley's wondrous art installation *Another Place*. It makes a dramatic starting point for exploring the many sand dunes, pinewoods and marshes of the Sefton Coast conservation area beyond, stretching 22 miles up to the Ribble estuary and home to sand lizards, red squirrels and natterjack toads (Europe's loudest amphibian!).

Download wildlife guides, view maps, and check activities and events in the area at www.seftoncoast.org.uk.

LOCAL RAMBLERS GROUPS... Merseyside and West Cheshire Area organises a programme of monthly guided walks open to the whole public, with pick-up points by coach from Liverpool and Birkenhead. Visit Liverpool Group's website (see p90) or ☎ 01695 421294 for further info... **The Lake District Area offers a self-catering chalet (The Gordon Walker Chalet) for up to 16 people in the Newlands Valley exclusively for Ramblers members or affiliated groups at only £4–£8 per night. Visit their website (see p89) or ☎ 01524 847868 for details...** A full route description for the scenic, waymarked 53km/33-mile Hyndburn Clog in Lancashire is available on Hyndburn Group's website (see p91).

MAP   195

BED & BREAKFAST

CHESHIRE

● **Congleton**
STAFFORDSHIRE WAY

Yew Tree Farm, North Rode, CW12 2PF ☎ 01260 223569 (Sheila Kidd)
www.yewtreebb.co.uk Map 118/890665
£30-£35 D1 T1 ✕ £16, 6pm
Ⓥ Ⓓ Ⓑ ⊛ 🐾🛁 ★★★★

● **Macclesfield**
PEAK DISTRICT

Ryles Arms
Hollin Lane, Higher Sutton, SK11 0NN ☎ 01260 252244 (Ian Brown)
www.rylesarms.com Map 118/939695
£45 D3 T1 F1 ✕ £11, 5:30pm
Ⓥ Ⓓ Ⓑ ⊛ 🐾🛁♿Ⓕ ★★★★Ⓦ

A true taste of Cheshire. This highly celebrated, long established 4-star traditional country inn is set on the Gritstone Trail and very popular with walkers.

Offering homemade food from traditional to the most contemporary alongside fine wine and real ale.
Boasts spectacular views of rolling Cheshire countryside only three miles from Macclesfield town centre and train station.

Luxury en-suite B&B accommodation in a historic barn conversion. Ample car parking available.

● **Rainow**
PEAK DISTRICT
STAFFORDSHIRE WAY

Common Barn Farm B&B
Smith Lane, SK10 5XJ ☎ 01625 574878
(Rona Cooper) www.cottages-with-a-view.co.uk
Map 118/968764
✕ Ⓓ Ⓑ ⊛ 🐾🚗!

A luxury barn conversion with en-suite facilities in all rooms, including power showers and under-floor heating. Fully accessible room with en-suite wetroom and wheelchair-friendly bathroom. Situated in the Peak District with unrivalled views across the Cheshire plain to the Welsh mountains.

● **Wilmslow**
The Croft, Gravel Lane, SK9 6LZ ☎ 01625 523435 / 07866 242010
(Sandra & Rick Megginson) sandramegginson@yahoo.co.uk Map 118/832798
£35-£50 D1 ✕ nearby 🚍(Wilmslow or Alderley Edge)
Ⓓ Ⓑ 🐾🚗!

● **Wincle**
PEAK DISTRICT

Hill Top Farm, SK11 0QH ☎ 01260 227257 (Susan Brocklehurst)
www.hill-top-farm.co.uk Map 118/965661
£28-£35 D1 T2 ✕ £15, 7pm Ⓥ Ⓓ Ⓑ ⊛ 🐾🛁! ★★★★

● **Wybunbury**

Lea Farm
Wrinehill Road, CW5 7NS ☎ 01270 841429 (Jean E Callwood)
www.leafarm.co.uk Map 118/716489
£29-£34 D1 T1 F1 ✕ nearby
Ⓓ Ⓑ ⊛ 🐾🛁🚗!🛁 ★★★

Charming farmhouse set in landscaped gardens with roaming peacocks. 150 acres of peaceful family farm. Delightful bedrooms. All amenities, some en-suite rooms. Snooker/pool table. Fishing available. Cheques and cash only please.
Email: leafarm@hotmail.co.uk

CUMBRIA

● **Alston**
PENNINE WAY

Lowbyer Manor Country House, Hexham Road, CA9 3JX ☎ 01434 381230
(Richard and Laura Elston) www.lowbyer.com Map 86/717469
£33 S1 D5 T2 F1 ✕ nearby
Ⓓ Ⓑ ⊛ 🐾🛁🛁 ★★★★

● **Ambleside**
LAKE DISTRICT
COAST TO COAST WALK & CUMBRIA WAY

Smallwood House Hotel
Compston Road, LA22 9DJ ☎ 015394 32330 (Anthony or Christine Harrison)
www.smallwoodhotel.co.uk Map 90/375044
£20-£50 S2 D4 T3 F3 ✕ £20, 6:30pm 🚍(Windermere)
Ⓥ Ⓓ Ⓑ ⊛ 🐾🛁🛁 ★★★★

Our central position is perfect for the many different walks which radiate from Ambleside.

Warm and comfortable rooms with underfloor heating in the en-suites, and all other amenities.

A full cooked breakfast with a variety of fruit and cereals.

After a long days walking return to the warmth and comfort of the Smallwood, maybe go and use the facilities of the Low Wood to unwind.

Packed lunches available, dogs welcome.

Croyden House, Church Street, LA22 0BU ☎ 015394 32209
(Sylvia & John Drinkall) www.croydenhouseambleside.co.uk Map 90/376043
£25-£40 S4 D6 T4 F2 ✕ nearby
Ⓓ Ⓑ ⊛ 🐾🛁

Lyndale Guest House, Lake Road, LA22 0DN ☎ 015394 34244
(Alison Harwood) www.lyndale-guesthouse.co.uk Map 90/377036
✕ ▣ Ⓑ ⊛ 🐾 🦮

Brantfell House, Rothay Road, LA22 0EE ☎ 015394 32239 (Chris & Jane Amos)
www.brantfell.co.uk Map 90/374041
£30-£50 D6 T2 ✕ nearby
▣ Ⓑ ⊛ 🖐 🦮 ★★★★

Nab Cottage
Rydal, LA22 9SD ☎ 015394 35311 (Liz & Tim Melling)
www.rydalwater.com Map 90/355064
£27-£30 S1 D3 T2 F1 ✕ £18, 7pm
▣ ▣ Ⓑ ⊛ 🐾🦮 🖐 🦮 ! 🦮 ★★★

A Grade II-listed 16th-century cottage overlooking Rydal Water. Once home of Thomas de Quincey and Hartley Coleridge. Superb walks in every direction. Delicious homecooked food. Informal atmosphere.
Email: tim@nabcottage.com

The Old Vicarage
Vicarage Road, LA22 9DH ☎ 015394 33364
www.oldvicarageambleside.co.uk Map 90/373044
£42.50-£120 D7 T4 F4 ✕ nearby
▣ Ⓑ ⊛ 🖐 🦮 ★★★★Ⓜ

High quality en-suite accommodation. Own indoor heated swimming pool, sauna and hot tub. Quiet location in central Ambleside, with parking. Ideal for getting out onto the fells. Dogs are very welcome.

● Appleby-in-Westmorland

Bongate House
CA16 6UE ☎ 017683 51245 (Mary & John Geary)
www.bongatehouse.co.uk Map 91/689200
£25-£35 S1 D3 T3 F2 ✕ nearby 🚶(Appleby)
▣ Ⓑ ⊛ 🐾🖐 🦮 ! 🦮 👟 Ⓕ ★★★

Quality accommodation in a fine Georgian House (built in 1760), with a warm and friendly welcome. Extensive gardens with ancient box hedges and fine views over the River Eden and Appleby Castle.
Farmhouse-style breakfasts using locally purchased produce.

● Arnside
Willowfield Hotel, The Promenade, LA5 0AD ☎ 01524 761354
(Janet & Ian Kerr) www.willowfield.uk.com Map 97/456788
✕ £16 🚶(Arnside)
▣ ▣ Ⓑ ⊛ 🐾🦮 🦮 ! ★★★★

Ye Olde Fighting Cocks, The Promenade, LA5 0HD ☎ 01524 761203
(Lesley Coop) www.fighting-cocks.co.uk Map 97/457789
£35 S2 D7 T1 F1 ✕ £6, 6pm 🚶(Arnside)
▣ ▣ Ⓑ 🐾🦮 🦮 🦮 !

● Bampton

Mardale Inn
Bampton, CA10 2RQ ☎ 01931 713244 (Sebastian Hindley)
www.mardaleinn.co.uk Map 90/514181
£30-£35 S2 D4 T4 F2 ✕ £8.95, 6pm
▣ ▣ Ⓑ ⊛ 🐾🦮 🦮 🦮 ! 🦮

Situated in the beautiful Lowther Valley, one mile from Haweswater, this recently refurbished inn affords great comfort and fantastic access to the Eastern Fells. Roaring log fire, quality real ale and fresh seasonal food ensures a great place to stay.

● Boot
Wha House, CA19 1TH ☎ 019467 23322 (Marie Crowe)
whahousefarm@aol.com Map 89/190009
£25 D2 T1 F1 ✕ nearby 🚶(Ravenglass & Eskdale) ▣ ⊛ 🐾🦮 🦮

● Borrowdale

Royal Oak Hotel
Borrowdale, CA12 5XB ☎ 017687 77214 (Neil Dowie)
www.royaloakhotel.co.uk Map 89/259148
£26-£41 S2 D5 T2 F5 ✕ £15, 7pm
▣ ▣ Ⓑ ⊛ 🐾🦮 🦮 ! 🦮 ★

A traditional Lakeland Hotel set in the heart of beautiful Borrowdale. Thick walls, snug bar, open fire and friendly service create a cosy and relaxed atmosphere.
All rooms are warm, comfortable and spacious; four have riverside views.

● Broughton-in-Furness
Middlesyke, Church Street, LA20 6ER ☎ 01229 716549 (David & Sarah Hartley)
www.middlesyke.co.uk Map 96/208876
£35 D2 ✕ nearby 🚶(Foxfield) ▣ Ⓑ ⊛ 🐾🦮 🦮 ! 🦮 Ⓜ

● Caldbeck

The Briars
Friar Row, CA7 8DS ☎ 016974 78633 (Dorothy H Coulthard)
Map 90/325399
£28-£30 S1 D1 T1
✕ ▣ Ⓑ ⊛ 🦮 !

Situated in Caldbeck village, overlooking Caldbeck Fells. Ideal for touring Lake District, Scottish Borders and Roman Wall. We are right on the Cumbria Way. Near Reivers cycle route. Tea-making facilities. Rooms ensuite with TV. Two minutes' walk to village inn.

NORTH WEST

Brownrigg Farm, Caldbeck, CA7 8EG ☎ 016974 78626 (Sally Vaux)
www.caldbeckvillage.co.uk Map 85/306403
£25 DI ▢ 🔧🛏☕🚗 Ⓜ

● Carlisle
HADRIAN'S WALL, CUMBRIA WAY, & PENNINE WAY

Angus Hotel & Almonds Bistro, 14 Scotland Road, Stanwix, CA3 9DG
☎ 01228 523546 www.angus-hotel.co.uk Map 85/400571
£40-£50 S3 D3 T4 F4 ✕ £15, 6pm ∿(Carlisle)
Ⓥ D B 🔧🛏☕!🍴 ★★★★

Knockupworth Hall, Burgh Road, CA2 7RF ☎ 01228 523531 (Patricia Dixon)
www.knockupworthdi.co.uk Map 85/370566
£36 D2 T2 FI ✕ £10, 7pm ∿(Carlisle)
Ⓥ D B ⊗ 🔧🛏☕🚗!

Abberley House, 33 Victoria Place, CAI IHP ☎ 01228 521645
www.abberleyhouse.co.uk Map 85/406561
✕, 5pm ∿(Carlisle) D B ⊗ !

Cambro House, 173 Warwick Road, CAI ILP ☎ 01228 543094 (David & Alice)
davidcambro@aol.com Map 85/412559
£25-£27.50 D2 TI ✕ nearby ∿(Carlisle)
D B ⊗ 🔧🛏☕! ★★★★

Howard Lodge Guest House, 90 Warwick Road, CAI IJU ☎ 01228 529842
(Charlotte Davies) www.howard-lodge.co.uk Map 85/407558
£30 S2 D2 T2 F2 ✕ nearby ∿(Carlisle)
D B 🔧🛏☕🍱 ★★★★

Cornerways Guest House, 107 Warwick Road, CAI IEA ☎ 01228 521733
(Steve & Be Coggan) www.cornerwaysbandb.co.uk Map 85/406559
£27.50-£32.50 S4 D2 T2 F2 ✕ nearby ∿(Carlisle)
D B ⊗ 🔧🛏☕!Ⓕ ★★★★Ⓦ

Queen's Arms Inn
Warwick-on-Eden, CA4 8PA ☎ 01228 560699 (Nadia)
www.queensatwarwick.com Map 86/464564
£30-£40 D3 T2 F2 ∿(Carlisle)
B ⊗ 🔧🛏🚗!🍱

Friendly guest house situated in Warwick-on-Eden just off A69, offering en-suite accommodation with Full English Breakfast. Conveniently located for walks with packed lunches, evening meals, garden/play area and large car park available. A warm welcome, excellent service and delicious food awaits.

● Cleator
COAST TO COAST WALK

Parkside Hotel
Parkside Road, CA25 5HF ☎ 01946 811001 (John Bruckshaw)
www.parksidehotelcumbria.co.uk Map 89/033154
£25-£35 S6 D3 T5 F3 ✕ £10, 7pm
Ⓥ D B ⊗ 🔧🛏🚗!

A perfect stop over for Coast to Coast walkers. Free pickup and drop off to the trail.
A friendly, affordable hotel, ideally situated on the edge of the Lake District National Park, near Cleator. Real ales and bar meals.

● Coniston
LAKE DISTRICT
CUMBRIA WAY

Beech Tree House
Yewdale Road, LA21 8DX ☎ 015394 41717
Map 96/302976
£32 D6 T2 ✕ nearby
D B ⊗ 🔧🛏☕🚗 ★★★★

Charming 18th-century house with attractive gardens situated 150m from the village centre and all amenities. Ideally situated for a walking holiday or overnight stay on the Cumbria Way. Good drying facilities, ample parking. En-suites available.

Lakeland House Guest House, Tilberthwaite Ave, LA21 8ED ☎ 015394 41303
(Sue Holland) www.lakelandhouse.com Map 96/304976
£30-£35 SI D4 TI F4 ✕ nearby
D B ⊗ 🔧🛏☕🚗!🍱 ★★★

Thwaite Cottage
Waterhead, LA21 8AJ ☎ 015394 41367 (Marguerite & Graham Aldridge)
www.thwaitcot.freeserve.co.uk Map 96/311977
£26-£32 D2 TI ✕ nearby
D B ⊗ ☕ ★★★★

Beautiful 17th-century cottage in peaceful wooded garden. Close to Coniston village and at the head of the lake. Central heating, log fires, old beams, panelling, slate floors. Rooms with private bathrooms or en-suite. Off-road parking. Non smoking.

Waverley, Lake Road, LA21 8EW ☎ 015394 41127 (Jenny Graham)
Map 96/302974
£25 SI DI TI FI ✕ nearby D B ⊗ 🔧🛏☕🍱

Orchard Cottage, 18 Yewdale Road, LA21 8DU ☎ 015394 41319
(Jean Johnson) www.conistonholidays.co.uk Map 96/302976
£27.50-£40 D2 TI ✕ nearby
D B ⊗ 🔧🛏☕🚗!★★★★Ⓦ Ⓜ

Wheelgate Country Guest House
Little Arrow, LA21 8AU ☎ 015394 41418 (Steve & Linda Abbott)
www.wheelgate.co.uk Map 96/290950
£39-£42 S2 D3 TI ✕ nearby
D B ⊗ ☕🚗 ★★★★★

17th-century farmhouse with beamed ceilings, spacious en-suite bedrooms and cosy bar. Excellent breakfasts cater for all tastes. Ideally situated for access to central lakes, with superb local walks to suit all ages and abilities.

Coniston Lodge, Station Road, LA21 8HH ☎ 015394 41201 (Mr & Mrs Robinson)
www.coniston-lodge.com Map 96/301975
£51.50 D2 T3 ✕ nearby
D B ⊗ 🔧🛏☕🚗! ★★★★★Ⓖ

● Dent
YORKSHIRE DALES
DALES WAY

Garda View Guest House, Main Street, LA10 5QL ☎ 015396 25209 (Rita Smith) rita@gardaview.co.uk Map 98/705870
£25 S1 D2 T1 ✗ nearby ☐D ☐B ⊛ 🐾♿ 🛁

● Eamont Bridge
CUMBRIA WAY

River View, 6 Lowther Glen, CA10 2BP ☎ 01768 864405 (Mrs C O'Neil) river-view.co.uk Map 90/524285
£30-£35 S3 D1 T1 ✗ nearby ⋘(Penrith) ☐D ☐B 🐾♿ 🛁

● Eskdale Green
LAKE DISTRICT

Forest How Guest House
CA19 1TR ☎ 019467 23201 (John & Diane Bromage)
www.foresthow.co.uk Map 96/136999
£28-£42 D5 T3 ✗ nearby ⋘(Ravenglass & Eskdale)
☐D ☐B ⊛ 🐾♿ 🛁

Secluded, warm, comfortable guest house.
Excellent home cooking.
Delightful gardens with spectacular views.
TVs, H&C, beverage trays.
Some en-suite. Parking.
Friendly and informal atmosphere.
Brochure available.

● Gilsland
HADRIAN'S WALL & PENNINE WAY

Tantallon House Bed and Breakfast, Tantallon House, Gilsland, CA8 7DA
☎ 01697 747 111 (Lorna and Roger Ashman)
www.hadrians-wall-bed-and-breakfast.co.uk Map 86/628666
£30 T2 ✗ nearby ☐D ☐B ⊛ 🐾♿ 🚗

Willowford Farm B&B
Willowford, Gilsland, CA8 7AA ☎ 016977 47962 (Lauren Harrison)
www.willowford.co.uk Map 86/624665
£35-£40 S2 D2 T4 F2 ✗ £15, 7:30pm
Ⓥ ☐B ⊛ 🐾♿ 🚗 ! 🛁♿ Ⓕ ★★★Ⓦ

We are a working farm offering comfortable accommodation and homecooked food.

Our land contains a large section of Hadrian's Wall and we are less than one mile from Birdoswald Fort and a day's walk from the other major Roman sites.

● Grasmere
LAKE DISTRICT
COAST TO COAST WALK & CUMBRIA WAY

Oak Lodge, Easedale Road, LA22 9QJ ☎ 015394 35527 (Alison Dixon)
www.oaklodge-grasmere.co.uk Map 90/331081
£30-£33 D2 T1 ✗ nearby ☐D ☐B ⊛ 🐾♿ 🛁

● Grayrigg
DALES WAY

Moresdale Barn Bed & Breakfast, Moresdale Barn, Lambrigg, LA8 0DH
☎ 01539 824463 (Joanna Parkins) j_parkins@hotmail.com Map 97/587958
£30-£35 D1 T1 ☐D ⊛ 🐾♿ 🚗 ♿

● Hesket Newmarket
LAKE DISTRICT
CUMBRIA WAY

Newlands Grange, CA7 8HP ☎ 016974 78676 (Mrs Dorothy Studholme)
studholme_newlands@hotmail.com Map 90/350394
£25-£27 S1 D1 T1 F2 ✗ £12, 6:30pm Ⓥ ☐D ☐B ⊛ 🐾♿ 🚗 ! 🛁

● Kendal
LAKE DISTRICT
DALES WAY

Hillside Bed & Breakfast, 4 Beast Banks, LA9 4JW ☎ 01539 722836
(Joanne Buchanan) www.hillside-kendal.co.uk Map 97/513925
£26-£31 S3 D2 T1 ✗ nearby ⋘(Oxenholme)
☐D ☐B ⊛ 🐾♿ 🚗 ★★★★

Sundial Guest House, Sundial House, 51 Milnthorpe Road, LA9 5QG
☎ 01539 724468 (Sue & Andrew McLeod) www.sundialguesthousekendal.co.uk
Map 97/516916
£24-£40 S2 D3 T3 F2 ✗ nearby ⋘(Oxenholme)
☐D ☐B ⊛ 🐾♿ 🚗 ! ★★★Ⓦ

The Glen (The Guest House under the 'Helm')
Oxenholme, LA9 7RF ☎ 01539 726386 (Chris Green)
www.glen-kendal.co.uk Map 97/534900
£35-£45 S1 D3 T2 F2 ✗ nearby ⋘(Oxenholme)
☐D ☐B ⊛ 🐾♿ 🚗 ! 🛁 ★★★★Ⓦ

Situated in a quiet location under 'Helm' (local walk and view point of Lakeland Mountains), but within a short walk of country inn and restaurant. Ideal for touring the Lakes & Yorkshire Dales. Relax in hot tub after your day walking.

Bridge House, 65 Castle Street, LA9 7AD ☎ 01539 722041 / 07813 679411
(Sheila Brindley) www.bridgehouse-kendal.co.uk Map 97/521930
£30-£35 D1 T1 ✗ nearby ⋘(Kendal) ☐D ☐B ⊛ 🐾♿ 🚗

● Kentmere
LAKE DISTRICT

Maggs Howe, LA8 9JP ☎ 01539 821689 (Christine Hevey)
www.smoothhound.co.uk/hotels/maggs Map 90/462041
£25-£30 S1 D1 T1 F1 ✗ £13.50, 7pm Ⓥ ☐D ☐B ⊛ 🐾♿ 🚗 ! 🛁

● Keswick
LAKE DISTRICT
CUMBRIA WAY

Hedgehog Hill, 18 Blencathra Street, CA12 4HP ☎ 017687 80654
(Shona & Keith Wiggle) www.hedgehoghill.co.uk Map 89/269233
£25-£29 S2 D3 T1 ✗ nearby ☐D ☐B ⊛ 🐾♿ ★★★★

Glencoe Guest House
21 Helvellyn, CA12 4EN ☎ 017687 71016 (Teresa Segasby)
www.glencoeguesthouse.co.uk Map 89/269233
£28-£30 S1 D5 T2 F1 ✗ nearby
☐D ☐B ⊛ 🐾♿ ★★★★

A warm friendly welcome awaits you at our Victorian home. Conveniently situated offering views of the local fells yet only a short stroll into Keswick and all its amenities. Free flask filling, maps, an excellent hearty breakfast and great hospitality.

NORTH WEST

Cumbria House

1 Derwentwater Place, Ambleside Road, CA12 4DR
☎ 017687 73171 (Mavis and Patrick Long)
www.cumbriahouse.co.uk Map 89/268232
£26-£35 S3 D5 T4 F1 ✕ nearby D B ⊗ ⛅ ⬆ ! 🌲 ★★★★

Mavis and Patrick welcome you to Cumbria House.

Situated within two minutes of the centre of Keswick in a quiet, scenic location opposite St Johns church.

Breakfasts cooked to order using quality local produce and Fairtrade beverages, homemade bread with luxury preserves, flasks filled for free.

Private car park, extensive library of walking and guide books in guests lounge, with log fire in winter months. Local weather forecast twice daily.

Badgers Wood

30 Stanger Street, CA12 5JU ☎ 017687 72621 (Anne Paylor)
www.badgers-wood.co.uk Map 89/265235
£30 S2 D4 T1 ✕ nearby
D B ⊗ ⛅ ⬆ ⛟ ! ★★★★

Quality accommodation and friendly welcome await at this traditional lakeland guest house situated in a quiet cul-de-sac just a two minute walk from the market square and bus station.

Our six en-suite bedrooms are furnished to a high standard and cleanliness of our new en-suite facilities is our trademark.

We gladly cater for special diets and are happy to share our 25 years' fell-walking experience with our guests.

Hazeldene

The Heads, CA12 5ER ☎ 01768 772106 (Helen Winter)
www.hazeldene-hotel.co.uk Map 89/264232
£32.50-£42.50 D5 T3 F2 ✕ nearby
D B ⊗ ⬆ ★★★★

A welcoming bed and breakfast establishment in a magnificent location.
Well appointed en-suite bedrooms, beautiful views and an excellent breakfast make Hazeldene the perfect haven for your visit to the Lake District. Games room.
Private parking for eight cars.

Need help with grid references? See pp68–71

Hawcliffe House

30 Eskin Street, CA12 4DG ☎ 017687 73250 (Diane & Ian McConnell)
www.hawcliffehouse.co.uk Map 89/270232
£25-£27 D4 T1 F1 ✕ nearby
B ⊗ ⛅ ⬆ ★★★★

- Family-run guest house.
- Warm welcome assured.
- Non-smoking.
- Packed lunches available on request.
- Short walk from town centre.
- Call Diane for more information.

Rivendell Guest House

23 Helvellyn Street, CA12 4EN ☎ 01768 773822
(Pat & Linda Dent & June Muse) www.rivendellguesthouse.com
Map 89/269233
£25-£27 S2 D6 T4 F2 ✕ nearby D B ⊗ ⛅ ⬆ ! 🌲 ★★★★ Ⓜ

A warm friendly welcome awaits you at our lovely Victorian home run by Ramblers' members.

Set in quiet location close to town centre and Fitz Park with lots of parking. Most rooms en-suite.

Pets and groups up to 15 welcome.

Cragside Guest House, 39 Blencathra St, CA12 4HX ☎ 01768 773344
(Wayne & Alison Binks) www.smoothhound.co.uk/hotels/cragside
Map 89/271234
£22.50-£25 D2 T1 F1 D B ⊗ ⬆ 🌲 ★★★★

Lincoln Guest House, 23 Stanger Street, CA12 5JX ☎ 017687 72597 (Joan Clark)
www.lincolnguesthouse.com Map 89/265236
£26-£38 S2 D3 T1 F1 ✕ nearby D B ⊗ ⛅ ⬆

Ouse Bridge House

Bassenthwaite Lake, CA13 9YD ☎ 017687 76322
(Katie Barrie) www.ousebridge.com Map 89/197312
£32-£35 S2 D6 T3 F2 ✕ £18.50, 7:30pm
D B ⊗ ⛅ ⬆ ★★★★ Ⓜ

Friendly guest house with amazing views over Bassenthwaite Lake and Skiddaw. Conveniently located for walks with packed lunches, evening meals, drying facilities and large car park available. A warm welcome, excellent service and delicious food in a stunning location.

Tarn Hows

3-5 Eskin Street, CA12 4DH ☎ 017687 73217 (Mr & Mrs T Bulch)
www.tarnhows.co.uk Map 89/270231
£30-£36 S2 D6 ✕ nearby
D B ⊗ ⛅ ⬆ ★★★★ Ⓢ

A beautifully appointed and decorated traditional Victorian residence. Within easy walking distance of town, parks, lakes and fells. Private off-street parking, residents lounge and drying facilities available.
Excellent, freshly prepared traditional English, vegetarian or continental breakfast.

Ferndene Guest Hoouse, 6 St John's Terrace, Ambleside Road, CA12 4DP
☎ 017687 74612 (Mr & Mrs Marsden)
www.ferndene-keswick.co.uk Map 89/268231
£30-£35 D5 T3 FI ✕ nearby Ⓓ Ⓑ ⊛ 🐾 👜 🛁

Derwent Bank

HF Holidays, Derwent Bank, Derwentwater, Portinscale, CA12 5TY
☎ 0845 470 7558 (Jean Crouch) Map 89/254228
www.hfholidays.co.uk/countryhousehotels/northernlakedistrict
£59-£69 S13 D6 T18 F5 ✕ £17, 7pm ₩(Penrith) Ⓥ Ⓓ Ⓑ 🐾 👜

This fine country house, situated on the banks of Derwent Water, promises a true taste of the Lake District.
A pleasant conservatory, landscaped grounds and a wealth of walks all close to hand. Single, twin and family en-suite rooms available.

● Kirkby Stephen

COAST TO COAST WALK

Redmayne House

Silver Street, CA17 4RB ☎ 017683 71441 (Mrs C J Prime)
Map 91/774088
£25 S1 D1 T1 FI ✕ nearby ₩(Kirkby Stephen)
Ⓓ ⊛ 🐾 👜 🛁

A spacious and attractive Georgian home set in a large garden. Glorious walking country.

Homemade bread and preserves, walkers' breakfasts, private sitting room, parking.
£25 - one price for all.

● Long Marton
PENNINE WAY & TEESDALE WAY

Broom House, CA16 6JP ☎ 017683 61318 (Sandra Bland)
broomhouseappleby.co.uk Map 91/666238
£27-£35 S1 D1 T1 FI ✕ nearby Ⓓ Ⓑ ⊛ 🐾 👜 🚗 ★★★★

● Patterdale
LAKE DISTRICT
COAST TO COAST WALK

Wordsworth Cottage, CA11 0NP ☎ 017684 82084 (Joan B Martin)
www.wordsworthcottage-ullswater.co.uk Map 90/400160
£30 D2 TI ✕ nearby Ⓓ Ⓑ ⊛ 🐾 👜 🚗 !

Old Water View

Patterdale, CA11 0NW ☎ 017684 82175 (Ian Moseley)
www.oldwaterview.co.uk Map 90/398157
£27.50-£39.50 D5 TI FI
✕ nearby Ⓓ Ⓑ 🐾 👜

Old Water View is a comfortable and charming Edwardian B&B, overlooking Goldrill Beck and surrounded by truly stunning mountain scenery in the village of Patterdale. An ideal base for the Eastern Fells, C2C Walk, Westmorland Way, Helvellyn & Striding Edge.

● Penrith

Motherby House

Motherby, CA11 0RJ ☎ 01768483368 (Jacquie Freeborn)
www.motherbyhouse.co.uk Map 90/429284
£24.50 F2 ✕ £17, 7pm
Ⓥ Ⓓ ⊛ 🐾 👜 🚗

- Warm friendly former 18th century farmhouse.
- Log fire in lounge.
- Excellent food for outdoor appetites.
- Drying room, muddy boots welcome.
- Secure bike storage.
- Ideal for exploring Blencathra, Helvellyn and the northern fells.

● Ravenglass
LAKE DISTRICT

Rose Garth, Main St , CA18 1SQ ☎ 01229717275 (Alex & Jean Blore)
rose-garth.co.uk Map 96/084964
£33-£36 S1 D4 TI FI ✕ nearby ₩(Ravenglass)
Ⓓ Ⓑ ⊛ 🐾 👜 ! 🛁 ★★★★

● Sedbergh
YORKSHIRE DALES
DALES WAY

Holmecroft, Station Road, LA10 5DW ☎ 015396 20754 (Mrs S Sharrocks)
www.holmecroftbandb.co.uk Map 97/650919
✕ 5pm Ⓓ ⊛ 🐾 🚗 !

Wheelwright Cottage, 15 Back Lane, LA10 5AQ ☎ 015396 20251
(Miss M Thurlby) antique.thurlby@amserve.net Map 97/659921
£24-£28 D1 TI ✕ nearby
Ⓓ ⊛ 🐾 👜 🚗 ! 🛁

Yew Tree Cottage, 35 Loftus Hill, LA10 5SQ ☎ 015396 21600 (Anne Jones)
www.sedbergh.org.uk Map 97/658917
£20-£25 D1 TI ✕ nearby Ⓓ ⊛ 🐾 👜 ! 🛁 ★★★

Brantrigg, Winfield Rd, LA10 5AZ ☎ 015396 21455 (Linda Hopkins)
www.brantrigg.co.uk Map 97/658923
✕ nearby Ⓓ Ⓑ ⊛ 🐾 🚗 Ⓜ

Thorns Hall

HF Holidays, Thorns Hall, Cautley Road, LA10 5LE ☎ 020 8905 9558
(Jean Crouch) Map 98/663921
www.hfholidays.co.uk/countryhousehotels/northernyorkshiredales
£59-£69 S10 D4 T10 F2 ✕ £17, 7pm ₩(Oxenholme) Ⓥ Ⓓ Ⓑ 🐾 👜

With its unique ambience and peaceful location Thorns Hall promises a relaxing retreat. A short walk from Sedbergh, at the foot of the Howgill Fells, it offers pleasant views and great walks. Single, twin and family en-suite rooms available.

● St Bees
COAST TO COAST WALK

Stonehouse Farm, Main Street, CA27 0DE ☎ 01946 822224 (Carole Smith)
www.stonehousefarm.net Map 89/971119
✕ ₩(St Bees) Ⓓ Ⓑ 🐾 👜 ! 🛁

1 Tomlin House, Beach Road, CA27 0EN ☎ 01946 822284
(Mr & Mrs Whitehead) id.whitehead@which.net Map 89/963118
✕ ₩(St Bees) Ⓓ Ⓑ ⊛ 🐾 🚗 🛁

● Threlkeld
LAKE DISTRICT
CUMBRIA WAY

Scales Farm Country Guest House, CA12 4SY ☎ 01768 779660
(Alan & Angela Jameison) www.scalesfarm.com Map 90/341268
£37 D3 T2 F1 ✕ nearby 🄓 🄑 ⊗ 🐾 ♨ 🚗 ⛰ ♿ 🄵 ★★★★Ⓢ

● Ulverston
CUMBRIA WAY

The Walkers Hostel, Oubas Hill, LA12 7LB ☎ 01229 585588 (Jan Nicholson)
www.walkershostel.co.uk Map 96/296787
✕ £10 ⅏(Ulverston) Ⓥ 🄓 ⊗ 🐾! ♨ Ⓜ

St Mary's Mount, Belmont, LA12 7HD ☎ 01229 583372 (Marlon Bobbett)
www.stmarysmount.co.uk Map 96/290788
✕ £17.50 ⅏(Ulverston) Ⓥ 🄓 🄑 ⊗ 🐾 🚗!

● Watermillock
LAKE DISTRICT

Land Ends Country Lodge
CA11 0NB ☎ 017684 86438 (Barbara Murphy)
www.landends.co.uk Map 90/433245
£40 S2 D5 T1 F1
🄓 🄑 ⊗ 🐾 ♨ ♿ ★★★

Enjoy peace and quiet in our converted farmhouse and barn close to Lake Ullswater set in attractive eight acre grounds with two lakes, pretty courtyard and fishpond. Rooms are modern in flavour, light and comfortable and breakfasts are substantial.

● Windermere
LAKE DISTRICT
DALES WAY

Holly Lodge, 6 College Road, LA23 1BX ☎ 015394 43873 (Anne & Barry Mott)
hollylodge20.co.uk Map 96/411985
£27-£35 S1 D4 F4 ✕ nearby ⅏(Windermere)
🄓 🄑 ⊗ 🐾 ♨ ★★★★

Lynwood, Broad Street, LA23 2AB ☎ 015394 42550 (Mrs F Holcroft)
www.lynwood-guest-house.co.uk Map 96/413982
£23-£30 S1 D2 T2 F3 ✕ nearby ⅏(Windermere)
🄓 🄑 ⊗ 🐾 ★★★★

LANCASHIRE

● Blackpool
Midland Hotel, 16 Rigby Road, FY1 5DE ☎ 01253 622735 (John Bogard)
www.midland-hotel.co.uk Map 102/306350
£25-£30 F7 ✕ nearby ⅏(Blackpool North)
🄓 🄑 ⊗ 🐾 ♨

FROM YOUR DOORSTEP!
Check out our new City Walks section and see a side of your town that you never knew existed, pp47–65.

● Chipping

Rakefoot Farm
Thornley Road, Chaigley, BB7 3LY ☎ 01995 61332 (Pat Gifford)
www.rakefootfarm.co.uk Map 103/663416
£25-£37.50 S2 D2 T2 F2
✕ £18, 7pm Ⓥ 🄓 🄑 ⊗ 🐾 ♨ 🚗! ♨ ★★★★

17th-century farmhouse and traditional stone barn on family farm. Original features, woodburners, homecooked meals/convenient restaurants, laundry, en-suite and ground floor available. Longridge Fell, Forest of Bowland, AONB and panoramic views. Transport available. See self-catering also.

● Clitheroe
RIBBLE WAY

Foxhill Barn
Howgill Lane, Gisburn, BB7 4JL ☎ 01200 415906 (Janet & Peter Moorhouse)
www.foxhillbarn.co.uk Map 103/843467
£35-£40 D1 T1 F1
🄓 ⊗ 🐾 ♨ 🚗 ⛰ ★★★★

A newly converted barn with beautiful panoramic views close to the Lancashire/Yorkshire border. Ribble Way and Pendle nearby. Many scenic walks in the surrounding area. After a day's rambling, the perfect place to relax and unwind.

The Red Pump Inn, Clitheroe Road, BB7 3DA ☎ 01254 826227 (Martina Myerscough) www.theredpumpinn.co.uk Map 103/695431
£35-£70 D1 T2 ✕ £10, 6pm ⅏(Clitheroe)
Ⓥ 🄑 ⊗ 🐾 ♨ ♿ ★★★★

● Preston

Parr Hall Farm
Parr Lane, PR7 5SL ☎ 01257 451917 (Mike & Kate Motley)
www.parrhallfarm.com Map 108/519174
£40-£45 S1 D10 T3 F1 ✕ nearby ⅏(Croston)
🄓 🄑 ⊗ 🐾 🚗!♿ 🄵 ★★★★

Quiet village location within easy walking distance of shops, public houses and restaurants. Local attractions: West Pennine Moors, Martin Mere, Rufford Old Hall, Southport and Formby Point. A good stopover for the Lake District and Scotland. M6 Junction 27.

● Silverdale
Spring Bank House, 19 Stankelt Rd, LA5 0TA ☎ 01524 702693 (Nancy Bond)
www.springbankhousesilverdale.co.uk Map 97/463749
£32.50 S1 D2 T2 ✕ nearby ⅏(Silverdale)
🄓 🄑 ⊗ 🐾 ♨ 🚗 Ⓜ

● Wycoller
Parson Lee Farm, BB8 8SU ☎ 01282 864747 (Pat Hodgson)
www.parsonleefarm.co.uk Map 103/937385
£22-£23 D1 T1 F1 ✕ £9, 7pm 🄓 🄑 ⊗ 🐾 ♨ 🚗!♨ ★★★

SELF-CATERING

CUMBRIA

● Ambleside
LAKE DISTRICT
COAST TO COAST WALK & CUMBRIA WAY

Ramsteads ☎ 015394 36583 (Gareth Evans)
www.ramsteads.co.uk Map 90/356034
£195-£425 Sleeps 4-6. 7 chalets. ⊛ Short breaks available

2 Lowfield ☎ 015394 32326 (PF Quarmby)
paulfquarmby@aol.com Map 90/356034
£140-£240 Sleeps 1-4. 1 garden flat. ⊛ 🛏

● Bassenthwaite
LAKE DISTRICT

Skiddaw View Holiday Park
☎ 016973 20919 (Philip Carr)
www.skiddawview.co.uk Map 89/181368
£176-£2038 Sleeps 2-18. 27 lodges, cottages, caravans.
⊛ 🛏 Short breaks available ★★★★

Four-star award-wining holiday park offering timber lodges and holiday static caravans. In the local area we also have cottages, houses and a very large house for groups. Excellent accommodation. Fantastic walking. Online Booking!

● Caldbeck
LAKE DISTRICT

Monkhouse Hill ☎ 016974 76254 (Jennifer or Andy Collard)
www.monkhousehill.co.uk Map 90/313393
£350-£2340 Sleeps 2-12. 9 cottages.
⊛ ♿ F 🛏 Short breaks available ★★★★

Newlands Grange ☎ 016974 78676 (Dorothy Studholme)
studholme_newlands@hotmail.com Map 90/313393
£100-£150 Sleeps 2-6. 1 caravan. ⊛ Short breaks available

● Cockermouth
LAKE DISTRICT

Wood Farm Cottages ☎ 01900 829533 (Mrs A Cooley)
www.woodfarmcottages.com Map 89/120301 ⊛ 🛏 Short breaks available

● Coniston
LAKE DISTRICT

Coniston Country Cottages
☎ 015394 41114 (Steve/Linda/Sharon) www.conistoncottages.co.uk
Map 119/251746
£230-£650 Sleeps 2-6. 14 cottages.
⊛ 🛏 Short breaks available ★★★

Cosy Lakeland cottages in superb surroundings.

Tastefully furnished and well equipped.

Easy access to central Lakes, with local walking to suit all ages and abilities.

● Eskdale
LAKE DISTRICT

Wha House ☎ 019467 23322 (Marie Crowe)
whahousefarm@aol.com143000 £245-£360 Sleeps 1-2. 1 cottage.
⊛ ♿ 🛏 Short breaks available

Irton Hall Country Cottages
☎ 0161 976 5440 (Steve Cottrell)
www.irtonhall.co.uk Map 89/104004
£125-£475 Sleeps 1-5. 2 cottages.
🛏 Short breaks available

These two-bedroomed cottages are built in traditional style and set within the grounds of the magnificent Irton Hall. Each cottage enjoys the benefits of this peaceful parkland setting, itself located in a quiet, yet particularly beautiful area of West Cumbria.

The Chalets
☎ 019467 23128 (Lisa & Philip)
www.thechalets.co.uk Map 89/179007
£250-£500 Sleeps 1-5. 4 timber cottages.
⊛ 🛏 Short breaks available ★★★★

Surrounded by stunning scenery, The Chalets has four immaculately presented cottages. Each cottage has two bedrooms, modern kitchen, pristine bathroom, large living/dining area and mature south facing riverside gardens. BBQ, charming pubs and spectacular walks from the door.

● Hawkshead
LAKE DISTRICT

Esthwaite Farm
☎ 015394 42435 (Ruth or Emma)
www.lakeland-hideaways.co.uk Map 96/351980
£235-£540 Sleeps 2-5. 11 apartments.
⊛ ♿ F 🛏 Short breaks available

Esthwaite Farm is on the edge of the pretty village of Sawrey made famous by Beatrix Potter – warm, comfortable cottage apartments – an excellent base for exploring low and high level walks of the Lake District. Walking groups welcome.

NORTH WEST

● Hayton
COAST TO COAST WALK & HADRIAN'S WALL

The Lodge, Hayton ☎ 016977 3444 (Colin Corlett)
www.the-lodge-holiday-cottages-cumbria.co.uk/ Map 86/512578
£410-£840 Sleeps 2-6. I cottage. & F Short breaks available

● Keswick
LAKE DISTRICT

CUMBRIA WAY

Birkrigg ☎ 017687 78278 (Mrs Beaty) Map 89/266235
£200-£350 Sleeps 1-4. I cottage.
Short breaks available ★★★

Hope Cottages ☎ 01900 85226 (Christine M England)
www.hope-farm-holiday-cottages.co.uk Map 89/266235
£240-£440 Sleeps 3-4. 2 cottages. ★★★

Brigham Farm
☎ 017687 79666 (N Green)
www.keswickholidays.co.uk Map 89/266235
£170-£405 Sleeps 2-4. 6 apartments.
Short breaks available ★★★★

 Quietly situated five minutes' walk from the town centre, former farmhouse converted to six spacious self-contained apartments. Handsomely furnished and well equipped, gas-fired CH, with garden and plenty of parking space. Carefully owner-maintained.

Email: selfcatering@keswickholidays.co.uk

The Studio
☎ 017687 79666 (N Green)
www.keswickholidays.co.uk Map 89/266235
£190-£365 Sleeps 2-4. I apartment.
Short breaks available

 Tasteful barn conversion in the lovely Vale of St Johns.

Well equipped, handsomely furnished with beautiful views. Five miles from Keswick.

Personally maintained.

Croft House Holidays
☎ 017687 73693 (Jan Boniface) www.crofthouselakes.co.uk
Map 89/266235
£280-£995 Sleeps 2-8. 5 cottages.
Short breaks available ★★★★Ⓦ

 Stunning, panoramic views. Peaceful rural settings in Applethwaite village — one mile from Keswick. Cottage and ground floor apartment in Victorian country house and three other cottages — including spacious barn conversion with snooker room. Open all year. Short breaks.

PUZZLED BY THE MAP REFERENCES?
See How to use a map and compass pp68–71

● Patterdale
LAKE DISTRICT

COAST TO COAST WALK

Patterdale Hall Estate
☎ 017684 82308 (Jon Holdsworth) www.patterdalehallestate.com
Map 90/396157
£168-£518 Sleeps 2-6. 17 lodges and cottages.
& F Short breaks available ★★

 Between Helvellyn and the pictuesque shore of Ullswater, the private 300-acre estate offers a range of 17 self-catering properties in an idyllic and relaxing setting with stunning views.

With its own foreshore, woodland and gardens, it is perfect for peaceful leisurely holidays and is an ideal starting point for many great Lakeland walks.

The estate's central location makes it a perfect base from which to explore the entire Lake District.

Wordsworth Barn
☎ 017684 82084 (Joan B Martin)
www.wordsworthbarn-ullswater.co.uk Map 90/400159
£295-£435 Sleeps 1-2. I converted barn.
Short breaks available ★★★★

 Idyllically located in quiet position with superb views but only 450m from the village amenities. This very well equipped 17th-century barn conversion offers a modern contemporary twist. Excellent walking to suit all abilities from the front door.

● Penrith
Howscales ☎ 01768 898666 (Mrs E Webster)
www.howscales.co.uk Map 90/523275
Short breaks available

Dukes Meadow
☎ 0121 705 4381 (Jane Hounsome)
www.dukesmeadow.co.uk Map 90/398350
£180-£450 Sleeps 1-6. I pine lodge.
Short breaks available ★★★

 Three-bedroomed holiday lodge, recently refurbished to a high standard (including D/W). Good base for the north Lakes and Eden Valley, and within easy reach of the excellent facilities in Penrith (15 mins). Mon-Fri and weekend lets available.
Email: janeandben@hotmail.co.uk

● Silverdale
CUMBRIA WAY

Challan Hall Mews ☎ 0114 2338619 (Dot McGahan)
haweswater-view@yahoo.co.uk Map 97/476766
£150-£350 Sleeps 1-5. I mews cottage. ⊗ Short breaks available Ⓜ

● Tebay

Ellerside House
☎ 07977 416576 (Caroline Davis)
www.ellersidehouse.co.uk Map 91/639053
£280-£480 Sleeps 2-6. I cottage/house.
⊗ & ⛱ Short breaks available

A 'home from home' cottage, very well equipped and in a perfect loaction for visiting the Lakes, Eden Valley and the Yorkshire Moors. Private parking and garden. Tastefully decorated. Wood burning stoves, spacious and relaxing. 1.5 miles from juntion 38 of M6. Short breaks available. Family friendly.

● Ulpha
LAKE DISTRICT

Chapel Cottage
☎ 01494 711202 (Vicky Treeby)
www.freewebs.com/chapelcottage-ulpha Map 96/204942
£450-£925 Sleeps 1-6. I cottage.
⊗ ⛱ Short breaks available

In the beautiful and quiet Duddon Valley, with some of the Lake District's finest fell walking right on its doorstep. Three bedrooms, two bathrooms, a fully equipped kitchen, large spacious living area, beautiful gardens with views of Caw and Stickle Fells.

● Watermillock
LAKE DISTRICT

Land Ends
☎ 017684 86438 (Barbara Murphy)
www.landends.co.uk Map 90/436221
£290-£550 Sleeps 1-5. 4 log cabins.
& ⛱ Short breaks available ★★★

Our four cosy log cabins are set in peaceful, pretty eight-acre grounds with two lakes close to Lake Ullswater and its dramatic scenery. Walk your dog from the doorstep and enjoy the birds, red squirrels and ducks from your verandah.

LANCASHIRE

● Chipping
Fell View ☎ 01995 61160 (Mrs J Porter)
www.fellviewchipping.co.uk Map 102/612427
£170-£220 Sleeps 1-2. I coach house.
⊗ ⛱ Short breaks available ★★★★

Rams Clough ☎ 01995 61476 (Oliver Starkey)
www.loudview.co.uk Map 102/637409
£250-£405 Sleeps 4-10. 2 cottages. ⊗ ⛱ ★★★★

Rakefoot Farm
☎ 01995 61332 (Pat Gifford)
www.rakefootfarm.co.uk Map 103/663416
£100-£649 Sleeps 2-22. 4 cottages in barn conversion.
⊗ ⛱ Short breaks available ★★★★

Past winner North West Tourist Board Silver Award. Original features with comforts of modern living. Woodburners, CH, panoramic views, garden, games room, homecooked meals service. Most bedrooms en-suite, some groundfloor, three properties interlinked when required. See B&B also.

● Wiswell
RIBBLE WAY

Manor Cottage Wiswell ☎ 01254 823097 (Nicola Fielden)
nicola@speechtherapy-children.co.uk Map 103/746372
£375-£585 Sleeps 1-8. I cottage. ⊗ Short breaks available ★★★★Ⓜ

GROUPS, HOSTELS, BUNKHOUSES, CAMPSITES & OTHERS

CUMBRIA

● Alston
PENNINE WAY

Nenthead Mines Bunkhouses, Nenthead Mines, Nenthead, CA9 3PD ☎ 01434 382037 (Tim Haldon) www.npht.com/nentheadmines Map 86/783435
SC £12-£12 per night Sleeps 1-18. Two bunkhouses. ⊗

● Ambleside
LAKE DISTRICT
CUMBRIA WAY

Smallwood House Hotel
Compston Road, LA22 9DJ ☎ 015394 32330 (Christine & Anthony Harrison)
www.smallwoodhotel.co.uk Map 90/375043
BB £30-£50 per night Sleeps 10-24. Group accommodation hotel.
Ⓥ Ⓓ ⊗ ⛱ ★★★★

We pride ourselves on a quality, friendly service in the traditional way. Special prices for groups of 11 or more — pay for ten and one stays free Sun-Thurs.

Do you want to organise a group but need help? Contact us for assistance.

All your walking needs catered for. Please telephone Anthony or Christine for a full brochure and tariff. enq@smallwoodhotel.co.uk

NORTH WEST

Ambleside Bacpackers Hostel
Ambleside Backpackers, Iveing Cottage, Old Lake Road, LA22 0DJ
☎ 015394 32340 (David Robbens) www.amblesidebackpackers.com
Map 90/377040
SC, BB £10-£17.50 per night Sleeps 1-65. Hostel. Ⓓ ⊗

Large traditional Lakeland Cottage in the heart of the Lake District.

Building has lots of character including a fine lounge, interesting dining room and large well-fitted kitchen.

Dorm-style bed rooms on the first and second floor with one ground floor dorm. Central heating, free internet access and just four minutes' walk from the centre of Ambleside make this a most convienient and comfortable base for walking in the Lakes.

Don't be put off by the dorms! We get lots of walkers who just love the place.

● Greengill

Big White House
Greengill, CA7 2RA ☎ 016973 20919 (Philip Carr)
www.bigwhitehouse.co.uk Map 89/105372
SC £930-£1848 per week Sleeps 10-18. Large house. ⋘(Aspatria)
Ⓓ ⊗ 🐾 ♨ ㊎ Ⓕ ★★★Ⓦ

Ideal for family parties, get-togethers and corporate meetings. Offering sole use for up to Eighteen in nine bedrooms, large grounds, drying room, secure bike storage. Activities and hot tubs. Catering can be arranged. See our website for full details.

● Windermere
LAKE DISTRICT
DALES WAY & CUMBRIA WAY
The Windermere Centre, Lake Road, LA23 2BY ☎ 015394 44902
(Amanda Moore) windermere.urc.org.uk Map 96/411979
BB, DBB, FB £30-£51.50 per night Sleeps 2-33.
Conference centre with accommodation.
⋘(Windermere) Ⓥ Ⓓ ⊗ 🐾 ㊎ Ⓕ

YORKSHIRE

Long Distance Paths

Cleveland Way CVL

Coast to Coast Walk C2C

Dales Way ....DLS

Nidderdale Way ....NID

Pennine Bridleway ....PNB

Pennine Way ....PNN

Ribble Way ....RIB

Teesdale Way ....TSD

Trans Pennine Trail ....TPT

Yorkshire Wolds Way ....WDS

See Paths & Access p25 for full details of LDPs and waymarks

National Parks

North York Moors
Yorkshire Dales

A LAVENDER-STREWN SECTION
OF THE CLEVELAND WAY

WALK...

...THE MEANWOOD VALLEY TRAIL

A slice of countryside in the heart of Leeds, this 11km/7-mile walk through a fabulous green corridor north-west of the city starts just a mile from the city centre by Hyde Park. Following the steeply forested Woodhouse Ridge along Meanwood Beck, it visits wildlife-rich parks, moors and woodland before arriving at the picturesque lakeview café in Golden Acre Park. Worthwhile detours include Breary Marsh and Meanwood Valley Urban Farm which serves excellent homemade snacks at the farmshop. The Dales Way can be joined by continuing the trail over the Otley Chevin.

A free leaflet is available from Leeds City Council. ☎ 0113 395 7400, email parks@leeds.gov.uk or search www.leeds.gov.uk for a downloadable map under the Meanwood Valley Local Nature Reserve section.

VISIT...   ...SHEFFIELD BOTANICAL GARDENS

Few gardens can claim to rival Kew, but Sheffield's 100-year-old botanical gardens can stake more of a claim than most since the multimillion-pound restoration of its Gardenesque-style grounds and majestic listed buildings to their original glory. It certainly trumps Kew for value, charging no admission for a stroll around 19 acres of colourful plant beds, ponds, woodland and hothouses, for which it was awarded a Green Flag last year.

Only a mile from the city centre, the gardens are well served by local buses. For more information, ☎ 0114 268 6001 or visit www.sbg.org.uk for a downloadable site-map and calendar of live events, including open-air theatre and concerts.

SEE...

...BARN OWLS AT HODGSON'S FIELDS

The struggling barn owl population in the East Yorkshire Wolds has received a big boost after a well-known local wildlife painter decided to stop painting his favourite bird and start saving it. Robert Fuller and his wife set up the Wolds Barn Owl Group last year with the aim of installing 50 nesting boxes each year and works with local landowners to protect the habitats of the owl's natural prey, such as mice and voles. Similar strategies are employed by the Yorkshire Wildlife Trust at Hodgson's Fields nature reserve near Easington, Humberside, and now visitors regularly see the stunning birds hunting over the wind-swept pastures.

For more about the Wolds project ☎ 01759 368355 or visit www.ywt.org.uk for details of local nature reserves.

LOCAL RAMBLERS GROUPS... Sheffield Group helps lead walks for the Sheffield Visually Impaired Walking Group on the second Wednesday and fourth Sunday of every month. For more info, visit www.sviwg.org.uk or ☎ 0114 234 1271... **Dearne Valley and Sheffield Groups both have free downloadable leaflets of some of their favourite walks on their websites or they are available by post for a small fee. See p107 and p108 for more details...** East Yorkshire & Derwent Area lists all open access land in the region with grid references on its website (see p87), covering over 4,000 acres in total.

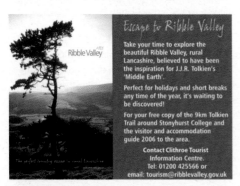

MAP 211

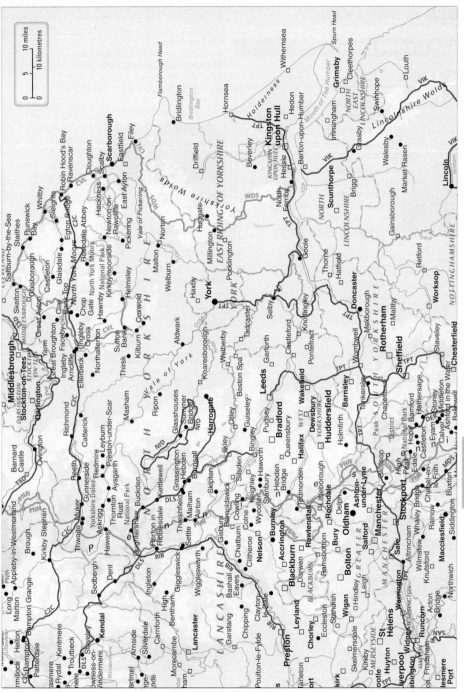

BED & BREAKFAST

EAST YORKSHIRE

● Bridlington

Rosebery House
I Belle View, Tennyson Avenue, YO15 2ET ☎ 01262 670336
(Helen Gallagher) helengallagher99@btinternet.com Map 101/186671
£32.50 D3 TI F3 ✕ nearby ⋙(Bridlington)
Ⓓ Ⓑ ⊗ 🍴👜🚿 ★★★★

Grade II-listed Georgian house.
Long garden and sea views. Amenities close by.
Ideal for walking and touring. Near Flamborough Head
and Bempton Bird Reserve.
High standard of comfort and friendliness.
All en-suite, CH, TV, tea/coffee facilities.
Some parking. Vegetarians/vegans welcome.

● Goole
TRANS PENNINE TRAIL

The Briarcroft Hotel, Clifton Gardens, DN14 6AR ☎ 01405 763024
www.briarcrofthotel.co.uk Map 105/739241
£48 S2 D3 T2 FI ✕ nearby ⋙(Goole Town)
Ⓓ Ⓑ ⊗ 🍴👜🚿 ★★★

● Huggate
YORKSHIRE WOLDS WAY

The Wolds Inn, Driffield Road, YO42 IYH ☎ 01377 288217 (John & Jane Leaver)
huggate@woldsinn.freeserve.co.uk Map 106/882550
£25-£38 S3 D2 TI ✕ £9, 6:30pm Ⓥ Ⓑ ⊗ 🍴👜 ★★★

● Millington
YORKSHIRE WOLDS WAY

Laburnum Cottage, YO42 ITX ☎ 01759 303055 (Maureen Dykes)
rogerandmaureen@labcott.fslife.co.uk Map 106/830517
£35 DI FI ✕ £10, 7pm
Ⓥ Ⓓ Ⓑ ⊗ 🍴👜🚗!🛁 ★★★

● North Ferriby
TRANS PENNINE TRAIL & YORKSHIRE WOLDS WAY

B&B at 103, 103 Ferriby High Road, HU14 3LA ☎ 01482 633637
(Margaret Simpson) www.bnb103.co.uk Map 106/999260
£20-£25 SI D2 TI ✕ nearby ⋙(Ferriby)
Ⓓ Ⓑ ⊗ 🍴👜🚗!🛁 ★★★

NORTH YORKSHIRE

● Askrigg
YORKSHIRE DALES

Milton House, DL8 3HJ ☎ 01969 650217 (Mrs B Percival)
www.miltonhousebandb.co.uk Map 98/948910
£25-£27 DI TI ✕ nearby Ⓓ Ⓑ ⊗ 🍴👜 ★★★★

Thornsgill House, Moor Road, DL8 3HH ☎ 01969 650617 (Wendy Turner)
www.thornsgill.co.uk Map 98/949912
£29-£31 DI TI FI ✕ nearby
Ⓓ Ⓑ ⊗ 🍴👜🚗!★★★★

● Barnard Castle
TEESDALE WAY

The Four Alls
Ovington, DL11 7BP ☎ 01833 627302 (John Stroud)
thefouralls-teesdale.co.uk Map 92/130146
£30 S2 DI T2 ✕ £10, 7pm
Ⓥ Ⓑ ⊗ 🍴👜🚗👜🛁 Ⓕ ★★★

Located in open countryside in Lower
Teesdale, the Four Alls offers
welcoming and comfortable
accommodation for the weary walker.
Recharge your batteries with excellent
home cooking and ales brewed on the
premises. Not to be missed!

● Buckden
YORKSHIRE DALES
DALES WAY

Romany Cottage, BD23 5JA ☎ 01756 760365 (Tim & Gwen Berry)
www.thedalesway.co.uk/romanycottage Map 98/942772
£25 SI DI T2 ✕ nearby Ⓓ ⊗ 🍴👜🚗!🛁

West Winds Yorkshire Tearooms, (nr. Buck Inn), BD23 5JA
☎ 01756 760883 (Lynn Thornborrow)
www.westwindsinyorkshire.co.uk Map 98/942772
£26 SI DI TI ✕ £8, 6pm Ⓥ Ⓓ ⊗ 🍴👜!

● Burnsall
YORKSHIRE DALES
DALES WAY

Wharfe View B&B, Wharfe View Farm, BD23 6BP ☎ 01756 720643
(Richard Hirst) www.burnsall.net Map 98/032614
✕ Ⓓ Ⓑ ⊗ 🍴👜!🛁

● Catterick Village
COAST TO COAST WALK

Rose Cottage Guest House, 26 High Street, DL10 7LJ ☎ 01748 811164
(Carol Archer) Map 99/249979
£28-£34 SI DI T2 ✕ £14, 6:30pm Ⓥ Ⓑ 🍴👜🛁🛁 ★★★Ⓜ

● Cowling
PENNINE WAY

Woodland House, 2 Woodland Street, BD22 0BS ☎ 01535 637886
(Susan Black) www.woodland-house.co.uk Map 103/973432
£25-£27.50 DI TI ✕ nearby Ⓓ Ⓑ ⊗ 🍴👜🚗!★★★★Ⓜ

● Egton Bridge
NORTH YORK MOORS
COAST TO COAST WALK

Broom House Country Guest House and Cottages
Broom House Lane, YO21 IXD ☎ 01947 895279 (David and Maria White)
www.egton-bridge.co.uk Map 94/796054
£35.50-£40 SI D4 TI FI ✕ nearby ⋙(Egton Bridge)
Ⓓ Ⓑ ⊗ 🍴👜🚗 Ⓕ ★★★★Ⓢ Ⓦ

Offering four-star, Silver accommodation in
picturesque village. Charmingly decorated en-
suite rooms. Superb choice of breakfast
featuring variety of fresh local produce.
Breathtaking scenery, great walking routes
from the doorstep. Highly Commended Tourism
Awards Guest Accommodation of the year 2006.

● Giggleswick
YORKSHIRE DALES
RIBBLE WAY

Harts Head Hotel
Belle Hill, BD24 0BA ☎ 01729 822086
www.hartsheadhotel.co.uk Map 98/812640
£40-£45 S2 D5 T2 F1 ✗ £8.95, 7pm ⋙(Settle)
Ⓥ Ⓓ Ⓑ ⊗ ⋙ ⅋ ! ★★★★Ⓦ

18th-century inn renowned for excellent, friendly service, food and real ales. Listed in Camra Good Beer Guide for last six years. All rooms en-suite. Wide choice of food. See website for more info: www.hartsheadhotel.co.uk

● Glaisdale
NORTH YORK MOORS
COAST TO COAST WALK

Red House Farm
YO21 2PZ ☎ 01947 897242 (Tom or Sandra Spashett)
www.redhousefarm.com Map 94/771049
£32.50-£40 S1 D2 T1 F1 ⋙(Glaisdale)
Ⓓ Ⓑ ⊗ ⋙ ⅋

Listed Georgian farmhouse, featured in Houses of the North Yorkshire Moors. Completely refurbished to highest standard retaining all original features. All bedrooms en-suite with CH, TV and tea-making facilities. Wonderful walking country. Coast to Coast Walk 400 yards.

● Grassington
YORKSHIRE DALES
DALES WAY

Lythe End, Wood Lane, BD23 5DF ☎ 01756 753196 (Andrew & Cynthia Colley)
www.grassingtonbandb.com Map 98/000647
£40 D1 F1 ✗ nearby Ⓓ Ⓑ ⊗ ⋙ ⅋ !

Bed & Breakfast, Yew Tree House, Scar Street, BD23 5AS ☎ 01756 753075
(Julie Taylor) www.yewtreehouse.org Map 98/003639
£30-£40 D3 T1 F1 ✗ nearby Ⓓ Ⓑ ⊗ ⋙ ⅋ ★★★★Ⓢ Ⓦ

● Great Ayton
NORTH YORK MOORS

Crossways, 116 Newton Road, TS9 6DL ☎ 01642 724351 (Sue Drennan)
susieds@crossways26.fsnet.co.uk Map 93/563115
✗ ⋙(Great Ayton) Ⓓ Ⓑ ⊗ ⋙ ⅋ !

● Gunnerside
YORKSHIRE DALES
COAST TO COAST WALK

Oxnop Hall, DL11 6JJ ☎ 01748 886253
(Mrs A I Porter) Map 98/931973
£33-£47 S1 D2 T2 Ⓓ Ⓑ ⊗ ⋙ ⅋ ★★★★

● Hackness
NORTH YORK MOORS

Hackness Grange Country House Hotel
Hackness, YO13 0JW ☎ 01723 374 374 (Central Reservations)
www.hacknessgrangehotel.co.uk Map 94/965900
£69-£89 S3 D14 T7 F7 ✗ £25, 6pm ⋙(Scarborough)
Ⓥ Ⓓ Ⓑ ⊗ ⋙ ⅋ ! ★★★

Built in the 18th century, this classic manor house provides the perfect retreat. Surrounded by endless scenery – from the Moors and Dales to the spectacular coastline – you can choose make your break as active, or relaxing, as you like.

● Harrogate
YORKSHIRE DALES

Barker's Guest House, 204 Kings Road, HG1 5JG ☎ 01423 568494
(Mrs E Barker) barkersguesthouse.co.uk
Map 104/304563
£30 S1 D1 T1 ⋙(Harrogate) Ⓓ Ⓑ ⊗ ⋙ ⅋

● Hawes
YORKSHIRE DALES
PENNINE WAY

Dalesview
East Marry, Gayle, DL8 3RZ ☎ 01969 667397 (Mrs S McGregor)
Map 98/871893
£26 D1 T1 ✗ nearby
Ⓓ Ⓑ ⊗ ⋙ ⅋

A modern comfortable bungalow situated in the picturesque village of Gayle, half a mile from the small market town of Hawes. 100m from Pennine Way. Lovely views, quiet location, an ideal centre for touring, cycling and walking in the Yorkshire Dales.

White Hart Inn
Main Street, DL8 3QL ☎ 01969 667259 (Judith Clark)
www.whiteharthawes.co.uk Map 98/875897
£30-£32.50 S1 D4 T2 ✗ £8.50, 5pm
Ⓥ Ⓓ ⊗ ⋙ ⅋ ! ⅋

A friendly family run inn, providing comfortable bedrooms and excellent home cooked food.

The Pennine Way passes within yards of the front door.

Drying facilities and packed lunches available. Dogs welcome.

Thorney Mire House
Appersett, DL8 3LU ☎ 01969 667159 (Mrs S Turner)
www.wensleydale.org/premier/62 Map 98/852899
£25-£32 S1 D2
Ⓓ Ⓑ ⊗ 🍴🛏🚗 ★★★★

Recommended in the Which? Good B&B Guide. A warm welcome awaits you at our traditional Dales House, surrounded by woods, fells and meadows: a place to unwind. Excellent walking, ideal for birdwatchers. Off road parking. Minimum stay two nights.

● Hubberholme
YORKSHIRE DALES
DALES WAY

Low Raisgill, Nr. Hubberholme, BD23 5JQ ☎ 01756 760351 (Mrs Susan Middleton) Map 98/905786
£30 S1 D1 T2 ✕ nearby Ⓓ Ⓑ ⊗ 🍴🛏🚗 ★★★★

● Ingleton
YORKSHIRE DALES

Riverside Lodge
24 Main Street, LA6 3HJ ☎ 015242 41359 (Andrew Foley)
www.riversideingleton.co.uk Map 98/691727
£36-£40 D2 T5 ✕ £15, 7pm
Ⓥ Ⓓ Ⓑ ⊗ 🍴🛏🚗 ★★★★

Beautiful riverside location, rooms with views of Ingleborough or wooded riverbank. Nearby waterfalls walk and Yorkshire Dales Three Peaks. Two ground floor rooms, all rooms en-suite with TV. Large residents lounge, pool/snooker table, sauna, Private car park.

Inglenook Guest House, 20 Main Street, LA6 3HJ ☎ 015242 41270 (Phil & Carolyn Smith) www.inglenookguesthouse.com Map 98/691727
£25-£28 D2 T2 F1 ✕ nearby Ⓑ ⊗ 🛏 ★★★★

● Kettlewell
YORKSHIRE DALES
DALES WAY

Lynburn, BD23 5RF ☎ 01756 760803 (Lorna Thornborrow)
lorna@lthornborrow.fsnet.co.uk Map 98/970720
£35-£40 D1 T1 ✕ nearby Ⓓ ⊗ 🍴🛏 ★★★

● Kirkbymoorside
NORTH YORK MOORS

Bitchagreen Cottage
Farndale East, YO62 7LB ☎ 01751 433250 (Shirley-Ann Collier)
www.farndalecottage.co.uk Map 94/674966
£22-£25 S1 T1 ✕ nearby
Ⓓ Ⓑ ⊗ 🍴

Lovely cottage in beautiful valley of Farndale. Safe parking. Breathtaking views. Own entrance, stairs, sitting/dining with comfort tray. Simple, clean, light, comfortable. Fine local food/home produce. River Dove, wild daffodils (spring), purple heather (August), peace (always). Good touring. Walker's paradise.

Mount Pleasant, Rudland, Fadmoor, YO62 7JJ ☎ 01751 431579 (Mary Clarke)
www.mountpleasantbedandbreakfast.co.uk Map 94/657917
£25 T1 F1 Ⓓ 🍴🛏🚗

● Leyburn
YORKSHIRE DALES

Golden Lion Hotel, Market Place, DL8 5AS ☎ 01969 622161 (Anne Wood)
www.thegoldenlion.co.uk Map 99/112905
£30-£38 S2 D5 T5 F2 ✕ £15, 6pm
Ⓥ Ⓓ Ⓑ ⊗ 🍴🛏🐾🚗 ★

● Malham
YORKSHIRE DALES
PENNINE WAY

River House Hotel
BD23 4DA ☎ 01729 830315 (Alex & Ann Roe)
www.riverhousehotel.co.uk Map 98/901628
£30-£50 D6 T2
Ⓓ Ⓑ ⊗ 🍴🛏🚗❗🐾🚭 Ⓕ ★★★★

A Victorian country house, with breakfast and dinner awards by the AA. An ideal base for walking in the Yorkshire Dales. Licensed restaurant, special diets catered for. Wood burning stove in the lounge bar. Group bookings welcome, midweek breaks avialable.

Beck Hall Guest House
Cove Road, BD23 4DJ ☎ 01729 830332 (Alice Maufe)
www.beckhallmalham.com Map 98/898631
£25-£60 S2 D8 T4 F3 ✕ £7.50, 5pm
Ⓥ Ⓓ Ⓑ ⊗ 🍴🛏❗🐾 ★★★Ⓦ

Family run 18th-century guesthouse welcomes all walkers. Midweek specials, huge breakfasts, packed lunches, lots of local walks and on the Pennine Way. Log fire for cold days and streamside patio for sunny days.

● Masham
Bank Villa Guest House, HG4 4DB ☎ 01765 689605 (Liz Howard-Barker)
www.bankvilla.com Map 99/224810
£45-£50 D2 T2 F2 ✕ £17, 7:30pm
Ⓥ Ⓓ Ⓑ ⊗ 🍴🚗❗

● Muker
YORKSHIRE DALES
COAST TO COAST WALK & PENNINE WAY

Bridge House, Muker, DL11 6QG ☎ 01748 886461 (John Slater)
www.bridgehousemuker.co.uk Map 98/909978
£32.50-£80 D2 T1 F1 Ⓓ Ⓑ ⊗ 🍴🛏🚗❗

● **Northallerton**
COAST TO COAST WALK

Somerset House Farm
Ingleby Arncliffe, DL6 3JP ☎ 01609 882555 (Nev or Ashley)
www.somersethousefarm.com Map 93/442004
£35-£40 S2 D2 T2 F2
D B ⊗ 🛏 🔥 ♿ ! ♿ ♿

Somerset House Farm is situated on the outskirts of the village of Ingleby Arncliffe with fantastic views towards the Cleveland Hills.

We are set in our own substantial landscaped grounds, with the large fish pond as the focal point. The deck to the side of the pond is a perfect place to sit and relax after a long days walking.

We offer B&B to a high standard, our rooms both contemporary and spacious. All our rooms have tea/coffee making facilities, freeview television and footspas. Full English Breakfast and packed lunches are available.

Kennel facilities for your four-legged friend.

● **Oughtershaw**
YORKSHIRE DALES
DALES WAY & PENNINE WAY

Nethergill Farm, Oughtershaw, BD23 5JS ☎ 01756 761126
(Fiona Clark) www.nethergill.co.uk Map 98/862822
£39 T1 ✕ £10, 7pm
V D B ⊗ 🛏 🔥 🚗 ★★★★

● **Pickering**
NORTH YORK MOORS

Bramwood Guest House
19 Hallgarth, YO18 7AW ☎ 01751 474066 (Marilyn Butler)
www.bramwoodguesthouse.co.uk Map 100/800840
£35 S2 D4 T1 F1 ✕ nearby ⋘(Pickering)
D B ⊗ 🛏 🔥 🚗 ! ★★★★⑤ Ⓦ

Elegant Georgian Grade II-listed building in quiet location close to town centre. All rooms are en-suite with TV and generous hospitality trays. Hearty breakfasts. Lounge with logfire and TV. Private parking. Charming walled garden. Steam railway nearby. See SC also.

● **Ravenscar**
NORTH YORK MOORS
CLEVELAND WAY

Brinka House Bed and Breakfast
2 Station Square, Ravenscar, YO13 0LU ☎ 01723871470 (Verity Henson)
www.brinkahousebedandbreakfast.co.uk Map 94/984013
£25 S2 D1 T1 F1 ✕ £12, 7:30pm ⋘(Scarborough)
V D B ⊗ 🛏 🔥 🚗 ! 🔥

Situated in Ravenscar, between Scarborough and Whitby. Ideal stop for Cleveland Way walkers (200yrds), Lyke Wake Walk and Coast to Coast. Bus service from door to Scarborough. Rooms en-suite, evening meal and packed lunch by arrangement. Warm welcome and tasty breakfast awaits.

● **Richmond**
YORKSHIRE DALES
COAST TO COAST WALK

Beechfield, 16 Beechfield Road, DL10 4PN
☎ 01748 824060 (Thelma Jackson)
www.beechfieldrichmond.co.uk Map 92/176015
✕ D B ⊗ 🛏

Frenchgate Guest House, 66 Frenchgate, DL10 7AG ☎ 01748823421
(Ralph Doy) www.66frenchgate.co.uk Map 92/173011
£30-£35 D4 T2 F2 ✕ nearby
D B 🛏 🔥 ! 🔥 ★★★★Ⓜ

● **Ripon**
Bishopton Grove House, HG4 2QL ☎ 01765 600888 (Susi Wimpress)
www.bishoptongrovehouse.co.uk Map 99/301711
£40 D1 T1 F1 ✕ nearby
D B ⊗ 🛏 🔥 🚗 🔥 ★★★

● **Rosedale Abbey**
NORTH YORK MOORS

Sevenford House
Thorgill, YO18 8SE ☎ 01751 417283 (Mrs Linda Sugars)
www.sevenford.com Map 94/724949
£27.50-£30 D1 T1 F1 ✕ nearby
D B ⊗ 🛏 🔥 🚗 ! ★★★★⑤

Originally a vicarage, built from the stones of Rosedale Abbey, Sevenford House stands in four acres of gardens in the heart of the Yorkshire Moors.

The tastefully furnished bedrooms overlooking Rosedale offer wonderful views of valley and moorland. Relaxing guests' lounge with a roaring log fire for colder evenings. Excellent base for exploring the regions: over 500 square-miles of open moorland, with ruined abbeys, Roman roads and steam railway. Email: sevenford@aol.com

YORKSHIRE

● Runswick Bay

NORTH YORK MOORS
CLEVELAND WAY

The Firs
26 Hinderwell Lane, TS13 5HR ☎ 01947 840433
www.the-firs.co.uk Map 94/791168
£45 S1 D4 T2 F4 ✕ £19.50, 6pm
Ⓥ Ⓓ Ⓑ 🐾 ⓑ 🦴 ★★★★

Situated at the top of the bank in the beautiful scenic coastal village of Runswick Bay. Ideal base for moors and coast, on edge of the North York Moors, Cleveland Way and Coast to Coast path. Five minutes from the beach.

● Saltburn-by-the-Sea

CLEVELAND WAY

The Rose Garden, 20 Hilda Place, TS12 1BP ☎ 01287 622947 (Anna Jastrzabek)
www.therosegarden.co.uk Map 94/661212
£40 D1 T1 ✕ nearby 🚶(Saltburn) Ⓓ Ⓑ ⓧ 🐾 ⓑ ★★★★

Sea Holly Guest House, 17 Pearl Street, TS12 1DU ☎ 01287 207284
(Sophie Mcintosh) www.seahollyguesthouse.co.uk Map 94/664215
£30-£35 D2 T1 ✕ nearby 🚶(Saltburn-by-the-Sea)
Ⓓ Ⓑ ⓧ 🐾 🦴 🚗 !

● Scalby

Wrea Head Country House Hotel
Barmoor Lane, Scalby, YO13 0PB ☎ 01723 374374 (Central Reservations)
www.wrea-head-hotel.co.uk Map 101/005911
£69-£89 S1 D12 T2 F2 ✕ £25, 6:30pm 🚶(Scarborough)
Ⓥ Ⓓ Ⓑ 🐾 ⓑ 🚗 ! ⓑ Ⓕ

Offering truly breathtaking, uninterrupted views across the Yorkshire countryside that must seen to be believed. Wrea Head makes an excellent choice for ramblers seeking to enjoy the many walks around Scarborough's coastline and countryside and the North Yorks Moors.

● Scarborough

CLEVELAND WAY

Russell Hotel, 22 Ryndleside, YO12 6AD ☎ 01723 365453 (Lyn Stanley)
www.russellhotel.net Map 101/033893
✕ £10 🚶(Scarborough) Ⓥ Ⓓ Ⓑ ⓧ 🐾 🚗 ! 🦴 ★★★★

The Royal Hotel
St. Nicholas Street, YO11 2HE ☎ 01723 374374 (Central Reservations)
www.royalhotelscarborough.co.uk Map 101/043885
£65-£95 S22 D34 T38 F16 ✕ £25, 7pm 🚶(Scarborough)
Ⓥ Ⓓ Ⓑ ⓧ 🐾 ⓑ ! ⓑ

Situated in an enviable location in the centre of town and overlooking South Bay, The Royal Hotel makes an excellent choice for ramblers walking the Cleveland Way and those seeking to enjoy the many walks around Scarborough's coastline and countryside.

The Ainsley Hotel, 4 Rutland Terrace, Queens Parade, YO12 7JB
☎ 01723 364832 (Mrs Mitchell) www.theainsleyhotel.co.uk Map 101/044890
£25 S3 D4 T1 ✕ nearby 🚶(Scarborough) Ⓑ ⓧ 🐾 ★★★

Cober Hill, Newlands Road, Cloughton, YO13 0AR ☎ 01723 870310
www.coberhill.co.uk Map 101/011953
£30-£55 S22 D6 T22 F14 ✕ £12, 7pm Ⓥ Ⓓ Ⓑ ⓧ 🐾 ⓑ 🦴 ⓑ Ⓕ ★★★

The Clifton Hotel
Queen's Parade, Northbay, YO12 7HX ☎ 01723 374374
www.clifton-hotel-scarborough.co.uk Map 101/039894
£45-£65 S17 D27 T15 F14 ✕ £20, 6pm 🚶(Scarborough)
Ⓥ Ⓑ ⓧ 🐾 ⓑ !

Set overlooking Scarborough's North Bay, the ever-popular Clifton Hotel has been a firm favourite with guests for many years. Offering some of the most amazing sea views in Scarborough, The Clifton makes the perfect base when visiting the Yorkshire Coast.

● Settle

YORKSHIRE DALES
RIBBLE WAY & PENNINE WAY

Golden Lion Hotel, Duke Street, BD24 9DU ☎ 01729 822203
www.yorkshirenet.co.uk/stayat/goldenlion Map 98/819635
£43 D7 T2 F2 ✕ £10, 6pm 🚶(Settle) Ⓥ Ⓓ Ⓑ ⓧ 🐾 ⓑ 🦴 ★★★★

● Skelton

CLEVELAND WAY

Westerland's Guest House, 27 East Parade, Skelton, TS12 2BJ
☎ 01287 650690 (Mrs B Bull) Map 94/655185
£23 S2 D3 ✕ £6, 6:30pm 🚶(Saltburn) Ⓥ Ⓓ Ⓑ ⓧ 🐾 ⓑ 🚗 ! 🦴 ★★

Whitefriars Country Guest House
Church Street, BD24 9JD ☎ 01729 823753
www.whitefriars-settle.co.uk Map 98/819637
£30-£35 S1 D4 T4 F1 ✕ nearby 🚶(Settle)
Ⓓ Ⓑ ⓧ 🐾 ⓑ ! ★★★★

Whitefriars is a delightful 16th-century, traditional family-run guesthouse, with original features. Set in spacious gardens and courtyard, just a stroll from the town centre and railway station. Ideal for exploring the Yorkshire Dales including the Three Peaks and Settle-Carlisle railway.

● Skipton

YORKSHIRE DALES

Low Skibeden House
Harrogate Rd, BD23 6AB ☎ 01756 793849 (Mrs Simpson)
www.yorkshirenet.co.uk/accgde/lowskibeden Map 104/012524
£26-£40 D4 T2 F2 🚶(Skipton)
Ⓓ Ⓑ ⓧ ⓑ

16th-century farmhouse. Quiet, country location set in private grounds. Beautiful views, gardens and parking. Offering 'home from home' comforts and little luxuries in guests' lounge. Close to many AONBs. Two minutes by car to the market town of Skipton.

● Staithes

NORTH YORK MOORS
CLEVELAND WAY

Brooklyn, Brown's Terrace, TS13 5BG ☎ 01947 841396 (Margaret Heald)
www.brooklynuk.co.uk Map 94/782187
£27.50 D2 T1 ✕ nearby ▣ ⊗ 🐾♨ ➔ ! ♨

● Summerbridge

NIDDERDALE WAY

Dalriada, Cabin Lane, Dacre Banks, HG3 4EE ☎ 01423 780512
(Mrs J E Smith) Map 99/196621
£27-£35 D1 T1 ✕ nearby ▣ ⊗ 🐾♨ ➔ ♨ ★★★

● Sutton Bank

NORTH YORK MOORS
CLEVELAND WAY

High House Farm, YO7 2HJ ☎ 01845 597557 (Mrs K M Hope)
Map 100/521839
£30 S1 D1 T1 F1 ▣ 🐾♨ ➔ ! ★★★

Cote Faw, Sutton Bank, YO7 2EZ ☎ 01845 597363 (Mrs J Jeffray)
Map 100/522829
£20-£22 S1 D1 T1 ✕ nearby ▣ ⊗ 🐾 ★★

● Threshfield

YORKSHIRE DALES
DALES WAY

Gamekeeper's Inn, Long Ashes Park, BD23 5PN ☎ 01756 752434
(Bill McKenzie) www.gamekeeperinn.co.uk Map 98/979648
£55-£60 D3 T1 F1 ✕ £20, 7pm Ⓥ Ⓑ ⊗ 🐾♨ ➔ !

● Whitby

NORTH YORK MOORS
COAST TO COAST WALK & CLEVELAND WAY

Ryedale House
156 Coach Road, Sleights, YO22 5EQ ☎ 01947 810534 (Pat Beale)
www.ryedalehouse.co.uk Map 94/866070
£28-£30 S1 D2 ✕ nearby ᴡᴡ(Sleights)
Ⓑ ⊗ 🐾♨ ★★★★

Welcoming home at foot of the moors in national park four miles from Whitby.

Magnificent scenery, superb walking, picturesque harbours, cliffs, beaches, scenic railways – it's all here! Beautifully appointed rooms, private facilities and many extras. Guest lounge, extensive breakfast menu served with panoramic views, facing large landscaped gardens. Local inn and fish restaurant just a short walk. Minimum booking two nights. Regret no pets/children. Exclusive to non-smokers.

Prospect Villa, 13 Prospect Hill, YO21 1QE ☎ 01947 603118 (J Gledhill)
janceeprospectvilla@hotmail.co.uk Map 94/894105
£26-£27 S2 T1 F2 ✕ nearby ᴡᴡ(Whitby) ▣ Ⓑ ⊗ 🐾♨ ★★★

Saxonville Hotel, Ladysmith Ave, YO21 3HX ☎ 01947 602631 (Richard Newton)
www.saxonville.co.uk Map 94/891113
£62.50 S4 D9 T8 F2 ✕ £12, 7pm ᴡᴡ(Whitby) Ⓥ ▣ Ⓑ ⊗ 🐾♨ ★★★Ⓢ

● York

TRANS PENNINE TRAIL

Ambleside Guest House, 62 Bootham Crescent, Bootham, YO30 7AH
☎ 01904 637165 (Keith Hugill) www.ambleside-gh.co.uk Map 105/598527
£60 D6 T1 F1 ✕ nearby ᴡᴡ(York) Ⓑ ⊗ ♨ ★★★

Ascot House
80 East Parade, YO31 7YH ☎ 01904 426826
(Mrs June Wood) www.ascothouseyork.com
Map 105/616525
✕ ᴡᴡ(York) Ⓑ 🐾♨ ⊗ Ⓢ

Family-run Victorian villa with four poster and canopy beds. 15 minutes' walk from historic city centre. Delicious English, Continental and vegetarian breakfast – generous helpings for hungry ramblers. Residential license and private enclosed parking.

WEST YORKSHIRE

● Guiseley

DALES WAY & EBOR WAY

Lyndhurst, Oxford Road, LS20 9AB ☎ 01943 879985 (Alison Button)
www.guiseley.co.uk/lyndhurst Map 104/190421
£30 D1 T1 ✕ nearby ᴡᴡ(Guiseley) ▣ Ⓑ ⊗ 🐾♨ ★★★Ⓜ

● Haworth

PENNINE WAY

Apothecary Guest House, 86 Main Street, BD22 8DP ☎ 01535 643642
(Mr N J Sisley) theapothecaryguesthouse.co.uk Map 104/030372
£25-£30 S1 D4 T2 F1 ✕ nearby ᴡᴡ(Haworth)
Ⓓ Ⓑ ⊗ 🐾♨ ★★

Aitches Guest House, 11 West Lane, BD22 8DU ☎ 01535 642501
(Philomena Evans) www.aitches.co.uk Map 104/030372
S2 D3 T1 F1 ᴡᴡ(Haworth) ▣ Ⓑ ⊗ 🐾♨ ➔ ! ♨ ★★★★

● Hebden Bridge

PENNINE WAY PENNINE BRIDLEWAY

White Lion Hotel
Bridge Gate, HX7 8EX ☎ 01422 842197 (Emma McCulloch)
www.whitelionhotel.net Map 103/993273
£48 D7 T1 F2 ✕ £10, 5pm ᴡᴡ(Hebden Bridge)
Ⓥ ▣ Ⓑ ⊗ 🐾♨ ➔ ! ♨ ★★★★Ⓦ

Traditional 17th-century coaching inn, riverside location. Good food, real ales, en-suite accommodation, friendly and relaxed atmosphere. Renowned for exceedingly good breakfasts. Walkers, climbers, cyclists and children friendly. Central Hebden Bridge, the town of little shops in superb walking country.

● Todmorden

PENNINE WAY

Highstones Guest House, Rochdale Road, Walsden, OL14 6TY
☎ 01706 816534 (Heather Pegg) Map 103/939208
£20 S1 D2 ✕ £10, 6:30pm ᴡᴡ(Walsden) Ⓥ ▣ ⊗ 🐾♨ ★★★

YORKSHIRE

SELF-CATERING

EAST YORKSHIRE

● Flamborough
YORKSHIRE WOLDS WAY & CLEVELAND WAY

Chalk Cottage ☎ 07766147391 (Chris Taylor)
www.chalkcottage.co.uk
£275-£575 Sleeps 1-6. 1 cottage. ⊗ Short breaks available ★★★★

NORTH YORKSHIRE

● Askrigg
YORKSHIRE DALES

Elm Hill Cottages ☎ 01969 624252 (Peter & Liz Haythornthwaite)
www.elmhillholidaycottages.co.uk Map 98/939900
£225-£485 Sleeps 4-6. 2 cottages.
⊗ Short breaks available ★★★

● Austwick
YORKSHIRE DALES

Spoutscroft Cottage ☎ 015242 51052 (Mrs.Christine Hartland)
www.spoutscroftcottage.co.uk Map 98/767672
£275-£450 Sleeps 1-3. 1 traditional dales cottage.
⊗ 🐾 Short breaks available ★★★★★ⓌⓌ

● Aysgarth Falls
YORKSHIRE DALES

Meadowcroft
☎ 01792 280068 (M C Mason)
www.meadowcroftcottage.co.uk Map 98/001865
£200-£376 Sleeps 1-5. 1 cottage.
⊗ 🐾 Short breaks available ★★★★

Wensleydale. Unspoilt village with pub and shop. Modern comfortable conversion of large traditional Dales barn in heart of the national park. Network of footpaths directly from cottage: a walker's paradise. Lovely views. Secure off-street parking and private paddock.

● Glaisdale
NORTH YORK MOORS

Red House Farm ☎ 01947 897242 (T J Spashett)
www.redhousefarm.com Map 94/771049
£250-£650 Sleeps 2-4. 2 cottages, and studio flat. 🐾

● Hawes
YORKSHIRE DALES
PENNINE WAY

Mile House Farm Country Cottages ☎ 01969 667481 (Anne Fawcett)
www.wensleydale.uk.com Map 98/870897
£250-£685 Sleeps 2-7. 4 cottages.
⊗ 🐾 Short breaks available

● Leyburn

Throstlenest Cottages
☎ 01969 623694 (Tricia Smith)
www.throstlenestcottages.co.uk Map 99/069891
£215-£460 Sleeps 1-6. 6 cottages.
⊗ ♿ Short breaks available ★★★

Six cosy, comfortable, well-equipped cottages converted from stone barns. All have a glorious panoramic view over Wensleydale and the high fells of Coverdale. Rural, yet town centre only half a mile. Sorry - no pets.

● Pateley Bridge
NIDDERDALE WAY

Edge Farm
☎ 01422 240829 / 07779 112246 (Michael O'Byrne)
www.edgefarm.co.uk Map 99/098770
£1400-£1450 Sleeps 6-12. 1 farmhouse.
⊗ Short breaks available ★★★★Ⓦ

Edge Farm is a spacious five-bedroom detached property set in the remote and picturesque Upper Nidderdale Valley. Refurbished to a very high standard, providing modern, well equipped and comfortable accommodation. The farm is ideal for families and walkers.

● Pickering
NORTH YORK MOORS

Keld Head Farm Cottages
☎ 01751 473974 (Penny & Julian Fearn)
www.keldheadcottages.com Map 94/801857
£190-£1038 Sleeps 2-8. 9 cottages.
⊗ ♿ Ⓕ Short breaks available ★★★★

In open countryside on the edge of the market town, a picturesque group of stone cottages with beamed ceilings and stone fireplaces.

Furnished with emphasis on comfort, some with four-poster bedrooms.
Large gardens with garden house, play and barbecue area.
Some single storey and one-bedroom cottages.
Excellent base for the York Moors, Heritage Coast, Cleveland Way, Wolds Way and Lyke Wake Walk.

See the virtual tour on our website.

Mel House Cottages ☎ 01751 475396 (John & Penny Wicks)
www.letsholiday.com Map 94/801857
£282-£790 Sleeps 1-19. 2 cottages & 2 apartments.
⊗ ♿ Ⓕ 🐾 Short breaks available ★★★★

Bramwood Cottages ☎ 01751 473446 (Marilyn Butler)
www.bramwoodguesthouse.co.uk Map 100/800840
£225-£500 Sleeps 2-4. 2 cottages. ⊛ Short breaks available ★★★★

● Settle
YORKSHIRE DALES

Selside Farm ☎ 01729 860367 (Mrs S E Lambert)
www.selsidefarmholidaycottage.co.uk Map 98/815651
£260-£480 Sleeps 2-6. 1 cottage. ⊛ Short breaks available ★★★★

● Skipton
YORKSHIRE DALES

Bankfoot Farm ☎ 07753 747912 (Peter Smith)
www.bankfootsutton.co.uk Map 103/961556
⊛ ⊛ Short breaks available

Aire View ☎ 0121 449 4593 (Harry Walkley)
Map 103/972500
£175-£350 Sleeps 2-5. 1 terrace cottage. ⊛ Ⓜ

● Staithes
NORTH YORK MOORS
CLEVELAND WAY

Seaways
☎ 01325320664 (Anthony Williams)
www.portmulgrave.com Map 94/795172
£240-£420 Sleeps 2-5. 1 cottage.
⊛ ⚭ Ⓕ ⚭

Seaways is a luxury cottage with spectacular sea and cliff views. Master bedroom, childs bedroom and large lounge have breathtaking sea views. The lounge has a bay window and French windows which open onto a decking area with spectacular sea views.
The long garden leads to a patio area with built in barbeque, you can dine alfresco while you watch the ships go by.
Cleveland Way runs past the garden.

● Wensleydale
YORKSHIRE DALES
PENNINE WAY & DALES WAY

Country Hideaways
☎ 01969 663559 (Nadine Bell)
www.countryhideaways.co.uk Map 98/939900
£173-£1166 Sleeps 2-10. 30 cottages.
⊛ ⚭ Short breaks available ★★★★

Unique watermill apartments, houses and cottages throughout Wensleydale and surrounding dales. Enjoy the timeless, unspoilt beauty of these wonderful dales, great for walking, touring, relaxing.
Visit our website and book on-line or call 01969 663559 for friendly help and advice.

● Whitby
NORTH YORK MOORS
COAST TO COAST WALK & CLEVELAND WAY

Grange Farm ☎ 01947 881080 (Denise Hooning)
www.grangefarm.net Map 94/929076
£760-£1665 Sleeps 2-14. 1 house.
⊛ Short breaks available ★★★★

GROUPS, HOSTELS, BUNKHOUSES, CAMPSITES & OTHERS

NORTH YORKSHIRE

● Kettlewell
YORKSHIRE DALES
DALES WAY

Scargill House, Kettlewell, BD23 5HU ☎ 01756 760234 (Marian Sloan)
www.scargillhouse.co.uk Map 98/977710
BB, DBB, FB £30-£59 per night Sleeps 10-80. Extended house.
Ⓥ Ⓓ ⊛ ⚭ ⚭ ! ⚭ Ⓕ

● Runswick Bay
NORTH YORK MOORS
CLEVELAND WAY

The Firs, 26 Hinderwell Lane, TS13 5HR ☎ 01947 840433 (Mandy Shackleton)
www.the-firs.co.uk Map 94/791168
BB £30 per night Sleeps 2-24. Bed & breakfast, group accommodation.
Ⓥ Ⓓ ⚭ ★★★★

● Whitby
NORTH YORK MOORS
COAST TO COAST WALK & CLEVELAND WAY

Whitby Backpackers, Harbour Grange, Spital Bridge, YO22 4EF
☎ 01947 600817 (Birgitta) www.whitbybackpackers.co.uk Map 94/901104
£12 per night Sleeps 1-24. Independent hostel. ⚭(Whitby) Ⓓ ⊛

Saxonville Hotel, Ladysmith Ave, YO21 3HX
☎ 01947 602631 (Richard Newton) www.saxonville.co.uk Map 94/892114
BB, DBB £42.50-£52.50 per night Sleeps 20-42.
Hotel, group accommodation. ⚭(Whitby) Ⓥ Ⓓ ⊛ ⚭ ★★★⑤

Sneaton Castle Centre
Castle Road, YO21 3QN ☎ 01947 600051 (Tony Holden)
www.sneatoncastle.co.uk Map 94/880106
BB, DBB, FB £24-£34 per night Sleeps 1-100. Hostel. ⚭(Whitby)
Ⓥ Ⓓ ⊛ ⚭ ⚭ Ⓕ ★★★

Excellent venue offering standard and en-suite accommodation in beautiful location in stunning castle grounds. Ideal for walking holidays, B&B and other events. Excellent home cooking, cosy licensed bar, ample parking. Perfect base for exploring the North York Moors and coastline.

YORKSHIRE

NORTH EAST

Long Distance Paths

**See Paths & Access p25 for full
details of LDPs and waymarks**

National Park

Northumberland

VIEW TOWARDS STEEL RIGG FROM
HADRIAN'S WALL IN NORTHUMBRIA

WALK...   ...THE LAKESIDE WAY

It's the biggest man-made lake in Europe surrounded by England's largest forest, and now the tranquil expanse of Kielder Water is to get an all-weather path along its 27-mile shoreline. Fourteen miles of the wheelchair-friendly Lakeside Way are currently open from Kielder Dam to the forest park's visitor centre – an 18th-century castle and former hunting lodge for the Duke of Northumberland. Situated in the remote Cheviot Hills, the park is a stronghold of the red squirrel and birds of prey, with a large roe deer population. For families, there's Leaplish Waterside Park where you can join a lake cruise or use the swimming pool and new mini golf course.

For details of 12 other walks and more about activities and events in Kielder, visit www.kielder.org or ☎ 01434 220643.

VISIT...   ...ALLEN BANKS AND STAWARD GORGE

This beautiful Victorian wild garden cuts through a large patch of ancient woodland in the North Pennines and is spectacularly situated above a gorge on the River Allen.

The hill and riverside habitat is rich in wildlife with a hundred acres designated a site of special scientific interest, and there are many delightful walks on offer. One woodland trail takes you to a dramatic promontory with the remains of a medieval pele tower, while another tours a reconstructed Victorian summerhouse and ornamental pond.

Contact the National Trust for opening times (www.nationaltrust.org.uk, ☎ 01434 344218) or search the North Pennines AONB website www.northpennines.org.uk for a free downloadable leaflet detailing the area's woodland trails.

SEE...   ...RED KITES AT DERWENT WALK

150 years after they last swooped across the region's skies, the red kite has triumphantly re-established itself in its former breeding grounds of the North East thanks to a high-profile reintroduction programme which comes to a close this year. Ninety-four kites have been released in Gateshead and the Derwent Valley since 2004, and last year six pairs successfully reared young in the Derwent Walk Country Park – one pair just 120m from a large comprehensive school!

Between Swalwell and Rowlands Gill, the park is adjacent to the Thornley Woodlands Centre (☎ 01207 545212) which offers up-to-date information on kite activities and their whereabouts for the best chance of viewing these magnificent creatures.

NORTH EAST

LOCAL RAMBLERS GROUPS... Crook and Weardale Group have helped create new walking routes around Wolsingham and Frosterley, in the Wear Valley, as part of the Minerals Valley Project to regenerate the environment and improve countryside access in the area. A series of walks leaflets will be available soon; visit www.mvp.org.uk for the latest updates... **Northumbria Short Circuits continues to be one of the country's fastest growing Ramblers Groups, offering walks of less than six miles every weekend. Their 2008 programme begins with routes around Great High Wood and Satley. Non-members can try three walks before joining. See p92 for more information.**

These routes were made for walking

Amazing, breathtaking, heart-stopping... round every corner there's another view. From the challenging North Pennines to beautiful dune-backed beaches, the sheer diversity of our landscape makes North East England a walker's paradise.

Of course when you choose to take a walking break, it's best to plan ahead, that's why we've a dedicated website packed with all the information you need. Visit our website to:

- Order your free copy of the walking guide
- View and print off the Walk of the Month
- Download walks direct to your iPod as a podscroll
- Find and book walker-friendly accommodation

Visit **www.visitnortheastengland.com/walking** for more details or call **0870 225 0128** quoting reference 3489/0.

Passionate about **walking**

north east england

MAP 223

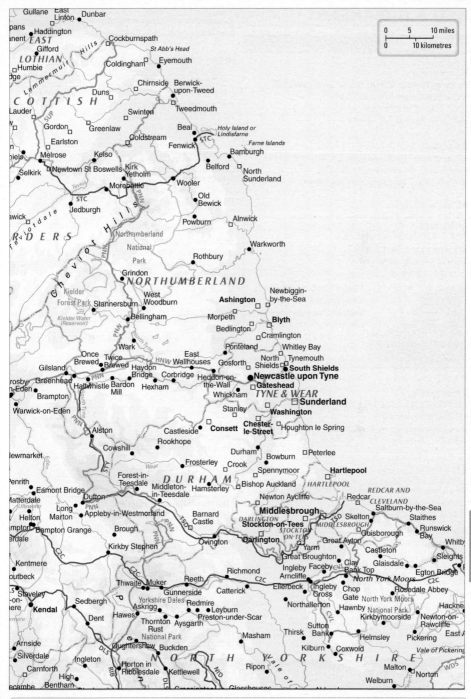

BED & BREAKFAST

DURHAM

● **Cowshill**
Low Cornriggs Farmhouse, DL13 1AQ ☎ 01388 537600 (Janet Elliott)
www.britnett.net/lowcornriggsfarm Map 86/845413
£35-£37 D1 T2 ✕ £16.50, 6:30pm
Ⅴ D B ⊗ ☜♨ ♿ F ★★★★

● **Durham**
Hillrise Guest House, 13 Durham Road West, DH6 5AU ☎ 0191 377 0302
(George Webster) www.hill-rise.com Map 93/306376
£30-£35 S1 D2 T2 F1 ✕ nearby D B ⊗ ♨ ★★★★

● **Durham City**

> **66 Claypath**
> DH1 1QT ☎ 0191 384 3193 (Richard Fletcher)
> www.66claypath.co.uk Map 88/276426
> £50 S1 D1 ✕ nearby ⋈(Durham)
> D ⊗ ☜♨ ★★Ⓦ Ⓜ
>
>
>
> A Grade II-listed Georgian town house,
> with a delightful secluded garden.
> Quality breakfasts prepared fresh to
> order. A short walk from Durham's
> market square, castle, cathedral and
> riverside paths. Ideally located for
> exploring all the North East has to offer.

● **Hamsterley**
Hamsterley Forest B&B, Ayhope Cottage, Redford, Hamsterley, DL13 3NL
☎ 01388 488420 (John and Julie)
www.hamsterleyforestbandb.com Map 92/072307
£27.50 D1 T1 ✕ £10, 7pm Ⅴ D B ⊗ ☜♨ ➡ !

● **Middleton-in-Teesdale**
PENNINE WAY & TEESDALE WAY
Belvedere House, 54 Market Place, DL12 0QA ☎ 01833 640884 (Mrs J A Finn)
www.thecoachhouse.net Map 91/947254
£25 D2 T1 ✕ nearby B ⊗ ☜♨ ♨ F ★★★★

Wemmergill Hall Farm, Lunedale, DL12 0PA ☎ 01833 640379 (Irene Stoddart)
www.wemmergill-farm.co.uk Map 91/901218
£25-£30 S1 D1 T1 F1 ✕ £15, 6:30pm
Ⅴ D B ⊗ ♨ ➡ ★★★★

Lonton South Farm, DL12 0PL ☎ 01833 640 409 (Irene Watson)
Map 91/954245
£27 S1 D1 T1 ✕ 5pm D ⊗ ☜♨ ★★★

Brunswick House, 55 Market Place, DL12 0QH ☎ 01833 640393
(Andrew & Sheila Milnes) www.brunswickhouse.net Map 91/946256
£40 D3 T2 ✕ £20, 7:30pm Ⅴ B ☜♨ ★★★★Ⓢ Ⓦ

NORTHUMBERLAND

● **Bardon Mill**
NORTHUMBERLAND NATIONAL PARK
PENNINE WAY & HADRIAN'S WALL
Twice Brewed Inn, Military Rd, NE47 7AN ☎ 01434 344534 (Brian Keen)
www.twicebrewedinn.co.uk Map 86/753669
£30-£50 S2 D6 T6 ✕ £7, 5pm ⋈(Bardon Mill)
Ⅴ B ⊗ ☜♨ ! ♿ ★★★

● **Bellingham**
PENNINE WAY
Riverdale Hall Hotel, NE48 2JT ☎ 01434 220254
www.riverdalehallhotel.co.uk Map 80/832834
£56-£65 S6 D20 T10 F8 ✕ £18.90, 6pm
Ⅴ D B ⊗ ☜♨ ♨ ! ♨ ♿ F ★★

● **Berwick-upon-Tweed**
Orkney Guest House, 37 Woolmarket, TD15 1DH
☎ 01289 331710 (Helen Rutherford)
orkneyguesthouse@yahoo.com Map 75/000528
£25-£28 D3 T1 F1 ✕ nearby ⋈(Berwick-upon-Tweed) B ⊗ ☜♨ ♨ ♨

● **Corbridge**
HADRIAN'S WALL
The Hayes, Newcastle Road, NE45 5LP ☎ 01434 632010 (Mrs M J Matthews)
www.hayes-corbridge.co.uk Map 87/996643
£29 S1 T1 F2 ✕ nearby ⋈(Corbridge)
D B ⊗ ☜♨ ➡ ! ★★★

● **East Wallhouses**
HADRIAN'S WALL
The Barn B&B, Military Road, NE18 0LL ☎ 01434 672649 (Brenda Walton)
www.smoothhound.co.uk/hotels/thebarn1.html Map 87/047683
£30 D1 T2 ✕ nearby ⊗ ☜♨ ! ♨

● **Fenwick**
ST CUTHBERT'S WAY

> **The Manor House**
> TD15 2PQ ☎ 01289 381016 (Kate Moore)
> www.manorhousefenwick.co.uk Map 75/066401
> £25-£40 D3 T1 F1 ✕ nearby
> D B ⊗ ☜♨ ♨ ! ★★★★Ⓦ
>
>
>
> Relax and unwind in the Manor
> House, built c.1750, the only four-star
> B&B in Fenwick actually on St
> Cuthbert's Way. Set in tranquil
> surroundings, only a short distance
> from Holy Island. Individually
> designed bedrooms with many extras.

Cherry Trees
TD15 2PJ ☎ 01289 381437
Map 75/066401
£25 D1 T1 F1 ✗ £12, 6pm
Ⓥ Ⓓ Ⓑ ⊛ 🐾 🛁 ⚲

Large detached house in large private grounds with ample parking. Ideally situated for St Cuthbert's Way, walking and touring. 6 miles to Holy Island. Spacious rooms, hospitality tray and countryside views.

● Gilsland
NORTHUMBERLAND NATIONAL PARK
HADRIAN'S WALL & PENNINE WAY

Brookside Villa, Hadrian's Wall, CA8 7DA ☎ 016977 47 300 (Denise Collins)
www.brooksidevilla.com Map 86/628666
£30-£33 D1 T1 F1 ✗ £12, 7pm ₥(Haltwhistle)
Ⓥ Ⓓ Ⓑ ⊛ 🐾 🚲 ⚲ ! 🐕 ★★★★Ⓖ

● Grindon
PEAK DISTRICT & NORTHUMBERLAND NATIONAL PARK
PENNINE WAY & HADRIAN'S WALL

Old Repeater Station
Military Road, NE47 6NQ ☎ 01434 688668 (Les Gibson)
www.hadrians-wall-bedandbreakfast.co.uk Map 86/816701
£25-£30 D1 T3 F1 ✗ £8, 7pm
Ⓥ Ⓓ Ⓑ ⊛ 🐾 🚲 ! 🐕 ⚬ Ⓕ ★★★Ⓦ

The 'Old Repeater Station' is a detached stone building near to the most scenic part of Hadrian's Wall.
The property makes extensive use of eco/green technology including geothermal heating and wood-burning stoves.

● Haltwhistle
PENNINE WAY & HADRIAN'S WALL & SOUTH TYNE TRAIL

Kellah Farm B&B
NE49 0JL ☎ 01434 320816 (Lesley Teasdale)
www.kellah.co.uk Map 86/659612
£35 D3 F2 ✗ £6, 7pm ₥(Haltwhistle)
Ⓥ Ⓓ Ⓑ ⊛ 🐾 🛁 ⚲ ! ★★★★Ⓦ

Farmhouse breakfasts using locally sourced produce, including our own free-range eggs. Comfortable accommodation with a warm welcome and stunning views of the Northumberland countryside will be our recipe for a relaxing stay at our newly refurbished Kellah Bed & Breakfast accommodation.

Chare Close Cottage Bed & Breakfast, Chare Close, Castle Hill, NE49 0EE
☎ 01434 322789 (Nick Wright) chareclose.com Map 86/716642
£25-£30 D2 T1 F1 ✗ nearby ₥(Haltwhistle) Ⓓ Ⓑ ⊛ 🐾 🛁 ⚲ ! Ⓕ

Hallmeadows, Main Street, NE49 0AZ ☎ 01434321021 (Heather Humes)
hallmeadows.co.uk Map 86/706640
£25-£27.50 S1 D1 T1 ✗ nearby ₥(Haltwhistle)
Ⓓ Ⓑ ⊛ 🐾 🛁 🚲 ★★★★

● Haydon Bridge
HADRIAN'S WALL

The Reading Rooms, 2 Church Street, NE47 6JQ ☎ 01434 688802
(Gill Valentine) thereadingroomshaydonbridge.co.uk Map 86/842643
£29-£39 D2 T1 F2 ✗ nearby ₥(Haydon Bridge)
Ⓓ Ⓑ ⊛ 🐾 🛁 🚲 ! ⚬ Ⓕ ★★★★Ⓦ

● Heddon-on-the-Wall
HADRIAN'S WALL

Ramblers' Repose, 8 Killiebrigs, NE15 0DD ☎ 01661 852419 (Mrs PA Millward)
pmillward155@btinternet.com Map 88/130665
£40 D1 T1 ✗ nearby ⊛ 🛁

Tyne Valley Views, 9 Killiebrigs, NE15 0DD ☎ 01661 853509 (Jillian Riddell)
www.j4online.co.uk Map 88/130665
£30 S1 D1 ✗ £6, 6pm ₥(Wylam) Ⓥ Ⓓ ⊛ 🐾 🛁 🚲

● Old Bewick

Old Bewick Farmhouse
NE66 4DZ ☎ 01668 217372 (Catherine Lister)
www.oldbewick.co.uk Map 75/069213
£30-£40 D1 F1 ✗ £12.50, 6pm
Ⓥ Ⓓ Ⓑ ⊛ 🐾 🛁 🚲 ! ★★★★★

A Georgian farmhouse situated in the unspoilt beautiful countryside of North Northumberland with panoramic views of the Cheviot Hills. An ideal location for walkers and cyclists of all abilities. We provide guided walks, packed lunches and evening meals on request.

● Rothbury
NORTHUMBERLAND NATIONAL PARK

Well Strand, NE65 7UD ☎ 01669 620794 (Helen & David Edes)
Map 81/056016
£22 S1 D1 T1 ✗ nearby Ⓓ ⊛ 🚲 ! 🐕

Beechy Hedge, 18 Cragside View, NE65 7YU ☎ 07896 061949 (Freda Bettany)
fredabettany@aol.com Map 81/054018
£19.50 S1 D1 ✗ £10, 6pm
Ⓥ Ⓓ ⊛ 🐾 🛁 🚲 Ⓜ

● Stannersburn
NORTHUMBERLAND NATIONAL PARK

The Pheasant Inn, NE48 1DD ☎ 01434 240382
www.thepheasantinn.com Map 80/721866
£50 D4 T3 F1 ✗ £12, 7pm Ⓥ Ⓑ 🐾 🛁 ! 🐕 ★★★★Ⓢ

NORTH EAST

● Wark
NORTHUMBERLAND NATIONAL PARK
PENNINE WAY

Battlesteads Country Inn & Restaurant
Battlesteads Hotel & Restaurant, NE48 3LS ☎ 01434 230209
(Richard & Dee Slade) www.battlesteads.com Map 87/860768
£45-£60 S1 D7 T7 F2 ✗ £15, 6:30pm
Ⓥ Ⓓ Ⓑ ⊗ 🍴 👤 🛏 ⌂ ! 🛁 🐾 Ⓕ ★★★★Ⓢ

Originally built as a farmstead in 1747, this stone-built inn and restaurant features a cosy open fire and a sunny walled beer-garden.Excellent bar meals and a la carte menus (including vegetarian) using fresh, local produce. Good choice of wines, three cask ales.
Friendly, family-run, country inn has 17 en-suite rooms. Ideally placed for exploring Hadrian's Wall, Kielder and Border Reiver country.
Good food, good wine list and good beer!

● Wooler
ST CUTHBERT'S WAY

Winton House
39 Glendale Road, NE71 6DL ☎ 01668 281362 (Terry & Veronica Gilbert)
www.wintonhousebandb.co.uk Map 75/991283
£35 D2 T1 ✗ nearby
Ⓓ Ⓑ ⊗ 🍴 👤 🛏 ! ★★★Ⓦ

Charming Edwardian house with spacious, comfortable rooms. Situated on quiet road close to village centre, just 250m from St Cuthbert's Way. Much praised breakfasts (early if required!) using local produce. Walkers (and cyclists) especially welcome. Personal knowledge of local walks.

Tilldale House
34/40 High Street, NE71 6BG ☎ 01668 281450 (Julia Devenport)
www.tilldalehouse.co.uk Map 75/990281
£28-£38 D3 T3 ✗ nearby
Ⓓ Ⓑ ⊗ 🍴 👤 🛏 ! 🛁 ★★★★Ⓢ

Our stone-built 17th-century home offers spacious comfortable en-suite bedrooms. An ideal base for walking, cycling, fishing, golf or riding. Located off the main road, 150 yards from St Cuthbert's Way. Further details on request.

TYNE & WEAR

● Whickham
DERWENT VALLEY HERITAGE WAY
East Byermoor Guest House, Fellside Road, NE16 5BD
☎ 01207 272687 (Christine Armstrong)
www.eastbyermoor.co.uk Map 88/193587
£40-£50 D3 T2 ✗ nearby 🚌(Metrocentre)
Ⓓ Ⓑ ⊗ 🍴 👤 🛏 🛁 ⌂ ★★★★

SELF-CATERING

DURHAM

● Barnard Castle
TEESDALE WAY

East Briscoe Farm Cottages
☎ 01833 650087 (Emma Wilson)
www.eastbriscoe.co.uk Map 92/006197
£165-£495 Sleeps 1-6. 6 cottages.
⊗ ⌂ Ⓕ 🛁 Short breaks available ★★★★Ⓦ

You'll find a superb base for walking at East Briscoe Farm Cottages. Set on a 14-acre estate in scenic Teesdale, the cottages are comfortable and well-equipped. Three cottages allow pets. Linen, towels and heating are included.

● Wolsingham
Mrs M Gardiner ☎ 01388 527538
Map 92/075374
⊗ 🛁 Short breaks available

NORTHUMBERLAND

● Bamburgh
Springhill Farm Holiday Cottages ☎ 01665 721820 (Sarah/Julie Gregory)
www.springhill-farm.co.uk Map 75/203318
£195-£1,060 Sleeps 2-6. 6 cottages. ⊗ 🛁 ★★★★★Ⓦ

● Berwick-upon-Tweed
Two, the Courtyard ☎ 01289 308737 / 07989 468008 (J Morton)
www.berwickselfcatering.co.uk Map 75/999529
£200-£750 Sleeps 1-12. 1 maisonette.
⊗ 🛁 Short breaks available ★★★Ⓦ

● Hexham
NORTHUMBERLAND NATIONAL PARK
HADRIAN'S WALL
Sammys Place ☎ 01434 604143 / 07903 038623 (Susan Sibbald)
www.sammyshideaways.com Map 87/934638
£270-£480 Sleeps 1-4. 3 apartments.
⊗ Short breaks available ★★★★

● Rothbury
NORTHUMBERLAND NATIONAL PARK

Bracken Lea Cottage ☎ 01670 519629 (Mr J Dalrymple)
www.brackenleacottage.co.uk Map 81/058017
£175-£385 Sleeps 1-3. 1 cottage. ⊗ ⚘ Short breaks available ★★★

Northumbria Byways ☎ 016977 46777 (Vicky Reed)
www.northumbria-byways.com Map 81/058017
£175-£2000 Sleeps 2-10. 150 cottages.
⊗ & F ⚘ Short breaks available ★★★★★Ⓦ

GROUPS, HOSTELS, BUNKHOUSES, CAMPSITES & OTHERS

NORTHUMBERLAND

● Bamburgh
Springhill Farm Caravan & Camping Site, Springhill Farm, NE68 7UR
☎ 01665 721820 (Sarah/Julie Gregory)
www.springhill-farm.co.uk Map 75/203318
£8-£18 per night Sleeps 1-25. Caravan & camping site. ⊗ ⚘

● Chatton
ST CUTHBERT'S WAY

Chatton Park Bunkhouse, Chatton Park Farm House, Chatton, NE66 5RA
☎ 01668 215247 (Jane Ord) www.chattonparkfarm.co.uk Map 75/066286
£12-£15 per night Sleeps 1-12. Bunkhouse. D ⊗ ! ⚘ & F Ⓦ

● Heddon-on-the-Wall
HADRIAN'S WALL

Houghton North Farm
NE15 0EZ ☎ 01661 854364 (Paula Laws)
www.hadrianswallaccommodation.com Map 88/126668
BB £23-£40 per night Sleeps 6-23. Hostel. ∿(Wylam)
D ⛍ 🚗 ! ⚘ & F ★★★★

Situated on Hadrian's Wall Trail, Houghton North Farm has 6 bunk-bedded rooms, 2 en-suite. With a fitted kitchen, lounge (TV and Internet), wood burning stove, laundry and drying room. continental breakfast, linen and towels are included in the price.

DID YOU KNOW?

Our website features accommodation along 100 Long Distance Paths, including many not listed in this guide.

You can also search by place name, postcode, town, county or national park.

Visit: www.ramblers.org.uk/accommodation

NORTH EAST

WALES

Long Distance Paths

Cambrian Way ....CAM

Clwydian Way ....CLW

Glyndŵr's Way ....GLN

Isle of Anglesey
Coastal Path ....ANC

Offa's Dyke Path ....OFD

Pembrokeshire
Coast Path ....PSC

Severn Way ....SVN

Valeways Millennium
Heritage Trail ....VMH

See Paths & Access p25 for full details of LDPs and waymarks

National Parks

Brecon Beacons
Pembrokeshire Coast
Snowdonia

REMAINS OF DOLWYDDELAN CASTLE IN
SNOWDONIA NATIONAL PARK

WALK...   ...THE NORTH BERWYN WAY

The Dee Valley is hoping to boost the number of walkers to this much overlooked and beautiful part of North Wales with this challenging new waymarked route. Trailing 15 miles over the wild North Berwyn Mountains from Llangollen to Corwen, it offers a bracing mix of walking along hilltop, moor, forest and riverside, much of it recently opened under right to roam legislation. Heather-clad ridges offer glorious views across the whole of Denbighshire, and the derelict buildings of old villages cling to the side of the mountains where a century ago its residents toiled for slate on perilous precipices.

An excellent downloadable leaflet is available from www.deevalleywalks.com (or call Llangollen TIC on ☎ 01978 860828) that details the area's rare flora and fauna, its history and shows maps of several other excellent walks in the area.

VISIT...   ...ELAN VALLEY

It's not hard to see why this beautiful and remote area of Powys to the west of Rhayader is often called the 'Welsh Lake District', with its complex of dammed lakes created at the turn of the last century. Now more than 80% of the 70-square-mile estate is designated a site of special scientific interest and walkers can enjoy most of its wildlife-rich scenery as open access. Several trails (one hard-surfaced) link up the numerous sites of interest, including the breached and overgrown Nant-y-Gro dam used by Barnes Wallis to test his bouncing bomb for the famous Dambusters raid in WW2, and Elan Village – the only purpose-built Arts and Crafts village in Wales.

Visit www.elanvalley.org.uk or ☎ 01597 810898 for more about activities and amenities in the area.

SEE...
...FEN ORCHIDS AT KENFIG DUNES

This spectacular nature reserve, near Bridgend in South Wales, was once part of a huge system of dunes stretching from the river Ogmore to the Gower peninsula. It is home to the UK's largest population of the exceptionally rare fen orchid, which makes up over half of all orchids found in Britain. Overlooking a 70-acre freshwater lake, the beautiful plants vie for your distraction with the wealth of birdlife and sand lizards darting through the undergrowth. And if they don't turn your head, then the top of a castle tower popping up through the sand certainly might – it is all that remains visible of an ancient town buried by sandstorms in the 16th century.

For more information, ☎ 01656 743386 or search Bridgend County Council's website www.bridgend.gov.uk.

WALES

LOCAL RAMBLERS GROUPS... Llanelli Group organises and hosts an annual festival of walks each spring bank holiday weekend, attracting walkers from all over the world. Dates this year are 24–26 May. Contact the Group for further details (see p96)... **Cardiff Group has an expanding number of local walks with accompanying maps on their excellent website (see p96) together with the text of two out-of-print books: *Capital Walks* and *More Capital Walks*.**

MAP   231

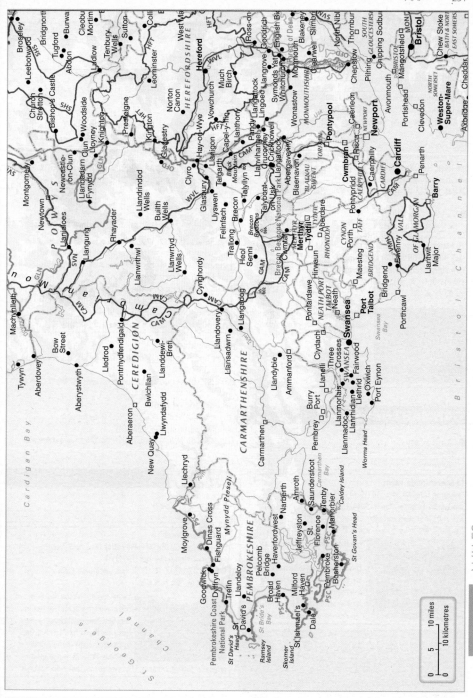

WALES

BED & BREAKFAST

ANGLESEY

● Holyhead

ISLE OF ANGLESEY COASTAL PATH

Quayside Guest House, 3 Stanley Crescent, LL65 1DD ☎ 01407 769202
(Ken Collett) quayside3@tiscali.co.uk Map 114/248827
£20-£25 D1 T4 ✗ nearby ⋙(Holyhead) Ⓓ ⊗ 🍴🛏🚗 ! 🛁

● Rhoscolyn

ISLE OF ANGLESEY COASTAL PATH

Glan Towyn, LL65 2NJ ☎ 01407 860380 (Carol Gough)
www.glantowyn-rhoscolyn.co.uk Map 114/272752
£25-£45 S1 D2 T2 ✗ nearby Ⓓ Ⓑ ⊗ 🍴🛏🚗 ! ★★★

● Valley

ISLE OF ANGLESEY COASTAL PATH

Ty Mawr
LL65 3HH ☎ 01407 740235 (Anne Lloyd)
www.angleseybedandbreakfast.co.uk Map 114/296784
£50-£58 D1 T1 ✗ nearby ⋙(Valley)
Ⓓ ⊗ 🛏🚗 🛁

A warm welcome awaits in our 19th-century
farmhouse, set in a lovely garden on our
300-acre dairy farm.

Close to the Anglesey Coastal Path, Ty Mawr
is an ideal place to stay for long or
short rambles.

CARMARTHENSHIRE

● Llandovery

BRECON BEACONS

CAMBRIAN WAY

LLanerchindda Farm
Cynghordy, SA20 0NB ☎ 01550 750274 (Lynn & Martin Hadley)
www.cambrianway.com Map 147/808429
£34 S1 D3 T4 F1 ⋙(Cynghordy)
Ⓓ Ⓑ ⊗ 🍴🛏🚗 ! 🛁🚶 ★★★Ⓦ Ⓜ

Family-run guest house with spectacular
views of the Brecon Beacons.
En-suite bedrooms, comfortable lounge
bar, excellent homecooked food, log fires
& drying room.
Ideal for exploring Mid & South Wales.
Self-catering cottages also available.

DID YOU KNOW?

Our website features accommodation
along 100 Long Distance Paths,
including many not featured in this guide.

Visit: www.ramblers.org.uk/accommodation

CEREDIGION

● Aberystwyth

Brynarth Country Guest House
Lledrod, SY23 4HX ☎ 01974 261367 (Ian & Cathy Campion)
www.brynarth.co.uk Map 135/665698
£27-£35 S2 D5 T2
Ⓓ Ⓑ ⊗ 🍴🛏🚗 ! 🛁 ★★★Ⓦ

17th-century farmhouse and converted barn set in stunning scenery within
the picturesque Ystwyth Valley, offering warm and comfortable accomodation
and excellent food using local produce.
Licensed snug bar and games barn, plus mature gardens with Cors Ian nature
reserve within 200 metres and Cors Caron within 10 mins' drive. Teifi Pools,
Devils Bridge and the Rheidol Valley close by.
Packed lunches, evening meals and drying facilities available!

● Bow Street

Garreg Lwyd, Penygarn, SY24 5BE ☎ 01970 828830 (Mrs A Edwards)
Map 135/625852
£25-£30 S1 D1 T1 F1 ✗ nearby ⋙(Aberystwyth) Ⓓ 🍴🛏🛁 ★★

● Llanddewi Brefi

Ffynnonddewi, SY25 6NZ ☎ 01570 493269 (Mary Pearce)
www.ffynnonddewi.net Map 146/645545
£35-£40 S1 D2 ✗ £15, 7pm Ⓥ Ⓓ Ⓑ ⊗ 🍴🛏🚗 ! ★★★★Ⓦ

CONWY

● Betws-y-Coed

SNOWDONIA/ERYRI

Fairy Glen Hotel
Beaver Bridge, LL24 0SH ☎ 01690 710269 (Mr & Mrs B Youe)
www.fairyglenhotel.co.uk Map 115/799547
£27-£30 S1 D5 T2 F1 ✗ £17.50, 7pm ⋙(Betws-y-Coed)
Ⓥ Ⓓ Ⓑ ⊗ 🍴🛏 ★★Ⓦ

A warm friendly welcome from Brian and
Enid as you arrive at our 17th-century,
Fairy Glen Hotel, overlooking the river
Conwy and Beaver Pool. Excellent, fresh,
homecooked cuisine and full British
breakfasts. Residents' lounge and bar,
private car parking, c/heating, CTV, beverage tray, clock radio, hairdryer.

Glan Llugwy Guest House, Glan Llugwy, LL24 0BN ☎ 01690 710592
(Graham & Jean Brayne) www.glanllugwy.co.uk Map 115/784565
£25 S1 D3 T2 ✗ nearby ⋙(Betws-y-Coed) Ⓓ Ⓑ ⊗ 🍴🛏🚗 ! ★★★Ⓦ

The Ferns Guest House
Holyhead Road, LL24 0AN ☎ 01690 710587 (Lynn & David Taylor)
www.ferns-guesthouse.co.uk Map 115/795562
£26-£40 S1 D6 F2 ✗ nearby ₥(Betws-y-Coed)
D B ⊗ ♨ ♨ ★★★★ⓦ

The Ferns Guest House is conveniently situated in the village of Betws-y-Coed. Nine comfortably-furnished en-suite rooms, including TV, beverage trays, clocks and hairdryers. Your hosts Lynn and David offer the warmest hospitality with an emphasis on service and comfort.

The Park Hill
Lanrwst Rd, LL24 0HD ☎ 01690 710540 (Jaap & Ghislaine Buis)
www.park-hill.co.uk Map 116/801565
£30-£39 D5 T4 ✗ £19, 7pm ₥(Betws-y-Coed)
V D B ⊗ ♨ ♨ ★★★★ⓦ

Highly recommended, traditionally built, Victorian guest house, with all mod-cons. Indoor heated swimming pool, Jacuzzi-type spa and sauna. Walkers, climbers and mountain bikers welcome. Free shuttle service to the nearest railway station. Secluded car park.

Garth Dderwen, Vicarage Rd, LL24 0AD ☎ 01690 710491
(Eifion and Frances Morris) www.garth-dderwen.co.uk Map 115/794563
£25-£28 S1 D2 T3 ✗ nearby ₥(Bets-y-Coed)
D B ⊗ ♨ ★★★

● Conwy
CAMBRIAN WAY

Glan Heulog Guest House
Llanrwst Road, LL32 8LT ☎ 01492 593845 (Stan & Vivien Watson-Jones)
www.walesbandb.co.uk Map 115/779772
£30-£40 S1 D4 T2 F1 ✗ nearby ₥(Conwy)
D B ⊗ ♨ ♨ ! ♨ ★★★

Beautiful Victorian house conveniently situated in the World Heritage town of Conwy. Non-smoking en-suite rooms, centrally heated with TV, beverage trays, clock radio and hairdryers. Lounge and conservatory to relax in. Car parking.

● Llandudno
CAMBRIAN WAY
Vine House, 23 Church Walks, LL30 2HG ☎ 01492 876493 (Amanda Jacob)
www.vinehouse.org.uk Map 115/778827
£25-£31 D2 F2 ✗ nearby ₥(Llandudno)
D B ⊗ ♨ ♨ !

The Moorfield Hotel, 15 Chapel Street, LL30 2SY ☎ 01492 876147
(Sharon Pugh) www.themoorfieldhotel.com Map 115/780823
£22-£25 S1 D2 T2 F4 ✗ nearby ₥(Llandudno)
B ⊗ ♨ ♨

● Llanfairfechan
SNOWDONIA/ERYRI
CAMBRIAN WAY

Rhiwiau Isaf
LL33 0EH ☎ 01248 681143 (Ruth Carrington)
www.rhiwiau.co.uk Map 115/678732
£27.50-£37.50 S1 D2 T2 F2 ✗ £12.50, 7pm ₥(Llanfairfechan)
V D B ⊗ ♨ ♨ ! ♨ ★★★ⓦ

Situated in secluded valley only 5 minutes from A55. Panoramic views of montains, Menai Straits and Anglesey. Walk through our 16 acres of woods to the Snowdonia National Park, Carneddau and North Wales Path. Own carpark. Afternoon tea on arrival.

● Trefriw
SNOWDONIA/ERYRI

Crafnant Guest House
LL27 0JH ☎ 01492 640809 (Mike & Jan Bertenshaw)
www.trefriw.co.uk Map 115/780631
£26.50-£30 D3 T1 F1 ₥(Llanrwst)
D B ⊗ ♨ ♨ ! ★★★★ⓦ

Whether you've discovered the mountain lakes which nestle above our village, conquered Snowdon or strolled around the stunning Conwy Valley, then rest assured of the comfort and warm welcome of Crafnant House. Traditional pubs & exceptional food on the doorstep.

GWYNEDD

● Aberdovey
SNOWDONIA/ERYRI
Awel y Mor, 4 Bodfor Terrace, LL35 0EA ☎ 01654 767058
(Jennifer Johnson) www.awelymor-aberdovey.co.uk Map 135/612959
£30-£35 S1 D2 T1 F3 ✗, 5pm ₥(Aberdovey) D B ⊗ ♨ ♨ ♨ ★★★

● Barmouth
SNOWDONIA/ERYRI
CAMBRIAN WAY
The Gables, Mynach Rd, LL42 1RL ☎ 01341 280553 (Mrs D Lewis)
Map 124/609166
£28 S1 D1 F1 ✗ nearby ₥(Barmouth) D B ⊗ ♨ ♨ ♨

Lawrenny Lodge
Aberamffra Road, LL42 1SU ☎ 01341 280466 (Toby & Chantal Simpson)
www.lawrennylodge.co.uk Map 124/617156
£32-£38 S1 D4 T2 F1 ✗ £10, 6:30pm ₥(Barmouth)
V D B ⊗ ♨ ♨ ★★ⓦ

Lawrenny Lodge is situated in a quiet area of Barmouth overlooking Cardigan Bay and the Mawddach estuary. Five minutes' walk from beach, town and harbour area. We offer 7 en-suite rooms with TV and tea/coffee-making facilities.

WALES

Ty'r Graig Castle
Llanaber Road, LL42 IYN ☎ 01341280470 (Janette & Khalid Osman)
www.tyrgraigcastle.co.uk Map 124/607167
£50-£55 SI D9 TI ✕ £20, 6:30pm ♨(Barmouth)
Ⓥ Ⓑ ⊛ 🐾👤♨

A landmark Victorian castle-hotel on the edge of Snowdonia National Park, overlooking Cardigan Bay. Approx' 1/2 mile out of Barmouth. For anyone wishing to explore the surrounding areas, it is a superb base situated between the mountains and the sea.

● Beddgelert
SNOWDONIA/ERYRI
CAMBRIAN WAY

Plas Tan Y Graig
Smith Street, LL55 4LT ☎ 01766 890310 (Tony Love or Sharon Sanders)
www.plas-tanygraig.co.uk Map 115/591482
£30-£35 D7 T6 F3
Ⓓ Ⓑ ⊛ 🐾👤 ★★★★Ⓜ

Plas Tan y Graig is a large Victorian detached house in the heart of Beddgelert. We provide an ideal base for outdoor pursuits, offering a friendly welcome and warm hospitality, with the emphasis on quality and high standards of service.

● Blaenau Ffestiniog
SNOWDONIA/ERYRI
CAMBRIAN WAY

The Don, 147 High Street, LL41 3AX ☎ 01766 831032 (Clare Abbott)
www.the-don.biz Map 115/706454
£26 S3 D3 TI FI ✕ £10, 8pm ♨(Blaenau Ffestiniog)
Ⓥ Ⓓ Ⓑ ⊛ 🐾👤🚗🏍♿ ★★Ⓦ

● Caernarfon
Tegfan B&B, 4 Church Street, LL55 ISW ☎ 01286 673703 (Philip Almond)
www.tegfanbb.co.uk Map 114/476628
✕ nearby Ⓑ ⊛ 🐾🚗 ★

● Dolgellau
SNOWDONIA/ERYRI
CAMBRIAN WAY

Ivy House
Finsbury Square, LL40 IRF ☎ 01341 422535 (M Bamford)
www.ivyhouse-dolgellau.co.uk Map 124/727177
£35 D3 T2 FI ✕ £17, 6:30pm
Ⓥ Ⓓ Ⓑ ⊛ 🐾👤🚗!🏍 ★★★

At the centre of an idyllic walking area, a country town guesthouse, offering homemade food: big breakfasts, evening meals and packed lunches. Fully centrally heated, all bedrooms have TV, hairdryers and tea/coffee making facilities, most ensuite.
Email: marg.bamford@btconnect.com

Dwy Olwyn
Coed-y-Fronallt, LL40 2YG ☎ 01341 422822 (Mrs N Jones)
www.dwyolwyn.co.uk Map 124/734183
£25-£35 DI TI F2 ✕ nearby
Ⓓ Ⓑ ⊛ 🐾👤 ★★★

"View of Cader Idris from Dwy Olwyn."
A warm welcome awaits in this comfortable guesthouse, set in an acre of landscaped gardens. Peaceful position, less than 10mins walk into town. Ideal for touring Snowdonia NP, sandy beaches, gauge railways, RSPB sanctuary and picturesque walks (including famous Precipice Walk above Mawddach estuary). Spacious bedrooms with colour TV, clock-radio, hairdryer. Lounge with selection of maps, guidebooks & leaflets. Clean and personable. Parking.

Einion House, Friog, LL38 2NX ☎ 01341 250644 (David Rowe)
www.einionhouse.co.uk Map 124/615122
£25-£35 SI D4 TI FI ✕ £12, 7pm ♨(Fairbourne)
Ⓥ Ⓑ ⊛ 🐾👤!

● Llanberis
SNOWDONIA/ERYRI

Mount Pleasant Hotel, High Street, LL55 4HA ☎ 01286 870395
www.waterton.org.uk/mph Map 114/577602
Ⓓ Ⓑ 🐾🚗!🏍

● Nefyn
Rhos Y Foel, Llannor, LL53 8PX ☎ 01758 614552 (Lynn Prescott)
www.rhosyfoel.co.uk Map 123/341389
£25-£30 D3 TI F2 ✕ £10, 6pm
Ⓥ Ⓓ Ⓑ ⊛ 🐾🚗!🏍

● Pant Glas
SNOWDONIA/ERYRI

Hen Ysgol (Old School)
Bwlch Derwin, LL51 9EQ ☎ 01286 660701 (Terry & Sue Gibbins)
www.oldschool-henysgol.co.uk Map 115/456474
£28 DI TI FI
Ⓓ Ⓑ ⊛ 🐾🚗!🏍♿ Ⓕ ★★★ⒼⓌ

A beautiful, historical 'Welsh Not' Country School provides a unique base for walking the re-opened network of paths linking Snowdonia with Lleyn Peninsular & Bardsey Island. Choice of Breakfast menu. Open all year. Terry & Sue offer a warm welcome.

● Pwllheli
SNOWDONIA/ERYRI

Neigwl Hotel & Restaurant, Abersoch, LL53 7DY ☎ 01758 712363 (Susan Turner) www.neigwl.co.uk Map 123/312279
£70-£80 SI D5 TI F2 ✕ £26, 7:30pm ♨(Pwllheli)
Ⓥ Ⓓ Ⓑ ⊛ 🐾👤🚗 ★★

● Talyllyn
SNOWDONIA/ERYRI
CAMBRIAN WAY

Dolffanog Fawr Country House, LL36 9AJ ☎ 01654 761247 (Lorraine Hinkins)
www.dolffanogfawr.co.uk Map 124/729104
£56 D2 T2 ✕ £20, 7:30pm
Ⓥ Ⓓ Ⓑ ⊛ 🐾 ♨ ⚘ ⛫ ★★★★★

MONMOUTHSHIRE

● Abergavenny
BRECON BEACONS
CAMBRIAN WAY

Park Guest House, 36 Hereford Road, NP7 5RA ☎ 01873 853715
(Neil & Julia Herring, Amanda Kromrei)
www.parkguesthouse.co.uk Map 161/303146
£25-£35 S1 D4 T1 F1 ✕ nearby 🚍(Abergavenny)
Ⓓ Ⓑ ⊛ 🐾 ♨ Ⓕ ★★Ⓦ

● Chepstow
OFFA'S DYKE

Upper Sedbury House, Sedbury Lane, Sedbury, NP16 7HN ☎ 01291 627173
(Christine Potts) www.smoothound.co.uk/hotels/uppersed.html
Map 162/547943 🚍(Chepstow) Ⓓ Ⓑ ⊛ 🐾 ♨ ⛫ ★★★

Southam, Welsh Street, Chepstow, NP16 5LU
☎ 01291 621162 (Maureen & Richard Langston)
maureenlangston@hotmail.com Map 162/527943
£32.50-£37.50 S2 D1 T2 F1 ✕ nearby 🚍(Approx 1 mile)
Ⓓ Ⓑ ⊛ 🐾 ♨ ⚘ ⛫ ★★★★

● Llanfihangel Crucorney
BRECON BEACONS
OFFA'S DYKE

Penyclawdd Farm, NP7 7LB ☎ 01873 890591 (Ann Davies)
www.penyclawdd.co.uk Map 161/312200
£30 S1 D1 T1 ✕ nearby 🚍(Abergavenny)
Ⓓ Ⓑ ⊛ 🐾 ♨ ⚘ ⛫ ★★★★

● Llangattock-Lingoed
BRECON BEACONS
OFFA'S DYKE

The Old Rectory, NP7 8RR ☎ 01873 821326 (Karen Ball)
www.rectoryonoffasdyke.co.uk Map 161/362201
£27.50-£30 S1 D2 T1 ✕ £12.50 Ⓥ Ⓓ Ⓑ ⊛ 🐾 ♨ ⚘ ⛫ ★★★Ⓦ

● Llanthony
BRECON BEACONS
OFFA'S DYKE & CAMBRIAN WAY

The Half Moon Inn, Llanthony, NP7 7NN ☎ 01873 890611 (George Lawrence)
halfmoon-llanthony.co.uk Map 161/287276
£26-£30 S4 D4 T4 F1 ✕ £5.50, 6pm 🚍(Abergavenny)
Ⓥ Ⓓ Ⓑ ⊛ 🐾 ♨ ⚘ ⛫

● Monmouth
OFFA'S DYKE & WYE VALLEY WALK

Penylan Farm, The Hendre, NP25 5NL ☎ 01600 716435 (Cathy & Dave Bowen)
www.penylanfarm.co.uk Map 161/445162
£38-£45 S1 D2 T2 F1 ✕ £18, 7:30pm
Ⓥ Ⓓ Ⓑ ⊛ 🐾 ⚘ ⛫ ★★★

Church Farm Guest House
Mitchel Troy, NP25 4HZ ☎ 01600 712176 (Rosey & Derek Ringer)
www.churchfarmmitcheltroy.co.uk Map 162/492103
£28-£33 S2 D3 T2 F3 ✕ £15, 7pm
Ⓥ Ⓓ Ⓑ ⊛ 🐾 ♨ ⚘ ⛫ ★★★Ⓜ

Set in large garden with stream, a 16th-century former farmhouse with oak beams and inglenook fireplaces. Excellent base for Wye Valley, Forest of Dean, Black Mountains. Central heating. Mainly en-suite bedrooms. Groups welcome (discounts available). Also self-catering unit.

Bistro Prego & Rooms, 7 Church Street, NP25 3BX ☎ 01600 712600
(Lynnette Bourgaize) www.pregomonmouth.co.uk Map 162/508129
£40 D5 T2 F1 ✕ £17.50, 6:30pm Ⓥ Ⓓ Ⓑ ⊛ 🐾 ♨

NORTH EAST WALES

● Bodfari
OFFA'S DYKE & CLWYDIAN WAY

Moel-y-Park, Mountain View, The Bungalow, Afon-Wen, CH7 5UB
☎ 01352 720338 (Mrs H L Priestley)
www.afonwen-guesthouse.co.uk Map 116/127716
£25 T3 ✕ nearby ⊛ 🐾 ♨ ⚘ ⛫

● Caerwys
OFFA'S DYKE

Plas Penucha, CH7 5BH ☎ 01352 720210 (Mrs N Price)
www.plaspenucha.co.uk Map 116/108733
£30-£33 S4 D2 T2 ✕ £17.50, 7pm Ⓥ Ⓓ Ⓑ ⊛ 🐾 ♨ ⚘ ⛫ ★★★

● Corwen
CLWYDIAN WAY

Corwen Court Private Hotel, London Road, LL21 0DP ☎ 01490 412854
Map 125/080434
£20 S6 D4 Ⓓ Ⓑ 🐾 ♨ ⚘

● Llangollen
OFFA'S DYKE & CLWYDIAN WAY

Oakmere
Regent Street, LL20 8HS ☎ 01978 861126 (Lyndsey Knibbs)
www.oakmere.llangollen.co.uk Map 117/218418
£30-£32.50 D4 T2 ✕ nearby
Ⓓ Ⓑ ⊛ 🐾 ♨ ⚘ ⛫ ★★★★

A large, faithfully restored Victorian house set in own grounds with splendid views, just a few minutes walk from the centre of Llangollen. Spacious bedrooms with either en-suite or with private facilities. Ideal base for exploring North Wales.

Plas Hafod, Abbey Road, LL20 8SN ☎ 01978 869225 (Margaret Richardson)
www.plas-hafod.co.uk Map 117/213423
£35-£40 S3 D3 T3 F3 ✕ nearby Ⓓ Ⓑ ⊛ 🐾 ♨ ⚘ ⛫ ★★★★

● Llangwm
Bryn Awel B&B, LL21 0RB ☎ 01490 420610 (Jenni Miller)
www.brynawelbnb.co.uk Map 125/963439 Ⓓ Ⓑ ⊛ 🐾 ♨ ⚘ ⛫ ★★

WALES

PEMBROKESHIRE

● Amroth
PEMBROKESHIRE COAST NATIONAL PARK
PEMBROKESHIRE COAST PATH

Ashdale Guest House, SA67 8NA ☎ 01834 813853 (Roy & Edith Williamson) Map 158/160071
£22.50-£24 S1 D4 T1 ✕ £10.50, 6pm ᎆ(Kilgetty) ⓋⒹⓈ 👍🛁🚗!

● Broad Haven
PEMBROKESHIRE COAST NATIONAL PARK
PEMBROKESHIRE COAST PATH

Albany Guesthouse, 27 Millmoor Way, SA62 3JJ ☎ 01437 781051 (Mrs Morgan) www.albanyguesthouse.co.uk Map 157/861138
£29-£34 S1 D1 T1 ✕ nearby ⒹⒷⓈ 🍺🛁!

● Cardigan
PEMBROKESHIRE COAST NATIONAL PARK
PEMBROKESHIRE COAST PATH & CEREDIGION COAST PATH

Pantygalchfa
Moylegrove, SA43 3BY ☎ 01239613787 (L & M Haslam) www.pantygalchfa.co.uk Map 145/138461
£30-£35 D2
ⒹⒷⓈ 🍺🛁🚗! ★★★★Ⓦ

We offer a warm welcome to our 19th-century former farmhouse set in 1.5 acres of gardens and woodland, stunning rural views. Ample secure parking available. Comfortable clean rooms, guests' lounge and use of garden. Self-catering accommodation also available.

● Dale
PEMBROKESHIRE COAST NATIONAL PARK
PEMBROKESHIRE COAST PATH

Allenbrook, SA62 3RN ☎ 01646 636254 (Elizabeth Webber) www.allenbrook-dale.co.uk Map 157/811059
£35 S1 D1 T1 F1 ✕ nearby
ⒹⒷⓈ 🍺🛁🚗! ★★★★

● Dinas Cross
PEMBROKESHIRE COAST NATIONAL PARK
PEMBROKESHIRE COAST PATH

Dolwern, Feidr Fawr, SA42 0UY ☎ 01348 811266 (Annette Keylock) annette-keylock@lineone.net Map 145/011390
£25-£30 S1 D2 ✕ nearby
ⒹⒷⓈ 🍺🛁🚗!🛁 ★★★Ⓦ

● Fishguard
PEMBROKESHIRE COAST NATIONAL PARK
PEMBROKESHIRE COAST PATH

Cartref Hotel, 15-19 High Street, SA65 9AW ☎ 01348 872430 (Kristiina Bjorkqvist) www.cartrefhotel.co.uk Map 157/956369
ᎆ(Fishguard Harbour) ⒹⒷ 🍺🛁!🛁 ★★

Avon House B&B, 76 High Street, SA65 9AU ☎ 01348 874476 (Sally Wilson) www.avon-house.co.uk Map 157/954367
£22.50 S1 D1 T1 ✕ nearby ᎆ(Fishguard Harbour)
ⒹⒷⓈ 🍺🛁!★★★Ⓦ

● Goodwick
PEMBROKESHIRE COAST NATIONAL PARK
PEMBROKESHIRE COAST PATH

Seaside Steps, 6 New Hill Villas, SA64 0DS ☎ 01348 874076 (Anne Strawbridge) seasidesteps@seasidesteps.plus.com Map 157/947385
£25 D1 F1 ✕ nearby ᎆ(Fishguard) ⒹⒷⓈ 🍺🛁🚗!🛁

Ivybridge, Drim Mill Dyffryn, SA64 0JT ☎ 01348 875366 (Colin Phillips) www.ivybridgeleisure.co.uk Map 157/942371
£35.50-£40 S1 D5 T4 F4 ✕ £15, 7pm ᎆ(Fishguard)
ⓋⒹⒷⓈ 🍺🛁🚗!🛁♿Ⓕ ★★★Ⓦ

● Haverfordwest

Cuckoo Mill Farm
Pelcomb Bridge, SA62 6EA ☎ 01437 762139 (Margaret Davies) www.cuckoomillfarm.co.uk Map 157/933172
£30 D2 T1 F1 ✕ £16, 6pm ᎆ(Haverfordwest)
ⓋⒹⒷⓈ 🍺🛁🛁 ★★★

Mixed farm in central Pembrokeshire. Country walking. Six miles to coastal path. Meal times to suit guests. Excellent home cooking. Cosy farmhouse. Warm, well-appointed rooms. En-suite facilities. Gold Welcome Host.

● Jeffreyston
PEMBROKESHIRE COAST PATH

Jeffreyston Grange, SA68 0RE ☎ 01646 650159 (Tony Hesslegrave) www.jeffreystongrange.co.uk Map 158/089065
£23.50-£27 S1 D3 T2 ✕ nearby ⒹⒷⓈ 🍺🛁🚗!♿Ⓕ

● Manorbier
PEMBROKESHIRE COAST NATIONAL PARK
PEMBROKESHIRE COAST PATH

B&B, Swanlake Farm Guest House, Westmoor, SA70 8QP ☎ 01834 871204 (Rayma Davies) info@swanlake-bay.co.uk Map 158/041985
£26-£30 S6 D6 T2 F2 ✕ £15, 6:30pm ᎆ(Manorbier)
ⓋⒹⒷⓈ 🍺🛁🚗!🛁♿ ★★★Ⓦ

● Moylegrove
PEMBROKESHIRE COAST NATIONAL PARK
PEMBROKESHIRE COAST PATH

Swn-y-Nant B&B, SA43 3BW ☎ 01239 881244 (Brendan & Ludka Powell) www.moylegrove.co.uk Map 145/117446 D2 T1 ✕ £15, 7pm
ⓋⒹⒷⓈ 🍺🛁🚗!Ⓕ ★★★★Ⓦ

● Pembroke
PEMBROKESHIRE COAST NATIONAL PARK
PEMBROKESHIRE COAST PATH

High Noon Guest House, Lower Lamphey Road, SA71 4AB ☎ 01646 683736 (The Barnikel Family) www.highnoon.co.uk Map 157/990011
£23.50-£39.50 S3 D3 T1 F2 ✕ nearby ᎆ(Pembroke)
ⒹⒷⓈ 🍺🛁🚗!🛁 ★★Ⓦ

● St Davids
PEMBROKESHIRE COAST NATIONAL PARK
PEMBROKESHIRE COAST PATH

Alandale Guest House, 43 Nun Street, SA62 6NU ☎ 01437 720404 (Rob & Gloria Pugh) www.stdavids.co.uk/guesthouse/alandale.htm Map 157/754256 ✕ ⒹⒷⓈ 🍺🛁!

Lochmeyler Farm Guest House
Llandeloy, Pen-y-Cwm, near Solva, SA62 6LL ☎ 01348 837724
(Mrs M M Jones) www.lochmeyler.co.uk Map 157/855275
£30-£55 S2 D4 T4 F2 ✗ £17.50, 7pm
Ⓥ Ⓓ Ⓑ ⊗ 🐾♨🐶 ★★★★★Ⓖ

On St David's peninsula. Accommodation with 12 en-suite luxury bedrooms. Explore countryside and Pembrokeshire Coastal Path. B&B £30 to £55. Optional evening dinner £17.50. Closed Christmas and New Year. 10% discount on inclusive dinner, B&B for 7 nights or more.

Glendower, 7 Nun Street, SA62 6NS ☎ 01437 721650 (J J Darby)
j.j.darby@btinternet.com Map 157/753253
£30-£40 S1 D3 T2 F2 ✗ nearby Ⓓ Ⓑ ⊗ 🐾♨🚗🐶 ★★

Pedwar Gwynt, Square and Compass, SA62 5JJ ☎ 01348 837032
(Claire Grimes) www.pedwargwynt.co.uk Map 157/851312
£35 D2 ✗ nearby Ⓓ ⊗ ♨🐶 ★★★Ⓦ

TYF Eco Hotel
Caerfai Road, SA62 6QS ☎ 01437 721678 (Philip Niemand)
www.tyf.com Map 157/758251
£35 S3 D3 T3 F3 ✗ £15, 7pm
Ⓥ Ⓑ 🐾♨🐶

Making customers happy, creating a sense of adventure, wonder and a balance for mind, body and spirit is at the heart of everything we do.

The beach, coast path and centre of St David's are all just a short walk away.

Delicious breakfasts, lunches and dinners are served in the hotel's popular organic restaurant. See website for more details.

● St Florence
PEMBROKESHIRE COAST PATH

Dove's Nest, St Florence, SA70 8LU ☎ 01834 871136 (Meurig Jones)
www.doves-nest.co.uk Map 158/083010
£25 D2 T1 ✗ nearby ₩₩(Manorbier)
Ⓓ Ⓑ ⊗ 🐾♨🚗❗♨ ★★★★Ⓦ

La Ponterosa
St. Florence, SA70 8LJ ☎ 01834 871674 (Jayne Reardon)
la-ponterosa.co.uk Map 158/081008
£25-£30 D3 T2 F1 ✗ £12, 5pm ₩₩(Tenby, 4 miles)
Ⓥ Ⓓ Ⓑ ⊗ 🐾♨🚗❗★★★Ⓦ

Family-run guest house set in 1.5 acres of mature gardens, with ample parking. In the picturesque village of St Florence, near Tenby.

Pembrokeshire offers spectacular coastline and fantastic beaches.

5-night breaks B&B £115 per person, October-March.

Flemish Court Guest House
Flemish Court, St Florence, SA70 8LS ☎ 01834 871413 (Maria Walsh)
www.flemishcourt.co.uk Map 158/082011
£25-£30 D2 T1 F1 ✗ £15, 6pm ₩₩(Manorbier)
Ⓥ Ⓓ Ⓑ ⊗ 🐾♨🚗❗Ⓕ ★★★★Ⓖ

Flemish Court Guest House is a friendly run, non-smoking, guest house in one of Pembrokeshire's prettiest villages. All ground floor en-suite bedrooms with beverage tray, TV/Video and a large selection of books and videos.

Excellent home cooking at affordable rates.

As many of our guests have commented, '4-star guest house with 5-star service'.

Special rates in March, April and May and October - 1 week's dinner, bed and breakfast £220. June July, Aug and September £250.

(Packed lunches available at £3 per day)

● Trefin
PEMBROKESHIRE COAST NATIONAL PARK
PEMBROKESHIRE COAST PATH

Bryngarw, Abercastle Road, SA62 5AR ☎ 01348 831211
(Anthony & Judith Johnson) www.bryngarwguesthouse.co.uk Map 157/842325
£38-£45 D4 T2 ✗ £20, 7pm Ⓥ Ⓓ Ⓑ ⊗ 🐾♨🐶 ★★★Ⓦ

Hampton House, 2 Ffordd-y-Felin, SA62 5AX ☎ 01348 837701
(Vivienne & Chris Prior) viv.kay@virgin.net Map 157/840324
£28-£30 S1 D1 T1 Ⓓ Ⓑ ⊗ 🐾🚗♨❗♨ ★★★Ⓦ

The Old School Hostel and B&B, Ffordd-yr-Afon, Trefin, SA62 5AU
☎ 01348 831 800 (Chris Clements and Sue Whitmore)
www.theoldschoolhostel.co.uk Map 157/841325
£11-£28 S5 D3 T4 F4 ✗ nearby Ⓓ ⊗ 🐾🚗❗★★★Ⓦ

● Brecon
BRECON BEACONS

The Grange, The Watton, LD3 7ED ☎ 01874 624038 (Meryl, Ian & John)
www.thegrange-brecon.co.uk Map 160/048283
£30-£40 D4 T1 F3 ✗ nearby Ⓓ ⊗ 🐾♨🐶 ★★★Ⓦ

The Beacon - Brecon's Smallest Guest House, 4 The Watton, LD3 7ED
☎ 01874 625862 (Joanna & Dafydd Jones)
www.beaconguesthouse.co.uk Map 160/048283
£27 T1 ✗ £8, 6:30pm Ⓥ Ⓓ Ⓑ ⊗ 🐾🚗🐶 ❗

WALES

The Old Mill
Felinfach, LD3 0UB ☎ 01874 625385 / 07909 743963
Map 161/091332
£30 D1 T2 ✕ nearby
Ⓓ Ⓑ ⊗ 🛏🐾 👤 ★★★★Ⓦ

A 16th-century converted corn mill, peacefully situated in its own grounds, Inglenook fireplace, exposed beams, TV lounge, beverage trays. Ideally situated for walks and touring the Brecon Beacons NP and Black Mountains or just relaxing. Local inn within walking distance.

● Capel-y-Ffin
BRECON BEACONS
CAMBRIAN WAY & OFFA'S DYKE
The Grange, NP7 7NP ☎ 01873 890215 (Griffiths Family)
www.grangeguesthouse.co.uk Map 161/251315
£27 S1 D1 T1 F2 ✕ £14, 7:30pm
Ⓥ Ⓓ Ⓑ ⊗ 🛏🐾 👤 ! 🐾 ★

● Crickhowell
BRECON BEACONS
CAMBRIAN WAY
Dragon Hotel, High Street, NP8 1BE ☎ 01873 810362 (Mr Ashley Nield)
www.dragonhotel.co.uk Map 161/217183
£40 S2 D10 T2 F1 ✕ £10, 6:30pm
Ⓥ Ⓓ Ⓑ ⊗ 🛏🐾 👤 ★★

Ty Croeso Hotel, The Dardy, NP8 1PU ☎ 01873 810573 (Linda Jarrett)
www.ty-croeso.co.uk Map 161/206183
Ⓓ Ⓑ ⊗ 🛏🐾 👤 ! Ⓜ

Ty Gwyn, Brecon Road, NP8 1DG ☎ 01873 811625 (Sue & Pete)
Map 161/216188
✕ Ⓓ Ⓑ ⊗ 🛏🐾 👤 ! ★★★★Ⓜ

Ty Tal B&B, 11 New Road, NP8 1AU ☎ 01873 812240 (Dinah & Brian Post)
tytalbedandbreakfast.co.uk Map 161/215184
£30 S1 D1 T1 ✕ nearby Ⓓ Ⓑ ⊗ 🛏🐾 👤 ! ★★★★Ⓦ

● Glasbury
WYE VALLEY WALK
Aberllynfi B&B, HR3 5NT ☎ 01497 847107 (Catherine Sturgeon)
www.hay-on-wye.co.uk/aberllynfi Map 161/179390
£25 S1 T2 ✕ nearby Ⓓ ⊗ 🛏🐾 👤 !

● Hay-on-Wye
BRECON BEACONS
OFFA'S DYKE & HEREFORDSHIRE TRAIL
La Fosse Guest House, Oxford Road, HR3 5AJ ☎ 01497 820613
(Bob and Annabel Crook) www.hay-on-wye/lafosse.co.uk Map 148/232423
£30 D3 T1 ✕ nearby Ⓓ Ⓑ ⊗ 🛏👤 ! 🐾

● Knighton
GLYNDWR'S WAY & OFFA'S DYKE
The Fleece House, Market Street, LD7 1BB ☎ 01547 520168 (Dana Simmons)
www.fleecehouse.co.uk Map 137/284723
£38-£43 T3 ✕ nearby ⋙(Knighton) Ⓓ Ⓑ ⊗ 👤 ! ★★★★

The Plough, 40 Market Street, LD7 1EY ☎ 01547 528041
sarahscotford@aol.com Map 137/284723
£22.50 S4 D1 T3 ⋙(Knighton) Ⓑ 🛏👤 🚗 ! 🐾

Travelly B&B, Knucklas Road, LD7 1UP ☎ 01547 528906 / 07855 143530
(Pam & Ivor Davies) pamjoandavies@aol.com Map 137/280725
£25-£30 D1 T1 F1 ✕ nearby ⋙(Knighton)
Ⓓ Ⓑ ⊗ 🛏🐾 🚗 !

Westwood, Presteigne Road, LD7 1HY ☎ 01547 520317 (Mrs Pat Sharratt)
www.knightonbedandbreakfast.co.uk Map 137/289717
£25-£30 D2 T1 ✕ nearby ⋙(Knighton)
Ⓓ Ⓑ ⊗ 🛏🐾 🚗 ! ★★★★Ⓦ

● Llandrindod Wells
WYE VALLEY WALK

Holly Farm
Howey, LD1 5PP ☎ 01597 822402 (Ruth Jones)
www.smoothhound.co.uk Map 147/049589
£30-£35 D2 T2 F1 ✕ £14, 7pm ⋙(Llandrindod Wells)
Ⓥ Ⓓ Ⓑ ⊗ 🛏🐾 👤 ★★★★

Tastefully decorated Tudor farmhouse on working farm in peaceful location.

En-suite bedrooms with breathtaking views over fields and woods. CTV and beverage trays. Two lounges, log fires, delicious cuisine using farm produce.
- Excellent area for walking, birdwatching or relaxing.
- Near red kite feeding station.
- Weekly reductions.
- Packed lunches.
- Safe parking.
- Call Mrs Ruth Jones for a brochure.

● Llangattock
BRECON BEACONS
CAMBRIAN WAY
Park Place Guest House, Park Place, The Legar, NP8 1HH ☎ 01873 810878
(Maxine Wheaton) www.parkplaceguesthouse.co.uk Map 161/215179
£25-£35 S2 D4 T3 F2 ✕ £8.95, 7pm
Ⓥ Ⓓ Ⓑ ⊗ 🛏🐾 👤 ! 🐾 ★★Ⓢ

● Llangurig
WYE VALLEY WALK
The Old Vicarage, SY18 6RN ☎ 01686 440280 (Margaret Hartey)
www.theoldvicaragellangurig.co.uk Map 136/912799
£25-£27 D3 T2 F1 ✕ £15, 5pm Ⓥ Ⓓ Ⓑ 🛏👤 🐾 ★★★★Ⓦ Ⓜ

● Llanidloes
GLYNDWR'S WAY & SEVERN WAY
Lloyds, Cambrian Place, SY18 6BX ☎ 01686 412284 (Tom Lines & Roy Hayter)
www.lloydshotel.co.uk Map 136/955844
£40 S2 D3 T2 F1 ✕ £33, 8pm Ⓥ Ⓓ Ⓑ ⊗ 👤 ★★★★

● Llanwddyn
GLYNDWR'S WAY
Gorffwysfa Guest House, Gorffwysfa, 4 Glyn Du, Lake Vyrnwy, SY10 0NB
☎ 01691 870217 (Diane Lewis)
vyrnwy-accommodation.co.uk Map 125/018189
£35-£45 D3 T1 F1 ✕ £20, 7pm Ⓥ Ⓓ Ⓑ 🛏🐾 👤 🚗 ! ★★★★Ⓦ

The Oaks
Lake Vyrnwy, SY10 0LZ ☎ 01691 870250 (Michael & Daphne Duggleby)
www.vyrnwyaccommodation.co.uk Map 125/017190
£30 D1 T2
D B ⊗ ❦ ♿ 🚗 ! 🛏 ★★★Ⓦ

Located by Lake Vyrnwy Dam
on Glyndwr's Way.
Ideal base for exploring and
walking locally.
Visit the the Berwyns or the
Arrans. Fantastic breakfast
to start the day's walking.

● **Llanwrtyd Wells**
Neuadd Arms Hotel, The Square, LD5 4RB ☎ 01591 610236
(Lindsay Ketteringham) www.neuaddarmshotel.co.uk Map 147/879467
£33 S5 D6 T9 ✕ £7, 6pm ₥(Llanwrtyd Wells) V D B ❦ ♿ ! 🛏 Ⓜ

● **Lloyney**
GLYNDWR'S WAY & OFFA'S DYKE
The Mill, Lloyney, LD7 1RG ☎ 01547 528842 (Marilyn Tippett)
www.lloyneymill.co.uk Map 137/245759
£25 S1 D2 ✕ nearby ₥(Knucklas) D ⊗ ❦ 🚗 ! F ★★★

● **Machynlleth**
GLYNDWR'S WAY
Maenllwyd, Newtown Road, SY20 8EY ☎ 01654 702928
(Margaret or Nigel Vince) www.maenllwyd.co.uk Map 135/752008
£40-£60 D4 T3 F1 ✕ nearby ₥(Machynlleth)
D B ⊗ ❦ ♿ 🚗 ! 🛏 ★★★

● **Montgomery**
OFFA'S DYKE
Dragon Hotel, SY15 6PA ☎ 01686 668359 (Mark & Sue Michaels)
www.dragonhotel.com Map 137/222964
£51-£61 S1 D13 T4 F2 ✕ £7, 7pm V D B ❦ ♿ 🚗 ! 🛏 ★★Ⓦ

Hendomen Farmhouse
Hendomen, SY15 6HB ☎ 01686 668004 (Jo & Bruce Lawson)
www.offasdykepath.com Map 137/218981
£25-£30 D2 T1
D B ⊗ ❦ 🚗 ! 🛏 ★★★Ⓦ Ⓜ

Stay in Montgomery and walk
the Dyke. Transport of walkers
can be arranged between
Knighton and Llangollen and
Glyndwr's Way. Discount for 3
nights. Owners are walkers.
Flexible breakfast times. 5 pubs (1 with pool) within a mile. Fabulous views.

● **Rhayader**
WYE VALLEY WALK & GLYNDWR'S WAY
Brynteg, East Street, LD6 5EA ☎ 01597 810052 (Mandy & Adrian Pearce)
bryntegbandb@hotmail.co.uk Map 136/972681
£24 S1 D2 T1 ✕ nearby D B ⊗ ❦ ♿ 🚗 ! ★★★Ⓦ

Ty Morgans Guest House, South Street, LD6 5BH ☎ 01597 811666
(Andrew Lewis) www.tymorgans.co.uk Map 136/972678
£33-£40 D4 F1 ✕ £15, 6pm
V D B ⊗ ❦ ♿ 🚗 ! ★★★★Ⓦ

● **Talybont-on-Usk**
BRECON BEACONS
Gethinog, LD3 7YN ☎ 01874 676258 (Christina & Roy Gale)
www.gethinog.co.uk Map 161/108233
£32 D1 T1 ✕ £16, 7pm V B ⊗ ❦ ♿

● **Trallong**
BRECON BEACONS

Beech Copse
2 Pentrebach Cottage, LD3 8HS ☎ 01874 636125 (Joy & Alan Bloss)
www.beechcopsebb.co.uk
Map 160/971297
D B ⊗ ❦ 🚗 ! ★★★Ⓦ

Comfort and tranquillity in delightful
cottage, northern edge of Brecon Beacons
National Park. Gorgeous countryside,
abundant wildlife. Excellent walking
nearby. Lifts provided. One double en-suite
room with additional single put-u-up.
Fully supported Walking Breaks also provided; see www.walkoverdale.co.uk

● **Welshpool**
GLYNDWR'S WAY, OFFA'S DYKE & SEVERN WAY
Tynllwyn Farm, SY21 9BW ☎ 01938 553175 (Jane Emberton)
www.tynllwynfarm.co.uk Map 126/215086
£27.50-£36 S4 D4 T4 F2 ₥(Welshpool)
D B ⊗ ❦ ♿ 🚗 ! ♿ ★★★★Ⓢ Ⓦ

Severn Farm, SY21 7BB ☎ 01938 555999 (Alun & Joyce Jones)
www.severnfarm.co.uk Map 126/231070
£25-£30 S3 D3 T3 F2 ₥(Welshpool) D ⊗ ❦ ♿ 🚗 !

SOUTH WALES

● **Blaenavon**
Oakfield B&B, 1 Oakfield Terrace, Varteg Road, NP4 9DS ☎ 01495 792 829
(Paul Scourfield) www.oakfieldbnb.com Map 161/252084
£35 D1 T2 ✕ nearby
D B ⊗ ❦ 🚗 ! ★★★★Ⓦ

● **Caerphilly**
Lugano Guest House, Hillside, Mountain Road, CF83 1HN ☎ 029 2085 2672
(Marian Dowson) citrus-67@hotmail.com Map 171/156863
£40 D1 T2 ✕ nearby ₥(Caerphilly)
D B ⊗ ❦ ♿ ★★★Ⓖ

● **Gower**
Old Stables Gower, Old Stables LLethryd Farm, SA2 7LH
☎ 01792 390743 (Layton James)
www.oldstablesgower.co.uk Map 159/531914
£60-£65 D3 F1 ✕ nearby D B ⊗ ❦ 🚗 ★★★★Ⓦ

● **Llanmadoc**
Forge Cottage, SA3 1DB ☎ 01792 386302 (Mike Downie)
www.forgecottagegower.co.uk Map 159/446932
£37.50 D2 F1 ✕ nearby
B ⊗ ❦ 🚗 ★★★★

WALES

● Llanrhidian

North Gower Hotel
Llanrhidian, SA3 IEE ☎ 01792 390042 (Reception)
www.northgowerhotel.co.uk Map 159/501919
£30-£45 D7 F10 ✕ £7, 7pm
Ⓥ Ⓓ Ⓑ 🍴🛏️🚗!🛁♿Ⓕ ★★Ⓦ

Our cental Gower location and range of guest facilities make us your ideal base, while exploring Gower.

For tailor-made group packages and prices – please call for details.

● Oxwich

Oxwich Bay Hotel
Oxwich Bay, SA3 1LS ☎ 01792 390329
www.oxwichbayhotel.co.uk Map 159/497865
£30 S6 D6 T7 F7 ✕ £7, 5pm
Ⓥ Ⓓ Ⓑ ✪ 🍴🛏️🛁

The only hotel located alongside the beach on the Gower Peninsular – Britain's first designated Area of Outstanding Natural Beauty. Oxwich Bay is named as "Britain's Best Beach". "A" Category rooms enjoy sweeping views of this spectacular bay.

● Pontypridd
BRECON BEACONS

Tyn-y-Wern
Ynysybwl, CF37 3LY ☎ 01443 790551 (Hermione Bruton)
www.tyn-y-wern.co.uk Map 170/065945
£30 D2 T1 ✕ nearby
Ⓓ Ⓑ ✪ 🍴🚗!🛁 ★★★Ⓦ

A Victorian mine manager's residence lovingly restored to its former glory, set in wonderfull grounds. A tranquil country retreat just 30 minutes from Cardiff. A great area for walkers and cyclists, on the edge of the Brecon Beacons.

● Wernffrwd
Ael-y-Bryn, Werffrwd, SA4 3TY ☎ 01792 850187 (Heather Bergfeld)
ael-y-bryn@tesco.net Map 159/514937
£26 D1 T1 F1 ✕ nearby Ⓓ Ⓑ ✪ 🍴🛏️🚗 🛁

SELF-CATERING

ANGLESEY

● Brynsiencyn
ISLE OF ANGLESEY COASTAL PATH

Cerrig Y Barcud Holidays ☎ 01248 430056 (Matthew & Annmarie Leonard)
www.cerrigybarcud.co.uk Map 114/480670
£185-£595 Sleeps 1-6. 5 cottages.
✪ Short breaks available ★★★★★

CARMARTHENSHIRE

● Newcastle Emlyn

Llainddu Farm Cottage
☎ 01559 371369 (Cath Abbott)
llainddu-farm.co.uk Map 145/350347
£145-£540 Sleeps 2-7. 1 cottage.
✪ 🛁 Short breaks available

Situated in stunning countryside on a 15-acre smallholding with private woodland and abundant wildlife, this delightfully refurbished spacious cottage provides a secluded rural retreat, perfect both for family groups and smaller parties. Provides quality accommodation of a high standard.

CEREDIGION

● Aberporth
Frances & Peter Miller ☎ 01239 810595
milldrove@aol.com Map 145/259510
£180-£350 Sleeps 1-4. 2 cottages. ✪ 🛁

● Cardigan
Y Cwm, Aberporth ☎ 01239810525 (Glynis Evans)
sian.evans1@virgin.net Map 145/253509
£350-£500 Sleeps 2-4. 1 apartment. 🛁 Short breaks available

● Llanilar
Nantclyd ☎ 01974 241543 (Liz Findlay)
www.nantclydorganics.co.uk Map 135/622744
£150-£180 Sleeps 1-6. 1 caravan. ✪ Short breaks available

● New Quay
Trem Y Môr ☎ 01545 580 565/ 580 713 (Mair Jones / Eleri Jones)
emyrll.jones@btopenworld.com Map 146/429590
£250-£580 Sleeps 1-6. 1 cottage.
✪ Short breaks available

Ty Hen Farm Cottages and Leisure Centre ☎ 01545 560346 (Roni Kelly)
www.tyhencottages.co.uk Map 145/359558
£250-£900 Sleeps 1-8. 8 cottages.
✪ 🛁 Short breaks available

Park Hall
☎ 01545 560996 (Carol Burgess)
www.park-hall.co.uk Map 200/827608
£1585-£2695 Sleeps 1-20. 1 large house.
Short breaks available ★★★★

Nestling within a beautiful valley, 300m from Cwmtydu Beach on the Ceredigion Heritage Coast, and set in 2.5 acres of lovely, lawned gardens.

Outstanding views of the sea. Spacious, comfortable and perfect venue for walking holidays, reunions, family holidays, special anniversaries and weddings. Eight bedrooms (7 en-suite), two lounges both with open fires and one with a piano. Large, sunny conservatory/dining room and games room.

Walking from the door, horse-riding, sea and fresh water fishing, clay pigeon shooting, canoeing, golf, bowls, tennis, quad-biking all within easy reach. Snowdon, Tenby and the Gower Peninsula within driving distance.

GWYNEDD

● Bangor
SNOWDONIA/ERYRI

Ogwen Valley Holidays
☎ 01248 600122 (Mrs Jill Jones)
www.ogwensnowdonia.co.uk Map 119/251746
£169-£589 Sleeps 2-6. 1 cottage, 1 flat.
Short breaks available ★★★★

Superb Snowdonia locations. Sunny positions, lovely gardens, fine views. Traditional Welsh Cottages, cosy all seasons. Three-bedroomed cottage for six. Cottage flat for 2 (+1 on fold-out). Convenient and accessible. Near River Ogwen and cyclepath. 15 mins' drive to coast and Anglesey.

● Beddgelert
SNOWDONIA/ERYRI
CAMBRIAN WAY

Coed Gelert Holiday Cottages ☎ 01766 890880 (Joan Firth)
www.snowdonia-cottages.net Map 115/590480
£320-£800 Sleeps 2-6. 5 cottage.
Short breaks available ★★★★★ Ⓦ

AROSFA ☎ 01766 890498 (Julie Owen)
www.arosfa-beddgelert.co.uk Map 115/591482
£230-£385 Sleeps 1-2. 1 cottage. ☺

● Betws Garmon
SNOWDONIA/ERYRI

Ystrad Isaf, Betws Garmon ☎ 01286 650552 (Veronica Owen)
josginwaun@hotmail.com Map 115/536575
£200-£600 Sleeps 2-5. 1 farmhouse.
☺ Short breaks available ★★★★

● Borth-y-Gest
SNOWDONIA/ERYRI

Sea Captain's House ☎ 020 7278 2539 (David Cole)
uk.geocities.com/davidygest Map 124/564373
£180-£510 Sleeps 2-7. 1 cottage.
Short breaks available ★★★

● Bronaber
SNOWDONIA/ERYRI

Trawsfynydd Holiday Village
☎ 01766 540219
www.logcabins-skiwales.co.uk Map 124/715319
£240-£510 Sleeps 4-8. 300 log cabins.
Short breaks available

Our elevated holiday village in the Snowdonia National Park overlooks the Rhinog Mountains and is an ideal base to explore the mountains between Cadair Idris and Snowdon. We offer self-catering log cabins sleeping 4-8 people and a bunkhouse sleeping 22.

● Caernarfon

Hafoty Farm Cottages
☎ 01286 830144 (Elaine Moss)
www.hafoty.com Map 115/501584
£210-£660 Sleeps 2-6. 6 cottages.
☺ Short breaks available Ⓦ

Set on the edge of Snowdonia, Hafoty Farm Cottages provide the perfect base for exploring Anglesey, the Llyn Peninsula, Caernarfon and the surrounding countryside. The cottages, converted from old farm barns, provide the highest standard in self-catering facilities.

WALES

● Dolgellau
SNOWDONIA/ERYRI
CAMBRIAN WAY

Mrs O Williams ☎ 01341 430277
Map 124/735192
£150-£180 Sleeps 1-6. 1 caravan. ⊛

Brynygwin Isaf
☎ 01341 423481 (Gilbert Gauntlett)
www.holidaysinwales.fsnet.co.uk Map 124/735192
£145-£750 Sleeps 2-24. 2 cottages.
⚑ Short breaks available

Two self-contained sections of family country house. Built 1806 with large, comfortably furnished rooms, superb views, extensive garden and character cottages. 1 mile from Dolgellau. Over 30 walk guidesheets provided. Log fires. Open all year. Children/pets welcome. Email: holidays_wales@onetel.com

● Llanberis
SNOWDONIA/ERYRI

Cadfan House
Llanberis ☎ 07879 452 624 (Kathryn Payne)
www.llanberisaccommodation.com Map 114/576603
£300-£400 Sleeps 5-7. 1 cottage.
⊛ ⚑ Short breaks available ★★★

Cadfan House is a self-catering house designed with the walker and activity lover in mind. The beds are comfy, the kitchen well equipped and the fire ready to toast your feet after a day in the Snowdonia mountains.

● Pwllheli
SNOWDONIA/ERYRI

10 West End Pwllheli ☎ 01291 673883 (Sherene Edwards)
gsjdedwards@tiscali.co.uk Map 123/369341
£449-£999 Sleeps 4-8. 1 apartment.
⊛ Short breaks available

● Tywyn
SNOWDONIA/ERYRI

Pant y Neuadd Cottages
☎ 01654711393 (Debra Stone)
www.pantyneuaddcaravanpark.co.uk Map 135/593005
£190-£470 Sleeps 2-4. 3 cottages.
⊛ ⚑ Short breaks available ★★★★★

Three cosy self-catering cottages offering top quality accommodation, conveniently located where the mountains meet the sea. A wealth of walking and bird watching opportunities right on our doorstep. Bedlinen, towels, heating and electricity included in the price.

MONMOUTHSHIRE

● Hendre
OFFA'S DYKE

Ciderhouse Cottage ☎ 01600 716435 (Cathy Bowen)
www.penylanfarm.co.uk Map 116/191678
£300-£575 Sleeps 1-7. 1 cottage. ⊛ ♿ Ⓕ Short breaks available ★★★★

NORTH EAST WALES

● Llangollen
OFFA'S DYKE & CLWYDIAN WAY

Tan Y Ddol
☎ 01206 855244 (Judith Watts)
www.tanyddol.co.uk Map 117/211423
£240-£390 Sleeps 1-4. 1 self-catering house.
⊛ Ⓕ Short breaks available ★★★★Ⓜ

This modern 2-bedroom property is situated on the outskirts of Llangollen, in a quite private mews. It is ideally situated for outdoor activities, hill and valley walking, canoeing, sightseeing and many other tourist attractions. Walking is straight from the door!

● Ruthin
OFFA'S DYKE & CLWYDIAN WAY

The Old Dairy at Penrhos Farm ☎ 01824 707641 (Diane Thomas)
www.penrhosfarm.com Map 116/136585
£215-£330 Sleeps 2-5. 1 cottage. ⊛ Short breaks available

The Cottage
☎ 07712659064 (Beverley Morgan-Davies)
www.thecottage-ruthin.co.uk Map 116/122614
£300-£450 Sleeps 1-4. 1 barn conversion/cottage.
⊛ Short breaks available

A walker's paradise! Beautiful 500yr-old luxury barn conversion nestled at the foot of the Clwydian mountain range in an AONB. 3 miles from the historic market town of Ruthin. 30mins Snowdonia National Park & wonderful North Wales coast.

PEMBROKESHIRE

● Broad Haven
PEMBROKESHIRE COAST NATIONAL PARK
PEMBROKESHIRE COAST PATH

St Bride's Bay View Apartment ☎ 01225 891090 (Denise Cooke)
www.stbridesbayview.com Map 157/861137
£225-£575 Sleeps 1-6. 1 apartment. ⊛ Short breaks available ★★★★

18 Puffin Way ☎ 01270 610752 (Sue price)
sue@priceharris.co.uk Map 157/862137
£295-£745 Sleeps 1-7. 1 cottage. ⊛ Short breaks available ★★★★★Ⓜ

● Haverfordwest

PEMBROKESHIRE COAST NATIONAL PARK

PEMBROKESHIRE COAST PATH

Caban Tawel ☎ 01348 840375 (Richard & Elizabeth James)
www.newtoneastfarm.co.uk Map 157/907189
£250-£450 Sleeps 1-6. 1 log cabin.
⊗ 🛏 Short breaks available ★★★★

Rock Cottage ☎ 07747 101024 (Ceri Crichton)
www.holidaylettings.co.uk/rentals/houghton/32293 Map 157/978082
£220-£475 Sleeps 1-5. 1 cottage.
⊗ 🛏 Short breaks available

● Moylegrove

PEMBROKESHIRE COAST NATIONAL PARK

PEMBROKESHIRE COAST PATH

Ty Newydd Cottage ☎ 01239 881280 (Dawn Cotton)
Map 145/118446
£325-£470 Sleeps 2-5. 3 cottages. 🛏 Short breaks available

● Rosebush

PEMBROKESHIRE COAST NATIONAL PARK

Coastal Cottages of Pembrokeshire
☎ 01437 765765 (Frances Edwards)
www.coastalcottages.co.uk Map 157/965159
£200-£2000 Sleeps 2-16. 550 cottages.
♿ F 🛏 Short breaks available ★★★★★ Ⓢ Ⓖ

Voted the "Best in Wales" at the National Tourism awards.

Coastal Cottages offer 550 Cottages along the Pembrokeshire Coast National Park.

Coastal Cottages have a free booking service for maps, books, restaurants and guided walks.

10% discount off-season if you mention the Ramblers' Association when booking. Please call 01437 765765 or visit www.coastalcottages.co.uk for all our live availability and online booking.

Preseli Holidays ☎ 01437 532495 (Sue Toogood)
www.preseliholidays.co.uk Map 145/059297
£215-£555 Sleeps 2-5. 4 cottages and log cabins. ⊗ Short breaks available

● St Dogmaels

PEMBROKESHIRE COAST PATH

Trenewydd Farm Cottages ☎ 01239 612370 (Tony and Linda Price)
www.cottages-wales.com Map 145/148446
£199-£990 Sleeps 2-13. 6 s/c cottages and B&B.
⊗ ♿ 🛏 Short breaks available

● St. Davids

PEMBROKESHIRE COAST NATIONAL PARK

PEMBROKESHIRE COAST PATH

Lower Porthmawr
☎ 07976 780928 (Debbie Henchoz)
debbiehenchoz@mac.com Map 157/735274
£300-£850 Sleeps 1-6. 1 cottage.
⊗ 🛏 Short breaks available

Lower Porthmawr is located in one of the most enviable positions in Pembrokeshire. Sitting above the internationally acclaimed Whitesands Beach with uninterrupted coastal views and only three minutes from the Pembrokeshire Coastal Path, you will want to return time and time again — as all of our guests do!

Even when the wind is howling you can snuggle in front of the wood burning stove and plan the next walk.

● Tenby

PEMBROKESHIRE COAST NATIONAL PARK

PEMBROKESHIRE COAST PATH

Fuchsias Annexe ☎ 01834 843057 (June Howell)
howell.penally@btinternet.com Map 158/115997
£150-£190 Sleeps 1-3. 1 bungalow annexe. ⊗ Short breaks available Ⓜ

POWYS

● Crickhowell

BRECON BEACONS

CAMBRIAN WAY

Westcombe House
☎ 01873 811759 (Lawrence Watts)
ljjw@crickhowell.fslife.co.uk Map 161/217183
£500-£950 Sleeps 2-10. 1 large detached house.
🛏 Short breaks available

Westcombe House is in the centre of Crickhowell, a small market town nestling beneath the Black Mountains and the Brecon Beacons. 300 yds from the award winning Bear Hotel and Nantyffin cider mill. Large utility/boot room ideal for walkers.

WALES

● Hay-on-Wye
BRECON BEACONS
OFFA'S DYKE

Glyn Farm Granary
☎ 01497851622 (Peter Holtorp)
www.hay-on-wye/accommodation/glyn farm granary Map 148/184466
£400-£500 Sleeps 4-6. I farmhouse annex.
Ⓧ Ⓢ Short breaks available ★★★★

Spacious and comprehensively equipped accommodation on a family-run working farm. 5 miles from Hay-on-Wye. Direct footpath access to the Radnorshire Hills, linking with Offa's Dyke path. Within easy reach of the Brecon Beacons and the Black Mountains.

● Lake Vyrnwy
SNOWDONIA/ERYRI
GLYNDWR'S WAY

Eunant
☎ 01691 870321 (Bronwen Davies)
www.terrafirmatravel.com Map 160/953227
£369-£595 Sleeps 1-7. I gite.
Ⓢ Short breaks available

Lovely self-catering accommodation; large farmhouse, woodburning stove, spacious conservatory. Fabulous walking, cycling and fishing in this area of outstanding natural beauty, on the edge of the beautiful Berwyn hills, not far from Snowdonia. Castles, beaches and more...

● Llanafan Fawr

Tyn-y-Beili Holiday Barn
☎ 01591 620697 (Caroline Cannons)
www.tyn-y-beili.com Map 147/935546
£150-£650 Sleeps 1-16. 3 converted barn.
Ⓧ Short breaks available

Lovely old barn converted into 3 holiday lets, surrounded by stunning scenery. Very peaceful. Lovely walks in local area, good pub serving great food and local shop 4 miles. Builth Wells 9 miles.

Pontbren Ddu
☎ 01981 540030 (Sarah Dean)
www.pontbren-ddu.co.uk Map 147/945574
£325-£650 Sleeps 1-4. I detached property.
Ⓧ Ⓢ Short breaks available

Quietly nestling in its own enclosed garden, surrounded by rugged hills and an unspoilt rural landscape, Pontbren is the last cottage on a single-track road leading onto 16,500 acres of National Trust countryside with wonderful walks literally on the doorstep.

● Llanidloes
GLYNDWR'S WAY & SEVERN WAY

Barn View Cottages ☎ 01686 413527 (Jon Phillips)
www.barnviewcottages.com Map 136/911849
£200-£420 Sleeps 1-11. 3 cottages.
Ⓧ Ⓢ Short breaks available Ⓦ

● Machynlleth
SNOWDONIA/ERYRI
GLYNDWR'S WAY

Lynn & John Williams ☎ 01654 702952 (Lynn & John Williams)
www.lynn.john.williams.care4free.net Map 135/768033
£170-£250 Sleeps 2-10. 2 cottages.
Ⓧ Ⓢ Short breaks available ★★★Ⓦ

● Rhayder
WYE VALLEY WALK

Wern Fach ☎ 0118 9862409 (Richard Green)
www.wernfach.co.uk Map 147/993648
£280-£350 Sleeps 1-6. I cottage. Ⓧ

● Welshpool
GLYNDWR'S WAY, OFFA'S DYKE & SEVERN WAY

Ty Gwyn Cottage
☎ 01516783966 (Mr & Mrs Campbell)
www.casitawales.co.uk Map 125/991106
£250-£490 Sleeps 5-6. I cottage.
Ⓧ Ⓢ Short breaks available

Nestling in elevated hillside location, beautiful tranquil surroundings, fabulous views across Banwy valley. Excellent local walks, easy reach of mid-Wales attractions. Walkers with dogs welcome. Fully equipped kitchen, bed linen provided. Ample parking, large conservatory, spacious lounge/dining room, wood burner.

SOUTH WALES

● Mumbles

Owen's Barn ☎ 01792368631 (Jane Grostate)
www.owensbarn.co.uk Map 119/251746
£280-£580 Sleeps 1-4. I cottage. Ⓧ Short breaks available ★★★★

● Pontypridd
BRECON BEACONS

Tyn-y-Wern Country House
☎ 01443 790551 (Mrs Hermione Bruton)
www.tyn-y-wern.co.uk Map 170/062945
£250-£250 Sleeps 2-4. 2 lodges.
Ⓧ Ⓖ Ⓕ Ⓢ Short breaks available ★★★★Ⓦ

Stylish conversion of an old building, offering modern facilities in a tranquil country retreat just 30 mins from Cardiff. Spectacular undiscovered walking and cycling area on the end of the Brecon Beacons. Well equipped, dishwasher, laundry room, price includes all linen.

● Port Eynon

Number 62
☎ 01527 576251 (Jules Evans)
www.number62.co.uk Map 159/463875
£250-£460 Sleeps 6. 1 bungalow.
& F ⚡ Short breaks available ★★★★

Really dog-friendly bungalow on the beautiful Gower Peninsula. Tiled and wooden floors throughout, fully fitted kitchen including dishwasher. Bathroom and separate shower room. Really easy to keep clean and near to beautiful coastal walks. Great for winter breaks.

GROUPS, HOSTELS, BUNKHOUSES, CAMPSITES & OTHERS

ANGLESEY

● Holyhead
ISLE OF ANGLESEY COASTAL PATH

Anglesey Outdoors, Porthdafarch Road, LL65 2LP ☎ 01407 769351
www.angleseyoutdoors.com Map 114/233803
SC, BB, DBB, FB £10-£15 per night Sleeps 2-80.
Hostel, bunkhouse and camping. Self-contained house.
🚶(Holyhead) V D ⊗ 🐾

CARMARTHENSHIRE

● Drefach Felindre

Ceridwen
Penybanc farm, Velindre, SA44 5XE ☎ 01559 370211 (Lottie Slater)
www.ceridwencentre.co.uk Map 145/362376
SC, DBB, FB £910-£1814 per week Sleeps 11-25. Converted smithy.
V D ⊗ 🐾 🍴 ! 🏇 ★★★

Sitting on a hillside and overlooking woodland in the Teifi valley, Ceridwen is full of traditional charm and character with modern facilities. Once the Welsh woollen industry capital, this fascinating area is littered with crumbling mills and old drovers roads.

GWYNEDD

● Beddgelert
SNOWDONIA/ERYRI
CAMBRIAN WAY

Hafod Y Llan Campsite, Hafod Y Llan, Nantgwynant, LL55 4NL
☎ 01766 510120 (Alison Ellis) Alison.Ellis@nationaltrust.org.uk
Map 115/632498
£2.50-£2.50 per night Sleeps 1-30. campsite. 🏇 &

Craflwyn
Beddgelert, LL55 4NG ☎ 01766 510120 (Eirian Jones)
www.craflwyn.org Map 115/596488
SC, DBB, FB £910-£2310 per week Sleeps 12-26. Bunkhouse and hall.
D ⊗ & F

Craflwyn is unique, located in the heart of Snowdonia. It is a place to get together and to get away from it all. Run by the National Trust, it offers a choice of a bunkhouse or a 19th-century Hall.

● Criccieth

Lion Hotel
Y Maes, LL52 0AA ☎ 01766 522460 (Sandra Burnett)
www.lionhotelcriccieth.co.uk Map 123/498381
BB, DBB, FB £32-£43 per night Sleeps 2-96. Hotel. 🚶(Criccieth)
V ⊗ 🐾 ! 🏇 & F ★★★ Ⓜ

The Lion Hotel dates back to the early 1700's when it was known as 'Ty'n y Maes' (the house on the green). This splendid hotel has the advantage of being centrally situated on the green where it commands spectacular views of the bay, mountains & castle.
Seperate annexe 'Castle View Cottage' houses twelve bedrooms.
A great base for walking in Snowdonia or the Llyn.
Packed lunches organised. Fully Licensed. Group rates available.

MONMOUTHSHIRE

● Abergavenny
BRECON BEACONS
CAMBRIAN WAY

Mulberry House Hostel
The Old Convent, Penypound, NP7 5UD ☎ 01873 855959
(Vivienne Compton) www.mulberrycentre.com Map 161/296146
BB, DBB, FB £21-£24 per night Sleeps 1-77. 3-star hostel.
🚶(Abergavenny) V D ⊗ 🐾 ★★★ Ⓜ

Situated on the edge of the Brecon Beacons National Park, Mulberry House is ideally situated as a base from which to explore the mountains, South Wales and the Welsh Borders.
Beautiful scenery and a warm welcome awaits visitors to Abergavenny.

PUZZLED BY THE MAP REFERENCES?
See How to use a map and compass pp68–71

WALES

POWYS

● Brecon
BRECON BEACONS

Canal Barn Bunkhouse, Ty Camlas, Canal Bank, LD3 7HH
☎ 01874 625361 (Ralph Day) bunkhouse-brecon-beacons-wales.co.uk
Map 160/051279
SC £12.50 per night Sleeps 6-24. bunkhouse. D Ⓔ ♨ ⅄ F ★★★★

● Crickhowell
BRECON BEACONS
CAMBRIAN WAY

Gliffaes Country House Hotel
NP8 1RH ☎ 01874 730 371 (Reception)
www.gliffaeshotel.com Map 161/170198
BB, DBB £78.50-£105 per night Sleeps 1-46. Country house hotel.
Ⓥ D Ⓔ ♨ ⅄ ! ♨ ⅄ F ★★★Ⓢ Ⓦ

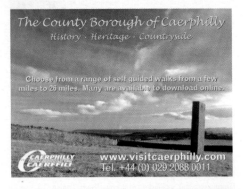

A comfortable base for you to explore the Brecon Beacons and Black Mountains. Come back to log fires and a great locally-sourced dinner before a quiet night's sleep. Fantastic riverside location with walks from the front door.

● Llanwrtyd Wells
Neuadd Arms Hotel, The Square, LD5 4RB ☎ 01591 610236
(Lindsay & Catherine Ketteringham) www.neuaddarmshotel.co.uk
Map 147/879467
BB £22 per night Sleeps 10-37. Group accommodation hotel.
₩(Llanwrtyd Wells) Ⓥ D 🐾 Ⓜ

● Rhayader
WYE VALLEY WALK & GLYNDWR'S WAY

Woodhouse Farm
Woodhouse, St Harmon, LD6 5LY ☎ 01597 870081 (Mr J Adams)
www.woodhouse-farm.org.uk Map 136/998750
SC, DBB £2.50-£15 per night Sleeps 1-20. Bunkhouse, campsite & tipi.
D Ⓔ 🐾 ⊶ ! ♨ ⅄ F

Woodhouse is a nature reserve alongside River Marteg in beautiful remote 'Red Kite' country. Camping and caravanning, secluded, level, electric hookups. Tipi to rent (sleeps 8). Bunkhouse (sleeps 20) nearing completion, opening 2008. Breakfast, meals and pickup service on request.

● Ystradfellte
BRECON BEACONS

Clyngwyn Bunkhouse, Ystradfellte Road, SA11 5US ☎ 01639722930
(Julie Hurst) www.bunkhouse-south-wales.co.uk Map 160/912106
SC, BB Sleeps 4-15. bunkhouse. D Ⓔ 🐾 ⊶ ♨ ★★★

Wales Valleys
Walking Festival

A variety of walks throughout the Valleys of Southern Wales to suit all abilities and interests.

5th - 21st September 2008

For further information on the festival and other walks throughout the year, please contact:-

Brochure or Bookings - 01495 355800
Information - 01495 355937

info@walkingwalesvalleys.uk2.net
www.wisdomandwalks.co.uk

SKYE, GLENBRITTLE

Holiday Cottage at the foot of the spectacular Cuillin mountains, close to lovely beach. Well equipped. Sleeps 5. Stunning views from cottage. Mountain and coastal walks direct from the door. From £240 per week.

Tel: 01883 715301

Email: cuillin.lodge@ntlworld.com
Web: www.cuillinlodge.co.uk

SCOTLAND

Long Distance Paths

Cateran Trail ....CAT

Cowal Way ....COW

Fife Coastal Path ....FFC

Great Glen Way ....GGN

Pennine Way ....PNN

Rob Roy Way ....RRY

Southern Upland Way ....UP

Speyside Way ....SPS

St Cuthbert's Way ....STC

West Highland Way ....WHL

**See Paths & Access p25 for full
details of LDPs and waymarks**

National Parks

Cairngorms
Loch Lomond & The Trossachs

MOONLIGHT OVER GLENCOE,
HIGHLAND

WALK...   ...THE ELIE CHAIN WALK

At Shell Bay the Fife Coastal Path splits. One way continues over the cliff to Kingcraig Point, and the other goes straight down on to the cliff-face in an exciting scramble along the UK's only 'via ferrata' (chain-assisted scramble). The steep, carved steps and eight vertical and horizontal chains take you on a dramatic route past wave-beaten volcanic rockpools and caves, requiring sturdy footwear and a cool head for heights. Allow 1.5 hours to go the distance at a comfortable rate, including time to look for 'eggs' at the Dragon's Nesting Ground.

See p28 for more about the Fife Coastal Path and always check with the local coastguard (☎ 01333 450666) that the tide is out before attempting the chain walk.

VISIT...   ...CAPE WRATH

Britain's most northwesterly point is named after the Norse for turning point, past which the Viking ships knew they were heading for home. Getting there from the mainland involves a ferry across the Kyle of Durness – where Common seals can often be seen – and then a long walk (or bus-ride) over some rough but magnificent scenery. An early 19th-century lighthouse stands at the cape. Other sights worth seeing include Kervaig House – a bothy overlooking a beautiful bay – and Clò Mór cliffs – the highest sea cliffs on mainland Britain at 620ft, and a major nesting site for birds.

For more information about walks in the area, transport and access restrictions due to MoD activity, visit www.capewrath.org.uk or ☎ 01971 511343.

SEE... ...RED DEER AT GALLOWAY FOREST

Britain's largest forest park at 300 square miles, Galloway Forest is so huge it's known as the 'Highlands of the Lowlands'. The sheer range of rugged and isolated terrain makes it a haven for some of our island's rarest species, including Golden Eagles, red squirrels and otters. But the only guaranteed wildlife encounter is at the Red Deer Range near Clatteringshaws Wildlife Centre, where guided walks and supervised handling of Britain's largest land mammal (and Scotland's most iconic) have been running for 30 years. The autumn tours are renowned for the awesome noise of the great stags roaring during the rut.

Contact the visitor centre on ☎ 01644 420285 or visit the Forestry Commission's website www.forestry.gov.uk for further information.

LOCAL RAMBLERS GROUPS... Helensburgh and West Dunbartonshire Group is recording red squirrel sightings on their walks to help the Scottish Squirrel Survey monitor the impact of the grey species on the native red. Visit www.scottishsquirrelsurvey.co.uk to learn more... **Bearsden and Milngavie Group has begun a short walks programme (between 3–4 miles, maximum two hours duration) open to members and non-members on alternate Wednesdays. Contact them for details (see p98)...** Monklands Group offers an A–Z guide to the best pubs, tearooms and chippies in Scotland on its website (see p98).

SCOTLAND

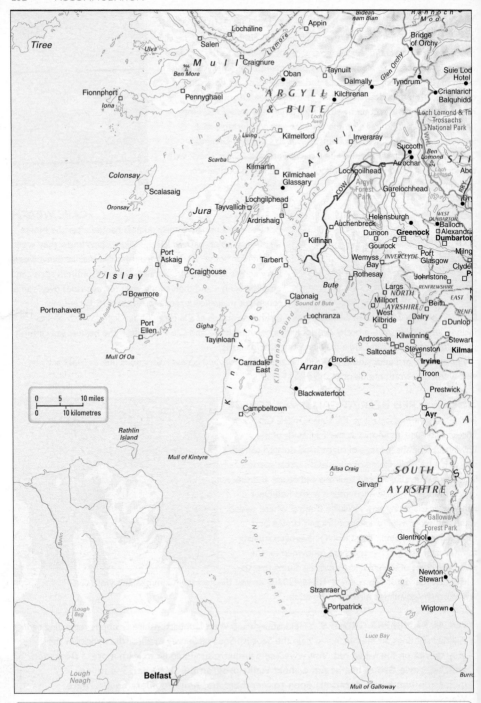

MAP 253

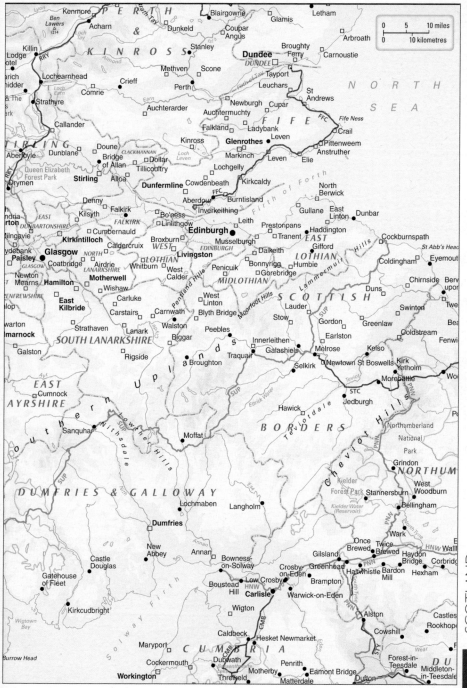

SCOTLAND

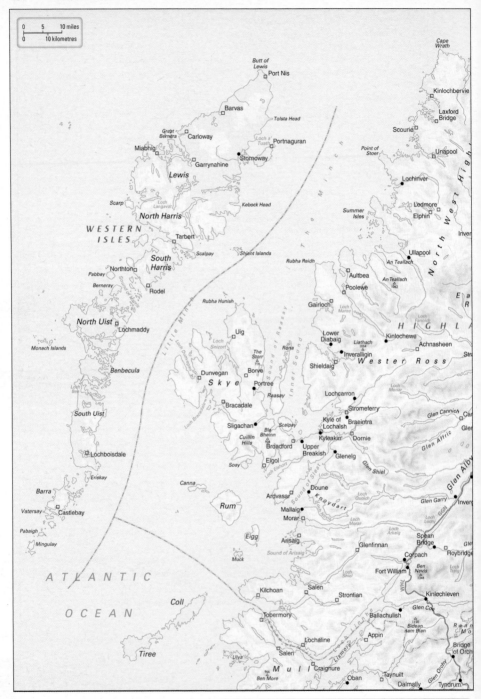

MAP 255

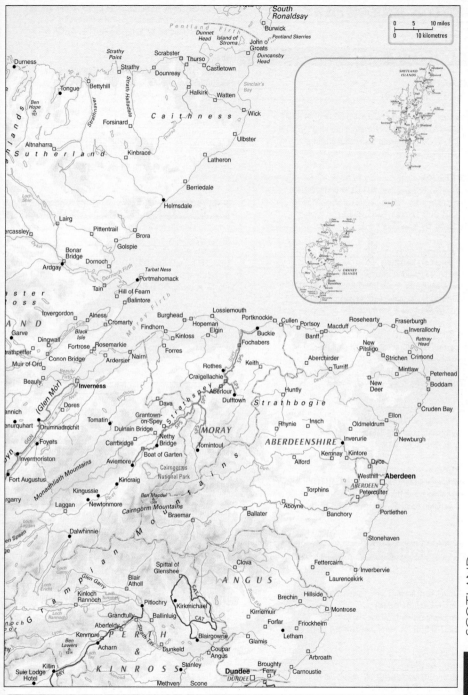

BED & BREAKFAST

ARGYLL & BUTE

● Arrochar
LOCH LOMOND & THE TROSSACHS
COWAL WAY

Ben Bheula Bed & Breakfast, Succoth, G83 7AL ☎ 01301 702184
(Barbara & Robert Webb) www.benbheula.co.uk Map 56/294049
£27.50–£40 D2 T1 ✕ nearby ⇜(Arrochar & Tarbet)
Ⓓ Ⓑ 🍴 👶 🚗 ! 🐾

● Dalmally
Craigroyston, Monument Road, PA33 1AA ☎ 01838 200234
(Sandra Boardman) www.craigroyston.com Map 50/158271
£22–£24 D1 T1 ✕ nearby ⇜(Dalmally)
Ⓓ Ⓑ 🛇 🍴 👶 🚗 🐾 ★★★Ⓦ

● Helensburgh
LOCH LOMOND & THE TROSSACHS

Balmillig, 64B Colquhoun Street, G84 9JP ☎ 01436 674922
(Anne & John Urquhart) www.balmillig.co.uk Map 56/297830
£32–£35 D2 T1 ✕ nearby ⇜(Helensburgh Central)
Ⓓ Ⓑ 🛇 🍴 👶 🚗 ! ★★★★Ⓖ Ⓦ

● Kilchrenan
Roineabhal, PA35 1HD ☎ 01866 833207 (Maria Soep)
www.roineabhal.com Map 50/033239
£45–£55 D2 T1 ✕ £32.50, 5pm
Ⓥ Ⓓ Ⓑ 🛇 🍴 👶 🚗 ! 👶 🚿 Ⓕ ★★★★

● Kilmichael Glassary
The Horseshoe Inn, PA31 8QA ☎ 01546 606369
www.horseshoeinn.biz Map 55/852930
£25 D2 T2 F1 Ⓑ 🛇 🍴 👶 🚗 🐾

● Oban
Kathmore, Soroba Road, PA34 4JF ☎ 01631 562104 (Mrs M Wardhaugh)
www.kathmore.co.uk Map 49/860292
✕ ⇜(Oban) Ⓓ Ⓑ 🛇 🍴 ★★★

CENTRAL BELT

● Edinburgh
Elderfields Guest House, 23 Spring Gardens, Holyrood, EH8 8HU
☎ 0131 6202222 (M Elderfield)
www.guest-houses-edinburgh.com Map 66/274741
£26–£32 S1 D2 T2 ✕ nearby ⇜(Wavereley) Ⓓ Ⓑ 🛇 🍴 👶

● Glasgow
WEST HIGHLAND WAY

Adelaide's, 209 Bath Street, G2 4HZ ☎ 0141 248 4970
www.adelaides.co.uk Map 64/584657
£32–£45 S2 D2 T2 F2 ✕ nearby ⇜(Glasgow Central)
Ⓓ Ⓑ 🛇 🍴 👶 ★★

Barrisdale Guest House, 115 Randolph Road, G11 7DS ☎ 0141 339 7589
(Ron Phillips) www.barrisdale-bnb.co.uk Map 64/546678
£30 S3 D3 T3 F1 ✕ nearby ⇜(Hyndland) Ⓓ Ⓑ 🛇 🍴 👶

● Haddington
Eaglescairnie Mains, Gifford, EH41 4HN ☎ 01620 810491
(Barbara Williams) www.eaglescairnie.com Map 66/516689
Ⓓ Ⓑ 🛇 🍴 🚗 🐾 ★★★★

● Leven
FIFE COASTAL PATH

Fluthers Wood B&B, Cupar Road, KY8 5NN ☎ 01333 351167
(Rosemary Lawson) www.flutherswood.freeuk.com Map 59/380043
£35 D2 ✕ £12, 6pm Ⓥ Ⓓ Ⓑ 🛇 🍴 👶 🚗 ! ★★★Ⓦ

DUMFRIES & GALLOWAY

● Glentrool
SOUTHERN UPLAND WAY

Lorien, 61 Glentrool Village, DG8 6SY ☎ 01671 840315 (Morag McIlwraith)
morag.lorien61@btinternet.com Map 77/358783
£20 T2 ✕ nearby Ⓓ Ⓑ 🛇 🍴 🚗 ! 🐾

● Langholm
Carnlea, 16 Hillside Crescent, DG13 0EE ☎ 013873 80284
(Meg Braithwaite) www.carnlea.co.uk Map 79/370839
£30 D1 T1 ✕ nearby Ⓓ Ⓑ 🛇 🍴 👶 🚗 🐾 ★★★

● Moffat
SOUTHERN UPLAND WAY

Morag, 19 Old Carlisle Road, DG10 9QJ ☎ 01683 220690 (Mrs L Taylor)
morag_moffat44@btopenworld.com Map 78/093046
£25–£29 S2 D2 T1
Ⓓ Ⓑ 🛇 🍴 👶 ★★★Ⓦ

North Nethermiln, Old Carlisle Road, DG10 9QJ ☎ 01683 220325
(Heather Quigley) Map 78/093046
£20–£25 S1 D2 T1 F1 ✕ £10, 6pm
Ⓥ Ⓓ 🛇 🍴 👶 🚗 !

> ### Bridge House
> Well Road, DG10 9JT ☎ 01683 220558
> www.bridgehousemoffat.co.uk Map 78/091057
> £45 D4 T2 F1 ✕ £23, 7pm
> Ⓥ Ⓓ Ⓑ 🛇 👶 ★★★★
>
>
> A fine Victorian property, Bridge House lies in attractive gardens in a quiet residential area on the fringe of the town. Family-run, the atmosphere is friendly and relaxed. The chef/proprietor provides excellent dinners for residents.

● Newton Stewart
Kilwarlin, 4 Corvisel Road, DG8 6LN ☎ 01671 403047 (Hazel Dickson)
hazel@kilwarlin.plus.com Map 83/409650
£24 S1 D1 F1 ✕ nearby Ⓓ 🛇 🍴 👶 🚗 ★★★Ⓦ

HIGHLAND

● Ardgay

Corvost B&B, Corvost, IV24 3BP ☎ 01863 755317
(Mrs Doreen Munro) Map 21/545915
£19 S1 D1 T1 ✕ £10, 7pm ⊛ 🍴🛏 ★★

● Aviemore
CAIRNGORMS
SPEYSIDE WAY

Ravenscraig Guest House, Grampian Road, PH22 1RP ☎ 01479 810278
(Jonathan Gatenby) www.aviemoreonline.com Map 35/895131
✕ ⚶(Aviemore) D B ⊛ 🍴🚗 ★★★

● Ballachulish
WEST HIGHLAND WAY

Park View, 18 Park Road, PH49 4JS ☎ 01855 811560 (Diana Macaskill)
www.glencoe-parkview.co.uk Map 41/080582
£25 S1 D2 T1 ✕ nearby D ⊛ 🍴🛏 ★★★Ⓦ

Fern Villa Guest House
Loanfern, PH49 4JE ☎ 01855 811393 (Catherine Susans)
www.fernvilla.org.uk Map 41/081580
£20-£37 D3 T2 ✕ nearby
D B ⊛ 🍴🛏🚗 ★★★

A friendly family-run guest house offering early cooked breakfasts. Pick up and drop off available for Kinlochleven and Kingshouse for the WHW. Ideally located for overnight stops or longer breaks. Plenty to do and see.

● Braeintra

Soluis Mu Thuath
IV53 8UP ☎ 01599 577219 (Margaret Arscott)
www.highlandsaccommodation.co.uk Map 24/864324
£23-£45 D1 T3 F1 ✕ £13.50, 7:30pm ⚶(Strome Ferry)
V D B ⊛ 🍴🛏🚗!🧺♿F ★★★

Situated in peaceful Strath Ascaig on the road to the north from Plockton Soluis Mu Thuath is ideal for walking in Kintail, Isle of Skye, Strath Carron and Torridon. Mu Thuath is a family-run guest house where a warm welcome awaits all walkers.

● Doune

Doune - Knoydart
PH41 4PL ☎ 01687 462667 (Martin Davies)
www.doune-knoydart.co.uk Map 33/705035
£68 S1 F3 ✕ £25, 7:30pm
V D B ⊛ 🍴🛏🚗! ★★★Ⓢ Ⓦ

Mountains, sea, wildlife, tranquillity, award-winning food, stunning sunsets & great walking. Located on the western tip of the remote Knoydart peninsula Doune provides a spectacular holiday setting for individuals, couples, families & small groups. (Price inc. all meals.)

● Fort William
WEST HIGHLAND WAY & GREAT GLEN WAY

Craig Nevis Guest House, Belford Road, PH33 6BU ☎ 01397 702023
www.craignevis.co.uk Map 41/108741
£22-£26 S2 D3 T3 ✕ nearby ⚶(Fort William)
D B ⊛ 🍴🛏♿F ★★

Alltonside Guest House, Achintore Road, PH33 6RW ☎ 01397 703542
(Elizabeth Ann Allton) www.alltonside.co.uk Map 41/085718
£18-£25 D3 T2 F1 ✕ £12, 7pm ⚶(Fort William)
V D B ⊛ 🍴🛏 ★★★

Ashburn House, Achintore Rd, PH33 6RQ ☎ 01397 706000
(Christine MacDonald) www.highland5star.co.uk Map 41/095732
£45-£55 S3 D4 ✕ nearby ⚶(Fort William)
D B ⊛ 🍴🛏 ★★★★★

● Kincraig
CAIRNGORMS

Insh House, PH21 1NU ☎ 01540 651377 (Nick & Patsy Thompson)
www.kincraig.com/inshhouse Map 35/836038
£26-£30 S2 D1 T1 F1 ✕ nearby D B ⊛ 🍴🛏🚗!🧺 ★★★

● Kingussie

Ardselma
The Crescent, PH21 1JZ ☎ 07786 696384 (Valerie Johnston)
www.kingussiebedandbreakfast.co.uk Map 35/757009
£20-£35 S1 D1 T3 F2 ✕ nearby ⚶(Kingussie)
D B ⊛ 🍴🛏🚗!🧺

Situated within the Cairngorms National Park, Ardselma is quiet and peaceful, set in its private grounds of three acres with ample parking and safe bicycle storage. Large bedrooms, log-fire sitting room, 5mins from train station and less from bus stop.

● Kinlochleven
WEST HIGHLAND WAY

Hermon, 5 Rob Roy Rd, PH50 4RA ☎ 01855 831383 (Miss MacAngus)
hughenamacangus@tiscali.co.uk Map 41/189622
✕ D B ⊛ 🍴🚗!🧺♿ ★★★Ⓦ

Tigh na Cheo Guest House, Garbhein Road, PH50 4SE ☎ 01855 831434
(Nicola Lyden) www.tigh-na-cheo.co.uk Map 41/182617
✕ V D B ⊛ 🍴🚗!

SCOTLAND

● Lochinver
Ardglas Guest House, IV27 4LJ ☎ 01571 844257 (Arthur & Meryl Quigley)
www.ardglas.co.uk Map 15/093231
£28 S3 D2 T3 ✗ nearby ⬛ ⊛ 🐾 🚗 ★★★Ⓜ

● Newtonmore
CAIRNGORMS

Craigerne House Hotel
Golf Course Rd, PH20 1AT ☎ 01540 673281 (David & Jane Adamson)
www.craigernehotel.com Map 35/716991
£28.50-£35 S1 D3 T6 F1 🚶(Newtonmore)
⬛ Ⓑ ⊛ 🐾 🍴 🚗 🐾

Detached Victorian villa with mature gardens, commanding magnificent views of the Monadhliath, Cairngorms and Spey Valley. 100 yards from Newtonmore centre – "The Walking Centre of Scotland". Recently refurbished. En-suite rooms with hospitality trays, hairdryers, TVs etc. Drying room available.

● Portmahomack
Caledonian Hotel, Main Street, IV20 1YS ☎ 01862 871345
(Bev Socas) www.caleyhotel.co.uk Map 21/915842
£35-£45 D2 T9 F3 ✗ £15, 6pm ⓋⒹⒷ ⊛ 🐾 🍴 🐾

● Spean Bridge
GREAT GLEN WAY
Inverour Guest House, PH34 4EU ☎ 01397 712218 (Lesley Brown)
www.inverourguesthouse.co.uk Map 34/223816
£27.50-£30 S2 D3 T1 F2 ✗ £12.50 🚶(Spean Bridge)
ⓋⒹⒷ ⊛ 🐾 🚗 ★★★Ⓦ

Distant Hills Guest House, Roy Bridge Road, PH34 4EU ☎ 01397 712452
(Peter McIntosh) www.distanthills.com Map 34/226818
£45-£70 D3 T4 F1 ✗ £22, 7pm 🚶(Spean Bridge)
ⓋⒹⒷ ⊛ 🐾 🚗 👤 ★★★★Ⓦ

● Torridon
Ben Bhraggie, Diabaig, IV22 2HE ☎ 01445 790268
(Mrs I Ross) Map 19/802605
£18 S1 D1 T1 ✗ £11, 7:30pm Ⓥ Ⓑ ⊛ 🐾 !

INNER HEBRIDES

● Kyleakin (Isle of Skye)

White Heather Hotel
The Harbour, IV41 8PL ☎ 01599 534577
(Gillian & Craig Glenwright) www.whiteheatherhotel.co.uk Map 33/753264
£30-£45 D5 T3 F1 ✗ nearby 🚶(Kyle Of Lochalsh)
⬛ Ⓑ ⊛ 🐾 🐾

A warm welcome awaits you at our cosy family-run hotel, nestled on the harbourside in the idyllic village of Kyleakin, near the Skye Bridge. All 9 bedrooms are en-suite & have digital TV, hairdryers & tea/coffee making facilities.

● Sligachan (Isle of Skye)

Sligachan Hotel
Sligachan, IV47 8SW ☎ 01478 650204 (Sligachan Hotel)
www.sligachan.co.uk Map 32/485298
£40-£54 S4 D6 T8 F3 ✗ £15, 5pm
Ⓥ ⬛ Ⓑ ⊛ 🐾 🚗 🐾

Ideal walking and touring base beside the Cuillin. 3-star accommodation, recently refurbished, with local cuisine and own brewery. Open fires in both peaceful McKenzies lounge or busy Seumas bar with all-day catering and over 200 malt whiskies.

ISLE OF ARRAN

● Blackwaterfoot
Lochside, KA27 8EY ☎ 01770 860276 (Marjorie Bannatyne)
george.bannatyne@virgin.net Map 68/903268
£28 S1 D2 T1 F1 ✗ £9, 6:30pm Ⓥ ⬛ Ⓑ ⊛ 🐾 🐾

● Brodick

Rosaburn Lodge
KA27 8DP ☎ 01770 302383
www.smoothhound.co.uk/hotels/rosaburn.html Map 69/009367
£30-£40 D3 T2 ✗ nearby
⬛ Ⓑ ⊛ 🐾 🚗 🍴 Ⓕ ★★★

Beautifully located on the banks of River Rosa. Nearest guest house to the Arran Hills.

Comfortable bedrooms and bathrooms. Excellent breakfasts. Private parking.

NORTH EAST SCOTLAND

● Forfar
Whinney-Knowe, 8 Dundee Street, DD8 2PQ ☎ 01307 818288 (Ellen Mann)
www.whinneyknowe.co.uk Map 54/525485
£20-£25 S1 D2 T1 ✗ £10, 7pm ⬛ Ⓑ ⊛ 🐾 🐾 ★★★

● Tomintoul
CAIRNGORMS
SPEYSIDE WAY
Morinsh, 26 Cults Drive, AB37 9HW ☎ 01807 580452 (Jean Birchall)
www.tomintoul-glenlivet.org Map 36/166189
✗ nearby ⬛ Ⓑ ⊛ 🐾 🚗 ! 🐾

PERTH & KINROSS

● Blairgowrie
CATERAN TRAIL
Shocarjen House, Balmoral Rd, PH10 7AF ☎ 01250 870525 (Shonaidh Beattie)
shocarjen@btinternet.com Map 53/180456
£30 D1 T1 F1 ⬛ Ⓑ ⊛ 🐾 🚗 ! 🐾 ★★★★

Glenisla Hotel
Kirkton of Glenisla, PH11 8PH ☎ 01575582223 (Warwick McKiever)
www.glenisla-hotel.com Map 44/212604
£45 S1 D2 T3 ✕ £17.50, 6pm
Ⓥ Ⓓ Ⓑ ⊛ 🐾 ♨ 🐕 ! 🌿

Glenisla hotel and restaurant, near Blairgowrie in the Angus Glens – the Heart of Scotland. Our aim is to offer you comfortable, enjoyable surroundings with excellent food, in this magnificent part of Scotland.

● Kirkmichael
CATERAN TRAIL

Strathardle Inn
PH10 7NS ☎ 01250 881224 (Tim Hancher)
www.strathardleinn.co.uk
Map 52/082599
Ⓓ Ⓑ ⊛ 🐾 🌿

The Cateran Trail runs in front of this cosy, family-run hotel set in the glorious Perthshire Highlands.

For the weary walker we offer plentiful refreshment, real ales, malts, open fires, lots of hot water, comfortable beds and drying facilities.

● Perth
Beeches, 2 Comelybank, PH2 7HU ☎ 01738 624486 (Pat & Brian Smith)
www.beeches-guest-house.co.uk Map 53/124245
£22-£27 S2 D1 T1 ✕ nearby ᴍᴍ(Perth)
Ⓓ Ⓑ ⊛ 🐾 🍵 ★★★

SCOTTISH BORDERS

● Eyemouth
The Brambles B&B, The Brambles, 1 Upper Houndlaw, TD14 5BU
☎ 018907 50281 (Sandra G Short)
daveshort@torness74.freeserve.co.uk Map 67/943641
£25 S1 D1 T1 ✕ nearby Ⓓ ⊛ 🐾 🍵 🌿

● Galashiels
SOUTHERN UPLAND WAY & ST CUTHBERT'S WAY
Ettrickvale, 33 Abbotsford Road, TD1 3HW ☎ 01896 755224 (Mrs S Field)
www.ettrickvalebandb.co.uk Map 73/499352
✕ £10 Ⓥ Ⓓ Ⓑ ⊛ 🐾 🌿 ★★★

● Jedburgh
ST CUTHBERT'S WAY

Ferniehirst Mill Lodge
TD8 6PQ ☎ 01835 863279 (Alan & Christine Swanston)
www.ferniehirstmill.co.uk Map 80/654171
£25 S2 D2 T4 ✕ £15, 5pm
Ⓥ Ⓓ Ⓑ ⊛ 🐾 🍵 ★

Just two and half miles south of Jedburgh, this chalet-style guesthouse is set in its own grounds of 25 acres besides Jed Water. Homecooking including vegetarian. Dogs welcome. A country-lover's paradise. Email: ferniehirstmill@aol.com

● Peebles
Whitestone House, Innerleithen Road, EH45 8BD
☎ 01721 720337 (Mrs M Muir)
www.aboutscotland.com/peebles/whitestone.html Map 73/251408
£26-£28 ✕ Ⓓ Ⓑ ⊛ ★★★Ⓜ

● Selkirk
Ivy Bank, Hillside Terrace, TD7 4LT ☎ 01750 21270 (Janet MacKenzie)
Iannet@aol.com Map 73/473286
£25 S1 D1 T1 ✕ nearby Ⓓ Ⓑ ⊛ 🐾 🍵 🐕 ! 🌿 ★★

● Traquair
SOUTHERN UPLAND WAY
The School House, EH44 6PL ☎ 01896 830425 (Mrs J A Caird)
www.old-schoolhouse.ndo.co.uk Map 73/331344
Ⓓ Ⓑ 🐾 🚗 ! 🌿 ★★

● Walston
Walston Mansion Farmhouse, ML11 8NF ☎ 01899 810334 (Margaret Kirby)
www.walstonmansion.co.uk Map 72/057454
£25 D1 T1 F2 ✕ £10, 7pm
Ⓥ Ⓓ Ⓑ ⊛ 🐾 🍵 🌿 ★★★

STIRLING

● Lochearnhead
LOCH LOMOND & THE TROSSACHS
ROB ROY WAY

Lochearnhead Hotel
Lochside, FK19 8PU ☎ 01567 830229
www.lochearnhead-hotel.com Map 51/596238
£45 D4 T5 F1 ✕ £12, 6pm
Ⓥ Ⓓ Ⓑ ⊛ 🐾 🍵 ★★

Enjoying wonderful views over Loch Earn. A family-run hotel with 10 en-suite bedrooms, lounge bar, restaurant and residents' lounge. Lots of wonderful walking in the vicinity of the hotel. There is ample parking with secure garage parking for motorcycles/bicycles.

SELF-CATERING

ARGYLL & BUTE

● Ballachulish
Sorcha Cottage ☎ 07751 105345 (Margaret Muir)
www.scottisholidays.co.uk Map 41/075583
£180-£450 Sleeps 2-6. 2 bungalows. ⊗ 🏠 Short breaks available ★★★

● Glendaruel
COWAL WAY

Home Farm Cottages
☎ 01463 229342 (Sarah Farquhar)
www.homefarms.co.uk Map 55/998869
£235-£600 Sleeps 1-6. 4 cottages.
⊗ F 🏠 Short breaks available ★★★★

This truly magical place offers adventure, tranquility, romance, beauty and some of the best walking in Scotland.

Home Farm Cottages run parallel with the Cowal Way and is regularly the 'end of day 2' for those who have set off from Glasgow.

There are many wonderful walks on your doorstep offering varying degrees of length and difficulty. Home Farms – until 1984 was a working dairy for 40 years. It is now made up of 'The Stables'; 'Home Farm Cottage'; 'The Byre' and 'The Dairy' and have been converted to a very high standard which affords our guests every comfort.

● Taynuilt

Airdeny Chalets
☎ 01866 822648 (Jenifer Moffat)
www.airdenychalets.co.uk Map 50/015278
£265-£685 Sleeps 4-6. 7 chalets.
⊗ & F 🏠 Short breaks available ★★★

Set in a peaceful natural habitat with stunning mountain views, one mile from Taynuilt and 12 miles from Oban, Airdeny Chalets provides an ideal base for walking, cycling, fishing, birdwatching, touring the Western Highlands and Islands or just relaxing.

The 7 two- and three-bedroomed chalets are furnished to a very high standard and immaculately maintained by the resident owner.

Each chalet enjoys its own privacy with parking and plenty of space for children to play safely.

An added bonus is that it is a 'midge-free zone'!

CENTRAL BELT

● Auchtermuchty
Pitcairlie ☎ 01337 827418/07831 646157 (Rosemary Jeynes)
www.pitcairlie-leisure.co.uk Map 58/238147
£250-£1040 Sleeps 2-21. 5 apartments, cottage.
⊗ & 🏠 Short breaks available ★★★★

DUMFRIES & GALLOWAY

● Moffat
SOUTHERN UPLAND WAY

Fran Considine
☎ 01784 740892 (Fran Considine)
www.holidayelegance.co.uk Map 78/092051
£250-£425 Sleeps 2-6. 1 apartment.
⊗ Short breaks available ★★★★

Spacious luxury apartment in recently refurbished Victorian villa, close to Moffat centre. Newly furnished, equipped & decorated to high spec. Described by tourist board as "excellent, elegant and thoroughly deserving of a four-star award". Private parking. Splendid views. Wonderful walks nearby.

HIGHLAND

● Aviemore
CAIRNGORMS
SPEYSIDE WAY

White Corries
☎ 07891 429929 (Steve Elliott)
www.aviemore-scotland.com Map 36/902132
£395-£750 Sleeps 1-10. 4-bedroom detatched house.
Ⓢ Short breaks available

4-bedroom detached house with garage. 10 mins walk from Aviemore village centre near to pubs, restaurants, shops nightlife. Ideal base to explore the Highlands for all Summer & Winter outdoor activities. Leisure pass available. Book online at our website.

● Fort William
WEST HIGHLAND WAY & GREAT GLEN WAY
Bunree Holiday Cottages/Caravans ☎ 01855821359
(Mary & Allan Maclean) www.holiday-homes.org Map 41/023631
£265-£715 Sleeps 1-6. 5 cottages.
Short breaks available ★★★★

● Nethy Bridge
Mondhuie ☎ 01479 821062 (David Mordaunt)
www.mondhuie.com Map 36/005201 🐾

INNER HEBRIDES

● Eabost (Isle of Skye)
Apple Blossom Cottage ☎ +44 (0)1599 534577 (Gillian Glenwright)
www.selfcateringisleofskye.co.uk Map 23/321390
£525-£650 Sleeps 1-4. 1 detached crofting cottage. Ⓢ

● Sligachan (Isle of Skye)
sligachan self catering ☎ 01478 650204 (sligachan hotel)
www.sligachansc.co.uk Map 32/485298
£440-£1200 Sleeps 8-14. 1 cottage & lodge. Ⓢ 🐾

● Torrin (Isle of Skye)
The Old Church ☎ 01422884276 (Nathaniel Le Pla)
www.theoldchurch-torrin.co.uk Map 32/577207
£625-£825 Sleeps 1-8. 1 cottage. Ⓢ 🐾 Short breaks available

ISLE OF ARRAN

● Blackwaterfoot
Lochside ☎ 01770 860276 (Mrs M Bannatyne)
george.bannatyne@virgin.net Map 68/898280
£220-£380 Sleeps 2-6. 2 cottages. 🐾

● Sliddery

Far Horizons Holiday Cottages
☎ 01770 870295 (Margaret Tait)
www.arran-far-horizons.co.uk Map 68/930229
£300-£425 Sleeps 2-4. 2 cottages.
Ⓢ Short breaks available

The Hayshed and Ploughman's Bothy are adjoining, beautifully converted, STB 3-star, two-bedroomed cottages, with spiral stairs set in a comfortable open-plan ground floor, all modern conveniences, satellite TV, sun terraces and private parking. Access down track to Arran's Coastal Way.

PERTH & KINROSS

● Crieff

Gamekeepers Cottage & Norwegian Lodges
☎ 01764 652586 (Stephen Brown)
www.monzievaird.com Map 52/848210
£400-£900 Sleeps 2-8. 24 lodges.
Ⓢ 🐾 Short breaks available ★★★★ⒼⓌ

Beautiful Highland estate, two miles west of Crieff, set in an historic designed landscape. Grounds of over 40 acres. Hidden away in a quiet location perfect for using as a base from which to discover the Highlands. Walks from your door.

● Killin

Morenish Mews
☎ 01567820527 (Ken Chew)
www.morenishmews.com Map 51/588348
£220-£370 Sleeps 1-3. 3 cottages, apartments.
Ⓢ Short breaks available ★★★★ⓌⓂ

Situated in a wooded hollow with superb outlook over Loch Tay. Ideal for couples. The summits of over 35 Munros lie within a 20-mile radius of Morenish, providing hill walkers with a wide range of walking challenges, summer and winter.

GROUPS, HOSTELS, BUNKHOUSES, CAMPSITES & OTHERS

HIGHLAND

Banavie
GREAT GLEN WAY & WEST HIGHLAND WAY

Chase The Wild Goose Hostel
Lochiel Crescent, Banavie, PH33 7LY ☎ 01397 772531
www.great-glen-hostel.com Map 41/114771
SC £9.95-£18 per night Sleeps 1-40. Independent hostel.
(Banavie) D ★★★★ W

Located in one of the the most beautiful parts of Scotland, you can see majestic Ben Nevis, the highest mountain in the UK, from the village.

Only 100m away is the famous 'Neptune's Staircase' on the Caledonian Canal.

We have a drying room equipped with de-humidifier, a secure cycle shed and a secure area to lock up your canoes. Pay-as-you-go internet access is available, with free Wi-Fi.

The Moorings Hotel and the Lochy Bar are just a short walk from the hostel for generous portion meals.

We offer comfort, in an out-of-town location, for a good night's sleep.

Doune

Doune - Knoydart
PH41 4PL ☎ 01687 462656 (Liz Tibbetts)
www.doune-knoydart.co.uk Map 33/705035
FB £50-£50 per night Sleeps 6-14. Lodge.
V D

Located on the western tip of the remote Knoydart peninsula Doune provides an ideal setting for walkers of all abilities. Mountains, wildlife, tranquillity, award-winning food and stunning sunsets combine for a unique adventure and enduring memories.

Dundonnell
Sail Mhor Croft Hostel, IV23 2QT ☎ 01854 633224
www.sailmhor.co.uk Map 19/064893
£11.50 per night Sleeps 1-16. Independent hostel. D

Fort William
WEST HIGHLAND WAY & GREAT GLEN WAY

Fort William Backpackers, Alma Road, PH33 6BH ☎ 01397 700711
www.scotlandstophostels.com Map 41/104738
SC £12-£15 per night Sleeps 1-38. Independent hostel.
(Fort William) D ★★

Kyleakin
Skye Backpackers, IV41 8PH ☎ 01599 534510
www.scotlandstophostels.com Map 33/750263
SC £9.50-£16 per night Sleeps 1-35. Independent hostel. (Kyle) D ★

Sligachan
Sligachan Bunkhouse, Sligachan, IV47 8SW ☎ 01478 650204 (Sligachan Hotel)
www.sligachansc.co.uk Map 32/485298
V D

CENTRAL BELT

Glasgow
WEST HIGHLAND WAY

Berkeley Globetrotters, 56 Berkeley Street, Charing Cross, G3 7DS
☎ 0141 221 7880 www.aubergeecosse.fr Map 64/577659
SC, BB £12.50-£18 per night Sleeps 1-60. Independent hostel.
(Charing Cross) D ★★

ISLE OF ARRAN

Kilmory
Kilmory Lodge Bunkhouse, KA27 8PQ ☎ 01770 870345 (Kirstin Napier)
www.kilmoryhall.com Map 68/960215
SC £230-£350 per week Sleeps 15-23. Bunkhouse. D ★★★

NORTH EAST SCOTLAND

Glenprosen
CATERAN TRAIL

Prosen Hostel
Glenprosen, DD8 4SA ☎ 01575 540 238 / 302 (Robert Witoslawski)
www.prosenhostel.co.uk
Map 44/328659
D F ★★★★

Opened in 2007 on the southern edge of the Cairngorms National Park. Ideal for groups (village hall nearby). Very comfortable (with linen included) & cosy (woodburning stove, internet etc.) Red squirrels outside, also new and upgraded footpaths to Glenisla & Glenclova.

PERTH & KINROSS

Pitlochry
Pitlochry Backpackers Hotel, 134 Atholl Road, PH16 5AB ☎ 01796 470044
www.scotlandstophostels.com Map 52/938582
SC £12-£37 per night Sleeps 1-88. Independent hostel.
(Pitlochry) D

SIGMA

OUR WORLD

Tim Matsui: Born in 1973 in California. Became a freelance photographer, after earning a degree in photojournalism, from the University of Washington. Established the FEAR Project, a non-profit media organisation creating documentaries about sexual violence, the environment and other vital social issues.

Photo data: Sigma 18-200mm F3.5-6.3 DC OS. 1/400-second exposure at f/6.3.

TIM MATSUI SHOOTS THE WORLD WITH A SIGMA LENS.

Traveling light for a high rugged climb, overlooking Oregon's Trout Creek, is made possible by Sigma's lightweight and compact optically stabilised lens.

Sigma's super-zoom lens for digital SLRs captured this reflective moment at twilight to perfection. The exclusive built-in Sigma Optical Stabiliser virtually eliminates the problem of camera shake that can otherwise mar telephoto photography in such low light conditions. SLD (Special Low Dispersion) glass and aspherical elements effectively eliminate aberrations whilst super multilayer coating cuts flare and ghosting. An impressive minimum focusing distance of 45cm/17.7in. throughout the entire zoom range gives a maximum reproduction ratio is 1:3.9. A matched petal-shaped lens hood is included and the non-rotating front element is ideal for accepting circular polarising filters.

NEW

*Vignetting (a darkening of the corners of the image) will occur if the lens is used with digital SLR cameras with image sensors larger than APS-C size or 35mm SLRs, and APS SLRs

● Available for:
Sigma SA, Canon EOS and
Nikon-D HSM digital SLRs

A high quality super-zoom lens for digital SLRs, with Sigma's exclusive Optical Stabiliser to minimise the effects of camera shake.

SIGMA 18-200mm F3.5-6.3 DC OS For DIGITAL

Σ Sigma Imaging (UK) Ltd, 13 Little Mundells, Welwyn Garden City, Herts. AL7 1EW. Tel: 01707 329 999 Fax: 01707 327 822
www.sigma-imaging-uk.com E-mail: sales@sigma-imaging-uk.com

WALKING HOLIDAYS
BRITAIN

The companies listed here have chosen to advertise with us and their inclusion should not imply any recommendation by the Ramblers' Association

ENGLAND

Footprints of Sussex, Pear Tree Cottage, Jarvis Lane, Steyning, West Sussex BN44 3GL Tel: 01903 813381
Email: footprintwalks@tinyworld.co.uk
Web: **www.footprintsofsussex.co.uk** Self-guided holidays along the South Downs Way with baggage transfers and lots of local knowledge. Covers: South Downs

Orchard Trails, 5 Orchard Way, Horsmonden, Tonbridge, Kent TN12 8JX Tel: 01892 722680 Fax: 01892 722680
Email Grabham@btinternet.com
Web: **www.kent-esites.co.uk/orchardtrails** Unescorted walking/cycling holidays. Kent and East Sussex. Luggage transported. Covers: Kent, East Sussex

ENGLAND

Everything you need to know ......
dartmooraccommodation.co.uk

North-West Frontiers, Viewfield, Strathpeffer IV14 9DS,
Scotland Tel/Fax: 01997 421474
Email: info@nwfrontiers.com Web: **www.nwfrontiers.com**
Since 1986 we have offered the widest range of quality small
group walking holidays in NW Scotland: Shetland, Orkney,
Sutherland, Western Isles and much more. Join the experts!

Pace the Peaks Guided Fell Walking in the Lake District - Local
knowledge is the secret to wonderful walking. Join Cathy for
guided walks or practical navigation. For groups or individuals I
tailor the walking just for you.
Cathy Colam, Keswick, Cumbria. tel 017687 74824 Web
www.pacethepeaks.co.uk

Skylark Holidays
Guided walks – classical Peak District and the new, ever-
changing National Forest. Walking activities – getting started with
Map reading. Responsible tourism with shared transport into
the Peak District National Park and supporting the National
Forest, the boldest environmental project in the UK.
Tel: 01283 701739 Web: **www.skylarkholidays.co.uk**

ENGLAND

THE ISLE OF WIGHT
WALKING FESTIVAL
3 to 18 MAY

20 08

The UK's Largest Walking Festival
10th Anniversary

www.isleofwightwalkingfestival.co.uk

WIGHT*link*
Ordnance Survey
RED FUNNEL
Millets
ISLE *of* WIGHT COUNCIL

Wight Walks
Discover the Isle of Wight

- Tranquil inland walks
- Stunning coastal path
- Magnificent scenery
- Cosy accommodation
- Unguided walks
- Luggage moved for you

Tel: 01983 281662
www.wight-walks.co.uk

WALES, SCOTLAND AND IRELAND

Beat a path to the rambling Island of ALDERNEY
so close, so different

A small slice of Britain with French dressing, that's Alderney. Fine food and wine, only 45 minutes by air from the south coast.

Tel: 01481 822333 Email: brochures@visitalderney.com
www.visitalderney.com

About Argyll Walking Holidays, Letters Lodge South, Strathlachlan, Argyll PA27 8BZ Tel/Fax: +44 (0)1369 860272
Email: info@aboutargyll.co.uk Web: **www.aboutargyll.co.uk**
Guided walking holidays designed for people who like to explore the beautiful countryside and discover the secrets of its history and wildlife.Covers: West Highlands & Islands of Scotland

WALES, SCOTLAND AND IRELAND

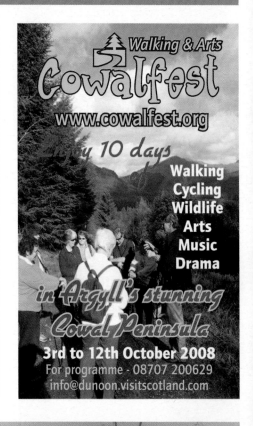

WALES, SCOTLAND AND IRELAND

Walk for twelve months without stopping.

At Plas y Brenin we run a full programme of courses and holidays which are ideal for hillwalkers throughout the year. You can unlock the mountains in winter by coming on one of our winter hillwalking or winter mountaineering courses, designed to give you the confidence to overcome the unexpected challenges Britain's mountains throw up in the depths of winter. Or you can simply develop your summer skills, improving your navigation technique, developing your GPS skills, or even moving onto steeper ground on one of our scrambling courses.

For the more experienced there's always the variety and scale of the Scottish Mountains. We run a full programme of Scottish Winter Hillwalking and Mountaineering courses from our base in Scotland. For those who'd like to try out their skills in the Alps, we have a wide range of Alpine mountaineering holidays and for the more ambitious we run a series of ski touring holidays, a great progression for hillwalkers who are also competent skiers.

One thing is for sure, whether you decide to join us in Wales, Scotland, France or Austria this year you'll be guaranteed the incredibly high standard of instruction, equipment, facilities and accommodation The National Mountain Centre has become famous for.

For a free 60-page colour brochure telephone us on 01690 720214, or e-mail us at brochure@pyb.co.uk.

> The **Professional's** Choice

www.pyb.co.uk

Plas y Brenin, The National Mountain Centre, Capel Curig, Conwy, Wales LL24 OET
Tel: 01690 720214 Fax: 01690 720394 www.pyb.co.uk Email: info@pyb.co.uk

Save
£370
on a walking
weekend*

SAVE a further 10% for
groups of 8 or more

Stunning countryside

Northamptonshire is nature's way. Only an hour from London,
yet situated in the very middle of prime English countryside.

Book now:
01604 731999
quoting reference 'WBHH07'

For more details visit:
www.growformiles.co.uk

To order your FREE 2008 visitor guide
Txt 'WALK' to 84880

*Two nights dinner, bed and breakfast, packed lunch,
thermos mug and afternoon tea.

Northamptonshire
let yourself grow.com

FOR LIFE'S UPS AND DOWNS

ROCLITE™ 390 GTX *para extreme*

"Lightest GORE-TEX® boot in the World"

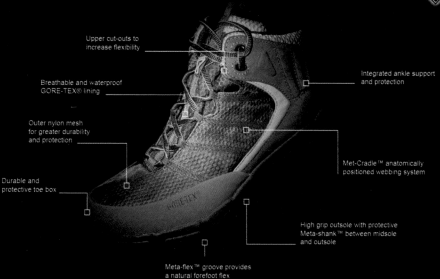

TRAIL "The most important innovation in hill footwear this century?"

GORE-TEX®

Upper cut-outs to increase flexibility

Breathable and waterproof GORE-TEX® lining

Outer nylon mesh for greater durability and protection

Durable and protective toe box

Integrated ankle support and protection

Met-Cradle™ anatomically positioned webbing system

High grip outsole with protective Meta-shank™ between midsole and outsole

Meta-flex™ groove provides a natural forefoot flex

The inov-8 philosophy has always been to design footwear around the natural function and precision shape of the foot, allowing the freedom to function as nature intended. We pride ourselves in leading the pack with original lightweight, flexible, high traction and low profile shoes that offer an intimate fit that's almost like running and walking barefoot.

inov-8.com
01388 744900

inov-8

  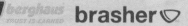

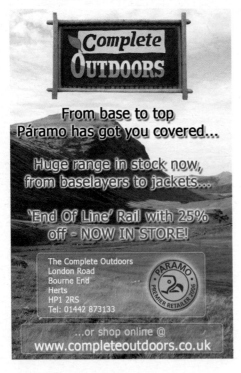

ADVERTISING INDEX

PHOTO CREDITS

p1 Whinstone Lee Tor, Peak District (britainonview/East Midlands Tourism/Daniel Bosworth)

p2-3 Dove Stones, South Pennines (Alastair Lee)

p4 Tor Bay, West Glamorgan (britainonview/Rod Edwards)

p5 Chris Smith at Torridon mountain, Wester Ross (Richard Else/Triple Echo Productions)

p8 Family Rambling Group in Dartmoor (Tony Carney)

p9 Little boy (Rebecca Barnham), SE Asian couple (Louise Hillyer), Anthony Sousa (Fred Agbah)

p10 New Forest, Hampshire (© Countryside Agency/Andy Tryner), Gated alley (Chris Ord), Dangerous crossing of A283 (Unknown)

p11 Ramblers staff outside House of Lords (Jacquetta Fewster)

p12 Martindale, Cumbria (www.britainonview.com), Vixen Tor, Dartmoor (Unknown)

p13 Deal beach, Kent (britainonview/Kent Tourism Alliance/Daniel Bosworth), Lake Buttermere, Lake District (britainonview/Martin Brent)

p14 View from Whinstone Lee Tor, Peak District (britainonview/East Midlands Tourism/Daniel Bosworth)

p15 767 landing (Zwitter/www.sxc.hu), Stansted expansion demo (Unknown), Brian Blessed at Ramblers protest, Weald AONB (Jancy Davies)

p16 An Caisteal, Loch Lomond & Trossachs (Nicholas Thomson), Hills above Greenock, Inverclyde (Inverclyde Ramblers)

p19 South Downs led walk (Jancy Davies), UYP Footpath Work Awards 2005 winners, Cardigan Bay (Unknown)

p24 Rhossili Bay, Swansea (britainonview/McCormick-McAdam)

p25 Whitesands Bay, Pembrokeshire (britainonview/Caravan Club/Rod Edwards)

p27 Cattersty Sands, Redcar & Cleveland (© Countryside Agency/Mike Kipling), Bodmin Moor (Unknown)

p28 Cleeve Hill, Glos (© Natural England/Jo Ward), Brackenbottom Scar, Pen-y-Ghent, Yorkshire Dales (Unknown)

p29 Urquhart Castle, Loch Ness (Jancy Davies), Ledbury, Herefordshire (www.britainonview.com), Ynys Llanddwyn, Anglesey (britainonview)

p30 Ilkley Moor, North Yorks (britainonview/McCormick-McAdam)

p31 Hunstanton Cliffs, Norfolk (© Natural England), Ceibwr Bay, Pembrokeshire (www.britainonview.com)

p33 Streatley, Berkshire (www.britainonview.com), Church Stretton, Shropshire (www.britainonview.com)

p34 Small Dole riverside, Sussex (James Ashford), Aviemore, Highland (www.britainonview.com)

p35 Barnard Castle, Durham (www.britainonview.com), The Round House, Lechdale, Glos (© Countryside Agency), Combestone Tor, Dartmoor (www.britainonview.com)

p36 Cerne Giant, Cerne Abbas, Dorset (www.britainonview.com), Symonds Yat, Herefordshire (britainonview/Adrian Houston)

p37 Boulby Cliffs, Redcar & Cleveland (britainonview/McCormick-McAdam)

p38 E9 fingerpost, Poole Harbour (Des de Moor)

p40 Newgale, Pembrokeshire (www.britainonview.com)

p41 Smeathe's Ridge, Wiltshire (Unknown)

p42 Torridon, Highland (www.britainonview.com)

p43 Whinstone Lee Tor, Peak District (britainonview/East Midlands Tourism/Daniel Bosworth), Stirling, Loch Lomond & Trossachs (britainonview/ANPA/McCormick-McAdam)

p55 View from Bilberry Hill, Lickey Hills County Park (CLS, www.wikipedia.org)

PHOTO CREDITS

p59 Hartshead Pike, Ashton-under-Lyne (Ashtonian)

p62 Roath Park, Cardiff (www.britainonview.com)

p69 Martindale, Cumbria (britainonview/Rod Edwards)

p75 Dry stone wall in Grange-over-Sands, Cumbria (britainonview/Rod Edwards)

p79 Snowdonia cwm climb (Unknown)

p86 Northumbria Walking Group above Derwentwater, Lake District (Unknown)

p88 Ramblers staff walk in Ashford, Surrey (Unknown)

p90 Offa's Dyke (Ian Smith/Disabled Ramblers)

p93 Northumbria Family Walking Group, Simonside, Northumbria (Richard Mann/Guzelian)

p94 Ramblers led walk in Western Weald AONB, Kent (Jancy Davies)

p110 Lodging at Gotten Manor, Chale, IOW (britainonview/McCormick-McAdam)

p113 B&B/tea shop in Dent, Cumbria (www.britainonview.com)

p116 Fisherman's Bay, Cornwall (www.britainonview.com)

p117 View from Birdlip Hill, Glos (© Countryside Agency/Nick Turner), Tyneham Village, Dorset (Chris Lewington/Alamy), Bottlenose dolphins in Cardigan Bay, Wales (Hanna Nuuttila)

p146 New Forest footpath (Dorset and the New Forest Tourism Partnership)

p147 Eltham Palace grounds, Greenwich (Coaster/Alamy), Samphire Hoe, Kent (britainonview/Kent Tourism Alliance/Daniel Bosworth), Cobstone Mill, Ibstone, Bucks (Greg Balfour Evans/Alamy)

p162 Thurne Dyke Wind Pump, Norfolk Broads (britainonview/Rod Edwards)

p163 St Alban's Cathedral, Herts (www.britainonview.com), Entrance to Top Lodge visitor centre, Fineshade, Northants (Isobel Cameron), Kingfisher

(© Gerald Downey)

p170 Stanage Edge, Derbyshire (britainonview/McCormick-McAdam)

p171 Tree-top trail, Salcey Forest, Northants. (Isobel Cameron), Well dressing in Hartington, Derbyshire (www.britainonview.com)

p192 Cauldron Snout, North Pennines (© Countryside Agency/McCoy-Wynne)

p193 Clitheroe Castle, Lancs (www.britainonview.com), View from Arnside Knott, Cumbria (Jon Sparks/Alamy), Crosby beach, Liverpool (Vic Pigula/Alamy)

p208 Moorland slabs, Redcar & Cleveland (© Countryside Agency/Mike Kipling)

p209 Golden Acre Park, Leeds (Janet Morrell), Sheffield Botanical Gardens (Pete Hill/Alamy), Barn owl in flight (Alan Williams/Alamy)

p220 Hadrian's Wall, nr Haltwhistle, Northumberland (britainonview/Rod Edwards)

p221 "Mapping" at Leaplish Waterside Park, Kielder, Northumberland (Forestry Commission), Allenbanks, North Pennines (www.britainonview.com), Red kite (© www.northeastwildlife.co.uk)

p228 Dolwyddelan, Conwy (britainonview/David Angel)

p229 16th-century Chain Bridge across River Dee, Llangollen, Denbighshire (www.britainonview.com), Garreg Ddu Viaduct, Powys (www.britainonview.com), Kenfig Dunes, Bridgend (alecstewart/Alamy)

p248 Glencoe, Highland (www.britainonview.com)

p249 Elie Chain Walk (Ashley Cooper/Alamy), Cape Wrath lighthouse (Stephen Finn/Alamy), Red deer stag, Galloway Forest (Forestry Commission)

Back cover (from top) – Stanage Edge, Derbyshire (britainonview/McCormick-McAdam), View from Birdlip Hill, Glos (© Countryside Agency/Nick Turner), Hadrian's Wall, nr Haltwhistle, Northumberland (britainonview/Rod Edwards), New Forest footpath (Dorset and the New Forest Tourism Partnership)

ACCOMMODATION INDEX

ACCOMMODATION INDEX

ACCOMMODATION INDEX

ACCOMMODATION INDEX

ACCOMMODATION INDEX

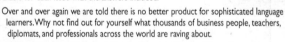